Nontoxic, Natural, & Earthwise

Nontoxic, Natural, & Earth*wise*

How to Protect Yourself and Your Family
from Harmful Products and
Live in Harmony with the Earth

DEBRA LYNN DADD

in collaboration with
Steve Lett and Judy Collins

JEREMY P. TARCHER, INC.
Los Angeles

Library of Congress Cataloging-in-Publication Data

Dadd, Debra Lynn.
    Nontoxic, natural, & earthwise: how to protect yourself and your family from harm-
ful products and live in harmony with the earth / Debra Lynn Dadd in collaboration
with Steve Lett.
        p.   cm.
    ISBN 0-87477-584-1: $12.95
    1. Environmental health–Popular works. 2. Environmentally induced diseases–
Prevention. I. Lett, Steve. II. Title. III. Title: Nontoxic, natural, and earthwise.
RA565.D34   1990   90-38920
363.19–dc20   CIP

Earthwise and the Earthwise logo ⊕ are trademarked by Debra Lynn Dadd.
Other companies using some variation of "Earthwise" in their business or brand name
are not associated with or endorsed by Debra Lynn Dadd, nor do they necessarily meet
the Earthwise standards outlined in this book.

Jeremy P. Tarcher, Inc.
5858 Wilshire Blvd., Suite 200
Los Angeles, CA 90036

Distributed by St. Martin's Press, New York

Manufactured in the United States of America
Revised edition
10 9 8 7 6 5 4 3 2 1

For Gaia, our Mother Earth

Come forth into the Light of Things,
Let Nature be your teacher.
WILLIAM WORDSWORTH

I have no other wish than a close fusion with nature
and I desire no other fate
than to have worked and lived
in harmony with her laws.
CLAUDE MONET

Contents

(Nonsoap) • Soap • Sponges • Suntan Lotion • Toilet Paper and
Facial Tissues • Toothbrushes • Toothpaste

❧ Acknowledgments

One of the most important things I have learned from writing this book is the value of working with others—something I believe we all need to do to heal our Earth. After working alone as an author for many years, I have now had the pleasure of coordinating the team that contributed to both the research and the writing in these pages.

Steve Lett has worked with me on this project since its inception, and brought to it many years of interest in and information about environmental issues—particularly the areas of energy, food and agriculture, and garbage. He also contributed to developing the standards used to evaluate products here.

Judy Collins is largely responsible for entering all the product information into the computerized database as well as typing all the manuscript corrections. I want to commend her for her efficiency, accuracy, and willingness to work long hours.

Racine Mason kept our files of catalogs and product information neat and up-to-date. By cheerfully and expertly handling all the subscription orders for my newsletter, *The Earthwise Consumer*, she made it possible for me to spend the long hours needed to write this book.

As always, Martha Casselman has been the best literary agent any writer could want. Once again, my publisher, Jeremy Tarcher, provided good support for my writing and allowed me to participate in the entire creative process and production of this book. My editor, Rick Benzel, was a big help in juggling schedules and keeping me focused. He also functioned perfectly as an average person interested in environmental and health issues and looking to this book for information. I knew I was on the right track when he told me one day that he went home and asked his wife to try some of the natural cleaning products listed here.

I would also like to thank Terry Mandel, Dave Smith, John Javna, and John Broomfield for supporting me in various ways during the writing of this book. And Marion—for always being there when we most needed her.

My husband, Larry Redalia, has been patient and supportive throughout all the research and writing. He deserves credit for all the evenings he spent waiting for me to finish typing; for listening to me; for feeding the cat, doing the grocery shopping, washing the dishes; for traipsing around foreign countries with me as I was looking for earthwise products; for saying, "Okay" with a smile every time I said, "But I have to work on my book now," instead of spending time with him. He has awakened in me a deeper love and awareness of nature all around us and set a good example of always working to make things better, regardless of how difficult the circumstances may seem. I ❤UQTπ.

And I also want to acknowledge everyone who is making and selling the products mentioned in this book, for having the courage to be leaders in the marketplace and acting to the best of their abilities for our common good.

Thank you, thank you, thank you all!

❦ Author's Note

As you are reading this book, please remember that I have written it, in good faith, as a consumer—not as a scientist, doctor, toxicologist, or even environmentalist. Think of me as a friend or neighbor who shares your interest in health and environmental issues, who has collected some information that not only might be useful to you personally but can also help make this world a better place for us all to live in.

All the information regarding products has come from written materials supplied by the manufacturer or retailer or from personal conversations with people who make and sell these products. If information is missing, it was probably not supplied in the written materials. Even when I called manufacturers with specific questions, I often couldn't find out such things as whether a product contained animal ingredients or where wood supplies came from.

So please think of the recommendations you find here as guidelines—not gospel. Like a map, they point the way to new things you might wish to explore for yourself, with *you* being a responsible explorer. Follow the suggestions given here with the same care you would use on a hike through a forest. Although a map allows you to choose your course with confidence as to the general terrain, as you walk you still need to watch out for boulders, the weather, poisonous snakes, and other hazards that the map cannot portray or prepare you for. (Certainly you'll also unexpectedly find such delights as wildflowers, deer, or a fallen tree bridging a creek.) Similarly, because of space limitations, I cannot possibly mention every item you might find in a mail-order catalog, so you are in for some wonderful surprises. In this book, as in the forest, only you can decide which path to take.

In order to help you choose products and to learn more about environmental issues and appropriate actions, I have included information about brand-name products, mail-order businesses, books, publications, and organizations. Buying these products, encouraging your friends and family members to buy them, and asking for them by name at your local stores will help guarantee their continued and increased availability. No advertising or promotional fees were accepted, and the inclusion of any product, business, book, publication, or organization here is not intended as an endorsement. If I occasionally mention that I use a product personally, this indicates only my preference; that item is not necessarily superior to other products mentioned.

To be an effective user or consumer of products means to take responsibility for the choices you make. Be as wary of blindly accepting the information presented here as you would of assuming that all products on the market are safe. Despite heroic efforts on my and the publisher's part to assure accuracy, we cannot guarantee *everything* to be absolutely correct, though we both have worked hard toward that goal. Specifically, we can make no representations about, and therefore cannot be responsible for:

incorrect or incomplete information regarding products;

changes in product ingredients or production methods;

substances or processes with toxicity or environmental destructiveness as yet undiscovered;

the continued availability of any item;

the effectiveness or any product or process listed; or

any adverse health of environmental effects caused by any product or process listed.

The assessment of products was made according to information available to all consumers; no independent testing was done by me. The products selected may contain as yet undisclosed harmful or environmentally destructive substances. Nevertheless, one can be fairly certain that these products are safer than those revealing contents known to be dangerous. It is my belief that products produced and sold by conscientious people truly are purer than those produced and sold by manufacturers unconcerned with the issues addressed here.

Throughout these pages, suggestions are made for using products in ways other than those for which those products were originally intended. Because government regulations do not allow manufacturers to recommend their products for certain uses without laboratory proof that they are indeed safe and effective for such uses (and then procuring government approval of the results), these alternate uses are not necessarily approved by the manufacturer. Not all of the suggestions given are tried and true, but all have been found to work for some people.

This book is designed to serve many people with different interests, budgets, spiritual and cultural beliefs, medical conditions, and lifestyles, and as such it may occasionally mention products or processes that are not appropriate for you personally. At these times, simply make an individual choice, and remember that the primary purpose of this book is to report on the availability of products that are generally good for our health and the environment.

And last but not least, the omission of a product from these pages should not imply that it isn't healthful or good for the Earth. In writing this book I was limited by space and time. My intention was to help consumers learn to choose appropriate products and give practical information, not to catalog every item in every store. It is my hope that, based upon the information you find here, you will make your own wise choices.

Explanatory Notes

Product categories are indicated in small caps. Example: Wash your clothes with plain SOAP. *Harmful materials, substances, or ingredients* that might be found in products are listed by name at the beginning of the entry for that product. See Appendix for information on their health and environmental effects. *Brand-name products* are in upper-and-lower-case Roman face, followed by the name of the manufacturer in parentheses. Addresses of manufacturers can be found in Mail-Order Sources. Example: Air Therapy (Mia Rose Products). *Mail-order catalogs* are in upper-and-lower-case *italic* face. Addresses of mail-order catalogs can be found in Mail-Order Sources. Example: *Seventh Generation.*

❧ Preface

> By the end of the next decade, the die will pretty well be
> cast . . . We do not have generations, we only have years
> to turn things around.   LESTER BROWN
>   PRESIDENT, WORLDWATCH INSTITUTE

This book grew from another book I wrote six years ago, *Non-toxic & Natural: How to Avoid Dangerous Everyday Products and Buy or Make Safe Ones*. I wanted to update it to include the many new nontoxic and natural products that have become available since then, and I wanted to expand it to address environmental issues as well. In this new edition of *Nontoxic & Natural*, the scope of consumer concerns is so much broader that we added a third adjective to the title: *Earthwise*.

The fundamental concept outlined in *Nontoxic & Natural* still holds true today: many products commonly used in our homes may be hazardous to our health. Labeling laws also make it difficult to know exactly what is in any product. *Nontoxic & Natural* listed many safe products that anyone could buy or easily make.

The reaction to that book was very positive. Indeed, today more and more people are recognizing the dangers of many products and choosing safer ones. Their actions are in turn bringing even more healthful and environmentally sound products to the marketplace. In fact, these products are proliferating so quickly that it is difficult to keep track of them all. Whereas in 1980 I began collecting information on nontoxic and natural products on three-by-five cards in a shoebox, I now compile product information using a large computerized database.

While reducing our personal exposure to toxics at home is an important step, there is a bigger issue at hand: we must also consider how our actions as consumers affect other people, other species, and the planet as a whole. Every time we make a purchase to fulfill our individual needs, we also make a choice that affects the environmental quality of the world we live in. Even if a product is relatively safe for us to use, its manufacture and disposal may harm the Earth. And this then affects our own health as the soil, air, and water that provide our sustenance become polluted.

For decades, numerous researchers have been telling us that we must consider the effects our modern lifestyles have on the living systems of the Earth. Recently, however, leading scientists have become increasingly concerned that we are not taking the concrete actions needed to reverse environmental destruction.

In September 1989, the Smithsonian Institution called together this country's foremost scientific authorities on global environmental problems, along with representatives of the media, to discuss the theme "The Global Environment: Are We Overreacting?" The consensus was that we were *not reacting enough* and that the general public was unaware of the magnitude of the problems we now face.

1

The scientists were perplexed that after years of warnings and increasing evidence to support them, there have been few changes in government policies or personal lifestyles. They suggested fundamental changes—not adjustments—in the way we live. "Global environmental change . . . is more deeply threatening than most people think," stated one expert. "And it is coming at us much faster than most people think . . . Advocates of delay are underrating the evidence of already existing harm." Thomas Lovejoy, assistant secretary for external affairs of the Smithsonian Institution, stated in 1988, "I am utterly convinced that most of the great environmental struggles will be either won or lost in the 1990s. And by the next century it will be too late."

Clearly, there is a genuine need to act *now*, but we need to know what to do. So in addition to pointing out the personal toxic dangers of household products, I have shown (to the best of my ability) how our daily consumer choices contribute to major environmental problems. So you'll get practical advice on making everyday consumer decisions that are healthful for you and your family, and are in harmony with the needs of the Earth.

All of us come to a turning point, a moment when we realize our responsibility to the Earth. My editor became concerned about the environment one day while carrying out yet another garbage can full of disposable diapers. Steve Lett, another associate, was greatly moved when he visited Native Americans in the Southwest and experienced their spiritual connection with the Earth. Each person makes the transition at his or her own pace.

I first began to realize the degree to which our consumer choices affect the Earth in 1987. I was reading a book called *Living Water: Viktor Schauberger and the Secrets of Natural Energy* which described a scientist's observations of water in its natural state. The water's cycle from the Earth to the atmosphere and back is somewhat more complex than the water-comes-down-as-precipitation-and-evaporates-back-up-to-the-sky version we all learned in science class. In the full cycle, the water falls to the Earth as precipitation, drains through the soil (rapidly cooling while sinking deeper and deeper) until it reaches a certain level (I'm leaving out the technical parts here), and then begins to rise, warmed by the Earth's heat. During this rise, the water is vitalized with various metals, salts, and gases, and bubbles to the surface as a spring. The full cycle can take place only where there is appropriate vegetation cover (such as forest) to allow the rain to penetrate deeply.

This made perfect sense to me, and as I was reading, I began to have a sinking feeling that the most healthful, energizing, optimal water we could possibly drink wasn't going to come from any of the water-purification devices I had been recommending in my books. The best we can do with water-purification devices is to remove pollutants from contaminated water. We can't make optimum water; only Nature can do that.

The more I thought about this, the more I realized that while the books I had written were helping many people choose safe and healthy products, I was not considering the natural world, the source of everything we need to be alive. I was assuming that the world was toxic and that we needed to somehow protect ourselves from it. This view was concerned only with what went on within the four walls that defined my home; now I saw that what goes on within those four walls always has an effect on what happens beyond them. *To take actions that destroy the ability of the Earth to provide its abundant natural gifts for us and then try to protect ourselves from our own destructive actions and make an artificial life ultimately doesn't work.* We are literally destroying the planet out from under ourselves. I knew then that I could no longer participate in the unthinking exploitation of our planet and its inhabitants, and I made a commitment to myself to live in harmony with the Earth as much as I could. On a deeper level, my whole outlook on life changed: I went from feeling isolated, defensive, protective, and fearful to wanting to experience connection, cooperation, openness, and love.

I could no longer ignore the fact that even though I lived the epitome of a nontoxic and natural lifestyle, I was still participating in the current general destruction of our planet. I had to find a better way to live that was good both for people and for the ecosystem of the Earth.

As I began to research this topic, I learned that our modern view of exploitation of the natural world is relatively recent. The industrial age began only about two hundred years ago. For most of our human experience on this planet, we have respected, preserved, and lived in harmony with Nature.

Indigenous peoples of the world hold a different view of life, one that has at its center a belief that all animals, plants, rocks, mountains, and oceans, the sky, and everything else in the universe are alive and have evolved from one spiritual source. All of Nature is considered to be a single, immense Great Chain or Web of Being in which each individual has its place.

People with this view perceive themselves as being intimately connected to everything around them, from the tiniest grain of sand to the motions of the sun, moon, and stars. As participants in the whole of life, they recognize that the Earth provides sustenance for humans, and that humans also have a reciprocal role in nurturing and sustaining the Earth. Not only are we dependent on the Earth's bounty, but the bounty of the Earth is also dependent on human cooperation.

To live with this view seems to be our *natural, original, intrinsic way of being.* The earliest archaeological records of Homo sapiens show an awareness of this cooperation with the living world. It is evident in the beliefs and values of all native peoples worldwide, and can also be found in peasant traditions, folk wisdom, and the writings of many ancient and modern philosophers, from Hippocrates to Emerson and Thoreau.

Ironically, scientists throughout this century have been developing new concepts of how the world works that are in agreement with these age-old beliefs. The Gaia hypothesis of the scientist James Lovelock, put forth in 1979, turned Buckminster Fuller's mechanical "Spaceship Earth" into a whole, *living* organism—a single integrated system united by universal principles, imbued with a governing intelligence, with all things related in an orderly way. From the world of quantum physics we learn that each of us is an integral part of the universe, and whether we acknowledge it or not, we are active participants in the functioning of all that happens. The new biology focuses on living organisms working together cooperatively for the survival of the whole balanced ecosystem. The more scientists discover about the way Nature works, the clearer our interconnection and interdependence with all Life becomes.

I became very inspired by this worldview and wondered how we might, today, apply this attitude in making choices in our lives. How might we live according to the wisdom of the Earth? How might we be *earthwise?*

We are all concerned about the current state of our environment, but where do we begin? What can we do that will really make a difference?

The changes that need to be made now are profound and will require the cooperation and action of government, industry, and individuals. Many writers have compared the modifications in lifestyle we as a society now face as being comparable in scale with the development of agriculture ten thousand years ago or the industrial revolution of the last two centuries. They affect every area of our lives and cut across all belief systems.

This book focuses on meaningful changes that each of us can make in the realm of consumer choices, and describes how to make these changes step-by-step. In chapter 1 I suggest a criterion for choosing products that will help you both recognize the benefits and identify the range of dangers—from immediate health and environmental effects to long-term hazards to our bodies and the planet that may take years to show up but which we cannot risk taking. Throughout the rest of the book, we'll explore a wide spectrum of products that we commonly use in our lives, and learn about both their potential harm to ourselves and the planet, and safe alternatives.

You will find some of the suggestions in this book simple and others surprising, for what we will explore is an enjoyable, fulfilling, and responsible way of living that is quite the opposite of the destructive and unhealthy lifestyle that is predominant in our society today.

I'm not a fanatic about this, but personally I have decided to take every step I can. I still drive my car and daily do hundreds of other things that are probably not good for my own health or the planet. But I have also made significant changes in my life that are for the betterment of myself and the Earth and will continue to do so as new options become available.

Each of you must decide for yourself what steps you are willing to take, and then take them at your own pace, in your own way.

That said, let me also stress that time is of the essence, and it is important that we all begin *now* to make as many changes as we can in our lives, as soon as possible. Just try new things one at a time. Start with something easy like switching to natural cleaning products or going to the hardware store to get low-flow faucet aerators and screwing them on your faucets. And remember, every change you make will be for your own good and the good of the planet.

I realize that the number of topics this book covers may seem overwhelming. I, too, feel overwhelmed at times by all the different and complex issues that consumers need to address. Making major changes can be difficult and confusing, and the right answers aren't always clear.

I tried to make this book readable and as simple as possible, so I didn't go into long, detailed discussions of environmental and health issues. I gave just enough information that you'll understand why and how things need to change. And I've also included lots of recommended books, organizations, and publications that can supply you with details on those subjects you have the most interest in; there are even more excellent resources awaiting your discovery.

We are living in a time of tremendous transition. As consumers, our choices and areas of concern are changing rapidly. I won't pretend that this book will give you all the definitive answers, but I can promise lots of hands-on, practical information that will move us all in the right direction. I plan to update this book every two years, and I also publish a newsletter. So if you have any comments or suggestions, please feel free to write to me at P.O. Box 279, Forest Knolls, CA 94933.

1 ❧ Nontoxic, Natural, & Earthwise

A thing is right when it tends to preserve the integrity, stability, and beauty of the biotic community. It is wrong when it tends otherwise.

ALDO LEOPOLD

This consumer guidebook is for everyone who is interested in how the products we use in our homes every day affect the environment and our personal health. Both of these issues are intertwined, for making changes that benefit the Earth will also contribute to our own well-being.

A 1989 market-research poll reported that 89 percent of Americans are concerned about the environmental impact of the products they purchase, and more than half of all Americans say they decline to buy certain products out of concern over their environment effects. Another poll, by Media General and Associated Press, indicated that the vast majority of Americans would accept mandatory trash recycling, higher electric bills, and other inconveniences to help clean up the environment.

Yet for all our good intentions, we still need specific information on how to make the best choices and take the best actions to live in a way that is good for humans and good for the Earth; we need to know how to be nontoxic, natural, and earthwise.

The biggest challenge for all of us is figuring out what really is good. Many new products in the marketplace claim to be healthy or environmentally sound when they really aren't. In Canada, for example, one large supermarket chain has designated a group of nearly one hundred products as being "green," among them hazardous chemical cleaning products with a bitter additive that prevents children from taking a second, perhaps fatal, swallow. A nice safety feature, but good for the environment? No. Another example is biodegradable plastic trash bags that break down into smaller and probably more dangerous bits of plastic and which produce toxic waste even in their manufacturing.

In some cases, intentionally misleading marketing maneuvers are used to give the impression that a familiar product has been improved to be safe for humans and the environment, when in fact only one aspect of the product has changed. These types of products include such items as dioxin-free disposable diapers; these are still made from rain-forest paper pulp and end up at the dump, where they don't biodegrade. Because these products take one step in the right direction, they give us the illusion that every other aspect of the product is environmentally sound as well.

Governments worldwide are now legislating new regulations and developing "seal of

5

approval" programs to designate products that are, in some way, better for the environment. It has been estimated that at least twenty-five countries will soon have "eco-labeling" programs. Many of the newer programs being developed in Canada, Japan, Norway, Sweden, Holland, France, here in America, and in other countries are based on the West German Blue Angel system. In effect since 1979, this program has approved 2,250 products in 50 categories and has achieved household recognition among 80 percent of consumers.

The main problem with these programs, however, is that they are all based on promoting the best of existing products that are widely available in the marketplace. They do not set *new standards* that take a creative leap into the realm of truly healthful and environmentally responsible products. Products that are only a little bit better often are rewarded, while the best alternatives are totally ignored. And because there are few perfect products, a single seal by its very nature cannot indicate the wide range of environmental, health, and ethical issues that must be considered for every product.

Coming up with workable and realistic standards for evaluating products is a complex task. The health effects and environmental impact of products must be considered throughout a product's entire span of existence, from cradle to grave, as the environmentalists say. Every product we use begins as a piece of the Earth, be it mineral, plant, or animal. We must look at the methods by which these so-called "resources" are removed from the ecosystem (mined, grown, raised, or harvested) as well as the processes used to manufacture the products and distribution methods, as well as product use and disposal.

resource → factory → warehouse → store → home → garbage can → landfill
[Earth]   [Earth]

The truth is, some very major changes need to take place in industry and government in order for truly good products to be available on a mass scale. We as consumers can help this transition along by supporting the businesses that are producing the best products, and when these aren't available using the next best, until there is greater availability of these products to all. More importantly, we can raise our expectations and demands for products that are safe for us and for the Earth.

FIVE KEY ISSUES TO CONSIDER WHEN CHOOSING PRODUCTS

Being a consumer in today's marketplace can be a frustrating experience as we face a bewildering array of issues. To make things a little simpler, I look at five key issues that give me useful indicators of the health and environmental integrity of products:

1. Product ingredients
2. Packaging
3. Energy use
4. Compassion to animals
5. Social responsibility

Let's take a look at each of these as they relate to our everyday purchasing decisions.

1. Product Ingredients

In evaluating the ingredients a product is made from, we need to consider the environmental impact of obtaining the raw materials from which it is made, the impact of the manufacturing and distribution processes, possible toxic exposure while we use it, and what happens to the product once we've finished using it.

HOW PRODUCT INGREDIENTS AFFECT OUR HEALTH

While there certainly have been instances of unhealthy products throughout history, we live in a unique time, when potentially hazardous substances pervade almost every item we might purchase. The chemical age really took off in the late 1940s thanks to technology developed during World War II. Today, synthetic chemicals, made primarily from crude oil, are used in nearly every industry and consumer product.

In 1987, the United States produced almost 400 billion pounds of synthetic organic chemicals, over four pounds of manmade substances for every person in this country each day. Worldwide, about seventy thousand synthetic chemicals are in use, with nearly one thousand new ones added every year. Some of these chemicals are considered safe for human use, but the vast majority have not been tested fully.

Next to nothing is currently known about the human toxic effects of almost 80 percent of the more than 48,000 chemicals listed by the United States Environmental Protection Agency. Fewer than 1,000 have been tested for immediate acute effects, and only about 500 have been tested for their ability to cause long-term health problems such as cancer, birth defects, and genetic changes. A National Research Council study found that complete health-hazard evaluations were available for only 10 percent of pesticides and 18 percent of drugs used in this country.

Almost no tests have been undertaken to evaluate the possible synergistic effects that occur when chemicals are combined in food, water, or air, or when chemicals interact with other chemicals in your body. The few studies that have been done indicate that such effects increase risks dramatically. Because scientists do not understand the ultimate effects of these chemicals, the government cannot begin to effectively regulate their use.

The average American home is literally filled with products made from these inadequately tested synthetic substances; we use more chemicals in our homes today than were found in a typical chemistry lab at the turn of the century. When professionals use chemicals in industrial settings, they are subject to strict health and safety codes; yet we use these same chemicals at home without guidance or restriction.

As further research is done, we are finding that many household products we assumed to be safe are actually toxic. A multitude of common symptoms can be related to exposure to household toxics, such as headaches and depression. Even ordinary wintertime flu symptoms might not be flu at all, but a reaction to the combustion by-products that are released when you turn on your gas heater. Insomnia might be a response to the formaldehyde resin used on your bedsheets to keep them wrinkle-free. Developmental and behavioral problems in children have also been linked to exposures to household toxics.

Every year 5 to 10 million household poisonings are reported as the result of accidental exposure to toxic products in the home. Some are fatal, and most of the victims are children. These poisonings are the result of accidental ingestion of common household products that, despite warning labels, are not kept out of children's reach.

But immediate poisonings are not the only problem presented by toxic substances. They are slowly affecting all of us, whether we become ill today or not. Numerous common household products can cause cancer—not an immediate effect because carcinogenic substances take twenty years or more to act. Other household chemicals are mutagenic: they can change genetic material and lead to health problems. Still others are known to be teratogenic, and the high incidence of birth defects continues to remind us that not all household substances have been tested for this danger.

The word *nontoxic* appears on many consumer products, but it is misleading. According to the federal regulatory definition, *nontoxic* doesn't necessarily mean "not at all toxic" or "absolutely safe," but can mean, for example, that up to half of the laboratory animals exposed to the product through ingestion or inhalation died within two weeks. A product can also be called nontoxic if no serious damage occurred through eye or skin contact. These tests reflect only short-term health effects that may be associated with the product. Long-term or chronic effects are not considered.

Determining the toxicity of any product is difficult because there are so many factors to consider. It's easy to identify some substances that are inherently unsafe, such as the bacteria that cause botulism—or benzene, which has clear harmful effects. Whether or not a substance is toxic can depend on the quantity of the substance you are exposed to, the strength of the substance (a small amount of one substance might be much more harmful than a large amount of another), and the method of exposure (ingestion, inhalation, or skin absorption). Some substances are safe to inhale, but not to eat or rub on your skin; others are damaging regardless of how you are exposed. How frequently you are exposed can also play a part in toxicity; many substances have a cumulative effect in the body and do not cause harm until a certain concentration is reached over repeated exposure. In short, human toxicity is very complex; the more we stay away from toxics, the better off we will be.

HOW PRODUCT INGREDIENTS AFFECT THE EARTH

Ecotoxicity.   Beyond the issue of human toxicity is, of course, the question of whether the more than seventy thousand synthetic chemicals in use are *ecotoxic*—toxic to other species in the environment and to the functioning in the Earth as a whole living organism. What may be safe for hardy humans can kill or harm more delicate species, and ultimately disrupt the balance of our ecosystem.

For example, the molecules of which biodegradable detergents are made contain a benzene unit that, when bound together in a chemical compound, is relatively harmless to humans. But when the molecules break down in a lake or stream, the benzene unit can be converted into toxic phenol, which can kill fish. Similarly, malathion (a pesticide used to kill the Mediterranean fruit fly) showed no immediate human health effects in studies done after aerial spraying from helicopters over residential areas in California, but the deaths of thousands of fish and the loss of many beneficial insects was linked to the chemical.

The ecotoxicity of a substance is generally determined by evaluating the inherent toxicity of the substance, its persistence in the environment, and its tendency to bioaccumulate up the food chain.

Establishing the inherent toxicity of a substance has a lot to do with the organism that is receiving the exposure—a flower, a tree, an insect, a fish, a bird, a whale. We know a tremendous amount about toxic exposure to experimental laboratory animals,

The human body as a toxic-waste dump.   This table of toxic substances found in the adipose-fat tissue of humans was compiled by the National Adipose Tissue Survey of the Public Health Service (a department of the Environmental Protection Agency). This is only a partial list; the entire list includes over one hundred chemicals, and is still growing.

Compound	Possible sources of exposure	Frequency in test subjects
Styrene	disposable cups, carpet backing	100% of people tested had this chemical in their fat
1, 4-Dichlorobenzene	mothballs, house deodorizers	100%
Xylene	gasoline, paints	100%
Ethylphenol	drinking water	100%
OCDD (dioxin)	wood treatment, herbicides, auto exhaust	100%
HxCDD (dioxin)	wood treatment, herbicides, auto exhaust	98%
Benzene	gasoline	96%
Chlorobenzene	drinking water	96%
Ethylbenzene	gasoline	96%
DDE	pesticide in produce	93%
Toluene	gasoline	91%
PCBs	air, water, food pollution	83%
Chloroform	drinking water	76%
Butylbenzyl phthalate	plastics	69%
Heptachlor	termite control	67%
DDT	food and air pollution (pesticide banned for use in the U.S. in 1972)	55%

but beyond that, our knowledge is limited to the toxic effects on only a few species of birds and fish.

Toxic synthetic chemicals have a tendency to persist in the environment because their molecular structures do not break down under the normal conditions. Once these artificial compounds are made, the environment does not have any way to decompose them and recombine them into other usable substances, and they become "pollution." Because we humans have recently had a strong desire to make goods that last forever, we have been working against those natural systems that constantly work to break things down.

For example, PCBs (an oil additive) were developed soon after the use of electricity became widespread, because electrical equipment needed oil that didn't break down. Now we find that PCBs are toxic and we cannot escape them because they persist in the environment. This is true for most other manmade substances as well.

Naturally occurring substances, on the other hand, break down efficiently into basic elements within the natural functioning of the biosystem: they are safely *biodegradable*. Unfortunately, the word *biodegradable* is frequently applied to products that generally aren't (such as detergents or plastics) and almost never used for products that generally are (such as soap or paper). Everything willl biodegrade eventually; even manmade compounds will eventually break apart after thousands of years. The deciding factor regarding biodegradability, then, is not whether a material or substance will eventually break down, but rather how fast and how easily the environment can assimilate it.

Persistent substances that are not easily broken down accumulate in organisms low on the food chain, which in turn are eaten by predators higher up. As you go up the food chain, each higher predator has a greater and greater accumulation. Humans are at the top of the food chain and are thus one of the most bioaccumulative organisms. The result is that we all carry around high levels of chemicals in our fat that in the environment are at much lower levels, and pass this accumulation to our offspring.

But even with all the money that might be spent on future environmental tests, we may still never be able to determine ecotoxicity accurately. Substances can bioaccumu-late in one organism with no visible effects yet be fatally toxic to its predator. Chemicals can subtly interfere with plant and animal behavior or reduce the population of a spe-cies, affecting the whole predator-prey relationship of an ecosystem.

Obviously, we could initiate complex programs that include multispecies tests, eco-logical testing preserves, and mathematical ecosystem models to give us accurate data, but is the effort worth it? Perhaps the health and environmental costs of using toxic manmade chemicals have already exceeded their benefits.

In November 1986, Congress passed the Emergency Planning and Community Right-to-Know Act, which was designed to help America's communities deal safely and effec-tively with the many hazardous substances that are used throughout our society. When the first annual report of toxic releases into air, water, and soil came out in spring 1989, EPA officials were startled at the unacceptably high figures. Manufacturing plants alone *legally* released 13 billion pounds of toxic waste, and this didn't include waste from sewage treatment, government facilities, gas stations, dry cleaners, transportation, or small companies that discharge less than ten thousand pounds per year—nor did it include toxic waste produced by the mining industry, which, according to the Sierra Club, generates *twice as much hazardous waste each year as all other industries and municipal landfills combined.*

Unfortunately, at present we cannot evaluate ecotoxicity on a product-by-product basis because we don't, as consumers, have adequate information on the toxics released when specific products are made. And in over two years of research I have been unable to locate a reference book that describes the ecotoxicity of various chemicals. For now, we'll just have to assume that a product that is toxic for us to use is also toxic for the Earth, and that if a product contains a known toxic substance, its manufacture probably produces toxic waste.

Sustainable use of resources.   Another aspect of assessing product ingredients is determining whether they are *sustainable.* This word is rapidly emerging as the most useful term to describe an attitude toward living that we all must begin to adopt.

The dictionary defines *sustainable* as "able to keep going, able to endure." Yet we are using up at a rapid rate resources that took the Earth millions of years to create. We must acknowledge the limits of the resources of this planet and begin using them in a way that assures continuous supply, maintains the integrity and diversity of the ecosystem, and shows respect for life. Our laws, our business practices, and our consumer choices must support this view.

Oil, coal, and natural gas, along with metals and minerals, form the foundation of our present technological age—all nonrenewable resources that are quickly becoming depleted. Thousands and thousands of products of every description are derived, either directly or indirectly, from crude petroleum oil. Sixty-three percent of all crude oil used in the United States goes into the making of gasoline for our automobiles; the rest goes to make other fuels, lubricants, greases, paraffin wax, solvents, detergents, synthetic fibers (nylon, polyester, acrylic), plastics, paints, garden hoses, food additives, cleaning products, pesticides, nail polish, lipstick, shampoo, and countless other items we use every day.

At our current rate of usage, we have enough crude oil and natural gas worldwide to last only about fifty years, with domestic sources running dry in thirty years.

Our minerals are also being depleted, both in quantity and quality. The hematite ores we used to mine in Minnesota contained 60 percent iron, but we have exhausted these and now must use lower-quality taconite ores, with a 25 percent iron content. A similar pattern is occurring with many of the Earth's metals.

To reverse this trend, we can use nonrenewable resources such as fossil fuels and metals as little as possible; when we do use them, they should be recycled.

But what will really make a difference is to use more resources that can be replenished. If used correctly, renewable resources could supply most of our needs without harming the Earth. For instance, most products and industrial chemicals could be derived from plants instead of fossil fuels. (Of course, we still need to create nontoxic chemical alternatives and recycle or biodegrade any pollutants.) Growing these plants in a sustainable way would also help detoxify the Earth.

Unfortunately, many of our renewable resources are being used up much faster than they are being replaced by us or can be replaced by nature, both from overuse and from practices such as the clear-cutting of forests and chemical agriculture. Already we are losing rain forests and turning grasslands into deserts. Untold numbers of species are becoming extinct as we turn their natural habitats into rangelands for cattle or parking lots for another shopping center. Even though we have renewable resources available to us, practices such as sustainable forestry, organic farming, and recycling must become commonplace in order for them to provide a continuous supply of resources.

Most of the products we refer to as *natural* are made primarily from renewable resources. The word *natural*, as it relates to consumer products, is actually meaningless, since every consumer product is made from the natural resources of the Earth. Because, as yet, there is no legal definition, *natural* has been both overused and misused in labels on many products.

In a world where much of what we use in our daily lives is vastly different from its original form, the common understanding of the word *natural* is that it refers to basic substances and materials "not made from petrochemicals," as in natural fibers (even though most have petrochemical dyes and finishes), natural foods (no petrochemical additives, but most are sprayed and grown with petrochemical pesticides and fertilizers), or natural cosmetics (where ingredients are synthesized primarily from plants, not petrochemicals). *Natural* is also understood to mean the opposite of *man-made*, where the substance or material is found in Nature and is therefore more generally compatible with the human body and the entire ecological system.

In place of the word *natural*, new terms are now beginning to be used that are more descriptive of the actual processes used to obtain and maintain resource supplies:

• *Sustainable* is being used as in "sustainable forestry," where wood is harvested by gently thinning the forest and maintaining the ecosystem, or in "sustainable agriculture" where the ongoing fertility of the topsoil is continuously improved instead of depleted.

• *Organically grown* generally means grown or raised without the use of petrochemical pesticides or fertilizers and using methods that build and maintain soil fertility. It is primarily used for food products, although it should also apply to other types of products, especially natural fibers and ingredients used in personal-care products. Another, similar term used on many imported products is *biodynamic*, which is a specialized form of organic agriculture.

• *Wildcrafted* plants are, as the term suggests, gathered from their natural, wild habitat, often from remote, pristine areas. When wildcrafting is done sustainably with proper respect, generally only the branches or flowers from plants are taken and the living plant is left, or if it is necessary to take the whole plant, seeds of the plant are placed in the empty hole from which the plant was taken.

Recycled resources.   Recycled materials are another good choice for products. In addition to saving resources, recycling also reduces pollution and litter, conserves energy, saves on packaging costs, and lowers community disposal bills.

Recycled materials originate in previous consumer products. They are made either by breaking down the material into a pulp or liquid that can be re-formed (such as paper, plastic, or metal), or by refashioning materials for a new use (such as an irrigation hose made from old tires).

In order for product recycling to be successful, the recyclable items must first be collected; they must then be delivered to and used by a manufacturer to make a new product; and the new product containing the recycled material must be purchased by a consumer. A discard is a discard until somebody figures out how to give it a second life *and* a market exists to give that second life economic value.

When looking for recycled products, there are two symbols and terms to watch for. *Recyclable* products are made from virgin materials that *can be recycled.* You'll see this symbol most frequently on plastic and paper products. *Recycled* products are made from materials that *have been recycled.* To keep the cycle going, both types of products need to be purchased and recycled in balance. Recycling doesn't work if you buy only recyclable products and never buy their recycled counterparts.

R *Recyclable*   ♲ *Recycled*

Despite its clear advantages, in the past recycling has not been widely adopted, primarily because the material generated by recycling has often exceeded the needs of manufacturers buying recyclable materials.

But our perceptions about recycling are rapidly changing as a new definition of recycling is emerging: our trash is now being recognized as a valuable source of raw materials. Recycling will soon become mandatory across the nation. It's up to each of us as consumers to keep the recycling loop flowing by putting recyclables in and taking recycled products out.

While searching for recycled products, I was surprised to find out how many products made with recycled materials are not labeled as such. Manufacturers believe that consumers assume recycled materials are inferior in performance and appearance to virgin materials. Manufacturers need to be bolder about using the word *recycled* on their products, so we can find them easily, admire their good quality, and expand the market.

Another way products can be given a second (or third or fourth life) is by being repaired, rebuilt, restored, or reconditioned and then reused: typewriter and computer-printer ribbon cartridges can be reinked or refilled, tires can be retreaded, cars can get new engines, etc.

Some products can be remade through what is known as "remanufacturing," an industrial process in which products are reassembled using old restored parts and a few new parts to produce a unit that is of the same quality as, if not superior to, the old. Currently automotive parts, industrial equipment, office machinery, and appliances form the largest market of remanufactured products.

2. Packaging

Packaging really needs to be evaluated separately from the ingredients in products because good products may come in bad packages, and bad products can come in good packages.

A lot of attention has been placed on packaging lately because of our garbage crisis and because putting an old product in a new package is one of the easiest ways for manufacturers to jump on the environmental-marketing bandwagon.

Packaging is like a second product that surrounds the product you are buying. It protects the product, holds a label that gives us information, and acts as a potent marketing device. But does a toxic cleaning product become environmentally safe because it is packaged in a recyclable plastic container? No. Nor does a sugar-coated cereal grown by chemical agriculture help restore polluted land, air, and water because it is in a recycled paperboard box. Choosing good packaging is an excellent first step to take to help the environment, but keep in mind the suitability of the product inside it. I consider packaging a secondary issue and couldn't, in good faith, include a questionable product here just because it had a good package.

Fifty percent (by volume) of all our trash is packaging. And according to the U.S. Department of Agriculture, we spent $32.3 billion on food packaging alone in 1988, up from $28 billion in 1986. Packaging accounts for a little over 10 percent of the price you pay for food, which is more than the farmer gets for growing it!

Approximately 90 percent of our nation's glass, 50 percent of our paper, 30 percent of our plastic, 11 percent of our aluminum, and 9 percent of our steel is used solely for packaging. Packaging also accounts for 30 percent of all ink usage; in comparison, books use only 2 percent.

THE BEST PACKAGES

From an environmental point of view, the best package is no package. But obviously there are many instances where packaging is not only practical, but necessary. When you do buy packaged products, choose packages that are reusable, recycled/recyclable, or biodegradable.

• Glass bottles and jars are reusable, recyclable, and often made of recycled glass. Take a look at the label, too, and make sure it is paper; some glass bottles have plastic labels that will need to be removed and disposed of separately before recycling.
• Aluminum cans are recyclable, and most are made of recycled aluminum. Aluminum cans are easily recognizable because they are seamless, have a rounded bottom, and have a rim only at the top. Most soda and beer cans are made of aluminum, as well as most tuna cans. Recently aluminum cans are being used for other food products, too.
• Paper and paperboard can be recycled and are biodegradable. According to the American Paper Institute, about half of the boxes used for cereals, detergents, pasta, and cake mixes are made of recycled paperboard (you can tell because they have a gray interior). Many also have the "recycled" symbol somewhere on their labels.
• Cellophane is made from plant cellulose and is biodegradable.

MARGINAL PACKAGING

Sometimes it will be necessary to purchase products that are not in optimal packages.

• Tin cans are recyclable, and many are made from recycled cans. If you buy products in tin cans, be sure to avoid those that are lead-soldered, since the food inside absorbs lead from the solder. The FDA has estimated that approximately 20 percent of the lead found in the average person's diet comes from canned foods. Lead-soldered cans can increase the amount of lead in canned food by 200 to 300 percent—even more if the food is stored in the can after opening. Lead-soldered cans have a top and bottom rim and an obvious, prominent side seam, which may also reveal traces of solder on the outside. If you run your finger around the top or bottom of the can near the rim, you will feel the lumpy seam. *Lead-free* welded cans have top and bottom rims with a very flat, narrow seam and a blue or black line running down the middle. I'm happy to report that during a recent survey of my local supermarket, most of the cans I found were lead-free. But even with a lead-free can, watch out for gold-colored can linings, which contain a phenol resin that may be absorbed by the food.
• Recycled plastic or plastic labeled as recyclable. Buying recycled or recyclable plastic will help reduce the amount of garbage we produce and reduce the amount of crude oil needed to make new plastic. But recyclable or not, plastic has inherent disadvantages.

PACKAGING TO AVOID

Unfortunately, the manufacturers of many products—even some of the products listed in this book—are still using packaging that is not good for our health or the environment.

• Avoid any type of packaging made from plastic or polystyrene. While plastic packaging amounts to only 4.3 percent of total packaging, it contributes almost 4 billion pounds of toxic trash each year. Polystyrene cups used by U.S. residents each year would form a chain circling the earth 436 times.

• Avoid complicated multimaterials packages that cannot be recycled or reused, and won't biodegrade or burn (for example, the aseptic cartons made of paper, foil, and plastic that are being used for juice, soy milk, and other liquid products, or potato-chip bags that are made with plastic and foil).

Environmental Action publishes an excellent book on plastics packaging called *Wrapped in Plastics: The Environmental Case for Reducing Plastics Packaging.* After you read this, you'll never want to buy another plastic package.

3. Energy Use

Energy use should also be of prime consideration in choosing products because of its enormous impact on the environment. But because we have so little information on the type or amount of energy used to make any product, it can be difficult to include this in our decision-making process.

The overwhelming majority of products in the marketplace today use vast amounts of energy in the production and harvest of raw materials, the manufacture of the product, its transportation to consumers, and its disposal. Add to this the energy used for heating, lighting, and running machinery and equipment at the manufacturing plant, warehouse, and retail stores; the energy used for packaging and advertising; and the energy that we as consumers use in our cars to go to the stores and buy the product. The total energy cost to keep our whole system of consumerism going becomes astronomical. And this doesn't include the energy we utilize at home when we use the product.

Almost all of the energy we currently use in this country comes from fossil fuels (coal, oil, and natural gas), with a small amount from nuclear power. As long as we continue widespread use of these forms of energy, very few products can qualify as being truly environmentally safe.

The use of fossil fuels as energy sources is the largest cause of climate change and air-quality problems. About 50 percent of the greenhouse effect and most acid rain and smog are the result of the burning of fossil fuels in industry, homes, and motor vehicles. The mining and transportation of fossil fuels causes tremendous environmental devastation as well, with oil spills such as the 1989 incident in Alaska being only one in a long list of examples. Nuclear power threatens us all with the risk of horrendous accidents, and with extremely dangerous waste products that currently cannot be disposed of safely and may pollute the environment for tens of thousands of years.

There are renewable sources of energy that can be used instead, such as solar power, biomass (plant and animal waste used to make fuel), solar-derived hydrogen fuel, ecologically sized hydroelectric power, and wind power. Although these sources aren't completely pollution-free in their manufacture and use, they are *dramatically* better than fossil fuels and can be equipped with control devices when needed. Some smaller businesses are beginning to employ these sources, and products already exist that make it possible to use them to power our own homes.

We also need to use our energy as efficiently as possible. Buildings can be made to heat and cool using a fraction of the energy now consumed; efficient motors can dramatically cut the energy needed to run them; lights and appliances can be made that require much less energy to run; cars could be made right now that would get over one hundred miles per gallon. In fact, by using already existing energy-efficiency measures, we can cut our total energy use *in half or better without affecting production or service.* Energy efficiency is the most cost-effective way to meet our energy needs and dramatically reduce pollution.

It is difficult, however, to consider these things when we are choosing products. In order to evaluate the energy appropriateness of a product, we would need to know how much energy was used in taking raw materials, as well as in its manufacture, transportation, use, and disposal. Except for efficiency-in-use ratings for some appliances, this information is not usually available.

Right now we can reduce the amount of total energy spent on our purchases by:

* making our homes as energy efficient as possible;
* buying products that can be powered manually;
* buying products with the most efficient energy-use ratings;
* buying locally produced products and buying by mail to reduce energy used in transportation; and
* organizing our shopping to make fewer trips.

4. Compassion to Animals

The issue of animal rights is a sensitive one, and for many people it is a factor in choosing products. Even within the animal-rights and protection movement, there is significant variety in the goals people are working toward, and in their motivations for doing so. The most predominant issue is the use of animals in testing frivolous consumer products such as cosmetics. For some people compassion to animals extends to not using products with animal ingredients or ingredients that come from animals such as beeswax or lanolin, not eating animal flesh, not eating milk or eggs, not wearing leather, and even not wearing silk and wool or using feathers.

In the United States, 65 to 100 million animals of all sizes and species are being used each year as test subjects in the laboratories of cosmetics companies and producers of household products and in hospital, university, and commercial research centers. Drug and chemical companies are the major users of research animals, and oil refineries routinely test their factory waste on fish before dumping it in waterways.

Standard methods of safety testing include the Lethal Dosage 50 Test (where the animals are force-fed large doses of a substance until 50 percent of the animals die), the Draize Eye Irritancy Test (in which the eyes of immobilized rabbits are clamped open and exposed to possibly irritating substances), and the Skin Irritancy Test (where test substances are applied to the skin of immobilized animals and covered with an adhesive plaster). The suffering of these animals is often intense, and unnecessary.

While this practice comes from the good intention of protecting humans against possible toxic products, it is not required by law, and there is considerable controversy about whether the tests are even effective indicators of potential human harm. The fertility drug thalidomine, for example, was deemed to be safe after years of extensive laboratory experiments, but then was banned after human use showed that it caused grotesque birth defects. In medical journals worldwide, doctors have spoken out against the validity of using data on effects in animals to predict effects in humans. With new and more accurate alternatives to animal testing now available, and natural products that are inherently safe to use, there is no good reason to continue this practice for consumer products.

The term "cruelty-free" is frequently used to indicate products that have not been tested on animals, but I have found the use of this term to be inconsistent and frequently misleading. A major international chain of body-care stores, and many cosmetics companies, too, call their products cruelty-free, yet they contain FD&C dyes from coal tar that have in the past been tested on animals and found to be carcinogenic. Upon inquiring, I was told that the products themselves hadn't been tested on animals, but that the ingredients used in the products might have been tested on animals at some time in the past.

Another difficult choice arises when we consider the cruelty-free standard as it applies to the entire company and not just to one of its products. It has been brought to my attention that the company that makes Arm and Hammer baking soda does animal testing—not on the baking soda, but on other products. Should we therefore not use baking soda, even though it is a less toxic alternative to other chemicals that *have* been tested on animals? My favorite all-natural and cruelty-free shampoo, which I've been using almost ten years now, was pulled from the shelves of all my local natural-food stores, because the company was bought by another that tests some products on animals, although this shampoo hasn't been tested. One of the major brands of natural pet food is made by a company that tests on animals. Where do we draw the line?

Another aspect of cruelty to animals concerns how animals are treated while they are being raised. Most meat, poultry, and animal products on the market today come from factory farms, where animals are confined in dark, crowded quarters, fed a diet high in drugs and chemicals, and deprived of exercise and fresh air. These animals are highly stressed, deformed, and diseased, and this method of raising them produces much environmental pollution and waste of resources, as well as inferior food.

Many animal-rights activists point out that the ultimate cruelty is to kill an animal and that by using animal products we support the abuse of animals. They argue that animals are living, feeling creatures that should not be used as product resources.

There are no easy answers to these issues. As much as possible I have tried to include products in this book that have not been tested on animals. But I have chosen to include animal products in this book because I realize that everyone is at a different point on the path to creating a healthful, environmentally safe, and ethical lifestyle. Some of you have taken the step to choose cosmetics that haven't been tested on animals, but you still eat flesh foods. Others eat a vegetarian diet yet wear leather. Some of you eat only organically grown foods and are not vegetarians. Making changes in our lives is a process, and as a consumer advocate, my job is to report on products appropriate for every step of the process. If you choose to eat meat, I want to let you know how to choose and buy the best meat possible.

While attempting to live a completely cruelty-free lifestyle is admirable, in our society right now it is nearly impossible. If you put gasoline in your car or ride gas-powered public transportation, you are using a product whose toxic refinery effluent is routinely tested on baby fish. If you eat non-organically grown food the pesticides used in raising it have been tested on animals (if they've been tested at all). The film in the movies you watch is made from gelatin from cows. It is very, very difficult to do anything in this modern world that doesn't involve animal products or animal testing. We can do our best to not contribute to animal exploitation, keeping in mind that this is a goal we are making progress toward.

The greatest controversy arises when we consider whether we should use animals at all. I have tremendous respect for life—human, animal, plant, mineral—and the whole ecosystem of the living Earth. When one takes a view that *all* species are alive and must be respected and cherished, and that all have a responsibility to give as well as receive, avoiding animal products altogether seems out of balance. It seems possible to me that with a cruelty-free ethic one could, for example, provide a waterfowl preserve and collect feathers from the ground for pillows, or shear sheep in a loving manner. I have been to llama farms where I have seen the llamas naturally shed their wool. Llamas are very affectionate, and to collect their wool with a friendly brushing seems like a pleasure to me for both human and animal. If one raises animals and cares for them well, when an animal dies a natural death, is it wrong to use its skin for shoes, or to eat its meat? Granted, most animals are not being treated this way now, but they could be in the future.

A majority of the indigenous peoples worldwide and throughout history who live in a way that preserves the Earth use some animals for their survival. Interestingly, in tropical regions, where native people have abundant fruits and vegetables, they eat and use fewer animals; in colder climes, where there is less vegetation, they eat more animals. When native people take the life of the animal for their own survival, it is done with ritual respect; they kill only those animals they need for survival, and all parts are used (meat, skin, and bones). While we can certainly look to their example, we can also envision a world where we are in harmony with the Earth and do not kill animals at all.

But I cannot join those in the cruelty-free movement who suggest that synthetic manmade materials be used as a replacement for animal products. I can't, for example, advocate the use of carcinogenic vinyl made from polluting and nonrenewable resources as a viable alternative to leather. What appears to be necessary is the development of new products that utilize safe, natural, and nonpolluting materials as alternatives to animals. Purses, luggage, belts, and other items are now being made from cotton; even cotton canvas-and-rope espadrilles are available.

I also can't highly recommend cruelty-free products that contain petrochemical derivatives (artificial colors and others) that disqualify them from my definition of nontoxic; and they certainly aren't natural. While all animal lovers may not agree with my views, they will find a compassionate sentiment throughout this book. See Recommended Resources at the end of this book.

5. Social Responsibility

The last issue I look at when assessing products is social responsibility. This term has been used for more than twenty years now to describe companies that support human values and contribute in some way to the resolution of social issues, rather than being exploitative or destructive.

But social responsibility means different things to different people, and no one company will meet the personal ethics of every person. We all have issues we cannot compromise on, and others we want to support.

Social responsibility can include many things: employee profit-sharing or ownership,

THE VALDEZ PRINCIPLES

The *Exxon Valdez* oil-spill disaster prompted shareholder groups to organize the Coalition for Environmentally Responsible Economies (CERES), dedicated to using their economic clout to influence corporate behavior. CERES devised the Valdez Principles for companies to use as guidelines for becoming more environmentally responsible; you can also use these guidelines when choosing companies to buy products from or invest in.

• *Protection of the biosphere.* We will minimize and strive to eliminate the release of any pollutant that may cause environmental damage to the air, water, or earth or its inhabitants.

• *Sustainable use of natural resources.* We will make sustainable use of renewable natural resources, such as water, soils, and forests.

• *Reduction and disposal of waste.* We will minimize creation of waste. We will dispose of all wastes safely and responsibly.

• *Wise use of energy.* We will make every effort to use environmentally safe and sustainable energy resources.

• *Risk reduction.* We will minimize environmental, health, and safety risks to employees and communities.

• *Marketing of safe products and services.* We will sell products or services that minimize adverse environmental impacts and that are safe as consumers commonly use them.

• *Damage compensation.* We will take responsibility for the harm we cause to the environment.

• *Disclosure.* We will disclose to our employees and to the public incidents relating to our operations that cause environmental harm or pose health or safety hazards.

• *Environmental directors and managers.* At least one member of the board of directors will be a person qualified to represent environmental interests. We will commit management resources to implement these principles.

• *Assessment and annual audit.* We will conduct and make public an annual self-evaluation of our progress in implementing these principles and in complying with all applicable laws and regulations throughout our worldwide operations.

women and minority advancement, disclosure of information, honest marketing. It can also refer to giving to charity and community outreach programs, not exploiting the people or resources of other countries, not carrying military contracts, not supporting nuclear power, or not doing business in countries where there is racial inequality. It can also mean not polluting the environment, or not testing on animals. Some people choose to avoid doing business with companies that sell alcoholic beverages or cigarettes.

In evaluating the businesses in this book, I looked for companies that:

• show a respect for life and the environment in their choice of products and respect for workers in their employment policies;

• have a positive commitment to building a sustainable economy;

• disclose information on ingredients in products and manufacturing practices, and have honest marketing policies;
• employ with equal opportunity women, senior citizens, the handicapped, minorities, and others who may be discriminated against;
• do not make nuclear or other military weapons or utilize nuclear compounds in their products; and
• do not exploit the labor or resources of Third World countries, and support building sustainable Third World economies.

While I cannot guarantee that every business mentioned in this book meets all of these criteria, in some ways each one qualifies as being socially responsible because they all sell products that are either good for or cause minimal harm to the environment. Many of them are small businesses; I can't imagine them being owned by a nuclear-weapons contractor, though they may buy their light bulbs from one.

Social responsibility becomes more of an issue when you are buying from multinational corporations or investing your money. In the past few years many socially responsible investment funds have come available. I had originally planned to devote a chapter in this book to socially responsible investing, but as I started doing research, I found the topic so complex that I decided to leave it for a future edition.

HOW I RATE THE PRODUCTS IN THIS BOOK

In light of the five key issues I've discussed, the ideal product would:

• be practical and durable, well made, with a timeless design;
• satisfy a functional and/or aesthetic need, and not be superfluous clutter;
• be made from either:
  ◦ renewable plants grown and harvested in an organic, sustainable way (or recycled) and processed in a manner that is environmentally benign;
  ◦ animals raised in a way that is environmentally benign and in a place where they are treated humanely; or
  ◦ recycled nonrenewable petrochemicals and metals (as opposed to mining new nonrenewables);
• be healthful for humans to use, and be biodegradable or recyclable;
• be made with renewable energy and be energy-efficient in manufacture and use;
• be responsibly packaged or not packaged at all;
• not be tested on animals; and
• be provided by businesses with socially responsible business practices.

My personal goal as a consumer advocate is to connect interested consumers with producers and sellers of products that meet the highest standards for human health and environmental integrity. There are very few products today that meet all these standards, but we are beginning to see a trend in this direction.

Throughout the book I've tried to give as much information as I could to help you make your own decisions based on your personal needs and ethics. To simplify the very complex task of evaluating products, I have used a new set of "earthwise" standards, based on living in a way that is continuously harmonious with our planet and balances human and nonhuman life. Since protecting ourselves and maintaining the equilibrium of life on Earth are so intertwined, it is almost impossible not to consider them as one. These standards are more stringent than any I've seen, but I believe it is vitally important to move in this direction.

The standards are set as reachable ideals that we can encourage manufacturers to work toward. Naturally, there are many types of products for which there are very few examples, or none, that meet the highest standard, so I have also, when necessary, included some products that are moving toward the ideal. By recognizing clearly where today's products stand, we can better see where improvements need to be made.

1. Product Ingredient Ratings

The most workable system I could come up with evaluates product ingredients on a gradient. Few products are perfect at this point; most fall somewhere between good and bad. If the perfect product isn't available, we'll want to use the next best one, so I've provided lists of products with varying degrees of personal and environmental safety.

This general rating system can be applied to any type of product. In each chapter these ratings are redefined according to the type of products discussed. I've been consistent in the ratings, though, so you'll know, for example, that an earthwise product will meet the same standards whether it is apple juice or a sweater. For those products for which no brand name received the highest rating, I defined the standard anyway, so that we can clearly acknowledge where we are and where we need to go.

Please keep in mind that these ratings are very, very general; don't take them too literally. They are meant to be loose guidelines, not absolute descriptions, and are based on information I was able to obtain from manufacturers and retailers. Remember always to evaluate products for yourself.

⊕ *Earthwise products.*   These products are the safest for us to use and the best for the environment. They are made from renewable natural resources taken in a sustainable way, or made of recycled materials. They do not create pollution when grown or manufactured and can be disposed of safely, being biodegradable for composting, or recyclable. Earthwise products are truly good for the Earth and for us; they are not merely the least harmful that happen to be available. For many product types, no earthwise products are currently available.

Examples of existing earthwise products are organically grown food, unbleached recycled paper, and skin-care products made from organically grown ingredients. New earthwise products could include all sorts of products made from organically grown plants, wood obtained by truly sustainable forestry methods, and products made only from recycled materials.

❧ *Natural products.*   While I use the word *natural* with reluctance, it seems to be the best term since the products in this category are those that we commonly refer to as natural—natural foods, natural fibers, natural cosmetics. The primary components of these products are natural and renewable, but they are not taken in a sustainable or nonpolluting way that maintains continuous supply or fertility of the local ecosystem (as in "natural" foods that are grown with toxic synthetic fertilizers and pesticides). While they are generally considered safe for human use, these products may be tainted with residues of petrochemical contaminants, and they produce toxic waste in their manufacture. Also included in this category are synthetic formulations that are made from nonpetrochemical sources—generally, plants or minerals. Think of these products as safer to use than average, perhaps better for the environment than average, but still needing improvement.

⊕ *Nontoxic products.*   Recognizing that we don't yet live in the best of all possible worlds, there will be times when there is no earthwise or natural product available. The next best alternative is a product that is relatively safe for human exposure and/or is marginally better for the environment than average products for a particular reason. These products are generally made from synthesized compounds that are derived from nonrenewable petrochemicals; they may produce toxic waste in their manufacture and disposal.

2. Packaging Ratings

In this book I have considered packaging secondary to products. Because not all of the good products mentioned here come in good packages, I have indicated good packaging separately. I used this icon only when I had information about packaging; frequently this is not noted in descriptions in mail-order catalogs or from manufacturers.

⊞ *Good packaging.*   These products are packaged in glass bottles, aluminum or un-leaded-tin cans, paper, and/or cellophane.

3. Product Energy Ratings

Rating products for their energy use is difficult at this time, primarily because there is so little information available. I will be giving information only when it is voluntarily offered by the manufacturer.

⚡ *Renewable, nonpolluting energy.*   These products are produced with renewable, nonpolluting sources of energy. An example is a wool pillow made from wool processed in a solar-powered wool mill.

▣ *Energy-efficient in use.*   Because there are no data available to evaluate energy efficiency in manufacturing a product, this icon will be used only to indicate products that are energy-efficient during use.

4. Compassion to Animals Ratings

Animal issues are rated separately to allow you to make your own ethical decisions. These symbols are used only when I had information to support them. *Lack of these icons does not mean that the product was tested on animals or that it contains animal ingredients.*

☻ *Cruelty-free.*   These products are not tested on animals.

⊘ *No animal ingredients.*   These products do not, to my knowledge, contain animal ingredients of any kind.

5. Social Responsibility Ratings

Because social responsibility has so many different facets, it is beyond the scope of this book to give a rating for the social responsibility of any given company. However, if a company makes a point of its own particular social ethics, I'll note it in the Mail-Order Sources directory.

SIMPLE LIVING IS IMPORTANT, TOO

In addition to choosing products appropriately, it is earthwise to simplify our lifestyles and buy less.

Many of us were born into a society that encourages excessive consumerism. After World War II, in an effort to stimulate the economy, products were specifically designed to be disposable and of inferior quality to force consumption. In the mid 1950s, marketing consultant Victor Lebow wrote in the New York *Journal of Retailing*, "Our enormously productive economy demands that we make consumption a way of life, that we convert the buying and use of goods into rituals, that we seek our spiritual satisfactions in consumption . . . We need things consumed, burned up, worn out, replaced, and discarded at an ever-growing rate."

In contrast, in the natural world all living things take from the surrounding environment only what they need to survive, and no more. The resources of the Earth can support us if we each take what we need to maintain a simple standard of living and do our part to give back to the ongoing continuum of life on Earth.

The concept of simple living is not new. Simplicity is an old and universal ethic; most of the world's great religions and philosophies have advocated some form of this lifestyle. It has been a predominant aspect of American thought since the landing of the *Mayflower*, and it was practiced for thousands of years before that by Native Americans and other indigenous peoples throughout the world.

The simple life is not so simple to define, however, or to live. The best definition I've found is that simple living is living in balance between poverty and excess, in a way that supports rather than entangles our existence as whole human beings. It requires learning the difference between our needs and wants, the necessary and the superfluous, the useful and the wasteful; it requires preserving what is vital and eliminating the extraneous. It means choosing what is deeply satisfying over passing whims. It necessitates considering what is good for the rest of humanity and the Earth as well as what is good for ourselves. When we identify what our true needs are and how we can satisfy those needs, we can begin to pare away the excess.

Living simply involves consuming quantitatively less, but it is not self-denying; rather it is life-affirming. Many products that appeal to those who live simply are of high quality and value, handcrafted and aesthetically pleasing, and can be considerably more expensive than mass-produced disposable products—and often more fulfilling. Material simplicity can mean a pattern of elegant "quality over quantity" consumption that will fit, with grace and integrity, your own standards of daily living, whether you live in a city, suburbia, or a rural area. On the other end of the spectrum, simple living can also mean spending very little money buying second-hand goods at flea markets.

Simple living means not only fewer products, but also simpler products. A loaf of bread made by a local baker from organically grown whole wheat and packaged in a paper wrapper is a simpler product than a loaf of bread made in an out-of-state bakery from pesticide-contaminated bleached wheat, packaged in a plastic bag, and trucked a thousand miles to your supermarket.

It has been said that to live simply is to live in a way that is outwardly simple and inwardly rich. Without the distractions of buying, interacting with, and storing super-fluous objects, and without taking the time to make money to buy or maintain these objects, there is more time for personal and spiritual endeavors, and for family and friends.

I began to live simply for two reasons. When I realized that every virgin product I buy costs a piece of Nature, I wanted to respect life by taking as little of it as possible. Also, when I discovered that I spent most of my waking hours working, for the sole purpose of making payments on my credit cards and on my house (which I had to buy to store all the things I wasn't using anyway), I decided that the effort needed to maintain all my material goods wasn't worth the sacrifices I was making in other areas of my life. By the time I sold everything I really didn't need, everything I owned fit in an eight-by-ten-foot storage locker and two suitcases. I don't miss any of the things I no longer have, and simple living feels so good that even though I buy new things, I continue to look for ways to reduce even further the amount of material goods I own. My life now actually is one of higher quality, even though there is less quantity.

While there is no set formula for simple living, people who live simply tend to:

• lower their overall level of personal consumption and pay more attention to what is functional, durable, and aesthetically pleasing—and good for themselves, the rest of humankind, and the planet;
• reduce unnecessary clutter and complexity in their personal lives by giving away or selling possessions that are seldom used and could be put to use by others;
• feel a sense of identity through development of the full spectrum of their physical, emotional, mental, and spiritual potentials, rather than feeling a sense of identity through their material goods;
• have survival feelings associated with the Earth as the source of all that sustains their lives, rather than having survival feelings attached to money;
• develop personal skills that contribute to greater self-reliance, such as cooking, gardening, and the ability to fix things around the house;
• take responsibility for themselves, the rest of humanity, and the Earth;
• approach problems in a challenging and creative manner; and
• prefer smaller-scale, human-sized living and working environments that foster community.

Before you buy an item, ask yourself:

Do I really want this? I always ask myself if I will still want to buy whatever it is in an hour. If the answer is definitely yes, I buy it. If I'm not sure, I say to myself, "If I really want this, I can come back and get it." Most of the time I forget all about it. Now I buy only things that will make my life more efficient or pleasurable and that feel satisfying to have.

Is it good for my own well-being and good for the environment? Your desire to buy a pretty polyester blouse might diminish somewhat when you remember that polyester is made from a nonrenewable resource and is not biodegradable, and you already have plenty of blouses.

Living simply and wisely can be the basis for developing your own satisfying lifestyle, one that is in harmony with your own needs and the Earth's.

2 ✹ Air

> I tried to define the physical boundaries of the body and
> began to realize they are virtually undefinable, for the air
> around any air-breathing creature from a weed to a whale
> is obviously a vital part of it even while it is also part of
> other creatures. The atmosphere in fact binds together all
> life on Earth . . . It is plain to see that we all breathe the
> same sky . . . it pours through our lungs and blood in a
> few minutes, then out again to mix and refresh itself in
> the earth.
>
> GUY MURCHIE

Air is the breath of life. I marvel at how Nature, in its wisdom, created such a balance that the oxygen produced by plants sustains humans and the other creatures of land and sea, and how our exhalations sustain plants.

Air brings us sweet smells and provides a medium for sound to travel through while remaining so clear that we can see right through it. Without the swirl of clean air around us, life would cease to exist.

HOW OUTDOOR AIR POLLUTION AFFECTS OUR HEALTH AND THE EARTH

We all produce air pollutants as we go about our daily lives. Air has the capacity to cleanse itself of a certain amount of pollutants through wind and rain, but as we progress through the current industrial age, we are producing more pollutants than can be assimilated by the air systems of our Earth. The results are smog, the thinning of the ozone layer, acid rain, and climate changes, which ultimately affect our own health.

Outdoor Air Pollution

Air pollution can affect our health by damaging tissues of the respiratory system, by poisoning the blood, and by altering DNA within the cells. It can cause emphysema, bronchitis, asthma, cancer, birth defects, and increased incidence of upper respiratory disease and heart disease; it may also be linked to various cancers, childhood retardation, and sudden infant death syndrome. Air pollution causes an estimated fifty thousand to two hundred thousand premature deaths each year.

On a more subtle level, air pollution can cause watery eyes, breathing difficulties, headaches, cough, and frequent upper-respiratory problems. Aggravation of chronic heart and lung disease, general poor health, and shortened life spans have also been connected with air pollution.

The quality of outdoor air has been regulated since 1970 by the federal Clean Air Act. Since its passage, outdoor air has become somewhat cleaner, but we still have a long way to go. In a major study released in 1989, the U.S. Office of Technology Assessment (OTA) said that over one hundred cities in this country are failing to meet the clean-air standards that were set by Congress *nearly twenty years ago*. In a similar report in 1988, the Environmental Protection Agency said 150 million United States citizens—60 percent of our population—lived in areas with higher levels of ozone or carbon monoxide pollution than it considered safe.

A study of data on toxic substances found that 2.4 billion pounds of hazardous chemicals were released by industry into our air in 1987 alone—the most common ones being two solvents that are used in many consumer products, toluene and xylene. One EPA spokesman has stated that the actual amount of toxic air emissions may be three times this amount (7.4 billion pounds) if pollutants from autos, hazardous-waste facilities, and dry cleaners are included. Understanding this number is difficult. Suffice it to say that Henry Waxman, chairman of the House subcommittee that released the study, said, "The magnitude of the problem exceeds our worst fears."

SMOG

We all know smog to be a common result of outdoor air pollution. Smog is created when sunlight acts on gaseous emissions such as the ubiquitous formaldehyde, on nitrogen oxide gases and hydrocarbons from fossil-fuel burning, on oil-refinery emissions, on evaporated solvents, and on gases released when forests and plants burn.

While smog used to be synonymous with Los Angeles, it is now found in rural and remote areas as well as in many cities. It hangs over the North Pole in the winter as a noxious brown cloud and over the Grand Canyon *all year*. Smog is damaging the foliage of trees in our forests, while the EPA estimates that smog reduces crop yields by as much as 30 percent in some areas and costs billions of dollars in lost production.

OZONE DEPLETION

The ozone molecule makes up only 0.0005 percent of our atmosphere. If all the ozone surrounding our Earth could be put into a pure single layer, it would be only a quarter inch think—yet this thin shield is all that stands between us and the potential destruction of most or all life on the planet.

Ozone plays a number of important roles in regulating the earth's temperature and also acts as a protective layer in the upper atmosphere that absorbs most of the harmful types of ultraviolet radiation from the sun that would be harmful to humans, animals, and plants.

Increased ultraviolet radiation leads to increased skin cancer, eye damage, and aging and wrinkling of the skin—an 83 percent increase over the past seven years in the United States. A 10 percent depletion of the ozone layer could result in almost 2 million additional skin cancers each year. It also appears that increased ultraviolet radiation damages the human immune system even at much lower doses than are required to induce cancer.

Both land and aquatic ecosystems would be affected as well. Of over two hundred plants studied, mostly crops, 70 percent were found to be sensitive to ultraviolet radiation. Ultraviolet radiation can also penetrate up to sixty feet or more into the sea. Studies show that phytoplankton, one-celled microscopic organisms that float on the ocean's surface and on which the entire marine food chain depends, decrease their productivity by about 35 percent with a 25 percent reduction in ozone.

A 10 percent reduction in ozone is likely to lead to about a 20 percent increase in harmful ultraviolet radiation. There were ozone losses over the Antarctic of 50 percent or more during the spring of 1987; this ozone "hole" alone covers 10 percent of the Southern Hemisphere and seems to be spreading. Ozone over the Arctic is being depleted up to 6 percent each winter. Worldwide, ozone levels fell roughly 2 percent between 1969 and 1986.

The ozone layer in our upper atmosphere is being depleted by manmade chlorine- and bromine-based chemicals that slowly rise from the Earth. As catalysts, chlorine and bromine destroy ozone without being altered themselves, and since many of these chemicals—particularly chlorofluorocarbons (CFCs)—remain in the atmosphere for over one hundred years, they can destroy a lot of ozone throughout their lifespan. One single molecule of chlorine can destroy 100,000 molecules of ozone. There are enough CFCs, for instance, embedded in one Styrofoam beer cooler to destroy all the ozone over an area as big as twenty football fields.

Chlorine-based chemicals account for about 80 percent of ozone depletion, and are found in such products as home and car air conditioners, refrigerators, foamed plastics (including cushions, carpet padding, foam insulation, and food containers), cleaning solvents, fire extinguishers, and hospital sterilants.

Volatile bromine compounds, which are about twenty times more potent than chlorine and currently account for about 20 percent of ozone depletion, are released from leaded gasoline, oil and gas recovery processes, fire extinguishers, and agricultural use. Another potentially large source may be the chlorine and bromine used in sewage and water treatment, swimming pools, spas, and hot tubs, and cleaning products.

The worst *known* stratospheric-ozone destroyers are CFCs (used in foams, aerosols, refrigeration, air conditioning, or as solvents), carbon tetrachloride (used to manufacture CFCs and as a pesticide), methyl chloroform (used as a cleaning solvent), and halons (used in fire extinguishers). In 1987, global production of these chemicals came close to 3 billion pounds, virtually all of it destined to end up in the atmosphere.

Unless we stop using them now, human-made chemicals are predicted to destroy enough ozone to allow at least 5 to 20 percent more ultraviolet radiation to reach populated areas of the Earth within the next forty years.

If all currently known technical control measures were used, total CFC and other ozone-destroying gases could be reduced by about 90 percent. The National Toxics Campaign warns: "The difference between stopping these chemicals by the year 2000 and stopping them now may be the difference between a minor global crisis and a completely unlivable planet."

ACID RAIN
Acid rain (which actually includes acid snow, fog, and dew) is also causing widespread environmental damage.

Acid rain occurs when sulfur dioxide and nitrogen oxide gases, which are emitted when fossil fuels are burned by factories and motor vehicles, undergo a chemical transformation in the atmosphere. Atmospheric reactions between formaldehyde and various hydrocarbons also seem to play a part in producing acid rain.

The average rain in the eastern United States is now as acidic as tomato juice, with nine thousand lakes and twenty-three hundred miles of streams estimated to be already affected. The average acidity of rainfall over much of the Northeast is about ten times normal.

Many other parts of our country are affected as well. In the Southeast, from Florida through Kentucky, rainfall having five to ten times the normal acidity has become increasingly frequent. In Minnesota and Wisconsin, thousands of lakes are in danger. In the Rocky Mountains, precipitation is increasingly found at acidities five times normal or greater. Mountain lakes in both Colorado and California are also becoming acidic, with potential loss in tourism and recreation industries as well as to ecosystems. Southern California has experienced acid fog, with acidity one thousand to two thousand times normal conditions.

In addition to damaging our aquatic life, acid rain has other deleterious effects. Acid waters running through soil tend to pick up increased amounts of aluminum; this interferes with the absorption rate of water and nutrients by tree roots. Acid rain is highly suspect as the cause of a 50 percent reduction in the growth rate of spruce trees in the United States between 1965 and 1979, and has damaged nearly one quarter of Europe's forests. The maple-syrup industry is facing possible extinction within the next ten to twenty years because of acid rain. Acid waters also tend to leach out important soil nutrients such as calcium and magnesium. Both the National Technology Policy panel have expressed concern that acid rain may cause long-term permanent damage to our soils.

Tourism, agriculture, and fishing are damaged, along with aquatic, forest, and soil ecosystems. Acid rain is also responsible for widespread corrosive damage to historic buildings and monuments—causing an estimated $20 billion in damage each year in Europe in this area alone.

CLIMATE CHANGES

Many scientists are warning that we are headed for an increase in average temperature, called the greenhouse effect, in which the gaseous pollution we are creating causes heat to be trapped in the atmosphere. Others say this effect is temporary and that our pollution is accelerating an ice age.

Whichever way it may go, WorldWatch Institute, in one of its publications, *State of the World 1989*, warns that the threat of severe climate change "can be compared with nuclear war for its potential to disrupt a wide range of human and natural systems . . ." This can include major shifts in weather patterns and agricultural zones, severe droughts, and rising sea levels that could drastically flood coastal areas.

Like smog and acid rain, our climate-change problems are mainly due to the burning of fossil fuels (coal, oil, and natural gas) and the destruction of our forests and plant life.

During the twenty-three thousand times we inhale each day, our lungs take in thirty-five pounds of oxygen. All of this oxygen comes from plants, much of it from forests and ocean algae. Forests and plants act as purifiers of the air we breathe by removing excess carbon dioxide and other gases. They also play key roles in maintaining worldwide weather patterns, creating rain, preventing soil erosion, and maintaining a diversity of wildlife. When we overcut forests and do not replenish them fully as mixed-species forests, the way nature grows them, we not only eliminate all these vital functions, we also release the carbon in the trees (either through burning or decay) back into the atmosphere as carbon dioxide. In the last fifty years alone, we have destroyed about 50 percent of our forests all over the world, and the pace of destruction continues to increase.

WHAT WE CAN DO ABOUT OUTDOOR AIR POLLUTION

While much needs to be done to change government policies and industrial practices to help clean up our outdoor air, there are many things we as individuals can do.

• Plant trees and regreen the Earth. To help restore our planet, set a goal of planting at least ten trees per year for the next ten years, or support tree-planting organizations (see Recommended Resources).
• Burn fewer fossil fuels (see Chapter 4). Drive less and take public transportation, use the best emissions-control devices available, and when you buy a car, buy one that's fuel-efficient. Try to make your home and place of work at least 50 percent more energy efficient.
• Use renewable energy rather than fossil fuels (see Chapter 4).
• Reduce use of coolants. One of the greatest releases of ozone-destroying CFCs occurs when coolants escape from refrigerators and air conditioners when they leak, are repaired, or are junked. Have your car, home, or office air conditioner and refrigerator-freezer checked periodically for leaks, and make sure the coolant is recycled when the appliance is repaired, recharged, or scrapped. Do not use Freon coolant for appliance or auto repairs.
• Try not to use your car air conditioner. If you do, replace the air-conditioner hose in your automobile every three years. For repairs, find an auto mechanic who has coolant-recycling equipment, or at least make sure your mechanic drains the coolant into bottles rather than letting it evaporate. When choosing a car, look for lighter exterior and interior colors, side vent windows, window glazings that slow solar absorption, sunroofs, and solar ventilation systems, which can reduce heat and lessen or eliminate the need for air conditioning.
• Use dry-chemical alternatives to CFC-based fire extinguishers.
• Don't buy toys such as CFC-propelled party streamers and horns.
• Use nonfoam alternatives for building insulation, natural fiberfill for cushioning, and paper for packaging and food containers.
• Use alternatives to chlorine cleaning products (see Chapter 7).

HOW INDOOR AIR POLLUTION AFFECTS OUR HEALTH

The level of toxic pollutants inside many modern buildings and houses is often higher than that of the air outside—sometimes even higher than the maximum allowable outdoor standards.

In one study in New Jersey, researchers chose 350 people and outfitted them with special test monitors that would continuously sample the surrounding air and measure their exposure to twenty separate organic chemicals. At the same time, they also monitored one hundred backyards for outdoor levels of pollutant. When they looked at the test data, they found that people living farther away from polluting industries did not show any less personal exposure than people who lived closer. The most important factor was *indoor* air pollution. In some homes pollutant levels were *one hundred times higher* than outdoors.

This study also pointed out another important fact: what we breathe travels throughout our bodies. Samples showed residues of gasoline on the breath of some people hours after they had filled their gas tanks, while a short visit to the dry cleaner resulted in tetrachloroethylene on the breath. Even taking a hot shower elevated breath levels of chloroform, which is released in the stream of chlorinated water.

Indoor air pollution has become a problem in the past decade because of the combination of sealing up our homes for energy efficiency without appropriate air-exchange equipment, and filling them with more and more toxic products. Particleboard furniture and cabinets, cleaning products, pesticides, plastics and synthetic fibers used in furnishing and construction, carpeting, drapes, scented items, gas appliances and heaters, and many other common items made from petrochemicals all contribute to an increase in indoor air pollution.

At present, many government agencies and private firms are studying indoor air pollution, its effects, and what to do about it. In 1988, the EPA released findings from a five-year study of ten buildings that identified nearly five hundred harmful chemicals— yet still no regulations are in effect to control these substances.

WHAT WE CAN DO ABOUT INDOOR AIR POLLUTION

• Avoid plastics entirely, if possible, as they are a major source of indoor and outdoor pollution. The plastics that create the least air pollution are hard plastics. To test plastic, try to bend it; use only those kinds you cannot bend or that would break if you applied enough pressure. If a plastic substance is at all pliable, it's giving off air pollutants. Remember, too, that plastic is made from a nonrenewable resource, creates toxic waste in its manufacture, does not biodegrade, and often cannot be recycled.
• Increase ventilation. Many people live and work in sealed buildings where there is little outside air. Open the windows (if you can) as much as the weather allows. If you need more ventilation but don't want to lose heat, use an air-to-air heat exchanger (see Chapter 4).
• Reduce pollutants at their source. Cut down or eliminate entirely:

  ° scented beauty and hygiene products
  ° cleaning products made from synthetic chemicals
  ° pesticides
  ° synthetic fibers and fabric finishes
  ° office supplies with volatile ingredients
  ° household furnishings made from synthetic materials
  ° gas appliances and heaters
  ° building materials made from formaldehyde

AIR FILTERS

Personal air filtration for your home or office is a relatively new field, and advances continue to be made. Yet air filters aren't the answer to indoor air pollution. No filter I have found can produce air such as might be found along a sparsely populated coastline or in the high mountains or in some desert areas. To act in harmony with the Earth, we would ideally reduce the amount of pollutants we produce as much as possible, so there would be no need to gather toxic pollutants in filters and then dispose of them somewhere else in the ecosystem.

There are times, however, when we need to protect our own health, and using an air filter makes good sense. Air filters are best used:

• When you are driving or riding in an automobile (this is probably the best use of an air filter).
• When all major sources of indoor air pollution have been removed and significant levels of pollutants are still present because of outdoor air pollution, or materials used inside the building (if this is the case, you might consider moving).
• When you absolutely have to use a toxic chemical and you want to give yourself some measure of protection.
• When you are very sensitive to all sorts of air pollutants (from chemicals to pollen) and cannot move someplace where there is outdoor air free from these contaminants.

Air filters can be purchased as portable models, or you can have them built into your central heating/air-conditioning system. An important point to remember is that the cleaning capabilities of any portable unit are generally limited to the air in the room in which it is being used. And as with air-conditioning, air cleaners are most effective if no outside air is entering from adjacent rooms, open windows, or a central air systems.

CHOOSING AN AIR FILTER THAT'S RIGHT FOR YOU

There is no one "best" air filter that is most appropriate for every person and every use. When evaluating air filters, you will want to consider:

1. Which pollutants you want to remove from the air and the effectiveness of pollutant removal.
2. The area you want to remove the pollutants from.
3. The cost of the filter.
4. The aesthetics of how the filter looks, and how much noise it makes.
5. What you need to do to maintain the filter.

WHAT'S IN YOUR AIR?

Air pollutants fall into two classes: gases such as misty vapors of volatile chemicals such as formaldehyde, plastics, paints, solvents, pesticides, and perfumes; and particulates such as bits of pollen, dust, mold, and animal dander. If you need to remove particles from the air, you'll proably know it because you'll be sneezing or you'll have other allergic symptoms. You'll need to remove gases if you have any of the products mentioned in this book as emitting volatile toxic chemicals.

If you want to have the air in your home tested, look in the Yellow Pages under "Laboratories—Analytical." Ask these places what testing they do and get estimates from several of them, because prices and services vary considerably.

There are also home tests for specific substances such as formaldehyde. These are available via mail order from *Allergy Resources, The Allergy Store, Baubiologie Hardware,* and *SelfCare Catalog.*

To remove pollutants, air-cleaning devices use one or more of four types of cleaning methods: activated carbon, mechanical filtration (HEPA), electrostatic filtration (precipitators, electret), and negative-ion generation. Each method works in a different way, and each removes different pollutants.

Activated Carbon

Activated carbon used in filters works by *adsorption,* a process by which pollutant gases are attracted by and stick to the carbon. There are several types of activated carbon; coconut-shell carbon is generally considered to be the highest quality.

In addition to plain activated carbon, filters can contain other filter media that have special qualities. Some coconut-shell carbon is impregnated to increase efficiency in removing formaldehyde. CI-impregnated carbon, also known as Formaldezorb, uses a copper-nickel salt; Formaldepure uses nonmetal salts. These special carbons can increase formaldehyde adsorption to up to 90 percent and beyond.

Most filters manufacturers recommend that carbon beds be at least one inch thick; anything less than that is practically useless. The small air cleaners found in most department, drug, and discount stores are inexpensive and convenient, but do not contain sufficient carbon to effectively clean the amount of air that passes through.

When choosing a carbon filter, also take into consideration the placement of the motor, which can produce objectionable fumes of its own. Some filters have the motor placed on top; others are inside. Motors can be lubricated, if necessary, with jojoba oil, available in natural-food stores.

In some activated-carbon units, the carbon is combined with Purafil, a nontoxic odoroxidant made of activated alumna impregnated with potassium permanganate. Purafil works by both absorbing and adsorbing gases and then destroying them by oxidation. This combination is more effective than carbon alone, but not as effective as impregnated carbon.

Mechanical Filtration

Mechanical filters work by trapping particles. High-Efficiency Particulate Arrestance (HEPA) filters are rated at 99.99 percent efficiency for particles .3 microns in size (dust, pollen, and plant and mold spores). Developed by the Atomic Energy Commission during World War II to remove radioactive dust from industrial exhausts, they are paperlike filters made of randomly positioned fibers that create narrow passages with many twists and turns. As the air passes through, particles are trapped, clogging holes and making the grid smaller, which enables the filter to be even more efficient with ongoing use. One disadvantage is that HEPA filters are generally bonded with polyvinyl acetate plastic, although nonpetrochemical HEPA filters are also available.

Electrostatic Filtration

Electrostatic filters attract particles by electricity. This is accomplished either by way of an electronic air cleaner (electrostatic precipitator) or with electronically charged plastic fibers (electret).

Generally, neither type is recommended. Electrostatic precipitators are rarely more than 80 percent efficient and can quickly drop to 20 percent efficiency. They also produce ozone and positive ions, and must be cleaned often with volatile petrochemical solvents. Electret, on the other hand, is extremely efficient for removing particles, but is a petrochemical product and gives off a strong odor.

Negative-Ion Generation

The biological advantages of negative ions are well known, but because negative-ion generators and ionizers cannot be sold to promote these health effects, they are often advertised as air cleaners.

As air cleaners, however, they are quite limited. The negative ions produced by the generator will precipitate only certain small particles. While practically useless for dust or pollen, these generators are very effective at removing the particles found in cigarette smoke and smog, cleaning the air so that it becomes clear and odorless. What they cannot remove are the invisible, odorless toxic gases that are also present in cigarette smoke and smog.

Negative-ion generators and ionizers should be purchased for their health benefits or for use with activated-carbon filters for removal of cigarette smoke, but not as broad-spectrum air cleaners. One problem with ion generators in the past has been a buildup of black particles on the walls and furniture around the generator. Newer

ionizers have built-in collection systems to trap these particles.

Room Size

Each unit is designed to effectively remove pollutants from the air contained in a certain measured space. The amount of filter media the unit contains, the rate at which the air flows through the media, the size of the motor, and all other aspects of the unit's design are geared to the designated room size. You may need several filters to continuously clean the air throughout the house, or a unit portable enough to be easily moved from room to room.

Price

In general, prices correspond to room sizes and the amount of filter media used. The more you get, the more you pay. But bigger is not necessarily better if it's more than

COMPARISON OF POLLUTANTS REMOVED BY AIR FILTERS

	Activated carbon	Mechanical filtration (HEPA)	Electrostatic filtration	Negative-ion generation
Particles (larger than .01 microns), e.g., asbestos dust, pollen, mold, animal hair, tobacco-smoke particles	No	Yes	Yes	No
Gases (smaller than .001 microns)				
Ammonia	Some	No	No	No
Carbon monoxide	No	No	No	No
Formaldehyde	Some	No	No	No
Lead	Yes	No	No	No
Nitrogen oxide	Some	No	No	No
Pesticides	Yes	No	No	No
Phenol	Yes	No	No	No
Plastic emissions	Yes	No	No	No
Sulfur dioxide	Some	No	No	No
Tobacco-smoke gases	Yes	No	No	No
Other organic chemicals	Yes	No	No	No

you need. Expect to pay around two hundred dollars to clean the air in your car or a small room, and up to one thousand dollars or more to have a unit built into your central air system.

Aesthetics

Style is an important factor in choosing an air filter because all portable units have to be sitting out in the room in order to be effective. Most filters are nondescript painted metal boxes or cylinders, but manufacturers are beginning to make them more aesthetically pleasing.

Metal housings are preferable and are standard on the units listed in this book. I don't recommend plastic housings because these often release a plastic smell of their own into the air.

The level of noise the motor makes is also a consideration. It's useless to have a filter if you don't run it because it's too loud. A filter with variable speeds will allow you to adjust noise levels as well as air flow.

Maintenance

Activated carbon and other filter materials must be changed regularly. How often you'll need to change them depends on how many hours a day the filter is used and how polluted the air is, so it is impossible to predict how long filter media will last. Manufacturers estimate that activated carbon will last about two thousand hours, or twelve hours per day for six months; under normal use, the carbon should last six to nine months. Prefilters are generally changed more frequently, and HEPA filters last for several years.

HOMEMADE ALTERNATIVES

Instead of a mechanical air filter, you can use nature's air filters—plants. Tests done by NASA have shown that common houseplants remove pollutants as they go through their natural process of photo-

synthesis; while plants draw in carbon monoxide, they also pick up airborne pollutants through small openings called stomates in the leaves. They are very effective at removing gases such as formaldehyde, carbon monoxide, carbon dioxide, benzene, cigarette smoke, and ozone, which are harmful for us to breathe but are a gourmet meal for a plant. Aloe vera, bamboo palm, common chrysanthemums, dracena palms, philodendrons, golden pothos, spider plants, and scheffleras make the best air filters. The only drawback is that it takes about fifteen to twenty good-sized plants to adequately purify the air in an average home, but you may enjoy the greenery.

At the Store/By Mail

Purchase an effective air filter by mail.

Activated-carbon air filters

Airoex Professional Series Model 45 (Aireox Research Corporation). Contains 4 pounds carbon or Purafil to clean a 12-by-12-foot room. Two speeds. Cylindrical style with environmentally safe finish on a metal housing. Weighs 14 pounds; measures 10 by 10 by 13 inches. *Aireox Research Corporation, The Allergy Store, N.E.E.D.S., Nigra Enterprise.*

Foust 160DT (E. L. Foust Company). Contains 2 to 3 pounds carbon or Purafil to clean a 12-by-12-foot office cubicle. Single speed. Cylindrical style with nickel-plated, painted steel housing. Weighs 10 pounds; measures 7 by 7 by 10 inches. *The Ecology Box, E. L. Foust Company, Environmental Purification Systems, The Living Source, N.E.E.D.S.*

Foust 160R2 (E. L. Foust Company). Contains 7 pounds carbon to clean a 20-by-20-foot room. Single speed. Cylindrical style with nickel-plated, painted steel housing. Weighs 18 pounds; measures 10 by 10 by 22 inches. *The Ecology Box, E. L. Foust Company, Environmental Purification Systems, The Living Source, N.E.E.D.S.*

*Activated-carbon
and particulate air filters*

AllerMed Airstar 5C (AllerMed Corporation). Contains 2 pounds carbon and a .3-micron HEPA filter to clean a 15-by-18-foot room. Also contains a negative-ion generator. Three speeds. Box style with baked-enamel steel housing. Weighs 19 pounds; measures 9 by 12 by 16 inches. *The Allergy Store, Allergy Relief Shop, Allergy Resource, AllerMed Corporation, Baubiologie Hardware, The Ecology Box, The Living Source, N.E.E.D.S., Nigra Enterprises, SelfCare Catalog.*

AllerMed CompanionAire (AllerMed Corporation). Contains impregnated carbon and a 1-micron particulate filter to clean an office cubicle. Three speeds. Box style with baked-enamel steel housing. Weighs 8 pounds; measures 7½ by 12 by 8 inches. *AllerMed Corporation, Baubiologie Hardware, Nigra Enterprises, SelfCare Catalog* (sold as SelfCare's desktop unit).

· AllerMed MartinAire VH300 (AllerMed Corporation). Contains 4 pounds Formaldepure and Carbomed and a .3-micron HEPA filter to clean a 15-by-15-foot room. Variable speeds. Box style with unpainted stainless-steel housing. Weighs 35 pounds; measures 12 by 12 by 24 inches. *Allergy Relief Shop, Allergy Resources, AllerMed Corporation Baubiologie Hardware, The Living Source, Nigra Enterprises.*

AllerMed Space Saver 400 (AllerMed Corporation). Contains 13 pounds carbon/Hydestop and a .3-micron HEPA filter to clean a 20-by-40-foot room. Variable speeds. Box style with unpainted stainless-steel housing with casters. Weighs 58 pounds; measures 12 by 25 by 27 inches. *Allergy Relief Shop, AllerMed Corporation, Nigra Enterprises.*

*Activated-carbon
and plant filter*

Bio-Safe PlantFilter (Bio-Safe). Contains a philodendron plant in a pot with a mixture of activated carbon and potting soil, along with a small fan. The plant leaves and roots and the charcoal act synergistically to remove large volumes of gas pollutants. One PlantFilter will filter the air as well as fifteen to nineteen regular plants. Recommended for an 18-by-18-foot room. Initially, the plant measures 2 by 2 feet; after one year it grows to about 43 inches and becomes even more efficient. *Bio-Safe.*

Auto air filters

Aireox Professional Series Model 22 Car (Aireox Research Corporation). Contains 2 pounds carbon. Two speeds. Cylindrical style with environmentally safe finish on steel housing. Weighs 8 pounds; measures 10½ by 10½ by 8 inches. *Aireox Research Corporation, The Allergy Store, N.E.E.D.S., Nigra Enterprises.*

AllerMed Auto Air 2 (AllerMed Corporation). Contains 2 to 3 pounds carbon. Two speeds. Square box style with baked-enamel steel housing. Weighs 10 pounds; measures 10 by 10 by 8½ inches. *The Allergy Store, Allergy Resources, AllerMed Corporation, Baubiologie Hardware, The Living Source, N.E.E.D.S., Nigra Enterprises, SelfCare Catalog.*

Foust 160A (E. L. Foust Company). Contains 2 to 3 pounds carbon. Single speed. Cylindrical style with nickel-plated and painted steel housing. Weighs 9 pounds; measures 9 by 7 by 16 inches. *Allergy Relief Shop, The Ecology Box, E. L. Foust Company, Environmental Purification Systems, The Living Source, N.E.E.D.S.*

Whole-house air filters

AllerMed Central System 2000 (AllerMed Corporation). A freestanding unit that can be used with gas or electric central air units. All-metal construction. You can run the unit independently or with heater or air-conditioner. Contains approximately 80 pound carbon and a .3-micron HEPA filter. *AllerMed Corporation, Nigra Enterprises.*

AllerMed Chairman 800 (AllerMed Corporation). Contains 10 pound carbon/ Hydestop mix and a .3-micron HEPA filter to clean a whole house (will clean up to 1,500 square feet in an open area, but will not pull air from hallways or adjacent separated rooms). Has slot for an extra tray of carbon. Variable speeds. Tall, rectangular style with unpainted stainless-steel housing with caster. Weighs 100 pounds; measures 25 by 24 by 29 inches. *Allergy Relief Shop, The Allergy Store, Aller-Med Corporation, The Living Source, Nigra Enterprises.*

CRSI 600H (Control Resource Systems). A freestanding unit that can be easily attached to gas central-air units. You can run the unit independently or with a heater or air conditioner. Contains a 3-inch bed or carbon and a .3-micron HEPA filter. *Environmental Purification Systems.*

Thurmond Air Quality Systems (Thurmond Air Quality Systems). Offers two units: IAQ-2000-DX heats, cools, and purifies air; IAQ-2000-F filters air only (can be retrofitted to your existing central gas or electric system). Both contain 52 to 60 pounds of your choice of carbon and a high-efficiency particulate postfilter (optional .3-mcron HEPA filter). Aluminum housing can be custom coated. *The Living Source, Thurmond Air Quality Systems.*

AIR FRESHENERS AND ODOR REMOVERS

Harmful ingredients: Aerosol propellants, colors, cresol, ethanol, formaldehyde, fragrances, naphthalene, phenol, xylene.

Air fresheners work in one of several ways: by using a nerve-deadening agent to interfere with your ability to smell, by coating your nasal passages with a unde-tectable oil film, by deactivating the offensive odor, or by covering up the odor with another. Most air fresheners do nothing to freshen the air; they only add more pollutants.

HOMEMADE ALTERNATIVES
• Keep things clean.
• Open the windows. This will also help reduce any buildup of toxic fumes that may be in your home.
• Empty the garbage frequently and clean the can when needed. One-half cup borax sprinkled in the bottom of the garbage can will help inhibit the growth of odor-producing molds and bacteria
• Distribute partially filled bowls of baking soda or white vinegar discreetly around the room to absorb odors.
• Make an air-freshening tea by adding herbs to boiling water to release their scent.
• Make citrus pomanders. Pierce a thin-skinned orange, lemon, or lime with cloves (if the cloves break while trying to pierce the skin, make small holes with a toothpick first). When the entire fruit is covered, roll in a mixture of 1½ teaspoons orris-root powder and 1½ teaspoons ground cinnamon. Wrap in tissue and store in a closed drawer, cabinet, or closet.

At the Store/By Mail
Buy herbal mixtures, essential oils, or one of the natural air fresheners listed below at your natural-food store.

⊕ *Earthwise air fresheners*
Clear Light Sachets & Cedar Mountain Mist (Clear Light). The cedar for the sachets comes from high in the New Mexico mountains, where the trees are not felled but trimmed in such a way that the trimming enhances the growth of the tree. Then the boughs are sun-dried and crumbled into cotton bags. The sachets can be used as an air freshener, bug re-

pellent, or effective mildew inhibitor. In addition, Clear Light also offers Cedar Mountain Mist, a tiny glass vial of cedar oil and a pump spray bottle, with instructions to fill the bottle with water, add some cedar oil, and spray. *Clear Light, The Hummer Nature Works.*

🐾 Natural air fresheners

+ *Fluir Herbals.* Potpourri blends with some organically grown herbs. 😊 ⊘

+ *Jeanne Rose Herbal BodyWorks.* Potpourris in a variety of herbal blends; organically grown herbs used when available. Beauty Without Cruelty seal of approval. 😊 ⊘

Air Therapy (Mia Rose Products). All natural ingredients, highly concentrated, in a nonaerosol spray mist. 😊 ⊘ *Allergy Resources, Carole's Cosmetics, The Compassionate Consumer, Ecco Bella, Earth Herbs, EveryBody Ltd., Humane Alternative Products, InterNatural, Karen's Nontoxic Products, Mia Rose Products, Seventh Generation.*

Aura Cacia Natural Air Freshener (Aura Cacia). Asian coin basket filled with fragrant flowers, herbs, and spices. 😊 ⊘ *Amberwood, Aura Cacia.*

Biozine II Air Deodorizer (Naace Industries). Made from plant enzymes and corn alcohol. Personal size comes in nonaerosol pump spray.

Carpet Stuff (Rathdowney Ltd.) Rids carpets of odors and fleas. *Seventh Generation.*

CitruScent (PRH & Associates). Made from fresh citrus-fruit extracts. Non-aerosol spray. 😊 ⊘ *Amberwood* (sold as Citrus Blend Air Fragrance), *Basically Natural* (sold as Citrus II Air Freshener).

G & W Supply. Sells Odor-Fresh, a natural volcanic mineral that is an adsorbent media for smoke, toxic gases, and bacterial odors. 😊 ⊘

Kettle Care Products. Potpourri blends. 😊 ⊘

Mountain Rose Herbs. Potpourri blends mix herbs, flower petals, spices, and essential oils.

Nichols Garden Nursery. Dry potpourri blends, as well as ingredients to make your own potpourris.

Vetcair Products: Animal Odor/Stain Eradicator, LitterCair, CageCair (Protech). Environmentally safe line of stain and odor eliminators includes an animal odor/stain eradicator, a spray for the cat-litter box, and a product for use with all caged animals. Works by naturally biodegrading the molecules of offending substances.

Wysong Citressence (Wysong Corporation). A natural odor counteractant. Comes in variety of forms. *InterNatural, Wysong Corporation.*

RADON

One of the more dangerous pollutants you may find in the air in your home is radon. Some scientists believe that radon poses the highest radiation threat to the American public. It is known to cause lung cancer in high concentrations, and the health effects at low levels of exposure are controversial. Even so, the EPA has estimated that exposure to radon may be the second leading cause of lung cancer, after cigarette smoking.

Radon is a natural radioactive gas that results from the decay of radioactive materials that may be present in rocks, soil, minerals, water, or natural gas. Soil and building materials containing radioactive substances are thought to be the major sources of radon in the home. The main risk is not from radon itself, but from its progeny, which you can inhale either directly or attached to other airborne particles. Two of the progeny emit alpha particles, which have the potential to inflict ten to twenty times the damage to biological tissue that similar doses of radiation from X rays can cause.

Studies have shown that indoor concentrations of radon are generally much higher than outdoor concentrations. Because it takes 1,602 years for only half the radon atoms to disintegrate, radon molecules tend to accumulate over time, causing concentrations to become higher.

The range of indoor radon concentrations found in homes is very broad, since concentrations are affected by the amount and rate of radon being produced by the particular conditions in your home, the volume of space in which it accumulates, and the rate of air exchange in your home. A *Consumer Reports* article told of a man in Pennsylvania who had absorbed so much radiation from the radon in his home that when he entered a nuclear power plant he set off the radiation alarm. Yet his neighbor's house had no radon at all. You will probably not be aware of its presence because radon cannot be detected by your senses and produces no immediate symptoms.

WHAT YOU CAN DO ABOUT RADON

The only way to know for sure if you have radon in your home is to get it tested. You can do this test yourself. Order radon-test kits from *Allergy Resources, The Allergy Store, Baubiologie Hardware,* and *SelfCare Catalog.* But before you rush to buy a test kit, contact your local EPA office to obtain a map showing areas with potentially high radon levels. Regardless of where you live, if large portions of your home are made of stone, brick, or concrete, it should be tested.

If your radon test is positive, you will need to take some action. Small concentrations can be handled with good ventilation; for higher levels, you will need professional help.

SMOKING

Warning labels:

"SURGEON GENERAL'S WARNING: Smoking causes lung cancer, heart disease, emphysema, and may complicate pregnancy.

SURGEON GENERAL'S WARNING: Quitting smoking now greatly reduces serious risks to your health.

SURGEON GENERAL'S WARNING: Smoking by pregnant women may result in fetal injury, premature birth, and low birth weight.

SURGEON GENERAL'S WARNING: Cigarette smoke contains carbon monoxide."

Cigarettes are probably the most toxic of consumer products. If you smoke and the health dangers have not yet convinced you to quit, consider also the environmental effects.

Tobacco, as a crop, ruins the soil on which it is grown. It depletes the soil of eleven times as much nitrogen as a food crop, thirty-six times as much phosphorus, and twenty-four times as much potassium. In addition, each year almost twenty thousand square miles of forest are cut down just to fuel the curing of tobacco. For more than one hundred Third World countries, tobacco occupies land that could be better used to grow food.

It's now common knowledge that cigarette smoke also poses a hazard to nonsmokers. Only 4 percent of the total smoke produced by a cigarette is actually inhaled by the smoker. The other 96 percent becomes sidestream waste, containing more than twice the concentrations of pollutants the smoker inhaled.

Possible symptoms for the *nonsmoker* who inhales this smoke include burning eyes, nasal congestion and drainage, sore throat, cough, headache, and nausea. It is a significant health hazard for infants, children, pregnant women and their yet-

to-be-born children, people with cardiovascular diseases, asthmatics, and others
with impaired respiratory function, heart
disease, lung disease, or allergies. Children of smoking parents have an increased incidence of upper-respiratory
infections, bronchitis, asthma, and pneu-
monia and a significant decrease in respiratory function.

Prolonged exposure to exhaled smoke
can increase the risk of disease in healthy
people who do not smoke, including
higher risk of lung cancer, respiratory infection, angina, decreased blood-oxygen
levels, decreased exercise tolerance, decreased respiratory function, bronchoconstriction, and bronchospasm.

In *The Health Consequences of Smoking:
Chronic Obstructive Lung Disease*, the for-
mer surgeon general of the United States
reports that there is very solid evidence
that nonsmokers suffer lung disease from
exposure to the smoke of those who do
use cigarettes.

Smokers will smoke, but the day is fast
approaching when smoking will be prohibited in most public places. Already
many restaurants have no-smoking sections—and some have even banned smoking altogether. Many hotels now have no-
smoking rooms, and smoking is now
against the law on domestic flights. We've
come a long way!

3 ❦ Water

Earth is the water planet. Other planets in our solar system
have little or no water—they have ammonia seas, carbon
dioxide ice, and methane steam—which would be inhospi-
table to life as we know it. Water appears to be relatively
scarce in the universe . . . Wherever there is water there
is life, and wherever there is life there is water. Pure, clean
natural waters, even raindrops, teem with microscopic life.
Water is not merely necessary for life, it is the essence
of life.

BEVERLY RUBIK

The frog does not drink up the pond in which he lives.

BUDDHIST PROVERB

Water is truly a remarkable and unusual substance, one on
which all life depends. By taking a few simple steps, we can make a big difference in
preserving our precious water supplies—and with a little effort, we can safeguard the
quality of water both in the environment and in our homes.

HOW WATER POLLUTION AFFECTS OUR HEALTH AND THE EARTH

Our municipal waterworks are doing their best to provide us with a safe and reliable
supply of high-quality water. For the most part, the water delivered to our taps does
meet existing drinking-water standards. But there are incidences of excessive levels of
dangerous substances in tap water, and even some substances that are routinely added to
our water supplies for our supposed benefit—such as fluoride and chlorine—can be
harmful to our health. Sometimes pollutants enter the water supply en route from the
water-treatment plant to our taps and cannot be controlled by our local waterworks.

According to Ralph Nader's Center for Study of Responsive Law, drinking water in
the United States contains more than twenty-one hundred toxic chemicals. Most mu-
nicipalities and water companies test for less than thirty, and only about fifty of our
nation's sixty thousand public water systems use modern treatment technologies that can
remove these chemicals, many of which cannot be tasted or seen. Some of these contaminants are known to cause cancer or inflict damage to vital organs such as kidneys,
the liver, the brain, and the cardiovascular system.

Most municipal water-treatment facilities were built in the early 1900s for the purpose of *disinfecting* water, not *purifying* it. The federal government estimates that it would
take billions of dollars and ten to fifteen years to upgrade our water-treatment facilities.

Most households are served by water systems regulated by the National Interim Primary Drinking Water Regulations, established in 1975. If your system has fewer than fifteen individual year-round hookups, or if your water comes from your own private well or spring, your water supply is not regulated.

Government regulations require water systems to sample water periodically for regulated substances. Depending on the number of customers served, from one hundred to five hundred samplings may be required per month. However, a survey done by the General Accounting Office found that over half of the community water systems fail to comply with federal testing requirements. These guidelines are designed only to *minimize* our risk, not to entirely eliminate the health threat.

Beyond our taps, water pollution is rampant throughout the world. It is caused by animal wastes, toxic chemicals from agriculture, energy production, industrial waste, and sewage-treatment plants that dump household toxics and human excreta untreated into leaking pipelines and into our waters after generally minimal processing.

About 40 trillion pounds of waste around the globe make their way into the sea each year, and an estimated 90 percent of this remains for years in coastal waters, interfering with the most productive breeding grounds of fish as well as polluting beaches. Persistent toxic chemicals such as PCBs, DDT, and heavy-metal compounds have spread throughout the world's ocean ecosystems, in part through gradual bioaccumulation in the food chain.

Approximately 80 percent of ocean-water pollution comes from sewage, industrial waste, and agricultural runoff. The other 20 percent comes from coastal mining, energy production and oceangoing vessels, much of it oil that has leaked or spilled. Tar balls, oil slicks, and sometimes high levels of heavy metals can be found along most of the major shipping routes, even in midocean—all of which are lethal for a variety of plankton, fish larvae, shellfish, and larger animals such as birds and marine mammals.

Our groundwater is also being polluted, and unlike surface water, it is neither renewable nor self-cleansing. Every year, 100 billion gallons of liquid hazardous wastes are absorbed into groundwater supplies. The EPA reports *serious* groundwater contamination in the continental United States from organic chemicals in forty-one states, inorganic chemicals in forty-four states, toxic metals in twenty-eight states, and pesticides in twenty-three states.

WE'RE RUNNING OUT OF WATER

It can be difficult to understand about water shortages when we know there is water all around us. We have streams, rivers, oceans, lakes, underground aquifers, and springs. It rains and snows. So how can we run out of water? The problem is not so much that there isn't any water. But between deforestation, global warming, poor agricultural practices, and more people using more water, less and less water is available to us for our daily needs.

Not all the water on this planet is usable to us. About 97.2 percent of the Earth's water is salt water. The remaining 2.8 percent—fresh water—is used for the natural functions of the planet or is flood runoff and quickly returns to the sea. About 2,376 trillion gallons a year can be captured for human use, which, according to a recent article in *Scientific American,* is enough to sustain 20 billion people *if* the water were evenly distributed. However, the total amount of water we use worldwide per year has risen since 1950 from about one-tenth this amount to close to half this amount in 1980. At this rate of increase in both population and per-person water use, we will exceed our capacity within ten to twenty years. Even with the world's present population of 5 billion, if everyone used as much water per person as we currently do in the United States (580,000 gallons per person per year), we would *already* be using more water than what is available worldwide!

Many areas are already experiencing water shortages. According to *WorldWatch*, underground water tables are falling in North America, Africa, China, the Soviet Union, and India. Groundwater levels are now falling between six inches and four feet a year in over one-quarter of the irrigated land in the United States; within the next forty years, over one-third of this land could dry up. Predicted climate changes could drastically reduce water availability even further.

Agriculture accounts for almost 75 percent of human use of water worldwide. The real water guzzler is raising animals, especially cows, for meat. In the United States it takes anywhere from three to one hundred gallons of water to produce one serving of most grain, vegetables, or fruit crops (rice takes about 250 gallons), whereas it takes twenty-six hundred gallons to produce a serving of steak, thirteen hundred gallons for hamburger, and four hundred gallons for chicken or pork. It takes less water to produce a *year's* food for a pure vegetarian than it takes to produce a *month's* food for a meat eater.

The distribution of water in the U.S. is similar to that in the rest of the world:

75 percent to agriculture (over 50 percent of *all* water use goes to grow livestock);

8.5 percent to industry;

7 percent to mining and thermoelectric-power processes;

7 percent to home use; and

2.5 percent to commercial use.

The amount used, however, varies greatly. The 580,000 gallons of water per person per year that we use is over seventy times the rate for Ghana and over four times the rate for Switzerland.

The loss of our forests has also played a major role in the loss of available water. Forests protect watersheds, protect soil from erosion, form windbreaks, and provide shade. Severe wind and rain erosion, the silting of rivers and irrigation systems, and the increasing severity of drought and floods around the world are the result of our loss of forest cover. When forests go, rivers often first flood and then dry up, since forests hold in moisture and recycle water back to the air through evaporation and transpiration.

WHAT WE CAN DO AT HOME

• Use water conservatively and efficienty to preserve water supplies for all life. See WATER CONSERVATION AND EFFICIENCY and WATER CONDITIONERS for tips and products that will allow you to meet all your water needs while using significantly less water.
• Purify water for drinking, bathing, and gardening with WATER PURIFICATION DEVICES.
• Drink BOTTLED WATER if you don't purify your water.
• Eat less meat or switch to a vegetarian diet. This can save more water than any other single act.

BOTTLED WATER

There are too many good bottled waters on the market to include a list of recommended brands here, but if you know what to look for, you can choose more wisely.

Bottled water is defined by the Food and Drug Administration as simply "water that is sealed in bottles or other containers and intended for human consumption." Many consumers, however, believe that bottled waters are of higher quality than tap water, although legally this need not be true. Federal regulations require that bottled waters marketed across state lines meet federal standards for drinking water. Those bottled waters sold only within individual states need meet only state requirements, which can vary from federal standards. Buying "pure" water in a plastic bottle defeats the purpose, because plastic quickly leaches into the water.

The purity of bottled water is controlled under the federal Food, Drug, and Cosmetic Act (mineral waters and soda waters are specifically exempt and thus are not regulated at all). Legally accepted sources for bottled water are wells, springs, and public water right from the tap. No requirements specify that the source of the water or any treatment it has undergone be listed on the label, but if any information is given at all, it must be truthful and not misleading. Manufacturers have an excellent selling point in telling if the water has come from a well or a spring, so if the source of the water is not revealed, chances are the water is treated tap water.

Bottled waters are divided into two types: still (without bubbles) and sparkling (with bubbles). Even though there are no state or federal regulations for the labeling of bottled-water containers, the labels do use certain generalized descriptive terms:

Drinking water. Tap or well water processed in some way before bottling.

Spring water. Water that emerges from the earth's surface under its own pressure, sometimes through a pipe. Water in bottles labeled "spring water" must come from a spring; "natural spring water," unlike plain spring water, may not be processed in any way before it goes into the bottle. Beware of companies with the word "spring" in the company name, rather than in the name of the product, or companies referring to the product as "spring-fresh," "springlike," or "spring-pure." Do not mistakenly assume that this water is from a spring.

Mineral water. Water containing a legally specified level of minerals. "Natural mineral water" is sparkling or still water, usually from a spring, which contains only the naturally occurring minerals. Regular "mineral water" may have had minerals added or removed. Mineral waters are specifically exempt from federal regulations for bottled waters.

Sparkling water. Water that contains bubbles made by carbon dioxide gas. "Naturally sparkling" water contains the bubbles when it is underground; when the water is drawn from the spring, the natural carbon dioxide is removed separately and reinjected during bottling. Some still waters are also carbonated, with either natural or manufactured carbon dioxide.

Club sodas and seltzer water are *not* controlled by federal regulations. Both are merely filtered and carbonated tap water; club soda also contains added mineral salts. The quality of these waters will differ greatly, depending on the local water and the method of filtration used. Many bulk waters that are home delivered in five-gallon bottles are also simply processed tap water.

According to tests done by Consumers Union in 1980, none of the thirty-eight brands of bottled waters tested for pesticides had detectable levels of trihalomethanes or other pesticides. Amounts of other pollutants, such as nitrates, cadmium, iron, and lead were well within federal limits, and none of the brands contained harmful quantities of bacteria. However, the tests did find a number of brands that had excessive levels of sodium and fluoride.

Still, bottled waters are not a recommended source of everyday drinking water because high pollutant levels are allowed based on an industry-wide assumption that bottled waters are consumed as a beverage—a health-conscious alternative to an alcoholic beverage or soda pop—and not as the primary source of drinking water. Also bottling water requires energy use and creates pollution at the bottling plant and in transportation, as well as creating a lot of empty bottles that need recycling.

Home-delivered bottled waters either come from a natural spring or are distilled or purified using reverse osmosis. Most come in plastic bottles nowadays, so you might not want to trust these, either, for your regular drinking water. If you can get clean spring water bottled in glass—great! When choosing a bottled water, the FDA suggests you select one that is controlled by federal regulations, preferably one that indicates its source. Most companies have a water-analysis report available for inspection that they should send on your request.

If you do want to drink bottled water occasionally, choose one bottled in glass directly from the natural source.

Gray Water

Gray water is the waste water that doesn't go down the toilet: water from your shower, bathroom sink, bathtub, dishwater, and washing machine. If you use a plain soap, gray water can be reused quite effectively for other purposes.

A gray-water recycling system will pump your wash water through a small filter and then make it available to flush toilets or water nonedible outdoor plants and the lawn reducing your new-water use by about 35 percent.

Using gray water isn't for everybody: setting up a collection tank and all the other apparatus takes time and can cost from two hundred to six hundred dollars. In many states it is illegal to use gray water, but where there are drought conditions, it may be acceptable.

At the Store/By Mail

Bi-Cep. Plans for a gray-water recycling system that recycles wash water into the toilet or out into the garden ($5.00 postpaid).

Robert Kourick. Water Cycle System is all set up to water your plants with laundry water at the turn of a knob. Also a great little book, *Gray Water Use in the Landscape: How to Use Gray Water to Save Your Landscape During Droughts* ($6.00 postpaid), that tells everything you need to know about the subject.

Water Conditioners

The purpose of a water conditioner is to soften hard water—not to make the water any safer to drink. You would want to use a water conditioner if you have a problem with soapy deposits in your bathtub or sinks, dull-looking laundry, spots on the dishes, scaly deposits on showerheads, or scale inside your water heater or pipes.

In the sixty-odd years that chemical water softeners have been on the market, the principle hasn't changed much. Essentially, the hard water flows through a tank filled with synthetic resin beads, each having millions of sodium ions loosely attached. The water exchanges its "hard" calcium and magnesium ions for the "soft" sodium ions—becoming much saltier in the process, of course. When the resin is saturated with hardness ions, salt water from a brine tank flows through the resin, regenerating the sodium supply as the resin exchanges its calcium and magnesium ions for the sodium ions. The waste brine then goes down the drain.

But there are other methods to soften water that do not increase the salt content or use chemicals and in the long run are more cost-effective and resource-efficient. Magnets are often used to soften water by suspending particles in water. One drawback to magnets, however, is that the effect only lasts 8–10 feet down the pipe. But with proper installation, they can work very well. Conditioned water also makes water use more efficient, thereby saving this resource.

At the Store/By Mail

Bricker's Organic Farm. Aqua-Purge magnetic water systems.

Care-free Water Conditioner (Carefree Water Products). "Conditions" water by passing it in a special flow pattern through a tube with a core composed of 16 different metals. This breaks up the adhesive qualities of the particles in the water and prevents scale from building up in pipes, water tanks, faucets, and toilets—even on the roots of plants. Benefits include reduction or elimination of water softening chemicals, higher yields with up to 50 percent less water needed to maintain lawns and gardens, up to 60 percent in pool chemical savings, and up to 50 percent less soap needed to wash clothes, do dishes, etcetera. Lett Company.

The Living Source. Rockett magnetic pipe descalers.

The Sprout House. The Magnetizer hard water conditioner.

Thunderstorm (Thunderstorm Corporation). Magnetic water conditioner.

WATER CONSERVATION AND EFFICIENCY

One of the most important things we can do to help the environment is to save water. Not only does it conserve our water resources, but it also reduces the amount of energy needed to heat water and process waste water. This doesn't necessarily mean fewer showers or withered gardens—just a more efficient use of water. Like any other resource, use what you need, but don't waste it. Here's how each of us typically uses a day's worth of water.

Indoors

Toilet flushing	24 gallons (30%)
Leaky toilets	4 gallons (5%)
Shower and bathing	24 gallons (30%)
Laundry	16 gallons (20%)
Dishwashing	3 gallons (4%)
Faucets	9 gallons (11%)
TOTAL	80 gallons

Outdoors (for homes with landscapes)

Lawn and shrubs	68 gallons (85%)
Garden	8 gallons (10%)
Car washing	4 gallons (5%)
TOTAL	80 gallons

WATER-SAVING TIPS

We can reduce the amount of water we use by at least half. Start by using a few water-saving devices that are generally inexpensive and easy to install. You can save a lot more water by changing a few habits. Once you get the hang of it, saving water will become second nature.

And remember, repair leaks immediately! One small leak—which is probably simple to fix—can waste seventy to one hundred gallons every day.

Read Your Water Meter

By reading your water meter, you can see how much water you are using and detect leaks. It takes only a minute and gives you feedback on how much water you're saving. You might want to take two meter readings one week apart to find out how much water you normally use. Then, after taking water-conserving measures, take another two readings to see how much water you're saving.

Step 1: Locate your meter. It is generally near the curb in front of your home, in a direct line with the main outside faucet. If you have any trouble locating it, call your local water-district office for help, they might even send someone out to show you if you ask.

Step 2: Read your meter. Carefully remove the lid by using a tool such as a large screwdriver. Reading a water meter is similar to reading the odometer on your car. There should be five numbers that count cubic feet; read the three to the left and ignore the rest.

Step 3: Calculate your water use. Subtract your previous meter reading from your current meter reading. One hundred cubic feet of water is equal to 748 gallons.

In the Bathroom

• Put a "displacement device" in your toilet tank to reduce the amount of water your tank will hold. Better than the bricks that were popular back in the sixties (small pieces can chip off and damage your plumbing system) are:

○ small plastic bottles. Reuse small juice or liquid-soap bottles. Just soak off the label, fill with water, and experiment a bit to get just the right balance between water savings and proper pressure for a good flush.

○ a displacement bag specifically designed for toilet tanks. I got one free from my local water department; they're also sold at hardware and plumbing stores.

These methods will save a gallon or two per flush. If you're buying a new toilet, get a water-saving model (see below).

• Consider not flushing the toilet every time it's used. Do what feels comfortable aesthetically.

• Take showers instead of baths. The typical shower runs about twenty-five gallons, the typical tub bath about sixty gallons.

• Use the minimal method to get clean: wet down, soap up without the water on, then rinse off. Or turn on the water less than full force.

• When brushing your teeth or shaving, turn the water on and off as needed instead of letting it run continuously. Saves ten to twenty gallons per brush or shave.

In the Kitchen

• Fill a sink or pan with soapy water to wash the dishes and then do the same with clean water to rinse them. Letting the water run constantly uses an average of 15.7 gallons.

• Dishwashers actually are pretty water-efficient. A study at Ohio State University showed that on the average, they use 9.9 gallons of water per normal load. To improve their water efficiency even further, remove excess debris from dishes before loading them (use a rubber scraper instead of holding them under running water). Then dishwashers can be set on short or light-soil cycles.

• Fill a pot with water to rinse fruits and vegetables in, and use a vegetable brush to remove debris instead of a forceful stream of water.

• Compost your kitchen scraps instead of using a garbage disposal.

• If you drink cold water, keep a bottle in the refrigerator instead of running the tap until cold water comes through.

• Thaw frozen foods in the refrigerator or sitting on the countertop instead of running them under hot water.

• Get an instant water heater (see RENEWABLE ENERGY) for your kitchen sink so you don't have to let water run while it heats up. Insulating hot-water pipes will also help hot water come up faster.

In the Laundry
• Run only full loads in the washer.
• Try running a full load with the water selector set to "medium load." If your clothes get just as clean, you've saved a few gallons.
• If you're in the market for a new clothes-washer (see APPLIANCES), choose one that conserves water and has a "suds saver" that reuses the rinse water in the next wash cycle. An efficient front-loading model can use 40 percent less water than a top-loading model.

At the Store/By Mail

Low-flow faucet aerators
Ask at your hardware or plumbing store for a low-flow faucet aerator (standard screen aerators won't do the same thing). Priced at less than four dollars each, these little gadgets combine a flow restrictor with a fine mesh screen. They work by reducing water flow and increasing pressure, then mixing air with the water as it comes from the tap. Even though you're using a lot less water, it will seem like the flow is stronger. Conventional faucets use five to fifteen gallons per minute; an aerated faucet reduces this to three gallons per minute.

Another option is to simply replace the faucet altogether. This is a little more expensive than buying a low-flow aerator, but new faucets flow at 2.75 gallons per minute or less.

Low-flow shower heads
These shower heads can reduce the amount of water used from five to seven gallons per minute to about three gallons per minute—and still give you the feel of a full shower. If you take a ten-minute shower, that's a savings of about thirty gallons each shower, or 10,950 gallons per year. And saving hot water also conserves the energy required to heat the water.

Unless you know you have a low-flow shower head, you probably have one that uses a lot of water, especially if you have an older model.

There are two types of low-flow shower heads. Aerated shower heads are the most popular. They reduce the amount of water in the flow, but maintain pressure by mixing air in with the water. Just like a regular shower head, they produce a steady, even spray. There have been some reports that the water cools down by the time it reaches your feet, but I haven't noticed that to be a problem. Many also have on-off levers that make it easy to restrict the flow while you're soaping up, then allow the water to come through full force when you want to rinse off.

The nonaerated variety simply reduces the flow. It gives a good, forceful spray, but the flow pulses like a massage shower head.

Low-flow shower heads can save about twenty-seven cents on water and fifty-one cents on electricity a day for a family of four—another way you can do something good for the Earth and save money, too. You might be able to get them free from your local water utility; if not, go to a good hardware or plumbing store or a bath-accessory shop, or order by mail.

Low-flush toilets
Toilets use more water in our homes (about 30 percent) than any other activity. A typical toilet will use 5 to 8 gallons per flush (gpf), whereas the new ultra-low-flush toilets use only about 1.5 gallons per flush. Ultra-low-flush toilets are reported to work as well as or even better than low-flush ones (which use 1.6 to 3.5 gallons per flush), and can cost as little as one hundred to two hundred dollars.

Composting toilets
Instead of wasting purified water and sewage systems to flush human wastes, we

could be using composting toilets. There is even an earthworm-composting toilet that works by vacuum flush and eliminates potential odor and insect problems. They require no water (or a very small amount) and leave you with rich compost for your garden. In addition to the listings below, Rocky Mountain Institute (see Recommended Resources) has an up-to-date listing of what's currently available in composting toilets.

Low-flow faucet aerators and shower heads

Ecological Water Products. Standard low-flow shower head.

New Alchemy Institute. Several models of low-flow shower heads.

People's Energy Resource Co-operative. Standard low-flow shower heads and faucet aerators.

Resources Conservation. Europa low-flow shower heads in a dozen decorator colors, plus matching bath fixtures. Also standard low-flow shower heads and a variety of faucet attachments.

Rising Sun Enterprises. Three low-flow shower heads with different spray textures and faucet aerators for the kitchen and bathroom.

Seventh Generation. Low-flow faucet aerators and one Europa low-flow shower head in several bright colors.

Vegan Street. Low-flow shower head.

Water Conservation Systems. Various faucet attachments and several brands of low-flow shower heads.

Ultra-low-flush toilets

Allegro / Cascade / Quantum (Mansfield Plumbing Products). 1.5 to 1.6 gallons per flush (gpf). *Resource Conservation Technology, Water Conservation Systems.*

Aqualine (U.S. Brass). 1.5 gpf.

Atlas (Universal-Rundle). 1.5 gpf or less.

CraneMiser/Economiser (Crane Plumbing). 1.6 gpf or less. *Water Conservation Systems.*

Hydro Miser (Peerless Pottery) 1.6 gpf. *New Alchemy Institute, People's Energy Resource Cooperative, Water Conservation Systems.*

Ifö Cascade Ultra Low Flush Toilets (Colton-Wartsila). *People's Energy Resource Cooperative, Real Goods Trading Company, Water Conservation Systems.*

Madera Aquameter/New Cadet Aquameter/Plebe Aquameter (American Standard), 1.5 to 1.6 gpf.

Microflush/Toto (Microphor). 0.5 gpf. *Resource Conservation Technology, Water Conservation Systems.*

Pearl (Water Conservation Systems). 1 cup per flush.

Santa Fe (Artesian Plumbing Supplies). 1.6 to 1.9 gpf.

Turboflush model 4700 (Briggs). 1.6 gpf.

Ultra Flush (Gerber Plumbing Fixtures). 1.6 gpf.

Ultra-One/G (Eljer Plumbingware). 1.4 gpf.

Vénéto (US 9710 Porcher). 1.5 gpf. *Resource Conservation Technology.*

Wellworth Lite (Kohler Company). 1.5 gpf.

Dry toilets

Bowli Composting Toilet (Sun-Mar). Electric and nonelectric models. Requires no septic system and uses no chemicals. *Backwoods Solar Electric Systems, Jade Mountain, Real Goods Trading Company, Water Conservation Systems* (also carries a variety of other brands from around the world).

Composting Toilet Systems. CTS composting toilets use no water, no chemicals, and have no adverse impact upon the environment. They utilize an air flush system and aerobic digestion to create compost in a separate tank.

Kansas Wind Power. Composting toilets.

WATER PURIFICATION

There is no question that in order to have the highest-quality water, we must produce it ourselves, in our own homes. In the future, home water-purification units may become standard household appliances. The health effects of tap water may be controversial, but common sense tells us that the cleaner the water, the lower the possible health risk.

No water-purification device can make your water 100 percent pure 100 percent of the time. Using current technology, we can reduce pollutants to a level that significantly lessens their health effects. When we choose a device, we are also choosing our level of risk.

Also, using a water-purification device protects us from harmful pollutants but does nothing to improve environmental conditions. Our ultimate goal needs to be clean water in the environment.

THE BEST DEVICE FOR YOU

Choosing a water-purification device can be confusing, but it's very important to choose the one that is right for your individual needs.

There are five factors to consider:

1. which pollutants need to be removed from your water;
2. how much it costs both to purchase the unit and to maintain it over time;
3. convenience;
4. what type of device to buy; and
5. effectiveness of pollutant removal.

Compromises will need to be made in each of these areas. The units that are most effective are not the least expensive. Are you willing to turn a unit on and off, or do you want purified water instantly at your tap? Do you want to remove just the pollutants found in your water supply, or do you want broad-spectrum removal to protect yourself from possible unknown contaminants?

WHAT'S IN YOUR WATER?

In theory, any molecule of any substance that is not a water molecule can be defined as a water pollutant. Some substances, such as minerals, are actually beneficial in some quantities because they give the water a pleasing taste or have a positive health effect. Others, such as carcinogenic organic compounds, are harmful in any amount and should be removed at all costs.

All water pollutants fall into five basic categories:

Microorganisms are microscopic plants and animals more commonly known as bacteria, viruses, protozoans, algae, and cysts. Not all are harmful, but many cause water-quality problems more frequently than any other pollutant.

Particulates include all the minute bits of material that do not dissolve in water: metals (such as lead), rust, dirt, sand, and other sediments.

Dissolved solids are solid materials like fluoride, nitrates, sulfates, and salts, which decompose in water.

Volatile chemicals include all nonparticulate substances that can be vaporized—chlorine, chloramine, chloroform, and other trihalomethanes, chlorinated hydrocarbons, pesticides (DDT, dialdrin, lindane, heptochlor), radon gas, benzene, carbontetrachloride, trichloroethylene, xylene, toluene, and hundreds of others.

Radioactive particles are minute bits of radioactive materials.

The first step is to find out which of these pollutants might be in your water and which you want to remove. If your water supply is regulated by the Safe Drinking Water Act, call city hall, your local water district, and your local department of health services to see if they have recent test results for the pollutants they require to be monitored.

One limitation to the water-quality data that come from your local waterworks is that the reports will tell you the quality of the water as it leaves the treatment plant, *not as it comes out of your tap*. The levels of chlorine, metals, bacteria, and particulates may have changed by the time the water is pumped through the distribution system to your home. For many years, the EPA failed to detect excessive lead in some drinking-water supplies; it was ultimately found by independent laboratories testing samples submitted by homeowners.

If your water supply is not regulated or if you would like to have your water independently tested, look in the Yellow Pages under "Laboratories—Analytical." Ask these laboratories what testing they do and get estimates from several, because prices and services can vary.

In response to consumer demand for home water-quality testing, there are now low-cost mail-order services specifically designed for homeowners. Contact *The Allergy Store, American Environmental Laboratories, Aqua Associates, Baubiologie Hardware, Hydro-Analysis Associates, National Testing Labs, SelfCare Catalog, Seventh Generation, Suburban Water Testing*, and *WaterTest Corporation* for information on their test kits.

But knowing what's in your water today is only part of the question. How will you know what will be in your water tomorrow? Do you want a device that removes only those specific pollutants known to be present in your water today, or do you want to invest in broad-spectrum protection against possible future pollutants?

COST OF WATER-PURIFICATION DEVICES

The cost of a water-purification device is a prime consideration for many people who want cleaner water. Units of varying effectiveness range in price from thirty-nine dollars to several thousand dollars. In general, it costs more to buy a more effective device, but not always. Almost any device is better than none at all, *if used properly*.

Buy the best you can afford, but remember to take into consideration the overall cost of the unit over time, including replacement components, if any.

CONVENIENCE

With convenience high on the priority list for choosing products these days, some people are willing to sacrifice water quality for having the water come right out of the tap or through an auxiliary faucet. Others are willing to turn devices on and off and collect drinking water in containers to have the purest water possible. If you aren't willing to keep up with the user participation and regular maintenance required in some devices, it's better to choose an automated device or one that requires less upkeep. Most units can actually pollute water if not properly maintained, so make sure you are willing to do what it takes to keep your unit operating optimally.

TYPES OF DEVICES

Water pollutants can enter our bodies in many ways, and all must be considered in choosing appropriate devices. In addition to exposure from actually drinking water and water used in cooking, studies have shown that significant exposures occur not only through skin absorption during bathing and swimming, but also through breathing fumes of certain pollutants released from running water.

According to the *American Journal of Public Health*, skin absorption may be an even greater avenue of exposure to water pollutants than the drinking of water. For a normal adult, taking a fifteen-minute bath can be equal to drinking a quart of the same water; a fifty-pound child can absorb up to ten times as much contamination from swimming in a pool for an hour as drinking a quart of water. An EPA report on indoor air pollution has identified carcinogenic chloroform, which is the result of evaporation from hot running shower water, as a major indoor air pollutant.

So the issue is no longer just clean water to drink, it's clean water to shower, bathe, soak, and swim in, too. For drinking water, you can simply use a point-of-use device that will purify water only at the point at which it is used. Point-of-use devices are also available to attach to shower heads and bathtub taps. Or you can choose a point-of-entry device that will purify water at the point at which it enters your house, providing clean water from every tap. Generally speaking, point-of-use devices produce drinking water of higher purity, and some people choose to use a combination of both.

POLLUTANT REMOVAL

Evaluating the efficiency of a water-purification device can be very difficult, primarily because much of the advertising for such devices is false and misleading. In many cases salespeople are unable to give accurate information on technical aspects of their devices, although I have consistently found that manufacturers and sellers of good-quality products are more than willing to reveal every detail about the devices they produce and represent. Beware of such sales tactics as refusing to give out information over the telephone, door-to-door salespeople wanting to sign you up for thousands of dollars' worth of equipment, phony "water officials" who call nights or weekends, and companies who will test your water for free, then try to sell you a unit.

There are only three basic methods of water purification used in devices designed to further decontaminate the already potable water that comes from your tap: activated carbon (in granular or block form), reverse osmosis, and distillation. Each has its limitations, and it's important to learn what each can, and cannot, do.

Activated Carbon

Activated carbon is the champion for removing volatile chemicals of all kinds, including chlorine and chlorine by-products such as trihalomethanes, chloramines, industrial solvents, pesticides, and radon gas. Used alone, it won't touch microorganisms, particulates, dissolved solids, or radioactive particles, although some of these may be removed as the water is strained through the carbon. If your water is chlorinated, you could benefit from using a carbon filter.

Activated carbon works through the process of adsorption. Each particle of carbon is like a honeycomb of minute pores that attract and trap pollutant molecules. As the water passes through and the micropores are filled, fewer and fewer pores remain vacant. As the pores become filled, the effectiveness of the carbon decreases. When the carbon becomes fully saturated, not only do the pollutant molecules flow right through the carbon, but some of the trapped pollutants are also released into the product water. For this reason, you *must* change the carbon regularly. How often you'll need to change the carbon depends on the size and amount of carbon in the unit and the volume of volatile chemicals in your water. All carbon units come with instructions to change the carbon after so many months or so many gallons, but a good way to gauge this for yourself is to purchase an inexpensive chlorine test kit (like you would use to test the chlorine in your swimming pool) and test your water periodically to find out exactly how long the carbon is effective with your water. Tests done by Rodale Product Testing Labs show that the effectiveness of contaminant removal declined sharply after about 75 percent of the rated life on all the filters tested. They suggest changing the carbon more often than recommended.

Another good reason to change your

carbon regularly is bacterial contamination. While there is no evidence that these bacteria are a common cause of disease when they enter the body via water passed through carbon units, there is no practical way to monitor the amount or type of bacteria that may be present in home filters. Some units offer a backwashing function to control bacteria growth, which involves switching a lever or attaching a separate device to flush hot water through the carbon in the reverse direction. Although backwashing will remove some bacteria, it is not as effective or reliable as changing the carbon completely. "Bacteriostatic" filters have been embedded with silver to control bacteria growth, but EPA studies have found that the silver does not actually perform this function. And as *Consumer Reports* says, "Bacteriostasis in a carbon filter is of little usefulness. Water supplied by municipal systems doesn't contain dangerous levels of bacteria."

There are several factors to consider when choosing a unit containing activated carbon. For maximum efficiency, you are looking for a good selection of micropore sizes within the carbon, an adequate amount of carbon (EPA studies showed that units with small amounts of carbon were only marginally effective at removing trihalomethanes, whereas units with larger

amounts removed trihalomethanes up to 98 percent), good contact time between the water and the carbon to allow the pollutant molecules to be adsorbed, and a smooth flow of water through the carbon. *Consumer Reports* found that pour-through pitcher-type filters removed only about half the pollutants after just twenty gallons—a practically worthless investment.

Activated-carbon units give you lots of choices when it comes to style and design: granular carbon or carbon block, plastic or stainless-steel housing, over-the-counter units that sit on countertops with diverter tubes to and from the tap, or undersink models that dispense filtered water through either the main or an auxiliary tap.

Carbon block is generally favored over granular carbon; because it is compressed more carbon fits in the same amount of space and provides more micropores for greater efficiency, there is a certain straining effect that removes some bacterial and heavy metals, and it tends to breed bacteria less easily than granular carbon.

There may not be much difference between a plastic and a stainless-steel housing in the outcome of the final product water. Plastics can release some polymers into the water as it flows by, but is is unknown exactly how much is released, or how much might then be adsorbed by the carbon. Stainless-steel housings might re-

COMPARISON OF POLLUTANTS REMOVED
BY WATER PURIFICATION METHODS

	Activated carbon (granular)	Activated carbon (block)	Distillation	Reverse osmosis
Asbestos	Some	Yes	Yes	Yes
Bacteria and viruses	Some	Yes	Yes	Some
Chlorine	Yes	Yes	No	No
Fluoride	No	Some	Yes	Yes
Heavy metals	No	Yes	Yes	Yes
Minerals	No	No	Yes	Yes
Nitrates	No	No	Yes	Yes
Organic chemicals	Yes	Yes	Some	Some
Salts	No	No	Yes	Yes

lease some infinitesimal amount of metals into the water, but again, how much of a danger this might be is unknown. Stainless-steel housings are recommended for individuals who have proven sensitive to petrochemicals.

Many of the most popular activated-carbon units have a single cartridge that is made up of a block of carbon surrounded by a sediment-prefiltering material. For both economy and efficiency, the preferred design is that which has two separate canisters—one for the sediment prefilter, the other for the carbon. Frequent change of inexpensive sediment filters can prolong the effective life of the carbon; with the single-cartridge design, the entire (expensive) cartridge must be replaced.

Reverse Osmosis

Reverse-osmosis units incorporate both activated carbon and a reverse-osmosis membrane. The membrane alone removes significant amounts of particulates, dissolved solids, and radioactive particles. Combined with the volatile-chemical-removal capability of carbon, a reverse-osmosis unit can provide good broad-spectrum removal of most common pollutants.

A typical reverse-osmosis system for use in the home consists of three canisters. The unit is installed under the sink and tapped into the incoming cold-water pipe. The water flows through a particulate prefilter in the first canister, then on to the reverse-osmosis membrane in the second. The membrane removes pollutants through a complex process that is not yet fully understood. What essentially happens is that the water molecules are pushed through the membrane, leaving the pollutant molecules behind. As each drop of water is purified, it drips down into a holding tank. When the holding tank is full, the unit automatically shuts off and stops producing water. When the pressure level in the holding tank falls, the unit once again begins to filter water.

To remove volatile chemical pollutants, the water passes through activated carbon in the third canister before being dispensed through an auxiliary gooseneck faucet.

Membranes will generally be one of three types of plastic—cellulose acetate, cellulose triacetate, or polyamid resin (thin film composite). Be sure to find out what type of membrane a unit has. Thin film membranes cannot be used with chlorinated water supplies, so in such an application a carbon prefilter must be used, and regularly changed. Cellulose acetate and triacetate membranes, on the other hand, require chlorinated water to prevent bacteria growth, which causes deterioration.

At best, most reverse-osmosis membranes will reject pollutant molecules at about 90 percent efficiency. The synthetic materials from which they are made can vary in consistency, and from day to day efficiency might further be diminished by changes in water pressure, the pH of the water, or the temperature of the water. The overall efficiency of pollutant removal will also diminish with use. Reverse-osmosis systems are made almost entirely of plastic, and store water in a plastic-lined holding tank. While some of the plastic is removed when the water flows through the carbon, this type of unit is not recommended for those who are especially sensitive to petrochemical pollutants.

Each component of the reverse-osmosis unit needs to be replaced periodically— the prefilter every few months as needed, the membrane once every two to five years, and the carbon every year or two.

A reverse-osmosis unit is ideal for someone who values convenience over effectiveness. It will remove significant amounts of almost all pollutants to some degree, hides under the sink, and gives over two gallons per day of somewhat purified water at the flip of a lever. If nothing else, it's better than drinking tap water.

If you choose a reverse-osmosis system, opt for one that has three separate can isteres for the three filtration methods. Some inexpensive models wrap the membrane around a core of carbon and have all three filtration steps in one unit. The three-canister models are more efficient, and you have more control over maintenance. When you first use your reverse-osmosis unit, it is very important to process at least twenty gallons of water through the system before drinking water from the system. Some membranes are preserved with formaldehyde which needs to be removed, and flushing water through will remove some plastic residues.

An environmental disadvantage to reverse-osmosis systems (besides the toxic manufacture and ultimate disposal problems of all the plastic) is that they waste a lot of water. Only 10 to 25 percent of the water passing through the system goes through the membrane; the rest goes down the drain. About 20 gallons each day is wasted by being flushed through the unit, even if you don't use any water.

Important note: If your chlorinated municipal water flows through galvanized pipes or if you don't have chlorinated water, you will have to take precautions to protect your reverse-osmosis membrane. "Spurs" build up inside galvanized pipes that are perfect breeding grounds for bacteria. While these bacteria are harmless to drink, they feed on the reverse-osmosis membrane, making it useless. To remedy this problem, either add about a teaspoon of chlorine bleach to the prefilter every month (a time-consuming and toxic procedure) or purchase a point-of-use ultraviolet unit to kill bacteria (available from *Nigra Enterprises*).

Distillation

Distillation has been used for years to remove microorganisms, particulates, dissolved solids, and radioactive particles from water. Because it removes 99.9 to 100 percent of contaminants, distillation is the method preferred by scientific laboratories. While the older distillers were not designed for volatile-chemical removal, newer models incorporate functions that remove significant amounts of these pollutants. Used in conjunction with carbon filtration, distillation gives the highest purity of all home units—consistently, gallon after gallon.

Water distillers remove pollutants by boiling water to turn it into steam, then condensing it. Boiling the water destroys bacteria and other living materials, leaving them behind in the boiling tank, along with particulates, dissolved solids, and radioactive particles that are too heavy to rise with the water vapor.

The major objection most people have to distillers is that they are inconvenient. Some have to be filled by hand; others have to be turned on and off manually. Regardless of the level of participation, in order to drink distilled water, you have to make it. Distillers cost money and energy to operate (about a dollar's worth of electricity to produce five gallons of water, but you never have to replace anything) and must be cleaned regularly (depending on water composition and size of distiller, once every two weeks to six months). They also waste water—about six to seven gallons for every gallon of distilled water it makes.

A distressing disadvantage that applies to almost all the distillers on the market is that stainless-steel distillers seem to add aluminum to the product water. In a laboratory test done by the Rodale Press Product Testing Department, all of the metal distillers tested produced water with at least traces of aluminum; some distillers actually *increased* the aluminum content of the water by up to 130 percent, bringing the level of aluminum to the limit of what is generally considered acceptable. Because aluminum exposure has been linked with nervous-system diseases and brain disorders such as Alzheimer's disease, the fact that stainless-steel distillers add this particular metal to the water is cause for concern. Rodale could not identify the source of aluminum in all distillers tested and did not test all distillers on the market. It may be that some stainless-steel distillers do not add aluminum to the product water, but at this time the question is unresolved. If you prefer to avoid this possible danger, choose a glass distiller.

RECOMMENDED
WATER-PURIFICATION DEVICES

There are over four hundred companies making water-filtration devices. Obviously, I can't list them all here. Nor would I want to. A water-filtration device is an important investment in your health, and a major financial expenditure. I wouldn't be doing my job if I didn't recommend some of the best ones I have found.

I have chosen representative brands for each device type that provide the most effective pollutant removal at a reasonable cost. A few more-expensive models are also included because of their unique and valuable features.

At the Store/By Mail

Activated carbon

There are many activated-carbon-block units on the market that are all about the same. They differ more in price than in performance. Compare Amway, Neo-life, Multipure, and Sears units with those listed below (be sure to consider both the original price of the units and the cost of replacement cartridges over time).

Aqua Clear SS (R.H. of Texas). 10 grams of granular activated carbon in a unique ceramic and stainless steel-cartridge. No plastic. Stainless-steel housing with optional stainless-steel output tubing. Counter-top and under-sink units. Removes bacteria and volatile chemicals. *An Ounce of Prevention, R.H. of Texas.*

EPS Drinking Water Filter (Environmental Purification Systems). Stainless-steel housing is filled with 1¾ pounds of loose granular coconut-shell carbon, without the plastic found in most carbon cartridges. Output tubing is copper or (at extra charge) stainless steel. Independent laboratory test shows removal of volatile chemicals to undetectable levels. *E.L. Foust Company, Environmental Purification Systems.*

Micron 1 (California Ecology). Has the same type of adsorptive structured matrix cartridge as the Seagull IV (see below), but is not as fine. For volatile-chemical removal it is just as effective as the Seagull IV, but it is less effective at removing the smaller particles. Housing is polypropylene. Removes 99 percent of volatile chemicals and has "absolute" retention of particles and microorganisms down to 1 micron in size. *An Ounce of Prevention, Nigra Enterprises.*

Seagull IV (General Ecology). An "enhanced carbon" filter made of a congealed, bonded mass of various activated carbons and other basic organic materials that optimizes the adsorption process by providing a multitude of different-sized micropores to match the molecule sizes of a wide variety of pollutants. This unique blend of materials not only adsorbs volatile chemicals more efficiently than any single carbon alone, but also maintains efficiency of pollutant removal for a longer period of time than carbon. Stainless-steel housing. Removes 99 percent of volatile chemicals and microorganisms. Can remove particulates, including heavy metals. *The Allergy Store, An Ounce of Prevention, The Living Source, Nigra Enterprises, The Pure Water Place.*

Water Safe OTC-500-TLC (Coast Filtration). An activated-carbon filter that sits on your countertop, with a special resin-core cartridge that removes lead in addition to volatile gases. Plastic housing with diverter valve that attaches to faucet. *Coast Filtration, Nigra Enterprises.*

Water-Safe TOC-200 (Coast Filtration). A two-canister activated-carbon filter with a 1-micron sediment prefilter and a 16-ounce activated-carbon block (a blend of two different carbons for broader-spectrum chemical removal). Hard-plastic housing. Ninety-nine percent volatile-chemical removal. *Baubiologie Hardware, Coast Filtration, Nigra Enterprises.*

Distillation

Rain Crystal 8 Water Distiller (Scientific Glass). The only Pyrex-glass distiller designed and marketed specifically for home use, with a two-stage process that double-distills the water. Removes 100 percent of all particulates and microorganisms, 99.9 percent of all dissolved solids (including fluoride), and 98 to 100 percent of volatile chemicals. *Environmental Purification Systems, Nigra Enterprises, Scientific Glass.*

Sunwater Solar Still (McCracken Solar Company). Personal portable and residential-size solar distillers since 1959. *McCracken Solar Company.*

Reverse osmosis

Water Safe WS/RO5 (Coast Filtration). A three-canister reverse-osmosis unit with a 1-micron particulate prefilter, a cellulose triacetate membrane and 16 ounces of crushed carbon (or carbon block). All membranes are tested for pollution-rejection rate; 94 percent is the accepted minimum, and some have rejection rates of up to 98 percent. Hard-plastic housings; holding tank is stainless steel with a neoprene plastic balloon. Removes 100 percent of all particulates, 91 to 99 percent of volatile chemicals, and 87 to 96 percent of dissolved solids (including fluoride). *Coast Filtration, Nigra Enterprises.*

Shower filters

Nigra Shower Filter (Nigra Enterprises). Fifteen ounces of granular carbon in a plastic housing with fittings to attach at shower head. Least expensive, most effective shower filter I know of. Proven chlorine removal from hot water. *Nigra Enterprises.*

Whole-house filters

Cuno AP600 (Cuno). Activated carbon with stainless-steel housing. Ninety-nine percent removal of volatile organic chemicals. *The Allergy Store, Nigra Enterprises.*

Spark L Pure (General Ecology). Same basic "structured matrix microfilter" as Seagull IV (see above). Stainless-steel housing with brass fittings. Ninety-nine percent removal of volatile chemicals and microorganisms. Can remove particulates. *The Allergy Store, Nigra Enterprises, The Pure Water Place.*

Water dispensers

Springwell Water Dispensers (Springwell Dispensers). Highest-quality porcelain dispenser with spigot. Sits on countertop or oak stand. *SelfCare Catalog.*

4 ✿ Energy

Most of the solar technologies we think are so new—
everything from solar steam engines to solar cells to make
electricity directly—are anywhere from a century to mille-
nia old . . . we're all just reinventing a very old wheel—
because, in the rush to burn up all that apparently cheap
oil and gas, we forgot about the sun.

ENERGY UNBOUND

Today, the burning of fossil fuels—coal, oil, and natural gas—provides us with almost 90 percent of the energy we use to run our industries, grow our food, live in our homes, and drive our cars. Unlike the natural energy of the sun, wind, and water, these petrochemicals are unhealthy, polluting, expensive, and nonrenewable. At our present rate of use, we have enough worldwide reserves to last only another thirty to fifty years. Sooner or later we're going to have to make major changes in our energy philosophy.

In the meanwhile, we need to learn all we can about how to use energy wisely and explore alternative sources of energy that are more abundant, inexpensive, healthful, and environmentally safe. Making small changes in the way we use and choose energy can help ease the transition.

HOW ENERGY AFFECTS OUR HEALTH AND THE EARTH

The production, use, and disposal of energy affects our health on two different levels, Directly in our homes or workplaces while we are using it, and indirectly as we live within the array of environmental problems caused by it.

Indoors, the greatest danger comes from the by-products of the burning of natural gas, kerosene, and wood for cooking and heating. The primary hazard is carbon monoxide, a poisonous gas that is produced when fuels do not burn completely. Early symptoms of carbon monoxide poisoning are much like flu symptoms and include sleepiness, headaches, dizziness, blurred vision, irritability, and an inability to concentrate. If you or anyone in your family seems to be sick all winter, you might want to check your heater. Carbon monoxide poisoning can be fatal.

Other combustion by-products produced by gas, kerosene, and wood-burning appliances include formaldehyde, nitrogen dioxide, sulfur dioxide, carbon dioxide, hydrogen cyanide, nitric oxide, and vapors from various organic chemicals. Many illnesses are known to result. People with emphysema, asthma, heart problems, or chemical sensitivities should be particularly cautious.

Natural gas, like gasoline, contains benzene, a carcinogen, which can be released if there are any gas leaks. Researchers at University of California's Lawrence Berkeley Laboratory found that cooking with a gas stove at 350 degrees Fahrenheit in a poorly ventilated kitchen could contaminate the room with as much carbon monoxide and nitrogen dioxide gas as the smoggy skies of Los Angeles.

Burning wood in stoves and fireplaces also produces toxic by-products such as carcinogenic benzo(a)pyrene. It is easy to tell if these pollutants are present in your home because they are extremely irritating to eyes, nose, throat, and lungs. Little research has been done on the effects of wood-combustion by-products on indoor air quality; however, some communities are banning the use of wood stoves for home heating because of the amount of outdoor air pollution produced.

And then there is the problem with electromagnetic fields—electrical and magnetic fields generated by the sun, the moon, and the planets, but also by our bodies, man-made electrical power-generating stations, and all electrical wiring and appliances. The activity of every living cell in our bodies is regulated by the flow of electromagnetic fields. Our metabolism is geared to the natural background levels of radiation and electromagnetic energies from the cosmos. The Earth's electromagnetic field pulses at the rate of 7.83 hertz, and our bodies' own bioelectrical systems pulse at about the same rate.

When electricity was first installed in American homes around one hundred years ago, we encased ourselves in invisible cages of electromagnetic energy pulsing at 60 hertz. At its introduction, electricity was thought to be perfectly safe. Now researchers are not as certain. While the scientific community is not yet completely convinced that exposure to electromagnetic fields from the electrical wiring and appliances in our homes (or from nearby power lines) poses any health threat, accumulating scientific evidence has convinced many that there is cause for concern.

Laboratory studies on animal cells have clearly shown that electromagnetic fields from sixty-hertz alternating current emit radiation that can interact with individual cells and organs to produce biological changes. Verified epidemiological studies found that children who lived near ordinary neighborhood electrical-distribution lines were twice as likely to develop cancer as those who did not. Results of such studies are encouraging a major worldwide research effort.

As for the environment, the burning of fossil fuels for electricity or direct use in our homes, industry, and motor vehicles is the primary cause of the major problems discussed in Chapter 2: smog, acid rain, and climate changes. The production and transportation of fossil fuels also causes a tremendous amount of pollution.

We all know about the tragic *Exxon Valdez* spill of 11 million gallons of oil in Alaskan waters that fouled more than one thousand miles of coastline, the four hundred thousand gallons of crude oil spilled just one and a half miles off the southern California coast, and other big oil spills. But there is much damage that we don't hear about. On the North Slope of Alaska alone, there are between four hundred and six hundred reported oil spills each year—*more than one every day*. In total, about .1 percent of the world's oil production, some 1.4 *billion* gallons, ends up in our oceans each year, killing marine life and coming back to us in our food supply.

A recent federal study found that 372 million barrels of toxic oil-drilling wastes, often laced with carcinogens such as arsenic, lead, and mercury, are dumped each year in unlined pits throughout U.S. oil-producing states, causing considerable damage to agricultural land, crops, animals, and people. An additional 21 billion barrels of water contaminated by the drilling process are dumped with little or no treatment into bodies of water, reducing life-supporting oxygen levels and harming aquatic life.

Energy from nuclear reactors has its own dangers. According to a study of the 1986 Chernobyl nuclear-power-plant accident in Russia conducted by the Lawrence Livermore National Laboratory in California, the accident released as much long-term radiation into the world's air, topsoil, and water as all the nuclear tests and bombs ever exploded. It has been estimated that one million people, half of them outside the Soviet Union, will develop cancer as a result, and that half of the cases will be fatal.

Although we in the United States were relatively lucky concerning radiation from the Chernobyl disaster, we haven't gone unscathed. According to the National Oceanic and Atmospheric Administration, fallout from Chernobyl could cover the United States for years. Rainwater samples taken in Oregon and Washington a few weeks after the accident showed elevated levels of radiation—twelve glasses of Washington rainwater contained radiation equal to that in a chest X ray.

When you look at the problems that have occurred at nuclear power plants, it is a wonder that we haven't had more Chernobyls. Two recent studies, one by Ralph Nader's Critical Mass Energy Project and the other by Massachusetts Representative Edward Markey, concluded that nuclear safety in the United States is worsening in regard to the number and severity of mishaps. An average of almost seven mishaps per day were filed with the Nuclear Regulatory Committee in 1984, and over eight mishaps a day were filed in 1985. There were one hundred operating reactors in the United States in 1986, providing just 3.5 percent of our total energy. According to the Nuclear Regulatory Commission, there is a 45 percent chance of a severe core-meltdown accident at one of these plants during the next twenty years.

WHAT WE CAN DO AT HOME

To minimize the dangers of exposure to the combustion by-products of natural gas, we can:

• Dilute pollutants with ventilation; open windows, flues, fans, and vents. Gases from combustion by-products concentrate initially in the area around the appliance and then spread to other areas of your home as the air circulates, so catch them at the source. During cooking, for example, a hood fan can remove up to 70 percent of pollutants produced.
• Check frequently to make sure your gas appliances are functioning properly. Clean clogged stove burners and blocked flues, fix cracks and leaks in pipes, and follow any maintenance routine suggested by the manufacturer. A poorly adjusted gas stove can give off thirty times the carbon monoxide of one that's well adjusted.
• Make sure you are using your appliances according to instructions.
• If possible, put your gas appliances in a space outside the living area, venting the fumes to the outside and placing a tight seal between the appliances and the living space to prevent gases from spreading throughout your home.
• Use a new-model gas stove with low-heat-input gas pilot lights and nongas ignition systems, which produce significantly fewer pollutants than do older stoves with pilot lights.

To minimize the dangers of exposure to the by-products of burning wood, we can:

• Make sure wood stoves and fireplaces are installed and fitted properly. Be certain that your fireplace was constructed to be used as a fireplace and is not just there for decoration. Have it inspected to make sure it has all necessary linings and clearances and that the flue is open.
• Always keep the damper opened properly while the fuel is burning.
• Have your chimney inspected for creosote buildup when the weather starts getting cold, or periodically throughout the year if you use your fireplace often. Creosote buildup can cause flue fires and may also block the chimney, preventing escape of toxic fumes.
• Leave a window open a crack to allow pollutants to escape.
• Fix cracks or leaks in the stovepipe and keep a regular maintenance schedule to keep the chimney and stovepipe clean and unblocked.
• Guard against negative air pressure indoors and watch for downdrafts, which will push pollutants into your living space instead of carrying them up the flue.

To reduce exposure to manmade electromagnetic fields in the home (which often pose a greater risk than exposures from outdoors), we can:

• Install shielded wire. Simply twisting wires for individual appliances around each other (one twist every two and a half inches) will reduce magnetic fields by about 80 percent.
• Install items that minimize the use of electricity—such as windows and skylights—to reduce the need for artificial lighting, climate-responsive heating and cooling to reduce the need for electric heating and air conditioning, and such things as a solar cooker instead of an electric stove—and a root cellar to replace the refrigerator. This will also help conserve energy.
• Use battery-powered appliances and electronics when possible. Batteries produce a weaker electromagnetic field, and rechargeable batteries can easily be recharged with solar energy.
• Use alternative energy sources (such as the sun or wind), which produce a lower voltage of electricity.
• Keep your distance from (or remove entirely) the most powerful emitters of electromagnetic fields in your home:

Dimmer switches	remove
Electric blankets	remove (or preheat bed, then unplug)
Photoelectric timer switches	remove
Microwave ovens	remove
Radiant heat installed in walls	don't use
Fluorescent lights	6 feet
Refrigerators and freezers	4 feet
Televisions and computers	3½ feet
Electric heaters	3 feet
Dial-faced electric clocks	3 feet
Blow dryer for hair	1 foot

• Unplug appliances and electronics when not in use (as long as they are connected, the wires are "hot," so that you can turn on the machine). At night, you may want to

shut off all the circuits in your house (except for the circuit that powers the refrigerator) as the wires in your walls are "hot" all the time as well. If you do shut off your power, keep a flashlight and battery-powered clock next to your bed.
• Make a special point to make your bedroom as electromagnetically safe as possible, as this is the room where you probably spend most of your time while at home and the room that needs to be most conducive to getting good sleep so your body can rejuvenate itself.

We can also use less energy. Each of us in the United States consumes about seventy barrels of fuel oil or its equivalent each year, compared with a world average of only about eleven barrels. With only five percent of the world's population, we guzzle 25 percent of the world's energy supply. The place we have the most room to change our energy use is in our homes and automobiles, which together use about 30 percent of total energy in this country.

We can reduce how much energy we use two ways: conservation (things such as turning off lights when you aren't in the room) and energy efficiency (things such as using energy-efficient light bulbs, which give you the same amount of light for less energy). By taking *already known* energy-conservation and efficiency measures, we can cut our total energy use in half or better (some estimates go as high as 80 percent) without affecting our quality of life.

Cutting our energy use will also reduce the energy pollution that causes smog, acid rain, climate change, and other environmental problems. Many simple tips for energy conservation and efficiency all around your home will be given throughout this chapter; they can help you achieve the goal of reducing fossil-fuel energy consumption in your home by 50 percent.

Although energy use varies depending on climate, here is a national-average breakdown of the way we use energy in our homes:

Space heating, 32 percent to 60 percent

Space cooling, 7 percent to 40 percent

Water heating (including clothes and dishwashers), 15 percent to 31 percent

Refrigeration/freezing, 8 percent to 12 percent

Lighting, 6 percent

Cooking, 4 percent

Dryer, 3 percent

Other appliances and electronics, 6 percent

The following actions *by themselves* have the potential to save *half* of your fossil-fuel energy use:

1. Insulate and weatherize your home.
2. Retrofit your home with energy-efficient space heating (and cooling if you need it).
3. Consider alternative energy sources such as a solar hot-water heater and solar electric panels.

All will pay for themselves over time and in some states qualify for tax rebates. Ask your local utility or energy organization to perform a free or low-cost energy audit to help you find out where and how you can save energy.

Remember that ultra-low-flow showerheads and faucets can also cut your hot-water heating bills and energy use.

A fully airtight house can lead to increased air pollution, so make sure you have good ventilation without losing heat (by using an air-to-air heat exchanger, for example).

APPLIANCES

Appliances (excluding WATER HEATERS) account for about 30 percent of the energy use in our homes. The most energy-efficient appliances currently on the mass market can reduce that figure by about one-third, saving you 10 percent or more on your total energy bill. Some appliances, such as a Sun Frost refrigerator, can reduce energy consumption by 80 percent.

Refrigerator/freezers take the most energy, followed by clothes washers, dishwashers, clothes dryers, cookers, and televisions. Gas appliances generally use up to 50 percent less energy than electric ones. If you do have electric appliances such as a dishwasher or washer and dryer, run them at off-peak hours, like late at night. To meet the demand during peak hours, utilities often must use backup generators that are even less energy-efficient.

Although replacing an appliance before it breaks may not be the most efficient use of resources, sometimes it can be energy- and cost-effective to do so. If everyone had a refrigerator that used 80 percent less energy, for example, we could shut down almost half of the country's nuclear power plants.

ENERGY-SAVING TIPS

Refrigerators
• Energy-efficient refrigerators put the motor on top rather than on the bottom (saving 50 percent of cooling costs), have good insulation and tight door seals, and are defrosted manually (saving two and a half times the energy, since frost-free refrigerators use an electric heater inside to melt frost).
• Keep your refrigerator at thirty-eight to forty degrees Fahrenheit and freezer compartment at five degrees Fahrenheit (zero degrees Fahrenheit for a separate freezer for long-term storage).
• With manual-defrost refrigerators, don't allow the frost to build up more than a quarter inch (frost buildup increases energy needed to run the motor). If you have an automatic ice maker, disconnect it and save a lot of energy.
• Place your refrigerator away from direct sun and provide good ventilation around it. Don't put it next to an oven.
• Test your door seals by closing the door over a piece of paper or dollar bill so it is half in and half out of the refrigerator. If you can easily pull the paper out, you may need to adjust the latch or replace the seals. Also clean the seals often.
• Open the refrigerator door as little as possible, as the cold air rushes out quickly. Don't leave the door open for long periods, either.
• Let hot foods cool to room temperature before putting them in the refrigerator, and cover foods to prevent condensation on the refrigerator walls.
• Clean the refrigerator coils, compressor, fan, and grill at least once a year (unplug it first). Use a vacuum and soap, water, and sponge. Besides saving a few dollars a month on your electric bill, this will extend the refrigerator's life.
• Most refrigerators use freon gas (an ozone destroyer) as the refrigerant, so make sure to recycle the refrigerant (and the refrigerator) when the refrigerator has died.

Clothes Washing
• Wash clothes in warm or cold water, and rinse in cold water.
• Use the right amount of detergent; over-sudsing makes the machine work harder.

• Presoak or use a soak cycle when washing heavily soiled clothes to avoid two washings.

Clothes Drying

• Use a clothesline whenever possible. Clothes dried outside often seem fresher and cleaner than those that are machine dried.
• When using a dryer, save up your laundry and run several loads back to back; a lot of energy goes to warming up the dryer each time you begin.
• Clean the lint screen between each use, as lint impedes the flow of air and makes the machine work harder.
• Save time and energy by "pressing" sheets and pillowcases on the warm top of your dryer and by hanging clothes in the bathroom while you're showering to let the steam remove the wrinkles.

Dishwashing

• Scrape rather than rinse dishes before loading. If you do rinse, use cold water.
• Run the dishwasher only when full, and use the energy-saving setting without heated drying.
• When doing dishes by hand, fill a container or the sink with soapy water rather than let the water run, and use a low-flow faucet or aerator for rinsing.

Cooking

• If you buy a gas stove, choose one with an electronic ignition instead of a pilot light; you'll save over 30 percent of gas use. Convection ovens are more efficient than are conventional ovens. Microwave ovens are more efficient than either, but may have potential health effects.
• Keep stove burners and reflector pans clean for better heat reflection.
• Use the stove top rather than the oven when you can, and cover pots for more efficient heating.

Television

• Unplug when not in use, since most new televisions draw up to ten watts standby power for the instant-on feature. The equivalent of one large power plant is used to power our televisions when they are turned off!

At the Store/By Mail

The American Council for an Energy-Efficient Economy (see Recommended Resources) puts out a yearly update of energy-efficient appliances you are likely to find in your local stores. I've included here some more unusual ones that you also might want to consider.

Stove/oven

Alternative Energy Engineering. Plans for building solar box cookers.

Bantam Sun Oven (Burns-Milwaukee). ▣ ⚡ Sun oven cooks entirely with the power of the sun. Use for baking bread, roasts, fish, chicken, casseroles, vegetables; anything you would bake in an oven. Portable. *Jade Mountain, Wendy & Cindy Originals.*

Spotlight Marketing. ▣ ⚡ Sells a ready-to-use portable, solid-wood solar cooker, a kit for building your own, and a plans booklet.

Tirolia Cook Stove (Gingerich Small Engines). ⚡ A combination stove and heater that cooks, bakes, and heats your water and home. Uses wood as the fuel, and can be used without electricity. *Gingerich Small Engines.*

Clothes washer

Jade Mountain. ▣ ⚡ A hand-operated washing machine that works totally without electricity. Washes normal-size loads.

Refrigerators

Sun Frost Refrigerators (Sun Frost) ⚡ "The world's most efficient refrigerator." Available in both AC and DC. *Alternative*

Energy Engineering, Backwoods Solar Electric Systems, Integral Energy Systems, Jade Mountain, Kansas Wind Power, Photocomm, Real Goods Trading Company, Sunelco.

AUTOMOBILES

Warning labels on gasoline pumps:
    "DANGER! Motor fuel.
    Harmful or fatal if swallowed.
    Vapors harmful.
    Long-term exposure to vapors has caused cancer in laboratory animals.
    May cause eye and skin irritation.
    Avoid prolonged breathing of vapors.
    Keep face away from nozzle and gas tank.
    Keep away from eyes and skin.
    Never siphon by mouth.
    Failure to use caution may cause serious injury or illness."

In the state of California:
    " WARNING. Chemicals known to the state of California to cause cancer, birth defects, or other reproductive harm are found in gasoline, crude oil, and many other petroleum products and their vapors or result from their use. Read and follow label directions and use care when handling or using petroleum products."

Gasoline- and diesel-engine exhausts are a complex mixture that contains hundreds of chemicals and is both mutagenic and carcinogenic.

A study released in 1990 by the American Lung Association and conducted by the University of California at Davis found that air pollution from motor vehicles alone could be linked to 50,000 to 120,000 premature deaths in the United States each year and is responsible for $40 to $50 billion in annual health-care costs.

Dr. Samuel Epstein, professor of occupational and environmental medicine at the University of Illinois Medical Center and a leading cancer researcher, has identified other health problems associated with fossil-fuel processing and refueling: leukemia and cancers among refinery workers and neighboring communities, leukemia and cancer from inhaling benzene during refueling, liver and kidney cancers related to evaporation and inhalation of unleaded gasoline. Consumers at self-serve gasoline pumps are routinely exposed to up to three times the level of benzene that the Occupational Safety and Health Administration (OSHA) requires workers to be warned and protected against.

ENERGY-EFFICIENCY TIPS
• Drive less. Walk, bicycle, join or form a carpool, use public transportation.
• Live closer to where you work to avoid commuting. See if you can do some of the work at home a few days a week; computers and modems are making this more possible.
• Choose a smaller, energy-efficient car. Both the Environmental Protection Agency and Consumers Union report yearly on the fuel efficiency of new cars. When you buy a used car, go to the library and look up the mileage ratings in publications from past years.
• Buy a used or restored car. There are many serviceable and relatively fuel-efficient used cars available. Manufacturing new cars requires a tremendous amount of energy and resources.
• Drive safely. Lower speeds, slower starts, and gradual accelerations improve fuel economy. Driving fifty miles per hour uses 8.1 percent more fuel than driving forty miles per hour. At sixty miles per hour, you use 11.3 percent more, and at seventy miles per hour another 17.3 percent.
• Maintain your automobile properly to increase fuel efficiency. Have regular tune-ups, keep adequate tire pressure, and change the oil frequently.

At the Store/By Mail

CAM2 Motor Oil (CAM2 Oil Products Company). Recycled motor oil. *Seventh Generation.*

Electro Automotive. Sells all the components you need to convert small cars (Hondas, VW Bugs, Chevettes, fiberglass kit cars) to electric cars that run on rechargeable batteries. ⚓ Also has a battery pack that can be recharged from solar cells.

KSA Jojoba. Jojoba-based automotive products include lubricants for standard and automotive transmissions and regular and high-performance two-cycle racing engines, plus an all-purpose industrial grease. These do contain some petrochemicals, but no animal by-products.

BATTERIES

Regular batteries cause a tremendous amount of heavy-metal pollution when disposed of, and they also can be used only once. Rechargeable batteries (nickel cadmium, or "ni-cad") can be used over and over, saving manufacturing energy and resources. You can also recharge them with a solar-powered battery charger and save electricity.

At the Store/By Mail

Seventh Generation. Designed for industrial use, their rechargeable batteries have a longer life than those sold in retail stores. Come in AA, C, and D, and can be recharged up to five hundred times. Also a portable solar battery charger that powers up to four AA nickel-cadmium batteries.

CANDLES

Harmful ingredients: colors, fragrance, paraffin.

While candles certainly are not going to supply all of our lighting needs, they are a peaceful, romantic source of light that can be made from natural materials. On occasions when you prefer candlelight, choose natural-color beeswax candles, which have a strong flame and a wonderful honey aroma, or bayberry wax candles.

At the Store/By Mail

Natural beeswax candles can be purchased at most candle shops and some natural-food stores.

Beeswax candles and candlemaking supplies

BeeDazzled Candleworks. Hand-dipped, rolled or molded beeswax candles in natural shade or colors. Tapers; menorah, votive, and hexagon styles. ⊞ Offers a five percent discount on candles ordered without the usual plastic packaging.

Cat Holler Farm. Handmade candles of pure beeswax with all-cotton wicking. ⊞ Hand-wrapped in tissue paper.

Del Mar Beeswax Candles (Knorr Beeswax Products). Beeswax candles. ⊞ Wrapped in cellophane. *Knorr Beeswax Products.*

Erwin's Bee Farm. Pure beeswax candles in molded shapes, ten-hour-burning colored hexagonal tapers, colored dipped tapers, rolled honeycomb in colors, and birthday candles. Also beeswax blocks for making your own candles, and oak candleholders.

Fluir Herbals. Hand-dipped six-inch beeswax candles.

Hearthsong. Beeswax-candle dipping kit allows you and your children to make inexpensive candles at home.

Illuminee du Monde. Rolled honeycomb beeswax candles in colors. Assorted sizes from tiny four-inch to twelve-inch tapers. Also special candles suitable for menorahs.

InterNatural. Natural-color beeswax candles.

Karen's Nontoxic Products. Beeswax candles colored with natural dyes.

Meadowbrook Herb Garden. Beeswax candles in six- and ten-inch tapers and ten inch hexagons.

Mountain Spirit. Beeswax candles.

Vermont Country Store. Bayberry wax candles. "Bayberries are harvested in the fall and boiled in water to release the wax, which floats to the top. It takes 1½ quarts of berries to make one candle! Hand-dipped 35 times, the ten-inch long tapers are green in color and delicate in fragrance, with no scent or color added.

Williams-Sonoma. Natural-color beeswax candles.

HEATING AND COOLING

Home heating is responsible for releasing carbon dioxide (the most prevalent gas contributing to the greenhouse effect), as well as sulfur dioxide and nitrogen oxide (the main causes of acid rain), into the atmosphere. An inefficient heating system can waste up to 50 percent of the energy it uses.

ENERGY-SAVING TIPS

• Use the most efficient heating or cooling system. Replacing or improving your present one can save you money in the long run. Choosing a system of the proper size for your home can also affect energy savings.

Home Heating

Electric heating systems are highly inefficient. If you do have one, consider installing a heat-pump system that uses thermal energy from outside air for both heating and cooling. The initial cost may be high, but such a system can cut your heating bill, by 40 to 60 percent.

If you want a gas furnace, choose one with an electronic ignition, as pilot lights waste energy. If your furnace has a pilot light, consult with your gas company about turning it off during the summer.

If you have a fireplace, install a woodstove or fireplace insert with doors or windows for the most efficient use. At the least, use a convective grate and install a well-fitting set of glass doors, and close them before retiring or when the fireplace is not in use. An open fireplace will let up to 8 percent of its heat go straight out the chimney. When using a fireplace, turn the house thermostat down to fifty to fifty-five degrees Fahrenheit, close all doors and warm-air ducts entering the room, and (unless the fireplace has an outside supply of air) open a window near the fireplace about an inch to keep warm air from being sucked from other parts of the house.

Wood stoves are better than fireplaces for heating but still can cause quite a bit of air pollution unless you use the best ones. Look for the most efficient and cleanest-burning models, which provide a secondary-burn chamber or catalytic device for reducing harmful emissions. The EPA rates wood stoves for both efficiency and emissions; their standards can be obtained from your local EPA office.

Heating only rooms actually in use with space heaters can be an efficient alternative to heating your whole house. Externally vented natural-gas-fueled space heaters can be safe and effective for room use. Again, electric space heaters for rooms use a lot of energy, often at peak times; they are not the best choice and may not even be more efficient than heating a larger area with other fuel sources. Among electric space heaters, radiant varieties such as quartz heaters are relatively more efficient since they work like the sun's radiant energy to warm people and objects rather than heating the air.

The best heat, of course, comes from renewable energy. Use add-on greenhouses, window-box solar room heaters, and super-efficient wood stoves.

Tune up your furnace. Gas furnaces should be tuned every two years and oil furnaces each year. Test your furnace for combustion efficiency and pollutants, clean it, and adjust it. A heating technician will do this for you for about forty to sixty dollars. With a forced-air system, change your filters (or better, clean reusable ones) once a month to save energy and minimize dust.

Install a programmable clock thermostat to keep the heat lower at night, and much lower during the day when you are away. This can save twenty to forty percent of energy use (10 to 14 percent at night). For each degree you lower the thermostat, you can obtain a fuel savings of 3 percent in cold climates, 6 percent in mild climates, and up to 11 percent in warm climates.

Wear layers of clothes made with closely woven natural fabrics to keep warm.

Plant evergreens to block winter wind, and deciduous trees to keep your home cool during the summer.

Use an air-to-air heat exchanger to effectively ventilate a closed house, with only 20- to 30-percent heat loss. Such a machine blows stale indoor air out of the house, which passes into close contact with fresh outdoor air that it is simultaneously being pulled in. This contact, occuring in many small, thin-walled tubes or channels, allows much of the indoor air's heat to be transferred to the incoming cold air so that warmth is retained.

Air is blown through a heat exchanger core that is made of metal, plastic, or treated paper. Tests at the Lawrence Berkeley Lab in California have found the metal core to work best at transferring heat. Metal cores also would release the fewest pollutants to the incoming air.

Heat exchangers are available in several sizes, from a window unit to full house systems that may require installation of ducting. Depending on the amount of pollution being produced, it could take up to five or six small units to adequately ventilate an average house.

When building new homes, there are many things you can do to drastically reduce your need for heating or cooling systems, including orienting the building to receive optimal sunlight, placing most or all of the windows on the sunny side, and building the home partially in the earth or with earth berms (mounds of soil) to block winter wind and keep in heat or coolness.

Home Cooling

Use open windows (opening more than one provides cross-ventilation) and fans instead of energy-guzzling and stale air-conditioning. A whole-house fan in your attic (or an upstairs window) will pull cool air into your home and blow warm air out, saving up to two-thirds of your cooling costs. Even if you have air-conditioning, it will pay to use the fan rather than air-conditioning when the outside temperature is below seventy-eight degrees Fahrenheit. Using a solar-powered fan has the advantage of running on the sun's free energy exactly when you need it to—when the sun is hottest.

Use trees, shrubs, hanging plants, overhangs, and window shades to keep out heat from direct sunlight. Properly planted, trees and shrubs can reduce air-conditioning energy use by as much as 50 percent.

During the hottest hours of the day, keep windows and doors closed and fans off. Keep lights low or off. Do your cooking and use other heat-generating appliances in the early morning and late evening. Turn off the furnace pilot light in summer, but make sure to relight it before you use the furnace again. Wear light, loose-fitting cotton clothes to keep cool.

If you do use an air-conditioner:

• Choose the most efficient model with the lowest capacity to meet your needs. Room air-conditioners can save energy over a central system.

• Insulate your cooling ducts, and keep the system well tuned with periodic maintenance. Clean or replace filters at least once a month, since a dirty fan has to run longer to move the same amount of air.

• Locate your air-conditioner thermostat away from direct sunlight and heat-generating appliances such as lamps or TV sets, which can cause the air-conditioner to run longer than necessary. Set the thermostat as high as possible (seventy-eight degrees or higher). Raising the temperature six degrees higher, say from seventy-two to seventy-eight degrees, will save from 12 to 47 percent of your cooling costs. Don't set the thermostat lower than normal when you first turn on the air-conditioner: it will not cool faster but will use more energy to cool to a lower temperature than you need.

• Set the fan speed to high except in very humid weather. Set the fan speed to low when it's humid; although you'll get less cooling, you will feel cooler since more moisture will be removed from the air.

• Turn off your window air-conditioner when you leave the room for a few hours. You will use less energy to cool it down later than you would use if you had left it on the whole time.

At the Store/By Mail

Air Changer (Preston-Brock Manufacturing Company). ⚡ Air-recovery heat exchanger (up to 78 percent efficient). *Memphremagog Heat Exchangers.*

Aldes Heat Recovery Ventilation Systems (Riehs & Riehs). ⚡ Air-recovery heat exchanger (70 percent efficiency). *Riehs & Riehs.*

Basilo Lepuschenko. ⚡ Offers plans for radiant-heat fireplaces. Known as Russian or Finnish fireplaces, they store 90 percent of the available heat from a fire in their own brick construction and then release it steadily to the surrounding air.

Black Jack Firebox (Leslie Manufacturing). ⚡ A waste-fueled heat plant composed of an iron box lined with firebrick, installed near the home to be heated, and connected to the home's existing heating system by water pipes or hot-air ducts. Can be used with several types of free fuel such as scrap wood, wastepaper, or agricultural by-products like wheat, straw, or corncobs. *Leslie Manufacturing.*

Conden Saver (Kim Supply Company). ⚡ Saves up to 27 percent on central air-conditioning. Makes your compressor coils work more efficiently by cooling them with a fine mist of completely pure water captured from your inside air-conditioning unit. *Kim Supply Company.*

Hearthstone Soapstone Stoves (NHC). ⚡ Soapstone stoves with 90 percent combustion efficiency.

Kachelofen (Kachelofen Group). ⚡ Ceramic-tile radiant heater that works with wood, gas, or electricity. *Baubiologie Hardware.*

Kickapoo Wood & Coal Furnaces (Kickapoo Diversified Products). ⚡ Wood- and coal-burning furnaces with up to 79 percent efficiency. *Kickapoo Diversified Products.*

Lennox Heating and Cooling Systems (Lennox). Heat pumps with up to 97 percent efficiency.

Pelonis Safe-T-Furnace (Del-Rain Corporation). Ceramic-disc heating element in a heavy-gauge-metal cabinet. Air filter cleans circulating air. *Allergy Relief Shop, The Living Source, Nigra Enterprises.*

Reggio Recessed Radiation System (Reggio Register Company). Recessed-radiation heating system, and attractive floor registers for forced-air heating systems. *Reggio Register Company.*

TESS Heat-Storing Fireplaces (Thermal Energy Storage Systems). ⚡ Applies age-old, proven design principles found in European masonry heaters to create an efficient masonry fireplace. Heat that would normally be lost up the flue in a conventional masonry fireplace is absorbed and stored in a massive heat-storage area, then released gradually and steadily for up to twenty-four hours after the fire has died out. You can choose from a number of exterior facing materials.

Tulikivi Wood Burning Fireplaces and Ovens. (Tulikivi Group North America) ⚡ Beautiful heat-retaining fireplaces and wood-burning ovens made of American soapstone, which has a phenomenal capacity for retaining heat. Heat is stored in the soapstone and released slowly and evenly into the room. Only one hot fire is necessary to radiate warmth for eight to twelve hours. "Tulikivi products don't waste energy or pollute the environment like ordinary stoves and fireplaces. The wood is thoroughly burned so the emissions are minimal." *Tulikivi Group North America.*

Whitfield Pellet Stoves (Pyro Industries). ⚡ These stoves release a fraction of the smoke and particulates wood stoves do, and are among the cleanest-burning today. Overall efficiency up to 82 percent. Wood pellets are made from lumber-industry waste—an environment-conscious, easy-to-use fuel.

Wirsbo-pePEX Radiant Hydronic Heating Systems (Wirsbo). ⚡ Radiant floor-heating system that can reduce energy use 25 percent or more compared with conventional heating systems.

INSULATION AND WEATHERIZATION

Insulating your home properly is the single most important thing you can do to reduce in-home energy use. It can save you up to 40 percent of your total energy use and often pays for itself in reduced costs within one or two years.

The type of insulation you use is very important, because insulation can be very toxic. Urea-formaldehyde foam insulation

(UFFI) is the most dangerous of all. The Consumer Product Safety Commission (CPSC) banned the use of UFFI in residences and schools in 1982, but one year later this ban was overturned by the United States Court of Appeals. The CPSC feels the court's decision was based on legal and factual errors and continues to warn consumers that available evidence indicates there are risks associated with this product. Reported symptoms include respiratory problems, dizziness, nausea, and eye and throat irritations—ranging from short-term discomfort to hospitalization.

Fiberglass batts are frequently used for insulation. These are generally considered to be relatively safe, although there is some speculation that inhalation of fiberglass fibers may cause adverse health effects similar to those from asbestos fibers, and they do contain a small amount of urea- and phenol-formaldehyde resin to keep them fluffy. Some also release fumes from asphalt impregnation, and foil-backed batts can interfere with the beneficial natural electromagnetic connections our bodies have with the Earth. If you do choose fiberglass batts, order them with paper backing.

Blown-in cellulose insulation is an acceptable alternative. It is made from recycled newspapers and sodium borate, is cheaper than fiberglass, and has greater insulating properties.

ENERGY-SAVING TIPS
• Fully insulate your attic (consider walls, too, which could save up to 20 percent energy), including ducts and places where there are gaps in insulation. Don't insulate over eaves, vents, or on top of recessed lighting fixtures or other heat-producing equipment on the attic floor, and keep insulation three inches away from the sides of these fixtures.
• Ask your utility to test for air leaks, or

do it yourself: on a windy day, move a lighted candle around door and window frames, cracks and holes in walls and ceilings, heating ducts, attic doors, sites where plumbing or wiring penetrates walls, and along the lines where floors, walls, and ceilings meet. If the candle flame flickers, there's a leak that needs to be fixed.

• Caulk and weatherstrip around doors, windows, cracks, and holes (inside and outside), and put gasket insulators behind all electrical outlets and switch plates (for a savings of up to 10 percent or more).

• Install storm windows, and insulate shades or curtains. Also, consider installing new windows, which can have the same insulative value as walls. These are double or triple glazed with low-emissivity or other coatings and may be filled with insulating gasses like argon or krypton. They can keep you warmer in winter and cooler in summer. As much energy leaks through our windows every year as flows through the Alaskan pipeline, so increasing the insulative value of your windows can make a big difference.

• Use kitchen, bath, and other ventilating fans sparingly, since in just one hour they can blow away a houseful of warm (or cool) air. Turn them off as soon as they have done their job.

At the Store/By Mail

☘ *Natural window blankets*
Crocodile Tiers. Heavy cotton window blankets to block sunlight and/or prevent temperature exchange. Fabric untreated; formaldehyde tested.

☘ *Natural caulks and joint sealants*
Auro No. 386 Natural Joint Filler (Auro). *Sinan Company.*
Livos Vedo Spackling Compound/Anavo Oil-based Spackle/Linseed Putty (Livos). *Livos Plantchemistry.*

⊕ *Nontoxic caulks and joint sealants*
AFM Joint Compound/Dyno Flex Caulking Compound/Spackling Compound (AFM Enterprises). AFM *Enterprises, Allergy Relief Shop, The Allergy Store, Baubiologie Hardware, The Ecology Box, The Living Source, Nigra Enterprises.*

⊕ *Nontoxic insulation*
Air-Crete Foamed-in-Place Insulation (Air-Crete). Cementitious magnesium-oxide foam that after application hardens to an inert hard sponge. Contains pink dye.
Perlite (Perlite Institute). Insulation made from perlite, a naturally occuring mineral.

LIGHTING

Over centuries, our bodies have become accustomed to being outdoors in natural light. Now most of us spend our days indoors under artificial lighting.

The problem with artificial lighting sources appears to be that the spectrum of the light they produce is not the same as that of natural sunlight. When forced to spend the majority of their time under artificial light, our bodies don't function quite as well.

Regular exposure to artificial light has been associated with fatigue, vision problems, hyperactivity, increased susceptibility to osteoporosis, and changes in heart rate, blood pressure, electrical brain-wave patterns, hormone secretions, and the body's natural cyclical rhythms. There is also a correspondence between mood and light, particularly between light and depression.

Artificial light also is generated with electricity, which generally comes from nonrenewable polluting nuclear or fossil-fuel sources.

Most of the major manufacturers of standard incandescent light bulbs also make nuclear weapons.

SPECIAL TIPS

It's important for our health to get as much natural daylight as possible—just as important as getting proper nutrition, sleep, and exercise. This doesn't mean staring at the sun, or even being in the sun; shaded light is preferable. The only criterion is that the source of the light be the sun. Using natural light benefits the environment, too, because this source is solar powered.

• Spend as much time outdoors as you can. If you have the space available, set up a work space on a screen porch or next to an open window, eat your meals outdoors, go for walks.
• Wear a sun visor or wide-brimmed hat for eye protection instead of sunglasses, which block the light from coming into your body through your eyes.

At the Store/By Mail

The perfect light bulb would be energy-efficient, have a long life, duplicate the spectrum of sunlight, contain no radioactive materials, and be manufactured by a company that doesn't also make nuclear weapons. Such a light bulb does not yet exist, to my knowledge, but there are some that satisfy one or more of these requirements. Regardless of the type of bulb you buy, check that the color of light produced is acceptable to you, as different bulbs have differing abilities to reproduce true color.

Compact fluorescent bulbs are the most energy-efficient, converting to light about 40 percent of the energy used, in contrast to a regular incandescent bulb, which converts to light only 10 percent of the energy used. So-called energy-saving incandescents are actually only 1 to 5 percent better. If we all used compact fluorescents in our homes and businesses, we could eliminate the need for all the nuclear power plants operating in the United States. They also last longer, with life-

spans ranging from 7,500 to 100,000 hours instead of the 750 to 1,000 hours of a standard incandescent bulb.

Some compact fluorescents use small quantities of radioactive material in them, so make sure the ones you buy do not. The U.S. Nuclear Regulatory Commission requires that the bulbs that do contain radioactive materials be so labeled, but this information may be in very fine print, so look carefully. Those that indicate they have electronic ballast are nuclear-free.

There are fluorescent bulbs available that can fit in regular incandescent-bulb sockets, as well as the usual long-tube varieties. An eighteen-watt compact fluorescent gives the same light as a seventy-five watt incandescent bulb and lasts thirteen times longer. Although these bulbs cost ten dollars to twenty-eight dollars, they are about half as expensive over their lifetime as incandescent bulbs because of the greatly reduced energy use.

Halogen bulbs also use less energy and last longer. About 15 percent of the energy used is converted to light, and they last about 2,000 hours. Best used for "spot" lights, because they give a bright white light.

Long-life incandescent bulbs will not save energy but do have greatly extended life spans.

Full-spectrum bulbs have a color that more closely duplicates sunlight.

Energy-efficient, full-spectrum, long-life, & nuclear-free light bulbs

Chromalux (Lumiram Electric Corporation). An incandescent bulb whose light is very close to natural sunlight. Rated to last about 4,000 hours. N.E.E.D.S., Simmons Company.

EcoWorks Ecological Lightbulbs (EcoWorks). ⚡ Incandescent bulbs that use 10 percent less energy and last three times as long. Made by a nuclear-free company. ⊞ Packaged in recycled materials printed with nontoxic ink. Nuclear Free America.

K Lighting Company. Long-life (2,100 hours) incandescent bulbs for residential and commercial uses. Also halogens and regular fluorescents.

New Alchemy Institute. Compact fluorescent bulbs.

Ott Light Systems. Full-spectrum fluorescent lights with special radiation-shielded fixtures.

People's Energy Resource Cooperative. Compact fluorescent and halogen bulbs.

Rising Sun Enterprises. ⚡ A good selection of compact fluorescents, and a knowledgable staff to help you choose the right ones for you. Also halogen lamps and fixtures.

Seventh Generation. Compact fluorescent bulbs in several shapes and sizes, with good background information to help you choose the best ones for you.

Vita-Lite (Duro-Lite Lamps). Fluorescent bulbs that nearly duplicate sunlight at high noon. Recommended by Nuclear Free America. *Simmons Company*.

RENEWABLE ENERGY

Although 30,000 homes in the United States already use solar energy as their primary energy source, switching to non-polluting and renewable sources of energy is now becoming a realistic option for many people.

I've listed here general alternative-energy catalogs that have a wide range of products that can help you convert to alternative energy either partially or entirely, or experiment with single appliances such as solar fans that can be powered by renewable energy.

Most alternative-energy systems use some kind of natural power to charge and recharge batteries that are then used as the power source. While the products available through each catalog vary, there are some basic components necessary to energy self-sufficiency that almost all the catalogs carry:

• large 12-volt batteries
• photovoltaic modules to capture sunlight (some catalogs have "starter kits" that can get you going for a relatively small investment)
• mounts and trackers to put your modules on (trackers pivot to follow the sun)
• controllers, meters, wire connectors, etc.
• windmills
• hydropower generators (use water for power)
• gas-powered generators (for when all else fails)
• inverters to convert 12-volt DC battery power to standard 120-volt AC power
• 12-volt energy-efficient light bulbs and appliances, including wireless telephones, telephone answering machines, electronic typewriters, television sets, refrigerators, and vacuums.

In addition, some catalogs also carry solar-powered items—such as small battery rechargers, wristwatches, and calculators—that are inexpensive, easy-to-use, fun ways to learn about alternative energy.

At the Store/By Mail
Look for local stores that may supply alternative-energy products, or order by mail.

⚡ Renewable energy
Alternative Energy Engineering. Photovoltaic systems (with helpful worksheets), portable solar generators, windmills, solar battery chargers and batteries, 12-volt appliances.

Backwoods Solar Electric Systems. This catalog gives good background information that is easy for the beginner to understand. Carries the basics needed for self-sufficiency. 🏠 Operates a home with a three desk office and a product construction shop with power tools on solar energy with wind power as a backup on stormy days when there is no sun. Because of their respect for animals and all life, they discourage using their equipment for electric fences that can harm animals.

Holly Solar Products. Solar panels, mounting packages and hardware.

Integral Energy Systems. A good selection of the basics, plus books on alternative energy.

Jade Mountain. A simple selection of the basics, including a starter kit, plus solar battery rechargers, solar-powered flashlights, and so on.

Kansas Wind Power. A wide assortment of items, including some, such as electric garden tractors, not found in other catalogs. Without pictures, and difficult to read.

Photocomm. A slick, full-color catalog with all the basics, toys, and novelties.

Real Goods. Nearly two hundred pages of catalog; not only includes every product imaginable, but also guarantees that the company will beat any price. Good reading, too.

Solar Components Corporation. Features glazing and kits for greenhouses and other passive installations, energy efficient skylights, solar hot-water systems, photovoltaics, and other serious solar collectors.

Solar Electric. A small, easy-to-read catalog with simple items such as a solar personal stereo, battery chargers, a solar starter kit, 12-volt appliances.

Sun Watt Corporation. A small company that makes hybrid solar modules that produce electricity and hot water at the same time, and small, inexpensive solar battery chargers with good-quality batteries. ▣ "We are operating out of a completely self-sufficient facility some distance from the nearest power line and use alternative energy in all our manufacturing processes."

Sunelco. The basics for solar power.

WATER HEATERS

Water heating consumes 15 to 30 percent of a home's energy. In a typical system, the storage-tank water must be reheated again and again throughout the day and night to maintain its temperature, whether you use it or not. New "instant" or "tankless" home water heaters are about one-fourth the size of conventional systems and heat only the water that passes through them when you turn on the hot-water tap. As an added bonus, you never run out of hot water because there is no holding tank. They can cut your water-heating bills up to 50 percent (or more if you have electric heat). Some models are very small and will fit under your kitchen sink or in the bathroom.

ENERGY-SAVING TIPS

• Use low-flow shower heads and faucets (see Chapter 3). These devices will often pay for themselves within six months.

• Install a solar water heater. There are attractive, well-designed ones available. You can use your existing water heater or a "tankless" one as a backup.

• Insulate your existing water tank. Hardware stores sell insulating jackets. Be careful not to block off air vents on gas-fired heaters. Also insulate all hot-water pipes, especially those in unheated spaces.

• Turn the water-heater temperature to low or 120 degrees. This can save 18 percent of the energy used at the usual 140-degree setting and still provide adequate hot water (lowering it to 130 degrees will save 6 percent). If you have a dishwasher without a hot-water booster, consult the owner's manual to see if you need to keep the water tank at a higher temperature.

• Put a timer on your water heater to turn it on for only a few hours a day in advance of when you need hot water. Even when off, the tank will keep water hot for several hours, depending on the insulation.

• Turn your water heater off if you go on vacation. If it is gas-fired with a pilot light, contact your gas company first.

• If you have a water-bed heater, it is using as much electricity as a large self-defrosting refrigerator. Insulate around and under the bed and put quilts and blankets over it when not in use.

At the Store/By Mail

E *Energy-efficient water heaters*

AquaStar Tankless Water Heaters (Controlled Energy Corporation). Tankless gas and electric water heaters—energy savings up to 50 percent. *Jade Mountain, Kansas Wind Power, Photocomm, Real Goods Trading Company.*

Copper Cricket Solar Water Heaters (Sage Advance Corporation). **E** Passive solar water heater—no motors, pumps, or valves.

Enro Heatsaver (Enro Manufacturing). Installs in your existing water heater and cuts bills 15 to 20 percent per month by capturing waste heat.

Heliodyne Solar Energy Systems (Heliodyne). Systems for home or pool hot-water heating. *Heliodyne.*

Instant-Flow Water Heater (Chronomite Laboratories). Compact point-of-use instant water heater.

Muck-Vac (Elemental Enterprises). Special vacuum for cleaning sediment from water heaters can make it more efficient and double heater life.

Myson Instantaneous Water Heaters (Myson). Undersink and whole-house gas or electric tankless water heaters.

Paloma Tankless Hot Water Heaters (Paloma Industries). Heats water instantaneously and continuously as it flows through the unit; fuel savings run more than 26 percent. *Real Goods Trading Company, Sunelco.*

Skylite Solar Water Heater (American Solar Network). **E** Solar water heaters with the aesthetic appearance of a skylight. *American Solar Network.*

Solahart Hot Water Systems (Solahart). Compact solar water heater that can save up to 80 percent of the energy your present water heater uses. *Solahart.*

5 ❧ Food

We as a nation are so removed from any real involvement
with the food we buy, cook, and consume. We have
become alienated by the frozen and hygienically sealed
foods. I want to stand in the supermarket aisles and
implore the shoppers, their carts piled high with mass-
produced artificiality, "Please . . . look at what you are
buying!" Food should be experienced through the senses,
and I am sad for those who cannot see a lovely,
unblemished apple just picked from the tree as voluptuous,
or a beautifully perfect pear as sensuous, or see that a
brown-spotted two-foot-high lettuce, its edges curling and
wilted, is ugly and offensive. It is a fundamental fact that
no cook, however creative and capable, can produce a dish
of a quality any higher than that of the raw ingredients.

ALICE WATERS

I've made a lot of changes in my diet throughout my life. I was
raised on TV dinners and fast food, then switched about ten years ago to a vegetarian
diet and a lot of "natural" convenience foods that were free from artificial colors,
flavors, and preservatives. I figured that as long as I wasn't eating the most toxic
additives and wasn't eating meat, I had a healthy diet.

Within the last year, I've made big changes. I have found the greatest epicurian
pleasure in eating mostly fresh, organically grown fruits and vegetables, whole grains,
nuts, tofu, and hardly any sweets. I feel better and have more energy than I ever had.

Making changes in how we eat can be difficult because we all have so many emotions
tied up with food. We want to socialize or do business over a meal, prepare old family
recipes, and be comforted by chocolate-chip cookies.

What most inspired me to change the way I eat was the simple realization that we
literally are what we eat. Food is both the fuel and the raw building material that keep
our body structures sound and functioning. Good, healthful food comes directly from
the plants of the Earth, which get their nutrients from the soil and air, their water from
the rain, and their energy from the sun. Would you rather have a body built from
pesticide-contaminated, processed, artificially colored, flavored, and preserved fried
potato chips, or luscious, vine-ripened, organically grown vegetables and fruits?

HOW OUR FOOD CHOICES AFFECT OUR HEALTH
AND THE EARTH

At the turn of this century, 80 percent of the people living in this country were
farmers. Agriculture was a way of life, and farming practices were based on centuries-

old methods that emphasized maintaining the fertility of the soil and being in harmony with nature's ways.

Today only about 2 percent of our citizens are farmers, and our food is grown by "agribusiness" corporations dependent on large inputs of petrochemicals, drugs, artificial fertilizers, toxic pesticides, and water. Our food is overprocessed, artificially colored, fumigated, and shipped long distances; now it is starting to be irradiated.

Current Agribusiness Practices

Most of our food supply is made up of malnourished plants fed limited nutrients from artificial fertilizers and sprayed with toxic pesticides.

In 1988, 270 billion pounds of artificial fertilizers were used in agriculture. In addition to providing inadequate nutrition for plants and destroying soil, fertilizers often leach through the soil into the groundwater rather than reaching the plant. A five-year study by the National Science Foundation found that 70 percent of the nitrogen applied to croplands as fertilizer ends up polluting the water table, salinizing the soil, and escaping into the atmosphere (where it depletes the ozone layer and contributes to acid rain). Another recent study in the scientific journal *Nature* estimated that as much as 25 percent of the greenhouse effect could be the result of using nitrogen fertilizers.

In the United States, almost 2 billion pounds of pesticides are applied to our land every year, including food crops. In 1987, an EPA report ranked pesticides in food as one of the nation's most serious health and environmental problems. Pesticides are among the most deadly of chemicals: according to a report from the National Academy of Sciences, 30 percent of commercially used insecticides, 50 percent of herbicides, and 90 percent of fungicides are known to cause cancer in animal studies. Ironically, pesticides aren't even doing their job. Since they were first developed after World War II, pesticide use has increased ten times; during that same period, crop losses due to insects has doubled. Often less than .1 percent of the chemicals applied to crops actually reach target pests.

Pesticides used in agriculture have contaminated nearly all the air, water, soil, and living beings of the entire planet. Almost all of us carry residues of toxic pesticides in the fat of our bodies.

The long-term human health effects of chronic, low-level exposures to pesticides currently used on our food are not known, but there are many reports of farmers and their families being poisoned by pesticides, and common sense tells us that to continuously put such substances into our bodies can't possibly be good for us.

Another problem with agribusiness methods is the use of hybrid seed (see Chapter 6). Most of the foods we eat today are not the same varieties provided by nature. They are bred for yield and uniformity of size rather than for taste or nutrition.

Food Processing and Nutrition

After agribusiness grows unhealthy, toxic plants, most of these are sent to a factory to be processed. There they are stripped of many of their nutrients, bleached, colored, flavored, preserved, and packaged with attractive labels. For example, if you buy peas in a can, 30 percent of the vitamins have been lost in cooking at the canning plant, and 25 percent have been lost in the sterilization process; 27 percent are discarded with the cooking liquid, and 12 percent are lost when you heat the peas after you open the can.

What's left? Squishy, tasteless little green balls with only 6 percent of their nutritional value. Frozen peas, after processing and cooking, are left with about 17 percent of the original vitamins. White flour loses up to ninety nutrients by milling, and only six nutrients are artificially added to "enrich" it.

Research suggests that a primary contributing factor to many of our modern diseases is our eating of processed, low-fiber, low-nutrition foods. Before 1900, degenerative diseases like cancer and heart disease were relatively rare. Now heart disease is the leading cause of death in the United States, and cancer hits one out of every three people during their lifetime. Together, cancer and heart disease cause 50 percent of all deaths in this country. Obesity was a problem that generally affected only the wealthy in eighteenth-century Europe, while today half of our population is overweight to some degree.

Studies of other cultures that eat traditional, whole, unrefined, unprocessed foods show a remarkable lack of illness. Yet study after study has found that people who switch from their native diet to a Western one gradually develop Western degenerative diseases.

Food also loses nutrition when it is stored. Yes, we have the convenience of apples all year long in the supermarket, but apples are kept in cold storage (which requires a lot of energy) and brought out as they are needed. The apple you eat in June was probably harvested the previous October. This is true for many other fruits and vegetables as well.

Artificial Colors, Flavors, and Preservatives

Because processing removes vital nutrients and alters food, artificial ingredients are often added to make the food more palatable, to help in the manufacturing process, or to give a product longer shelf life. The average person in this country consumes five thousand different synthetic chemicals in his or her day-to-day diet for a total of six pounds of preservatives and artificial compounds each year.

Since 1972, thirty-five widely used food additives have been found to be unsafe and have been removed from the FDA-approved list. Many of these cause cancer. In 1980, the National Toxicology Council contracted with the National Research Council and the National Academy of Sciences to investigate one hundred substances from a list of 8,627 food additives. Of these, it was possible to completely assess the health hazards of only 5 percent.

Regardless of the results of the toxicity tests for single food additives, the real issue is how they interact, because that is how we consume them. Food additives can have a synergistic effect and become more harmful as they combine. This was clearly demonstrated in a study by Dr. Benjamin Ershoff at the Institute for Nutritional Studies in California. Rats were given different combinations of three common food additives: sodium cyclamate, Red Dye No. 2, and polyoxyethelene sorbitan monostearate. At first the rats were fed only one of the three additives, and nothing happened. Then the test animals were given sodium cyclamate and Red Dye No. 2; they stopped growing, lost their hair, and developed diarrhea. When the rats were finally given all three additives, they lost weight rapidly and died within two weeks.

Irradiation

A relatively new threat to our food supply is irradiation. While the FDA proclaims its safety and has already authorized the irradiation of fruits, vegetables, pork, herbs, spices, teas, and seeds, the Department of Energy and the Pentagon have refused to release their research into its long-term effects.

Food irradiation is done by zapping food with a dosage of radiation almost 60 million times that of a chest X ray. Gamma rays (radioactive by-products of the nuclear industry) or X rays are used to kill insects and bacteria, prevent sprouting, and slow rotting. While the process does not make the food itself radioactive, the chemical structure of the food is altered, and there are a number of animal studies that show negative health effects.

The facilities where irradiation takes place also pose health and environmental problems to workers and the general population. Supporters of food irradiation hope to put one thousand irradiation facilities into operation in the United States by 1995, an average of twenty in each state. Besides potential problems with transportation of radioactive materials, there have already been several radiation leaks and contaminations in existing plants, as well as numerous safety violations.

And, like other harmful food practices, irradiation may not even be effective. Researchers reported in the British medical journal *Lancet* that "irradiation confers no advantage over heat processing in respect of bacterial toxins." Another study, in *New Scientist*, examined irradiated coconuts and found that while the process killed fungi that affect the taste of the coconut, other bacteria had flourished, including a variety that can cause food poisoning.

So far, spices are the mostly widely irradiated food in the United States, with 200 million pounds irradiated in 1986. The FDA requires whole foods that have been irradiated to display on the label and international logo of a flower in a circle and the words "treated by [or with] irradiation." However, when irradiated foods or spices are used in processed foods, that fact does not have to be indicated on the label.

Animals

There are many very important environmental reasons to eat a lot less animal food than we do (currently, about 5 billion animals are slaughtered each year for food in this country). Roughly one-third of the world's annual grain harvest is fed to livestock, and more fish is fed to livestock in the United States than is consumed by humans. The least efficient livestock product is beef: it takes about seven pounds of grain to produce a pound of meat.

Raising livestock takes over half of all cropland in this country and produces much less food than if we directly ate the crops used to feed the animals. We waste 90 percent of the protein, 99 percent of the carbohydrates, and 100 percent of the dietary fiber by cycling grain through livestock. Twenty pure vegetarians can be fed on the same amount of land it takes to feed one person on a meat-based diet. John Robbins, author of *Diet for a New America*, points out that the 60 million people around the world who starved to death in 1989 could have adequately been fed by the grain saved if Americans reduced their intake of meat by only 10 percent.

Similar statistics can be shown for the enormous amount of fossil-fuel energy and water used to produce meat compared with the requirements for plant food crops (see Chapters 3 and 4)—as well as the enormous amount of animal excrement that is not recycled but ends up contaminating our water supply.

About 50 percent of the destruction of the world's rain forests is due to clearing of land for export agriculture, especially cattle ranching. This then pushes peasants to clear more land for firewood and subsistence farming. In the United States, about one-third of our original forest land has been converted to land used to feed animals. For each acre of American forest cleared to make room for parking lots, roads, houses, shopping centers, and the like, seven acres of forests are cleared to raise livestock feed or for grazing.

The evidence also is overwhelming that vegetarians and those who eat little animal food are far healthier than those who eat the supermarket meats of today, although the healthiest indigenous people worldwide ate wild animals of both land and sea and considered them essential to their health. Perhaps meat in itself is not a health problem, but rather the quality of today's flesh foods and the large quantity that we eat. Because of genetic manipulations, we are now sold animals that grow bigger and faster but are of poorer quality. Hens are laying more eggs than ever before, but these are far inferior to eggs from barnyard chickens.

Beyond the health and environmental effects of raising and eating animals, there is the ethical question of how they are treated while being raised and whether we should kill animals for food. It can be emotionally wrenching to see or even read about the crowded, disease-prone cages that our farm animals are currently forced to occupy during their lifetimes. Far from being "contented cows" and "happy hens" growing up on a family farm, about 90 percent of all animals used for food in the United States are raised in barren, cramped, overcrowded, and unnatural facilities—factory farms. They are often fed antibiotics and other drugs to keep them alive and make them gain weight by adding fat or retaining water until slaughter time. Studies have shown that, in addition to causing immeasurable stress on the animals, factory farming leads to human health problems and contamination of soil, water, and air.

Imported Food

Many of the foods we find in our supermarket are grown in Third World countries—everything from bananas to wheat. The enormous debt we encouraged Third World countries to undertake and our current payback policies have forced these countries to grow export crops and overmine their resources. The result is that growing crops for export to America often leaves little land available for growing food for the local people.

Food that comes from far away loses its nutrition and unnecessarily wastes energy resources, in addition to causing even more pollution. In our current system of food growing and distribution, for every two dollars spent on growing food, we spend one dollar to move it somewhere else. This happens not only with food from foreign countries, but within the United States as well, where food that is shipped across the country could easily be grown locally. The average food in this country travels fourteen hundred miles before it reaches your grocery store.

EATING IN HARMONY WITH OUR BODIES AND THE EARTH

There are many diets and approaches to eating and food combining. Here are some basic practices that will have a great effect on our own and the Earth's health.

• *Eat whole, fresh, unprocessed foods.* This is probably the most important step you can take toward getting more nutrition and avoiding artificial additives. You can also make

many convenience foods much more healthfully at home, such as applesauce, soups, cookies, and even ketchup.
• *Buy organically grown foods as much as possible.* Organically grown foods are free from artificial fertilizers and pesticides. Instead, the soil is nourished to produce healthy, nutritious plants. Right now about 100,000 farms (out of 2 million) use organic methods without any government assistance. Many studies show that yields and profits from these farms can be as high as from those using toxic, artificial chemical systems. The National Academy of Sciences recently confirmed this in a study and said that federal policies actually encourage poor soil-conservation practices and the overuse of agricultural chemicals. If your supermarket doesn't carry organically grown food (few do, but the practice is becoming more common), visit your local natural-food store, or order by mail.
• *Eat locally grown foods as much as possible, and foods that are in season for your local area.* You may have to do a little research to find out what's local and in season. Check your library for garden books that say when foods are in season (you'll also be able to find out which foods grow in and are native to your area), and make up a chart for your future reference.
• *Eat less meat or become a vegetarian. If you do eat meat, make sure it is healthfully and humanely raised.* There are many other sources for dietary protein besides meat: grains, nuts, seeds, beans, and soy products such as tofu or tempeh. There are many good vegetarian cookbooks with delicious recipes; check your natural-food store. There are now some farms and ranches that use more humane and healthy rearing practices. They allow plenty of room indoors and free-range access outdoors, natural social contact (including time for mothers and their offspring to be together), and range feeding or feeding from organically grown whole foods. They take no part in genetic engineering, do not force animals to overproduce, and do not use antibiotics, hormones, or other drugs and pesticides.
• *Grow your own food.* You can grow bushels of healthful, luscious food in your own yard (see Chapter 6 for details).

READING LABELS

Fresh Organically Grown Foods

Buy *certified* organically grown produce, which is certain to have been grown by true organic methods: *without* synthetic fertilizers, pesticides (including herbicides, insecticides, fungicides), artificial ripening processes, growth stimulators and regulators such as hormones, or antibiotics and other drugs; only those materials and practices that are allowed by the certification agency can be used. In addition, organically grown foods must also be processed, packaged, transported, and stored *without* the use of chemicals such as fumigants, artificial additives, and preservatives, and *without* food irradiation. Depending on the certification agency, a farm usually must have been using organic growing methods for one to three years before it can be certified.

National standards are currently being proposed to empower the United States Department of Agriculture (USDA) to certify organically grown foods, but legislation has not been enacted yet. At this time, one-third of the states have legal definitions for organically grown food. In California, food sold as organic must carry the statement:

GROWN AND PROCESSED IN ACCORDANCE WITH SECTION 26569.11 OF THE CALIFORNIA HEALTH AND SAFETY CODE.

Biodynamically grown food is a special type of organically grown food that meets or exceeds all organic growing standards. The aim of this practice is to produce the highest-quality nutrition for both humans and animals, while developing a self-contained farm ecosystem that regenerates land, plants, animals, and people. Less known in this country than in Europe, biodynamic methods may help establish a new standard of farming as greater consumer education develops (see Chapter 6).

There are also private certification organizations and growers' associations that evaluate farms and give a seal of approval according to their individual criteria. Your local natural-food store should be able to refer you to the certifying organizations in your area.

Not all fresh food and food products offered at natural-food stores will be certified, however. Foods may be labeled with a variety of descriptive terms, some of which may be misleading. Consumers should note the following:

"Certified Organically Grown" means grown by organic methods and certified by an independent organization or association of organic growers who verify that the farm meets particular criteria. The name of the certifying organization should accompany this label, and many have logos that are easy to recognize. This is the best assurance that the food is organically grown.

"Organically Grown" or "Organic" by itself is generally meaningless, unless the store has its own definition posted near the produce bin. Sometimes this term is used by stores that have signed statements from the grower, describing the precise growing practices. In these cases, the store must take the grower's word as truth, for there is neither time nor money to send knowledgeable people to inspect the farms, run pesticide tests, or perform all the other necessities to certify the produce.

"Represented" or "Claimed Organic" is generally used when the farmer has told the store that the produce is organic, but nobody has checked on it. Usually no signed statement of growing practices has been submitted.

"Transitional Organic" usually means the farm is growing organically but hasn't been doing it for the required one- to three-year period to be able to meet state or private certification.

"Unsprayed" simply indicates that the food has not been sprayed with pesticides. It is also usually not colored, gased, or waxed, but probably does not come from a farm with a soil building program, and probably has not been carefully harvested or packaged. Artificial fertilizers have probably been used.

"IPM" (Integrated Pest Management) or "Ecologic" means grown on a farm that is using Integrated Pest Management (whereby a lesser amount of pesticides is used) or that may be in the process of converting to organic methods.

Your natural-food store should provide some explanation of what its terms mean. If you don't see adequate labeling, ask! Find out how insects, weeds, and diseases were controlled, and what fertilizers were used. Become acquainted with the produce buyer, and encourage informative labeling and responsible buying practices.

Try to avoid imported foods. They may have been sprayed with pesticides long since banned in the United States, and have certainly been fumigated before being allowed into the country (even fruits from Hawaii are fumigated before they are allowed to enter the mainland). Coffee, cocoa, papayas, mangos, guavas, pineapples, bananas, and other tropical fruits fall into this category.

Packaged Foods

Realistically, I know that most of us will still buy some packaged products and not make everything from scratch. To fill this market niche, there are a growing number of packaged foods made from organically grown ingredients.

To find good additive-free and organically grown packaged foods, bypass all the advertising hype that may be on the front of the label and read the ingredient list. There you should find recognizable foods ("whole wheat," for instance, or "organically grown apples"). Beware of ingredients that are processed foods themselves, such as margarine or ham; any additives that are in ingredients in these foods need not be on the label. If an ingredient is indicated as "organically grown," it should also state by what standards.

HOW I RATE FOODS AND FOOD PRODUCTS

Foods and food products are among the very few products in this book that get the earthwise rating; this is because there are increasing numbers of organically grown foods available.

Although many of the foods listed here are rated earthwise because they are organically grown, it is important to note that not all organic growing methods are the same. As we move to safer and more nutritious food, "organically grown" will come to mean not just "grown without artificial chemicals," but grown with fully mineralized and composted soils, using soil-, water-, and energy-conserving practices that truly regenerate the land. It will also mean using seed varieties that are naturally nutritious and tasty. We aren't there yet, but we are on the way. Our support of organic farmers will make it happen.

⊕ **Earthwise** foods:
• are healthy to eat;
• are nonpolluting in their manufacture, use, and disposal (except for energy use);
• are whole foods grown or raised without artificial fertilizers or pesticides and with methods that build soil fertility; and
• contain no artificial additives.

Note: Foods gathered from the wild or grown from open-pollinated seed are indicated with a plus sign. Multiple-ingredient food products in which most of the ingredients are organically grown but a few minor ones (such as spices) are nonorganic are indicated with a minus sign.

🍂 **Natural** foods:
• are relatively healthy to eat;
• are whole foods grown or raised by methods that use artificial fertilizers or pesticides that may leave residues; and
• contain no artificial additives.

Note: Multiple-ingredient food products whose *prime ingredient* is organically grown but which contain a number of nonorganic ingredients are indicated with a plus sign.

⊞ means the product comes in responsible packaging.

Most of the foods listed in this chapter are organically grown. Because nonorganic, additive-free food products are so prevalent and easy to find in any natural-food store, I have instead focused on those that are made from organic ingredients. There are no desserts listed, to allow more room for truly nutritious foods. Many of the catalogs listed do carry sweet treats, as do natural-food stores.

Although I do not list homemade alternatives in the product sections below, remember that the healthiest meals are those you prepare yourself from fresh, whole foods. Natural-food stores carry many books with delicious recipes.

APPLESAUCE

Harmful ingredients: pesticide residues, sucrose.

At the Store/By Mail
Most applesauce is free from additives. Look for the organically grown brands listed here at your natural-food store, or at least choose one of the natural unsweetened brands packaged in glass that are sold at your supermarket.

⊕ Earthwise applesauce
Santa Cruz Natural Organic Applesauces (Santa Cruz Natural). Apple, gravenstein apple, apple blends (blackberry, dark sweet cherry, raspberry, strawberry). *Mountain Ark Trading Company, Natural Lifestyle Supplies, Organic Foods Express.*

Sonoma Gold Organic Applesauce (Appleseed Orchards). *Gold Mine Natural Food Company.*

BAKING MIXES

Harmful ingredients: BHA/BHT, hydrogenated oil, pesticide residues, sucrose.

At the Store/By Mail
Choose a whole-grain, sugar-free baking mix, available at natural-food stores and supermarkets.

⊕ Earthwise baking mixes
+ *Cross Seed Company.* Amaranth pancake and biscuit mixes made from certified, open-pollinated grain.

Community Mill & Bean. Certified mixes include Belgian waffle, buckwheat pancake, buttermilk flapjack, corn bread, gingerbread, and wheat-free muffin.

Diamond K Enterprises. Barley, buckwheat, corn, and whole-wheat pancake mix.

Shiloh Farms. Buckwheat and whole-wheat pancake mix.

Special Foods. Pancake mixes: white sweet potato, cassava, malanga, lotus, amaranth, and milo.

− David's Goodbatter Pancake Mixes (David's Goodbatter). Whole-wheat buttermilk, wheat-free buttermilk, buckwheat buttermilk, rice and oats, premium almond, and premium pecan. *Simply Delicious.*

− Eagle Agricultural Products. Blueberry and buttermilk pancake and muffin mix.

− Fiddler's Green Farm. Baking mixes include pancake and muffin, wheat-free oats 'n barley pancake and baking, bread and biscuits, and buttermilk spicecake and cookie. ⊞

− Walnut Acres High Lysine Corn Bread Mix (Walnut Acres). *Walnut Acres.*

🍃 Natural baking mixes
+ *Helmuth Country Bakery.* Amaranth and Wheat Base Mix flours are certified organically grown.

+ Native Blue Corn Muffin Mix (Arrowhead Mills). *Arrowhead Mills, Simply Delicious.*

+ Walnut Acres Baking Mixes (Walnut Acres). Pancake mixes: rice, twelve-grain, whole wheat with soy, unbleached white, wheatless, Hi Bran, and buttermilk. Muffin mixes: bran, corn, maple granola, blueberry, and cherry. Quick-bread mixes: date nut, apricot nut, spicy apple nut, banana nut, and wheat-free raisin cinnamon. *Walnut Acres.*

Butte Creek Mill. Pancake/waffle mix, bran-muffin mix, corn-bread mix, biscuit mix, oat-bran-muffin mix—all made from stone-ground grains. ✠ Paper. ⚡ Water-powered mill.

BARBECUE SAUCE

Harmful ingredients: benzyl alcohol/sodium benzoate, flavors, sucrose.

At the Store/By Mail
Choose an additive-free barbecue sauce from your supermarket.

🌿 Natural barbecue sauce
+ Señor Felipe's Barbeque Sauce (Señor Felipe's).

Gorilla Sauce (Whole Food Marketing Company). Five percent of the profits are used to benefit gorillas.

BEANS

Harmful ingredients: pesticide residues, sucrose.

At the Store/By Mail
Buy additive-free, organically grown beans at a natural-food store or by mail.

⊕ Earthwise beans
+ *Cross Seed Company.* Open-pollinated, certified, adzuki and mung beans, whole green peas, lentils, soybeans, and pinto, garbanzo, and black turtle beans.

Allergy Resources. Adzuki, black turtle, kidney, navy, and pinto beans, chickpeas, and green lentils.

Arrowhead Mills Beans (Arrowhead Mills). Anasazi, garbanzo, mung, soy, and pinto beans. *Arrowhead Mills, Millstream Natural Health Supplies.*

Community Mill & Bean. Certified black turtle, garbanzo, great northern, red kidney, mung, navy, and pinto beans, lentils, and green split peas.

Country Life Natural Foods. Adzuki, black turtle, cranberry, garbanzo, great northern, kidney, lima, mung, navy, pinto, soy, and red beans, green lentils, and green and yellow split peas.

Deer Valley Farm. Adzuki, black turtle, marrow, mung, soy, and navy beans; yellow split peas.

Eagle Agricultural Products. Anasazi, pinto, great northern, soy, garbanzo, black turtle, small red, black soy, navy, red kidney, adzuki, and baby lima beans, green split peas, whole green peas, yellow split peas, and green lentils.

Eden Foods Beans (Eden Foods). Adzuki, black turtle, garbanzo, kidney, great northern, navy, soy, and pinto beans, green lentils, and green split peas. *Millstream Natural Health Supplies.*

Gold Mine Natural Food Company. Adzuki, black soy, anasazi, bolita, pinto, and garbanzo beans; green lentils.

Green Earth Natural Foods. Adzuki, black turtle, kidney, navy, and pinto beans, chickpeas, lentils, and split peas.

Jaffe Brothers. Adzuki, black turtle, garbanzo, great northern, and red kidney beans, lentils, baby lima, mung, and navy beans, black-eyed and green split peas, and soy and pinto beans.

Krystal Wharf Farms. Adzuki, black turtle, garbanzo, great northern, kidney, lentil, mung, navy, soy, pinto, and red chili beans; green and yellow split peas.

Living Farms. Black turtle, mung, soy, and pinto beans.

Mountain Ark Trading Company. Adzuki, black turtle, garbanzo, pinto, soy, and anasazi beans, green and red lentils, green split peas, and black-eyed peas.

Natural Lifestyle Supplies. Adzuki, black turtle, kidney, pinto, black soy, and navy beans; lentils.

Natural Way Mills Beans (Natural Way Mills). Soy and pinto beans. Certified.

Organic Foods Express. Black turtle, garbanzo, great northern, navy, and pinto beans, lentils, and green split peas.

Rising Sun Organic Produce. Adzuki, garbanzo, great northern, and kidney beans, lentils, mung and navy beans, green split peas, and pinto beans. All organically or biodynamically grown.

Shiloh Farms. Adzuki, garbanzo, red kidney, lima, mung, navy, pinto, soy, black turtle, and great northern beans, lentils, black-eyed peas, and yellow and green split peas.

Simply Delicious. Adzuki, red kidney, pinto, soy, and black turtle beans, green lentils, green split peas, and chickpeas.

Specialty Grain Company. Certified adzuki, black turtle, small red chili, garbanzo, great northern, and kidney beans, lentils, mung and navy beans, black-eyed peas, green and yellow split peas, and soy and pinto beans.

Totally Organic Farms. Black, kidney, soy, navy, pinto beans, lentils, and whole peas.

Walnut Acres. Kidney, navy, pinto, garbanzo, soy, and great northern beans, green and red split lentils, and split peas.

BREAD

Harmful ingredients: BHA/BHT, colors, flavors, hydrogenated shortening, mineral oil, MSG, pesticide residues.

Food standards allow more than eighty ingredients to be included in a loaf of bread without being listed on the label.

At the Store/By Mail
In addition to the national brands and mail-order varieties listed here, you may find other locally baked breads on the shelves of your natural food store. Check labels carefully for breads that are made with organic, unbleached, or whole-grain flour and that do not contain additives. Most French breads are additive free. Your natural-food store will carry whole-grain,

additive-free breads, and can perhaps recommend a local bakery where you can purchase fresh-baked bread.

⊕ Earthwise breads
Baldwin Hill Bakery. Real sourdough bread made by traditional methods from whole, unrefined ingredients. Whole wheat is grown on compost-fertilized fields; flour is stone-ground at a cool temperature. The bakery is located on a twenty-one-acre farm in central Massachusetts and takes water from an eighty-foot-deep well. ⚡ Baked in a brick oven fueled with local New England hardwoods.

Bread Alone. Specialty breads handmade from stone-ground grains. Varieties include Sour Rye with caraway, Mixed Grain, traditional French Miche, Raisin Pumpernickel, and Whole Wheat Walnut. ⚡ Baked on the hearth of wood-fired brick ovens.

Deer Valley Farm. Stone-milled grains, fresh eggs, milk, and raw honey are used in baking their breads; varieties include whole wheat, whole-grain rye (contains wheat), whole-grain raisin, and three-grain (sprouted wheat, rye, and oats), as well as whole-wheat frankfurter and hamburger rolls.

Eden Foods Organic Mochi (Eden Foods). A breadlike rice product.

French Meadow Breads (French Meadow Bakery). Eighteen varieties of naturally leavened breads. Voted one of the top ten breads in the United States by *Bon Appétit* magazine. *Gold Mine Natural Food Company, Mountain Ark Trading Company.*

Harvest Moon Mochi (Harvest Moon Mochi Company). A breadlike rice product. Lifestream Essene Breads (Lifestream Natural Foods). Certified.

Millstream Natural Health Supplies. Whole-wheat and Italian bread. Rye Essene bread with sprouted grains; pocket bible bread.

Nokomis Farms. Sourdough breads handmade from stone-ground biodynamically grown grains: wheat, wheat/sesame, wheat/rye, rye, wild rice, muesli. Also yeasted breads.

Ohsawa Organic Brown Rice Mochi (Ohsawa America). A breadlike rice product. *Gold Mine Natural Food Company.*

Organic Foods Express. An assortment of breads including whole wheat, eight-grain, and sourdough rye.

Organic Wheat-Free Muffins (Sprout Delights). Oat bran and millet.

Ponce Bakery Breads (Ponce Bakery). Variety of naturally leavened breads with organically grown grains. Sprouted rye, wheat, seven-grain, wheat-free, gluten, whole wheat, whole-wheat raisin, and oat bran. *Ponce Bakery, Shiloh Farms.*

Still House Bakery. Sprouted-wheat or -rye Essene breads made from organically grown grains and spring-fed well water. Plain or with seeds or fruits.

Special Foods. Bread varieties include white sweet potato, cassava, malanga, lotus, amaranth, and milo. Also flour tortillas made with white sweet potato, cassava, malanga, yam, artichoke, lotus, amaranth, and milo.

Sprouted Organic Breads (Sprout Delights). Plain and raisin wheat, wheat-free rye, and rye veggie, wheat fruit cake.

Sprouted Organic Rolls (Sprout Delights). Wheat sesame seed and wheat cinnamon raisin.

Sun-Rais Breads (The Prepared Gourmet). Regular and with flaxseed. *Gemma Wenger.*

Totally Organic Farms. Sprouted breads include oat, wheat, raisin, fruit nut, and eight-grain.

− Alvarado Organic Sprouted Breads (Alvarado Street Bakery). Barley, sourdough, wheat, and oat berry. Also dinner rolls, bagels, and tortillas.

❖ Natural breads

+ Col. Sanchez Tortillas (Col. Sanchez Foods). Blue-corn and red-chili tortillas made with stone-ground organically grown corn.

+ Tree of Life Breads (Tree of Life). Whole wheat, salt-free whole wheat, millet, eight-grain, cracked wheat, soya sunflower, sprouted wheat, sprouted seven-grain, sourdough rye, whole-wheat raisin. Made with organic flours when possible.

BUTTER

Harmful ingredients: BHA/BHT, colors, pesticide residues.

Hydrogenation (bubbling hydrogen gas in the presence of nickel through a tank of liquid polyunsaturated oil) is used to solidify cheap liquid vegetable fats such as corn oil and safflower oil into products such as margarine. The process turns these polyunsaturated fats into saturated fats. So when you think you are getting a polyunsaturated fat in your margarine, you are actually getting the very saturated fats the margarine sellers claim they are helping you avoid.

The debate about saturated versus unsaturated fats is a heated one. It is important to cut down on *all* fats, since the average American diet gets about 40 percent of its calories from fat—forty times more than necessary, according to the National Research Council. The Japanese, who get only about 10 percent of their calories from fat, have about one-tenth the U.S. rate of heart attacks.

Many brands of domestic butter are colored seasonally in order to maintain a consistent color year-round. Dairies may use artificial colors or the "natural" colors annatto and carotene (which may be preserved with BHA and BHT) without listing them on the label as ingredients. It is therefore nearly impossible to tell whether any particular brand of domestic butter at any particular time contains artificial additives.

Butter is higher in pesticide residues

(including DDT) than are other milk products because the pesticides in milk get stored in the fat. Butter also contains residues of antibiotics, hormones, and tranquilizers used in milk production.

At the Store/By Mail
Buy sweet (unsalted) butter from France or a domestic unsalted butter sold in bulk in specialty gourmet shops, or in the frozen-food department of your supermarket or natural-food store. These usually do not contain added color.

CEREAL

Harmful ingredients: BHA/BHT, colors, pesticide residues, sucrose.

At the Store/By Mail
Additive-free cereals can be found in natural-food stores and supermarkets.

⊕ *Earthwise cereal*
Little Bear Koko Cereal (Little Bear Organic Foods). Stone-ground brown rice and barley. *Krystal Wharf Farms.*

Arrowhead Mills Cereals (Arrowhead Mills). Cracked-wheat cereal; barley, rye, triticale, and wheat flakes; wheat bran. *Arrowhead Mills.*

Bioforce Breakfast Muesli (Bioforce of America). Prepared with biologically grown grains, dried fruit, and nuts. *Bioforce of America.*

Deer Valley Farm. Soybean grits, wheat middlings, wheat cereal.

Diamond K Enterprises. Brown rice, corn grits, cracked wheat, steel-cut oats, seven-grain, soy grits.

Eagle Agricultural Products. Brown-rice cream, wheat bran, yellow and white corn grits, cracked wheat, oat bran, wheat flakes, rye flakes, barley flakes, soy flakes, and rolled oats.

Eden Foods Organic Cereals (Eden Foods). Rice cream, seven-grain.

Fiddler's Green Farm. Hot-cereal mixes: oat bran and brown rice, four grain, and oatmeal.

Gold Mine Natural Food Company. Rolled oats.

Green Earth Natural Foods. Granola, rolled oats, and muesli; oat, wheat bran.

Health Valley Blue Corn Flakes (Health Valley Natural Foods). *Millstream Natural Health Supplies, Mountain Ark Trading Company, Simply Delicious.*

Lima Rizli (Eden Foods). Rice, apples, raisins, hazelnuts; all certified.

Lundberg Creamy Rice Cereal (Lundberg Family Farms). Oven-roasted, stoneground brown rice. *Krystal Wharf Farms, Lundberg Family Farms, Simply Delicious.*

Mountain Ark Trading Company. Brown-rice cream, white corn grits, rolled oats, Belgian muesli.

Natural Way Mills Cereals (Natural Way Mills). Certified cracked wheat, cream of wheat, Scotch barley, millet, rye grits, flax meal, corn and barley grits, and wheat bran.

Nu-World Amaranth. Puffed amaranth and toasted amaranth bran.

Organic Foods Express. Rolled oats and quick oats, oat bran, muesli, granola, creamy rice and rye, and twelve-grain.

Paul's Grains. Stone-ground cereals include corn, oat, and wheat bran; buckwheat groats; cornmeal; barley, corn, and soy grits; oatmeal; and rye, cracked wheat, and seven-grain.

Shiloh Farms. Fourteen-grain seed-nut mix, seven-grain, barley grits, cornmeal, rolled oats, bulghur wheat, cracked wheat, honey-oat, raisin-nut, and seven-grain granolas, bran, and wheat germ.

Simply Delicious. Rolled oats, rice cream.

Special Foods. Cereals include cream of white sweet potato, cassava, malanga, yam, artichoke, lotus, amaranth, and milo. Also crispy shreds of white sweet potato, cassava, malanga, yam, artichoke, and lotus.

Specialty Grain Company. Certified rolled grain flakes include barley, oats, rye, soy, and wheat.

Summa Organic Cereals (Purity Foods). Wheat and rice; instant baby cereal. *Simply Delicious, Walnut Acres.*

Totally Organic Farms. Rolled oats.

Tree of Life Organic Oat Bran (Tree of Life).

Walnut Acres Hot Cereals (Walnut Acres). Oatmeal, wheat, twelve-grain, four-grain, rye, Indian meal, bran flakes, and hearty cereal. Also corn, rice, and soy grits, millet, and brown-rice cream. *Walnut Acres.*

− Back to Nature Rice Bran Flakes (Organic Milling Company). Contains organically grown rice and oat bran, brown rice, and oat flour. Sweetened with malted barley, fruit-juice concentrate, and malt syrup.

− Erewhon Cereals (U.S. Mills). Regular and low-sodium crispy brown rice, raisin bran, fruit and wheat, and wheat flakes. *Millstream Natural Health Supplies, Natural Lifestyle Supplies.*

− Lima Muesli (Eden Foods). Contains organically grown grains.

🌿 **Natural cereal**

+ American Prairie Cereals (Mercantile Food Company). Eight varieties of cereals including regular and wheat-free muesli, plus hot cereals. *Krystal Wharf Farms, Natural Lifestyle Supplies.*

+ Barbara's Cereals (Barbara's Bakery).

+ *Krystal Wharf Farms.* Granola and muesli.

+ Manna Flakes Cereals (Nature's Path Foods). Multigrain with oat bran, millet rice (wheat-free), and multigrain with raisins and oat bran. *Krystal Wharf Farms, Millstream Natural Health Supplies, Natural Lifestyle Supplies.*

Butte Creek Mill. Sixteen cracked and rolled whole-grain cereals made from wheat, rye, corn, oats, barley, and triti-

cale—all stone-ground. 🔋 Water-powered mill. ⊞ Paper.

CHEESE

Harmful ingredients: aerosol propellants, BHA/BHT, colors, flavors.

Labels on cheeses need state only the presence of benzyl peroxide, a petrochemical-derived bleaching agent that is generally considered safe as a food additive but is toxic when inhaled.

Pesticide residues (including DDT) are greater in high-fat cheeses than in other milk products because pesticides in milk get stored in the fat. Cheeses can also contain residues of antibiotics, hormones, and tranquilizers used in milk production.

At the Store/By Mail

Avoid processed cheeses, flavored specialty cheeses, and cheeses in aerosol cans. Choose fresh, natural cheeses instead. Raw-milk cheeses usually do not contain any additives.

To minimize pesticide concentrations, choose cheeses made from organic milk, which are carried in many natural food stores. Some varieties of cheese are made with whole milk or skimmed milk. Ask at your local cheese shop for undyed cheese make from skimmed milk.

⊕ **Earthwise cheese**

Brier Run Farm Goat Cheeses (Brier Run Farm). Seven varieties of award-winning goat-milk cheeses. *Brier Run Farm.*

Coulee Region Organic Produce Pool. Organic cheeses made from pasteurized or raw milk. Certified.

Deer Valley Farm. Imported Italian romano cheese from raw sheep's milk.

Dutch Mill Cheese Shop. Amish cheese made with milk from traditional Amish farms. Clotted with a vegetable enzyme and colored with vegetable color.

Morningland Dairy. Raw-milk vegetarian cheeses from cows grazed in organic pastures and hayfields. Fifteen varieties.

North Farm Organic Cheese (North Farm Cooperative). Seven varieties, made from certified unpasteurized milk.

Organic Foods Express. Cheddar cheese.

Rising Sun Organic Produce. Cheddar, Gouda, and Swiss made from organically or biodynamically raised cow's milk.

Shelburne Farms. Farmhouse cheddar cheese made from fresh milk produced by their herd of Brown Swiss cows. Descended from stock raised for cheesemaking in the Swiss mountain villages, these cows are noted for their high-protein, moderate-fat milk. The cheese is made in small batches by hand and ripened at cool temperatures.

Tree of Life Organic Cheese (Tree of Life). Seven varieties.

❧ Natural cheese substitutes

+ NuTofu Soy Cheeses (Cemac Foods Corporation). Made with organically grown soy milk.

+ Tofu Cream Chie (21st Century Foods). Cream-cheese substitute made with organically grown soy milk.

CHIPS

Harmful ingredients: BHA/BHT, colors, hydrogenated oil, MSG, pesticide residues.

At the Store/By Mail

Additive-free and organically grown chips can be purchased at natural-food stores and supermarkets.

⊕ Earthwise chips

Special Foods. Chips made from white sweet potatoes, cassava, or malanga.

Westbrae 100 percent Organic Russet Potato Chips (Westbrae Natural Foods).

❧ Natural chips

+ Arrowhead Mills Blue Corn Curls/ Yellow Corn Chips (Arrowhead Mills). Baked, not fried. *Arrowhead Mills.*

+ American Natural Snacks Organic Potato Chips (Tree of Life).

+ Barbara's Oat Bran Pretzels (Barbara's Bakery). Whole-wheat flour and over 30 percent oat bran.

+ Barbara's Organic Blue Corn Tortilla Chips (Barbara's Bakery). *Millstream Natural Health Supplies.*

+ Barbara's Organic Yellow Corn Tortilla Chips (Barbara's Bakery).

+ Bearito's Organic Corn Chips/ Nacho Chips (Little Bear Organic Foods). Stone-ground corn. *Eagle Agricultural Products, Millstream Natural Health Supplies.*

+ Cascadian Farm Organic Potato Chips (Cascadian Farm). *Cascadian Farm, Krystal Wharf Farms, Millstream Natural Health Supplies.*

+ Col. Sanchez Corn Mother Blue Corn Chips (Col. Sanchez Foods). Made with stone-ground blue corn.

+ *Country Life Natural Foods.* Corn chips.

+ Garden of Eatin' Black Bean Tortilla Chips/Blue Corn Chips/Sesame Blues (Garden of Eatin'). *The Ecology Box, Mountain Ark Trading Company.*

+ *Jaffe Brothers.* "Mother Earth" tortilla chips.

+ Little Bear Organically Grown Yellow & Blue Corn Chips (Little Bear Organic Foods).

+ Maine Coast Sea Chips (Maine Coast Sea Vegetables). Seaweed-flavored tortilla chips made with organic stone-ground yellow corn, canola oil, dulse, kelp, onion, and garlic. Sea vegetables wildcrafted from the Gulf of Maine. *Maine Coast Sea Vegetables.*

+ Mexi-Snax California Organic Tortilla Chips (Mexi-Snax).

+ *Organic Foods Express.* Regular and blue-corn chips, plus potato chips.

+ Wysong Health Chips (Wysong Corporation). Made with Native American blue corn. *Wysong Corporation.*

COFFEE

Harmful ingredients: flavors, hexane, methylene chloride, pesticide residues, sucrose, trichloroethylene.

Most coffee sold in the United States is grown in foreign countries that often use pesticides that have been banned here. Coffee drinking may contribute to a higher incidence of cancer of the pancreas, the fourth most common cause of cancer deaths in America. Although no physiological studies have been done, scientists at the Harvard School of Public Health have made a statistical link to support this theory.

The caffeine in coffee is responsible for many ills, including increased incidence of heart attacks, headaches, indigestion and ulcers, insomnia, anxiety, and depression. Pregnant women should limit their intake of caffeine; in large quantities it has contributed to the incidence of miscarriages, premature births, and birth defects.

Bleached white coffee filters can contain trace amounts of dioxin.

At the Store/By Mail
Limit your consumption of coffee, and avoid instant and flavored coffees, which contain many chemical additives. Instead, brew the (preferably organically grown) coffee in a nonplastic container from freshly ground beans. If you prefer decaffeinated coffee, use steam- or water-processed varieties to avoid the hexane and methylene chloride used in the decaffeinating process.

Drink herb tea or noncaffeinated hot beverages with flavors similar to coffee (see "Coffee Substitutes," below).

Organically grown coffee can be purchased in natural-food stores. Most specialty shops that sell coffee beans carry water-processed decaffeinated beans.

Purchase unbleached paper coffee filters or cotton cloth filters, or invest in a "press pot" (such as those made by Melior) that self-filters the coffee grounds.

⊕ *Earthwise coffee*
Cafe Altura Coffees (Terra Nova). Regular or decaf, both dark and regular roast. Berries are picked by hand when ripe, soaked in rainwater to remove the outer husks, and dried in the sun. Beans are of the Arabica variety, which are used only for the world's best coffee and have a caffeine content of slightly less than one percent (half the caffeine of common grocery-store coffees). *Eagle Agricultural Products, Earth Herbs, Green Earth Natural Foods, Natural Lifestyle Supplies, Mountain Ark Trading Company.*

Cafe Tierra Certified Organic Coffee Products (Cafe Tierra). Certified. Uses Arabica beans (up to 50 percent less caffeine than other beans). Also water-processed decaffeinated. *Ecco Bella, Eagle Agricultural Products, Fiddler's Green Farm, Green Earth Natural Foods, Monterey Bay Gourmet Natural Foods, Walnut Acres.*

Organic Foods Express. Regular and decaffeinated coffees.

Organic Peruvian Coffee (Equal Exchange). From the Ashaninkas cooperative in the highlands of Peru. Certified. *Mountain Ark Trading Company, Pueblo to People.*

− Cafe Tierra Naturally Flavored Certified Organic Coffees (Cafe Tierra). Fifteen varieties of regular and five varieties of water-process decaffeinated coffees. *Eagle Agricultural Products.*

⊕ *Earthwise coffee substitutes*
Bioforce Bambu (Bioforce of America). Contains chicory, figs, wheat, malted bar-

ley, and acorns. *Bioforce of America, Deer Valley Farm.*

— Lima Yannoh (Eden Foods). Made with barley, rye, malted barley, chicory, and acorns. *Gold Mine Natural Food Company, Mountain Ark Trading Company.*

🍂 Natural coffee substitutes

Cafix Coffee Substitute (Richter Bros.). Made from whole grains; has no caffeine. *Country Life Natural Foods, Deer Valley Farm.*

Dacopa (Dacopa Foods/California Natural Products). Juice of the roasted dahlia tuber. No caffeine or gluten. *Allergy Resources, Earth Herbs.*

Herb T. Company Macro Grain Coffee Substitute (Muramoto). *Gold Mine Natural Food Company.*

Pero Coffee Substitute (Alpura). Made from whole grains; has no caffeine. *Country Life Natural Foods, Deer Valley Farm.*

🍂 Natural coffee filters

C.A.R.E Paper Coffee Filters (Ashdun Industries). Made with paper bleached with an environmentally friendly non-chlorine process.

Eco-Filter (Earthen Joys). A 100 percent cotton filter that lasts over one year. Available in sizes to fit popular styles of drip coffeemakers. *Allergy Resources, Earthen Joys, Ecco Bella, Natural Lifestyle Supplies.*

Melitta Natural Brown Coffee Filters (Melitta North America). Made from unbleached paper. Available in supermarkets, department stores, and specialty stores.

Natural Brew Coffee Filters (Natural Brew Coffee Filters). Unbleached. *Fiddler's Green Farm, Green Earth Natural Foods, Natural Lifestyle Supplies, Mountain Ark Trading Company, Seventh Generation.*

DRIED FRUITS

Harmful ingredients: methyl bromide, sulfur compounds.

At the Store/By Mail

Purchase unsulfured dried fruits at your natural-food store. These can be easily recognized because they are usually darker in color than sulfured fruits. They are also drier and tougher, but they taste like the fruit instead of sulfur dioxide. Unsulfured fruits that are water processed or dipped in honey are softer and retain the original color of the fruit. Sulfured fruits are brightly colored.

⊕ Earthwise dried fruits

Ahlers Organic Date & Grapefruit. Dates since 1955. Picked as they ripen, cured and preserved in clean desert air and hot sun.

Country Life Natural Foods. Turkish apricots, currants, dates (pitted or with pit), date pieces in oat flour, date-coconut rolls, date-nut rolls, date-pecan logs, and raisins.

Covalda Date Company. Eight varieties of dates grown on the company's own land. Also dried apples, apricots, figs, peaches, pears, and raisins.

Deer Valley Farm. Dried apples, apricots, figs, sun-cured prunes, raisins, and dates, plus datelets (chopped dates and coconut) and date confection (with almonds and coconut).

Diamond K Enterprises. Raisins and dates.

Eagle Agricultural Products. Raisins and large prunes.

Green Earth Natural Foods. Apricots, currants, dates, figs, pears, peaches, persimmons, pitted prunes, and raisins.

Jaffe Brothers. Apples, apricots, cherries, figs, dates, mixed fruit, nectarines, peaches, pears, jumbo prunes, pitted prunes, raisins, currants, and persimmons.

Krystal Wharf Farms. Apples, apricots, cherries, currants, dates, figs, peaches, pears, pitted prunes, and raisins.

Millstream Natural Health Supplies. Raisins and dates.

Monterey Bay Gourmet Natural Foods. Sun-dried apricots, pears, bing cherries, persimmons, dates, and coconut-date rolls.

Mountain Ark Trading Company. Apples, apricots, raisins, peaches, prunes, figs, cherries, and mixed fruits.

Organic Foods Express. Apricots, dates, figs, prunes, and raisins.

Rising Sun Organic Produce. Apples, apricots, cherries, currants, dates, figs, peaches, pears, pitted or whole prunes, and raisins. All organically or biodynamically grown.

Shiloh Farms. Raisins and apricots.

Simply Delicious. Mixed fruit, raisins.

Sonoma Dried Fruits (Timber Crest Farms). Unsulfured apples, apricots, cherries, dates, figs, peaches, pears, prunes, and raisins. *Simply Delicious, Timber Crest Farms, Walnut Acres, The Ecology Box.*

Special Foods. Fruit leathers made from papaya, mango, pomegranate, and star fruit.

Specialty Grain Company. Certified dried apples, peaches, pears, prunes, and raisins.

Starr Organic Produce. Dried apples, bananas, and papaya.

Three Sisters. Certified raisins and currants.

Totally Organic Farms. Apples, apricots, currants, dates, figs, papaya, pears, peaches, pineapple, prunes, and raisins.

Tree of Life Organic Raisins (Tree of Life). *Natural Lifestyle Supplies.*

Van Dyke Ranch. Sun-dried apricots and bing cherries. Certified.

Walnut Acres Hunza Dried Fruit (Walnut Acres). Apricot halves, apricots, mixed fruits and nuts, white mulberries, fruit mix. All grown and sun-dried in northern Pakistan. *Walnut Acres.*

Food dryers

Bee Beyer's Natural Food Dryers (Bee Beyer). All-steel, with baked enamel finish. Stainless-steel mesh trays. *Bee Beyer.*

FISH AND SEAFOOD

Harmful ingredients: benzyl alcohol/sodium benzoate, hydrogen peroxide, nitrates/nitrosamines.

Along the Pacific coast from southern California to Chile, dolphins that swim over tuna are often caught and killed along with tuna in the huge, sometimes mile-long nets used by fishing crews. From 100,000 to 200,000 dolphins are estimated to be killed worldwide each year. In April 1990, three of the United States' largest tuna canners, bowing to consumer pressure, pledged to stop buying tuna that is caught with practices that harm dolphins; make sure the tuna you buy carries a label documenting it as such. Even so, these particular brands still contain additives, so you might want to check your natural-food store for additive-free brands.

Fish and seafood also contain contaminants (including DDT and other pesticides) that are present in the waters from which they were taken. Fish can contain pollutants two thousand times more concentrated than the amounts present in the waters where they were found. In less than one month fish can store up to nine million times the PCB levels in surrounding waters.

At the Store/By Mail

Choose deep-water ocean fish, as there is a better chance that they will come from less-polluted waters. According to Dr. Ronald Schmid, in *Traditional Foods Are Your Best Medicine,* the best varieties include herring, sardines, and anchovies; smaller salmon such as pink, coho, sockeye, and Atlantic; some types of cod, such as scrod, hake, haddock, and pollock; and mackerel, pompano, red- and yellowtail snapper, striped bass, butterfish, squid, and octopus. Tuna, bluefish, swordfish, and king salmon are best when taken from nonindustrialized coastal waters.

Purchase fish and seafood fresh, wrapped in paper, from a fish market or butcher; check to see if any additives were applied.

⊕ *Earthwise fish and seafood*
Aquaculture Marketing Service. Fresh and canned rainbow trout that have been raised in pollution-free spring water. All their trout are carefully selected from farmers who practice an all-natural culture and conform to the organic standards of California.

Bandon Sea-Pack Salmon/Tuna (Bandon Sea-Pack). Salmon and albacore tuna caught off the Oregon coast in cold, clean water. Cut by hand from uncooked fresh fish to ensure that it does not touch plastic pans or cutting boards, then packed by hand in jars with no additives and cooked in its own natural juices. ⊞ Glass jar. *Bandon Sea-Pack.*

Deep Sea Tongol Tuna (Deep Sea). Smaller variety of tuna that doesn't swim with dolphins and porpoises.

Deer Valley Farm. Frozen Icelandic cod, perch, turbot, scallops, and shrimp.

Green Earth Natural Foods. Preservative-free and kosher fish include cod, haddock, red snapper, and albacore tuna.

Magic Garden Produce. Rainbow trout raised in untreated, perfectly balanced natural spring water and fed only natural grains.

Mountain Springs. Rainbow trout fillets from fish grown in fresh, cold, pollutant-free spring water. ⊞ No-lead can.

Walnut Acres. Salmon caught from pristine Alaskan waters. ⊞ Glass jar.

FLOUR

Harmful ingredients: chlorine, formaldehyde, pesticide residues.

At the Store/By Mail
Purchase unbleached whole flours, preferably made from organically grown grains, in natural-food stores.

⊕ *Earthwise flours*
+ *Blue Corn Trading Company.* Native American-grown blue-corn flour (with recipes).
+ *Deer Valley Farm.* Open-pollinated yellow-corn flour, stone milled fresh, daily.

Allergy Resources. Amaranth, soy, barley, buckwheat, corn, millet, oat, rice, quinoa, rye, and navy-bean flours.

Arrowhead Mills Flours (Arrowhead Mills). Amaranth, garbanzo, brown-rice, triticale, and whole-wheat flours, plus blue and yellow cornmeal. *Arrowhead Mills, The Ecology Box.*

Community Mill & Bean. Certified buckwheat, whole-cornmeal, oat, soy, whole-rye, whole-wheat bread, and whole-wheat pastry flours.

Country Life Natural Foods. Barley, buckwheat, rye, white (with germ), whole-wheat, whole-wheat pastry, and gluten flours.

Deer Valley Farm. Barley, graham, rice, rye, soy, wheat, and unbleached white flours, stone milled fresh, daily.

Diamond K Enterprises. Barley, brown-rice, buckwheat, millet, multigrain, oat, pastry, rye, and soy flours, plus flax meal, corn flour and meal, and pumpernickel mix (wheat, rye, and cornmeal).

Eagle Agricultural Products. Stone-ground flours milled to order: whole wheat, unbleached white, barley, millet, wheat pastry, brown rice, buckwheat, rye, and yellow and white corn. Also meal from yellow, blue, and white corn.

Eden Foods Flours (Eden Foods). Brown-rice, buckwheat, rye, and whole-wheat flours, plus yellow cornmeal.

Fiddler's Green Farm. Whole-wheat pastry, whole-wheat bread, unbleached white, and brown-rice flours, yellow cornmeal, and wheat bran. All grains stone-ground to order.

Green Earth Natural Foods. Whole-wheat flour and cornmeal.

Jaffe Brothers. Amaranth flour, yellow cornmeal, rye flour, pastry wheat flour, and whole-wheat flour.

Krystal Wharf Farms. Brown-rice, rye, whole-wheat bread, whole-wheat pastry, and unbleached white flours, plus cornmeal.

Lundberg Organic Brown Rice Flour (Lundberg Family Farms). *Lundberg Family Farms.*

Maskal Teff Flour (Maskal Forages). Teff is an ancient grain of Ethiopia. Specify that you want organically grown teff flour. *Maskal Forages.*

Mountain Ark Trading Company. Whole-wheat and unbleached white flours, plus yellow cornmeal.

Natural Way Mills Flours (Natural Way Mills). Whole-wheat, rye, whole-wheat pastry, millet, barley, buckwheat, amaranth, corn, soy, gluten, graham, and brown-rice flours, plus cornmeal. Certified.

Nu-World Amaranth. Amaranth flour, plus custom bread-making flour blends: wheat/amaranth, rice/amaranth, rye/amaranth, oat/amaranth, and corn/amaranth.

Organic Foods Express. Whole-wheat bread and pastry flours, plus unbleached white flour and cornmeal.

Paul's Grains. Stone-ground flours include barley, bran-removed, buckwheat, corn, millet, oat, pastry, rice, rye, soy, whole wheat, and seven-grain.

Purity Foods Vita-Spelt Flour (Purity Foods). Spelt flour.

Rising Sun Organic Produce. Barley flour, organically or biodynamically grown.

Shiloh Farms. Barley, buckwheat, rice, oat, rye, soybean, triticale, unbleached, whole-wheat, and whole-wheat pastry flours.

Simply Delicious. Barley, brown-rice, buckwheat, corn, oat, rye, soy, whole-wheat, whole-wheat pastry, and unbleached white flours. Also yellow cornmeal.

Special Foods. Flours include white sweet potato, cassava, malanga, yam, artichoke, lotus, amaranth, milo, and water chestnut. Recipes are included.

Walnut Acres Flours (Walnut Acres). Whole-wheat bread, unbleached bread, whole-wheat, unbleached wheat, Deaf Smith whole-wheat, twelve-grain, soy, graham, corn, millet, rye, amaranth, Cornell-bread, and barley flour. Also cornmeal. *Walnut Acres.*

Natural flours

Butte Creek Mill. Stone-ground whole-wheat bread, whole-wheat graham, whole-wheat pastry, rye, corn, soy (organically grown), brown rice, barley, oat, millet, and triticale flours. Water-powered mill.

FOOD STORAGE

Harmful ingredients: plastic.

At the Store/By Mail

Clothcrafters. Cotton cheesecloth bags for storing salad greens; greens keep better in these than in plastic. Washable and reusable.

Dona Designs. Clear cellophane in rolls.

Earth Care Paper Company. Cellulose food-storage bags in three sizes.

The Ecology Box. Cellophane bags in assorted sizes. Also in rolls.

Janice Corporation. Cellophane bags in three sizes.

Seventh Generation. Cellulose sandwich, freezer, and storage bags.

Special Foods. Cellophane bags in various sizes. Also in rolls.

The Sprout House. Cellulose bags in several sizes.

GRAINS

Harmful ingredients: pesticide residues, talc.

In addition to the grains most of us use (such as rice, wheat, rye, oats, barley, and corn), there are a number of grains that are gaining popularity and starting to be grown domestically. These traditional varieties are quite nutritious, and some have the advantage of being more digestible or less allergenic.

Amaranth. Together with corn, this highly nutritious grain formed the basis of the Aztec diet in ancient Mexico. It contains the essential amino acid lysine that is lacking in most other grains, is high in vitamins, minerals, and fiber as well as protein, and is low in gluten. It is also naturally pest resistant.

Buckwheat. Technically a fruit, buckwheat looks like a grain. It is a very good source of protein, rich in vitamin E, and is a good blood-building food. Dark buckwheat flour, which contains more of the hull than the light variety, also has the amino acid lysine. Kasha (roasted buckwheat groats) is a traditional dish of eastern European countries.

Job's tears. An Asian staple, this is also one of the few nonhybridized grains available today.

Millet. One of the oldest foods, millet is commonly used in China, Africa, and India. It is a good source of protein and is high in minerals; it is the only grain that is alkaline when cooked, even when no salt is added.

Quinoa. Cultivated in South America since at least 3,000 B.C., quinoa is high in protein, iron, calcium, and phosphorus.

Sorghum. Ranked as the third-most-used grain in the world, sorghum is extremely hardy and can be freshly ground and cooked as a porridge.

Spelt. Popular with health-conscious Europeans, this ancient grain is high in protein, vitamin E, and fiber, and has a nutty taste. Some people who are allergic to wheat are able to eat spelt.

Teff. A highly nutritious grain that has been the mainstay in the Ethiopian diet for thousands of years. According to a supplier, it contains seventeen times more calcium than whole wheat or barley.

At the Store/By Mail

Buy organically grown whole grains at natural-food stores or by mail. They are often sold in bulk.

⊕ Earthwise grains

+ *Deer Valley Farm.* Buckwheat, open-pollinated yellow corn, long- and short-grain rice, rye, sweet rice, soft and hard wheat kernels, and triticale.

+ *Eden Foods Job's Tears* (Eden Foods).

+ *Gold Mine Natural Food Company.* A variety of traditional Native American open-pollinated corns, such as Hopi blue, black Aztec sweet, and multicolored.

+ *Mountain Ark Trading Company.* Brown rice, wild rice, pearled barley, white barley, buckwheat groats, hopi blue corn, sweet white corn, open-pollinated yellow corn, spelt.

+ *Northern Lakes Wild Rice Company.* Wild rice hand-harvested in Minnesota.

+ *Paul's Grains.* Open-pollinated corn.

Allergy Resources. Brown rice, barley, quinoa, flaxseed, millet, rice, and buckwheat grits.

Arrowhead Mills Grains (Arrowhead Mills). Pearled barley, brown rice, blue and yellow whole corn, millet, yellow popcorn, triticale, and wheat. *Arrowhead Mills, Millstream Natural Health Supplies.*

Community Mill & Bean. Certified pearled barley, hulled millet, yellow popcorn, and brown rice.

Cooperative Trading. Wild rice hand-harvested from natural stands by native ricers.

Country Life Natural Foods. Barley

(hulled, hulless, and rolled cereal), buckwheat groats, corn meal (yellow and whole), hulled millet, rolled oats, yellow popcorn, lone pine rice (long, short, and broken brown), rye berries, triticale flakes, wheat bran, cracked wheat, cream of wheat (with bran and germ), and wheat berries (soft and hard).

Cross Seed Company. Certified whole barley, rye and oats, hulled oats, hard red winter wheat, soft white winter wheat, triticale, whole buckwheat, whole millet, golden amaranth, and popcorn.

Diamond K Enterprises. Barley, buckwheat (groats and grits), yellow corn, millet, oats, popcorn, and short-, medium-, and long-grain brown rice.

Eagle Agricultural Products. Hard red winter wheat, soft wheat, barley, millet, brown rice, rye, wild rice, buckwheat groats, buckwheat, amaranth, oat groats, quinoa, and yellow, blue, and white corn, Also a unique tri-colored miniature popcorn without the hulls.

Eden Foods Grains (Eden Foods). Pearled barley, brown rice, whole buckwheat, popcorn, yellow millet, rye, wheat, and blue, flint, and yellow corn.

Fiddler's Green Farm. Whole-grain brown rice and Native American wild rice.

Gold Mine Natural Food Company. Quinoa, whole barley, millet, oats, rye, wheat, and pastry wheat. Also Job's tears.

Green Earth Natural Foods. Barley, buckwheat, bulgur, corn, millet, oats, brown rice, wild rice, wheat berries, and cracked wheat.

Jaffe Brothers. Amaranth, hulled barley, buckwheat groats, multigrain cereal, whole-kernel yellow corn, millet, rolled and hulled oats, oat bran, quinoa, long-and short-grain brown rice, rye berries, pastry-wheat berries (soft), and wheat berries.

Krystal Wharf Farms. Barley, buckwheat, corn, millet, popcorn, brown basmati rice, rye berries, wheat berries.

Living Farms. Whole buckwheat, buckwheat groats, corn, flax, millet groats, popcorn, rye, hard red spring wheat, hard red winter wheat, and soft white winter wheat.

Lundberg Organic Short & Long Grain Brown Rice (Lundberg Family Farms). *Lundberg Family Farms, Simply Delicious.*

Maskal Teff (Maskal Forages). Specify that you want organically grown grain. *Maskal Forages.*

Natural Lifestyle Supplies. Barley, buckwheat, millet, oats, popcorn, sweet rice, and wheat.

Natural Way Mills Whole Grains (Natural Way Mills). Wheat, rye, amaranth, corn, brown rice, barley berries. Certified.

Nu-World Amaranth. Whole-seed amaranth.

Ohsawa Brown Rice (Ohsawa America). *Gold Mine Natural Food Company.*

Organic Foods Express. Barley, kasha, millet, popcorn, wheat berries, white and brown basmati rice, and long- and short-grain brown rice.

Paul's Grains. Barley groats, buckwheat, flax, millet, oat groats, brown rice, rye berries, and wheat berries.

Purity Foods Hulled Vita-Spelt (Purity Foods). Spelt.

Rising Sun Organic Produce. Amaranth, barley, buckwheat, corn, millet, oats (groats, rolled, old-fashioned), popcorn, quinoa, rice, rye, wild rice, and wheat berries. All organically or biodynamically grown.

Shiloh Farms. Barley, buckwheat, and oat groats, popcorn, millet, rice, rye, triticale, and wheat.

Simply Delicious. Amaranth, barley, buckwheat groats, yellow popcorn, corn grits, millet, oat groats.

Special Foods. Amaranth, quinoa, and milo.

Specialty Grain Company. Certified amaranth, barley, buckwheat, flax, millet, popcorn, rice, rye, wheat, and blue, field, and white corn. All in fifty-pound quantities except roasted buckwheat (twenty-five-pounds).

Totally Organic Farms. Barley, flax, wheat berries, brown rice, and popcorn.

Walnut Acres Grains (Walnut Acres). Wild rice, popcorn, buckwheat groats, wheat, barley, and millet. *Walnut Acres.*

HERBS AND SPICES

Harmful ingredients: artificial color, BHA/ BHT, MSG, pesticide residues.

Most herbs are fumigated one or more times with phostoxin, methyl bromide, or ethylene oxide, and may now also be irradiated.

At the Store/By Mail

Purchase whole dried herbs and spices (preferably organically grown) at supermarkets, natural-food stores, and gourmet shops (make sure they have not been irradiated) and then grind them yourself at home. The flavor will be much fresher, and you'll know you won't be getting the fillers and anticaking ingredients sometimes found in preground seasonings.

⊕ *Earthwise herbs and spices*

Allergy Resources. Earth salt; high in minerals.

Bioforce Herbamare Herb Seasoning/ Trocomare Spicy Herb Seasoning (Bioforce of America). Fresh, organically grown herbs combined with natural sea salt. *Bioforce of America, Natural Lifestyle Supplies.*

Celtic Grey Sea Minerals (Grain and Salt Society). Hand-harvested by traditional craftspeople in Brittany. *Gold Mine Natural Food Company.*

Eagle Agricultural Products. Comfrey, peppermint, sage, spearmint, oregano, and lemongrass.

Eden Foods Gomasio (Eden Foods). Sesame salt.

Jack's Sun Isles Spices (Jack's Honey Bee Products). Organically grown spices include basil, cilantro, dill weed, paprika, parsley, sage, tarragon, and thyme, plus garlic and onion (chopped and powdered). *Jack's Honey Bee Products.*

Jaffe Brothers. Unrefined natural sea salt.

Krystal Wharf Farms. Wildcrafted herbs include red clover, yarrow, red raspberry leaves, heal-all, mullein, red sumac, goldenrod, wintergreen, and peppermint.

Lima Sea Salt (Eden Foods). Pure, unrefined, mineral-rich sea salt. *Gold Mine Natural Food Company, Mountain Ark Trading Company.*

Lost Prairie Herb Farm. Over three hundred varieties of organically grown herbs.

Maine Coast Sea Seasonings (Maine Coast Sea Vegetables). Seasonings include dulse-garlic, kelp-cayenne, and nori-ginger, and dulse, kelp, and nori granules. From sea vegetables wildcrafted from the Gulf of Maine. *Maine Coast Sea Vegetables, Natural Lifestyle Supplies.*

McFadden Farm Organic Spices (Tree of Life). America's only all-organic spice line. Basil, bay leaf, garlic powder, lemon thyme, marjoram, oregano, rosemary, sage, summer savory, tarragon, and thyme. ⊞ Glass jars. *Simply Delicious.*

Meadowbrook Herb Garden. Biodynamically grown culinary herbs and salt-free culinary mixtures for fish, hamburger, poultry, salads, and soups. Also imported spices, none of which are fumigated or irradiated.

Monterey Bay Gourmet Natural Foods. Garlic and dried elephant-garlic slices.

Mountain Butterfly Dried Culinary Herbs (Mountain Butterfly Herbs). Certified. Dried whole herbs. *Mountain Butterfly Herbs.*

Muramoto Sea Salt (Muramoto). Very high in trace minerals, this salt is handprocessed from pollution-free waters of Baja California. *Gold Mine Natural Food Company, Mountain Ark Trading Company, Natural Lifestyle Supplies.*

RealSalt (American Orsa). Made from rock salt from a deposit near Redmond, Utah. Hand selected, crushed, screened, and packaged.

Trout Lake Farm. Certified dried culinary herbs.

Walnut Acres Dried Herbs (Walnut Acres). Basil, celery, chives, dill leaves, fish herbs, marjoram, oregano, parsley, poultry seasoning, rosemary, sage, salad herbs, savory, soup herbs, tarragon, and thyme. *Walnut Acres.*

Wysong Whole Salt & Garlic Whole Salt (Wysong Corporation). Over seventy naturally chelated trace minerals including iodine. Naturally occurring salt is not subjected to chemical treatments or purification processing. Garlic salt contains organically grown garlic. *Wysong Corporation.*

JAMS, JELLIES, AND PRESERVES

Harmful ingredients: colors, pesticide residues, saccharin, sucrose.

At the Store/By Mail
Most brands of jams, jellies, marmalades, and preserves are additive free but do contain sugar. Choose one that is either unsweetened or sweetened with honey, natural fruit sweeteners, or rice syrup, and preferably organically grown. Sugar-free fruit spreads can be purchased at natural-food stores and supermarkets.

⊕ *Earthwise fruit spreads*
Cascadian Farm Fruit-Sweetened Conserves/Honey-Sweetened Conserves (Cascadian Farm). Fruits are organically grown or wildcrafted. *Cascadian Farm, Mountain Ark Trading Company.*

Fiddler's Green Farm. Wild Maine blueberry syrup made from blueberries raked from a nearby hill, then boiled down with raspberry, lemon juice, and a dash of cornstarch. Wild Maine blueberry jam simmered with honey and pectin. Orange-rhubarb butter with raisins and honey. Organic apple butter with honey, cider, cinnamon, and spices.

Jaffe Brothers. Jam made from organically grown fruit, honey, lemon juice, and pectin. Also apple butter.

Special Foods. Unsweetened jams made from papaya, mango, guava, pomegranate, and star fruit.

Walnut Acres Jams & Preserves (Walnut Acres). Jams: strawberry, black raspberry, wild elderberry, wild blackberry. Also blueberry preserves. Sweetened with honey. *Walnut Acres.*

− A. Vogel's Fruit Spreads (Bioforce of America). From organically grown fruit, concentrated under vacuum at low pressure. Sweetened with European granulated fructose. *Bioforce of America.*

JUICES

Harmful ingredients: colors, BHA/BHT, glycols, pesticide residues.

At the Store/By Mail
"Reconstituted" juices or those made from concentrate may contain polluted tap water. Pure juices can be purchased at natural-food stores and supermarkets. Juices in bottles or cans have been pasteurized, thus destroying enzymes and vitamins.

⊕ *Earthwise juices*
After the Fall Organic Juices (After the Fall). A vareity of juices, nectars, and punches. ⊞ Glass. *Simply Delicious, Walnut Acres.*

Bioforce Vegetable Juice (Bioforce of America). Mixed-vegetabled juice (beets, carrots, and raw sauerkraut). ⊞ Glass. *Bioforce of America.*

Deer Valley Farm. Grape juice. ⊞ Glass.

Heinke's Organic Juices (Heinke's). Apple (Granny Smith, gravenstein, pippin), apricot, nectarine, pear, and apricot juices; boysenberry, peach, and strawberry ciders. Also fruit blend. ⊞ Glass.

Jaffe Brothers. Apple, apricot, and prune juices. ⊞ Glass.

Knudsen Organic Juices (Knudsen & Sons). Apple, concord grape, pear. ⊞ Glass.

Santa Cruz Natural Organic Juices (Santa Cruz Naturals). Apple, apple blends (blackberry, boysenberry, raspberry, strawberry), Kauai punch, apricot nectar. Lemonade and lemonade blends (concord grape/wild blackberry, dark sweet cherry, raspberry, strawberry, and strawberry guava). ⊞ Glass. *Natural Lifestyle Supplies, Organic Foods Express.*

Tree of Life Organic Tomato Juice (Tree of Life). From concentrate. ⊞ Glass.

♣ Natural juices

+ Walnut Acres Juices (Walnut Acres). Vegetable-juice cocktail, apple juice, purple grape juice, and unsweetened and honey-sweetened cranberry nectar. ⊞ Glass. *Walnut Acres.*

Triomphe de Normandy Genuine Draft Cidres (First American Marketing Group). Claims to be the only naturally sparkling juice on the U.S. market. No preservatives or citric acid (flavor enhancer) added. ⊞ Glass.

KETCHUP

Harmful ingredients: pesticide residues, sucrose.

At the Store/By Mail

Honey-sweetened ketchup is sold in natural-food stores. It may be called imitation ketchup or be spelled a different way, because federal standards of identity require that ketchup contain a sucrose sweetener. (Despite this, some products not containing a sucrose sweetener still label themselves as ketchup.)

♣ Natural ketchup

+ Walnut Acres Ketchup (Walnut Acres). ⊞ Glass. *Walnut Acres.*

Westbrae Un-ketchup (Westbrae Natural Foods. Unsweetened. ⊞ Glass. *Natural Lifestyle Supplies.*

LEAVENING

Most baking powders contain aluminum salts. While little research has been done on the actual amounts of these salts we are exposed to from this source, we do know that aluminum salts are toxic. A letter to the *New England Journal of Medicine* points out the connection between aluminum and such brain disorders as dementia, Alzheimer's disease, behavior abnormalities, poor memory, and impaired visual-motor coordination.

At the Store/By Mail

Leaven breads with nonaluminum baking powders, sourdough starters, or tequezquite, a naturally occuring mixture of mineral salts created by the decomposition of volcanic rocks due to the biological action of microalgae that has been used by Native Americans for hundreds of years (it also enhances the flavor and deepens the color of corn and cooked vegetables.

⊕ Earthwise leavening

Gem Cultures. Fresh rye sourdough starter maintained on organically grown flour for many generations; guaranteed to be wheat free.

Gold Mine Natural Food Company. Tequezquite natural leavening.

Mountain Ark Trading Company. Tequezquite natural leavening.

Special Foods. Baking powders in many varieties, including white sweet potato, cassava, malanga, yam, artichoke, lotus, amaranth, milo, water chestnut, rice, oat, barley, millet, rye, mung bean, and buckwheat.

Walnut Acres. Baking powder, baking yeast, and sourdough starter. All aluminum free.

🌣 *Natural leavening*

Allergy Resources. Baking powder free of starch, sodium, and potassium.

Sourdough International. Sourdough cultures from San Francisco, France, Austria, Egypt, Bahrain, Saudi Arabia, and the Yukon, plus a book, *World Sourdoughs from Antiquity,* that traces the history of bread making and shows how easy making sourdough bread can be.

MAYONNAISE

Harmful ingredients: EDTA, hydrogenated oil.

At the Store/By Mail
I know of no standard-recipe mayonnaise made from organically grown ingredients, but there are a couple of "imitation" mayonnaises that do use such ingredients.

⊕ *Earthwise imitation mayonnaise*

Special Foods. Imitation mayonnaise with safflower or sunflower oil in the following flavors: white sweet potato, cassava, malanga, yam, artichoke, lotus, amaranth, and milo.

🌣 *Natural imitation mayonnaise*

+ Nayonaise (Nasoya Foods). Tofu-based mayonnaise substitute made with organically grown soybeans. Cholesterol free. *Natural Lifestyle Supplies.*

MEAT, POULTRY, AND EGGS

Harmful ingredients: artificial colors, nitrates/nitrosamines, pesticide residues, plastic residues (polyethylene, polystryrene).

Over 140 drugs (including antibiotics, stimulants, and tranquilizers) and pesticides have been identified by the General Accounting Office as being likely to leave residues in meat and poultry. Of these, forty-two are suspected human carcinogens, twenty may be teratogens, and six may be mutagens. Approximately 14 per-

cent of all meat and poultry sold may contain illegal amounts of these chemicals. This contaminated food makes its way to the consumer because results of tests for contamination are sometimes not available until after the meat and poultry have been purchased and consumed.

Several human carcinogens are commonly added to flesh foods. Arsenic is used in 90 percent of all chicken feed, and diethyl stilbesterol (DES) in 80 to 85 percent of all beef-cattle and lamb feed; also, high levels of PCBs can be found in most fish-based feed, which further contaminates animals.

Eggs contain, in addition to pesticide residues and colors, residues of antibiotics, hormones, stimulants, tranquilizers, and fumigants from feed that is given to the mother hens. And after the eggs are laid, they are washed with detergents and sprayed with a petrochemical oil or solvent to extend shelf life.

In addition to chemical contaminants, the animals and birds themselves are stressed and weak as a result of their factory farm conditions. About 90 percent of all animals used for food are currently raised in barren, overcrowded facilities.

Veal calves are perhaps the most cruelly raised animals of all. Newborn dairy calves are considered by-products of the dairy industry. They are taken from their mothers, kept in darkened, windowless barns in crates too small for them to turn around in or lie down comfortably, and often tied at the neck to prevent them from licking the stall's metal bars for iron. They are given a diet consisting solely of skim milk, dried whey, starch, fats, sugar, vitamins and high levels of antibiotics. They are denied essential iron to keep them anemic so their meat will be white (the euphemistically called "milk fed" veal).

SPECIAL TIPS
• Eat fewer flesh foods and more organically grown fruits, vegetables, nuts, and

whole grains. Flesh foods contain higher concentrations of pesticides than do foods lower down on the food chain, and are more healthful as a smaller portion of the diet.

• If you do buy meat, be sure it comes from organically grown and humanely raised animals.

• If you can't find organically grown meat, avoid eating liver, sweetbreads, and other organ meats, as toxins tend to accumulate there; remove fat before cooking, as pesticides tend to accumulate there; avoid processed meats (bacon, sausage, salami, luncheon meats, frankfurters, and so on).

• Remove the purple-inked USDA stamp from all meats before cooking.

• Purchase meat, fish, and poultry fresh, cut to order, and wrapped in paper from a butcher; avoid heat-sealed plastic containers.

MEAT SUBSTITUTES

There are now other protein foods that have the bulk and texture of meat, but are made from plant sources, which are often grown organically.

Tofu is made by boiling soybeans, mashing the beans through a sieve to make "soy milk", adding a coagulant to the milk, and then pressing the water from the curdled milk. It is available in hard or soft firmnesses and has a bland taste that, though unappealing when eaten alone, can be combined successfully with many flavors.

Tempeh is also made from soybeans. After they are hulled and split, they are cooked, spread into trays, and undergo a fermenting process similar to yogurt-making, which turns the soybean mash into a firm, fuzzy cake. When fried, it tastes somewhat like chicken. It is very high in vitamin B12, a nutrient that is often lacking in vegetarian diets.

Seitan is made from whole wheat. Water is added to wheat flour, and it is kneaded and rinsed until all the bran and starch is washed away and only the gluten remains. It is frequently used in vegetarian Chinese restaurants as a meat substitute.

At the Store/By Mail

Organically grown meat that is humanely raised and free of chemicals can be purchased at natural-food stores or ordered by mail.

Buy eggs either from a local farm whose growing practices you are familiar with or from your natural-food store in cartons that clearly state: "No Antibiotics, No Artificial Stimulants." Fertile eggs often are grown by natural methods, but the word *fertile* alone on the carton simply means that baby chicks can hatch from the eggs; it does not mean the eggs are all-natural, unless there is also some other indication. (Brand names are not listed here because all eggs are sold locally).

⊕ *Earthwise meat and poultry*

Brae Beef. Beef. Their ground beef contains two-thirds less fat than most lean ground beef.

Buffalo Gal. American buffalo meat, "raised on a diet of lush grass, natural grains, and sun-cured hay." Buffalo has 35 percent more protein, 50 percent less cholesterol, and 70 percent less fat than beef, and half the calories of beef. Steaks, ground meat, sausage, canned meat. USDA inspected. Also elk and wild boar.

Coleman Ranch Organic Beef (Coleman Natural Beef). The only beef in the United States to carry a USDA label stating that the animals have never been fed antibiotics or stimulants and have never received hormones. The label also states that there are no artificial or synthetic ingredients and that the USDA does not permit preservatives. Certified

Czimer Foods. Wild game meats and birds, including pheasant, duck, partridge, quail, wild turkey, Canada goose, squab, venison, buffalo, elk, bear, wild boar, moose, reindeer, antelope, camel, hippopotamus, water buffalo, lion, mountain sheep, wild goat, llama, kangaroo, zebra, giraffe, alligator, rattlesnake, beaver, raccoon, and rabbit. Also some smoked meats and unusual fish and seafoods.

David Feldman Drug-Free (Organic) Meats. Beef and pork raised on a fourth-generation organic farm.

Deer Valley Farm. Beef, pork, and poultry products. Also non-nitrate-cured sausages, ham, and bacon processed in their own plant, plus fertile eggs from chickens raised on organically grown grains.

Green Earth Natural Foods. Organically raised beef, lamb, and chicken. Also biodynamically raised pork.

Millstream Natural Health Supplies. Chicken.

Nokomis Farms. Biodynamically raised beef and pork.

Organic Cattle Company. Beef.

Rising Sun Organic Produce. Eggs from chickens fed organically grown grains. Beef, chicken, lamb, and pork.

Roseland Farms. Beef.

Special Foods. Beef, lamb, pork, chicken, and turkey. ⊞ Cellophane wrapped.

Walnut Acres. Ground beef.

Wolfe's Neck Farm. Lean beef and lamb.

🐄 Natural meat and poultry

Coleman Ranch Alpine Lamb (Coleman Natural Beef). Raised on home-grown alfalfa, grasses, and grain.

Coleman Ranch Natural Beef (Coleman Natural Beef).

Dakota Lean Meats. Low-fat and low-cholesterol beef raised on South Dakota prairie grass and ranch-grown grains. No hormones or antibiotics.

Lean and Free Beef (Lean and Free Products). From cattle raised, without antibiotics or synthetic growth stimulants, in small groups in healthy environments, with plenty of room to exercise. *Lean and Free Products.*

Pacific Pastures Veal (International Foods Specialty Company). Veal Raised humanely; graded USDA Choice.

Shelburne Farms. Fully-cooked hams and bacon, from hogs raised without steroids, antibiotics, or growth hormones. Smoked slowly over maple and corn cobs. Available without nitrites upon request.

Shelton's Turkey (Shelton's Poultry). Birds are raised without antibiotics, under natural sunlight on the ground in cages that are larger than average, but not as large as those recommended by humane-farming groups.

Summerfield Farm. Veal from calves raised the old-fashioned way, in large open spaces and on whole milk directly from the cow, and with no medication, hormones, or additives. Also young lamb and fresh pheasants.

⊕ Earthwise meat substitutes

Gold Mine Natural Food Company. Seitan.

Island Spring Tofu (Island Spring). Traditional firm, pressed silken, high fiber, extra firm.

Lima Seitan (Eden Foods). Wheat based. *Gold Mine Natural Food Company.*

Lima Tempeh (Eden Foods). Organic soybeans. *Gold Mine Natural Food Company.*

Tree of Life Tofu (Tree of Life). Raw, baked, and savory, all made with organically grown soybeans. *Millstream Natural Health Supplies.*

21st Century Foods Organic Tofu/Soy Tempeh/Soy Millet Tempeh (21st Century Foods).

White Wave Tofu, Water Pack Style (White Wave Soyfoods).

– Island Spring Tofu Burgers (Island Spring). Italian, Mexican, and Oriental flavors.

❧ *Natural meat substitutes*

+ 21st Century Foods Tempeh Burgers/ Tofu Burgers/Soylami (21st Century Foods).

+ White Wave Meatless Health Franks (White Wave Soyfoods).

+ White Wave Tempeh/Tempeh Burger (White Wave Soyfoods). Amaranth, five-grain, lemon broil, original soy, quinoa, sea veggie, sesame peanut, sloppy joe, soy rice, barbecue, burger, chili, cutlet, teriyaki burger.

MILK

Harmful ingredients: BHT/BHT, formaldehyde, glycols, paraffin residues, pesticide residues, plastic residues.

About 98 percent of all the milk we drink in the United States comes from factory farms. Normally cows live fifteen to twenty years, but because of genetic engineering, the constant stress of having calves taken away shortly after birth, and having to produce ten times more milk than normal, dairy cows are slaughtered at an early age—five or six years—when they no longer can produce milk.

Milk can also contain residues of antibiotics, hormones, and tranquilizers that have been fed to the cows, as well as residues of antiseptic solutions used to clean cow udders before milking. "Fortification" with vitamin A or D adds propylene glycol, alcohols, and BHT. All milk contains pesticide residues; no milk available in the United States today is free from them.

Most milk is pasteurized and homogenized before it reaches the consumer. Pasteurized milk has been heated to destroy bacteria, and in the process some nutrients are destroyed, too. Homogenized milk has been mixed under pressure to reduce fat particles to a uniform size and texture.

There is evidence that the process of homogenizing milk contributes to heart disease by breaking down the milk's fat globules. This releases a substance called xanthine oxidase, which then passes through the intestine into the circulatory system, where it deposits in the artery lining and destroys a substance called plasmalogen. People who have heart attacks or serious arteriosclerosis have a marked decrease in plasmalogen. The increased incidence of heart attacks in the United States and other countries very closely parallels the increased use of homogenized milk.

At the Store/By Mail

Drink raw milk, the unprocessed liquid that comes direct from a cow or goat. It is graded according to levels of bacteria found in it. Grade A has the lowest bacteria count and in addition cannot, by law, contain detectable antibiotic residue. "Certified milk—raw" means that the milk conforms to the latest requirements of the American Association of Medical Milk Commissions. Since pesticides are stored in milk fat, it follows that low-fat or nonfat milk would contain lower levels of them.

If possible, buy milk in glass bottles. Some local dairies will deliver milk in glass bottles to your door. Milk in paper cartons would be a second choice—milk in bleached paper cartons has been found to contain a minute amount of dioxin, a cancer-causing agent, which migrated from the carton. Milk in plastic bottles is not recommended.

Look for unfortified milk. Fortified milk will list vitamin A or vitamin D on the label. Raw milk, buttermilk, cream, and half-and half are usually not fortified, and you may be able to get unfortified whole, low-fat, and nonfat milk from your local dairy.

Try soy milk, which can be made from organic soybeans, or amazake, a milk substitute made from rice.

Milk is sold regionally, so check with your natural-food store for the brand of raw milk sold in your area, and for soy milk.

⊕ *Earthwise milk substitutes*

Deer Valley Farm. Soy-milk powder.

Eden Foods Edensoy (Eden Foods). Made with well water, organically grown soybeans, and malted cereal. *Natural Lifestyle Supplies, Simply Delicious.*

Island Spring Soymilk (Island Spring).

Westbrae WestSoy Soy Drinks/Soy Milk (Westbrae Natural Foods). *Natural Lifestyle Supplies.*

MUSTARD

Harmful ingredients: benzyl alcohol/sodium benzoate, EDTA, flavors.

At the Store/By Mail
Plain mustard is usually free of additives, but beware of flavored gourmet mustards, which often contain them. Look for organically grown mustard at your natural-food store.

⊕ *Earthwise mustard*

Tree of Life Organic French Mustards (Tree of Life). Dijon and whole grain.

NUTRITIONAL SUPPLEMENTS

Harmful ingredients: BHA/BHT, artificial colors, artificial flavors, mineral oil, sulfites, talc, plastic.

"Let your food be your medicine, and your medicine be your food," said Hippocrates. One of the most important and basic things you can do for your health is to get good nutrition. The optimum way is to eat fresh, whole, unprocessed, organically grown or biodynamically grown food from well-mineralized soils, but since this isn't possible much of the time, you may want to consider supplementing your diet with additional nutrients. Also, when you are under stress or your body defenses are down, you can use specific nutrients to help your body come back into balance.

Regardless of why you might want to take nutritional supplements, the first step is to consider whether to take vitamins derived from natural sources or synthetic vitamins made from petrochemicals such as coal tar.

Even though many people claim that natural and synthetic supplements are chemically identical, natural supplements do have molecular, biological, and electromagnetic differences that produce greater levels of biological activity; they are better utilized by the body than synthetic forms.

In some cases, synthetic vitamins have entirely different chemical structures than their natural counterparts as found in food. In his book *The Body Electric*, Robert O. Becker, M.D., states, "All organic compounds . . . are identified by the way they bend light in solution. The dextrorotatory (D) forms rotate it to the right, while levorotatory (L) isomers refract it to the left. All artificial methods of synthesizing organic compounds yield roughly equal mixtures of D and L molecules. However, living things consist of either D or L forms, depending on the species, but *never both.*" Besides, environmentally, we need to move away from being reliant on making things (especially things we put in our bodies) from petrochemicals.

There are twelve pharmaceutical manufacturers in the world (five in the United States) that make vitamins. Almost all the distributors of the few thousand vitamin brands you see on the market buy their vitamins from these giant companies, which produce them according to internationally accepted standards. In most cases they are all synthetic and artificial. Most "natural" vitamins on the market today either are fortified (a *very* small amount of low-potency natural vitamins mixed with high-potency synthetic vitamins) or are synthetic vitamins in a *very* small amount of natural base (the label will say something like "in a natural base containing . . .").

The only truly natural vitamins are those that come from foods. They are available in nutritional supplements as:

• highly nutritious, concentrated foods (such as bee pollen);
• powdered concentrates of foods and herbs with the moisture removed (as in barley-juice powder); and
• an isolated component of a food (wheat germ, for example).

Herbs are becoming an increasingly popular natural way to cleanse, nourish, and strengthen the body to maintain good health. Many people take herbs as nutritional supplements for preventive health care, as herbs are oftten a good souce of minerals, vitamins, and other nutrients. (For a listing of herbal extracts, see FIRST AID in Chapter 9.)

At the Store/By Mail
Natural food supplements available at your local natural-food store include alfalfa- and barley-juice powder, bee pollen, bone meal, brewer's yeast, chlorophyll, wheatgrass juice or powder, cod-liver oil, desiccated liver, kelp, flaxseed oil, lecithin, freshwater algae (blue-green algae, chlorella, spirulina), sea vegetables such as kelp, enzymes, wheat-germ oil, and minerals from ancient sea, clay, or vegetation beds. Also, certain combination herb supplements are available that give a range of vitamin, mineral, and other nutrients. If they are organically grown, biodynamically grown, or wildcrafted, all the better.

The vitamin supplements listed below are all from nonsynthetic sources, either as whole-food or herb concentrates or derived from plants. The minerals are mostly naturally amino-acid chelated or in a colloidal form, which the body can easily assimilate and utilize.

⊕ *Earthwise nutritional supplements*
Allergy Resources 100 Percent Certified Organic Extra Virgin Flax Oil (Allergy Resources). Good source of essential fatty acids.

Aura I (Integrated Health Network). Blend of ancient-seabed minerals and certified organically grown herbs. *Integrated Health Network.*

Barley Green (American Image Marketing). Powder from the juice of organically grown young barley leaves.

Bee Pollen Products (Mr. Bee Pollen). Air-dried pollen from high-desert pesticide-free areas.

Bioforce Blutenpollen/Gelee Royale/Vegetable Juice Concentrates/Vitaforce Tonic (Bioforce of America). *Bioforce of America.*

Cell Guard (Biotec Foods). Enzyme complex combining three strains of unique sprouts.

China Chlorella (Natrol). Organically grown in manmade ponds.

Comvita Pure Bee Products (Pacific Resources International). A wide variety of bee products "from nuclear-free New Zealand."

Gaia Herbs. Nutritional supplementation through elixirs from organically grown or ecologically wildcrafted plants.

Golden Pride. Barley-juice powder and several bee-pollen products.

Green Magma (Green Foods Corporation). Dried juice from young barley plants, with brown rice. *The Ecology Box.*

Hawkhaven Greenhouse. Fresh-frozen

wheat-grass juice from wheat grown in composted, sea-kelp-reinforced topsoil. Certified organic; bacteriologically safe as tested at a local hospital laboratory.

Herbal Melange (Alpine Spirit Company). Refined black moor earth from Austria that contains over three hundred plants "identified as beneficial to the gastrointestinal system."

Herbal Traditions Organic Herbals (The Herb Shop). *The Herb Shop.*

High Desert Bee Pollen. (C.C. Pollen) Cold-processed high-desert bee-pollen products.

Kyolic Super Formula 100 (Wakunaga of America Company). Sodium- and yeast-free odorless garlic. *The Ecology Box.*

Le Tan Flower Pollen (Le Tan). European food supplement that contains all major vitamins, minerals, amino acids, and enzymes, as well as hundreds of micronutrients. Gathered by hand in Spain (not by bees) from pollution-free fields of specially grown plants. Allergy free. *Le Tan.*

Liquid Trace Minerals/Trace Mineral Tablets (Marine Minerals). Low-sodium, concentrated sea-water minerals from the Great Salt Lake. *Marine Minerals.*

Maharishi Amrit Kalash (Maharishi Ayurveda Products International). Blend of rare herbs and fruits based on India's ancient Ayurvedic medical tradition. Herbs are hand-gathered from the Himalayan mountains. *Maharishi Ayurveda Products International.*

Microlight Hawaiian Grown Spirulina (Microlight Nutritional Products). Grown in a pristine environment, with no agricultural chemicals within thirty miles, and fed a volcanic-rich source of waterborne mineral nutrients.

Mineral Gold (Vibrant Life). Liquid minerals from a prehistoric deposit of vegetation in Utah.

Mineral Toddy (The Rockland Corporation). Liquid minerals from a prehistoric deposit of vegetation.

Montana Big Sky Bee Products (Montana Naturals International). A complete line of bee products: bee pollen, propolis, royal jelly, and several herbal/bee-product combinations. (Herbs are not organically grown.) Their pollen comes from the Big Sky region of Montana—the cleanest and most sparsely populated area in the continental United States—and is processed the way the bees do it; in total darkness, in special cold-air dryers. ⊞ Glass. *Montana Natural International.*

Nutri-Flax (Allergy Research Group). Organic cold-pressed flaxseed oil. *Allergy Research Group.*

Optimin Mineral Supplement (Integrated Health Network). An aqueous extract of minerals and trace minerals from the clay of an ancient seabed. *Integrated Health Network.*

Oxybliss (Helios). An organic mineral supplement made primarily of magnesium and calcium in combination with 21 essential minerals and 190 trace minerals. Minerals are obtained from uncontaminated underground mines in ancient seabeds. *Helios.*

Pine's Wheat Grass Powder (Pine's International). Dehydrated or frozen juice from grass grown naturally outdoors and harvested at its maximum nutrient level. *The Ecology Box, Pines International.*

Premier One Royal Jelly (Premier One Products). Royal jelly from bees preserved in honey and pollen only.

2nd Opinion. "Balance" multivitamin/mineral supplement from organically grown or wildcrafted plant and herb sources. Contains a full range of vitamins, minerals, enzymes, amino acids, pigments, trace elements, lipids, cell salts, and nucleic acids.

Super Blue Green Algae (Cell Tech). Harvested from a 140-square-mile lake that is rich in minerals washed from miles of volcanic soil in southern Oregon. *Cell Tech.*

Veg-Omega-3 (Spectrum Naturals). Organic cold-pressed flax oil.

Wachters' Organic Seafood Supplements (Wachters' Organic Sea Products). Blend of sea plants containing sixty-one elements, vitamins, enzymes, amino acids, cell-growth stimulators, plant hormones, and many other micro–food factors. *Natural Lifestyle Supplies, Wachters' Organic Sea Products.*

Wala-Elixirs (Dr. Hauschka Cosmetics). Nine food-supplement elixirs made from wildcrafted plants and organically cultivated fruits.

Wysong Chelamin (Wysong Corporation). Naturally chelated complex containing over seventy-four trace minerals supplied in tablet form. Derived from naturally composted sediment of an ancient seabed. *Wysong Corporation.*

– Nature's Sunshine Herbs and Herbal Extracts (Nature's Sunshine Products). Organically grown or wildcrafted whenever possible.

NUTS, SEEDS, AND BUTTERS

Harmful ingredients: BHA/BHT, colors, glycerin, hydrogenated oil, pesticide residues, sucrose.

Avoid red pecans and pistachios, which are colored with coal-tar dyes.

At the Store/By Mail
Buy nuts and seeds in the shell, or buy unroasted and unsalted shelled nuts and seeds; buy organically grown peanut butter and other nut and seed butters. All are available at natural-food stores or by mail.

⊕ Earthwise nuts and seeds
+ *Cross Seed Company.* Certified, open-pollinated sunflower seeds.

Allergy Resources. Flaxseed.

Arrowhead Mills Seeds (Arrowhead Mills). Amaranth, flax, sesame, and quinoa seeds. *Arrowhead Mills, Millstream Natural Health Supplies.*

Blue Heron Farm. Four varieties of almonds, and Hartley walnuts; available at fall harvest. Certified.

Community Mill & Bean. Sunflower seeds.

Country Life Natural Foods. Amaranth, flax, and sunflower seeds.

Covalda Date Company. Pecans grown on their own land; available in February. Also almonds and English walnuts.

Deer Valley Farm. Walnuts in shells.

Diamond K Enterprises. Sunflower and flaxseeds.

Eagle Agricultural Products. Hulled sunflower seeds, sesame seeds, and whole almonds.

Green Earth Natural Foods. Almonds, peanuts, walnuts, and sunflower seeds.

Jaffe Brothers. Shelled nuts (almonds, filberts, peanuts, pecans, and walnuts), as well as in-shell nuts (almonds, filberts macadamias, pecans, and walnuts). Seeds include flax, sesame, and hulled and in-shell sunflower.

Krystal Wharf Farms. Almonds, filberts, walnut halves; alfalfa, sesame, and sunflower seeds.

Monterey Bay Gourmet Natural Foods. Almonds, raw macadamias, raw pistachios, and walnuts.

Mountain Ark Trading Company. Almonds, pecans, sesame seeds, and sunflower seeds.

Natural Way Mills Seeds (Natural Way Mills). Certified flaxseed.

Organic Foods Express. Sesame and sunflower seeds, plus almonds and walnuts.

Rising Sun Organic Produce. Raw, whole nuts include almonds, filberts, peanuts, pine nuts, and walnuts. Also roasted pistachios. Seeds include flax, sesame, and sunflower. All organically or biodynamically grown.

Shiloh Farms. Almonds and raw red-skin peanuts.

Simply Delicious. Almonds and sesame seeds.

Specialty Grain Company. Sesame and sunflower seeds, plus almonds and walnuts. All certified.

Totally Organic Farms. Almonds, cashews, filberts, macadamias, peanuts, pecans, pine nuts, and walnuts. Also pumpkin and sunflower seeds.

Walnut Acres Seeds (Walnut Acres). Amaranth seeds and flaxseed. *Walnut Acres.*

⊕ **Earthwise nut and seed butters**

Allergy Resources. Almond butter.

Arrowhead Mills Peanut Butter/Sesame Tahini (Arrowhead Mills). *Arrowhead Mills, The Ecology Box, Mountain Ark Trading Company, Natural Lifestyle Supplies, Simply Delicious.*

Baugher Ranch Organic Almond Butter (Baugher Ranch).

Eden Foods Pralima (Eden Foods). Sweet hazelnut spread. *Gold Mine Natural Food Company.*

Jaffe Brothers. Almond butter, peanut butter, and sesame tahini.

Maranatha Organic Nut & Seed Butters (Maranatha Natural Foods). Roasted-almond and raw-sesame tahini.

Monterey Bay Gourmet Natural Foods. Almond butter.

Open Sesame Organic Nut & Seed Butters (Open Sesame.) Crunchy roasted almond, sunflower.

Organic Foods Express. Almond butter.

Rejuvenative Foods Nut & Seed Butters (Rejuvenative Foods). Tahini, halvah, sesame butter, and nut and seed blends. ⊞ Glass jar.

Special Foods. Imitation nut butters made from white sweet potatoes, cassava, malanga, yam, lotus, amaranth, and milo. Also pecan and pumpkinseed butters.

Westbrae Sesame Butter & Tahini (Westbrae Natural Foods). *Natural Lifestyle Supplies.*

OILS

Harmful ingredients: BHA/BHT, EDTA, pesticide residues, sulfur compounds.

Most common oils found in supermarkets have been extracted using hexane, a petrochemical solvent. They have then been bleached, filtered, and deodorized, making each variety virtually indistinguishable from the other.

At the Store/By Mail

Purchase *unrefined* "pressed" or "expeller pressed" oils, squeezed from organically grown vegetables, nuts, and seeds by a mechanical process that does not use chemicals. These oils retain colors, flavors, and aromas from the original sources, so take care to use an oil compatible with whatever food it is being used to prepare.

Pressed olive oils are designated as "extra virgin" (from the first pressing) or "virgin" (from the next pressing). "Pure" olive oil has been solvent extracted from either the pit or the remaining fruit pulp.

Beware of labels that say "cold-pressed." This has become meaningless health-food-store jargon with no legal definition. Often cold-pressed oils are solvent extracted, and should be avoided unless the label clearly states that the oil has been pressed at a temperature less than 100 degrees Fahrenheit.

If you prefer a refined oil, choose one that does not contain preservatives.

Natural-food stores and gourmet food shops will have a good selection of many different kinds of oils. Look for the organically grown brands listed here, which are also available by mail.

⊕ **Earthwise oils**

+ Greek Gourmet Extra Virgin Olive Oil (Greek Gourmet). Used at Chez Panisse, the highly acclaimed restaurant of cookbook author Alice Waters. *Greek Gourmet* (case only).

Allergy Resources. Organic flaxseed oil.

Arrowhead Mills Sesame Oil (Arrowhead Mills). *Arrowhead Mills, Natural Lifestyle Supplies.*

Flora Organic Oils (Flora Laboratories). Flax, pumpkinseed, sunflower, safflower, sesame, peanut, canola, and extra-virgin olive oil.   ⊞ Glass.

Gaeta Itri Organic Olive Oils (Gaeta Imports). Regular and extra virgin. *Gaeta Imports.*

Jaffe Brothers. Crude sesame oil from naturally grown seeds. Organic olive oil.

Loriva Supreme Extra Virgin Organic Sesame Oil (Loriva Supreme Foods).

Mitoku Macrobiotic Authentic Sesame Oil (Mitoku Company). Made by hand.

Montserrati Organic Extra Virgin Olive Oil (Santa Barbara Olive Company). Certified; imported from Spain. *Santa Barbara Olive Company.*

Mountain Ark Trading Company. Canola and extra-virgin olive oil.

Organic Foods Express. Olive, safflower, and sesame oil.

Sciabica Organic 100% Extra Virgin Olive Oils (Nick Sciabica & Sons). Pressed from fully ripe black olives. *Monterey Bay Gourmet Natural Foods, Nick Sciabica & Sons.*

Spectrum Naturals Organic Oils (Spectrum Naturals). Extra-virgin olive, unrefined sesame, and fresh flax oils. Certified.

Tree of Life Organic Oils (Tree of Life). Olive and sunflower.

OLIVES

Harmful ingredients: pesticide residues.

At the Store/By Mail

Olives are generally free of additives, but most are packed in leaded cans. Choose a brand from your supermarket or natural-food store that is packed in a glass jar or unleaded can.

⊕ *Earthwise olives*

Gaeta Itri Organic Olives (Gaeta Imports). From their family estates in Italy. *Gaeta Imports.*

Jaffe Brothers. Tree-ripened canned olives. Also sun-dried Greek black olives and pitted Italian olives.

PASTA AND PASTA SAUCES

Harmful ingredients: pesticide residues.

At the Store/By Mail

Although most have pesticide residues, pastas are generally additive-free. Below I've listed brands that are organically grown, whole grain, or for special diets.

⊕ *Earthwise pastas*

Country Life Natural Foods. Whole-wheat varieties, such as alphabets, elbows, flats, lasagna, shells, spaghetti, and spirals. Also whole wheat with additions such as artichoke, brown rice, rainbow veggies, sesame, soy, and spinach. Contains no eggs or dairy products.

DeBoles Organic Whole Wheat Pastas (DeBoles Nutritional Foods). Made with certified durum whole wheat. Spaghetti, shells, elbow, lasagna, and ribbons. ⊞ *DeBoles Nutritional Foods.*

Deer Valley Farm. Whole wheat pastas in a variety of shapes including linguini, elbows, and lasagna; also spinach fettuccine and linguini.

Eden Foods Whole Wheat Pastas (Eden Foods). Spaghetti, vegetable spirals, sesame-rice spirals, and spinach ribbons. *Fiddler's Green Farm.*

Jaffe Brothers. Whole-wheat pasta in a variety of shapes.

Krystal Wharf Farms. Flats, lasagna, shells, spinach flats, spinach spaghetti, veggie elbow, veggie spirals, and chow mein noodles.

La Maison de Soba Soba/Udon (La Maison de Soba). Made with stone-ground flours.

Mitoku Macrobiotic Organic Noodles (Mitoku Company). Shizen soba, whole-wheat udon, brown-rice udon, whole-wheat somen, mugwort soba, and kagoshima authentic kuzu. Made by hand. *Natural Lifestyle Supplies.*

Monterey Bay Gourmet Natural Foods. Organic soba noodles of finely milled buckwheat and whole-wheat flours.

Mountain Ark Trading Company. Whole-wheat noodles and spaghetti, sesame-rice and wheat spirals.

Ohsawa Organic Noodles (Ohsawa America). *Gold Mine Natural Food Company.*

Organic Foods Express. Whole-wheat pastas include elbow, shells, and spaghetti; also spinach spaghetti and veggie spirals.

Purity Foods Vita-Spelt Organic Pasta (Purity Foods) Spelt spaghetti, elbow, shells, and egg noddles. *Mountain Ark Trading Company.*

Special Foods. Pasta varieties include white sweet potato, cassava, malanga, yam, lotus, amaranth, milo, quinoa, oat, barley, millet, rye, and lentil.

Tree of Life Pasta (Tree of Life). Angel-hair and fettuccine in a variety of flavors.

Walnut Acres Pastas (Walnut Acres). Whole-wheat elbow macaroni, spaghetti, shells, spirals, and rigatoni. *Walnut Acres.*

Westbrae Pastas (Westbrae Natural Foods). Whole-wheat spaghetti, elbows, lasagna, and veggie bows, plus spinach spaghetti and lasagna. Also Japanese noodles: whole-wheat udon, genmai udon, and whole-wheat somen.

− Eden Foods Sifted Wheat Pastas (Eden Foods). Ribbons, plain, with vegetables, or herbed. *Fiddler's Green Farm.*

− Walnut Acres Pastas (Walnut Acres). Vegetable elbow macaroni and whole-wheat vegetable spirals. *Walnut Acres.*

Natural pastas
+ Walnut Acres Pastas (Walnut Acres). Whole-wheat and sesame spiral macaroni, and whole-wheat egg noodles. *Walnut Acres.*

DeBoles Corn Pastas/Jerusalem Artichoke Pastas/Jerusalem Artichoke Spinach Pastas (DeBoles Nutritional Foods). Spaghetti, shells, and elbow. ⊞ *DeBoles Nutritional Foods, Simply Delicious.*

Natural pasta sauces
+ Señor Felipe's Pasta Sauce (Señor Felipe's).

+ Tree of Life Pasta Sauce (Tree of Life). From vine-ripened, organically grown tomatoes. ⊞ Glass. *Natural Lifestyle Supplies.*

+ Walnut Acres Pasta Sauces (Walnut Acres). Marinara and spaghetti. ⊞ Lead-free cans. *Walnut Acres.*

PÂTÉ

Harmful ingredients: pesticide residues.

At the Store/By Mail
Organically grown vegetable pâtés can be found at natural-food stores or ordered by mail.

Earthwise pâtés
Eden Foods Vegetable Pâté with Lentils (Eden Foods).

URD Vegetarian Pâtés (Threefold International Company). Biodynamic. ⊞ Glass. *Threefold International Company.*

Natural pâtés
+ Lima Spreads and Pâtés (Eden Foods). Chickpea spread, hearty vegetable pâté and spread, wheat-and-vegetable spread, and lentil-and-onion spread. *Gold Mine Natural Food Company.*

+ 21st Century Foods Vegetarian Pâté (21st Century Foods). Soy based.

PICKLES

Harmful ingredients: benzyl alcohol/sodium benzoate, colors, EDTA, sulfur compounds, sucrose.

At the Store/By Mail

Natural-food stores and supermarkets carry additive-free natural pickles. Natural-food stores also carry organically grown pickles. Or order them by mail.

⊕ *Earthwise pickles*

Cascadian Farms Organic Pickles (Cascadian Farms). Sweet relish, kosher dills. ⊞ *Cascadian Farms, Natural Lifestyle Supplies, Walnut Acres.*

John Wood Farms Dill Pickles (John Wood Farms). *The Ecology Box.*

Ohsawa Organic Pickles (Ohsawa America). *Gold Mine Natural Food Company.*

— *Jaffe Brothers.* Sweet-pickle relish and low-salt kosher dill pickles.

— Walnut Acres Dilled Zucchini Spears/ Zucchini Relish (Walnut Acres). *Walnut Acres.*

PRODUCE

Harmful ingredients: colors, detergent residues, mineral oil, paraffin, pesticide residues, phenol, plastic residues, sulfur compounds.

Buy organically grown foods as much as possible. But if it is not regularly available to you, follow these tips for choosing the best commercial produce:

• Avoid produce that has been artificially dyed: some oranges (all Florida citrus sold before January); some red "new" potatoes (regular potatoes dyed to resemble the more expensive variety); some red "yams" (really altered sweet potatoes). How to tell if they're dyed? It is often not possible, but one is more likely to get dyed produce from a supermarket than from a natural-food store.

• Avoid potatoes and onions that have been treated with maleic hydrazide, a potential human carcinogen. Treated potatoes and onions tend to sprout on the inside instead of the outside, so if you slice one open and see it sprouting or beginning to brown, you know it has been treated. Test a potato and an onion from the store you regularly buy from by keeping it several weeks and then slicing it open when you see no exterior signs of sprouting. You can assume that store's potatoes and onions to be consistent—one way or the another—since grocers repeatedly buy from the same source.

• Buy tomatoes, bananas, oranges, lemons, cantaloupes, persimmons, and pears in season only; off season they may be ripened artificially with ethylene gas.

• Remove peels from produce that may be coated with paraffin: carrots, oranges, lemons, limes, apples, pears, plums, peaches, melons, parsnips, eggplants, summer squash, potatoes, tomatoes, green peppers, rutabagas, turnips, cucumbers, grapefruits, and tangerines. This will help to some degree, but paraffin cannot be completely removed since it sticks to cut surfaces. In addition to their carcinogenic impurities, paraffin food coatings entrap pesticide, dye, and gas residues.

• Eat foods that are less likely to be contaminated by pesticide sprays: carrots, white potatoes, beets, turnips, celery root, radishes, onions, parsnips, mushrooms, sweet potatoes, and yams.

• Remove pesticide residues as much as possible. Some pesticides can be removed by washing and peeling, but keep in mind that while these methods might remove the pesticide *residues* on the *outside* of the fruit or vegetable, produce is sprayed repeatedly, and nothing can remove the pesticides inside.

• Encourage your local markets to furnish paper instead of plastic bags to hold your selected produce in, and reuse paper and plastic bags by bringing them from home.

At the Store/By Mail

Check your natural-food store and supermarket for organically grown produce. It can also be ordered by mail. All mail-order sources listed have produce available only *seasonally,* and may require ordering in advance.

⊕ **Earthwise produce**

Arjoy Acres. Elephant and regular garlic, shallots, pinto and red kidney beans, and jerusalem artichokes—all grown organically on a farm in the mountains of central Arizona. ⊞

Blue Heron Farm. Washington navel oranges. Certified.

Covalda Date Company. Pink grapefruit, oranges.

Deer Valley Farm. Macintosh, spy, cortland, red delicious, and winesap apples, plus oranges, grapefruits, and lemons.

Ecology Sound Farms. Oranges, kiwis, Asian pears (a crisp, juicy, sweet cross between an apple and a pear), persimmons, and plums, grown "in the spirit of restoring our land and life-sustaining resources for future generations."

Fiddler's Green Farm. Organic Yukon gold potatoes.

Green Earth Natural Foods. A comprehensive selection of fruits and vegetables, including sun-dried tomatoes.

Green Knoll Farm. Certified kiwis.

Hardscrabble Enterprises. Shiitake mushrooms.

Jaffe Brothers. Dehydrated vegetables, including sliced mushrooms and sun-dried tomato halves.

Magic Garden Produce. Seasonal produce.

Millstream Natural Health Supplies. Wide variety of certified fruits and vegetables.

Monterey Bay Gourmet Natural Foods. Fresh citrus including mandarin oranges, tangerines, tangelos, lemons, and limes, plus fresh kiwis, sun-dried regular and cherry tomatoes, and Roma tomato halves.

Mountain Ark Trading Company. Dried mushrooms.

Mountain Butterfly Herbs. Shallots and garlic; certified.

Organic Foods Express. Wide variety of fruits and vegetables.

Starr Organic Produce. Oranges, tangelos, tangerines, grapefruits, and limes, plus avocados, papayas, and bananas.

Texas Ruby. Tree-ripened grapefruits and oranges.

Totally Organic Farms. Huge variety of fresh fruit and vegetables.

Valley Cove Ranch. Navel and Valencia oranges, lemons, mandarins, grapefruits, and avocados.

Weiss's Kiwifruit. Certified kiwis.

SALAD DRESSING

Harmful ingredients: BHA/BHT, colors, EDTA, flavors, glycols, hydrogenated oil, pesticide residues, sucrose, sulfur compounds.

At the Store/By Mail

Additive-free salad dressings are sold in supermarkets and natural-food stores.

⊕ **Earthwise salad dressings**

Duggan's Organic Dressings (Duggan's). Crazy Carrot, Summer Scallion, Sweet Beet. *Simply Delicious.*

❧ **Natural salad dressings**

+ Island Spring Salad Dressings (Island Spring). Contain organically grown soybean oil, tofu and fructose. Ranch, blue cheese, fruit.

+ Nasoya Vegi-Dressings (Nasoya Foods). Tofu-based salad dressings in several flavors; made with organically grown soybeans. Cholesterol free.

SALSA

Harmful ingredients: pesticide residues.

At the Store/By Mail

Additive-free natural salsas can be found in natural-food stores and supermarkets. Organically grown salsas are sold in natural-food stores and by mail order.

⊕ *Earthwise salsas*
—Enrico's Organic Salsa (Ventre Packing Company).

� *Natural salsas*
+ Tree of Life Salsa (Tree of Life). From organically grown tomatoes.

SAUERKRAUT

Harmful ingredients: pesticide residues, sulfur compounds

At the Store/By Mail
Purchase organically grown and natural sauerkraut at natural-food stores.

⊕ *Earthwise sauerkraut*
Cascadian Farm Organic Sauerkraut (Cascadian Farm). Contains only organic cabbage and sea salt. ⊞ Glass. *Cascadian Farm, Natural Lifestyle Supplies.*
Eden Foods Sauerkraut (Eden Foods). *Mountain Ark Trading Company.*
Jaffe Brothers. Low-salt sauerkraut.
Walnut Acres Sauerkraut (Walnut Acres). ⊞ Lead-free can. *Walnut Acres.*

SEA VEGETABLES

Eating sea vegetables may seem odd at first, but they are a nutritious wild food that many people find delicious—neither salty nor fishy. The Japanese have been eating them for centuries.

You can collect sea vegetables yourself or buy them dried. Your local natural-food store will probably have literature that can introduce you to sea vegetables, as well as cookbooks with recipes using them.

At the Store/By Mail
Dried sea vegetables can be purchased at natural-food stores or by mail.

⊕ *Earthwise sea vegetables*
Eden Foods Sea Vegetables (Eden Foods). Grown in environmentally clean waters, harvested at their nutritional peak, and processed using traditional techniques.

Emerald Cove Imported Sea Vegetables (Great Eastern Sun). *Natural Lifestyle Supplies.*
Fiddler's Green Farm. Sea vegetables including dulse and kelp.
Maine Coast Sea Vegetables (Maine Coast Sea Vegetables). Four varieties wildcrafted from the Gulf of Maine. *Maine Coast Sea Vegetables, Natural Lifestyle Supplies.*
Mendocino Sea Vegetables (Mendocino Sea Vegetable Company). Types include nori, wakame, kombu, sea-palm fronds, dulse, sea-whip fronds, flaked nori, sea lettuce, and Mendocino grapestone. Wildcrafted from wild growth along the Mendocino County coastline, an essentially pollution-free area. *Mendocino Sea Vegetable Company* also offers *Sea Vegetable Gourmet Cookbook and Forager's Guide,* with information on locating, identifying, harvesting, rinsing, drying, storing, and cooking with the wild seaweeds growing on the Pacific and Atlantic coasts.
Mountain Ark Trading Company. Japanese and American sea vegetables.
Ohsawa Organic Seaweeds (Ohsawa America). *Gold Mine Natural Food Company.*

SOUP

Harmful ingredients: BHA/BHT, colors, hydrogenated shortening, MSG, pesticide residues.

In addition to more familiar soups, you might try miso, a fermented soybean product said to have beneficial health effects. It can also be added to other soups as a flavor enhancer.

At the Store/By Mail

⊕ *Earthwise soup mix*
Fiddler's Green Farm. Dried bean-soup mix.
— Lima Soups (Eden Foods). Lentil and sweet pumpkin.

— Walnut Acres Meat & Chicken Soups/Organic Vegetable Soups/Seafood Chowders/Soup Bags/Organic Bean Soup Mix (Walnut Acres). A wide variety of canned soups and chowders, plus soup herbs and a mixture of organic beans with its own recipe. ✠ Lead-free can. *Organic Foods Express, Walnut Acres.*

⊕ *Earthwise miso soup*
    Eden Foods Miso (Eden Foods). *Gold Mine Natural Food Company.*
    Mitoku Macrobiotic Organic Miso (Mitoku Company). Mansan soy and johsen brown rice. Made by hand. *Natural Lifestyle Supplies.*
    Mountain Ark Trading Company. Japanese misos.
    Natural Lifestyle Supplies. Many varieties of domestic and imported organic misos.
    Ohsawa Unpasteurized Miso (Ohsawa America). *Gold Mine Natural Food Company.*
    South River Miso (South River Miso Company). Varieties include barley, black soy barley, golden millet, chickpea, adzuki rice, brown rice, and black soybean. *Gold Mine Natural Food Company, Mountain Ark Trading Company, South River Miso Company.*
    Westbrae Misos (Westbrae Natural Foods). Brown-rice, white, and red misos.

SOY SAUCE

Harmful ingredients: pesticide residues, sucrose.

At the Store/By Mail
Organically grown and natural soy sauces are sold at supermarkets and natural-food stores.

⊕ *Earthwise soy sauce*
    Eden Foods Organic Shoyu (Eden Foods).
    Mitoku Macrobiotic Organic Soysauces

(Mitoku Company). Sakae shoyu and mansan tamari. Made by hand. *Natural Lifestyle Supplies.*
    Mountain Ark Trading Company. Shoyu and tamari.
    Ohsawa Lima Soy Sauce (Ohsawa America). ✠ Glass. *Gold Mine Natural Food Company.*
    Westbrae Organic Soy Sauce (Westbrae Natural Foods).

SPROUTS

Sprouts are becoming more popular. In addition to mung beans and alfalfa, all kinds of seeds, beans, and grains are now being sprouted; many fresh sprouts are available at your natural-food store.

Sprouts may be the ultimate "live" organic food. As the little sprouts grow, they are packed with vitamin C and B-complex vitamins, and the protein content also increases.

Sprouts continue to grow and create fresh vitamins until the moment you eat or cook them. Simply soak seeds overnight, then drain and place in a wide-mouth jar with cheesecloth fixed over the top with rubber bands (or you can buy sprouting kits at your natural-food store). Rinse and drain several times a day and watch your sprouts grow.

Many different types of seeds can be used. Try cabbage, clover, radish, or sunflower seeds; beans such as black-eyed peas, garbanzos, mung beans, soybeans, or lentils; or even whole corn or wheat berries. Each has its own distinct flavor. There is some concern that alfalfa seeds may have harmful concentrations of a natural pesticide during the sprouting stage, so you may want to avoid them.

At the Store/By Mail
Your natural-food store carries seeds appropriate for sprouting, or you can order organically grown seeds by mail.

⊕ *Earthwise seeds for sprouting*

+ *Cross Seed Company.* Open-pollinated, certified, adzuki, black turtle, garbanzo, mung, soy and pinto beans, lentils, green peas, alfalfa, barley, buckwheat, yellow clover, red clover, turnip, Chinese cabbage, millet, oat, rye, black mustard, fenugreek, wheat, and radish seeds.

Allergy Resources. Buckwheat seeds.

Deer Valley Farm. Alfalfa seeds.

Diamond K Enterprises. Alfalfa, buckwheat, and sunflower seeds; mung beans.

Jaffe Brothers. Barley, whole-kernel buckwheat, red clover, millet, oats, whole peas, red radish, and wheat berries.

Living Farms. Alfalfa, red clover, black mustard, and radish seeds.

Organic Foods Express. Alfalfa seeds.

Shiloh Farms. Alfalfa, flax, pumpkin, sesame, and sunflower seeds.

Specialty Grain Company. Certified alfalfa, red clover, and radish seeds.

The Sprout House. "The world's finest selection of certified organic sprouting seeds": alfalfa, crimson clover, red radish, turnip, kale, fenugreek, Chinese cabbage, black mustard, buckwheat, whole sunflower, shelled sunflower, Alaskan green pea, sprouting corn, hard wheat, soft white wheat, rye, triticale, mung, lentil, adzuki, soy, chia, garbanzo, sprouting peanut, quinoa, and flaxseed, plus a raw-linen sprouting bag (just dip to rinse and hang to grow) and all-natural, untreated bamboo sprouters. Also sprout recipes and booklets.

Totally Organic Farms. Alfalfa seeds.

SWEETENERS

Harmful ingredients: BHA/BHT, pesticide residues, sucrose.

Warning label:
"Use of this product may be hazardous to your health. Contains saccharin, which has been determined to cause cancer in laboratory animals."

For many years saccharin has been widely used as an artificial sweetner, despite the fact that it can cause cancer in humans. After several attempts to ban this substance, it is still on the shelves in some products, such as dehydrated ice tea mix.

More popular now is aspartame (sold as NutraSweet and Equal). It's a so-called "natural" sweetener made of phenylalanine and aspartic acid, and containing "nothing artificial." In your body, these naturally occuring substances break down into the same amino acids found in any protein food.

The primary problem with aspartame is overconsumption. Large doses of phenylalanine are toxic to the brain and can cause mental retardation and seizures in people with a particular genetic disorder called phenylketonuria. Other people experience headaches, depression, mood swings, high blood pressure, insomnia, and behavior problems as a result of chemical changes in the brain caused by the sweetener. Aspartame is not recommended for use by pregnant women as it is known to cause birth defects. With aspartame now being used in every food product from breakfast cereals to vitamin pills, it's easy to ingest too much.

More diseases have been linked to eating sugar (sucrose) than to any other aspect of nutrition. One of the most important characteristics of sugar to consider is that as a simple carbohydrate it cannot be digested, assimilated, or utilized by the body without the help of other nutrients that must be provided from somewhere else. So in order to accommodate sucrose, the missing nutrients must be taken from nutritious food in your diet, from nutrients in your blood, and even from nutrient reserves stored in your bones.

Sugar also inhibits the ability of the white blood cells in your immune system to curb bacteria. This effect lasts for about four hours, so if you eat sugar for breakfast, lunch, and dinner, this is likely to leave your body vulnerable to bacteria most of the time. Among the ailments sucrose consumption is likely to aggravate, if not cause, are tooth decay, diabetes, hypoglycemia, coronary disease, obesity, ulcers, high blood pressure, vaginal yeast infections, osteoporosis, and malnutrition.

Sugar has many names: Barbados molasses/sugar, blackstrap molasses, brown sugar, cane sugar/syrup, corn syrup, dextrose, invert sugar, invert sugar/syrup, maple sugar/syrup, muscavado sugar, raw sugar, ribbon cane syrup, sorghum syrup, and turbinado sugar. They may come from different sources, look different, and taste different, but they are all sucrose.

Fructose is often used as a substitute for sucrose in health-food products. Even though its name suggests it might be healthier, the fructose used in commercial products bears about as much resemblance to the natural sugar found in fruits as refined white sugar does to sugarcane. Generally manufactured from corn syrup, it, too, is a simple carbohydrate. Although it is easier to metabolize than sucrose and you need to use less (its sweetening power is almost twice that of sucrose), fructose cannot be relied upon as a substitute sweetener because it usually is in the form of a high-fructose corn syrup that contains 55 percent sucrose.

Refined white sugar is the most heavily contaminated of the sucrose sweeteners, having been sprayed with multiple pesticides, processed over a natural-gas flame, and chemically bleached. Beet sugar, additionally, is processed with BHA or BHT, and both beet and cane sugar contain residues of sulfur compounds.

Instead of sugar, eat naturally sweet foods. Add fruit juices or fresh or dried fruits to dishes that need to be sweetened, or use one of the many sweeteners that do not rely on sucrose as their sweetening agent.

Aguamiel
The naturally sweet, nutritious sap of the century plant, used for centuries as a food, tonic, and sweetener. It tastes like a blend of honey and molasses, though is less sweet than honey. Use like you would honey, rice syrup, or barley malt syrup.

Barley malt
This natural sweetener, composed mainly of maltose, is made by soaking and sprouting barley to make malt, then combining it with more barley and cooking this mixture until the starch is converted to sugar. The mash is then strained and cooked down to syrup or dried into powder.

Barley-malt syrup is only about 40 percent as sweet as sucrose, so substitute two cups of syrup for each cup of sugar in a recipe. Since it is a liquid sweetener, decrease the liquid in the recipe by one-fourth cup for each three-fourths of a cup of syrup used.

Barley-malt powder, on the other hand, is 2000 percent sweeter than sucrose. Be very careful when cooking with it. Use only two to two and one-half teaspoons of barley-malt powder per cup of sugar.

Date sugar
This sweetener is made by dehydrating dates to two percent moisture and grinding them very finely into granules. This natural fructose sweetener is equal to sugar in its sweetening power and so can be substituted for white sugar cup for cup. It is especially good in recipes that call for brown sugar.

Fig syrup
Made from figs and water, it works very well as a substitute for molasses when substituted cup for cup.

Fruit sweetener
A thick syrup made from a blend of fruits which are concentrated by removing water,

natural fruit acids, and strong flavors. It can be used as a syrup like honey, or substituted cup for cup for sugar (reduce liquid in recipe by one-third).

Honey

Composed of glucose and fructose, honey generally is the least chemically contaminated sweetener because bees exposed to pesticides usually don't make it back to the hive.

Legally, for a bottle to be labeled honey it must contain "the nectar and floral exudations of plants gathered and stored in the comb of honeybees." Honey is always honey, regardless of how it is labeled. "U.S. Grade A" or "Fancy" refers to the level of filtration and does not give any indication of quality or freedom from chemical contamination.

The best processing is the least processing; avoid honey that has been subjected to heat or chemicals or that comes from beehives that are sprayed with antibiotics or other chemicals. Since some honey is diluted with corn syrup, choose a brand whose label states that it is undiluted.

There are many different types of honey. The lighter-colored honeys usually are more delicate, while darker-colored honeys have a very strong, distinct flavor. For sweetness without too much flavor, try clover, star-thistle, mountain-wildflower, or orange-blossom honey. Iron-bark-tree honey tastes like butterscotch. Tupelo is best for baking. Other types of honey include alfalfa, black-eyed bean, buckwheat, cabbage, conifer, grapefruit, Hawaiian wild lava plum, hawthorne, heather, lime, lemon blossom, manzanita, mesquite, rosemary, safflower, and thyme.

Honey is 140 percent as sweet as sugar, so replace each cup of sugar with one-half to three-fourths of a cup of honey and reduce the liquid in the recipe by one-fourth cup for each three-fourths of a cup of honey used.

One problem is that the flavor of the honey may come through in the finished product even when a light honey is used. By using less honey than is called for in the recipe, you will get the sweetness without as much of a honey taste.

Maple syrup/sugar

Along with honey, maple syrup has been a mainstay natural-food sweetener for years, as it is simply boiled-down maple sap. Unfortunately, its sweetness comes from sucrose; but because its method of processing does not add the contaminants found in cane and beet sugars, it is the best sucrose sweetener to use. You might want to limit your consumption, however, and save it for Sunday pancakes while using some other alternative for your all-purpose sweetener.

Maple trees are grown without fertilizers or pesticide sprays, but in America the law permits injection of the trees with formaldehyde pellets to increase the flow of sap and does not require this to be stated on the label. The Canadian Food and Drug Directorate, on the other hand, does not allow this practice.

Government regulations stipulate that all maple syrup be maple-sap syrup, be free from foreign material, and weigh not less than eleven pounds per gallon. The syrup is then graded by color according to U.S. color standards; the lighter the syrup, the higher the quality and the more delicate the flavor. Grade Fancy—Light Amber is the highest quality, the first syrup made each season. Grade A—Medium Amber is produced in greatest quantity, with a medium maple flavor. Grade B—Dark Amber has the strongest maple flavor, which really comes through in recipes.

Rice syrup

A natural sweetener composed mainly of maltose, rice syrup is made by combining barley malt with rice and cooking it until all the starch is converted to sugar. The mash is then strained and cooked down to syrup.

Rice syrup is best used just as it comes from the jar, on pancakes, waffles, toast, and rice cakes, or in cooking when only a touch of sweetness is needed. Because it is only 20 percent as sweet as sugar, it is impractical as a sugar substitute in recipes.

Stevia

Stevia Rebaudiana is a South American herb with a slight licorice taste that is eighty to one hundred times as sweet as sugar. Yet one serving that equals the sweetness of two tablespoons of sugar contains less than one calorie. Stevia has been researched extensively since 1899 and found to be completely nontoxic, which would make it an ideal substitute for saccharin and other artificial sweetening agents. Traditional use of Stevia has shown it to be beneficial to the pancreas and of great value in treating the symptoms of diabetes, high blood pressure, and infections. Stevia does not break down under heat, and because of its beneficial virtues it is an excellent substitute for sugar in baking and sweetening beverages.

Experiment with Stevia leaves, powder, or extract to find out how to use it to please your own sweet tooth. You can use a pinch of Stevia to sweeten beverages, or make a tea with the herb by dissolving one rounded teaspoon into one cup of water, then use four to five drops to equal one teaspoon of sugar. This handy liquid sweetener will keep several days when refrigerated.

At the Store/By Mail

Look for natural sweeteners in your natural-food store, or order by mail.

⊕ *Earthwise sweeteners*

2nd Opinion. Stevia. Also a book, *Sugarfree Cooking*, by Nicole J. Walker.

Allergy Resources. Aguamiel (with a booklet of recipes) and Stevia.

Cascadian Farm Organic Fruit Sweetener (Cascadian Farm). ⊞ *Cascadian Farm.*

Deer Valley Farm. Buckwheat, Champlain Valley, comb, tupelo, and wildflower honey.

Dial Herbs. Stevia.

Domaine de Donadei Honeys (Schoonmaker/Lynn Enterprises). Liquid and crystallized honeys. Hives are treated with vitamin C instead of antibiotics. *Schoonmaker/Lynn Enterprises.*

Eden Foods Barley Malt Syrup (Eden Foods). *Gold Mine Natural Food Company.*

Eden Foods Organic Amazake (Eden Foods). Sweetener made from organic brown rice. *Gold Mine Natural Food Company.*

Eden Foods Organic Sorghum Molasses (Eden Foods).

Erwin's Bee Farm. Oregon wildflower honey.

Fiddler's Green Farm. Raspberry honey.

Jack's Honeys (Jack's Honey Bee Products). Variety of delicious-sounding honeys, "not filtered with chemical agents, uncooked, and undiluted—just pure honey purchased directly from local beekeepers we know and trust." *Jack's Honey Bee Products.*

Jaffe Brothers. Honey from the flowers of southern California. Vermont country maple sprinkles, an all-natural granulated sweetener.

Uncle Joel's Maple Syrup. Pure Wisconsin maple syrup.

Lundberg Sweet Dream Brown Rice Syrup (Lundberg Family Farms). *Lundberg Family Farms.*

Mountain Ark Trading Company. Maple syrup.

Organic Foods Express. Brown rice and maple syrup.

Rising Sun Organic Produce. Maple syrup from trees grown by organic or biodynamic methods.

Shelburne Farms. Maple syrup produced without additives.

Shiloh Farms. Honey.

Smoot Honey Company. Variety of honeys from some of the most pollution-free areas remaining in this country.

Sucanat Organic Sugar (Pronatec International). Evaporated cane juice contains up to three percent mineral salts and can be used cup for cup as sugar substitute. Certified by independent testing to be free of pesticides. *Millstream Natural Health Supplies, Pronatec International, Rising Sun Organic Produce, Simply Delicious.*

Sweet Cloud Barley Malt Syrup and Rice Syrup. (Great Eastern Sun). Made with sprouted barley and water, and brown rice, sprouted barley, and water. *Natural Lifestyle Supplies.*

Walnut Acres Honey (Walnut Acres). Unadulterated honeys produced without the use of chemicals include wildflower, tupelo, and orange blossom. *Walnut Acres.*

Westbrae Organic Brown Rice Syrup (Westbrae Natural Foods). Light butterscotch flavor. *Natural Lifestyle Supplies.*

🌱 Natural sweeteners

Lima Barley Malt Syrup (Eden Foods). *Gold Mine Natural Food Company.*

Rice Nectar Natural Rice Syrups (T & A Gourmet). Made with brown rice and sweetened with fruit. *Gold Mine Natural Food Company.*

Wax Orchards Fruit Sweet (Wax Orchards). A blend of all natural fruit juices concentrated to produce a richness not found with other sweeteners or refined sugar; use for baking and cooking. *Wax Orchards, Walnut Acres.*

TEA

Harmful ingredients: pesticide residues.

Loose tea is generally fresher and has a better flavor than tea in bags because it is in its more natural leaf or flower form, rather than being ground into tiny particles. Also, tea bags may contain bleaches and dyes in the paper and be held together with heat-sealant adhesives.

If you want to avoid caffeine, you'll want to choose herbal tea rather than black tea.

At the Store/By Mail

Buy loose tea and brew it using metal tea balls, bamboo strainers, or cotton tea bags. Many natural-food stores have herbs for tea in their bulk-herb section, and there are many organically grown herbal teas that can be ordered by mail.

✺ Earthwise herbal tea

Mountain Ark Trading Company. Bancha twig tea bags.

Bioforce Teas (Bioforce of America). From organically grown or wildcrafted herbs. *Bioforce of America.*

Eden Foods Mu Tea (Eden Foods). *Gold Mine Natural Food Company.*

Fiddler's Green Farm. Kukicha tea.

Herb T. Company Roasted Barley Tea (Muramoto). *Gold Mine Natural Food Company.*

Meadowbrook Herb Garden. Tea herbs biodynamically grown or gathered wild. Also tea blends and assorted fine tea utensils.

Mitoku Macrobiotic Organic Twig Tea (Mitoku Company). Made by hand. *Natural Lifestyle Supplies, Mountain Ark Trading Company.*

Mountain Butterfly Herbs. A variety of herbal teas, all certified.

Natureland Organically Grown Teas (Natureland Teas). The first British organically grown tea.

Ohsawa Organic Teas (Ohsawa America). *Gold Mine Natural Food Company.*

Rosetta Teas. Loose herbal teas to "refresh, rejuvenate, and remedy" from "ancient herbal traditions that span the planet." Organically grown and harvested wild whenever possible. Also bamboo tea strainers, cotton tea bags, and steel-mesh tea balls.

Satori Organic Teas (Satori). Comfrey, lemongrass, peppermint, and spearmint, all certified and grown at Trout Lake Farms, Washington.

Trout Lake Farm. Certified dried herbs.

Wahatoya Herbal Teas (Wahatoya Herb). Primarily wildcrafted or organically grown. *Wahatoya Herb.*

VINEGAR

Harmful ingredients: pesticide residues.

At the Store/By Mail

Because of their acidic nature, vinegars do not need preservatives and so are as safe as any other nonorganic, additive-free food. Flavored vinegars contain natural herbs, spices, and fruits. So enjoy yourself, and let the many different varieties add a lift to your menus. The vinegars listed here are organically grown and for that reason particularly recommended.

⊕ *Earthwise vinegars*

Dach Ranch. Organic apple-cider vinegar.

Eden Foods Organic Brown Rice Vinegar (Eden Foods). *Gold Mine Natural Food Company, Simply Delicious.*

Mitoku Macrobiotic Kyushu Organic Brown Rice Vinegar (Mitoku Company). *Natural Lifestyle Supplies.*

Ohsawa Organic Vinegar (Ohsawa America). *Gold Mine Natural Food Company.*

Walnut Acres "Ole Time" Organic Apple Cider Vinegar (Walnut Acres). From "biologically" grown apples. *Walnut Acres.*

WINE AND BEER

Harmful ingredients: ammonia, asbestos residues, colors, EDTA, flavors, glycerin,

hydrogen peroxide, lead residues, methylene chloride, mineral oil, pesticide residues, plastic (PVP), sulfur compounds. (These additives have not been tested for safety in the presence of alcohol or on animals whose detoxification systems have been weakened by long-term alcohol consumption.)

Warning label:

"CAUTION: The Surgeon General has determined that consumption of alcoholic beverages during pregnancy can cause serious birth defects. Alcohol can also impair driving ability, create dependency or addiction, and can contribute to other major health hazards."

Alcoholic beverages are regulated by the Bureau of Alcohol, Tobacco, and Firearms (BATF), not the FDA. Although the Food, Drug, and Cosmetic Act of 1938 does not exempt alcoholic beverages, no agency is enforcing this law, and ingredients are not listed on labels.

One or two drinks a day may not be harmful, but once this limit is passed, problems begin. Alcoholism can cause heart disease, hepatitis, cirrhosis of the liver, decreased resistance to disease, shortened life span, nutrient deficiencies, cancer, fetal alcohol syndrome, brain damage, stroke, phlebitis, varicose veins, and a reduced testosterone level that in males can cause sexual impotence, loss of libido, breast enlargement, and loss of facial hair.

Unfortunately, the harmful effects of alcohol do not stop with the body of the drinker. Alcohol is responsible for many needless deaths caused by drunk drivers and is a factor in more than half of all the homicides, rapes, and sexually aggressive acts in this nation. Many alcoholics also die from falling, inability to escape during a fire, drowning, and suicide.

If you want to avoid alcoholic beverages, beware of so-called nonalcoholic or dealcoholized wines and beers. Many still contain the same additives as alcoholic beverages (some even declare them on the labels) and under federal law can also contain up to .5 percent alcohol, without stating so on the label. Better to choose a varietal grape juice (made from the same varieties of grapes as wine, but not fermented). Sparkling "wine" can be made by mixing varietal grape juice with carbonated mineral water. Sparkling apple juice is a good substitute for champagne.

At the Store/By Mail
Since the law does not require ingredients of alcoholic beverages to be listed, look for brands that voluntarily reveal the purity of their ingredients.

I know of no beers that use organically grown hops or malt, but there are many natural beers. All German beers are protected by a law called the *Reinheitsgebot* ("law of purity"), that makes it a crime to brew beer with ingredients other than hops, malt, and water. In addition, many of the popular beers such as Coors, Budweiser, and Pabst are additive-free, and you might want to look for beers from small local breweries, which generally use the finest of natural ingredients.

There are, however, many wines made from organically grown grapes. Some can be ordered by mail; look for others at your natural-food store, or ask your wine dealer to stock them.

⊕ *Earthwise wines*
Ask your local wine merchant or natural food store to order these wines for you.

Bellrose Vineyard Wine (Bellrose Vineyard). Cabernet Sauvignon since 1984.

The Boston Wine Company. French, German, and Italian wines.

Chartrand Imports. Currently offers over twenty organic wines, including a line of California wines from Fitzpatrick Winery. All are certified organic by independent third-party verification. Will mail-order if you can't find their wines in stores.

Domaine de la Bousquette (The Organic Wine Company). Red and white French wines.

Fitzpatrick Wines (Fitzpatrick Winery). Organic wines include Eire Ban, chardonnay, and Sierra Dreams. Member of the California Organic Wine Alliance. *Fitzpatrick Winery.*

Four Chimneys Farm Winery. A varied selection of red and white wines including a Catawba-grape wine and "Eye of the Bee," a Concord-grape wine made with honey. Also imports organically grown French, German, and Italian wines.

Frey Vineyards Organic Wines (Frey Vineyards). California's largest organically grown wine producer. French colombard, gray riesling, sauvignon blanc, chardonnay, pinot noir, zinfandel, and cabernet sauvignon.

H. Coturri & Sons Wines (H. Coturri & Sons). Some wines made with organically grown grapes. All made with traditional methods and no sulfites added.

Hidden Cellars Wine (Hidden Cellars). Chardonnay.

Las Montanas Wines (Las Montanas). One of California's oldest wine producers. Zinfandel and Cabernet Sauvignon with no added sulfites.

Octopus Mountain Wines (Octopus Mountain).

Olson Wines (Olson Vineyards).

Organic Vintages. Distributor of a number of California wines and several French wines, all organically grown. Some with no added sulfites.

The Organic Wine Works Wines (The Organic Wine Works). Sauvignon Blanc and Semillon with no sulfites added.

Paul Thomas Wines (Paul Thomas). Crimson Rhubarb wine with no sulfites added.

Robert Kacher Selections. Two estate wines from Provence.

Terry Theise Selections. Several German wines.

Vineyard Brands/Robert Haas Selections.

Imports three organically grown French wines—one made with biodynamically grown grapes.

Weygant-Metzler Importing. Small estate French burgundies.

⊕ *Earthwise nonalcoholic beverages*

Olde Norfolk Punch (Traditional Products). Nonalcoholic beverage made from a medieval monastic recipe that contains over thirty herbs and spices pounded by hand with a mortar and pestle and steeped in natural underground waters.

YOGURT AND KEFIR

Harmful ingredients: colors, flavors.

All brands of plain yogurt are free from artificial additives, but harmful ingredients are often found in flavored yogurts. Buy plain yogurt and add your own sweeteners and toppings, or buy an additive-free brand.

Most yogurts are made with regular milk, which contains residues of pesticides and other harmful substances; buying nonfat yogurt minimizes your exposure to pesticides. There is at least one brand I know of that is made with milk from cows raised on a biodynamic farm.

Kefir, though similar to yogurt, is a liquid and is made from a different culture. Kefir cheese has had some of the water removed and tastes like sour cream mixed with cream cheese.

At the Store/By Mail

Look for yogurt and kefir at your natural-food store.

⊕ *Earthwise yogurt*

Seven Stars Farm Biodynamic Yogurt (Seven Stars Farm). From a four hundred-acre farm that uses biodynamic herbal preparations to enhance the vitality of its composted soil, plants, and animals. Cows exclusively fed home-grown biodynamic hay and grains.

6 ❧ Lawn & Garden Supplies

What was paradise but a garden
An orchard full of trees and herbs
Full of pleasures and nothing there but delights.
ANONYMOUS

As we all move toward living in harmony with the Earth, organic gardening is a skill many of us will cultivate. Whether we grow sprouts on our windowsills, flowers in window boxes, strawberries on the deck, or vegetables in our backyards—or have acres of countryside or a city block to farm—gardening brings us back in touch with the Earth and its cycles in a way no other domestic activity can.

Gardening can also provide a significant portion of our food. A home garden can yield two to four times more food per acre than commercial agriculture; in a single season the average home garden can provide over six hundred dollar's worth of food. We can increase that yield further with raised beds and biointensive organic methods. Of even greater value is the quality of the food itself—fresher, tastier, and more nutritious.

Whether you grow food, flowers, grass, or trees, you can garden without toxic, polluting chemicals.

HOW GARDENING PRODUCTS AFFECT OUR HEALTH AND THE EARTH

Chapters 5 and 8 cover many issues pertaining to the dangers of using toxic pesticides and fertilizers. These same issues apply to home gardening as well. In many ways our gardens are microcosms of agricultural methods; the same pesticides and fertilizers used by agribusiness are on our local nursery shelves, in smaller bottles with prettier labels. According to the National Academy of Sciences, "suburban gardens and lawns receive heavier pesticide applications than most other land areas in the United States," including agricultural areas.

When we use pesticides and fertilizers in our gardens, the problem is not only with residues in our food; we also contaminate the land in our own yards, pollute our own water, and create invisible clouds of poison in our own air. A 1987 study under the auspices of the National Cancer Institute found that children who lived in households where outdoor pesticides were regularly used were six to nine times more likely to develop some forms of childhood leukemia; the figure increased four times when indoor pesticides were regularly used. In addition, our children or pets can accidentally ingest stored pesticides, with possibly fatal results.

One of the most common pesticides used in home gardens is 2,4-D, one of two chemical components of the defoliant Agent Orange, used widely in Vietnam with disastrous results. According to the National Cancer Institute, farmers exposed to this chemical for more than twenty-one days each year are more likely to fall victim to lymphatic cancer. Other garden pesticides have similar dangers.

ORGANIC GARDENING

The alternative to chemical pesticides and fertilizers is organic gardening, or "eco-gardening." Organic gardening methods are based on an understanding of how nature creates healthy plants. The natural method is a dynamic living process that includes biological, chemical, and electromagnetic processes, as well as no doubt many others we don't even know of yet.

The ultimate goal of sustainable organic gardening is to have a healthy living plant/soil ecosystem that does not need added pesticides of any kind, artificial or natural. Organic gardening uses natural biological methods to build soil fertility and healthy, insect-resisting plants. The needed raw materials are taken in a sustainable way from local plant and mineral sources.

Within the realm of eco-gardening there are some philosophies and specialized systems you might want to learn more about.

Permaculture—short for "permanent agriculture"—is a way of designing and maintaining farms and gardens (or whole communities) that have the diversity, stability, and resilience of natural ecosystems. This involves an integrated approach in which, as in nature, plants, animals, land, people, and houses all serve to support a sustainable, multiuse ecosystem. Providing a framework in which many organic methods can be integrated, permaculture incorporates ways to store rainfall, create microclimates to increase available land on which useful crops can be grown. It also involves using tree crops, forest agriculture, edible landscaping, biological pest control, organic-waste recycling, and water/energy efficiency to their fullest potential by working with, not against, nature.

Biodynamic gardening was originally developed by the scientist-philosopher Rudolph Steiner in the 1920s. Literally meaning "forces of life," biodynamics considers the soil to be the foundation of health for plants, animals, and humans. Special compost preparations and sprays are used to enhance the biological life of the soil. In Europe, biodynamically grown food is considered to be among the best. The shelf life and flavor of vegetables is better, and animals have a preference for biodynamically grown grain when given a choice. Biodynamic methods have been used to regenerate over 1 million acres of farm and ranch land in Australia.

Biointensive gardening methods have roots that go back to ancient Chinese and Greek agriculture. Raised, cultivated beds are used to grow a lot of food in a small area—two to ten times more than what conventional mechanized agriculture can grow. At the same time, to grow food this way takes one-third to one-thirtieth the water and one one-hundredth the human and mechanical energy needed for more common methods.

CREATING YOUR GARDEN

Creating an earthwise organic garden takes a little more planning and research than just going down to your local nursery and picking out the prettiest flowers or whatever vegetable plants their buyer thought would sell. Here are some ways to plan a garden that use resources wisely and follow nature's ways.

• *Landscape with edible plants.* Fruit and nut trees, flowers, herbs, and other edible plants can be very attractive and provide shade, windbreaks, and food—all at the same time. They are a way to extend your garden and food supply to a larger area.
• *Design a water-efficient garden.*
  ○ Create a "xeriscape" by using plants that need little watering. Check with your local college, gardening groups, water district, or gardening centers (or consult with mail-order seed companies) to find out about plants that can live on the rainfall levels that are common for your area and require little or no additional water from you. Plants from open-pollinated seed (see SEEDS) are usually less demanding of water than those from hybrid seed.
  ○ Use a drip irrigation system (see TOOLS FOR ORGANIC GARDENING), which can save 60 to 80 percent ot the water used in your garden.
  ○ Use a WATER CONDITIONER. Some gardeners have found that using a water conditioner can reduce scale deposits on plant roots and greatly facilitate the ability of plants to take in water and nutrients, reducing the amount of water needed.
  ○ Use squeeze nozzles on hoses.
  ○ Reuse GRAY WATER.
  ○ Water in the evening to minimize evaporation. And let the water run slowly so the soil can absorb it thoroughly.
• *Use native plants.* These are the plants that have evolved naturally in the areas we live in. In many cases they are threatened with extinction by plants imported from other regions. Native species usually are better suited to the ecology of the region. In addition, they are already adapted to the climate and generally need fewer resources to maintain. You can also create lawns of native grass instead of the typical water-guzzling grass varieties.
• *Encourage beneficial wildlife.* Your garden can be a virtual haven for all sorts of wild creatures—from butterflies and birds to squirrels and salamanders.
• *Create windbreaks with trees, bushes, and other plants.* This can help protect your garden from harsh winds and improve the yield and quality of your food, as well as attract beneficial birds and insects. You can even create "living fences" instead of wood or metal ones.
• *Use companion planting methods.* Organize your garden to bring together plants that support their neighbors by providing benefits such as shade, insect deterrence, and/or growing support.
• *Stay away from plastics as much as possible.* Make soil blocks instead of using plastic trays for seedlings, use paper mulch instead of plastic mulch, etc.

HOW I RATE GARDENING SUPPLIES

Most of the items listed in this chapter are not rated, since in many cases not enough information was available about the mining practices used to obtain minerals or the source of plant materials used in making compost, etc. Ratings are given for SEEDS and are described in that section.

COMPOST, FERTILIZER, AND OTHER SOIL AMENDMENTS

Artificial fertilizers are made up of NPK: nitrogen, phosphorous, and potassium. While this sounds natural enough, the form of the chemicals used in artificial fertilizers is often detrimental to you, the soil, and plants.

One of the most widely used forms of nitrogen fertilizer is anhydrous ammonia, a chemical that can burn the skin and lungs. In soil, it reduces beneficial microorganisms while at the same time creating an environment in which harmful organisms thrive.

Muriate of potash (potassium chloride), the most commonly used potassium fertilizer in the United States, creates hypochlorous acid—the main chemical used in swimming-pool disinfectants—in the soil, which inhibits beneficial bacteria, and chlorine gas (a suspected ozone-depleting gas that evaporates into the air). Its use produces mineral-deficient crops and eventually turns the land into a desert.

In addition, plants need more than these three minerals for optimal growth. Some 16 elements are now commonly considered essential, and over 56 have been detected in plant life. While using artificial NPK fertilizer can give plants an impressive jolt of growth, it does nothing to address the more important issue of providing full biological and nutritional support for the plant—and for all of us who eat them.

What is needed is fertile soil. Plants grown in good soil resist pests, diseases, and contain more nutrients. Fertile soil, healthy plants, and no pesticides add up to good health for us and the Earth.

Good soil is one with a rich humus layer that contains a complete balance of mineral nutrients and is full of essential microorganisms, earthworms, and other beneficial critters. Humus is the life of the soil, concentrated in the top five to seven inches. Made from decaying plant and animal matter, humus provides a base of support, energy, and nutrients for the soil's microorganisms, which perform many functions essential to healthy soil and plants, such as the conversion of minerals and other elements into forms usable by the plants.

There are many natural ways to maintain good soil fertility. These include *fertilizers,* which give the soil and plants the necessary major and minor nutrients, and *soil amendments,* which can also be fertilizers but have other qualities that help develop good soil structure, texture, drainage, and organic matter. Natural fertilizers include chicken, turkey, and other animal manure, bracken ferns, wood ash (also good for pest control), bat guano (make sure it's certified to be free of rabies), bone meal, fish emulsion and meal, greensand, hoof and horn meal, kelp meal, lime and oyster shell, various kinds of rock-dust minerals, and soft phosphate. Natural soil amendments include compost and manures, cocoa hulls, oakleaf mold, potting mixes, rice hulls, shredded bark, and horticultural sand.

As a general rule, soil and plants need good organic matter and a variety of minerals, which can be added to the soil or sprayed directly on the plant.

Compost

Compost is Nature's most nearly perfect plant food and soil conditioner. It improves your soil's structure and texture and helps it retain essential nutrients, air, and water. Compost controls erosion and the leaching away of nutrients, protects against drought and weeds, and regulates the pH of your soil. Compost provides nutrients to your plants exactly as they need them, and stretches the growing season in both spring and fall. One forestry project had a tenfold increase in growth when using compost.

You can make your own compost at home, or buy it ready-made (when buying, consider the quality of the raw materials that the compost is made from). There are many types of compost bins that can be purchased, as well as starters that get the process going.

Worm composting—called vermicomposting—is becoming more popular, as a way to both increase soil fertility and process plant-based "garbage." Earthworms play an invaluable role in soil fertility. They aerate the soil, transform elements into usable forms for plants, make the soil more livable for beneficial microorganisms, increase soil water-holding and buffer capacity, and reduce the toxicity of both natural and human-made toxic substances. They also convert organic matter into worm castings, one of the best fertilizers in the world. The United States Department of Agriculture has stated that earthworm castings contain over five time the available nitrogen, seven times the phosphorus, three times the exchangable magnesium, eleven times the potash, and one and a half times the lime (calcium) found in good topsoil.

Minerals
Nature's minerals, including trace minerals, are another key to healthy soils. According to testimony before the Senate Nutrition Committee, many plant foods we eat today are deficient in trace elements needed to produce proteins and amino acids in our own bodies. As an example, the soil in thirty-two states lacks zinc, one of the vital trace elements.

The best fertilizers are those that give a full range of minerals in the same basic proportions as Nature. These can be obtained from sea minerals, ancient seabed or clay mineral deposits, and "rock dust"

made from local mixed gravel or granite that is ground to a powder.

Natural mineral sources can be added to your compost or directly to the soil. Farmers and gardeners who use them often find that fully mineralized soils and plants have no insect problems, and the taste of their food improves.

Beneficial plant sprays
Beneficial plant sprays can also enhance the yield, nutrition, and natural pest-control ability of plants. These sprays can give nutrients to the plant through tiny openings on the leaves, called stomata, which plants constantly use to exchange gases and mists with the surrounding air. The best time to use these sprays is in the morning, when the stomata are stimulated to open to their maximum by the sounds of nearby birds (another reason to have birds around), allowing the plants to take in their early-morning drink of dew and nutrients.

Biodynamic sprays are made from a combination of herbs and other plants, some animal products including composted cow manure, and some minerals.

Mineral sprays are often a mix of minerals from seaweed or other sources. These sprays may also contain enzymes, plant hormones, and other biologically active ingredients.

Hydrogen peroxide can also be used in very small amounts: sixteen drops of 35 percent food-grade hydrogen peroxide in one quart of water for plants (for larger gardens, use eight ounces of 35 percent in ten gallons of water per half acre of crops). Hydrogen peroxide plant sprays have been getting enthusiastic endorsements from farmers and gardeners who have tried them. The Amish have apparently been using hydrogen peroxide for years.

COMPOST-MAKING TIPS

The simplest way to compost is to layer your food wastes and yard clippings in a box or a pile in your yard. Turn the pile frequently to allow air to circulate. Make sure the pile is covered to keep animals out. Keep the pile moist but not soggy. Add worms to the compost for faster decomposition and better-quality compost. Finished compost is rich, dark, and crumbly, and will have lost its heat.

Use a variety of materials for a higher nutrient content. Fallen leaves, for example, are one of the most concentrated sources of nutrients available, carrying 50 to 80 percent of the nutrients that a tree extracts from the soil and air. Fresh grass and plant trimmings are a rich source of nitrogen. Wastes that can be composted include:

- food scraps;
- lawn and garden wastes, including grass clippings, weeds, leaves, sawdust, and shredded bushes;
- chipped untreated wood;
- natural-fiber discards;
- newspapers;
- wood ashes;
- straw and hay; and
- feathers.

The smaller the pieces, the faster they decompose.

Don't compost meat, fat, or grease.

Keep herbicides, pesticides, and other toxic substances out of the pile.

At the Store/By Mail

Compost and compost-making supplies, fertilizers, minerals, soil amendments, and plant sprays

Azomite (Azome-Utah West). Mined clay with heavy concentration of minerals and trace elements.

BioBin (BioBin). Backyard composting unit constructed of scrap wood from milled second-growth cedar trees. *BioBin.*

Bioterra Organic Soil Enhancer (Bioterra). Made exclusively from fruit and vegetable matter. Approved for certified organic growers in Oregon and California. *Nichols Garden Nursery.*

Black Bat Soil Conditioner. Organic bat-guano soil conditioner from Carlsbad, New Mexico.

Bricker's. Cricket manure, compost, compost starter, and other soil conditioners.

Chase Organics Herbal Compost (Chase Organics). From England. *Nichols Garden Nursery.*

D. Senften. Instructions for building your own composter and making compost in fourteen days.

Deer Valley Farm. Natural fertilizers and soil conditioners.

Dirt Cheap Organics. Organic fertilizers, and a type of worm which they say is unsurpassed in its ability to condition and detoxify the soil.

Ecology Action. Basic single soil amendments, fertilizers, worm compost.

Erth-Rite (Erth-Rite). Composted soil builders made from various natural organic raw materials; biodynamic compost starter. *Harmony Farm Supply, Karen's Nontoxic Products, Erth-Rite.*

Evergreen Bin (Evergreen Bin). Backyard composting unit made of sawmill seconds from second-growth western red cedar trees. *Harmonius Technologies.*

Flowerfield Enterprises. Sells the book *Worms Eat My Garbage;* offers supplies for setting up your own worm composting system at home.

Garden-Ville. Basic soil conditioners.

Gardener's Supply. Several kinds of composting bins, compost starter and thermometer, shredders, organic fertilizer, earthworm castings, cover crops, and other soil conditioners.

Gardens Alive! Cover crops, humus, compost starter, organic plant foods, and soil conditioners.

Harmony Farm Supply. Biodynamic compost, compost starter and field spray, bat guano, seaweeds, earthworm castings, and other soil conditioners.

Humboldt Composting Company. Seabird and bat guano, earthworm castings, and compost mixes of all three fertilizers. Has instructions on earthworm composting.

Integrated Fertility Management. Natural soil amendments and seaweed. Also foliar-spray fertilizers and mineral sprays.

Kemp Company. An eighteen-bushel drum composter that creates high temperatures to accelerate composting time. Also sells a shredder-chipper.

Live Earth Compost (Erth-Rite). *Erth-Rite, Harmony Farm Supply.*

Livingstone's Living Earth Topsoil Production Centers. Earthworm humus and an organic potting mix of earthworm humus and peat moss for houseplants.

Maxicrop Liquefied Seaweed (Maxicrop USA & Company). Seaweed plant spray. *Erth-Rite, Karen's Nontoxic Products.*

Meadowbrook Herb Garden. Organic fertilizers and compost starter.

Medina Organic Soil Amendments (Medina Agriculture Products). Includes soil activators to increase the growth of beneficial organisms in the soil and liquid humus. *The Living Source, Medina Agriculture Products.*

Mountain Ark Trading Company. Rock dust from an ancient-seabed mineral deposit in central Colorado.

Necessary Trading Company. Compost thermometer, compost starter, and trace minerals.

Nitron Industries. Enzyme soil conditioners and all-purpose natural fertilizer, seaweeds, bat guano. Also organic compost, earthworm castings, wire compost bin, compost starter, shredder, and minerals and trace elements.

Nutra-Min. Humuslike material from an old seabed in Nevada that contains almost all known trace elements.

Organic Soil Treatment (Dr. & Mrs. J.M. Summers). *The Living Source.*

Peaceful Valley Farm Supply. Earthworm castings, biodynamic compost and compost starter, chipper/shredder. Also many natural soil amendments, trace minerals, cover crops, and seeds.

Pinetree Garden Seeds. Seaweed, earthworm castings, compost starter.

Ringer Natural Lawn and Garden Fertilizers (Ringer). A number of varieties for different purposes, with balanced nutrients and microorganisms that aerate soil. *Ringer, Pinetree Garden Seeds.*

Ringer. Compost, compost starters, shredders, and compost tools.

Shur-Crop (Hi-Bar). Concentrated liquid-kelp soil conditioner and plant spray for lawns and gardens. *Lett Company, Peaceful Valley Farm Supply.*

Sonic Bloom (Scientific Enterprises). Combines the benefits of an organic spray (fifty-five trace minerals and amino acids) with a special sound that opens the plant's pores and stimulates much greater absorption of nutrients. Reported to increase both yields and nutrition in plants. Dan Carlson, the inventor, is in the Guinness Book of World Records for growing the world's longest Purple Passion plant (1300 feet) using Sonic Bloom. *Scientific Enterprises.*

Stone Flour Products. Rock-dust minerals from a quarry in Arkansas.

Sustane Natural Organic Fertilizer (Sustane Corporation). Organic compost fertilizer, dehydrated and granulated for ease of shipment and application. *Sustane Corporation.*

The Natural Gardening Company. Natural-redwood compost bin, compost turner, compost book, biodynamic compost starter, and seaweeds.

Unco Night Crawlers (Unco Industries). Produces millions of night crawlers and eggs, primarily for bait, composting, and soil-regeneration purposes. *Unco Industries.*

Wiggle Worm Soil Builder (Unco In-dustries). Organic worm castings. *Unco Industries.*

LAWN CARE

Harmful materials: pesticides.

Over 4 million American households pay up to two hundred dollars a year to have their lawns maintained with hazardous chemicals.

The $1.5-billion lawn-care industry has grown dramatically in the last few years, thanks to the tanker spray truck. By premixing pesticides and fertilizer in large quantities and applying them from a nozzle, lawn-care companies can treat dozens of lawns each day during the entire season. This means that more pesticides and fertilizers than ever before are being applied on a regular basis within immedi-ate neighborhoods. The chemicals evapo-rate into the air during and even after ap-plication, contaminating land and local water supplies.

Because lawn-chemical spraying is not just a personal hazard, but a community hazard as well, many communities are adopting right-to-know ordinances that require the company that sprays to notify residents before spraying will take place and after spraying has occurred. Because of such ordinances, industry is beginning to voluntarily post signs.

Pesticides commonly used on lawns are the insecticides chloropyrifos and diazinon (common name Dursban and others), the herbicides 2,4-D and banvel, and the fun-gicides benomyl and daconil. The adverse health effects associated with these pesti-cides are numerous.

Considering the health and environ-mental effects of lawn-care chemicals, it's ironic that chemical lawn care is not even good for the health of the lawn. While you may see improvement for the first two to four years, the lawn later begins to disintegrate.

SPECIAL TIPS

You might want to share these tips with your neighbors to help stop pesticide spraying in your neighborhood altogether.

• *Let your grass grow.* Close and frequent mowing weakens grass plants. Grass that is two and a half to three inches tall shades weed seedlings (preventing their growth) and holds moisture in the soil. Mow grass when it is dry and in the eve-ning or the cool of the day, and keep your mower blade sharp. Leave nitrogen-rich grass clippings behind to degrade into soil-building compost. Rake up any large clumps to use for compost or mulch.

• *Fertilize naturally.* Grass clippings, com-post, and manure return needed bacteria and enzymes to the soil along with nu-trients. Include clover or other nitrogen-fixing plants in your lawn to make it self-fertilizing.

• *Cut dandelions* at the root, several inches below the ground and reseed bare spots. Despite the advertising to the contrary, most won't grow back. Or just learn to live with them. They look bad only twice a year, and a quick mowing will solve that.

• *De-thatch* in late spring or early summer, then reseed.

• *Dry out fungus,* de-hatch, add soil bacte-ria, and reseed. Fungus grows only in wet, thatchy, overfertilized lawns.

• *Aerate* twice a year (compacted soil pro-motes weeds). Add a soil loosener like com-post or gypsum, then reseed.

• *Reseed* bare spots and thinning lawns to prevent weed growth.

• *Water* in the evening, deeply and infre-quently. Allow the grass to dry thoroughly between waterings.

• *Choose the right species.* An eighty-twenty mix of fescue and rye grows well in most areas, although it is best to choose a

grass native to your area. Pick varieties that resist drought and disease, need little mowing, fertilizer, or water, and are suited to available light and traffic.
• Use your lawn space to grow a wildflower meadow, an organic edible garden, or anything else you'd like.

At the Store/By Mail

Check your local nursery for natural lawn-care products; also ask if they know of a lawn-care company that uses natural methods. Or order lawn-care products by mail. Many of the previous COMPOST, FERTILIZER, AND OTHER SOIL AMENDMENTS products can be applied to lawns as well. Here are some companies that have special lawn products.

Gardens Alive! Natural lawn-care products and seeds.

Necessary Trading Company. Instructions and fertilizers for natural lawn care. Also a two-page pamphlet describing the basics of chemical-free lawn care, with a monthly lawn-management schedule.

Ringer. Natural fertilizers, seeds, lawn-mowers, and a booklet on growing a healthy lawn the natural way.

Nichols Garden Nursery. "We confess to a lasting desire for soft green patches for children and adults to sit and play upon, but a reluctance to get involved with intensive mowing, spraying, fertilizing and irrigating schedules. We feel our new Ecology Lawn Mixes are the answers to this continuing dilemma. Carefully blended turf mixtures, combining grass, sweet clovers, wildflowers and herbs. They present an attractive appearance between mowings, the quality of the turf is such that it will not be subject to thatch buildup, and it is both drought and shade tolerant."

PEST CONTROL FOR ORGANIC GARDENS

We spend a lot of time and money, and create a lot of toxic dangers, trying to eradicate what we think of as garden pests, but actually many pests are beneficial. Insects seem to be Nature's way of picking up the garbage. Attracted by odors and electromagnetic signals put out by nutrient-deficient, weakened, and diseased plants, they remove them from the food chain. Fully healthy plants give signals that are generally unappealing to these creatures.

Virtually all healthy plants can produce their own natural pesticides, which usually make up about 5 to 10 percent of a plant's dry weight. These include inhibitors to block the protein-digesting enzymes of the attacking pest; enzymes that can dissolve part of the outer skin of insects; and powerful antibiotics than can kill viruses, bacteria, fungi, and nematodes.

Fifty years ago, soil scientist William Albrecht did a classic experiment in which he grew two plants in different pots next to each other. The soil in the pots was identical except that some of the minerals had been removed in one. As the two plants grew they were wrapped around each other. The plant in the deficient soil developed fungus and insect problems, while the plant in the fully mineralized soil grew healthily, with no insect problems or disease—even with the weakened and diseased plant wrapped around it.

Weeds, too, appear to be Nature's way of correcting deficiencies. They help to create conditions that return missing elements back to the soil. If you know how to read what weeds are telling you about the health of the soil, you can work with Nature and correct the imbalance a lot faster than it will take the weeds. Just getting rid of the weeds will not solve the fundamental problem of deficient soil and food.

So the first thing to do to control all the helpful things we consider to be pests is to create healthy soil (see COMPOST, FERTILIZER, AND OTHER SOIL AMENDMENTS). Until that is achieved, you can use several natural and harmonious ways to handle unwanted insects, animals, and plants. These include traps, companion plants that deter harmful insects, natural repellents, beneficial insects and organisms, and natural botanical pesticides and repellents.

Natural botanical pesticides are less toxic than their synthetically derived counterparts, but they do need to be used with care and as a last resort. Here's a rundown on the health and environmental effects of the most popular botanical pesticides:

• *Nicotine* is extracted from the tobacco plant. It is a violent poison that injures the human nervous system and is also toxic to other mammals, birds, and fish.
• *Rotenone* is moderately toxic to humans and many animals, and highly toxic to fish and other aquatic life.
• *Pyrethrins* are extracted from the seeds of a type of chrysanthemum. They are relatively nontoxic to humans, but slightly toxic to fish and other wildlife.
• *Sabadilla* (Red Devil Dust) comes from the seeds of the South American lily. Generally toxic only on contact, but harmful to bees.

If you do use natural pesticides, use them sparingly. Because they are marketed as being nontoxic, safe and organic, there is a danger that we will assume they are not harmful at all and end up using them in even greater quantities than artificial pesticides.

At the Store/By Mail
Look for natural pest controls at your local nursery or organic-garden store, or order them from the mail-order catalogs listed here.

⚒ Natural pest controls
Attack Garden Insect Controls (Ringer). For flying and crawling insects. *Ringer.*

Baubiologie Hardware. Biological insect control.

Beneficial Insectary. Good range of beneficial insects and organisms. Knowledgeable staff.

BioSafe Lawn & Garden Insect Control (Biosys). Effective broad-spectrum garden insecticide that kills pests with natural microscopic agents. *Beneficial Insectary, Harmony Farm Supply, Integrated Fertility Management, Johnny's Selected Seeds, The Natural Gardening Company, Necessary Trading Company, Peaceful Valley Farm Supply, Rincon-Vitova.*

Bricker's. Botanical insecticides.

Brody Enterprises. Copper snail/slug banding material; traps for rats, chipmunks, gophers, and moles; bird netting. Also attractants to make trapping easier.

Deer Valley Farm. Nontoxic, effective sprays for insect control.

Dirt Cheap Organics. Beneficial insects.

Ecology Action. A variety of natural pest controls.

Fairfax Biological Laboratory. Spore powder for control of Japanese-beetle grubs.

Foothill Agricultural Research. Beneficial insects and organisms.

Garden-Ville. Assorted natural pest controls.

Gardener's Supply. Repellents, traps, and other natural pest controls.

Gardens Alive! Repellents, nets, traps, and botanical pesticides.

Green Ban for Plants (Green Ban). Repellent and plant food in a spray. Safe for edibles. *Basically Natural, Baubiologie Hardware, Eco-Choice.*

Harmony Farm Supply. Beneficial insects, traps, and repellents. Also, a useful chart listing a variety of pests and products that help control them.

Hartmann's Plantation. "Scare-Eye" bird deterrent for frightening crop- or garden-damaging birds such as starlings, grackles, crows, and pigeons.

Integrated Fertility Management. Nice charts on using natural pest controls, plus trapping kits, botanical pesticides, and predators.

Johnny's Selected Seeds. Offers a variety of biological and botanical insect controls.

The Natural Gardening Company. Barriers, traps, repellents, beneficial organisms.

Natural Pest Controls. Beneficial insects and organisms.

Nature's Control. Beneficial insects and organisms.

Necessary Trading Company. Pheromone traps, insect traps, beneficial organisms, botanical insecticides.

Organic Pest Management. Beneficial organisms, predators, pheromone traps, botanical pesticides, dusts, live traps, and more.

Peaceful Valley Farm Supply. Pages and pages of pest controls, plus a clear chart that tells how to use beneficial organisms and a good selection of them; biological insecticides, traps, barriers, repellents, insect-identification books, and tools for monitoring pests.

Pinetree Garden Seeds. Traps, netting.

Rincon-Vitova. Beneficial insects and organisms.

Ringer. Botanical pesticides, repellents, traps.

Safer Botanical Insecticides (Safer). Contain pyrethrins. *Gardener's Supply, Harmony Farm Supply, Integrated Fertility Management, Johnny's Selected Seeds, The Natural Gardening Company, Necessary Trading Company, Nitron Industries, Peaceful Valley Farm Supply, Pinetree Garden Seeds.*

Safer Insecticidal Soaps (Safer). Made of fatty-acid salts; contain no petroleum additives. *Eco-Choice, Gardener's Supply, Harmony Farm Supply, Integrated Fertility Management, Johnny's Selected Seeds, The Natural Gardening Company, Necessary Trading Company, Nichols Garden Nursery, Nitron Industries, Peaceful Valley Farm Supply, Pinetree Garden Seeds.*

Trio Aluminum Birdhouses (Nature House). Aluminum birdhouses that attract purple martins, which can eat ten thousand mosquitoes a day. *Nature House.*

Unique Insect Control. Beneficial insects and organisms.

Weiss Brothers Nursery. Gopher traps.

SEEDS

Seeds are the foundation of our food supply. Yet its diversity is seriously threatened by the almost exclusive use of new patented seed varieties. Today we use less than 3 percent of the vegetable varieties that we used in 1900.

Over billions of years, Nature evolved plant types that were ideally suited to the various climates and soil conditions around the world. In the last ten thousand years, farmers have been selecting those varieties that produce the hardiest plants and best foods for local growing conditions, and carefully saving the finest specimens for seed stock. Throughout this natural selection, all the plants were naturally open-pollinated and each was slightly different, having its own unique combination of genes.

At the turn of this century, new biological discoveries allowed scientists to make deliberate crosses between two varieties of the same species. Instead of allowing the plants to cross-pollinate with each other as they would in a garden, hybridizers hand-pollinate each flower with pollen from the same plant. This inbreeding is repeated for as many as ten or twelve generations and results in many weak or deformed plants, which are weeded out until the breeders have a generation of acceptable plants that are genetically uniform. When seeds from the inbred line are planted, they produce identical plants, but they are often sterile and never display the productivity of their parents.

Ninety-nine percent of the seeds used today by agribusiness, organic farmers, and home gardeners are hybrids. In addition to their inferior quality, many of these seeds are coated with fungicides that are so toxic that the yearly leftover packaged seeds cannot be burned because the emissions will not pass EPA requirements. Such seeds should not be handled by children (though you won't see this warning on the label).

Patented hybrid varieties are usually bred for "commercial" values such as yield, long shelf life (thicker skin), and uniformity of harvest time, size, and looks—everything but the most important values to consumers: *nutrition and taste.*

Preliminary tests show *two to four times* greater nutritive value (in a range of vitamins and minerals) in the food grown with open-pollinated seed from Seeds of Change, a seed-preservation group and seed/farm business in Gila, New Mexico, than is found in commonly used hybrid varieties. Adolph Steinbronn of Fairbanks, Iowa grew both a hybrid and an open-pollinated variety of corn and had them tested. His open-pollinated corn contained 19 percent more crude protein, 35 percent more digestible protein, 60 percent more copper, 27 percent more iron, and 25 percent more manganese than the hybrid corn.

Genetic engineering of plants and other life forms is the next step beyond hybridization. One example of genetic engineering is the attempt to create disease- or pest-resistant plants. Unlike hybridization, which allows us to manipulate traits only within a species, genetic engineering gives us the capability of taking from one species a gene (or set of genes) that controls a trait and inserting it into the same or a different species. We now have the ability to erode the differences both within and between species that give each life form and species its uniqueness and place within the web of Nature.

The danger of genetic engineering is probably not so much that any one newly created organism will seriously hurt us or the environment (although we won't know this for sure until after the damage has been done). Most likely the more serious threat is that releasing hundreds of thousands of altered life forms will degrade the natural intricate workings of life on this planet which already give us an abundance of all that we need. Once they are in the environment, we can't say "Oops, we made a mistake" and recall them. The altered living form will interact with other life forms, reproduce, and proliferate.

We do not need new, human-made plants; rather we need to restore our soil, create better growing conditions, and save and use the incredibly abundant variety of plants already available. By using open-pollinated seeds in your garden, you can help the dedicated groups and seed companies that are working to keep alive our rich heritage of seeds. Unlike hybrid seeds, seeds from plants grown from open-pollinated seed can be saved and used from year to year. These seeds are often more nutritious, tastier, hardier, more disease resistant, and need less water and other resources to grow. Using open-pollinated seeds helps preserve one of our most precious resources—a diverse food supply.

HOW I RATE SEEDS

⊕ Earthwise seeds are made from natural, renewable plants that are organically grown or harvested from the wild in a sustainable way.

🌿 Natural seeds are made from natural, renewable plants which have been grown with artificial fertilizers or pesticides.

At the Store/By Mail

Buy open-pollinated and organically grown seeds by mail, as they are not yet a common item in stores and nurseries. All seed companies listed here sell untreated seeds, unless otherwise noted. A plus sign before the name of the catalog indicates that that company carries open-pollinated seeds.

⊕ *Earthwise seeds*

+ *Abundant Life Seed Foundation.* Open-pollinated, untreated seeds, focusing on cool-climate heirloom vegetables, old-fashioned flowers, medicinal and culinary herbs, and native plants of the Cascadian and nearby bioregions. Most seeds come from homegrown and wildcrafted sources. Many edible flowers and other edible landscape plants. Wonderful selection of garden books that inspire the spirit of gardening. Not all seeds are organically grown, but they are committed to providing them as they are available.

+ *Bear Creek Nursery.* Specializes in unusual and unique varieties: cold- and drought-hardy new and antique apples, rootstocks, nut-tree seedlings and cultivars, living fences with multipurposes, and stocks for gardens, orchards, windbreaks, wildlife conservation, and permaculture plantings.

+ *Corns.* Free distribution of organically grown, open-pollinated corn seed to those who are willing to grow the seed out and return seeds for further distribution. Corns is "dedicated to the production and preservation of the genetic diversity of open-polllinated corn varieties" and have several hundred varieties on hand—some rare—and access to several hundred more.

+ *Ecology Action.* Offers untreated, open-pollinated heirloom seeds, mostly from Chase Seeds of England, a pioneer in the organic movement.

+ *The Fragrant Path.* Open-pollinated, untreated, organically grown seeds for fragrant, rare, and old-fashioned plants.

+ *Garden City Seeds.* Both the seeds and production fields are certified as organic. A good selection of open-pollinated, northern-acclimated vegetable seeds plus beans, strawberries, and sunflowers. Has good information on safe pest-control methods and offers some organic fertilizer and pest-control products.

+ *Goodwin Creek Gardens.* Organically grown herbs, everlasting flowers, and fragrant plants, including a large number of native American herbs. Potted plants and seeds.

+ *Halcyon Gardens.* Rare and common organically grown herb seeds and an herb nursery for growing herbs indoors.

+ *J. L. Hudson, Seedsman.* An impressive variety of all types of seeds from around the world. "From the beginning I have stressed open-pollinated seeds and the preservation of our genetic resources. You should all take note that the supplies of many species are tenuous at best. Many species are collected or grown by only one person in the world, sometimes an elderly man or woman, and a year never goes by that we do not hear that one of our old friends has died. The sanctions against South Africa cut off supplies from that part of the world. Flooding in a remote part of India destroyed the only plantings of several species. So you can see that though a seed is listed this year, it may be gone the next."

+ *Johnny's Selected Seeds.* All the standard vegetable seeds, with heirloom varieties noted. Also flowers especially suited for cutting and easy to grow from seed, with edible varieties noted. All seeds untreated (unless otherwise noted) and grown primarily on the company's farm. You can specify "untreated only" on your order.

+ *Living Tree Centre.* Historic apple trees. Also persimmon, apricot, and pear trees.

+ *Livingstone's Living Earth Topsoil Production Centers.* Sells seeds encapsulated in earthworm humus, which protects the seeds from birds as well as providing initial nourishment. Simply toss these ready-to-use seed capsules along the road and/or in your garden. Wildflower, home-flower, and vegetable-garden mixes.

+ *Maplewood Seed Company.* Rare maple-tree seeds only, open-pollinated and organically grown.

+ *Moon Mountain.* All kinds of wild-flower seeds; varieties sold singly and in mixtures. Most are field-grown from seeds gathered in the wild.

+ *Native Seed Foundation.* Native conifer, shrub, nut and fruit seeds that are collected from hardy stands in the Pacific Northwest.

+ *Native Seeds/SEARCH.* The catalog of a nonprofit seed-conservation organization working to preserve the traditional native crops of the U.S. Southwest and northwest Mexico. Contains over two hundred varieties of native crops for spring, summer, and fall gardens.

+ *The Natural Gardening Company.* Gourmet-vegetable and herb seedlings, gourmet-heirloom-vegetable seeds, bulk seeds for single wildflowers, and seed potatoes.

+ *Northplan/Mountain Seed.* Wild-flower, shrub, tree, grass, and legume seeds for disturbed land restoration.

+ *Northwoods Nursery.* Offers fruit, nut, and shade trees; fragrant and flowering shrubs; ground covers, bamboo, and other windbreaks. Some items, like fruit trees, are organically grown; others, like berries, are not.

+ *Nu-World Amaranth.* Amaranth seed.

+ *Peace Seeds.* An excellent and educational catalog offering open-pollinated seeds that are organically grown or wild-crafted. They also publish research papers and a journal about plants, genetic kingdoms, and diversity.

+ *Rex and Susan Mongold.* Offers rare, unusual, and gourmet seed potatoes. The stock is all organically grown on the Mongold's isolated, high-desert farm.

+ *Ronniger's Seed Potatoes.* Small, family-operated organic seed-potato and vegetable farm nestled in the north-easternmost part of Idaho. Over one hundred varieties of seed potatoes grown in fertile soil using natural fertilizers, cover crops, rotations, and composting.

+ *Seeds of Change.* Operates a seed bank that contains over sixty-five hundred native varieties that have not been exposed to synthetic and petrochemical products. Many native seeds are drought-tolerant and pest-resistant. Catalog lists hundreds of open-pollinated and organically grown varieties.

+ *Sonoma Antique Apple Nursery.* Over one hundred varieties of flavorful antique apples and pears, plus some other fruit trees. Organically grown trees are marked.

+ *Southern Oregon Organics.* Vegetable and herb seeds.

+ *Spring Valley Gardens.* Three hundred varieties of organically grown herbs, perennials, everlastings, and alpine and prairie plants.

+ *Synergy Seeds.* Cool- and hot-weather crops; peppers, tomatoes, vine crops; Inca, Aztec, and Hopi corns.

+ *Talavaya Seeds.* Catalog offered by a nonprofit organization that has collected more than thirteen hundred strains of open-pollinated seeds for its seed bank in Espanola, New Mexico. These organically grown seeds are hardy, drought- and insect-resistant, and rich in vitamins, minerals, and protein.

+ *The Tomato Seed Company.* They try to offer as many varieties of tomato seeds as they can. All hybrids are marked as such.

Burbank Gourmet Gardens. Organically grown gourmet seedlings from European, American, and Asian seed stock. Salad greens, vegetables, herbs.

Butterbrooke Farm. Seeds for common vegetables; chosen for rapid maturation in a short growing season.

Companion Plants. Over five hundred herb plants and almost three hundred varieties of herb seeds. Many suitable for companion planting.

The Good Earth Seed Company. Mostly open-pollinated Oriental food seeds.

Meadowbrook Herb Garden. Seeds for

culinary use, as well as dye plants, those with insecticidal and medicinal properties, and those that attract butterflies or hummingbirds. Also books on biodynamic and organic gardening.

Tinmouth Channel Farm. Organic herb seeds and plants.

Wilton's Organic Certified Potatoes. Organic seed potatoes from high-altitude potatoes, making them crisper, firmer, more prolific, and more flavorful.

❧ Natural seeds

+ *D. Landreth Seed Company.* Oldest seed house in America. Offers seeds, bulbs, and roots. Untreated, mostly open-pollinated seeds; hybrids are listed as such.

+ *Good Seed Company.* Open-pollinated and heirloom vegetable, flower, herb, and cover-crop seeds, plus some shrubs and trees.

+ *Heirloom Gardens.* Unique collection of old-time culinary and ornamental flowers. Open-pollinated and untreated.

+ *Heirloom Seeds.* Open-pollinated varieties of vegetables, beans, and some fruits and flowers.

+ *High Altitude Gardens.* Offers varieties of seeds (mostly open-pollinated) that have proven themselves not only vigorous, early maturing, and tolerant of harsh climate, but also exceptionally tasty or beautiful in bloom. Many gardeners at lower elevations report excellent results. Seeds are untreated unless otherwise stated.

+ *Nichols Garden Nursery.* Many open-pollinated seeds (hybrids are noted) for interesting and unusual vegetables and flowers.

+ *Ornamental Edibles.* "We specialize in the seeds for a truly international, imaginative and beautiful garden filled with wholesome gourmet delights." Over four hundred varieties of vegetable seeds,

green starts, and trees from around the world. Many are open-pollinated, and some are organic.

+ *Peaceful Valley Farm Supply.* Wildflower mixes.

+ *Pinetree Garden Seeds.* Carries over six hundred different open-pollinated and hybrid varieties of vegetable, herb, cover-crop, and flower seeds.

+ *Plants of the Southwest.* Native grasses, wildflowers, herbs, trees and shrubs, and early American vegetables.

+ *Redwood City Seed Company.* Open-pollinated vegetable and herb seeds, mostly old-fashioned, pre-1900 varieties.

+ *Seeds Blüm.* Works with small-scale seed growers to offer an array of otherwise unavailable open-pollinated varieties.

+ *Select Seeds.* Open-pollinated flower seeds from Europe and the United States, many not available elsewhere.

+ *Southern Exposure Seed Exchange.* Located in the foothills of the Blue Ridge Mountains of central Virginia, they serve the entire U.S., with an emphasis on varieties adapted to the Mid-Atlantic region. They offer vegetable, herb, fruit, and flower seeds, including many heirloom and rare varieties enjoyed for their unique taste, color, adaptability, or usefulness.

+ *Stock Seed Farms.* Native grass seeds for "care-free" lawns, as well as wildflower seeds and literature on prairie grass lawns.

+ *Sunnybrook Farms.* Good selection of herbs, ornamental ivies, scented geraniums, perennials, and hostas.

+ *Sunrise Enterprises.* Offers a variety of Oriental vegetable and flower seeds, with information on how to grow them.

+ *Territorial Seed Company.* Offers vegetable varieties for maritime Northwest gardeners, where the summers are cool and the winters are mild and rainy. Sells both open-pollinated and hybrid varieties.

+ *Westwind Seeds.* Over 175 open-pollinated varieties of vegetable, flower, and herb seeds. They specialize in short-season and heat- and drought-resistant varieties.

Seed starters

Gardener's Supply. PaperPot System is a honeycomb of biodegradable paper pots held together with a water-soluble glue. Holds moisture; creates vigorous root systems.

The Natural Gardening Company. Soil-block makers, which eliminate the need for plastic seed-starter trays.

TOOLS FOR ORGANIC GARDENING

Having the right tool for the job always makes things easier. Here are some catalogs that carry everything from hoes, shovels, rakes, and trowels, to seed-starting kits, watering systems, plant supports, cloches and cold frames, and books.

At the Store/By Mail

Gardening tools

Acres, U.S.A. Large selection of books on eco-gardening and agriculture.

agAccess. A comprehensive offering of books on all aspects of growing plants. Has good sections on organic gardening and landscaping, sustainable agriculture, water conservation, and soil fertility.

Ecology Action. Many books geared toward home organic gardening.

Gardens Alive! Drip irrigation kits (including one made from recycled tires), birdhouses, and bird food. Lots of educational information.

Gardener's Supply. Tools and aids for gardening, including soaker hoses and other watering equipment, and a cold frame finished with a natural wood preservative.

Harmony Farm Supply. Extensive selection of drip and sprinkler irrigation equipment.

The Kinsman Company. Beautiful English watering cans, plant supports, arch systems, birdhouses, English gardening tools, and sturdy tool hooks.

Langenbach. Fine gardening tools from Europe and America.

Medina Agriculture Products. Special dual-pressure drip irrigation system with no emitters to plug up.

The Natural Gardening Company. Soaker hose made from recycled tire trimmings, Gardena watering systems, English gardening tools. Drip irrigation system designed by Robert Kourick, one of the nation's leading drip irrigation experts.

Nitron Industries. Irrigation-hose system.

Peaceful Valley Farm Supply. Watering equipment, sprayers, carts, gardening tools, books.

Pinetree Garden Seeds. Hand tools such as trowels, pruners, and a seed dispenser that eliminates wasted seeds by dispensing them one at a time. Watering systems, landscape aids, and a nice selection of gardening books.

Ringer. Garden watering systems, plant supports, bird feeders.

The Urban Farmer Store. Drip irrigation systems.

Wade Manufacturing Company. Drip irrigation systems.

Walt Nicke Company. Tools for the home gardener, many imported from England. Includes an inexpensive hand-powered paper shredder that recycles newspapers into garden mulch.

Water Conservation Systems. Drip irrigation systems.

Weiss Brothers Nursery. Drip irrigation systems.

7 & Cleaning Products

Cleaning your house while your kids are still growing
Is like shoveling the walk before it stops snowing.
PHYLLIS DILLER

When people ask me what the easiest thing to change is, I always tell them to start with cleaning products. You can get everything in your house just as clean with natural commercial products, or by using common substances that you probably already have in your kitchen, as you can with the "new and improved" products from the supermarket. By choosing natural and nontoxic cleaners you can reduce the amount of toxic waste that goes into the environment and protect yourself from many toxic substances. With homemade cleaners you don't have to pay for advertising, add another plastic bottle to a landfill, or buy a different product for every cleaning need. This one simple change is a big one, for cleaning products are among the most toxic products you'll find in your home.

HOW CLEANING PRODUCTS AFFECT OUR HEALTH AND THE EARTH

Cleaning products can cause a wide variety of health problems—from a simple skin rash while washing dishes or burning eyes from a whiff of ammonia to death from an accidental swallow of drain cleaner. Despite the fact that labels on nearly all cleaning products clearly state "Keep Out of Reach of Children," accidental poisonings frequently occur, especially among infants and children who cannot read the warnings.

Many of these products also give off volatile hazardous fumes. Not only are you exposed to these during use, but they stay trapped inside your home until they can escape through an open window. During seasons when you keep windows closed, and especially if you have a year-round air-heating and -cooling system, fumes can build up undetected and create dangerously high levels of pollutants.

Whether or not you have an obvious reaction to a cleaning product, it's best not to unnecessarily expose yourself to such potentially harmful substances day in and day out over years.

Cleaning products also produce tons of toxic waste in their use, manufacture, and disposal. Each *day* Americans pour more than 32 million pounds of household cleaning products down the drain (that's almost 12 billion pounds per year). Most of these products contain toxic substances that are not processed by sewage and septic systems and eventually pollute our groundwater, streams, rivers, and oceans. Leftover cleaning products turn refuse sites into toxic-waste dumps, jeopardizing the health of sanitation workers and polluting the Earth and groundwater. All this is in addition to the toxic waste produced by manufacturers as the chemicals that go into these products are synthesized.

Chlorine, one of the most common chemicals that we use, may be depleting our ozone layer. One scientist at the University of California believes that when chlorine (or bromine, which is used instead of chlorine in some cases) mixes with water it can form active vapors that rise into the upper atmosphere and destroy ozone, much as CFCs do (see Chapter 2).

"Biodegradable" synthetic detergents have several disadvantages also. They are made from nonrenewable resources, and the synethic surfactants in the detergents tend to become more toxic for human use as they are made more biodegradable for the environment. Almost nothing is known about the possible mutagenic effects of these synthetic chemicals on other life forms, and the benzene in most synthetic detergents—before they completely biodegrade into harmless substances in aquatic systems (which can take two to four weeks)—can be converted to phenol (carbolic acid), a substance toxic to fish.

READING LABELS

Cleaning products are the only household products regulated by the Consumer Product Safety Commission under the 1960 Federal Hazardous Substances Labeling Act. This means that cleaning products that can hurt you must carry various warnings on their labels. If a cleaning product contains a chemical that is hazardous, it must by law specify the hazard. Look at your cleaning product labels and see if you find any of these words:

• **Toxic/Highly Toxic** (poisonous if you happen to drink it, if you breathe the fumes, or if it gets absorbed through your skin)
• **Extremely Flammable/Flammable/Combustible** (can catch fire if exposed to a flame or an electric spark)
• **Corrosive** (will eat away your skin or cause inflammation of mucous membranes)
• **Strong Sensitizer** (may provoke an allergic reaction)

Hazardous cleaning products must also prominently display one of the following signal words:

• **DANGER** (or POISON, with skull and crossbones)—could kill an adult if only a tiny pinch is ingested.
• **WARNING**—could kill an adult if about a teaspoon is ingested.
• **CAUTION**—will not kill until an amount from two tablespoons to two cups is ingested.

At one time these signal words accurately indicated the dose required to cause a toxic effect, but because of poor labeling practices, these words now give only a general degree of danger.

Another flaw in the system: the Hazardous Substances Labeling Act focuses only on the *immediate* effects the product can have if not used according to instructions. Labels warn against accidental ingestion, eye contact, prolonged skin contact, or breathing concentrated fumes but don't mention that the chemicals used in these products can also have *long-term* effects. And even if you do follow directions on the label to the letter, most cleaning products can still be harmful during use. This is not mentioned on the label, either, because it is not required by law.

The real safety or danger of cleaning products is difficult to assess because manufacturers are not required to list exact ingredients on the label. You can't look at a label to be sure, for instance, that a certain furniture polish doesn't contain nitrobenzene (a substance commonly used in furniture polish that could be fatal if swallowed), or that a mold-and-mildew cleaner is free from pentachlorophenol (another commonly used deadly substance). The products we trust on our supermarket shelves may contain any number of toxic chemicals, but we have no way of finding out what they are. Even the government and poison-control centers cannot break the code of trade secrecy surrounding cleaning products.

The best information we can get from poison-control centers is general lists of the chemicals commonly used in specific categories of products, but which brand-name products do or do not actually contain these substances is anybody's guess, unless the manufacturer voluntarily reveals the product's ingredients.

Cleaning-product manufacturers are also not required to include in label warnings the type of hazard associated with using the product, nor must they warn against product use by those who are at high risk because of specific medical conditions. For example, the American Lung Association cautions that the mists from aerosol sprays can aggravate existing lung conditions such as asthma, yet product labels do not reflect these specific concerns.

Some people think cleaning products are safe to buy, use, and keep around the house because their labels have clear instructions on what to do in case of poisoning. However, a study done by the New York Poison Control Center found that 85 *percent of the product warning labels they studied were inadequate.* Some labels list incorrect first-aid information, and others warn against dangers that don't even exist. I hope that after reading this chapter you will remove any toxic cleaning products from your home. But if you do not and have an accidental poisoning, please call your local poison-control center for correct information before administering first aid.

The environmental effects of cleaning products are not required on the label.

HOW I RATE CLEANING PRODUCTS

When I evaluate a cleaning product, I first look to see how natural the ingredients are and if they have been tested on animals. But because cleaning products are designed to cut through heavy grease and grime, they often aren't very gentle to our health or the environment.

⊕ **Earthwise** cleaning products are:
• safe to use;
• nonpolluting in their manufacture, use, and disposal;
• made from natural, renewable ingredients that are organically grown or harvested from the wild in a sustainable way—devoid of petrochemical ingredients; and
• biodegradable.

🔳 **Natural** cleaning products are:
• safe to use;
• made from natural (but not organically grown), renewable ingredients that may have residues of petrochemicals used in growing or processing, or small amounts of nontoxic petrochemical ingredients; and
• biodegradable.

Note: A plus sign before the name of a natural product indicates that it contains some earthwise ingredient(s) such as organically grown herbs.

⊕ **Nontoxic** cleaning products are:
• relatively safe to use;
• made of synthetic ingredients formulated from petrochemical or natural sources; and
• biodegradable.

There are few earthwise cleaning products on the market at this time. Most of the products you'll find in your natural-food store meet the natural criteria, and there are a few good nontoxic products that can be used when natural products are unavailable.

I'm frequently asked about Amway, Neo-Life, and Shaklee products. You may notice that they are conspicuously absent from these pages. There are two reasons for this. For many years I have been trying to get ingredient lists for the cleaning products made by these companies, and I finally got a list for one of the companies. Without going into detail, the general ingredients were synethetic detergents, optical brighteners, some animal ingredients, fragrances, and artificial colors. Also, there is some question as to whether these companies test on animals. Some animal-rights organizations say yes, others no. Since there are plenty of other cleaning products available that have more natural ingredients and clearly don't test on animals, I have listed those instead.

Your local natural-food store should have a good selection of the brand-name products listed in this chapter, or you can order from mail-order catalogs.

MY EARTHWISE AND NATURAL CLEANING KIT

The very best recommendation I can make is to suggest that you make most of your cleaning products at home. It's simple, inexpensive, effective, and reduces the amount of packaging you have to throw away.

For almost ten years now I have done *all* my cleaning with a squirt bottle of 50-50 vinegar-and-water mix, liquid soap, and a can of Bon Ami cleaning powder. You might need a few more items, though, to accomplish your own specific cleaning needs. In the sections that follow, I'll give formulas as we discuss each specific cleaner. Here's a list of natural substances you might want to have on hand:

• *Baking soda.* A naturally occurring mineral. Available in bulk at natural-food stores.
• *Salt.* Another naturally occurring mineral. Any table salt will do.
• *Distilled white vinegar.* Made by distilling vinegar made by bacterial fermentation of apple cider or other fruit juice, wine, malt, or barley. Any brand is fine, preferably packaged in a recyclable glass bottle.

• *Lemon juice.* Squeeze it yourself to save on unnecessary packaging and factory energy use. Use organically grown lemons or grow your own, if possible.

• *Liquid soap* (see SOAP).

• *Borax.* A naturally occurring mineral that has no toxic fumes and is safe for the environment, but does carry a warning label that says, "Irritating to eyes and skin; harmful if swallowed; keep out of reach of children." It can be purchased in the cleaning-products department of every supermarket.

• *Scouring powder* (see SCOURING POWDER).

• *Trisodium phosphate* (TSP) and *Sodium Hexametaphosphate.* Both are naturally occurring minerals that are nontoxic to humans but may have environmental effects because they are phosphates. Phosphates widely used in laundry detergents are a nutrient and have been linked to excessive algae growth in waterways, which then depletes oxygen in the water and causes fish to die. I included these minerals as alternatives to other, toxic substances. Even in areas where phosphate detergents have been banned, neither of these has been banned. To my knowledge there are no environmental effects associated with their use. I feel comfortable using them judiciously.

TSP can be purchased at any hardware, variety, or paint store. While the label does warn that it is for external use only, it is a skin irritant, and it should be kept out of reach of children. I have found it to be relatively mild for the heavy-duty cleaning power it offers, and absolutely odorless.

Order sodium hexametaphosphate by mail from *Allergy Resources, The Allergy Store, The Ecology Box, The Living Source, Nigra Enterprises.*

AMMONIA AND OTHER ALL-PURPOSE CLEANERS

Harmful ingredients: ammonia, artificial dyes, detergents, fragrances.

Warning labels: Manufacturers seem to be confused about what type of warning to put on ammonia bottles. Here are two examples:

"POISON: May cause burns. Call a physician. Keep out of reach of children."

"CAUTION: Harmful if swallowed. Irritant. Avoid contact with eyes and prolonged contact with skin. Do not swallow. *Avoid inhalation of vapors. Use in a well-ventilated area.*"

HOMEMADE ALTERNATIVES

• Mix one teaspoon liquid soap or borax into one quart warm or hot water. Add a squeeze of lemon juice or a splash of vinegar to cut grease. Experiment, and you'll find which combinations work best.

• Mix three tablespoons washing soda in one quart warm water.

• For heavy-duty cleaning, mix a half cup borax, a half teaspoon liquid soap, and two teaspoons TSP into two gallons warm water.

At the Store/By Mail

⊕ *Earthwise all-purpose cleaners*

Shur Kleen Hi-Bar. Organic enzymatic cleaner made from naturally dried, certified food-grade Icelandic kelp. *Clean Country.*

❧ *Natural all-purpose cleaners*

+ Natural Bodycare Citrus Organic Cleaner (Natural Bodycare). Contains citrus, coconut extract, and organically grown herbs. *Earth Herbs.*

Auro Cleansing Emulsion (Auro). Highly concentrated plant soap for very soiled surfaces. Natural ingredients. *Sinan Company.*

Auro Wax Cleaner (Auro). Highly concentrated plant soap for very soiled surfaces. Natural ingredients. *Sinan Company.*

Bon Ami Cleaning Cake (Faultless Starch/Bon Ami Company). Contains animal fat. *The Ecology Box, The Living Source.*

Cloverdale (Cloverdale). Patented biodegradable cleaner that contains a quaternary ammonium compound derived from coconuts. Removes animal, vegetable, and petroleum oils and greases, and deodorizes. *The Sprout House.*

Dr. Bronner's SAL Suds (All-One-God-Faith).

Eco-Bright All-Purpose Cleaner (Clean Environments). Contains primarily nontoxic, biodegradable glycol ether and grapefruit oil. ⊞ Glass gallon jug. *Clean Environments.*

Ecover Cream Cleaner (Mercantile Food Company). Nonabrasive; suitable for all household surfaces, including acrylic, fiberglass, stainless steel, and chrome. ☺ Ⓐ *Amberwood, Clean Country, Ecco Bella, Eco-Choice, Karen's Nontoxic Products, Seventh Generation, Walnut Acres.*

Heavenly Horsetail All-Purpose Cleaner (Infinity Herbal Products). *InterNatural, Natural Lifestyle Supplies.*

Jurlique Sparkle (Jurlique). Highly concentrated liquid. ☺ *Jurlique.*

Life Tree Liquid Home Soap (Life Tree Products). Biodegradable, pH balanced, superconcentrated. *Eco-Choice, Sunrise Lane.*

Naturall Multipurpose Spray Cleaner (Naturall). ☺ Ⓐ

Sweet & Clean Lightning. Organic cleaner for wood, metal, leather, chrome, porcelain, floors, and walls. Removes odors and stains. Contains citrus oils, organic emulsifiers, and purified water. *Karen's Nontoxic Products.*

⊕ *Nontoxic all-purpose cleaners*

AFM Super Clean (AFM Enterprises). Unscented. For rapid removal of grease, dirty oil, film, and scum. ☺ *AFM Enterprises, Allergy Relief Shop, Allergy Resources, The Allergy Store, Baubiologie Hardware, The Ecology Box, The Living Source, Nigra Enterprises, Seventh Generation.*

Allen's Naturally All-Purpose Cleaner (Allen's Naturally). No dyes or fragrance. Concentrated cleaner for heavily soiled floors, clothes, etc. ☺ Ⓐ *Allen's Naturally, Baubiologie Hardware, Eco-Choice, The Ecology Box, EveryBody Ltd., My Brother's Keeper.*

Allen's Naturally Multi-Purpose Spray Cleaner (Allen's Naturally). No dyes or fragrance. Cleans most washable surfaces such as countertops, walls, whitewall tires. ☺ Ⓐ *Allen's Naturally, Baubiologie Hardware, Carole's Cosmetics, Eco-Choice, Janice Corporation, Sunrise Lane.*

Fuller Brush. Fulsol degreaser, biodegradable and phosphate-free.

Granny's All-Purpose Cleaner (Granny's Old Fashioned Products). Contains coconut-oil derivatives, aloe vera, vegetable glycerine, and salt. ☺ Ⓐ *Baubiologie Hardware, The Allergy Store, Granny's Old Fashioned Products.*

Home Service Products Company. Professional Super All-Purpose Spray Cleaner. Approved by Beauty Without Cruelty, People for the Ethical Treatment of Animals, and the National Antivivisection Society. ☺

Kleen All-Purpose Cleaner (Mountain Fresh). Honeysuckle fragrance. ☺ Ⓐ *Amberwood, The Compassionate Consumer, EveryBody Ltd., Green Earth Natural Foods, Humane Alternative Products, Mountain Fresh, Sunrise Lane, Terra Verde Products.*

BASIN, TUB, AND TILE CLEANERS

Harmful ingredients: aerosol propellants, ammonia, detergents, ethanol, fragrances.

Warning labels: There are no warning labels on basin, tub, and tile cleaners.

HOMEMADE ALTERNATIVES
Use a nonchlorine SCOURING POWDER.

BLEACH

Harmful ingredients: chlorine, lye, artificial dyes, detergents, fluorescent brighteners, synthetic fragrances.

Environmental alert: Chlorine fumes contribute to depletion of the ozone layer.

Warning labels:
"CAUTION: Keep out of reach of children. May be harmful if swallowed or may cause severe eye irritation. *Never* mix chlorine bleach with cleaning products containing ammonia, or with vinegar. *The resulting chloramine fumes are deadly.* It also should not be used on silk, wool, mohair, leather, spandex, or on any natural fiber that is not colorfast as it can damage or discolor the fabric, and cause colors to run."

The main hazardous ingredient in bleach is sodium hypochlorite (chlorine added to a liquid solution of lye). Product labels warn only against drinking liquid bleach, but toxicology books report that chlorine is "toxic as a [skin] irritant and by inhalation." Even though the amount of fumes released is well within recognized safety limits, many people report adverse reactions to chlorine fumes even at these low levels, and to chlorine residues left in fabrics after laundering.

SPECIAL TIPS
• Make your whites whiter and your brights brighter by using a WATER SOFTENER or WATER CONDITIONER that prevents mineral deposits and soap scum from sticking to fabrics and making them look dull and dingy. Then you won't need bleach at all.
• If you have years of accumulated soap or detergent film on your laundry that needs to be removed, use a WATER SOFTENER and run the items through a whole wash cycle using twice as much softener as you would normally use, and no soap or detergent.

At the Store/By Mail

🍃 *Natural bleach*
Ecover Alternative Bleach (Mercantile Food Company). Contains no chlorine. ⊞ ☺ Ⓐ
Winter White Powdered Bleach (Mountain Fresh). ☺ Ⓐ *Mountain Fresh, Sunrise Lane, Terra Verde Products.*

💧 *Nontoxic bleach*
Home Service Products Company. Professional All-Fabric Bleach. Contains no chlorine. Approved by Beauty Without Cruelty, People for the Ethical Treatment of Animals, and the National Antivivisection Society. ☺
Winter White Non-Chlorine Liquid Bleach (Mountain Fresh). ☺ Ⓐ *Carole's Cosmetics, Mountain Fresh, Terra Verde Products.*

DISHWASHER DETERGENT

Harmful ingredients: chlorine, dyes, detergents, fragrances.

Warning labels:
"CAUTION: Injurious to eyes. Harmful if swallowed. Avoid contact with eyes, mucous membranes, and prolonged skin contact. Keep out of reach of children."

HOMEMADE ALTERNATIVES
Use sodium hexametaphosphate, the same amount as you would use of dishwasher detergent. It is probably the best substance you could use in your dishwasher. Not only does it cut grease and leave dishes spotless, it also acts as a scale inhibitor and will actually clean your dishwasher with each washing.

SPECIAL TIPS
Never use dishwashing liquid or liquid soap as a substitute in a dishwasher, as the bubbles can clog the drain and inhibit the action of the water spray.

At the Store/By Mail

❦ *Natural dishwasher detergent*
Allen's Naturally Automatic Dishwasher Detergent (Allen's Naturally). Made from naturally occurring minerals that soften water, prevent spotting of glassware, and cut grease. ☺ Ⓐ *Allen's Naturally, Baubiologie Hardware, Carole's Cosmetics, Eco-Choice, The Ecology Box, EveryBody Ltd., My Brother's Keeper.*
Cal Ben Soap Company. "Destain" Automatic Dish Machine Compound. ☺ Ⓐ
Ecover Dishwashing Machine Powder (Mercantile Food Company).
Naturall Dishwasher Compound (Naturall). ☺ Ⓐ *Humane Alternative Products.*

⊕ *Nontoxic dishwasher detergent*
Home Service Products Company. Professional Automatic Dishwashing Compound. Approved by Beauty Without Cruelty, People for the Ethical Treatment of Animals, and the National Antivivisection Society. ☺
Kleer II Automatic Dishwashing Detergent (Mountain Fresh). Lemon scented. ☺ Ⓐ *Baubiologie Hardware, Carole's Cosmetics, The Compassionate Consumer, EveryBody Ltd., Mountain Fresh, Sunrise Lane, Terra Verde Products.*
Kleer III Automatic Powdered Dishwashing Detergent (Mountain Fresh). ☺ Ⓐ *Mountain Fresh, Terra Verde Products.*

DISHWASHING LIQUID

Harmful ingredients: liquid detergent, artificial dyes, fragrances, ethanol.

Warning label: Even though they are not labeled with warnings, it is best to keep all detergents out of reach of children. Their fruity smells are particularly attractive, and detergents cause more household poisonings than any other product in an average home.

There appear to be no regulations for the safety of dyes used in dishwashing liquids. I am concerned about these dyes in particular since many homemakers soak their hands in dishwater three times each day. Considering the fact that the FDA allows artificial colors in foods, drugs, and cosmetics even though they are known to cause cancer, perhaps we should not assume they are safe until we have more information about them.

HOMEMADE ALTERNATIVES
• Use a plain liquid SOAP.
• Rub your sponge with bar soap. But be careful: some bar soaps I have tried are a bit slipperier than liquids, so don't drop the plate you're washing!

SPECIAL TIPS
• *To cut grease:* Add a few slices of fresh lemon or a few tablespoons vinegar along with the soap in your dishwater.
• *To prevent water spotting:* Dissolve two teaspoons sodium hexametaphosphate in a sinkful of hot water, then add about half the amount of soap you would normally use. Wash glassware, dishes, and silver, rinse with hot water, and dry in a dish drainer.
• *To disinfect without soap:* If you cannot use sufficiently hot water while washing, clean the food off with a sponge or brush, then pile dishes in a sink and fill it with water hotter than you can touch.
• *To wash bottles:* Put sand and water in the bottle, cover the opening with a lid or your hand, and shake vigorously.
• *To clean breadboards, cutting boards, wooden salad bowls and butcher blocks:* Rub half a cut lemon or lime over the surface, rinse, dry with a cloth, and cover with salt

to absorb moisture, or use a paste of baking soda and water.

• *To wash fine crystal:* Clean gently with warm, soapy water; then rinse in a solution of one part white vinegar and three parts warm water.

• *To remove stains on enamel-finish cookware:* Use a paste of salt and white vinegar.

• *To remove burned-on food:* Sprinkle pot or pan with baking soda and moisten with water. Let sit for a few hours, and food should lift right out.

• *To remove sediment from tea kettles:* Mix together one and a half cups apple-cider vinegar, one and a half cups water, and three tablespoons salt in the kettle and boil for fifteen minutes. Let sit overnight, then rinse with clear water.

At the Store/By Mail

🔋 **Natural dishwashing liquid**

Cal Ben Soap Company. Seafoam Dish Glow, a soap-based cleaner. Can be used on floors, as an all-purpose cleaner, as liquid hand soap, and for fine washables. ☺

Ecover Dishwashing Liquid (Mercantile Food Company). Made from pure biodegradable coconut-based cleaner. Chamomile and calendula oils stimulate healing of small cuts and scratches. Biodegradable preservative. ☺ ⊗ *Karen's Nontoxic Products, Walnut Acres.*

Life Tree Dishwashing Liquid (Life Tree Products). With aloe vera and calendula. *Eco-Choice, Sunrise Lane.*

North Farm Dish Detergent (North Farm Cooperative). *Green Earth Natural Foods.*

🌀 **Nontoxic dishwashing liquid**

Allen's Naturally Dishwashing Liquid (Allen's Naturally). No dyes or fragrances. ☺ ⊗ *Allen's Naturally, Baubiologie Hardware, Eco-Choice, The Ecology Box, EveryBody Ltd., Green Earth Natural Foods, Jan-*

ice Corporation, My Brother's Keeper, Sunrise Lane.

Granny's Aloe Vera Dish Liquid (Granny's Old Fashioned Products). ☺ ⊗ *Baubiologie Hardware, Carole's Cosmetics, Granny's Old Fashioned Products, Green Earth Natural Foods, The Living Source.*

Home Service Products Company. Professional Dishwash Detergent. Approved by Beauty Without Cruelty, People for the Ethical Treatment of Animals, and the National Antivivisection Society. ☺

Kleer Dishwashing Detergent (Mountain Fresh). Lime fragrance. ☺ ⊗ *Amberwood, Baubiologie Hardware, Carole's Cosmetics, The Compassionate Consumer, EveryBody Ltd., Humane Alternative Products, Mountain Fresh, Sunrise Lane, Terra Verde Products.*

Dish drying rack

If you're in the market for a dish drying rack, forgo the plastic or plastic-covered metal variety and choose a biodegradable wooden one, available at most import and gourmet cooking stores.

DISINFECTANTS

Harmful ingredients: cresol, phenol, ethanol, formaldehyde, ammonia, chlorine, artificial dyes, synthetic fragrances.

Warning labels:

"CAUTION: Keep out of reach of children. Keep away from heat, sparks, and open flame. Keep out of eyes. Avoid contact with food."

If you believe the television commercials, we all need disinfectants to "kill odor-causing germs." Or we might have some on hand to kill germs when a family member is ill. There are other ways to disinfect, though, that are less toxic and actually work better. In fact, disinfectants don't even kill all the germs. Yes, they will "kill germs on contact"—some of them. They can *reduce* the number of germs, but they will not kill all the germs present. To make something totally germ free, you have to sterilize it with boiling water.

HOMEMADE ALTERNATIVES
• Clean regularly with plain soap and water. Just a hot water rinse kills bacteria.
• Keep things dry (bacteria, mildew, and mold cannot live without dampness).
• Use borax. Long recognized for its deodorizing properties, it is also a very effective disinfectant. One hospital experimented with using a solution of a half cup borax to one gallon hot water for one year. At the end of that period, the monitoring bacteriologist reported that the borax solution satisfied all the hospital's germicidal requirements.

DRAIN CLEANERS

Harmful ingredients: petroleum distillates, sulfur compounds.

Warning labels:

"POISON ☠ CALL POISON CENTER, EMERGENCY ROOM, OR PHYSICIAN AT ONCE. Causes severe eye and skin damage; may cause blindness. Harmful or fatal if swallowed."

The primary component of drain cleaners is lye, an extremely corrosive material that can eat right through your skin. Even a drop spilled on your skin or a dry crystal that falls on wet skin can cause damage. When ingested, lye quickly burns through internal tissues, damaging the esophagus, stomach, and entire intestinal tract. The internal damage may be irreparable for those who survive lye poisoning.

If you change only one cleaning product in your home, this is it. Drain cleaners get my vote for the most dangerous unnecessary product in the house.

HOMEMADE ALTERNATIVES
• Use a plunger or a mechanical snake (small metal snakes can be purchased inexpensively at hardware stores; large motorized ones can be rented from hardware or equipment-rental stores).
• Pour a handful of baking soda and a half cup of white vinegar down the drainpipe and cover tightly for one minute. The chemical reaction between the two will cause pressure in the drain and dislodge any obstructive matter. Rinse with hot water and repeat as needed.
• Pour a half cup salt and a half cup baking soda down the drain, following by six cups boiling water. Let sit for several hours or overnight, then flush with water.
• If the above methods don't work, try pouring a quarter cup 35 percent hydrogen peroxide down the drain. Wait a few minutes, then plunge. Repeat a second time if needed. This can open clogged drains that have defied other methods.

SPECIAL TIPS
• You can prevent clogged drains and eliminate the need for a drain cleaner by using a drain strainer to trap food particles or hair that might cause a clog.
• Remember not to pour grease down the drain (dump it in the garbage or into a "grease can" to be reused instead; better yet, cut down on fried foods).

At the Store/By Mail

⊕ *Earthwise Drain Cleaner*
Shur Go (Hi-Bar). Organic enzymatic cleaner of naturally dried, certified food-grade Icelandic kelp. *Clean Country.*

❧ *Natural Drain Cleaner*
Medina Agriculture Products Company. Sells Actina, which produces digestive organisms that liquefy grease and waste solids and reduce or eliminate odors. For drains, pipes, and septic tanks.

DRY CLEANING

Harmful ingredients: detergent, perchloro-ethylene, benzene, chlorine, formalde-hyde, naphthalene, toluene, trichloro-ethylene, xylene.

The EPA has listed fumes from slightly damp dry-cleaned items as a common in-door air pollutant. In addition, the plas-tic bag in which every dry-cleaned item comes wrapped is made from a non-re-newable resource, produces toxic waste, and is not biodegradable or recyclable. Many babies and children have suffocated while playing with plastic bags from the dry cleaners.

WASH YOUR CLOTHES INSTEAD
While dry-cleaned fabrics won't shrink or stretch, dyes won't fade or run, delicate fabrics won't tear or waterspot, and wools won't mat, some of your clothing marked "dry clean only" really doesn't need dry cleaning; manufacturers just recommend dry cleaning out of fear that consumers will complain about garments after they wash them incorrectly. Even professional dry cleaners agree that you can wash al-most anything without harm—if you know how to do it. And you can always take a clean garment in for a professional press-ing if you like.

IF YOU ABSOLUTELY MUST HAVE AN ITEM DRY-CLEANED
Of course, I'm not suggesting that you throw your wool blazers or sequined eve-ning dresses in the washing machine. For those occasions when you must dry-clean, remove the plastic covering as soon as you get home, and hang the item in a well-ventilated area (preferably outdoors) to encourage evaporation of the solvent. This could take up to a week; the warmer it is, the faster the solvent will dry. If you must dry-clean regularly, you might want to set up a space where items that have just been dry-cleaned can be hung, near a small space heater. Close the door to keep fumes out of the rest of the house, and open windows in that room to ventilate the solvent fumes. This will protect you from toxic exposure, but is not especially good for the environment. It's best not to dry-clean at all.

AVOID DRY CLEANING ENTIRELY
In the future when you buy clothing, choose fabrics and styles that do not re-quire dry cleaning. This may require a slight or major change in your wardrobe, but it can be done, and stylishly, too (see CLOTHING).

FABRIC SOFTENERS

Harmful ingredients: aerosol propellants, ammonia, artificial dyes, very strong syn-thetic fragrances.

Warning labels:
"CAUTION: Keep out of reach of chil-dren."

Fabric softeners are designed to reduce static cling in *synthetic fabrics* and are un-necessary with natural fibers. Fabric soft-eners leave a residue on fabrics to control static cling. They never really wash out, so you are exposed whenever you are in con-tact with a treated fabric. Residues can be very irritating to skin, causing allergic re-actions such as stuffy nose and watery eyes.

At the very least, go through your closet, separate natural fibers from syn-thetics, and refrain from using fabric soft-ener in your natural-fiber laundry. If you have lots of natural/synthetic blends, try laundering them without fabric softener and see if you really need to use it.

HOMEMADE ALTERNATIVES
To make natural-fiber fabrics softer, pour one cup white vinegar into the final rinse water.

At the Store/By Mail

⚕ *Natural fabric softener*

Ecover Fabric Conditioner (Mercantile Food Company). Suitable for all types of fabric, for both hand and machine washing. Biodegradable preservative. ☺ ⊗ *Ecco Bella, Karen's Nontoxic Products, Walnut Acres.*

Soft-n-Fresh Fabric Softener (Mountain Fresh). Cedar fragrance. Biodegradable. Reduces static cling. ☺ ⊗ *Amberwood, Baubiologie Hardware, Carole's Cosmetics, The Compassionate Consumer, EveryBody Ltd., Humane Alternative Products, Mountain Fresh, Seventh Generation, Sunrise Lane, Terra Verde Products.*

Allen's Naturally Anti-Static Concentrated Fabric Softener (Allen's Naturally). Biodegradable. No phosphates, dyes, or fragrance. ☺ ⊗ *Allen's Naturally, Baubiologie Hardware, Eco-Choice, The Ecology Box, My Brother's Keeper.*

Home Service Products Company. Professional Pre-Add Fabric Softener. Approved by Beauty Without Cruelty, People for the Ethical Treatment of Animals, and the National Antivivisection Society. ☺

⊕ *Nontoxic fabric softener*

Choose the unscented sheet variety that goes into the dryer (available at every supermarket) rather than a liquid added to the wash (which might be accidentally swallowed) or an aerosol spray that is applied to dry clothes (which could end up on your skin or in your eyes or lungs).

FURNITURE AND FLOOR POLISH

Harmful ingredients: aerosol propellants, ammonia, detergents, synthetic fragrance (particularly lemon), nitrobenzene, phenol, acrylic and polystyrene plastics.

Warning labels:
"DANGER: Harmful or fatal if swallowed. Keep out of reach of children."

Both accidental ingestion and inhalation of fumes during normal use of furniture polish can be harmful, especially if an aerosol spray is used. In addition, some of the more toxic ingredients can be easily absorbed through the skin. The primary danger is from exposure during use, but once it's on the furniture, polish can continue to give off residual fumes, sometimes for months.

HOMEMADE ALTERNATIVES
Use a soft cloth to apply one of the following old-fashioned, tried-and-true mixtures to furniture (don't worry, any odor will go away after absorption and drying):

• Wipe with mayonnaise.
• Rub with a cloth dipped in cool tea.
• Mix together one teaspoon olive oil, juice of one lemon, and one teaspoon water (one teaspoon brandy or whisky optional). Make fresh each time.
• Mix three parts olive oil and one part white vinegar.
• For oak: boil one quart beer with one tablespoon sugar and two tablespoons beeswax. When mixture is cool, wipe onto wood. When dry, polish with a dry chamois cloth.
• For mahogany: mix equal parts white vinegar and warm water; wipe onto wood, then polish with a chamois cloth.
• Use plain mineral oil (the active ingredient in most commercial polishes). Buy it at any drugstore and apply sparingly with a soft cloth. Mineral oil is a petrochemical product that is relatively safe to use, although it is a nonrenewable resource. It's odorless and (like the other alternatives listed above) is absorbed right into the wood. If you like lemon-scented polish, add one teaspoon lemon oil (available at hardware stores) to two cups mineral oil.

SPECIAL TIPS
• *For grease spots:* Pour on salt immediately to absorb grease and prevent staining.

• *For scratches:* Mix equal amounts of lemon juice and vegetable oil. Rub this mixture into scratches with a soft cloth until they disappear.

• *For water spots:* Mix ten drops lemon oil into two cups vodka. Dampen one corner of a soft cloth with this mixture and lightly rub the spots. Dry immediately with the dry end of the cloth.

At the Store/By Mail

🌱 *Natural furniture and floor polish*

Ecover Floor Soap (Mercantile Food Company). For all types of floors. Regular use will give floor a deep natural shine as small pores become filled with saponified oils. ☺ Ⓐ *Ecco Bella, Karen's Nontoxic Products, Seventh Generation, Walnut Acres.*

Livos Floor Wax (Livos). Use on wood, stone, brick, terra-cotta tile, and linoleum. Ⓐ *Karen's Nontoxic Products, Livos Plant Chemistry.*

Livos Waxes—Liquid and Paste (Livos). Beeswax, for use on wood, stone, metal, and plastic laminates. Ⓐ *Karen's Nontoxic Products, Livos Plant Chemistry, Seventh Generation.*

🌐 *Nontoxic furniture and floor polish*

AFM All-Purpose Polish and Wax (AFM Enterprises). To clean and preserve most surfaces, including furniture and most floors. In liquid and paste form. ☺ *AFM Enterprises, Allergy Relief Shop, Allergy Resources, The Allergy Store, Eco-Choice, Nigra Enterprises, Baubiologie Hardware, The Ecology Box, The Living Source.*

AFM One-Step Seal and Shine (AFM Enterprises). Sealer and polish for hard surfaces and floors. ① *AFM Enterprises, Allergy Relief Shop, Baubiologie Hardware, Eco-Choice, The Ecology Box, The Living Source, Nigra Enterprises.*

GLASS CLEANERS

Harmful ingredients: ammonia, artificial dye, aerosol propellants.

Warning labels: Glass cleaners have no warning labels at all, yet many ammonia bottles are labeled "POISON." The small amount of ammonia in glass cleaners is certainly not as harmful as a bottle of straight ammonia, but glass cleaners can still release highly irritating fumes and can cause eye damage if accidentally sprayed into the eye. Glass cleaners dispersed with aerosol propellants are even more likely to be inhaled or float into your eyes.

HOMEMADE ALTERNATIVES

My favorite glass cleaner: half vinegar and half water, applied with a soft cloth or pump spray bottle. This works so well that some big corporations are selling it in the supermarket in a plastic bottle with a little green dye.

SPECIAL TIPS

• If vinegar and water streaks terribly the first time you use it, it is because you have been using a type of glass cleaner that has left years of buildup that will have to be removed. Use a little rubbing alcohol to get it off.

• Never wash windows when the sun is shining directly on them; the cleaning solution will dry too fast and streak.

• When washing, use side-to-side strokes on one side and up-and-down strokes on the other so you can tell which side might need some extra polishing.

• *For foggy windows:* Wash windows with plain soap rubbed directly onto a soft, damp cloth. Rinse and dry. The soap will leave a transparent film that will make the water molecules bead up instead of sticking to the glass as a mist.

• *For scratches:* Rub with toothpaste and a soft cloth.
• *To clean cut glass:* Use baking soda sprinkled on a damp rag. Rinse with clean water.

At the Store/By Mail

🌸 *Natural glass cleaners*

Allen's Naturally Glass Cleaner (Allen's Naturally). No dyes, fragrances or phosphates. Biodegradable. ☺ Ⓧ *Allen's Naturally, Baubiologie Hardware, Eco-Choice, The Ecology Box, EveryBody Ltd.*

Glass Mate with Willards Water (Mountain Fresh). ☺ Ⓧ *Mountain Fresh, Terra Verde Products.*

Naturall Spray Glass Cleaner (Naturall). ☺ Ⓧ *Humane Alternative Products.*

LAUNDRY DETERGENT

Harmful ingredients: detergents, ammonia, fluorescent brighteners, ethanol, fragrance, naphthalene, phenol.

Warning labels: Manufacturers don't agree on how harmful laundry detergents might be. Look at a number of different laundry detergents and you'll find a variety of warnings (some detergents have no warnings):

"DANGER. In case of eye contact, get prompt medical attention. Keep out of reach of children."

"WARNING: Harmful if swallowed, irritating to eyes and skin. Keep out of reach of children."

"CAUTION: May be harmful if swallowed."

It can't be said too often that detergents cause more household poisonings than any other household products, frequently when children accidentally ingest colorful powders packaged in easy-to-open boxes. Lesser hazards come from detergent residues left on clothing and bed sheets that can cause skin rashes, and from fragrances that linger long after articles have been laundered.

Detergents were developed *especially to clean synthetic fibers*, and are unnecessary on natural fibers such as cotton, linen, silk, and wool. These fabrics can be washed using compounds that are good for your health and the Earth.

HOMEMADE ALTERNATIVES
• Use a plain powdered or liquid SOAP. Bar soap can also be grated and added to laundry. One problem with soap that our grandmothers experienced was that it leaves a residual scum on fabrics. This can be eliminated by using a WATER SOFTENER, or, preferably, a WATER CONDITIONER.
• You don't always need to use soap to get clothes clean. Often the purpose of laundering is not so much to dispel dirt as to freshen clothing and remove perspiration and odors. For this you can use about one cup of plain baking soda, white vinegar, or borax per load of clothes.

HOW TO WASH NATURAL-FIBER FABRICS
• *Cotton:* Throw into the washing machine with natural soap, borax, baking soda, and/or sodium hexametaphosphate. Wash whites in hot water. Wash colors in warm water to prevent fading; about a tablespoon of white vinegar per tub of laundry will also help keep items colorfast. Using borax in the wash will help retard the formation of mildew. Dry cotton items using medium heat to prevent shrinking and remove them from the dryer the moment they are dry to minimize wrinkles.
• *Linen:* Throw in the washing machine. If it is a very delicate weave, you might want to wash it by hand; otherwise, just pretend it's cotton. Remove from the dryer and press while the fabric is still damp.

• *Silk:* Washing silk fabrics in the washer or by hand is generally discouraged, but I've been washing my silk shirts by hand for ten years and have never had a problem. Wash each item separately by swishing it around in a basic of very cold water with a bit of mild soap. Do not rub. Rinse with cold water and gently remove excess water by rolling the fabric in a towel. I let my silk garments drip-dry in the shower stall and then press them with a warm (not hot), dry iron.

• *Wool:* Hand-wash in cool or lukewarm water (to prevent shrinkage) with mild soap or a few tablespoons of vinegar. Sweaters and knits should be reshaped on a towel to their original size while still damp. Roll up the sweater in the towel to absorb excess moisture, then dry by hanging it over the back of a wooden chair or over a towel bar.

• *Items containing down or feathers:* Wash in your bathtub with warm water and a mild soap or baking soda. Dry in a tumble dryer at a cool temperature, with a sneaker to help renew the fluff.

At the Store/By Mail

💐 *Natural laundry soaps*

Amytis Washing Liquid for Wool & Silk (Walter Rau Gmbh & Company Speickwerk). Cleansing agents derived from coconut oil, with natural protein. Unscented. 1️⃣ ⊗

Arm & Hammer Unscented Super Washing Soda (Church & Dwight Company).

Cal Ben Soap Company. Seafoam All-Temperature Laundry Soap, a concentrated natural soap-based laundry compound. Light fragrance. ⊞ ☺

Ecco Bella. Laundry Booster and Whitener, and Suds Soap.

Ecover Laundry Powder (Mercantile Food Company). ⊞ ☺ ⊗ *Ecco Bella, Karen's Nontoxic Products, Walnut Acres.*

Ecover Liquid Laundry Soap (Mercantile Food Company). ☺ ⊗

Ecover Wool Wash Liquid (Mercantile Food Company). ☺ ⊗ *Ecco Bella, Eco-Choice, Karen's Nontoxic Products, Seventh Generation, Walnut Acres.*

Jurlique Gentle (Jurlique). Liquid soap for all fabrics, especially silk, wool, and baby clothes. ☺ *Jurlique.*

Life Tree Premium Laundry Liquid (Life Tree Products). Biodegradable, phosphate free, concentrated. *Eco-Choice, Sunrise Lane.*

Sierra Dawn Silke Suds (Life Tree Products). For hand washing silk and silk-blend fabrics. *Sunrise Lane.*

White King Laundry Soap (Huish Chemical Company). Made with tallow from beef and lamb. ☺

⊕ *Nontoxic laundry detergents*

Allen's Naturally Liquid Heavy-Duty Laundry Detergent (Allen's Naturally). No dyes, fragrances or phosphates. Biodegradable. ☺ ⊗ *Allen's Naturally, Baubiologie Hardware, Eco-Choice, The Ecology Box, EveryBody Ltd., Green Earth Natural Foods, Janice Corporation, My Brother's Keeper, Sunrise Lane.*

Cool Wash with Aloe (Mountain Fresh). For hand washables. ☺ ⊗ *Mountain Fresh, Terra Verde Products.*

Granny's Power Plus Laundry Concentrate. (Granny's Old Fashioned Products). ☺ ⊗ *The Allergy Store, Baubiologie Hardware, Carole's Cosmetics, Granny's Old Fashioned Products, Green Earth Natural Foods, The Living Source.*

Home Service Products Company. Concentrated powder and liquid compounds. Approved by Beauty Without Cruelty, People for the Ethical Treatment of Animals, and the National Antivivisection Society. ☺

North Farm Liquid Detergent/Powder Detergent (North Farm Cooperative). *Green Earth Natural Foods.*

Winter White Laundry Detergent (Mountain Fresh). Cedar fragrance. Biodegradable; no phosphates. 😊 Ⓐ *Amberwood, Baubiologie Hardware, Carole's Cosmetics, EveryBody Ltd., Green Earth Natural Foods, Humane Alternative Products, Mountain Fresh, Natural Lifestyle Supplies, Seventh Generation, Sunrise Lane, Terra Verde Products.*

LAUNDRY STARCH

Harmful ingredients: formaldehyde, phenol, pentachlorophenol, aerosol propellants.

Warning labels: Spray starch is not generally considered an especially toxic product, and the label warning reflects this, pointing out only the dangers of the aerosol can.

"CAUTION: Contents under pressure. Keep out of reach of children."

HOMEMADE ALTERNATIVES
Dissolve one tablespoon cornstarch in one pint cold water. Place in pump spray bottle. Shake before using.

At the Store/By Mail
Choose a dry powdered starch rather than one in an aerosol can, or consider not starching your clothes at all. Your local dry cleaners can give your clothes a good stiff pressing with their professional irons; be sure to specify no starch.

🌿 *Natural laundry starch*
Faultless Starch (Faultless Starch/Bon Ami Co).

MOLD AND MILDEW CLEANERS

Harmful ingredients: formaldehyde, phenol, pentachlorophenol, kerosene.

Warning label:
"DANGER: Eye irritant. Keep out of reach of children. Use only in well-ventilated area."

SPECIAL TIPS
• Mold grows in dark, damp places, so keep rooms dry and light. During wet winters you may have to keep the heat on instead of wearing sweaters, if you live in a shaded area that gets little sun, or next to a creek, or in any location that is especially moist.

• Allow air to circulate to help keep things dry. Hang clothes so there is space between them, and if you don't launder clothing that is damp with perspiration, at least allow it to dry before putting it back in the closet.

• Hang wet towels after bathing to let them dry before throwing them in the hamper. If you have the space in your bathroom, get in the habit of hanging your wet towel on the towel rack after bathing, then replacing it with a fresh one right before your next bath or shower.

• Check the walls behind the furniture to see if mold is growing there and if necessary, rearrange the furniture to allow plenty of air flow. Small fans can increase air flow, if needed.

• Place a piece of charcoal in bookcases to help absorb dampness. If books are musty, you can "bake" an open book dry in the oven for a few minutes at a low temperature.

HOMEMADE ALTERNATIVES
• Mold and mildew cleaner: Mix borax or vinegar with water in a spray bottle. Spray it on and the mold wipes right off. Borax also inhibits mold growth, so you might try washing down the walls in your bathroom with a borax solution and just leaving it on, or sprinkling borax in damp cabinets under the sink.

• For major mold problems, use heat. Though this is not the most energy-efficient method, it will definitely solve the problem. Put a portable electric heater in the room, turn it to the highest setting, close the door, and let it bake all day or overnight. The mold will dry up into a powder that brushes right off. For concentrated areas, use a hand-held hair dryer to dry the mold in just a few minutes.

At the Store/By Mail

⊕ *Nontoxic mold and mildew cleaners*
AFM Safety Clean (AFM Enterprises). An active cleaner with antibacterial properties for any area conducive to bacterial growth. Will remove existing mildew. Nontoxic synthetic formulation from petrochemical sources. ☺ *AFM Enterprises, Allergy Relief Shop, Allergy Resources, The Allergy Store, Eco-Choice, The Ecology Box, Nigra Enterprises, Baubiologie Hardware, The Living Source.*

AFM X158 Mildew Control (AFM Enterprises). A safe, high-potency liquid cleaner that provides mildew resistance and preservation against microbial attack. Nontoxic synthetic formulation from petrochemical sources. ☺ *AFM Enterprises, Allergy Relief Shop, Allergy Resources, The Allergy Store, The Ecology Box, Nigra Enterprises, Baubiologie Hardware, The Living Source.*

Oven Cleaners

Harmful ingredients: ammonia, detergents, synthetic fragrances, aerosol propellants.

Warning labels:
"DANGER: CONTACT WILL CAUSE BURNS. Avoid contact with skin, eyes, mucous membranes and clothing. Do not take internally. Wear rubber gloves while using. Contains lye. If taken internally or sprayed in eyes call a physician. Keep out of reach of children. Irritant to mucous membranes. Avoid inhaling vapors. Contents under pressure. Recommended for use only on porcelain, enamel, iron, stainless steel, ceramic, and glass surfaces. Do not get on exterior oven surfaces such

as aluminum and chrome trim, baked enamel, copper tone, or painted areas, or on linoleum or plastics. For gas ovens, avoid spraying on pilot light. Keep spray off electrical connections such as door-operated light switch, heating element, etc."

The greatest danger comes from lye, which can eat right through your skin, and ammonia. Oven cleaners dispersed with aerosol propellants are particularly dangerous because the spray sends tiny droplets of lye and ammonia into the air, where they can be easily inhaled or land in your eyes or on your skin.

Be especially cautious about oven cleaners that advertise "no fumes." While it is true that these products have no *aerosol* fumes, they are still strong-smelling substances that require excellent ventilation.

SPECIAL TIPS
• It is possible *never* to have to clean your oven if you are very careful to keep things from spilling. You can prevent spills by cooking food in proper-sized containers, and by putting a cookie sheet on the lower rack to catch spills.
• If after all your preventive measures food does end up at the bottom of the oven, clean it as soon as the oven has cooled to prevent it baking on even more.

HOMEMADE ALTERNATIVES
The very best way to clean your oven, one that professionals use, is to mix together in a spray bottle two tablespoons liquid soap (not detergent), two teaspoons borax, and warm water to fill the bottle. Make sure the salts are completely dissolved to avoid clogging the squirting mechanism. Spray it on, holding the bottle very close to the oven surface so the solution doesn't get into the air (and into your eyes and lungs). Even though these are natural ingredients, this solution is designed to cut heavy-duty oven grime, so

wear gloves and glasses or goggles if you have them. Leave the solution on for twenty minutes, then scrub with steel wool and a nonchlorine SCOURING POWDER. Rub baked-on black spots with pumice, available in stick form at hardware stores.

IF YOU MUST USE AN OVEN CLEANER

If you have an extremely dirty oven layered with years of baked-on grease, you may have to use a chemical oven cleaner *once* to get it clean before you can begin your nontoxic maintenance. For this *one* application, choose a nonaerosol product and follow these precautions from the Consumer Product Safety Commission for safer use of oven cleaners:

• Read and follow the directions before each use.
• Wear protective gloves for your hands and goggles for your eyes.
• Open windows in the kitchen and be sure that children [and pets] and other members of the family are out of the room.
• If you use an oven cleaner that requires boiling water, place the can in the oven before adding boiling water, so that you will not be overcome by ammonia fumes.
• If the fumes begin to irritate you, close the oven door, leave the room, and get fresh air.

RUG, CARPET, AND UPHOLSTERY SHAMPOO

Harmful ingredients: perchloroethylene, naphthalene, ethanol, ammonia, detergents, fluorescent brighteners, artificial colors, synthetic fragrances.

Warning label:
    "CAUTION: Do not take internally. In case of eye contact, flush thoroughly with water. Keep out of reach of children."

SPECIAL TIPS
• Clean spills on your rugs and carpets immediately, before they become stains.
• Keep carpets fresh with regular vacuuming.

HOMEMADE ALTERNATIVES
To deodorize: Sprinkle baking soda liberally over entire carpet, making sure carpet is dry. Use several pounds for a nine-by-12-foot area. Wait fifteen minutes or longer, then vacuum. For persistent odors, wait overnight before vacuuming. Repeat procedure if necessary.

To brighten colors: Vacuum first to remove dust. Mix together 1 quart white vinegar and 3 quarts boiling water. Apply to rug with a wet rag, taking care not to saturate backing. Dry thoroughly and air until dry. Then rub the surface with warm bread crumbs and vacuum.

To remove stains:
• *Blood:* Gently sponge the stain with cold water, and dry with a towel. Repeat until stain is gone.
• *Grease:* Cover with baking soda, rubbing lightly into the rug. Leave on for one hour, then brush off. Repeat as needed.
• *Grease and oil:* Cover spots with cornstarch. Wait one hour, then vacuum.
• *Ink:* Put cream of tartar on the stain and squeeze a few drops of lemon juice on top. Rub into the stain for a minute, brush off the powder with a clean brush, and sponge immediately with warm water. Repeat if needed. If the ink is still wet, immediately put a mound of table salt on the wet spot. Let it sit for a few moments, then brush up and continue to reapply and remove until all moisture is absorbed and the stain is bleached out.
• *Soot:* Cover thickly with salt, then sweep it up carefully.
• *Urine:* Rinse with warm water, then apply a solution of three tablespoons white vinegar and one teaspoon liquid soap. Leave on for fifteen minutes, then rinse and rub dry.

At the Store/By Mail

⊕ *Nontoxic rug and carpet shampoo*

AFM T38 Carpet Shampoo (AFM Enterprises). Rug and carpet shampoo for all types of floor coverings. Provides effective germicidal properties. ☺ *AFM Enterprises, Allergy Resources, Nigra Enterprises, Eco-Choice, The Ecology Box, Baubiologie Hardware.*

Granny's Karpet Kleen Carpet Shampoo (Granny's Old Fashioned Products). ☺ Ⓐ *The Allergy Store, Baubiologie Hardware, Granny's Old Fashioned Products, Green Earth Natural Foods, My Brother's Keeper.*

SCOURING POWDER

Harmful ingredients: dry chlorine bleach, detergents, artificial dyes. Some brands may also contain talc, which can be contaminated with carcinogenic asbestos.

Warning label: There are no warning labels on scouring powders.

HOMEMADE ALTERNATIVES
Sprinkle baking soda, borax, or dry table salt on the surface to be cleaned or on a sponge, then scour and rinse.

At the Store/By Mail

🌣 *Natural scouring powder*

Bon Ami Cleaning Powder (Faultless Starch/Bon Ami Co.). Soap-and-feldspar formula.

⊕ *Nontoxic scouring powder*

Bon Ami Polishing Cleanser (Faultless Starch/Bon Ami Co.). Non-chlorinated, detergent-based formula.

SHOE POLISH

Harmful materials: aerosol propellants, ethanol, methylene chloride, nitrobenzene, perchloroethylene, trichloroethane, trichloroethylene, xylene.

Never use shoe polish while drinking alcoholic beverages or immediately afterward, as the toxic effects of nitrobenzene are compounded by the presence of alcohol in the system.

SPECIAL TIP
Wear suede or canvas shoes that do not require polishing.

At the Store/By Mail

🌣 *Natural shoe polish*

Auro Leather Care Cream (Auro). Natural ingredients. *Sinan Company.*

Livos Bertos—Leather Seal (Livos). All natural. *To waterproof leather clothing, shoes, and boots.* Ⓐ *Livos Plant Chemistry, Seventh Generation.*

Livos Snado—Leather Polish (Livos). Made from nonsynthetic waxes, plant oils, and earth pigments. Ⓐ *Livos Plant Chemistry, Karen's Nontoxic Products, Seventh Generation.*

⊕ *Nontoxic shoe polish*

AFM E-Z Shoe Polish (AFM Enterprises). No obnoxious odor. Does not contain petroleum distillates. Brown, black, white. ☺ *AFM Enterprises, Allergy Relief Shop, Allergy Resources, The Allergy Store, Baubiologie Hardware, The Ecology Box, The Living Source, Nigra Enterprises.*

SILVER POLISH AND OTHER METAL CLEANERS

Harmful ingredients: ammonia, petroleum distillates, ethanol, synthetic fragrance, sulfur compounds.

Warning label:
"DANGER: Harmful or fatal if swallowed. Combustible. Irritating to eyes. Contains petroleum distillates and ammonia. If swallowed, do not induce vomiting. Call physician immediately. Keep out of reach of children. Keep away from heat and flame."

HOMEMADE ALTERNATIVES

Brass and Copper Polish

• Use lemon juice or a paste of lemon juice and salt, or a slice of lemon sprinkled with baking soda. Rub with a soft cloth, rinse with water, and dry.
• Make a paste of lemon juice and cream of tartar. Apply, leave on for five minutes, then wash in warm water and dry with a soft cloth.
• Make a paste of salt, white vinegar, and flour. Apply the paste, let it set for an hour, then rub off, rinse, and polish with a soft cloth.
• Rub with hot buttermilk or sour milk.
• Rub with tomato juice.
• Brass will look brighter and need less polishing if rubbed with olive oil after each polishing.
• If copper is tarnished, boil article in a pot of water with one tablespoon salt and one cup white vinegar for several hours. Wash with soap in hot water, rinse, and dry.

Chrome Polish

• Wipe with a soft cloth dipped in undiluted cider vinegar.
• Rub with a lemon peel, rinse, and polish with a soft cloth.

Gold Polish

Wash in lukewarm soapy water. Dry with a cotton cloth, then polish with a chamois cloth.

Silver Polish

The best way to clean silver is to *magnetize* tarnish away! The basic ingredients needed are aluminum (in the form of either a pot, a pan, or aluminum foil) and some kind of salt (table salt, rock salt, sea salt, and baking soda all work fine). In the salty water, the aluminum will act as a magnet and attract the tarnish away from the silver. After submerging the pieces of silver for a few minutes in water containing both the aluminum and the salt, you can literally wipe them dry and the tarnish will be gone (badly tarnished silver may need to go through the process several times).

For large items, such as trays or candelabra, run very hot water into your kitchen sink and add a sheet of aluminum foil and a handful of salt. Let sit for two or three minutes, then rinse and dry.

For silverware, put a sheet of aluminum foil in the bottom of a pan, then add two or three inches of water, one teaspoon salt, and one teaspoon baking soda. Bring to a boil and add silver pieces, making sure water totally covers them. Boil for two or three minutes, then remove from pan, rinse, and dry.

For small items such as jewelry, fill a glass jar half full with thin strips of aluminum foil. Add one tablespoon salt and cold water to fill the jar. Keep covered. To use, simply drop small items into the jar for a few minutes, then remove, rinse, and dry.

At the Store/By Mail

🌸 *Natural silver polish*

Nitron Industries. Natural enzyme formula cleans fine jewelry. Contains no ammonia.

SOAP FOR CLEANING

Soap is made from animal or vegetable fat and an alkali such as sodium hydroxide or ashes. It has been used for centuries and is absolutely safe and biodegradable. As a chemical-engineering textbook from the sixties states, "There is absolutely no reason why old-fashioned soap cannot be use for most household and commercial cleaning."

A WATER SOFTENER or WATER CONDITIONER will improve the performance of soap, eliminate soap scum, and allow you to use less soap to do the same cleaning job.

Don't be concerned if natural soaps don't foam up like detergent products. Some cleaners have extra foaming additives that create more bubbles. Plain soap cleans just as well.

SPECIAL TIP
Save the ends of bar soap in a jar with a little water. When you've accumulated enough, they will have dissolved down into a good cleaning soap.

At the Store/By Mail

☘ *Natural soap for cleaning*
Allen's Naturally Liquid Soap with Aloe (Allen's Naturally). No scent or dyes. Contains coconut-based cleaners, oil of almond, and an unidentified preservative. ☺ ⊗ *Allen's Naturally.*
Auro Organic Soap (Auro). Highly concentrated milk cleanser for all surfaces. Natural ingredients. *Sinan Company.*
Dr. Bronner's Pure Castile Soaps (All-One-God-Faith). ⊗ *Amberwood, Earth Herbs, Karen's Nontoxic Products, Natural Lifestyle Supplies, Simply Delicious.*
Lifeline Biodegradable Natural Cleaner (Lifeline Natural Soaps).
Livos Latis—Natural Soap (Livos). Liquid soap for general-purpose cleaning. Made from pure plant ingredients. ⊗ *Livos Plant Chemistry.*

☘ *Natural hand cleaner*
+ Hewara Cosmetic Hand Cleanser (Walter Rau Gmbh & Company Speickwerk). Cleans hands effectively after work in kitchen, shop, office, or garden. Biologically or biodynamically grown herbal extracts. Scented with essential oils. ☺ ⊗ *Meadowbrook Herb Garden.*
Homesteaders Hand Soap (Homesteader & Arnold Company). Soft-soap-and-pumice compound removes grease, ink, paint, and dirt without harming your skin. Contains lanolin. ☺ *Green Earth Natural Foods, InterNatural.*
Ringer. Natural hand cleaner with lemon oil and lanolin.

SPOT REMOVER

Harmful ingredients: perchloroethylene, ammonia, benzene, chlorine, synthetic fragrances, naphthalene, toluene, trichloroethylene, aerosol propellants.

Warning label:
"CAUTION: Eye irritant. Vapor harmful. Keep out of reach of children."

SPECIAL TIP
Spots are easiest to remove the minute they occur, so get in the habit of attacking them immediately, before they become stains.

HOMEMADE ALTERNATIVES
• *Blood:* Soak fabric in cold water, then wash with soap and cold water. If necessary, bleach white fabrics in a solution of a quarter cup borax and two cups water, then wash as usual.
• *Cocoa, chocolate, and coffee:* Sponge stain with cold water, then with a solution of one tablespoon borax in two cups water. Wash as usual.
• *Fruit and fruit juice:* Stretch the fabric over a basin and pour boiling water over the stain. Wash as usual.
• *Grass:* Rub with glycerin soap and let sit for one hour. Wash as usual.
• *Ink:* Soak fabric in cold water, then wash as usual. If stain has set on a white fabric, wet fabric with cold water, then apply a paste of cream of tartar and lemon juice and let sit for one hour. Wash as usual.
• *Mildew:* Wash in hot, soapy water. Rinse and dry in the sun.
• *Milk:* Soak fabric in warm water and rub gently with glycerin soap. Then wash in cooler soapy water, rinse, and dry.

• *Mud:* Brush off excess dried mud with a soft brush, then rub the stain with water left over from boiling potatoes, or a solution of two tablespoons borax in two cups water. Rinse well and wash as usual.

• *Perspiration:* Sponge stains with a weak solution of white vinegar or lemon juice and water.

• *Tea:* Stretch the fabric over a basin and pour boiling water over the stain. Wash as usual.

• *Urine:* Sponge the stain with a solution of baking soda and water, then rinse in warm water and wash as usual.

• *Water:* Hold fabric in hot steam until damp, shaking frequently; then press with a warm iron.

At the Store/By Mail

⊕ **Nontoxic spot remover**

Granny's Soil Away Stain Remover (Granny's Old Fashioned Products). ☺ ⊘ *The Allergy Store, Baubiologie Hardware, Carole's Cosmetics, Granny's Old Fashioned Products, Green Earth Natural Foods, The Living Source, My Brother's Keeper.*

Winter White Pre-Wash (Mountain Fresh). ☺ ⊘ *Mountain Fresh, Terra Verde Products.*

TOOLS FOR CLEANING

Harmful ingredients: Sponges: plastics, including polyurethane foam. Scouring pads: detergent, artificial dyes, synthetic fragrances, plastic.

NATURAL SPONGES

Use biodegradable sea sponges—large, soft corals gathered from the ocean. They are soft and spongy, and come in many sizes. Sea sponges are sold in most natural-food stores and bath shops.

As a second choice, go to your local hardware or paint store and get natural beige-colored sponges made from processed natural cellulose.

NATURAL SCOURING PADS

Use biodegradable loofas—long, stiff sponges made from gourds. They are naturally a light golden beige in color; avoid those that are dyed bright colors. To make little scouring pads, cut loofas into one inch slices. For added cleaning power, use a loofa scrubber with SCOURING POWDERS. Loofas are sold in most natural-food stores and bath shops.

At the Store/By Mail

Berea College Student Craft Industries. Wide variety of broom styles made by hand from natural broomcorn.

Earthen Joys. Sponges and sponge cloths made of cellulose.

Fuller Brush. Natural-fiber brooms with hardwood handles in all-purpose and push styles. Also a scrub brush with natural Tampico-hemp bristles and a detachable handle, a sheep's wool wax applicator, cotton-yarn dust and wet mops, natural cellulose sponges, stainless-steel scrubbers, and real feather dusters, plus garbage cans made of fire-safe galvanized steel.

Natural Lifestyle Supplies. Compressed cellulose sponges, and cellulose sponge cloths to use instead of paper towels.

Seventh Generation. Stainless-steel scrubbers, cellulose sponges.

Williams-Sonoma. Cotton dishcloths and dust cloths; cellulose sponges.

WATER SOFTENERS

Harmful ingredients: fragrance.

Warning label:
   "CAUTION: May be harmful if swallowed. Eye irritant."

Water softeners are necessary when using soap to clean and prevent soapy deposits in bathtubs and sinks and soap-scum that dulls laundry. They work by adding some type of salt to the water, which exchanges the "hard" calcium and magnesium ions in water for "soft" sodium ions, so actually any salt will do.

HOMEMADE ALTERNATIVES
• The best salt-based water softener I've found is sodium hexametaphosphate. Use a quarter cup to one cup sodium hexametaphosphate per five gallons of water, depending on water hardness, to prevent dull film from forming. If you don't know how hard your water is, start with one-eighth cup sodium hexametaphosphate and keep adding until the water feels slippery between your fingers. Add soap after the sodium hexametaphosphate, and use only half as much as you normally would.
• Use baking soda (sodium bicarbonate) or borax (sodium borate).

SPECIAL TIP
Instead of adding salt to soften water, use a magnetic or catalytic water conditioner, which will work indefinitely once it's installed. See WATER CONDITIONERS in Chapter 3 for more information.

8 ❧ Household Pest Control

> . . . The house soon had a wide variety of life in it, many
> forms taking advantage of the space, the materials, the
> amenities not being used by man. Some forms competed
> directly with him for these—for instance the mice ate
> much the same food as he did and used wool and fur for
> nests, but none of the animals ate exactly the same things
> and required exactly the same accommodation as man.
> This was fortunate both for him and for them . . . Had
> mice and men both needed exactly the same supplies one
> or another would have vanished, and it need not neces-
> sarily have been the mice.
>
> GEORGE ORDISH

I haven't used a chemical pesticide in over ten years, and you don't have to, either. Most household pest problems can be solved with such simple things as a sprinkle of cayenne pepper, a few squirts of strong mint tea, some honey on a sheet of bright yellow paper, or a vacuum cleaner. Even tough pest problems can be remedied by natural or nontoxic means, though they might take more effort.

The word *pesticide* comes from the Latin *pestis*, which means "plague," and *cida*, "to kill." Literally, pesticides are designed to kill unwanted insects, plants, fungi, rodents, bacteria, and other pests. More than thirty-four thousand pesticides, derived from about six hundred basic chemical ingredients, are currently registered by the EPA for use in this country.

I was astonished to find out that *suburban homeowners use more pesticides per acre than farmers use on their fields.* Sales of home pesticides are estimated at $1 billion annually. Around 91 percent of all American households apply some 300 million pounds of these poisonous substances (about 20 percent of total pesticide use) in and around their homes, most frequently in the kitchen and bedroom. We use insecticides (insect killers), acaricides (mite killers), and rodenticides (rodent killers). In our gardens we also use nematocides (nematode worm killers), fungicides (fungus killers), and herbicides (weed and brush killers).

HOW HOUSEHOLD PESTICIDES AFFECT OUR HEALTH AND THE EARTH

Pesticides are the number-two cause of household poisonings in the United States. About 2.5 million children and adults are affected each year by such common household items as fly spray, ant and roach bait, and insect repellents. According to poison-control-center reports on pesticide exposures, 70 percent of the incidents involve children under five years of age, and over half of those who die from pesticide-related incidents are children.

Household pesticides can harm us both from breathing the pesticide directly while we're applying it, and from breathing the residues. Pesticides are specially formulated to resist natural decomposition processes. When used indoors, protected from sun and wind, they last even longer. Pesticides can remain actively airborne for days or weeks, even up to thirty years.

When more than one pesticide is used, the combination can become even more toxic. Multiple exposures are frequently encountered in homes, offices, and public buildings, and from pets, water, air, and soil.

The immediate health effects from inhaling some common household pesticides during use include nausea, cough, breathing difficulties, depression, eye irritation, dizziness, weakness, blurred vision, muscle twitching, and convulsions. Many pesticides can be stored in body fat, sometimes accumulating to toxic levels. Although long-term effects are not fully known, long-term exposure from repeated use and lingering residues can damage the liver, kidneys, and lungs, and can cause paralysis, sterility, suppression of immune function, brain hemorrhages, decreased fertility and sexual function, heart problems, and coma.

Infants, children, and adults with certain chronic illnesses are more susceptible to pesticide poisoning than are healthy adults.

Pesticides are regulated by the federal Insecticide, Fungicide, and Rodenticide Act, last amended by Congress in 1972. This act gives federal control to all pesticide applications and regulates both intrastate and interstate marketing of pesticides.

Since October 1977, the EPA has required laboratory safety tests at the manufacturer's expense before any new pesticide is allowed on the market. Included must be tests for acute-exposure effects, the lethal dose in animals, and chronic-exposure tests for cancer, genetic mutations, birth defects, and fertility.

Pesticides that were in use before 1977, however, have not undergone such testing and still continue to be used. A further complication is that many of the safety tests on which earlier registrations were based were sloppy or fraudulent. In the early 1980s, Industrial Bio-Test, the nation's leading pesticide-testing laboratory at the time, was found to have faked many of its test results. So we can't even be sure of the safety of the pesticides that have supposedly been tested. In 1987, Consumers Union examined the EPA's records of fifty common household pesticides to see if the agency had enough data to determine their safety. In 72 percent of the cases, the EPA lacked this crucial information.

The job of the EPA in regulating pesticides is to weigh the health and environmental risks against the benefits of using the pesticide. Since there are safe, workable, and cost-effective alternatives available that make it unnecessary in most cases to use toxic pesticides at all, zero pesticides should be our goal.

Perhaps the most toxic part of pesticide products is their inert ingredients—extremely toxic substances whose identity is protected by trade secrecy. Even poison-control centers don't know what the inert ingredients are, so if you end up at the hospital with pesticide poisoning, the doctors won't always know exactly what to treat you for. The EPA keeps a listing of possible inert ingredients that includes 57 chemicals of "immediate toxicological concern"—28 of which are suspected carcinogens. Xylene, a popular inert ingredient, is known to be used in 2,216 pesticide products.

The environmental effects of pesticides used on crops are well known, and many of these same dangers apply to household use as well. While it's unlikely that you might kill a songbird while spraying for flies, pesticides are still made from polluting, non-renewable petrochemicals that produce toxic waste.

Pesticides by their very nature are cruel to animals. Not only are they extensively tested on animals (when they are tested at all), but they also indiscriminately kill a wide variety of living creatures that are not pests but play integral and important parts in our ecosystem.

READING LABELS

Pesticide product labels give us very little information. All that must be listed is the *active* ingredients that actually function as poisons. Generally, their names are long and intimidating (even to me!) and give us no information as to their safety.

The simplest way to assess the danger of a pesticide might be to look at the signal-word warnings on the label:

• Those marked with DANGER—POISON, with skull and crossbones, could kill an adult if only a tiny pinch is ingested.
• Those marked with WARNING could kill an adult if about a teaspoon is ingested.
• Those marked with CAUTION will not kill until an amount ranging from two table-spoons to two cups is ingested.

But, as with cleaning products, these signal words are not used properly. Our best bet is to simply use the highly effective natural alternatives that are available.

LIVING NATURALLY WITH PESTS

When we begin to feel like responsible participants in the natural world and realize that every other species has a vital role to play in maintaining the balance of life on Earth, it radically changes our approach to dealing with what are generallly considered pests.

In nature, living things coexist by establishing their territories and honoring those established by others. Establish your territory with insects by pest-proofing your home.

The key to success in any natural pest-control program is to prevent pests from entering your home in the first place and to make it impossible for them to live there. If you have pests, you are probably providing them with perfect living conditions.

The first thing to do is figure out how pests are getting into your home, and do something to keep them out. If you have ants, follow the line of ants to see where they're coming from, then seal up the hole with white glue (it's less toxic than caulk). They're sure to find another way to get in, but after a few days of keeping a sharp lookout, you'll fill all the holes and eliminate the ant problem for good. Also you might want to invest in screens on your windows to block flying insects. And it's a good idea to look for and fill holes and cracks in your building that mice can crawl through.

Second, make your home an unpleasant place for pests to be. Here's how:

• Take away their food supply by keeping living areas clean. Be especially careful to sweep up crumbs, wipe up spills when they happen, wash dishes immediately, and

deposit leftover food in its proper place. Store food in tightly closed, impenetrable metal or glass containers. Empty garbage frequently into outside garbage cans (or better yet, compost) to eliminate the enticing odors of decaying food. Disposable diapers attract pests; don't use them, or if you do, rinse the liner in the toilet prior to disposal.
• Dry up their water supply. Repair leaky faucets, pipes, and clogged drains.
• Get rid of any clutter they can hide in. Clean out your attic, basement, and closets. Remove piles of old clothing, newspapers and magazines, and boxes. Check out-of-the-way places (under stairwells, for example) where unused items often get tossed.

ELIMINATING PESTS

• First, identify the pest. Reference books such as field guides or gardening books are a good place to look, or call a pesticide dealer.
• Decide how many pests you can tolerate. There is no way to totally eliminate all the creatures we think of as pests from the world. Many pests are actually beneficial; for instance, house centipedes eat flies. But often we see any creature as an invader to our territory and get out the pesticides, instead of doing something as simple as shooing it, taking it outdoors, or vacuuming it up. A true pest is one that is doing damage or presenting a health threat. If rats are chewing through your electrical wires, that's a very different situation than a moth resting on your wall.
• Try the most natural, least toxic methods of control first.

HOW I RATE PEST-CONTROL PRODUCTS

To be consistent, I have rated pest-control products according to their ingredients; however, I want to note that to be truly earthwise we would live in balance with insects and animals, even those in our homes, and not try to exterminate them at all costs.

⊕ **Earthwise** pest controls are:
• safe to use;
• nonpolluting in their manufacture, use, and disposal;
• made from natural, renewable ingredients that are organically grown or harvested from the wild in a sustainable way—devoid of petrochemical ingredients; and
• biodegradable.

❧ **Natural** pest controls are:
• safe to use;
• made from natural (but not organically grown), renewable ingredients that may have residues of petrochemicals used in growing or processing, or small amounts of nontoxic petrochemical ingredients; and
• biodegradable.
    Note: A plus sign before the name of a natural product indicates that it contains some earthwise ingredient(s) such as organically grown herbs.

⊕ **Nontoxic** pest controls are:
• relatively safe to use;
• made mainly of synthetic ingredients formulated from petrochemical or natural sources;
• biodegradable.

INSECTICIDES

Harmful materials: pesticides.

Warning labels:

"CAUTION: Keep out of reach of children. Use only when area to be treated is vacated by humans and pets. Not to be taken internally by humans or animals. Hazardous if swallowed or absorbed through skin. Do not get on skin, in eyes, or on clothing. Avoid breathing of vapors or spray mist. Do not smoke while using. Should not be used in homes of the seriously ill or those on medication. Should not be used in homes of pollen-sensitive people or asthmatics. Do not use in any rooms where infants, the sick, or aged are or will be present for any extended period of confinement. Do not use in kitchen areas or areas where food is prepared or served. Do not apply directly to food. In the home, all food-processing surfaces and utensils should be covered during treatment or thoroughly washed before use. Remove pets and cover fish aquariums and delicate plants before spraying."

Many multipurpose household insecticide sprays contain pyrethrum, a natural insecticide extracted from the seeds of a species of chysanthemum flower. Commercial formulations containing pyrethrum should not be used because they contain toxic inert ingredients. You can use pure, natural pyrethrum. Remember that while it is relatively nontoxic to humans, it is toxic to honeybees, many beneficial insects, fish, and animals.

HOMEMADE ALTERNATIVES

Ants
One of the most frequent reasons pesticides are sprayed around the home is to control ants.

• Keep things clean; don't leave any crumbs or garbage around.

• Wipe up a line of ants with a wet sponge so that other ants will not follow. Wipe up any stray ants that may be out looking for food or others.
• Sprinkle powdered chili pepper, paprika, dried peppermint, damp coffee grounds, or borax where ants are coming in. Or squeeze the juice of a lemon at the entry spot and leave the peel there.
• Plant mint around the outside of the house to discourage ants from entering, or spray them with strong mint tea in a squirt bottle.
• Spray ants and ant trails with a biodegradable soap, both inside and outside your house.

Cockroaches and Silverfish
Over half of all pesticides sold for home use are cockroach killers. While they aren't particularly appealing to live with, it might be comforting to remember that cockroaches really aren't a pest. The World Health Organization does not include cockroaches on its list of insects that are hazardous to health (fleas, bedbugs, lice, mites, scorpions, and some spiders are included), and there are no reported instances in the scientific literature of roaches transmitting human disease.

• Mix equal parts powdered oatmeal or flour with plaster of paris. Spread on the floor of infested area.
• Mix equal parts baking soda and sugar. Spread around infested area.
• Mix by stirring and sifting one ounce trisodium phosphate, six ounces borax, four ounces granulated sugar, and eight ounces flour. Spread on the floor of infested area. Repeat after four days and again after two weeks to kill newly hatched roaches.
• Mix two tablespoons flour, one tablespoon cocoa powder, and four tablespoons borax. Spread around infested area.
• Use cucumber rinds in infested area.
• Use bay leaves in infested area.

• Trap them: set an uncapped one-quart mason jar upright, with grease on the inside of the neck and a piece of banana inside for bait. Place a tongue depressor against the outside of the jar so they can walk up and fall, trapped, into the jar.

Flies
• Hang clusters of cloves in a room.
• Make flypaper by spreading honey thinly onto bright yellow paper (yellow is the favorite color of flies).
• Use a fly swatter.
• Scratch the skin of an orange and leave it out; the citrus oil released will repel flies.

Food-Storage Pests (Beetles and Weevils)
• Put a bay leaf in each container of cereal, crackers, cookies, flour, and other grain products.
• Kill them manually when you see them.
• Store flour and grains in a cool cabinet, or preferably in the refrigerator. This will also help keep whole grains and whole-grain flour fresh.
• Hang small cloth sacks of black pepper in your food bins.

Mosquitoes
• Put screens on windows and doors.
• When you see them sitting on walls at night, vacuum them up with the long attachment on the vacuum cleaner.

Spider Mites
• Put fresh banana peels in infested areas. Keep adding fresh peels to the old ones to repel all the mites.
• Mix four cups wheat flour and a half cup buttermilk with five gallons water. Spray on plants to get rid of mites.

Spiders
Every house should have a few spiders because they help keep the population of other insects under control. The bites of some spiders, however, can be poisonous. Find out from your local library or poison-control center about poisonous spiders that might live in your area and learn to identify them. If you see a friendly spider, leave it be.

A HUMANE TIP
If you don't want to kill a pest that is already in your home, cover it with a glass jar, slip a piece of paper under it, and take it outdoors. Or use a small, hand-held vacuum to wisk it up, and then dispose of it in an outdoor location.

At the Store/By Mail
Safe retail products include herbal repellents (which work well for moths and some other bugs) and adhesive pest traps.

Insect traps and repellents
Allergy Resources. Fly traps, moth kits. Also pure pyrethrum powder and diatomaceous earth, which kills roaches and fleas in the carpet.

Big Stinky Fly Trap (J. L. Price). *Necessary Trading Company.*

Black Flag Roach Motel Traps (Boyle-Midway).

Brody Enterprises. Traps for cockroaches, fleas, and other insects, sticky fly traps, and flea combs.

D-Con Roach Traps (D-Con Company/Sterling Drug). *Walnut Acres.*

EcoSafe Zap (EcoSafe Products). Dried pyrethrum flowers.

Fly Stik Fly Trap (Farnam Companies).

Fly Trap Fly Catcher Strip (Willert Home Products).

Gardens Alive! Pheromone traps, boric-acid powder, roach-killing bait stations.

Air Therapy (Mia Rose Products). Natural ingredients, highly concentrated, in a nonaerosol spray mist, effective in eliminating fleas, flies, ants, and crickets. ⊕ *Allergy Resources, Humane Alternative Products, Mia Rose Products.*

Stick-A-Roach Roach Glue Traps (J. T. Eaton Company).

Thermal Pest Eradication (Isothermics). Process for killing household insects using heat. Nontoxic, safe, nonpolluting; faster and more effective than fumigants, and safer for workers. Available from licensed professionals.

INSECT REPELLENTS

Harmful ingredients: pesticides.

Warning labels:

"CAUTION: Harmful if swallowed. Avoid contact with eyes and lips. Do not allow children to rub eyes if hands have been treated. Do not apply on or near: rayon, spandex, or other synthetics. May damage furniture finishes, plastics, leather, watch crystals, and painted or varnished surfaces including automobiles."

I don't know about you, but I don't think I'd want to rub something on my skin that could take the paint off my car.

The most commonly used pesticide in insect repellents is DEET. According to the British medical journal *Lancet*, exposure to DEET has been reported to cause brain disorders, slurred speech, difficulty walking, tremors, and even death. *Consumer Reports* has documented at least a dozen cases of acute neurotoxicity in children who had been exposed to or accidentally swallowed DEET; some of the children died.

While everyone who uses a DEET-based insect repellent obviously won't suffer these effects, it makes you think twice, especially since almost 10 percent of the DEET applied to the surface of your skin can be absorbed within twelve hours.

HOMEMADE ALTERNATIVES

• The quickest and easiest repellent: splash a little vinegar on exposed skin, or dab it on with a cotton ball.

• Dilute oil of citronella or oil of pennyroyal with vodka or vegetable oil (a few drops to one ounce of either) and then apply at strategic points (like perfume). Be very careful with these: even though they are natural, they have strong fragrances and can produce rashes when applied directly to the skin, and they can irritate your eyes if rubbed in accidentally.

• Eat lots of garlicky food and/or rub garlic on your skin; mosquitoes hate the smell of garlic.

• Wear protective clothing. Depending on the insect, this may mean using big rubber bands to tighten pant cuffs around boots, a cotton turtleneck shirt, a hat with protective netting, a silk balaclava for your face, and cotton work gloves. This is, of course, overkill for most people, but putting on a loose-fitting shirt on summer evenings will keep some insects off your skin. Some outdoor outfitters, like *L. L. Bean,* carry insect-protective clothing.

• Put mosquito netting around your bed.

At the Store/By Mail

Order natural insect repellents by mail.

❧ *Natural insect repellents*

+ *Willow Rain Herbal Goods.* Repellent with oils of pennyroyal, anise, citronella, cedarwood, and eucalyptus in an olive oil base.

EcoSafe Skeeter Shooo (EcoSafe Products). Repellent for mosquitoes, fleas, and flies. *Earth Herbs, EcoSafe Products.*

Edna's Insect Rejector (Edna's). Contains citronella, pennyroyal, and essential oils. *The Ecology Box.*

Green Ban for People (Green Ban). Essential oils in a calendula-oil base. No harsh chemicals. *Basically Natural, Baubiologie Hardware, Eco-Choice, InterNatural.*

Naturpath. Beat It!—a natural herbal insect repellent for humans and pets.

No Common Scents. (No Common Scents). Liquid insect repellent. ☺ ⊘ Humane Alternative Products.

North Country Citronella Soap (North Country Soap). Soap with pleasant citrus fragrance that is naturally offensive to mosquitoes, gnats, and other flying insects. Beauty Without Cruelty seal of approval. ⊞ ☺ *North Country Soap.*

Royal Guard Bug-A-Way (Laurel Canyon Herbs). Insect repellent containing Australian tea-tree oil, pennyroyal, citronella, and other essential oils in a vegetable base. *Karen's Nontoxic Products, Motherwear.*

Weeds of Worth (Weeds of Worth). Natural insect repellent. *Amberwood, Karen's Nontoxic Products.*

LICE SHAMPOO

Harmful materials: At one time the most common treatment for head lice was a shampoo that contained lindane, a very toxic chemical easily absorbed through the skin. One child's death was reported to have been the result of lindane poisoning after treatment for head lice, and lindane is now known to cause convulsions, seizures, and cancer in laboratory animals. None of the half dozen brands of lice shampoo available at my local drugstore contain lindane, but it is still used in many popular brands, so read labels carefully.

More frequently the active ingredient nowadays is pyrethrin. As with general-purpose pesticide sprays, the toxicity problem lies not with the pyrethrin, but with the added inert ingredients, in this case petroleum distillates, which frequently are not identified. I would hesitate to put chemicals of unknown toxicity on my child's scalp, especially since the scalp area is very porous, and chemicals put on the hair are easily absorbed into the bloodstream.

HOMEMADE ALTERNATIVES
A very effective, and much less toxic, alternative is to use a combination of sham

pooing, soaking, and combing with a nit-removing comb especially designed to eliminate lice (available at your local pharmacy). Here is the procedure:

1. Wet hair thoroughly with warm water and apply a coconut-based shampoo or soap. Coconut oil contains dodecyl alcohol, which is deadly to adult lice. (Any shampoo that lists sodium lauryl sulfate as an ingredient contains coconut oil. Or you can use a bar soap that has a coconut-oil base.) Work the soap or shampoo into a thick lather, covering the entire head and all the hair.
2. Rinse with warm water and repeat the lathering process, this time leaving suds on hair. Tie a towel around the lathered hair and leave it on for thirty minutes.
3. Remove the towel and comb the soapy hair with a regular comb to remove tangles; then use the nit-removing comb on one-inch sections of hair (following the instructions that come with the comb). If the hair dries during combing, dampen it with water. Depending on the length of hair, the combing can take two hours or more. Very curly or woolly hair can take even longer.
4. After removing lice, wash the hair a third time, rinse, and dry. Inspect the hair when dry for any lice you missed and remove them.

Everyone in the household must be treated when one member of the family has head lice. Lice don't care which head of hair they live in, and family members can spread lice back and forth. During the elimination process, everyone must comb their dry hair daily to check for lice. Also, vacuum upholstered furniture daily, and launder pillowcases, bed sheets, and clothes. As an extra precaution, you might want to run pillows and blankets through your clothes dryer.

Check after seven to ten days to see if

any missed lice nits have hatched; if so, you have to go through the whole process again.

Another alternative is to use a treatment of warm coconut oil. Heat coconut oil to make it fluid, then pour slowly over the child's hair, massaging it in (make this a pleasant before-bed activity). Cover the child's head with a cotton knit cap that ties under the chin and put him or her to bed for the night. The coconut oil will loosen both lice and eggs.

In the morning wash twice with shampoo, then comb to remove eggs. Repeat weekly until the infestation is gone.

At the Store/By Mail
Brody Enterprises. Berbac head-lice kit includes a fine-toothed metal comb to trap nits and a specially formulated pine-tar soap that makes the comb work easier.

MOTHBALLS

Harmful materials: paradichlorobenzene.

Warning label:
"CAUTION: May be harmful if swallowed. Avoid prolonged breathing of vapor or repeated contact with skin. Keep out of reach of children."

I would find the warning on mothballs amusing if it weren't so alarming: it clearly states, "Avoid prolonged breathing of vapor," yet how can you use mothballs without breathing the fumes? The odor of mothballs hidden in a closet can permeate your entire home and increase to high levels if there is not adequate ventilation. The vapors from mothballs are also absorbed by clothing and blankets, and can be very strong when you use these items.

HOMEMADE ALTERNATIVES
• Don't worry about moths if you can see them. The moths that cause damage are a specific variety of clothes moth that is too small to notice. It is the larvae of these moths that eat fabric.
• Kill moth eggs before they hatch by placing items in the sun or by running them through a warm clothes dryer. This should be done when the item is first purchased and at periodic intervals while being stored.
• Protect uninfested items by storing them in airtight containers, such as paper packages or cardboard boxes, with all edges carefully sealed with paper tape.
• Store items in a clean condition; moth larvae especially love areas soiled with food stains.
• Washing destroys all forms of the moth.
• Using cotton, linen, or silk fabric, make sachets of dried lavender or equal parts of dried rosemary and mint, and place in drawers and closets.
• Use whole peppercorns.
• Use cedar oil or chips.

At the Store/By Mail

⊕ *Earthwise moth repellents*
The Hummer Nature Works. Cedar mothballs, hangers, closet fresheners, and small cutouts in nature shapes, all fashioned only from deadwood that has been air drying for ten years or more, or trees that have fallen because of weather conditions or disease.

♣ *Natural moth repellents*
+ *Fluir Herbals.* Fragrant herbal potpourri to keep with linens and wools. ☺ ⊗
+ *Jeanne Rose Herbal BodyWorks.* Potpourri moth and bug repellent using organically grown herbs when available. ☺ ⊗
Brooks Brothers. Cedar blocks and eggs.
Fuller Brush. Cedar chests, panels for drawers or closets, shoe racks, sweater racks, and cedar-filled hanging shoe and sweater bags.

L. L. Bean. Assorted cedar accessories for storage and protection of wool clothes and blankets.

Lillian Vernon. Cedar blocks and hangers to repel moths.

Orvis. Cedar mothballs, and cedar sachets with cotton covers.

Seventh Generation. Cedar blocks and drawer liners.

The Company Store. Cedar blocks.

Vermont Country Store. Natural moth repellent made of herbs, spices, and oils.

Walnut Acres. Cedar drawer liners, mothballs, storage blocks, hangers, and modular shoe racks.

RAT & MOUSE KILLERS

Harmful materials: pesticides.

Warning labels:

"CAUTION: Keep out of reach of children. May be harmful or fatal if swallowed. Keep away from humans and domestic animals and pets."

"ENVIRONMENTAL HAZARD: Keep out of lakes, streams, or ponds. Toxic to fish, bird, and wildlife—can pose a secondary hazard to birds to prey and mammals."

HOMEMADE ALTERNATIVES
• Use mousetraps.
• Get a cat. I had a kitten once who eliminated all the mice in my house within the first two weeks after she came to live with me.
• Starve them by making sure no food is left in open places (including food in unopened cardboard containers; they'll eat right through them). Keep garbage in tightly covered metal containers.
• Remove their shelter by keeping storage spaces orderly and keeping stored items off the floor. Seal holes around the bottom of walls.
• Keep them out of the house by closing any holes in exterior walls and keeping doors closed.

• Make a mixture of one part plaster of paris, one part flour, and a little sugar and cocoa powder, and sprinkle where rats and mice will find it.

At the Store/By Mail

❧ *Natural rat and mouse killers*

Brody Enterprises. Glue boards or bulk glue to make your own boards, plus a variety of mousetraps, including live traps.

Gardens Alive . . . Vitamin D rat and mouse bait.

Stick-Em Rat & Mouse Glue Traps (J. T. Eaton Company).

TERMITICIDES

Harmful materials: pesticides.

The two questions regarding pesticides that I am most often asked have to do with termite treatments—how toxic are they, and what can be done for nonchemical treatment?

Termites play an essential role in nature by helping to clear the forest of dead trees. Since large areas of our homes are made from dead wood, it's not surprising that termites are responsible for structural damage in excess of $750 million each year in the United States alone.

Since World War II, the most popular method of termite control has been to spray potent, long-lasting pesticides—such as chlordane, aldrin, dieldrin and heptachlor—directly onto or into the soil around a building's foundation, and in the crawl space or basement. Chlordane has been found in the soil of treated areas thirty years or more after treatment. After persistent health and environmental problems became associated with the use of these pesticides—poisoned fish ponds, contaminated well water, seepage into the indoor air of treated homes—several states banned them. The EPA discovered that 90 percent of the homes *properly* treated with termiticides still had detectable residues in the air one year later. Under public pressure, the manufacture of these pesticides ceased in 1987, and since April 15, 1988, their sale has been prohibited.

The new popular termiticide is chlorpyrifos (commonly known as Dursban, Lorsban, or Pyrinex). Injected underground, it can continue to be effective for almost twenty years. Consumers Union found that chlorpyrifos has not been adequately tested to determine if it causes cancer, genetic mutations, or nerve damage. It is extremely toxic to fish, birds, and aquatic invertebrates.

TERMITE-PREVENTION TIPS
The best way by far to control termites is to make your home unattractive or inaccessible to them.

• Subterranean termites need food, warmth, and moisture in order to survive. Keep the area under your house cold and dry, and they'll look elsewhere for food.
• Do an annual inspection. It takes a well-established termite colony almost three months to eat a pound of wood, so catching them early can make it easier to control any problems that do arise.
• Use copper or galvanized-steel termite shields. Properly installed, these shields prevent termites from reaching the woodwork from the Earth. Use them at basements, crawl spaces, or chimney foundations; on concrete piers with saddle and wood posts; and at entrances with wood steps or floors. Buy termite shields ready-made, or buy a roll of sheet metal at a building-supply store. Unroll the sheet metal over foundation walls and bed edges down at a forty-five-degree angle. If this sounds too confusing, call a few contractors and see if you can find an experienced person locally to help you with this.

• When building or remodeling, there are a few preventive measures you can take. Some of these tips can also be applied to already-existing structures:
• Design and construct foundation walls and supporting piers in a way that minimizes the possibility of future cracks or fissures through which termites can attack.
• Wood in contact with the ground should be heart tidewater red cypress or heart redwood or treated with a natural wood preservative (see Livos Plantchemistry and Sinan Company catalogs).
• Provide good cross-ventilation for unexcavated areas under the house.
• Screen all openings for ventilation under the house and in the attic with eighteen-mesh metal screening.
• Remove all wood scraps and stumps from the soil surrounding the house.
• Wooden floor joists should be at least twenty-four inches above the ground, and wooden construction on the exterior of the house should be at least six inches above the ground.

TO GET RID OF TERMITES WITHOUT TOXIC CHEMICALS
• Bake them out by using heat. Either close up the area and heat it up with a space heater, or keep a small area at 140 degrees Fahrenheit for ten minutes with a heat lamp.
• Cut out and replace infested wood.

At the Store/By Mail

⊕ Nontoxic termite control
Electro-Gun (Etex Ltd.). Zaps termites to death with electrical charge. Call 800-543-5651 for the name of a local trained technician.

9 ❧ Personal Care

The beauty that addresses itself to the eye is only the spell of the moment; the eye of the body is not always that of the soul.

GEORGE SAND

I used to be one of those women who wouldn't leave the house without complete makeup on, and my hair done perfectly and sprayed. But now my beauty regime is much simpler.

I've come to know that true beauty comes from within: the glow of healthy skin and the sparkle in happy eyes can't be duplicated by any cosmetic. For daily grooming, I use only a few basic products. My hairstyle comes from a good haircut instead of out of a can. And when it's important to dress up, I use only natural cosmetics, very sparingly. My husband actually thinks I look better without makeup at all.

For many years, people thought that the skin was impenetrable, but now we know that everything we put on our skin goes directly into our bodies. Modern medicine now uses skin patches in some cases to administer drugs, for doctors know that what is absorbed through the skin eventually travels to every part of the body. Since we are applying beauty and hygiene products to some of the most sensitive and thin-skinned parts of our bodies, it makes good sense to use only the purest natural products we can.

HOW PERSONAL-CARE PRODUCTS AFFECT YOU AND THE EARTH

Thousands of different ingredients are used in the manufacture of beauty and hygiene products. They are derived from either petrochemicals or natural animal, vegetable, or mineral sources. The most common problem with the use of these products is, of course, skin rash, but there are some ingredients commonly used that can cause cancer.

Many beauty products for sale may be unsafe because cosmetics are not legally required to be tested for safety. The FDA can take action only after a cosmetic is on the market and enough evidence exists to prove in court that it is hazardous, after which the FDA may halt its production and sale.

The ingredients used to make many cosmetic items are derived from nonrenewable petrochemicals that can be harmful to use and create toxic waste in their manufacture. Commonly used petrochemical ingredients that you may want to avoid include aerosol propellants, alcohol, ammonia, artificial colors and flavors, BHA and BHT, EDTA, ethanol, fluoride, formaldehyde, fragrance, gylcerol, glyceryl, hexachlorophene, isopropyl alcohol, methyl ethyl ketone, mineral oil, nylon, paraffin, phenol, anything that begins with PEG- or PPG-, PVP, quaternium 15 (releases formaldhyde), saccharin, and talc.

174

Even so-called natural personal-care products are often made from plant ingredients that are grown with pesticides and artificial fertilizers, or from ingredients derived from animals. So once again, its a good idea to only use what we need.

READING LABELS

Natural beauty and hygiene products are becoming big business, yet there is no official legal definition of the term *natural* as it relates to these items. Even though the FDA requires a complete listing of ingredients on all domestic cosmetics packaged after April 17, 1977, itemized in decreasing order by weight and using standardized language, there are still some problems with the system.

Some items commonly considered by consumers to be cosmetics do not need to have their ingredients listed at all, because the FDA considers them over-the-counter drugs. According to the FDA definition, a cosmetic is anything that can be "rubbed, poured, sprinkled, or sprayed on, introduced into, or otherwise applied to the human body . . . for cleansing, beautifying, promoting attractiveness, or altering the appearance without affecting the body's structure or functions." If a product claims to affect the body's structure or function (such as fighting tooth decay), it is considered an over-the-counter drug. Hygiene items *not* covered by cosmetics labeling requirements include deodorant soaps, fluoridated toothpastes, antiperspirants, sunscreens, and antidandruff shampoos.

For those cosmetic items that do list their ingredients, everything is not necessarily revealed on the label. Trade secrets such as fragrance or flavor formulas are not divulged. Nor do the labels tell you whether the ingredients in "natural" beauty products are actually derived from natural sources. Some clever manufacturers create "natural" formulas by adding natural-sounding ingredients such as honey or herbs or jojoba oil, instead of actually making a more natural formula by removing unnecessary artificial colors, fragrances, and preservatives.

If you have allergies, beware of products labeled "hypoallergenic." No one product can be truly hypoallergenic to everyone. *Hypoallergenic* simply means that some of the most *common* allergens have been removed—fragrance, lanolin, cocoa butter, cornstarch, cottonseed oil. These products still contain ingredients to which you may be allergic, especially if you are sensitive to petrochemicals.

Cruelty-free is another legally meaningless term that is used on many cosmetic and hygiene products. Within the animal-rights movement, *cruelty-free* generally means that the product itself has not been tested on animals, though it may contain ingredients such as artificial colors, sodium laurel sulfate, and methyl and propyl paraben—all of which have had animal tests. Some cruelty-free products contain animal products such as animal tallow, collagen, honey, beeswax, or lanolin. In this book I've marked cruelty-free products as such. For a list of companies that don't do animal tests or use animal ingredients, contact the animal-rights organizations in Recommended Resources.

HOW I RATE PERSONAL-CARE PRODUCTS

As more people become aware that what they put *on* their bodies should be as pure as what they put *in* them, the number of natural personal-care and beauty products is increasing. Some people are even beginning to use organically grown or wildcrafted in-gredients.

⊕ **Earthwise** personal-care products are:
- safe to use;
- nonpolluting in their manufacture, use, and disposal;
- made from natural, renewable ingredients that are organically grown or wildcrafted—devoid of petrochemical ingredients; and
- biodegradable.

Note: Personal-care products that are *primarily* made from organically grown ingredients but have a few minor nonorganic ingredients are indicated with a minus sign.

🍃 **Natural** personal-care products are:
- safe to use;
- made from natural, renewable ingredients that may have residues of petrochemicals used in growing or processing, or trace amounts of nontoxic petrochemical ingredients, particularly the preservatives methyl and propyl paraben (some products rated as natural will contain ingredients that have been derived from natural sources but are not in their natural state, such as sodium laurel sulfate, which is derived from coconut oil; products made from powdered minerals get the natural rating because generally nothing is known about the mining process); and
- biodegradable.

Note: Personal-care products that contain organically grown or wildcrafted herbs but few other organically grown ingredients are indicated with a plus sign. Keep in mind that most ingredients in these products are natural, but not organically grown.

If a product is scented, I have indicated its scent, when known. Products advertised as unscented are also noted as such.

Most of the products listed in this chapter are natural, although a good number are earthwise. I have not included some of the most popular products that are advertised as cruelty-free because they contain artificial colors or preservatives. You will see that there are plenty of products that are natural and cruelty-free, too.

Look for the products listed in this chapter at your local natural-food store, or order them by mail. You can also make many of your own cosmetic items at home. In addition to the formulas listed throughout this chapter, your natural-food store and local library should have some books on this subject.

ANTIPERSPIRANTS & DEODORANTS

Harmful ingredients: aerosol propellants, colors, ammonia, ethanol, formaldehyde, fragrance, glycerin.

In the past ten years, more than eight different ingredients have been banned by the FDA or voluntarily removed from anti-perspirants and deodorants because they posed a hazard to users.

The most common symptom from use is skin irritation, often severe enough to require medical attention. This is caused by the mixing of the antisweat compound (aluminum chlorohydrate or, in non-aerosol products, zirconium compounds) with perspiration.

Although little research has been done on the actual amount of aluminum salts we are exposed to from the aluminum chlorohydrate in antiperspirants, it is known that aluminum salts are toxic. A letter to the *New England Journal of Medicine* points out the connection between aluminum and brain disorders such as dementia, Alzheimer's disease, behavior abnormalities, poor memory, and impaired visual-motor coordination.

Nonantiperspirant deodorants may contain the bactericide triclosan, which can cause liver damage when absorbed through the skin.

HOMEMADE ALTERNATIVES

For deodorant, use pure, dry baking soda. This works better than anything else, even for those who have a problem with perspiration odor. If desired, mix baking soda with corn starch, wheat starch, rice starch, or fragrant dried herbs. After a bath or shower, just sprinkle baking soda onto fingertips and apply to underarm.

At the Store/By Mail

Look for aluminum-free zirconium-free antiperspirants and deodorants in natural-food stores and drugstores.

Natural antiperspirants and deodorants

+ *Jeanne Rose Herbal BodyWorks.* Herbal deodorant powder made from organically grown herbs when available. Beauty Without Cruelty Seal of Approval ☺ ⊗ ⊞

+ Speick Deodorant (Walter Rau Gmbh & Company Speickwerk). Biological or biodynamically grown herbal extracts and thermal spring water in a grain-alcohol base. Scented. Stick or spray. ☺ ⊗ *Meadowbrook Herb Garden*

+ Weleda Natural Sage Deodorant (Weleda). Contains biodynamically grown herbs. ☺ ⊗ *Amberwood, Deer Valley Farm, EveryBody Ltd., Humane Alternative Products, InterNatural, Meadowbrook Herb Garden, Naturpath, Sunrise Lane, Vega Street, Weleda.*

Alvera Natural Aloe Vera Deodorant Aloe Products. Contains herbal and vegetable derivatives. No aluminum. Unscented and herbal scent. *Home Health Products.*

Aubrey Organics Anti-Perspirants & Deodorants (Aubrey Organics). Vitamins and herbs in a rosewater-and-grain-alcohol base. Pump spray bottle. ☺ ⊗ *The Allergy Store, Aubrey Organics, Humane Alternative Products, Karen's Nontoxic Products, Natural Lifestyle Supplies, Vegan Street.*

Le Crystal Naturel (French Transit). Natural deodorant salts in crystal form ☺ ⊗ *The Allergy Store, Earth Herbs, The Ecology Box, EveryBody Ltd., Home Health Products, Karen's Nontoxic Products, The Living Source, 2nd Opinion, SelfCare Catalog, Simmons Handcrafts.*

Nature de France Deodorants (Nature de France). Aluminum and alcohol free. ☺ ⊗ *Amberwood, The Compassionate Consumer, EveryBody Ltd.*

Nature's Gate Deodorant Sticks (Levlad). Herbal or spice scent. ☺ ⊗ *EveryBody Ltd., Vegan Street.*

Orjene Natural Cosmetics Deodorant Sticks (Orjene Natural Cosmetics). No alcohol, aluminum salts, or artificial colors. Mint, citrus, and herbal scent. ☺ ⊗ *The Compassionate Consumer.*

Paul Penders Deodorant (Paul Penders). ☺ ⊗ *Basically Natural, InterNatural, My Brother's Keeper, Natural Lifestyle Supplies, Sunrise Lane*

Queen Helene Deodorants (Para Labs). Mint julep, vitamin E, and aloe vera, in stick form. ☺ ⊗ *EveryBody Ltd.*

Simple Anti-Perspirant (Simple Soap). Unscented. *The Living Source*

Tom's Natural Deodorants & Antiperspirants (Tom's of Maine). Deodorants in roll-on or stick. ☺ Ⓧ *Amberwood, The Compassionate Consumer, Ecco Bella, Eco-Choice, Humane Alternative Products, InterNatural, My Brother's Keeper, Naturally Ewe, Natural Lifestyle Supplies, Seventh Generation, Simply Delicious.*

Wysong Deodorant (Wysong Corporation). Natural fragrance. No aluminum or preservatives. ☺ Ⓧ *InterNatural, Wysong Corporation*

ASTRINGENTS & TONERS

Harmful ingredients: colors, ethanol, fragrance, glycerin.

HOMEMADE ALTERNATIVES
Instead of bottled astringent, try using the following:

• Vodka
• Club soda
• White vinegar
• Buttermilk, applied to skin and allowed to dry for ten minutes before rinsing

Here are a number of simple, homemade potions; after processing the ingredients, pour into a glass spray bottle and store under refrigeration.

• Boil dark-leaved lettuce leaves for ten minutes in enough water to cover. Let cool and strain.
• Brew strong chamomile or mint tea.
• Combine two-third cup pure water, two tablespoons vodka, and three-quarter cup borax in a blender until borax is dissolved.
• Blend two ounces lemon juice, two ounces lime juice, two ounces pure water, and one ounce vodka.

At the Store/By Mail
Check your local natural-food store for natural astringents.

❧ *Natural astringents and toners*
+ Alexandra Avery Toner (Alexandra Avery). Natural scent of biodynamically grown herbal ingredients. ☺ Ⓧ *Alexandra Avery, Earthen Joys, InterNatural*

+ Jeanne Rose Herbal BodyWorks. Vinegar-based herbal astringents using organically grown herbs when available. Beauty Without Cruelty Seal of Approval. ☺ Ⓧ

Aubrey Organics Herbal Facial Astringent/Facial Toner/Complexion Mist (Aubrey Organics). ☺ Ⓧ *The Allergy Store, Aubrey Organics, The Compassionate Consumer, Humane Alternative Products, InterNatural, Karen's Nontoxic Products, Natural Lifestyle Supplies.*

Earth Science Aloe Vera Complexion Toner & Freshener/Clarifying Herbal Astringent (Earth Science). ☺ Ⓧ *Earth Science, EveryBody Ltd.*

Home Health All-Natural Facial Moisturizing Mist/Natural Skin Freshener (Home Health Products). ☺ Ⓧ *Home Health Products.*

Kiss My Face Astringents & Toners (Kiss My Face). ☺ Ⓧ *Amberwood, Eco-Choice, EveryBody Ltd., Kiss My Face.*

Nature's Gate Toner (Levlad). ☺ *EveryBody Ltd.*

O'Naturel Floral Water (O'Naturel). Chamomile, rose, or lavender scent. ☺ Ⓧ *Amberwood, InterNatural.*

Paul Penders Men's Natural Skin Toner (Paul Penders). ☺ Ⓧ *InterNatural, My Brother's Keeper, Natural Lifestyle Supplies*

Tonialg Toning Lotion (Tonialg). Seaweed based; natural fragrance. ☺ Ⓧ *Eco-Choice, EveryBody Ltd.*

BATH PRODUCTS

Harmful ingredients: colors, detergents, ethanol, fragrance, glycerin, mineral oil.

Bubble-bath preparations present the greatest hazard of all bath products. The FDA receives many complaints about urinary-tract, bladder, and kidney infections, as well as genital injuries, skin rashes, and irritations that seem to have been caused by these products. This is particularly true for children, who have extrasensitive skin.

HOMEMADE ALTERNATIVES
• Add one of the following to a tubful of warm bathwater:

a half cup or more baking soda

one quart whole or skim milk

slices and juice of several lemons

a quarter cup white vinegar

juice of one large grapefruit

• Place five to ten chamomile, mint, or other type of tea bags in very hot water in the bathtub. Steep five to ten minutes and add the rest of the bath water at normal temperature.

• While standing in the bathtub, rub your entire body with your favorite warm oil. Scrape it off with a damp loofa sponge. Follow with a hot bath.

• Dissolve one cup honey in one cup boiling water; add two cups milk. Dissolve one half cup sea salt and two tablespoons baking soda in warm bathwater, and add honey/milk mixture.

At the Store/By Mail

⊕ *Earthwise bath products*

Alexandra Avery Bath Herbs (Alexandra Avery). Fragrant herbs and flowers to steep by the handful; grown biodynamically. ☺ ⊗ *Alexandra Avery, Earthen Joys*

Aphrodite's Bath Sponge (Alexandra Avery). Biodynamically grown herbs, ground oats, and almonds in a cotton muslin bag. Steep in the bag for a bath, or use as a soapless scrub in the shower. ☺ ⊗ *Alexandra Avery.*

Mountain Spirit. Herbal blends for the bath.

🌿 *Natural bath products*

+ Dr. Hauschka Bath Concentrates (Dr. Hauschka Cosmetics). Lavender,

lemon, rosemary, and pine. Essential oils; no detergents. ☺ ⊗ *InterNatural, Meadowbrook Herb Garden*

+ *Fluir Herbals.* Steam-distilled plant oils with almond and olive oils. ☺ ⊗ ⊞ Glass

+ *Jeanne Rose Herbal BodyWorks.* Herbal bath mixtures, using organically grown herbs when available. Also scented bath and body oils. Beauty Without Cruelty Seal of Approval. ☺

+ Jurlique Shower Gel (Jurlique). Plant materials grown organically. ☺ *Jurlique*

+ *Oak Valley Herb Farm.* Scented bath oils with herbs. ⊞ Amber glass bottles.

+ Speick Bath Skin Cleansers (Walter Rau Gmbh & Company Speickwerk). Plant oils with biological or biodynamically grown herbal extracts. Scented. ☺ ⊗ *Meadowbrook Herb Garden.*

+ Weleda Bath Oils (Weleda). Contain biodynamically grown herbs. ☺ ⊗ *Amberwood, EveryBody Ltd., InterNatural, Meadowbrook Herb Garden, Naturpath, Weleda.*

Abracadabra Bath Products (Abracadabra). Mineral bath salts combined with aloe vera. ☺ ⊗ *Amberwood, Earth Herbs, InterNatural*

Alba Botanica Sparkling Mint Body Bath (Alba Botanica Cosmetics). ☺ *EveryBody Ltd., InterNatural, Sunrise Lane*

Anton Hubner Therapeutic Bath Oils (Baudelaire). Up to 40 percent essential oils in a pure vegetable-oil base. ☺ ⊗ *Basically Natural, InterNatural.*

Aubrey Organics Bath Products (Aubrey Organics). Herbs, vitamins, and aloe vera in coconut oil. ☺ ⊗ *Aubrey Organics, The Compassionate Consumer, InterNatural, Karen's Nontoxic Products, My Brother's Keeper, Natural Lifestyle Supplies, Vegan Street.*

Aura Cacia Aromatherapy Bath Products (Aura Cacia). Scented with natural essential oils. ☺ ⊗ *Aura Cacia, InterNatural, Laren's Nontoxic Products.*

Bellmira Herbal Health Bath (Brant Corporation). Contains herbs from the Bavarian Alps. *Earth Herbs.*

Body Love Love Mitts (Body Love). Cotton pouches filled with herbs, grains, and essential oils to cleanse, soothe, and tone. ☺ ⊗ *The Compassionate Consumer, Earthen Joys.*

Earth Science Body Satin Bath Oil (Earth Science). ☺ ⊗ *Earth Science.*

Gregory's Mixable Bath Oils (Baudelaire). ⊗ *InterNatural.*

Kettle Care Products. Bath herbs. ☺ ☺

KSA Jojoba. Jojoba spray mist for after the shower.

Living Earth (Norimoor Company). Natural mineral bath from the world-famous Neydharting Spa of Austria.

Miracle of Aloe Aloe Bubble & Body Treatment (Aloe Products). Aloe-vera gel and herbal extracts including chamomile; gardenia scent. *Home Health Products.*

Mountain Rose Herbs. Bath herbs and mineral salts.

Natural Bodycare Aloe-Herb Body Wash for Bath and Shower (Natural Bodycare). *Earth Herbs.*

Nature's Gate Foaming Bath Oils (Levlad). ☺ *EveryBody Ltd.*

O'Naturel Bath & Shower Foams (O'Naturel). ☺ ⊗ *InterNatural.*

Olbas Bath Liquid (Penn Herb Company). Stimulates and invigorates painful muscles. ☺ *EveryBody Ltd., Meadowbrook Herb Garden.*

Patricia Allison Roman Oil Beauty Bath (Patricia Allison). ☺ *The Living Source.*

Paul Penders Bath Oil/Shower Gel (Paul Penders). High percentage of natural essential oils. ☺ ⊗ *Basically Natural, Carole's Cosmetics, The Compassionate Consumer, InterNatural, My Brother's Keeper, Natural Lifestyle Supplies.*

Queene Helene Batherapy (Para Labs). ☺ *EveryBody Ltd.*

Rainbow Bubble Bath (Rainbow Research Corporation). ☺ ⊗ *Amberwood, My Brother's Keeper, Vegan Street.*

Sunfeather Herbal Bath Products (Sunfeather Herbal Soap Company). Herb and mineral bath salts scented with essential oils. Also bath and facial herbs in a cotton bath pouch. ☺ ⊗ ✠ *Sunfeather Herbal Soap Company*

Tonialg Bath & Shower Products (Tonialg). Foaming bath gel; bath and shower gel. Seaweed based; natural fragrance. ☺ *Eco-Choice, EveryBody Ltd.*

BODY & MASSAGE OIL

Harmful ingredients: mineral oil, fragrance.

At the Store/By Mail

⊕ **Earthwise body and massage oils**

Avena Botanicals. Organically grown and wildcrafted sweet-scented herbs; organically grown cold-pressed olive-oil base.

Dr. Hauschka Body and Massage Oils (Dr. Hauschka Cosmetics). Oils of birch, chamomile, cowslip, eucalyptus, lavender, lemon balm, rose, rosemary, and more. ☺ ⊗ ✠ Glass.

Willow Rain Herbal Goods. Individual and combination essential oils for massage, bath, or body oil.

🌿 **Natural body and massage oils**

+ Alexandra Avery Massage Oils (Alexandra Avery). Biodynamically grown herbal ingredients. ☺ ⊗ *Alexandra Avery, Earthen Joys, InterNatural.*

+ Aubrey Organics Sea Herbal Massage Lotion (Aubrey Organics). ☺ ⊗ *Aubrey Organics, Humane Alternative Products.*

+ Jeanne Rose Herbal BodyWorks. Made of organically grown herbs, vegetable oils, and essential oils. ☺ ⊗

+ Jurlique Body Care Oil (Jurlique). Contains plant materials grown organically. ☺ Ⓧ *Jurlique*.

+ *Mountain Rose Herbs*. Herbal extracted oils for body and bath.

+ *Mountain Spirit*. Massage oils come unscented or scented with lavender, orange, amber, or orange-amber. Also herbal body oils for massage.

+ *Oak Valley Herb Farm*. Massage oils with herbs and spices. ✠

+ *Simple Wisdom*. Blend of organic essential oils. Contains lanolin. Handmade; highly concentrated. ☺

+ Speick Skin & Massage Oil (Walter Rau Gmbh & Company Speickwerk). Soy-oil base. Biological or biodynamically grown herbal extracts scented with essential oils ☺ Ⓧ *Meadowbrook Herb Garden*.

+ Weleda Body and Massage Oils (Weleda). Contain biodynamically grown herbs. ☺ Ⓧ *Amberwood, The Compassionate Consumer, Deer Valley Farm, EveryBody Ltd., Humane Alternative Products, InterNatural, Meadowbrook Herb Garden, My Brother's Keeper, Naturpath, Weleda*.

Aura Cacia Aromatherapy Massage & Bath Oils/Massage Butter (Aura Cacia). Scented with essential oils. Sweet almond oil comes unscented; can be scented with your choice of essential oils. ☺ Ⓧ *Aura Cacia, Earth Herbs, InterNatural*.

Bindi Massage and Body Oil (Pratima). *InterNatural*.

Cloudworks Body Oils (Cloudworks). Scented. ☺ Ⓧ *InterNatural*.

Community Soap Factory Pure Coconut Oil (Community Soap Factory). Unscented. ☺ Ⓧ *Vegan Street*.

Edgar Cayce Aura Glow Skin Lotion (Home Health Products). Scented and unscented. ☺ Ⓧ *Home Health Products, InterNatural*.

Egyptian Massage Oil (Home Health Products). ☺ Ⓧ *Home Health Products, InterNatural*.

Gregory's Skin Oils (Baudelaire). Pure fragrance in a blend of natural oils. ☺ Ⓧ *InterNatural*.

Kettle Care Products. Massage oils. ☺ Ⓧ

KSA Jojoba. Jojoba oil.

Patricia Allison Vitamin Massage Oil (Patricia Allison). ☺ Ⓧ *The Living Source*.

Rainbow Body & Massage Oils (Rainbow Research Corporation). Scented or unscented. Contains lanolin. ☺

Simmons Handcrafts. Almond and grapeseed oils, scented and unscented.

Swasthya Ayurvedic Massage Oils (Auromere). Ayuervedic herbs in a sesame-oil base. Natural scent of herbal ingredients. ☺ Ⓧ *Auromere*.

BODY POWDERS

Harmful ingredients: fragrance, talc.

HOMEMADE ALTERNATIVES

• Use cornstarch or oat powder.

• Mix ten ounces corn or rice starch with one ounce borax.

• Rinse and dry eggshells thoroughly, then crush to a fine powder in a blender or food processor.

At the Store/By Mail

Look for body powders at your natural-food store.

🌿 *Natural body powders*

+ *Jeanne Rose Herbal BodyWorks*. Herbal body powder contains herbs in an eggshell base, organically grown herbs when available. Beauty Without Cruelty Seal of Approval. ☺ ✠

+ Jurlique Silk Dust Powder (Jurlique). Plant materials grown organically in unpolluted, mineral-rich soil. ☺ *Jurlique*.

Alexandra Avery Moonsilk Body Powder (Alexandra Avery). Talcless powder made with arrowroot, baking soda, powdered sandalwood, myrrh, and spices.

☺ ⊘ *Alexandra Avery, Earthen Joys, InterNatural.*

Aura Cacia Natural Body Powders (Aura Cacia). Powdered herbs and essential oils in a cornstarch base. ☺ ⊘ *Amberwood, Aura Cacia, Basically Natural, Humane Alternative Products, InterNatural, Sunrise Lane, Vegan Street.*

Dr. Hauschka Body Powder (Dr. Hauschka Cosmetics). Pure ground silk. ☺ *Meadowbrook Herb Garden.*

Fluir Herbals. Arrowroot, white clay, orris root; lavender, rosemary oils. ☺ ⊘ ⊞ Cardboard container.

Herbomineral Ayurvedic Bathpowder (Auromere). ☺ ⊘ *Aura Cacia, Auromere.*

Kettle Care Products. Herbal body powder. ☺ ⊘

Nature de France White Clay Dusting Powder (Nature de France). ☺ ⊘ *Amberwood, The Compassionate Consumer.*

Sunfeather Herbal Soap After-Shower Flower Powder (Sunfeather Herbal Soap Company). Talc-free powder made of cornstarch, herbs, and essential oils. ☺ ⊘ ⊞ *Sunfeather Herbal Soap Company.*

Terra Flora Herbal Body Powder (Terra Flora). White clay; rose fragrance. ☺ ⊘ *InterNatural.*

CLEANSING GRAINS

Harmful ingredients: colors, fragrance, glycerin, mineral oil.

Homemade Alternatives

• Grind almond to a fine powder. Splash water on face and rub with a handful of almond powder. (Store powder in an airtight container.)

• Grind two tablespoons almonds in a blender or coffee grinder until crunchy. Add one or two teaspoons whole milk and a half teaspoon flour. Mix until a thick paste is formed. Rub into skin for a few minutes, then rinse. Also try adding a half teaspoon honey.

At the Store/By Mail

❧ *Natural cleansing grains*

Alba Botanica Gentle Body Smoother (Alga Botanica Cosmetics). ☺ *EveryBody Ltd., InterNatural, Sunrise Lane.*

Aubrey Organics Men's Stock Ginseng Face Scrub (Aubrey Organics). ☺ ⊘ *Aubrey Organics, Ecco Bella, Humane Alternative Products.*

Body Love Amazing Grains (Body Love). ☺ ⊘ *The Compassionate Consumer, Earthen Joys, InterNatural, My Brother's Keeper.*

Desert Essence Jojoba-Aloe Vera Facial Scrub (Desert Essence Cosmetics). Contains jojoba meal and oil. ☺ ⊘ *Desert Essence Cosmetics, Ecco Bella.*

Earth Science Mild Apricot Facial Scrub (Earth Science). ☺ ⊘ *Earth Science, EveryBody Ltd.*

Kettle Care Products. Facial scrubs for all skin types. ☺ ⊘

KSA Jojoba. Facial scrub with jojoba. ☺ ⊘

Mountain Rose Herbs. Cleansing grains containing almonds, white clay, ground oats, cornmeal, and pure herbal essence.

Nature's Gate Scrub (Levlad). ⊘ *EveryBody Ltd.*

CONTRACEPTIVES

Harmful ingredients: colors, ethanol, formaldehyde, fragrance, plastic (polyurethane).

Contraception is an important environmental issue because it is vital that we keep our population within the limits defined by the resources of the Earth. While populations are increasing worldwide, in this country we are maintaining our current population level. Because many contraceptive methods have unhealthful side effects, it's important to choose a method that is healthful as well as effective.

CONTRACEPTIVE METHODS

Oral Contraceptive Pills

Detailed warnings on possible side effects are required with every prescription of oral contraceptives in the United States. Symptoms can include weight gain, nausea, inflammation of the optic nerve (leading to loss of vision, double vision, and eye pains), headaches, depression, loss of sex drive, heart attacks, high blood pressure, birth defects, ectopic pregnancy, cancer, breast tumors, menstrual irregularities, postpill infertility, infections, and many others.

The FDA warns that the pill should be avoided by women who have or have had blood clots in their legs or lungs, have pains in their heart or have had a heart attack or stroke, know or suspect they have cancer of the breast or sex organs, have unusual vaginal bleeding that has not yet been diagnosed, or know or suspect they are pregnant. If you choose to take the pill, the FDA warns that you should be closely supervised by a doctor if you have a family history of breast cancer; have breast nodules, fibrocystic disease of the breast, or an abnormal mammogram; have diabetes; have high cholesterol; get migraine headaches; have heart or kidney disease; are frequently depressed; or if you smoke.

Intrauterine Devices (IUDs)

FDA-approved IUDs are made of polyethylene plastic infused with a small amount of barium. Some have added copper wires or synthetic progesterone. Since polyethylene is a weak carcinogen for rats, the possibility should not be ignored that IUDs may have a cancer-causing potential in humans. As of yet, no studies prove this.

Complications include increased menstrual flow coupled with heavy cramps and backaches, fatal infection, perforation of the uterus or cervix resulting in a possible hysterectomy, miscarriage (a 30 to 50 percent chance if pregnancy does occur), and ectopic pregnancy (which usually causes sterility when the IUD is surgically removed).

You should not use an IUD if you have had a recent pelvic infection or have had pelvic infections in the past, an abnormal Pap smear, an ectopic pregnancy, abnormal thickening of the uterine lining, rheumatic heart disease, diabetes, abnormal blood clotting, have taken medications that lower your resistance to infection, or do not have immediate access to emergency care.

Diaphragms

Can cause vaginal irritation, swelling, or blistering as an allergic reaction to the spermicide that must be used with them, or to the latex rubber from which they are made.

Condoms

Allergic reactions can occur from the latex rubber they are made of, or from the chemicals in the lubricants that most are treated with.

Vaginal Spermicides: Foam, Creams, Jellies, Suppositories, Foaming Tablets

Even though few side effects beyond irritation have been reported from the use of these contraceptives, there is a suspected correlation betweeen their use and a higher incidence of birth defects and spontaneous abortions requiring hospitalization. An FDA advisory review panel could find only a very few out-of-date studies that evaluated the safety of spermicides. No studies have assessed the direct effects of active spermicides on an unborn baby carried in the womb or on future generations through genetic mutation, nor have possible carcinogenic or toxic repercussions been examined. Inactive ingredients have not been evaluated at all.

Only active ingredients need to be listed on the labels of vaginal contraceptives, making it impossible for the consumer to know exactly what is contained in the product in addition to the spermicide. Inactive ingredients may include alcohol, benzethonium chloride, boric acid, butylparaben, formaldehyde, glycerin, methylbenzethonium chloride, methylparaben, methylpolysiloxane, perfume, preservatives, and propylparaben.

Contraceptive Sponges

Approved for general use by the FDA in June 1983, the contraceptive sponge (marketed under the name Today) is made of polyurethane plastic infused with Nonoxynol-9, the same active ingredient used in vaginal spermicides. Studies by the World Health Organziation showed a high frequency of cancerous conditions in mice given daily insertions of polyurethane-sponge tampons. The Consumer Federation of America recommends that the contraceptive sponge not be used until its safety is demonstrated through further testing. The FDA is monitoring the sponge because of reports linking it to toxic shock syndrome.

HOMEMADE ALTERNATIVES

Use one of the natural birth-control methods. Collectively called the fertility-awareness method or natural family planning, these approaches are increasingly being investigated by women who want to act more in harmony with the cycles of Nature within their own bodies and have the freedom to make love without chemicals of questionable safety. The Catholic church is now promoting natural family planning as a replacement for the less reliable rhythm method.

Natural birth-control methods are all based on abstinence during calculated fer-

tile times. Since it is much easier to determine when ovulation is actually occurring than it is to predict when it will occur, effectiveness for all methods increases if unprotected intercourse occurs only on the days *after* ovulation.

Fertile times can be determined in several ways. The Billings (or ovulation) method relies on vaginal mucus changes to signal hormonal changes A World Health Organization study showed that over 90 percent of women can learn to recognize their mucus changes within the first month. (Some women may have difficulties with this method if they have regular vaginal discharges due to chronic yeast infection.)

Changes of body temperature can also indicate fertile times. If you take your temperature each morning at the same time with a basal body thermometer and record it on a chart you will notice a slight rise following ovulation. When your temperature is .4 degrees higher for three days, you know ovulation has occurred. The problem is that other body changes (such as infection or allergic reaction) can also affect your temperature, so a change in temperature alone is not always an accurate indication that the fertile time has passed.

After several months of checking mucus and/or taking temperatures, many women notice subtle symptoms at the time of ovulation that they had not previously been aware of: mood change, skin oiliness or dryness, limp hair, weight gain. Natural birth control works best if you use as many indicators as possible to tell that your fertile time has passed.

Natural birth control is most effective when both partners understand the method thoroughly and cooperate in its practice. I recommend reading several books on the subject; best of all, take a class. Contact your local women's health clinic, or ask your doctor for more information.

At the Store/By Mail

If you need to use a contraceptive device, use condoms (unlubricated are preferable), or a diaphragm with an unscented contraceptive jelly. Both are available in drugstores.

Natural birth control

Naturpath. Ovulation package includes ovulation thermometer, fertility charts, and the book *Co-operative Method of Natural Birth Control*.

COSMETICS

Harmful ingredients: ammonia, BHA-BHT, colors, flavors, fragrance, glycerin, mineral oil, paraffin, plastics (nylon, PVP), saccharin, talc.

HOMEMADE ALTERNATIVES

• *Lip Gloss.* Melt a quarter cup beeswax in the top of a double boiler. Remove from heat and add one quarter cup castor oil, two tablespoons sesame oil, and two tablespoons liquid lanolin. Tint to desired shade with carmine, beet juice, or berry juice, or leave it clear. Pour into small jars and cool.

• *Lip Color.* Rub a piece of raw beet over your lips and cover with a clear gloss, if desired.

• *Blusher.* Rub a piece of raw beet over skin until desired shade is reached. This works best if beet color is applied to bare skin and powder is applied on top.

• *Face Powder.* In a dry skillet, brown oat flour, cornstarch, rice flour, or white clay to desired shade. Store in a tighly covered jar and apply with a cotton ball. Will be transparent when applied, but gives the skin a soft look and a smooth finish.

At the Store/By Mail

Unscented cosmetics containing a minimum of petrochemical derivatives are sold in natural-food stores and department stores. All the brands listed below are unscented, except as noted.

Natural blusher

+ *Oak Valley Herb Farm.* Mountain Rose Cheek Glow, made with alkanet root and safflower oil.

Dr. Hauschka Lip and Cheek Shades (Dr. Hauschka Cosmetics). Contain natural oils, colors, and beeswax. ⊞ ☺ *InterNatural, Meadowbrook Herb Garden.*

Ida Grae Creme Rouge (Nature's Colors). Contains beeswax and lanolin. ☺ ⊞ *The Allergy Store, Carole's Cosmetics, Earth Herbs, InterNatural, Karen's Nontoxic Products, Nature's Colors.*

Ida Grae Earth Rouge (Nature's Colors. Natural silicates and iron oxides. ☺ ⊗ ⊞ *The Allergy Store, Carole's Cosmetics, Earth Herbs, Humane Alternative Products, InterNatural, Karen's Nontoxic Products, Nature's Colors.*

Paul Penders Blusher (Paul Penders). ☺ ⊗ *Amberwood, The Compassionate Consumer, InterNatural, My Brother's Keeper, Natural Lifestyle Supplies, Sunrise Lane, Vegan Street.*

Natural makeup remover

Aubrey Organics Herbessence Makeup Remover and Complexion Oil (Aubrey Organics). ☺ ⊗ *Aubrey Organics, The Compassionate Consumer, Humane Alternative Products.*

Ecco Bella. Eye makeup remover pads.

Paul Penders Eye Makeup Remover (Paul Penders). ☺ *The Allergy Store, Amberwood, Basically Natural, Carole's Cosmetics, My Brother's Keeper, Natural Lifestyle Supplies, Sunrise Lane.*

Natural eyebrow pencils

Paul Penders Eyebrow Pencils (Paul Penders). ☺ ⊗ *The Allergy Store, Basically Natural, Carole's Cosmetics, The Compassionate Consumer, Earth Herbs, InterNatural, Karen's Nontoxic Products, My Brother's Keeper, Natural Lifestyle Supplies, Sunrise Lane.*

🐾 *Natural eyeshadow*

Dr. Hauschka Eyelid Tone (Dr. Hauschka Cosmetics). Contains beeswax and pigments derived from plants. ☺ ⊞ *Meadowbrook Herb Garden.*

Ida Grae Earth Eyes (Nature's Colors). ☺ ⊗ *The Allergy Store, Carole's Cosmetics, Earth Herbs, Humane Alternative Products, InterNatural, Karen's Nontoxic Products, My Brother's Keeper, Nature's Colors.*

Paul Penders Cream Eye Color (Paul Penders). ☺ ⊗ *The Allergy Store, Amberwood, The Compassionate Consumer, InterNatural, My Brother's Keeper, Natural Lifestyle Supplies, Sunrise Lane, Vegan Street.*

Viva Vera Aloe Soft Eye Color (Viva Vera). ☺ ⊗ *Amberwood.*

🐾 *Natural face powder*

Aubrey Organics Silken Earth (Aubrey Organics). Silk powder colored with earth minerals. ☺ *Aubrey Organics, Karen's Nontoxic Products.*

Ida Grae Earth Translucent Powder (Nature's Colors). Silk powder. ⊗ ⊞ *The Allergy Store, Earth Herbs, InterNatural, Karen's Nontoxic Products, Nature's Colors.*

🐾 *Natural foundation makeup*

Aubrey Organics Natural Translucent Base (Aubrey Organics). Translucent silk powder with aloe vera and henna. Scented with natural flower oils. ☺ *Aubrey Organics, Karen's Nontoxic Products.*

Dr. Hauschka Colored Day Creams (Dr. Hauschka Cosmetics). Made with natural oils and colors, plus beeswax and lanolin. ☺ *Meadowbrook Herb Garden.*

Ida Grae Creme Foundation (Nature's Colors). ☺ ⊗ ⊞ *The Allergy Store, InterNatural, Karen's Nontoxic Products, Nature's Colors*

Paul Penders Makeup Cream (Paul Penders). ☺ ⊗ *Amberwood, Carole's Cosmetics, The Compassionate Consumer, Humane Alternative Products, InterNatural,*

Karen's Nontoxic Products, My Brother's Keeper, Natural Lifestyle Supplies, Vegan Street.

Viva Vera Aloe Oil Free Foundation (Viva Vera). ☺ ⊗ *Amberwood*

🐾 *Natural lip products*

+ Jurlique Lip-Care Balm (Jurlique). Contains plant materials grown organically. ☺ *Jurlique.*

+ *Oak Valley Herb Farm.* Lip balm containing almond oil, beeswax, vitamin E, vanilla, and peppermint. Flavored.

+ *Special Foods.* Lip balms made with your choice of avocado, sunflower, cottonseed, coconut, olive, eucalyptus/sunflower, cottonseed, coconut, olive, alfalfa/soy, thistle/safflower, buckwheat, orange blossom/sesame, holly/grape, or honeydew/sunflower oils. ⊞

Alexandra Avery Lip Balm (Alexandra Avery). Contains natural oils, honey, and beeswax. ☺ *Alexandra Avery, Earthen Joys, InterNatural, Sunrise Lane.*

Aubrey Organics Lipsilks (Aubrey Organics). Lip balms with jojoba oil, wheatgerm oil, aloe vera, and vitamins. Cinnamon (red) or peppermint (clear). ☺ ⊗ *Aubrey Organics, Natural Lifestyle Supplies.*

Aubrey Organics Natural Lips (Aubrey Organics). Lip balms. Sun Protection Factor (SPF) 15. ☺ ⊗ *The Allergy Store, Amberwood, Aubrey Organics, Humane Alternative Products, Karen's Nontoxic Products.*

Autumn Harp Lip Balm (Autumn Harp). SPF 15. Flavored and unflavored. ☺ *The Compassionate Consumer.*

Autumn Harp Lip Sense (Autumn Harp). Lip balms. SPF 18. Flavored and jojoba aloe vera. ☺ *Ecco Bella, InterNatural, My Brother's Keeper, Natural Lifestyle Supplies, Sunrise Lane.*

Autumn Harp Ultra Care (Autumn Harp). ☺ *Carole's Cosmetics, Ecco Bella, InterNatural, Natural Lifestyle Supplies, Sunrise Lane.*

Desert Essence Jojoba–Aloe Vera Lip Balm (Desert Essence Cosmetics). Contains beeswax. ☺ *Desert Essence Cosmetics.*

Dr. Hauschka Lip and Cheek Shades (Dr. Hauschka Cosmetics). Contain natural oils, colors, and beeswax. ☺ ⊞ Glass.ʼ *InterNatural, Meadowbrook Herb Garden.*

Earth Science Lip Protector (Earth Science). ☺ ⊞ *Earth Science.*

Ednaʼs Lip Gloss with Comfrey/Aloe Vera (Ednaʼs). Made with plant oils, beeswax, essential oils, PABA, and cinnamon. *The Ecology Box.*

Erwinʼs Bee Farm. Beeswax lip balm with cold-pressed olive oil and vitamin E.

Fluir Herbals. Lip balm with an almond and wheat-germ-oil base. Four essential-oil scents. Contains beeswax.

Ida Grae Earth Eye/Lip Cream (Natureʼs Colors). Contains lanolin and beeswax. ☺ *The Allergy Store, Earth Herbs, InterNatural, Karenʼs Nontoxic Products, Natureʼs Colors.*

Kettle Care Products. Lip balm with almond oil, aloe, vitamin E, and beeswax. ☺

KSA Jojoba. Jojoba lip balm. Orange scent. ☺ Ⓧ

Lip Shtick Lip Balms (Lip Shtick). Blends of natural oils, beeswax, and natural flavor.

Mountain Ocean Lip Trip SPF-15 (Mountain Ocean). Lip balm. Contains beeswax and lanolin. ☺

Mountain Rose Lip Balm (Mountain Rose Herbs). Flavored or unflavored. Contains beeswax, honey, almond oil, and essential oils. *Mountain Rose Herbs, Simmons Handcrafts*

Paul Penders Lip Color/Lip Pencils (Paul Penders). ☺ Ⓧ *The Allergy Store, Amberwood, Basically Natural, Caroleʼs Cosmetics, The Compassionate Consumer, Earth Herbs, InterNatural, Karenʼs Nontoxic Products, My Brotherʼs Keeper, Natural Lifestyle Supplies, Sunrise Lane.*

Real Purity Lipstick (Real Purity). *Karenʼs Nontoxic Products.*

Viva Vera Lipmender (Viva Vera). Lip balm. ☺ Ⓧ *Amberwood.*

🐾 Natural mascara

Bare Escentuals Mascara (Bare Escentuals). May contain talc. *The Allergy Store.*

Paul Penders Mascara (Paul Penders). ☺ Ⓧ *The Allergy Store, Amberwood, Basically Natural, Caroleʼs Cosmetics, The Compassionate Consumer, InterNatural, Karenʼs Nontoxic Products, My Brotherʼs Keeper, Natural Lifestyle Supplies, Sunrise Lane, Vegan Street.*

Real Purity Mascara (Real Purity). *Karenʼs Nontoxic Products.*

DENTURE CLEANERS

Harmful ingredients: benzyl alcohol/sodium benzoate, colors, EDTA, isopropyl alcohol, plastic (PVP).

Warning labels:

"DANGER: injurious to eyes. Harmful if swallowed. Keep out of reach of children."

HOMEMADE ALTERNATIVES

• Soak dentures overnight in a mixture of a quarter teaspoon trisodium phosphate (TSP) and a half glass of water.

• Mix together thoroughly ten ounces TSP, five ounces sodium perborate, and five ounces salt. Soak dentures overnight in one quarter teaspoon of this mixture dissolved in one half glass of water.

• Mix five ounces TSP with seven drops essential oil of cinnamon by shaking them vigorously in a bottle until thoroughly blended. Soak dentures overnight in one quarter teaspoon of this mixture dissolved in one half glass of water. Rinse with plain water.

DOUCHES

Harmful ingredients: ammonia, colors, detergents, EDTA, fragrance, glycerin, phenol.

Douching commonly causes irritation, allergic reactions, and chemical vaginitis from the strong chemicals often used in the douche solutions. Douches can also affect external tissues, producing swelling, inflammation, and other symptoms of dermatitis. Toxic chemicals are easily absorbed through delicate vaginal skin.

An FDA advisory review panel says there is no need to douche and blames "tradition, ignorance, and commercial advertising" for the practice. Do, however, rinse the vaginal area with plain water regularly when bathing. Use a mild soap externally if desired, but do not use soap inside, as it may cause irritation for you or your sexual partner.

In addition, avoid clothes and undergarments that are tight and constricting in the crotch area. Wear cotton undergarments that absorb moisture and allow perspiration to evaporate.

If unusual genital odors, itching, or discharge develops, see your doctor; it could be a sign of a medical problem.

HOMEMADE ALTERNATIVES
• Use one- and-a-half teaspoons vinegar mixed in one quart water.
• Use one teaspoon baking soda mixed in one pint water.
• To ease itching, crush one garlic clove and add to one cup yogurt. Let set for several hours. Boil one cup water, add to yogurt, and shake until yogurt dissolves. Strain through cheesecloth to remove garlic, and apply.

At the Store/By Mail

☘ *Natural douches*
+ *Jeanne Rose Herbal BodyWorks.* Herbal douche using organically grown herbs when available. Beauty Without Cruelty Seal of Approval. ☺ ⊗

Bee Kind (Withers Mill Company). Douche with honey, aloe vera, myrrh, and yarrow. ☺ ⊗ *Allergy Resources, Beauty Naturally, Eco-Choice, Mountain Ark Trading Company, Naturally Ewe.*

Hygenia Cleansing Douche (Nature's Own). Natural douche with lactobacillus-acidophilus yogurt cells in a special medium of natural dry vinegar. Helps promote normal vaginal-flora balance. *Home Health Products.*

EYEDROPS

Harmful ingredients: ammonia, EDTA, glycerin.

HOMEMADE ALTERNATIVES
• Apply fresh, cold cucumber slices, chilled wet teabags, or grated raw potato wrapped in cotton gauze to closed eyelids.
• Dissolve one sixteenth teaspoon baking soda in one cup distilled water. Decant into glass dropper bottle.
• Dissolve seventh eighths teaspoon salt in one pint warm water. Decant into glass dropper bottle.

FACIALS

Harmful ingredients: colors, ethanol, fragrance, glycerin, talc.

HOMEMADE ALTERNATIVES

Facial Steam Bath
Boil two quarts water with two tablespoons fresh or dried herbs of your choice for five minutes. Pour into a large bowl. Drape a large towel over your head and put your face over the bowl, so that the towel forms a tent over you and the bowl. Allow the steam to penetrate your skin for five to ten minutes, then rinse with very cold water to close the pores.

Masks
Mix any of the following groups of ingredients, then prepare for the mask by cleansing your face and taking a facial

steam bath (see above), or by moistening your face and neck with warm water. Apply mask to skin, avoiding area around eyes; allow to dry for the specified time, then rinse with warm water, followed by cold water to close the pores, Masks should be freshly made for each use; if necessary, however, larger quantities of those masks containing produce items may be made in advance, then frozen into cubes and thawed as needed.

There are many recipes for facial masks; check your natural-food store for books on making your own beauty products and herbal recipes. Here are just a few recipes to try.

• Peel and slice half a cucumber. Place in blender or food processor and puree. Mix in one tablespoon yogurt. Leave on for 20 minutes.
• Puree a half cup fresh mint leaves and three ice cubes (made from pure water) in blender. Strain liquid and apply. Leave on until dry.
• Puree one ripe avocado in blender or food processor. Apply as is or combine with an equal amount of sour cream or yogurt, or a half cup honey and two tablespoons peanut or olive oil, or one teaspoon honey and the juice of half a lemon. Leave on for fifteen to thirty minutes.
• Make a smooth paste of oatmeal and water. Apply and leave on until it dries completely. Remove by rubbing off with your fingers. Rinse.
• Mix one tablespoon raw wheat germ with two tablespoons pure warm water, adding one egg yolk to form a heavy dough. Leave mask on for ten to fifteen minutes.

At the Store/By Mail

⊕ Earthwise facial steam baths

Alexandra Avery Facial Steam (Alexandra Avery). Natural scent of herbal ingredients grown biodynamically. ☺ Ⓐ *Alexandra Avery, Earthen Joys.*

Jurlique Facial Steam Bath Concentrate (Jurlique). Contains plant materials grown organically in unpolluted, mineral-rich soil. ☺ *Jurlique.*

Mountain Rose Herbs. Facial steam baths.

🌿 Natural masks and facial steam baths

+*Blue Corn Trading Company.* Facial masks traditionally used by Native Americans. Contain blue corn, herbs, and clays from sacred lands. ☺ Ⓐ

+ *Fluir Herbals.* Facial-sauna herbal mix. ☺ Ⓐ

+ *Jeanne Rose Herbal BodyWorks.* Herbal facial-steam mixtures, plus herbal facial masks in two types: a gritty, herbal oatmeal/clay mixture that can be used as a scrub, and a honey-based mixture that is used for massage or as a mask. Both made with organically grown herbs when available. Beauty Without Cruelty Seal of Approval. ☺ Ⓐ ⊞

+ *Oak Valley Herb Farm.* Aromatherapy facial kit contains facial waters, sauna, silk sponge, cosmetic clay, herbal soap, and instructions.

Simplers Botanical Herbal Facial Kit (Simplers Botanical Company). Herbal steam, oatmeal scrub, clay mask, and nutritive mask. Made with organically grown and wildcrafted herbs. ☺ Ⓐ *Mountain Rose Herbs, Simplers Botanical Company.*

Allergy Resources. Pure kaolin clay.

Aubrey Organics Amino Derm Gel/Jojoba Meal & Oatmeal Facial Scrub & Mask/Meal 'N Herbs/SeaClay (Aubrey Organics). ☺ Ⓐ *Amberwood, Aubrey Organics. The Compassionate Consumer, Humane Alternative Products, Karen's Nontoxic Products, Natural Lifestyle Supplies.*

Aztec Secret Mask (Aztec Secret Health and Beauty Products). Indian healing clay facial of pure sun-dried bentonite. ☺ Ⓐ *Aztec Secret Health and Beauty Products, Earth Herbs, InterNatural.*

Body Love Herbal Facial Steams (Body Love). ☺ ⊘ *The Compassionate Consumer, My Brother's Keeper.*

Desert Essence Jojoba–Aloe Vera Facial Mask (Desert Essence Cosmetics). French clay, jojoba oil, and honey. ☺ ⊘ *Desert Essence Cosmetics, Ecco Bella.*

Earth Science Mint Tingle Mask (Earth Science). ☺ ⊘ *Earth Science.*

Earthen Joys. Herbal facial steams. ☺ ⊘

Fluir Herbals. Almond facial mask with natural cosmetic sponge. ☺ ⊘ ⊞

Kiss My Face Daily Scrub/Weeky Masque (Kiss My Face). ☺ ⊘ *Eco-Choice, EveryBody Ltd., Kiss My Face, My Brother's Keeper.*

Magick Mud (Magick Mud). ☺ ⊘ *InterNatural.*

Nature de France French Green Clay Powder/French Rose Clay Mask Powder (Nature de France). Pure, natural clay in superfine powder form. Unscented. ☺ ⊘ *Amberwood, EveryBody Ltd.*

Nature's Gate Mask (Levlad). ☺ ⊘ *EveryBody Ltd.*

Pascalite. Pure, cream-colored clay containing natural antibiotics. ☺ ⊘

Skin Zyme/Clean Zyme (Enzyme Health & Beauty Products of Hawaii). Mask for removing spent cells and encouraging new cell activity, made of green-papaya concentrate. ☺ ⊘ *Beauty Naturally.*

Suncare Facial Masque (Sunrider International). Redmond clay, flower essence, and chrysanthemum. ☺ ⊘ *Allergy Resources.*

Tonialg Exfoliating Masque (Tonialg). Seaweed-based; natural fragrance. ☺ ⊘ *Eco-Choice, EveryBody Ltd.*

FEMININE PROTECTION

Harmful ingredients: formaldehyde fragrance, plastics (acrylonitrile, polyester).

Over 20 percent of the respondents in a *Consumer Reports* magazine survey had been warned by their doctors not to use deodorant tampons or pads. Even people who are not normally sensitive to perfume can, over time, develop irritations from or allergic reactions to these deodorant scents. Bleached paper in the pads may contain dioxin.

All brands of tampons have, in addition, been associated with toxic shock syndrome, so approach the use of any tampon with caution.

SPECIAL TIPS

• Use reusuable menstrual pads made from cotton. Reusable pads are less convenient since they have to be washed, and since they obligate you to carry soiled or damp pads with you when you are away from home, but they don't pile up in land-fills or waste resources in their manufacture and they feel much softer next to your skin. You can make your own, or purchase them in natural-food stores or by mail.

• Use small, soft, natural sea sponges, which can be inserted like a tampon. The main disadvantage is that they tend to leak during a heavy flow if left in too long. They can be rinsed and reinserted, and must be sterilized often.

Federal regulations prohibit the marketing of sponges "to insert into the body," so you will not find any sponges that suggest they be used as a tampon. If you choose to use sponges for this purpose, there are a few precautions to take. First, prepare the sponge by rinsing it several times in clean running water, and then sterilize it by dropping it into a pot of boiling water, letting it boil for thirty seconds, and allowing it to sit in the water for a minute after turning off the heat.

Always wash your hands before removing or inserting the sponge. After removal, rinse the sponge well and squeeze it dry. It can then be reinserted. Store your sponge between periods in a clean, airy location. Do not put a damp sponge in a plastic or airtight container. If your sponge develops an odor, soak it overnight in a solution of white vinegar and water. Sponges should be resanitized before each period.

Frequent removal and rinsing of your sponge is recommended, as is alternating use with napkins. If the sponge is too big and fits too tightly, it can be cut to size. If it is too small, you may need two sponges. If you have trouble removing your sponge, tie a piece of silk thread or dental floss around the sponge to help pull it out.

At the Store/By Mail

Use a pad or tampon made with natural fibers. In a study reported in the *American Journal of Obstetrics and Gynecology,* it was found that the presence of synthetic fibers dramatically increased the production of the bacterium that causes toxic shock syndrome, and that bacterium production *decreased* when cotton fibers were used.

With the exception of tampons, which are readily available in supermarkets and drugstores, feminine-protection products made from natural fibers may be hard to find. Ask your local natural-food store to carry them, or order them by mail. Suitable small sponges may be available at both shops and import stores.

🍃 Natural menstrual pads

Arco Iris. The original washable and reusable all-cotton menstrual pad. Handmade of highly absorbent layered white cotton flannel inside a white soft cotton knit sleeve. Hand quilted to retain its shape. With proper care will last two years or longer. Three sizes. ⊘

Seventh Generation. Pads and liners made with a new technology that requires

half the trees generally needed to make these items. Bleached with hydrogen peroxide. ⊞

🌐 Nontoxic menstrual pads

New Cycle Menstrual Pads (New Cycle). Cotton; three sizes. Red on red, or red on pink roses. *New Cycle.*

🍃 Natural tampons

Note: Manufacturers are not required by law to list tampon ingredients. The information listed here has appeared publicly in articles and advertisements. These are the only unscented brands that are made from natural fibers and claim to be chemically untreated.

Kotex Security Tampons (Kimberly-Clark Corporation). Cotton and rayon in a plastic applicator. "No superabsorbent materials."

O.B. (Johnson & Johnson). Cotton and rayon.

Tampax Original Regular Tampons (Tambrands). All cotton.

FIRST AID

Warning label:

"WARNING: Keep this and all medications out of the reach of children. In case of accidental overdose, contact a physician or poison-control center immediately. As with any drug, if you are pregnant or nursing a baby seek the advice of a physicain before using this product."

Our medicine chests are filled with first-aid items to grab for a cut finger or to take for a headache. While some of these are as harmless as a cotton swab, others are over-the-counter drugs: pain killers, antacids, allergy medicines, cough syrups, laxatives, sleeping pills . . . you name it.

The biggest danger with most of these drugs is the risk of accidental poisoning from overdose. Children are attracted to brightly colored pills and can easily and quickly consume too many.

And many over-the-counter drugs have dangerous side effects. I'm not going to get into listing them here, but if you are taking one on a regular basis, or are considering taking one, you might want to go to the library and look it up in the *Physician's Desk Reference* a guide to over twenty-five hundred popular pharmaceuticals. Another good reference is *The Essential Guide to Nonprescription Drugs* by David R. Zimmerman, which is written more for the layperson.

Only the active ingredients are required to be listed on the labels of over-the-counter drugs and medications. Most contain other ingredients that you may not want in your body, such as alcohol, caffeine, artificial colors and flavors, sugar, saccharin, preservatives, and many other useless and possibly harmful ingredients: there is no way of knowing if these additives are in the product.

Since 1962, the FDA has been reviewing the active ingredients used in over-the-counter drugs and has found in many cases that, while they may be safe, *they are not effective at doing what the consumer believes the drug is supposed to do.* The most common over-the-counter drugs taken are pain killers for headaches, yet an FDA investigation found that over-the-counter pain relievers are inappropriate to treat the cause of nine out of ten headaches. They are appropriately used to treat a headache caused by a fever or a hangover—not for migraine or hypertension headaches or headaches caused by inflammation or anxiety, worry, depression, or other emotional states.

First-aid products are meant to provide *temporary* relief for *minor* ailments on an *occasional* basis, and not to be used regularly. "If symptoms persist, see your doctor," say the labels. You may have a serious illness.

Symptoms are signals from our body that something is wrong and that our body is doing something about it. When we run a fever, our body is heating up to kill germs; we cough to clear our lungs; a headache may be a sign that we are under too much stress and should take more leisure time for ourselves.

To be more comfortable while your body is healing itself, there are some natural things you can do.

The oldest form of medicine, as well as the basis of modern pharmacology, is the use of herbs and plants. Herbs and medicinal plants can be taken in many forms, including tinctures (the most concentrated form, usually in an alcohol base), teas, pills, and pressed juices for internal use, and ointments and shampoos for external use.

Homeopathic remedies are another choice. Homeopathy is a medicinal system that stimulates our own innate healing and immune processes by using the energetic essences of plant, mineral, and animal substances captured by a water-based pharmaceutical process. One of the main principles of homeopathy is that like cures like, which means that a substance that creates a specific set of symptoms in a healthy person when given in a large dose will cure similar symptoms in a sick person when given in a specially prepared minute dose. Almost every pharmacy in France carries homeopathic medicines, and in Germany 16,000 physicians use this medically recognized system.

When you need more extensive health care, consider exploring alternative therapies that can be used either alone or in conjunction with modern medical practices. Acupuncture, ayuvredic medicine, chiropractic, bodywork, and many other holistic modalities are worth looking into.

While most insurance companies don't support alternative health services, there are many that do give discounts to non-smokers. And there are a couple that pay for chiropractic and acupuncture. Contact *Alternative Health Insurance Service* and *Co-op America Health Insurance* for more information.

HOMEMADE ALTERNATIVES

Cuts and Scratches
Run under cold water to stop bleeding, then dab on a little honey and cover with a bandage.

Constipation
• Check out what you're eating. A diet of fresh whole foods should digest right through.
• Take large doses of vitamin C.
• Take psyllium seed, the active ingredients in drugstore laxatives (available at your natural-food store).

Diarrhea
Let everything in your intestines come out; your body probably wants to get rid of something you put in it. Sip warm water to keep from getting dehydrated.

Fever
• First decide if you really want to lower the fever (if it's over 102 degrees it requires immediate medical attention). In many cases fever can be beneficial, as it can enhance the ability of your white blood cells to kill germs. If you reduce the fever prematurely, you're interfering with your body's natural healing process and it might take longer for you to get well.
• Put a cold washcloth on your forehead and keep replacing it with a new one as it absorbs heat from your skin. For a serious fever, overall sponging of the body with cool water, taking a cool bath or shower, or wrapping the patient in a wet sheet for short periods of time will help.
• Add hot red cayenne pepper to food or drink, or fill a couple of gelatin capsules with cayenne and take them with a glass of water.
• Drink a tea of boneset, yarrow, vervain, or barberry leaves.
• Drink lots of water with lemon juice.

Headaches
• Drink a cup of strong peppermint tea and take a short nap. Or try tea made from rosemary, catnip, or sage.
• Gently massage the area where the ache is.
• Relax your head by letting your neck droop forward, then turning it gently in large circles.
• Lie in a warm bath with a cold washcloth on your head to draw the blood (and the pain) away from your head.
• If you have persistent headaches, they might be due to food allergies or a toxic chemical in your home, car, or office. Try changing your diet and removing potentially toxic things.

Insomnia
• Determine if you really have insomnia. Perhaps your body doesn't need a full eight hours's sleep. If you stay awake because something is bothering you or you are under a lot of stress, handle the problem or learn to relax.
• Drink a cup of chamomile tea. Other herbs known to relax you into sleep are valerian root, hops, passionflower, catnip, basil, and lemon verbena.
• Use all-cotton bed sheets. Polyester/cotton sheets are coated with formaldehyde, which is a substance known to cause insomnia.

Poison Ivy
Reduce the effects of poison ivy by prompt treatment after exposure. As soon as pos-

sible, wash the area that came into contact with the plant with copious amounts of cold water; using a small amount of water could just spread the oil, and warm water allows the oil to penetrate more and speeds up the body's reaction. Don't use soap; it removes skin lipids that offer some protection against the oil.

Sore Throat
• Suck on any type of hard candy. Check your natural-food store for those sweetened with honey, rice syrup, or other natural sweeteners.
• My old family recipe for coughs, sore throat, and laryngitis: slice a whole yellow onion in a bowl, cover it with lots of honey, then put a plate on top of the bowl and let it sit. After a few hours, the onion will release its juice. Take a couple of teaspoons of this juice every few hours until cured (this generally works in less than twenty-four hours).

Stomach Upsets
• Drink ginger ale.
• Drink raspberry-leaf or basil tea.

At the Store/By Mail

☘ *Natural first-aid products*
    Avena Botanicals. Healing oils and salves made from certified organically grown and wildcrafted herbs in organically grown cold-pressed olive oil. For relief of minor cuts, skin irritations, burns, abrasions, bruises, stressed muscles, earache, and diaper rash. ☺ Ⓧ ⊞
    + *Bioforce Herbal Cough Syrups and Drops* (Bioforce of America). From organically grown or wildcrafted herbs. ☺ Ⓧ *Bioforce of America*
    + *Dry Creek Herb Farm.* Herbal balms, and oils hand made with organically grown and wildcrafted herbs.
    + *Fluir Herbals.* Wildflower salve; non-greasy, with a minty fragrance. Contains

beeswax. Also a vapor/rub balm for chest and nasal congestion that contains pure spice oils in a base of olive oil and beeswax. ☺ ⊞
    + *Mountain Spirit.* Herbal salves, tinctures, and essential oils.
    + *Oak Valley Herb Farm.* Sierra Wonder Salve, with nine healing herbs.
    Alfalco Alfalfa Tonic (Boericke & Tafel). A homeopathic tonic to tone your system, relieve mental fatigue, and induce quiet, restful sleep. ⊞ Glass. *Auro Trading Company, Boerike & Tafel.*
    Arnica Ointment (Boiron Borneman). For muscle aches and pains. *Boiron Borneman, SelfCare Catalog.*
    Arniflora Arnica Gel/Lotion/Ointment/Oil (Boericke & Tael). Homeopathic pain relief for muscle and joint pain and swelling, and black and blue marks from bruises, injuries, blows, and accidents. ⊞ *Auro Trading Company, Boerike & Tafel, Ecco Bella, InterNatural.*
    Aubrey Organics Calal (Aubrey Organics). Calamine-aloe lotion to soothe rashes, burns, and bites. Contains collagen. ☺ *Aubrey Organics.*
    Aubrey Organics NSR Natural Sports Rub (Aubrey Organics). Herbs and vitamins specially chosen to heal, calm, and reduce inflammation; blended in a coconut-oil base. ☺ Ⓧ *Aubrey Organics.*
    Boericke & Tafel Cough & Bronchial Syrup (Boericke & Tafel). Homeopathic relief for cough and bronchial irritation. Ⓧ *Boericke & Tafel.*
    Calendula Ointment (Boiron Borneman). Natural antibacterial for skin irritations, burns and rashes. *Boiron Borneman, SelfCare Catalog.*
    Califlora Calendula Gel/Cream/Lotion/Oil/Ointment (Boericke & Tafel). Homeopathic skin protectants for minor cuts, wounds, burns, and scrapes, as well as sunburn, windburn, and dry, chapped skin. ⊞ *Auro Trading Company, Boericke & Tafel, Ecco Bella, InterNatural.*

The Charis Company. First-aid kits that include Chinese herbal formulas in pill form and homeopathic remedies.

Cloudworks Green Gold Herbal Salve (Cloudworks). With comfrey, calendula, plantain, goldenseal, and vitamin E in a pure olive-oil base. Contains beeswax. ☺ *InterNatural*.

Desert Essence Tea-Tree Oil (Desert Essence Cosmetics). Safe, effective germicide, fungicide, and antiseptic. ☺ Ⓐ *Desert Essence Cosmetics, Earth Herbs, Ecco Bella, Mountain Ark Trading Company*.

Deva Magic Herbal First-Aid Kit (Deva Magic). Contains heal-all salve, swelling salve, bleeding powder (to stop bleeding), antiseptic tincture, tincture for bites and stings, burn gel, bandage strips, gauze pads, and metal tweezers. Comes in cotton carrying case. *Deva Magic*.

Ear Candles (Bobalee Originals). For removing wax build-up from the ear. *Quality Health Products*.

Eucalyptamint Ointment (Naturopathic Laboratories). The active ingredients are natural menthol and eucalyptus oil. Contains lanolin. For pain, and muscle aches and strains. *SelfCare Catalog*.

Home Health Products. A variety of herbal and homeopathic remedies.

InterNatural. A good selection of first-aid ointments, creams, and herbal and homeopathic remedies.

Karen's Nontoxic Products. Everything from basic medicine-chest supplies to Chinese herbs and homeopathic medicines.

Kettle Care Products. Herbal muscle rub. ☺ Ⓐ

KSA Jojoba. Jojoba propolis, an ointment-type product that contains propolis, a substance that bees use at the opening of the hive to sterilize anything entering it. ☺ Ⓐ

Longevity Pure Medicines (Longevity Pure Medicines). Homeopathic medicines for pain, colds, sore throat, headache, etc. *Longevity Pure Medicines*.

Olbas Cough Syrup/Oil/Pastilles/Pocket Inhaler/Salve (Penn Herb Company). *EveryBody Ltd., Meadowbrook Herb Garden*.

Red Tiger Balm (Prince of Peace Enterprises). Analgesic salve from China. ☺ Ⓐ *Simmons Handcrafts*.

Rhus Toxicondendron (Boericke & Tafel). Homeopathic relief for poison ivy. *Boericke & Tafel*.

SelfCare Catalog. A collection of tools to help you take charge of all aspects of your health. Includes self-tests, natural remedies, home health-care products, and informative books.

SSSStingStop Soothing Gel (Boericke & Tafel). Homeopathic relief for insect bites and stings—plus an all-natural insect repellent. *Auro Trading Company, Boericke & Tafel, Ecco Bella, InterNatural, Meadowbrook Herb Garden*.

Thursday Plantation Tea-Tree Oil/Antiseptic Cream (Teaco International). Powerful bactericide that kills a broad spectrum of bacteria and some stubborn fungi such as candida and athlete's foot. Safe for healthy tissue, and doesn't inhibit normal cell growth and rejuvenation. Also a natural solvent that will disperse pus in pimples or infected wounds, and neutralize the venom of most minor insect bites. Fragrance free. *InterNatural, Karen's Nontoxic Products, Teaco International*.

Triflora Analgesic Gel (Boericke & Tafel). Homeopathic relief from chronic muscle and joint pain. ⊞ *Auro Trading Company, Boericke & Tafel, InterNatural*.

Zand HerbaLozenge (McZand Herbal). Herbal cough drops sweetened only with natural rice syrup. *Karen's Nontoxic Products*.

⊕ Nontoxic first-aid products

Ivy Shield (Interpro). Skin cream that helps prevent poison-ivy and poison-oak dermatitis by forming an insoluble layer over the skin. Doesn't wash off with water or perspiration, but wears off after about twelve hours. *Interpro*.

Tecnu Poison Oak-N-Ivy Cleanser (Tecnu Enterprises). Prevents and relieves allergic reactions to poison oak and poison ivy. *The Kinsman Company, Nichols Garden Nursery, SelfCare Catalog.*

⊕ **Earthwise herbal remedies**

Avena Botanicals. Wildcrafted and certified organic herbs extracted into pure grain alcohol. More than fifty simple extracts, plus healing-compound extracts and extracts for women.

Bio-Botanica Herbal Extracts (Bio-Botanica). Low-alcohol and no-alcohol wildcrafted herbal extracts. All kosher certified. *Earth Herbs, Penn Herb Company.*

Bioforce Herbal Extracts (Bioforce of America). From organically grown or wildcrafted herbs. *Bioforce of America.*

Blessed Herbs. Fresh bulk herbs, cut and sifted, or powdered.

Dial Herbs. Full range of herbal tinctures and tablets, all organically grown or wildcrafted. Offers special veggie tabs, a combination of twenty-seven herbs and vegetables.

Earth Essences (Botanical Pharmaceuticals). Ninety-eight different herbal tinctures available generally, plus sixty-six others by special order. Imported from the United Kingdom. *Botanical Pharmaceuticals.*

Eclectic Herbs (Eclectic Institute). Freeze-dried organically grown herbs. *The Ecology Box.*

Flora Laboratories Herb Extracts (Flora Laboratories). Prepared from fresh, undried herbs whenever possible. Herbs are either wildcrafted or grown organically. *Trinity Herb.*

Gaia Herbs. Extracts of herbs that are either ecologically wildcrafted or certified organically grown in pollution-free environments. Hand-harvested during the appropriate season and at the proper time of day to insure maximum effectiveness.

Herb-Pharm Herbal Tinctures (Herb-Pharm). All herbs are wildcrafted or or-

ganically cultivated. *Herb-Pharm, Mountain Rose Herbs.*

Herbalist & Alchemist. Over one hundred herbal extracts, oils, and ointments, all organically grown or wildcrafted. Also Chinese herbs and traditional tea blends that are not fumigated when entering the U.S.

Mountain Ark Trading Company. Herbal extracts from the Ozarks. Wildcrafted or organically grown.

Mountain Rose Herbs. A full list of herbs, many organically grown or wildcrafted. Also has books and videos about herbs.

Nature's Herbs Certified Organic Herbs (Nature's Herbs).

Nature's Way Herbs/Herbal Medicines (Nature's Way Products). Large selection of single and combination herbs—mostly in capsules, some in bulk. Organically grown or wildcrafted herbs are clearly labeled. *Earth Herbs, The Ecology Box, Nature's Way Products.*

Rainbow Light Herbal Concentrates (Rainbow Light Nutritional Systems). Extracts prepared from fresh, undried herbs whenever possible. Herbs either wildcrafted or organically grown. *Trinity Herb.*

Rainbow Light Native Herb Liquid Extracts (Rainbow Light Nutritional Systems). *Sun Mountain.*

2nd Opinion. Organically grown or wildcrafted Brazilian herbs, liquid extracts, and teas.

Simplers Botanical Liquid Compound Formulas & Single Plant Extracts (Simplers Botanical Company). Liquid herbal concentrates from organic and wildcrafted herbs—simples and compounds, infusions in organic olive oil. ☺ ⊗ *Mountain Rose Herbs, Simplers Botanical Company, Trinity Herb.*

Trinity Herb. Organically grown herbal extracts.

Trout Lake Farm. Dried medicinal herbs (leaves, flowers, roots) certified organically grown or wildcrafted.

Willow Rain Herbal Goods. Organically grown and wildcrafted herbal tinctures and salves.

🌺 Natural herbal remedies

+ *Jeanne Rose Herbal BodyWorks.* Herbal-tea blends and an herbal medicinal oil made from sixty-five herbs that is effective for cuts, scratches, burns, itches, and hurts. Also an herbal inhaler for stuffy nose and headache. All made from organically grown herbs when available. Beauty Without Cruelty Seal of Approval. 😃

+ *Oak Valley Herb Farm.* Fresh herbal extracts and medicinal tea blends made from fresh plants. ⊞ Extracts in glass bottles.

+ *Terra Firma Botanicals.* Individual herbal tinctures, combination tinctures, herbs in glycerine, and flower oils—all made with organically grown or wildcrafted herbs. 😃 Ⓐ

🌺 Homeopathic remedies

Boericke & Tafel Home Medicine Chest (Boericke & Tafel). Twenty-eight homeopathic remedies for common family health problems. Comes complete with home medical guide that gives instructions for using homeopathy. *Boericke & Tafel.*

Boericke & Tafel Homeopathic Remedies (Boericke & Tafel). For every type of bodily discomfort. ⊞ *Auro Trading Company, Boericke & Tafel.*

BHI Homeopathic Remedies (Biological Homeopathic Industries). A full range of homeopathic medicines.

Bioforce Homeopathic Medicines (Bioforce of America). From organically grown or wildcrafted herbs. *Bioforce of America.*

Boiron Borneman Homeopathic Kits (Boiron Borneman). Homeopathic remedies and kits, cell salts, and books. *Auro Trading Company Boiron Borneman, SelfCare Catalog.*

Ellon Bach Homeopathic Remedies (Ellon Bach USA). Exclusive representa-

tive for the Bach Centre in England. The Bach remedies were developed over fifty years ago by a renowned British physician and scientist, Dr. Edward Bach. Strictly homeopathic remedies, they contain the essence of flowers in a small percentage of alcohol to prevent spoilage. *Ellon Bach USA, InterNatural.*

Homeopathic First-Aid Kits (Boiron Borneman). *Auro Trading Company, Boiron Borneman, SelfCare Catalog.*

Hyland's Homeopathic Products (Standard Homeopathic Company). A full line of homeopathic remedies and cell salts. *Auro Trading Company, Standard Homeopathic Company.*

Similasan Homeopathic Remedies (Similasan Corporation).

FRAGRANCES

Harmful ingredients: aerosol propellants, benzyl alcohol, colors, ethanol, formaldehyde, fragrance (synthetic and natural), glycerin, phenol, trichloroethylene.

There has been very little scientific study of the health effects of synthetic fragrances beyond their ability to cause skin irritation. Nevertheless, many people report a variety of ill effects.

Use essential oils for a natural scent. But please use them *sparingly* for the benefit of those who are sensitive to all fragrances. There are three types of essential oils:

1. Natural—from a plant source; the fragrance is that of the plant (for example, a lemon yielding a lemon scent).
2. Synthetic—from a plant source; the fragrance is different from that of the plant (for example, a geranium yielding a lemon scent).
3. Artificial (also called "perfume oil")—from petrochemicals.

When buying essential oils, make sure they have been obtained from natural plant sources. All natural essential oils are made from plants that have not been sprayed with pesticides.

Essential oils are usually removed by steam distillation. Those labeled "true," "absolute," or "concrete" are pure oils; extracts and tinctures have had grain alcohol added; and extended oils contain dipropylene glycol or diethyl phthalate (a plasticizer).

Caution: Use essential oils carefully, as they are extremely potent. Do not apply directly to skin without dilution, and do not apply to mucous-membrane areas at all.

HOMEMADE ALTERNATIVES

To make perfume, add a few drops of essential oil to one ounce of vegetable oil or vodka (100 proof if possible).

At the Store/By Mail

⊕ **Earthwise essential oils**

Alexandra Avery Perfumes (Alexandra Avery). *Alexandra Avery, Earthen Joys, Sunrise Lane.*

Aroma Vera. Essential oils extracted by steam distillation or scarification from wildcrafted or organically grown plants as much as possible ⊞

Aura Cacia Essential and Perfume Oils (Aura Cacia). ☺ ⊘ *Aura Cacia, InterNatural, Vegan Street.*

Bindi Essential Oil (Pratima). Created from Eastern Indian recipes ultilizing the principles of ayurvedics, an ancient Eastern Indian system of living in harmony with nature. ⌶ Glass bottle. *Earth Herbs, InterNatural.*

Ida Grae Earth Fragrance (Nature's Colors). Solid perfume made with flower essences and colors. Contains beeswax and lanolin. ⊘ ⊞ *Nature's Colors.*

Jeanne Rose Herbal BodyWorks. Aromatherapy oils containing organically grown herbs when available. ☺ ⊞

KSA Jojoba. Natural perfumes containing jojoba oil instead of animal products. ☺ ⊘ ⊞ Glass bottle.

Madini Oriental Perfume Essences (Talisman). Exotic essential oils made by the Madini family of Tangiers. Recipes have been passed down for four hundred years. ⊞ Glass. *Carole's Cosmetics, Talisman.*

Mountain Rose Herbs. Pure essential oils. ⊞

Oak Valley Herb Farm. A wide offering of essential oils. ⊞

Original Swiss Aromatics (Original Swiss Aromatics). Essential oils that are wildcrafted or organically cultivated in Switzerland. Ask for organic-product list. ⊡ *Original Swiss Aromatics.*

Santa Fe Perfume Oils (Santa Fe Fragrance Company). Botanically pure perfume oils. *Karen's Nontoxic Products, Santa Fe Fragrance Company.*

Simplers Botanical Company. Organically grown or wildcrafted essential oils. ⊞

HAIRBRUSHES & COMBS

Harmful ingredients: plastics (nylon PVC/vinyl chloride, and others).

At the Store/By Mail

Choose hairbrushes with wood handles and natural bristles, and use wood combs. Not only are they natural, but they are free of the static electricity produced by plastic brushes and combs.

🌸 *Natural-bristle hairbrushes and wooden combs*

Brooks Wooden Comb (Traditional Products Company). Traditional Oriental comb. *Earth Herbs, Janice Corporation, Natural Lifestyle Supplies, Traditional Products Company.*

Fuller Brush. A variety of natural boar-bristle brushes for men and women, hand sanded and hand finished. Also genuine

French combs of Australian and Argentine horn.

InterNatural. Italian combs made of ash wood.

Karen's Nontoxic Products. Wooden and cow-horn combs from China.

Mother Hart's Natural Products. All-natural boar-bristle brushes with hardwood handles, made in China.

Sierra Legacy. Handmade hardwood combs. Fourteen different wood varieties.

Simmons Handcrafts. Handmade hardwood combs from China.

Widu Wooden Bristle Brushes (DCM Industries). Ash handles; wooden bristles set in rubber cushions. Antistatic. *InterNatural, Karen's Nontoxic Products.*

HAIR COLOR

Harmful ingredients: ammonia, colors, detergents, EDTA, ethanol, fragrance, glycols, lead, mineral oil, sulfur compounds.

Warning labels:

"WARNING: Contains an ingredient that can penetrate your skin and has been determined to cause cancer in laboratory animals." (Proposed FDA warning that does not appear on hair-dye labels because of loopholes in regulations.)

The FDA has no jurisdiction over hair dyes, which are mutagenic and suspected human carcinogens. Many hair-dye chemicals, which can easily penetrate the scalp and enter the bloodstream, are not even tested for safety. One study suggests that women over the age of fifty who have used hair dyes for ten or more years have an increased risk of breast cancer.

Medical consultants for *Consumer Reports* magazine recommend that women avoid hair dyes entirely when pregnant or of childbearing age.

If you must use chemical dyes, *Consumer Reports* has some tips to help minimize the risk: don't use hair dyes more often than necessary, don't leave the dye on your head for any longer than necessary, flood your scalp thoroughly with water afterward, use a technique that involves minimal contact between the dye and your scalp, and put off using any hair dye to as late in life as possible.

HOMEMADE ALTERNATIVES

Use henna, the dried powdered leaves of a small tree native to southwest Asia and north Africa. Many different shades of this natural coloring agent are available to darken or highlight. Henna gives hair a semipermanent protein coating, protecting it from sun damage and air pollution; it washes out gradually over a six-month period.

For best results, be sure to use pure henna—without metallic bases, "henna enhancers," or chemical dyes. On henna labels, "100 percent natural henna" doesn't necessarily mean "100 percent *pure* henna." There is some controversy about the different shades of henna. Several sources claim that any shade that is not orange-red may also contain chemical dyes.

You can also intensify the color by adding other ingredients. Use paprika, beet juice, or red zinger tea to bring out red; for brown, use ginger, nutmeg, or hot coffee instead of water. Gold is accentuated with black tea, chamomile, or onion juice. To tone down the orange-red, add one part chamomile flowers to two parts henna.

Never use henna on eyebrows, eyelashes, or facial hair, or if you already have a chemical dye on your hair or are about to get a permanent.

You can take on temporary hair color with natural rinses made from plant materials. Because they are not as strong as chemical dyes, these rinses cannot effect drastic color changes, but they certainly can enrich your natural color and, when used repetitively, continue to be absorbed more and more into your hair. Because they are not permanent, they should be renewed occasionally to prevent the color from fading.

Pour liquid produced by the following formulas through hair fifteen times, catching it in a basin and rerinsing. Wring out excess and leave in hair for fifteen to twenty minutes before finally rinsing it out with clear water.

Blond

Note: The effects of any blond rinse will be heightened by drying your hair in the sun.

• Mix one tablespoon lemon juice with one gallon pure warm water. Use for final rinse.
• Pour three cups hot water over four tablespoons chopped rhubarb root and simmer fifteen minutes.
• Steep a half cup chamomile flowers or any other yellow-blossomed flower or herb (calendula, yellow broom flowers, saffron, turmeric) in one quart boiling water for a half hour. Strain and let cool.
• Mix flower or herb tea for blond rinse (see above) with an equal amount of lemon juice. Thicken by adding arrowroot to the warm mixture and stirring over heat until it forms a gel. Apply to hair and sit out in the sun for an hour. Rinse with plain water.

Brown

• Cook an unpeeled potato. Dip a cotton ball into the cooking water and saturate hair. Keep away from skin to prevent discoloration.
• Use strong black tea or black coffee for final rinse.

To Cover Gray

• Simmer a half cup dried sage in two cups water for thirty minutes. Steep

several hours. Pour strained liquid over clean hair fifteen or more times, leave on hair until hair dries; then rinse and dry hair again. Apply weekly until desired shade is achieved, then monthly to maintain color.
• Crush walnut hulls in a mortar, cover with boiling water, add a pinch of salt, and soak for three days. Add three cups boiling water and simmer in a glass pot for five hours, replacing water as needed. Strain, then simmer liquid to one-quarter of its original volume. Cool and add one teaspoon ground cloves or allspice and steep in the refrigerator for one week, shaking the mixture every day. Strain and use. *Caution:* this solution will stain everything you touch, so wear gloves and try to avoid skin contact.
• Mix one tablespoon apple-cider vinegar with one gallon pure warm water. Use for final rinse.

Red

• Mix together one tablespoon each of henna, chamomile flowers, and vinegar, then steep in boiling water for fifteen minutes. Cool and strain before using.
• Use a strong tea of rose hips or clove.
• Use strong black coffee for final rinse.

At the Store/By Mail

Natural hair color

Helix Henna (Helix Corporation). *Earth Herbs.*

Paul Penders Color Conditioners (Paul Penders). ☺ ✪ *InterNatural, Natural Lifestyle Supplies.*

Rainbow Henna (Rainbow Research Corporation). ☺ ✪ *Amberwood, Eco-Choice, InterNatural, My Brother's Keeper.*

VitaWave Creme Color (Vita Wave Products). Vegetable-dye hair coloring (contains natural spirits of ammonia). ☺ ✪ *Allergy Relief Shop, Beauty Naturally, The Compassionate Consumer, Ecco Bella, Humane Alternative Products, Karen's Non-*

toxic Products, My Brother's Keeper, Sunrise Lane.

VitaWave Hair Lightener Set (Vita Wave Products). ☺ ⊗ *Beauty Naturally, Ecco Bella, Sunrise Lane.*

HAIR CONDITIONERS

Harmful ingredients: aerosol propellants, ammonia, colors, fragrance, formaldehyde glycols.

HOMEMADE ALTERNATIVES

For Normal Hair
• Use neutral henna as directed on package.
• Saturate hair with olive, sesame, or corn oil. Make *hot* towels by running hot water over towels in washing machine and putting them through the spin cycle. Wrap head in aluminum foil and apply hot towels. Leave on for twenty minutes. Shampoo.

For Dry Hair
• Heat one cup olive oil and one quarter cup honey until warm. Pour into a bottle and shake well. Apply one or two tablespoons to scalp; massage. Cover head with a towel for several hours or wrap a hot damp towel around head for ten minutes. Wash hair.
• Apply one half cup mayonnaise to dry hair. Cover with a cellophane bag and wait fifteen minutes. Rinse and shampoo.
• Puree one ripe avocado in blender or food processor. Massage into hair and wrap with a towel. Wait one hour before shampooing.

For Split Ends
• Massage scalp and hair ends with warm olive or avocado oil. Wrap head with a cotton towel, scarf, or diaper and leave on for eight to twelve hours (all day or all night). Shampoo with regular shampoo to which one egg yolk has been added. Rinse with diluted lemon juice or vinegar.

• Massage one small carton plain yogurt into hair and comb through. Rinse well.
• Mash one whole cucumber in a blender or food processor, adding a little water if necessary to make a paste. Apply to shampooed, towel-dried hair and leave on for ten minutes. Rinse well.

At the Store/By Mail

⊕ *Earthwise hair conditioners*
Alexandra Avery Rosemary Hair Oil (Alexandra Avery). Rosemary, lavender, and olive oil. Herbs grown biodynamically. ☺ ⊗ *Alexandra Avery, Earthen Joys, InterNatural.*
Simple Wisdom. Organic almond-oil hair conditioner. Handmade; highly concentrated. ☺ ⊗

🍃 *Natural hair conditioners*
+ Dr. Hauschka Neem Hair Lotion and Oil (Dr. Hauschka Cosmetics). Contains biodynamically grown herbal extracts. ☺ *InterNatural, Meadowbrook Herb Garden.*
+ Giovanni Conditioners (Giovanni Cosmetics). Contain organically grown ingredients whenever possible. ☺ ⊗ *Eco-Choice, Vegan Street.*
+ Jeanne Rose Herbal BodyWorks. Aromatic herbal-vinegar hair rinse containing organically grown herbs when available. Beauty Without Cruelty Seal of Approval. ☺
+ Jurlique Verbena Conditioners (Jurlique). Strengthens hair and helps prevent split ends. Contains plant materials grown organically. ☺ *Jurlique.*
+ Weleda Conditioners/Rosemary Hair Oil (Weleda). Contain biodynamically grown chamomile or rosemary. ☺ *Deer Valley Farm, EveryBody Ltd., InterNatural, Meadowbrook Herb Garden, Naturpath, Weleda.*
Aubrey Organics Hair Rinses and Conditioners (Aubrey Organics). ☺ ⊗ *The Allergy Store, Aubrey Organics, Ecco Bella,*

Humane Alternative Products, Karen's Non-toxic Products, Natural Lifestyle Supplies.

Desert Essence Jojoba Nutrient Conditioner (Desert Essence Cosmetics). ☺ ⊗ Desert Essence Cosmetics.

Earth Science, Conditioners (Earth Science). ☺ ⊗ Earth Science, Every-Body Ltd.

Golden Lotus Conditioners (Mountain Fresh). Natural scents. ☺ ⊗ Carole's Cosmetics, Mountain Fresh, Seventh Generation, Sunrise Lane, Terra Verde Products.

Granny's Soft 'N Silky Hair Conditioner (Granny's Old Fashioned Products). Unscented. ☺ ⊗ Allergy Resources, The Allergy Store, Granny's Old Fashioned Products, The Living Source.

Home Health Hair Conditioners (Home Health Products). ☺ ⊗ Home Health Products.

Kiss My Face Olive and Aloe Conditioner (Kiss My Face). ☺ ⊗ Eco-Choice, EveryBody Ltd., Kiss My Face, My Brother's Keeper.

KSA Jojoba. Jojoba cream rinse. ☺ ⊗ Mountain Rose Herbs. For light or dark hair.

Natural Bodycare Aloe-Herb Conditioner (Natural Bodycare). All-natural formula with vitamins. Earth Herbs.

Natural Bodycare Herbal-Satin Natural Hair Revitalizer (Natural Bodycare). Earth Herbs.

Nature de France Natural French Clay Conditioners (Nature de France). For all hair types. ☺ ⊗ Amberwood, The Compassionate Consumer, EveryBody Ltd., My Brother's Keeper.

Nature's Gate Herbal Conditioner (Levlad). ☺ ⊗ EveryBody Ltd., Vegan Street.

Patricia Allison Shimmer Hair Treatment (Patricia Allison). ☺ ⊗ The Living Source.

Paul Penders Chamomile Hair Conditioners (Paul Penders). ☺ ⊗ Basically Natural, Carole's Cosmetics, The Compassionate Consumer, InterNatural, My Brother's

Keeper, Natural Lifestyle Supplies, Sunrise Lane.

Rainbow Conditioners (Rainbow Research Corporation). ☺ ⊗ Amberwood, My Brother's Keeper, Vegan Street.

Simple Hair Conditioner (Simple Soap). The Living Source.

Thursday Plantation Tea-Tree Oil Hair Conditioner (Teaco International). Inter-Natural, Teaco International.

Tonialg Restorative Conditioner (Tonialg). Seaweed based; natural fragrance. ☺ Eco-Choice EveryBody Ltd.

Wysong Rinseless Conditioner (Wysong Corporation). InterNatural, Wysong Corporation.

HAIR-REMOVAL PRODUCTS

Harmful ingredients: aerosol propellants, fragrance, mineral oil, paraffin.

HOMEMADE ALTERNATIVES
• Shave
• Tweeze
• Melt a small amount of beeswax in a small pan until very warm, but still cool enough to touch. After dusting skin with a body powder, apply warm wax to skin with a wooden spatula. Allow wax to dry for a few seconds, then remove quickly with a light tapping. The hairs will be removed with the wax. Soothe with a bit of cream or lotion.

HAIR-SETTING LOTION

Harmful ingredients: ammonia, colors, formaldehyde, fragrance, mineral oil, plastic, (PVP).

HOMEMADE ALTERNATIVES
• Dissolve one teaspoon gelatin in one cup warm water. Use as a liquid, or chill and use as a gel.
• Use stale beer.
• Comb milk through hair to coat each strand.

At the Store/By Mail

🌀 Natural hair-setting lotions

Aubrey Organics Natural Body Highlighter mousses (Aubrey Organics). Non-aerosol mousses that hold, moisturize, and highlight hair with natural gums and colors. 😃 Ⓧ *Aubrey Organics, The Compassionate Consumer, Humane Alternative Products, My Brother's Keeper.*

+ Giovanni Styling Products (Giovanni Cosmetics). Contain organically grown ingredients whenever possible. 😃 Ⓧ *Carole's Cosmetics, Vegan Street.*

HAIRSPRAY

Harmful ingredients: aerosol propellants, colors, ethanol, formaldehyde resins, fragrance, plastic (PVP).

The use of hairspray has long been associated with lung disease. In 1958, the lung disease thesaurosis was attributed to chronic inhalation of hairspray; symptoms include shortness of breath, breathing difficulties, and reduced lung capacity. In most cases, the symptoms disappear after hairspray use is discontinued.

HOMEMADE ALTERNATIVES

Chop one lemon (or one orange for dry hair). Place in a pot and cover with two cups pure, hot water. Boil until only half remains. Cool and strain. Add more water if needed. Refrigerate in a fine spray bottle. If desired, add one ounce vodka per cup of hairspray.

SPECIAL TIP

Consult your hairdresser to find a style that doesn't need to be held in place with hairspray.

At the Store/By Mail

🌀 Natural hairspray

⊦ Giovanni Hair Sprays (Giovanni Cosmetics). Contain organically grown

ingredients whenever possible. 😃 Ⓧ *Eco-Choice, Vegan Street.*

Aubrey Organics Hair Sprays (Aubrey Organics). Plant ingredients in natural grain alcohol. Pump spray bottle. 😃 Ⓧ *The Allergy Store, Amberwood, Aubrey Organics, The Compassionate Consumer, Humane Alternative Products, Karen's Nontoxic Products, My Brother's Keeper, Natural Lifestyle Supplies, Vegan Street.*

Earth Science Hair-Setting Products (Earth Science). 😃 Ⓧ *Earth Science, EveryBody Ltd.*

Earth Science Hair Sprays (Earth Science). Nonaerosol sprays. 😃 Ⓧ *Carole's Cosmetics, Earth Science.*

VitaWave Proteinized Hairspray (Vita Wave Products). Nonaerosol. 😃 Ⓧ *Vegan Street.*

LOTIONS, CREAMS, & MOISTURIZERS

Harmful ingredients: ammonia, colors, EDTA, ethanol, fragrance, glycols, mineral oil, phenol.

HOMEMADE ALTERNATIVES

• Melt together four ounces almond butter (make by grinding almonds in a food processor or blender until butter is formed, or purchase at a natural-food store), four ounces natural glycerin or honey, and two ounces coconut oil. In a separate pot, heat sixteen ounces distilled water and dissolve one teaspoon borax in it. Slowly add to the oil mixture. Beat well by hand, or mix in blender or food processor. Place in bottles. Keep refrigerated.

• Simmer one cup rolled oats in six cups pure water for thirty minutes. Strain. Massage small amount of lotion into clean skin.

• Beat two eggs in a chilled bowl. While beating, slowly add one cup oil. When mixture begins to thicken, add one tablespoon fresh lemon juice or one tablespoon apple-cider vinegar. Refrigerate in a covered glass container.

At the Store/By Mail

Natural and unscented lotions, creams, and moisturizers can be purchased at drugstores and natural-food stores.

⊕ Earthwise lotions, creams, and moisturizers

Alexandra's Dream Cream/Herbal Balm (Alexandra Avery). An extra-rich emulsion formulated for dry and aging skin. Natural scent of biodynamicaly grown herbal ingredients. ☺ Ø *Alexandra Avery, Earthen Joys, InterNatural.*

Mountain Rose Herbs Lotions. Made from wildcrafted or organically grown herbs and organic cold-pressed olive oil.

�});Natural lotions, creams, and moisturizers

+ Alexandra Avery Almond Cream (Alexandra Avery). For daily moisture and protection. Natural scent of biodynamically grown herbal ingredients. ☺ Ø *Alexandra Avery, Earthen Joys.*

+ Fluir Herbals. Hand and body lotion with an almond-oil base. Ø ✚

+ *Jeanne Rose Herbal BodyWorks.* Skin creams made with organically grown herbs when available. Contain honey and lanolin. ☺

+ Jurlique Creams and Lotions (Jurlique). ☺ *Jurlique.*

+ *Oak Valley Herb Farm.* Mountainrose facial cream. Contains lanolin and beeswax.

+ Speick Hand Care Cream (Walter Rau Gmbh & Company Speickwerk). Biological or biodynamically grown herbal extracts. Scented with essential oils. Contains thermal spring water rich in silica. ☺ *Meadowbrook Herb Garden.*

+ Speick Skin Care Lotion (Walter Rau Gmbh & Company Speickwerk). With coconut oil, natural protein, and thermal spring water. Biological or biodynamically grown herbal extracts. Scented

with essential oils. ☺ Ø *Meadowbrook Herb Garden.*

+ Weleda Iris Face Oil/Moisturizing Cream/Night Cream/Hand Cream (Weleda). Contains biodynamically grown herbs. ☺ Ø *Amberwood, The Compassionate Consumer, Deer Valley Farm, EveryBody Ltd., InterNatural, Meadowbrook Herb Garden, Weleda.*

Alba Botanica Facial Care Complex/Very Emollient Body Lotion (Alba Botanica Cosmetics). ☺ *EveryBody Ltd., InterNatural, Sunrise Lane.*

Allergy Resources. Pure lanolin. ☺

Aqualin (Micro Balanced Products). Moisturizing water gel. ☺ Ø *Beauty Naturally, Carole's Cosmetics, InterNatural, Micro Balanced Products, Quality Health Products.*

Aubrey Organics Lotions, Creams, and Moisturizers (Aubrey Organics). ☺ Ø *The Allergy Store, Aubrey Organics, The Compassionate Consumer, Ecco Bella, Humane Alternative Products, InterNatural, My Brother's Keeper, Natural Lifestyle Supplies.*

Beebalm (Old World Honey Company). Beeswax hand cream. *Meadowbrook Herb Garden.*

Autumn Harp Aloe Rose Body Lotion (Autumn Harp). Almond, olive, and peanut oils. *InterNatural.*

Bindi Moisturizing Cream (Pratima). Created from ancient Indian recipes and utilizing the principles of ayurvedics. *Earth Herbs, InterNatural.*

Cloudworks Rose Cream (Cloudworks). For hands, face, and body. ☺ Ø *InterNatural.*

Desert Essence Jojoba Oil/Hand & Body Lotion/Moisture Cream (Desert Essence Cosmetics). 100% pure. ☺ Ø *Desert Essence Cosmetics.*

Earth Science Lotions, Creams & Oils (Earth Science). ☺ Ø *Earth Science, EveryBody Ltd.*

Edna's Unscented Body Moisturizer

(Edna's). Made with olive, apricot, vitamin E, sunflower, beeswax, essential oils and rose water. No chemicals or perfumes. *The Ecology Box.*

Fluir Herbals. Rose cream for day or night, with almond- and apricot-kernel oils. Also lemon-scented hand cream. Both contain lanolin and beeswax. ☺ Ⓐ

Garden Empress Lotions/Moisturizing Cream (Garden Empress). Rich moisturizing lotions, scented with gardenia, lotus, and vanilla, or unscented. Contains beeswax. *Simmons Handcrafts.*

Golden Lotus Ginseng & Aloe Moisturizing Lotion (Mountain Fresh). ☺ Ⓐ *Amberwood, Mountain Fresh, Seventh Generation, Sunrise Lane.*

Granny's Moisture Guard (Granny's Old Fashioned Products). Unscented moisturizer for hands, face, and body. ☺ Ⓐ *The Allergy Store, Granny's Old Fashioned Products, The Living Source.*

Home Health Skin Lotions (Home Health Products). ☺ *Home Health Products.*

Ida Grae Earth Venus Moisturizer (Nature's Colors). Unscented. Contains lanolin and beeswax. ☺ ⊞ Glass jars. *The Allergy Store, Carole's Cosmetics, Earth Herbs, InterNatural, Nature's Colors.*

Kettle Care Products. Herbal lotions and moisturizers. Herbal moisturizing cremes including a "Creative Creme" of soy oil, purified water, and beeswax that allows you to make your own custom creme. Comes with directions and suggestions. ☺ Ⓐ

Kiss My Face Moisturizers/Moisture Creams (Kiss My Face). ☺ Ⓐ Offers protection from the sun. *EveryBody Ltd., Kiss My Face.*

Kiss My Face Moisture Creams (Kiss My Face). Both All-Day and All-Night formulas. ☺ Ⓐ *Eco-choice, EveryBody Ltd., Kiss My Face, My Brother's Keeper.*

Kiss My Face Moisturizers (Kiss My Face). Olive and aloe. Also oil-free. ☺ Ⓐ *Eco-Choice, Kiss My Face, My Brother's Keeper.*

KSA Jojoba. Jojoba foot lotion and body cream. ☺ Ⓐ

Mountain Ocean Cream Moisturizer/ Skin Trip Coconut Moisturizer (Mountain Ocean). Contains lanolin.

Natural Bodycare Aloe-Herb Skin Rejuvenating Mist (Natural Bodycare). All-natural formula with NaPCA, a natural moisturizer found in all human skin that is lost with age. *Earth Herbs.*

Nature's Gate Moisture Cream (Levlad). Provides natural sunscreen. ☺ *EveryBody Ltd.*

Nature's Second Skin (Lanocre Laboratories). Pure lanolin for extremely dry skin. *Lanocare Laboratories.*

Patricia Allison Vita Balm Lotion/Vita Magic Night Cream (Patricia Allison). ☺ *The Living Source.*

Paul Penders Body Lotions, Creams and Moisturizers (Paul Penders). ☺ Ⓐ *Basically Natural, Carole's Cosmetics, InterNatural, My Brother's Keeper, Natural Lifestyle Supplies, Vegan Street.*

Rainbow Creams and Lotions (Rainbow Research Corporation). ☺ Ⓐ *Amberwood, My Brother's Keeper, Vegan Street.*

Simple Lotions & Creams (Simple Soap). Unscented. *The Living Source.*

Swedish Pollenique Body Silk Moisturizer (Third Day Botanicals). ☺ Ⓐ *Sunrise Lane.*

Tonialg Creams & Lotions (Tonialg). Seaweed-based, natural fragrance. ☺ *Eco-Choice, EveryBody Ltd.*

Vermont Country Store. Pure lanolin to protect and heal.

Vicco Turmeric Ayurvedic Complexion Cream. (Auromere). ☺ Ⓐ *Aura Cacia, Auromere, Earth Herbs.*

Wysong Extraordinary Skin Moisturizer (Wysong Corporation). With aloe, jojoba, and rosehip oils. *InterNatural, Wysong Corporation.*

LUBRICANTS

Petroleum jelly is generally considered harmless, but it is a nonrenewable petrochemical product and should be approached with caution by anyone who is sensitive to petrochemical derivatives.

At the Store/By Mail

🌿 *Natural lubricants*

Autumn Harp Un-Petroleum Jelly (Autumn Harp). Made with pure vegetable oils, beeswax, vitamin E, and extracts of calendula and comfrey. Unscented. ☺ *InterNatural, Seventh Generation.*

Miracle of Aloe V-loe Vaginal Cream & Lubricant (Aloe Products). Contains 70 percent aloe vera in a cream base. Unscented. *Home Health Products.*

Vegelatum (Mountain Fresh). Unscented vegetable jelly. ☺ ⊗ *Amberwood, Earth Herbs, My Brother's Keeper, Simply Delicious, Sunrise Lane, Vegan Street.*

MOUTHWASH

Harmful ingredients: aerosol propellants, ammonia, colors, cresol, ethanol, flavors, formaldehyde, glycols, phenol.

HOMEMADE ALTERNATIVES
• Prevent bad breath with good dental hygiene, including regular brushing and flossing.
• Use plain or salted warm water to rinse loose food from your mouth.
• Use one teaspoon baking soda in one glass pure water.
• Use sage, birch, or mint tea.
• Add one half teaspoon essential oil of peppermint (or other essential oil) to one quart water in a two-quart bottle. Shake the bottle every other minute for fifteen minutes. Let the mixture sit, covered, for twelve hours or longer, then filter through wet filter paper. Dissolve one teaspoon salt and one half teaspoon baking soda in the peppermint water.

At the Store/By Mail

🌿 *Natural mouthwashes*

+ Weleda Mouthwash Concentrate (Weleda). ☺ *The Compassionate Consumer, Earth Herbs, EveryBody Ltd., InterNatural, Meadowbrook Herb Garden, My Brother's Keeper, Naturpath, Sunrise Lane, Weleda.*

Aubrey Organics Natural Mint Mouthwash & Breath Freshener (Aubrey Organics). Herbal oils and vitamins in distilled water. ☺ ⊗ *Aubrey Organics, Humane Alternative Products, Karen's Nontoxic Products, Vegan Street.*

Desert Essence Tea-Tree Oil Mouthwash (Desert Essence Cosmetics). With lavender and peppermint oils. ☺ ⊗ *Desert Essence Cosmetics.*

Glyco Thymoline Mouthwash & Gargle (Kress & Owens Company). *Home Health Products.*

Home Health Peri-Dent (Home Health Products). Herbal gum massage and mouthwash. ☺ ⊗ *Home Health Products.*

Ipsadent Mouthwash (Heritage Store Products). *InterNatural, Karen's Nontoxic Products.*

Merfluan Mouthwash Concentrate (American Merfluan). Essential-oil formula; contains no alcohol or artificial ingredients. ☺ ⊗ *InterNatural.*

Nature's Gate Mouthwash (Levlad). With vitamin C and aloe vera, in cinnamon, anise, or mint flavor. ☺ *EveryBody Ltd.*

Tom's Natural Mouthwashes (Tom's of Maine). "Cinnamint" and spearmint. ⊗ *Amberwood, Carole's Cosmetics, The Compassionate Consumer, Ecco Bella, Eco-Choice, My Brother's Keeper, Naturally Ewe.*

PERMANENT WAVES

Harmful ingredients: ammonia, colors, fragrance, glycols, mineral oil.

SPECIAL TIP
Consult with your hairdresser to find a style appropriate for the natural wave in your hair.

At the Store/By Mail

♣ *Natural permanent waves*
VitaWave Perms (Vita Wave Products). Home perms that provide natural body and/or curls. Contain natural spirits of ammonia. ☺ ⊗ *Allergy Relief Shop, Allergy Resources, Beauty Naturally, The Compassionate Consumer, Ecco Bella, Humane Alternative Products, Karen's Nontoxic Products, My Brother's Keeper, Sunrise Lane.*

SHAMPOO

Harmful ingredients: ammonia, colors, cresol, detergent, EDTA, ethanol, formaldehyde, fragrance, nitrates/nitrosamines, plastic (PVP), sulfur compounds.

In addition to the above, antidandruff shampoos contain coal-tar solutions or other toxic ingredients. Selenium sulfide, for example, can cause degenerative lesions of the liver, kidney, heart, spleen, stomach, bowels, and lungs if swallowed. Another toxic chemical used in antidandruff shampoos, recorcinol, is very easily absorbed through the skin.

HOMEMADE ALTERNATIVES
• Use liquid soap.
• Blend one cup liquid castile soap (can be made from castile bar soap by grating bar and mixing with pure water in a blender or food processor) with one quarter cup olive, avocado, or almond oil. Add one half cup distilled water. Place in bottles. Use sparingly.

• Mix one egg with one cup liquid castile soap in a blender until well beaten. Store in refrigerator. For added protein, as you blend pour in one package unflavored gelatin, a small amount at a time, until mixed. Store in refrigerator no longer than two weeks.
• Use baking soda. Simply rub a handful of dry baking soda into wet hair and rinse. For the first several weeks of use, hair will be drier than normal, but then the natural oils will begin to make your hair very soft. Great for dandruff.

To remove dulling soap film, add one teaspoon sodium hexametaphosphate (see page 144) to one gallon warm water. Wet hair thoroughly with this solution, then wash hair with soap or shampoo. Rinse with what's left of the solution, then with plain water.

At the Store/By Mail

♣ *Natural shampoos*
+ Giovanni Shampoos (Giovanni Cosmetics). Contain organically grown ingredients whenever possible. ☺ ⊗ *Eco-Choice, Vegan Street.*
+ *Jeanne Rose Herbal BodyWorks.* A variety of shampoos for all types of hair, containing organically grown herbs when available. Beauty Without Cruelty Seal of Approval. ☺ ⊗
+ *Simple Wisdom.* A blend of coconut-based soaps and organically grown almond oil. Handmade; highly concentrated. ☺ ⊗
+ Speick Hair Shampoo (Walter Rau Gmbh & Company Speickwerk). From coconut and castor oils, with natural protein and biological or biodynamically grown herbal extracts. Scented with essential oils. ☺ ⊗ *Meadowbrook Herb Garden.*
+ Weleda Shampoos (Weleda). Shampoos with biodynamically grown cham-

omile or rosemary. ☺ *Deer Valley Farm, EveryBody Ltd., InterNatural, Meadowbrook Herb Garden, Naturpath, Vegan Street, Weleda.*

AFM Satin Touch Hair & Body Shampoo (AFM Enterprises). Unscented, concentrated shampoo. Formulated especially for the chemically sensitive. ☺ Ⓐ *AFM Enterprises, Allergy Relief Shop, Baubiologie Hardware, The Living Source, Nigra Enterprises.*

Aubrey Organics Shampoos (Aubrey Organics). ☺ Ⓐ *The Allergy Store, Aubrey Organics, The Compassionate Consumer, Ecco Bella, Humane Alternative Products, Karen's Nontoxic Products, My Brother's Keeper, Natural Lifestyle Supplies, Vegan Street.*

Cal Ben Soap Company. Gold Star Shampoo Concentrate, a gentle protein shampoo. Can also be used as bubble bath. ▦

Community Soap Factory Shampoos (Community Soap Factory). Herbal scent. ☺ Ⓐ *Amberwood, Carole's Cosmetics, InterNatural, Sunrise Lane, Vegan Street.*

Desert Essence Jojoba Spirulina Shampoo (Desert Essence Cosmetics). Scented. ☺ Ⓐ *Desert Essence Cosmetics, Ecco Bella.*

Earth Science Shampoos (Earth Science). ☺ Ⓐ *Earth Science, EveryBody Ltd.*

Golden Lotus Shampoos (Mountain Fresh). Natural scent. ☺ Ⓐ *Amberwood, Carole's Cosmetics, Mountain Fresh, Sunrise Lane, Terra Verde Products.*

Granny's Rich & Radiant & Gently Yours Shampoos (Granny's Old Fashioned Products). Unscented. ☺ Ⓐ *The Allergy Store, Allergy Resource, Granny's Old Fashioned Products, Green Earth Natural Foods, The Living Source.*

Hofel's Shampoos (Baudelaire). Peach and almond, nettle and rosemary, and clove and dandelion. *InterNatural.*

Home Health Oliva Shampoo/Everclean Pine Tar Dandruff Shampoo/Chamovera Shampoo (Home Health Products). ☺ Ⓐ *Home Health Products, InterNatural.*

J.R. Liggett's Old-Fashioned Bar Shampoo (J.R. Liggett). All-natural shampoo bar comes with attractive wooden drainage stand. ⊞ *InterNatural, Seventh Generation.*

Jacob Hooy Shampoos (Baudelaire). *InterNatural.*

Jurlique Shampoos (Jurlique). Contain plant materials grown organically. ☺ *Jurlique.*

Kiss My Face Olive & Aloe Shampoo (Kiss My Face). ☺ Ⓐ *EveryBody Ltd., Kiss My Face, My Brother's Keeper.*

KSA Jojoba. All-natural jojoba shampoo with aloe vera; also jojoba shampoo for frequent users. ☺ Ⓐ

Mountain Rose Herbs. Rosemary and chamomile shampoos.

Natural Bodycare Aloe-Herb Shampoo (Natural Bodycare). All-natural formula with vitamins. *Earth Herbs.*

Nature de France Natural French Clay Shampoos (Nature de France). ☺ Ⓐ *Amberwood, The Compassionate Consumer, EveryBody Ltd., My Brother's Keeper.*

Nature's Gate Herbal Shampoo (Levlad). ☺ Ⓐ *EveryBody Ltd., Vegan Street.*

O'Naturel Shampoos (O'Naturel). ☺ Ⓐ *InterNatural.*

Orjene Kelp Sea Protein Shampoo (Orjene Natural Cosmetics). ☺ *The Compassionate Consumer.*

Patricia Allison Rose Petal Luxury Shampoo (Patricia Allison). ☺ *The Living Source.*

Paul Penders Shampoos (Paul Penders). Peppermint, rosemary, and jasmine. ☺ Ⓐ *Basically Natural, Carole's Cosmetics, The Compassionate Consumer, InterNatural, My Brother's Keeper, Natural Lifestyle Supplies, Sunrise Lane.*

Rainbow Shampoos (Rainbow Research Corporation). A henna shampoo, and a sports shampoo for extra protection against chlorine. ☺ Ⓧ *Amberwood, My Brother's Keeper.*

ShiKai Shampoos (ShiKai Products). Formula based on an extract from the *shikai* tree of the tropical Far East. *InterNatural, Simmons Handcrafts, Sunrise Lane.*

Simple Shampoo (Simple Soap). *The Allergy Store, The Living Source.*

Sunfeather Herbal Shampoo Bars (Sunfeather Herbal Soap Company). Comes in sandalwood and lavender, forest fern and moss, and rosemary and lemon. ☺ Ⓧ ⊞ *Sunfeather Herbal Soap Company.*

Thursday Plantation Tea-Tree Oil Shampoo (Teaco International). *InterNatural, Teaco International*

Tom's Natural Shampoo with Aloe & Almond (Tom's of Maine). ☺ *Amberwood, Humane Alternative Products, My Brother's Keeper, Seventh Generation.*

Tonialg Restorative Shampoo (Tonialg). Seaweed based; natural fragrance. ☺ *Eco-Choice, EveryBody Ltd.*

Wysong Shampoos (Wysong Corporation). *InterNatural, Wysong Corporation.*

SHAVING CREAM

Harmful ingredients: aerosol propellants, ammonia, BHA/BHT, colors, ethanol, fragrance, mineral oil, phenol, talc.

Instead of using an electric razor, use a safety razor, with soap applied with a natural-bristle shaving brush, or a natural shaving cream, available at your natural-food store.

At the Store/By Mail

🐱 *Natural shaving cream*
+ Jurlique Birch-Essence Shave Gel (Jurlique). Contains plant materials grown organically. ☺ *Jurlique.*

+ Speick Shaving Products (Walter Rau Gmbh & Company Speickwerk). Contain biodynamically grown herbal extracts; scented with essential oils. Some contain beeswax and honey. ☺ *Meadowbrook Herb Garden.*

Alba Botanica Shaving Products (Alba Botanica Cosmetics). ☺ *EveryBody Ltd., InterNatural, Sunrise Lane.*

Aubrey Organics Shaving Products (Aubrey Organics). ☺ Ⓧ *Amberwood, Aubrey Organics, The Compassionate Consumer, Ecco Bella, Humane Alternative Products, Natural Lifestyle Supplies, Vegan Street.*

Earth Science Shaving Products (Earth Science). ☺ Ⓧ *Earth Science, EveryBody Ltd.*

Paul Penders Men's After-Shave Lotion (Paul Penders). Plant oils and carrageenan in an alcohol base. ① Ⓧ *Carole's Cosmetics, InterNatural, My Brother's Keeper, Natural Lifestyle Supplies, Sunrise Lane, Vegan Street.*

Sunfeather Herbal Mr. Spicey (Sunfeather Herbal Soap Company). High-lather shaving soap. ☺ Ⓧ ⊞ *Sunfeather Herbal Soap Company.*

Tom's Natural Shave Cream (Tom's of Maine). ☺ *Amberwood, The Compassionate Consumer, Ecco Bella, Humane Alternative Products, My Brother's Keeper, Natural Lifestyle Supplies, Seventh Generation, Simply Delicious.*

Wysong Shaving Gel (Wysong Corporation). With natural moisturizers and lubricants. *InterNatural, Wysong Corporation.*

SKIN-CARE SYSTEMS

Harmful ingredients: BHA/BHT, colors, ethanol, fragrance, mineral oil, talc.

There are a number of skin-care lines now that have very pure ingredients; groups of products are designed to work together to nourish the skin and encourage the natural renewal process. Rather than list all the products in each line, I've grouped them together.

At the Store/By Mail

⊕ *Earthwise skin-care systems*

Alexandra Avery Skin-Care Products (Alexandra Avery). All of the herbs are grown biodynamically. The oils used are organically grown, except for almond oil. All ingredients are whole and natural; no derivatives are used. All scents, colors, and preservatives come from the ingredients themselves. ☺ *Alexandra Avery, Earthen Joys, InterNatural.*

Annemarie Börlind Skin-Care Systems (Börlind of Germany). These products have been manufactured and sold in Europe for over twenty-five years. All plant materials are organically grown. Water comes from a spring-fed well. Colors and fragrances come from natural plant and mineral sources; the first pressing of oils is used exclusively. Creams and lotions do contain preservatives; the parabens are less than .3 percent of the product. ☺ *Eco-Choice, SelfCare Catalog.*

Dr. Hauschka Skin-Care System (Dr. Hauschka Cosmetics). All plants used in Dr. Hauschka's formulations are biodynamically grown. Because of special processing, they do not need preservatives. All ingredients are active; no extraneous colors or fragrances are added. Products are based on the work of Rudolph Steiner and have been on the market for thirty-five years. ☺ *The Allergy Store, InterNatural Meadowbrook Herb Garden, N.E.E.D.S., Weleda.*

Dry Creek Herb Farm. Simple skin care products made with organically grown and wildcrafted herbs.

Gajee Skin-Care Products (The Gajee Company). Most of the ingredients are organically grown in the Himalayas; the remainder are organically grown or wild-

crafted in other parts of the world. All products are handmade. Only first-pressed oils are used, and all products are made with whole plants. ☺ *Denise Blythe.*

Jurlique Skin-Care Products (Jurlique). Made in Australia. All plant materials used are grown organically; all other ingredients meet the same standards for purity. No preservatives, colors, or fragrances are added. ☺ *Jurlique.*

Paul Penders Skin-Care System (Paul Penders). Extracts are made from herbs grown without pesticides or fertilizers. ☺ Ⓐ *Amberwood, Basically Natural, Carole's Cosmetics, The Compassionate Consumer, InterNatural, My Brother's Keeper, Natural Lifestyle Supplies, Sunrise Lane.*

Rejuvaderm Skin-Care System (Monda Belle de Vienne). Natural herbal and organically grown ingredients. *Monda Belle de Vienne.*

SKIN CLEANSERS (NONSOAP)

Harmful ingredients: colors, ethanol, fragrance, mineral oil.

HOMEMADE ALTERNATIVES

Cleansing Cream
Whip plain sweet (unsalted) butter. Can be stored at room temperature, but keep away from heat since butter melts easily.

Cold Cream
• Combine ten ounces apricot-kernel oil, two ounces cocoa butter, and two ounces beeswax. Melt in a double boiler until completely dissolved. Beat the mixture with a wooden spoon until cold, and put into jars. Keep refrigerated.
• Melt four ounces beeswax and add two cups almond oil. In a separate pan, warm five ounces water and dissolve in it one and one half teaspoons borax. Mix borax solution with beeswax/oil mixture, stirring constantly until cool. Store in a cool place.

• Beat together two tablespoons aloe vera gel and three ounces almond oil in the top of a double boiler. Add one ounce lanolin and melt together. Remove from heat and add two ounces plain water or rose water. Beat continuously until mixture has cooled, and spoon into a jar.

At the Store/By Mail

⊕ **Earthwise skin cleansers**

Alexandra Avery Complexion Care (Alexandra Avery). Natural scent of biodynamically grown herbal ingredients. ☺ Ⓧ *Alexandra Avery, Earthen Joys, Inter-Natural.*

♣ **Natural skin cleansers**

+ Weleda Iris Cleansing Lotion (Weleda). ☺ *Deer Valley Farm, Every-Body Ltd., InterNatural, Meadowbrook Herb Garden, Weleda.*

Almond Sun Three-in-One Cleanser, Moisturizer, Mask (Almond Sun). Pure enough to eat. ☺ Ⓧ *InterNatural*

Aubrey Organics Cleansers & Cleansing Creams (Aubrey Organics). *The Allergy Store, Amberwood, Aubrey Organics, The Compassionate Consumer, Humane Alternative Products, Karen's Nontoxic Products, Natural Lifestyle Supplies.*

Bindi Herbal Facial Cleanser (Pratima). Created from ancient Indian recipes. *Earth Herbs, InterNatural.*

Earth Science Facial Cleansers (Earth Science). ☺ Ⓧ *Earth Science, Every-Body Ltd.*

Home Health Facial Cleansing Gel (Home Health Products). ☺ Ⓧ *Home Health Products.*

Kettle Care Products. Lemon cleansing cream. Contains beeswax. ☺

Kiss My Face Olive & Aloe Cleanser (Kiss My Face). ☺ Ⓧ *Amberwood, Eco-Choice, EveryBody Ltd., Kiss My Face, My Brother's Keeper.*

Nature's Gate Cleanser (Levlad). ☺ *EveryBody Ltd.*

Paul Penders Men's Natural Skin Cleanser (Paul Penders). ☺ Ⓧ *The Compassionate Consumer, InterNatural, My Brother's Keeper, Natural Lifestyle Supplies.*

Tonialg Cleanser (Tonialg). Seaweed based; natural fragrance. ☺ *Eco-Choice, EveryBody Ltd.*

SOAP

Harmful ingredients: ammonia BHA/BHT, color, formaldehyde, fragrance, glycols, phenol.

Soap is not considered a cosmetic and therefore is not affected by the cosmetic labeling laws requiring ingredients to be listed. Although a few companies voluntarily disclose ingredients, most do not.

Basically, soap is made from a combination of an animal or vegetable fat and sodium hydroxide. Natural glycerin, a by-product of this combination, is also used as a base for soap. Herbs, scents, colors, and other ingredients can be added to either type of soap.

The most popular and most heavily advertised soaps are the antimicrobial "deodorant" soaps. An FDA advisory review panel has questioned the safety of using these potent germ killers on a regular day-to-day, year-after-year basis. There is concern about possible dangerous consequences when these substances are absorbed through the skin and accumulate in the liver and other organs. As a result, the panel has declared "not safe" or "not proved safe" those deodorant soaps containing chloroxylenol (PCMX), cloflucarban, phenol, triclocarban, or triclosan. Some other substances that have been banned for over-the-counter sales are still used in prescription soaps.

The panel could find no evidence that these potentially hazardous substances actually helped stop body odor any more effectively than did plain soap, and also warned that deodorant soaps should not be used on infants under six months of age.

In nondeodorant soaps, the most common and troublesome ingredient is synthetic fragrance. The fragrances in deodorant and luxury toilet soaps are clearly recognizable, but some of the other soaps commonly regarded as "pure" also contain added synthetic fragrance. Moreover, some soaps represented as "natural" contain synthetic fragrance (of, say, coconut or oatmeal) to enhance the scent of the natural ingredient. Not only are fragrances totally unnecessary to the effectiveness of soap, they are often irritating and can cause dry skin, redness, and rashes. Scented soaps usually also contain fixatives to keep you smelling "springtime fresh" all day. From an aesthetic point of view, these scents might clash with any natural fragrance you may choose to apply separately.

At the Store/By Mail
Buy pure, plain, unscented, uncolored soap from natural-food stores, bath shops, or drugstores, or order by mail.

Some advertisers claim that soap is drying to the skin. This is true for some soaps, especially those made primarily from coconut oil, so if dry skin is a problem, choose a glycerin soap or one made from olive oil.

☘ *Natural soap*
+ Alexandra Avery Vegetable-Oil Soaps (Alexandra Avery). Natural scent of herbal ingredients from biodynamically grown herbs. ☺ Ⓧ *Alexandra Avery, Earthen Joys, InterNatural, Sunrise Lane.*

+ Simmons Pure Vegetarian Soaps/Pure Castile Soaps (Simmons Handcrafts). Natural glycerin and vitamin E, lightly scented with essential oils. Seven varieties. ☺ Ⓧ *Mountain Rose Herbs, Simons Handcrafts.*

+ Speick Soap (Walter Rau Gmbh & Company Speickwerk). Biological or biodynamically grown herbal extracts. Scented with essential oils. Contains beeswax and honey. ☺ *Meadowbrook Herb Garden.*

+ Weleda Soaps (Weleda). Lightly scented with plant oils and herbal essences, such as iris, rose, and rosemary. ☺ Ⓧ *The Allergy Store, Amberwood, The Compassionate Consumer, Deer Valley Farm, EveryBody Ltd., Humane Alternative Products, InterNatural, Meadowbrook Herb Garden, Naturpath, Sunrise Lane, Vegan Street, Weleda.*

The Allergy Store. Unscented French olive-oil soap.

Amytis Natural Plant-Oil Soap (Walter Rau Gmbh & Company Speickwerk). Contains coconut, palm, and olive oils. ☺ Ⓧ

Aubrey Organics Herbal Liquid Body Soap (Aubrey Organics). Contains collagen (a beef by-product) and herbal extracts and oils in a coconut-oil base. ☺ *Aubrey Organics, Karen's Nontoxic Products.*

Aubrey Organics Honeysuckle Vegeta Soap (Aubrey Organics). Palm kernel, coconut, and peanut oil, with honeysuckle fragrance. ☺ Ⓧ *Aubrey Organics, The Compassionate Consumer, Humane Alternative Products, InterNatural, Vegan Street.*

Aura Cacia Aromatherapy Bath Soaps (Aura Cacia). Cocoa butter and many essential oils. ☺ Ⓧ *Aura Cacia, InterNatural.*

Brookside Oatmeal & Almond Soap (Brookside Soap Company). Handmade all-vegetable soap with coconut, palm, and olive oils and natural fragrance. Ⓧ ⊞ Paper.

Cal Ben Soap Company. Pure Soap, an extra-hard soap made from white tallow and pure cocoa-butter oil. Very light almond scent. ⊞ ☺

Canada's All Natural Soaps (Trianco Corporation). Handmade aloe vera, cucumber, oatmeal, and honey-glycerin soaps. ☺ Ⓧ *Trianco Corporation.*

Chambers. Fragrance-free vegetable-oil-based glycerin soap brick.

Chandrika Ayurvedic Soap (Auromere). Produced in India with pure vegetable oils and herbal extracts. Natural scent of ingredients. ☺ Ⓧ ⊞ *Aura Cacia, Auromere, Basically Natural, Earth Herbs, InterNatural, Vegan Street.*

Chef's Soap (Beh Housewares Corporation). Unscented. Made from tallow. ⊞ *Allergy Resources, The Allergy Store, The Ecology Box, Janice Corporation.*

Clearly Natural Glycerin Soaps (Clearly Natural). Sixteen fragrances and colors. Profits from their "Save the Whales" Soap are donated to Greenpeace. ☺ *EveryBody Ltd., InterNatural, Vegan Street.*

Community Soap Factory Natural Castile Soaps (Community Soap Factory). Plain, peppermint, or almond. Made with coconut and olive oils and lecithin. ☺ Ⓧ *Amberwood, Carole's Cosmetics, InterNatural, Janice Corporation, Karen's Nontoxic Products, Sunrise Lane, Vegan Street.*

Desert Essence Tea-Tree Oil Castile Soap (Desert Essence Cosmetics). With coconut and olive oils. ☺ Ⓧ *Desert Essence Cosmetics.*

Glycerin Creme Soaps (Sappo Hill) made with palm-oil and coconut-oil by an old-fashioned kettle process, then air dried and hand cut. With or without fragrance; some with no added color. ⊞ *Earthen Joys.*

Earth Science Aloe-Gel Lathering Hand Cleanser (Earth Science). ☺ Ⓧ *Earth Science, EveryBody Ltd.*

The Ecology Box. Pure almond-oil castile soap and unscented olive oil soap.

Faith in Nature Soaps (Faith Products). Pure vegetable-oil soap ☺ Ⓧ ⊞ *Basically Natural, InterNatural.*

Fluir Herbals. Natural olive-oil soaps in four fragrances. Ⓧ

Grandpa's Pine Tar Soap (Grandpa Soap Company). Pure soap and vegetable tar oil. *Earth Herbs.*

Granny's Body Satin (Granny's Old Fashioned Products). Liquid body soap. ☺ Ⓧ *Allergy Resources, The Allergy Store, Granny's Old Fashioned Products, Green Earth Natural Foods, The Living Source.*

Gregory Soaps (Gregory Soaps). English soaps with natural scents. Ⓧ *Earth Herbs, InterNatural, SelfCare Catalog.*

Heavenly Soap. Pure soaps made of olive, soy, coconut, palm, and cottonseed oils. Available with or without scent or color. Contain honey and beeswax. ☺ ⊞

Home Health Almond Glow Nourishing Beauty Bar (Home Health Products). Pure vegetable soap. ☺ Ⓧ *Home Health Products.*

Indian Creek Natural Soaps (Indian Creek Naturals). Contain 50 percent olive oil and vitamin E. ☺ Ⓧ *Earth Herbs.*

Jaffe Brothers. Jaybee liquid soap, made from potassium solution and coconut, olive, and peppermint oils. Can also be used as a shampoo.

Kiss My Face Soaps (Kiss My Face). Olive, olive and aloe, and olive and herbal. ☺ Ⓧ *Amberwood, Carole's Cosmetics, Ecco Bella, The Ecology Box, Eco-Choice, EveryBody Ltd., Janice Corp., Kiss My Face, My Brother's Keeper.*

KSA Jojoba. Jojoba glycerine soap in liquid or bar. Also jojoba liquid soap without glycerin. ☺ Ⓧ

Livos Lavenos—Hand Soap (Livos). Made from pure plant ingredients. ☺ Ⓧ *Karen's Nontoxic Products, Livos Plantchemistry.*

Loanda Herbal Soaps (Loanda Products Corporation). *Earth Herbs, InterNatural, Kettle Care Products, Sunrise Lane.*

McClinton's Barilla Soap (E. McCormack & Company). Unscented, uncolored vegetable soap made since the 1800s. ☺ Ⓧ *Basically Natural, InterNatural, SelfCare Catalog.*

Melos Cosmetic Plant-Oil Soap (Walter Rau Gmbh & Company Speickwerk).

Contains coconut, palm, and olive oils, beeswax, and honey. ☺

Nature de France Natural French Milled Soaps/Verite Facial Cleansing Bar (Nature de France). Scented. ☺ ⊘ *Amberwood, The Compassionate Consumer, EveryBody Ltd., Karen's Nontoxic Products, My Brother's Keeper, Natural Lifestyle Supplies.*

North Country Glycerin Soaps (North Country Soap). Fragrant soaps, handmade in small batches. Four fragrances have no animal products; others contain lard, lanolin, or honey. ☺ ⊘ ⊞ *North Country Soap.*

Physicians & Surgeons Soaps (Sigma Pharmaceutical Corporation). All natural; fragrance and color free. *Janice Corporation.*

Phytokosma Pure Plant-Oil Soaps (Walter Rau Gmbh & Company Speickwerk). Avocado, aloe vera, and jojoba soaps contain coconut, palm, and olive oils. ☺ ⊘

Rainbow Bar Soaps (Rainbow Research Corporation). Aloe-oatmeal, golden moisture, and clay cleansing. ☺ ⊘ *Amber-wood, My Brother's Keeper, Vegan Street.*

Rokeach Coconut-Oil Soap (I. Rokeach & Sons). *The Ecology Box.*

Seventh Generation. Unscented soaps in four varieties: aloe vera, camomile, cucumber, and oatmeal.

Simple Soap (Simple Soap). Unscented. *The Allergy Store, The Ecology Box, The Living Source.*

Sirena Soaps (Tropical Soap Company). ☺ ⊘ *The Allergy Store, Amberwood, Janice Corp.*

Sunfeather Herbal Soaps (Sunfeather Herbal Soap Company). Handcrafted olive-oil soaps in many herbal blends, including blue lilac, comfrey and aloe, jasmine, lemon verbena, and a cleansing soap with ground corn and oats. ☺ ⊘ ⊞ *Sunfeather Herbal Soap Company.*

The Soap Factory. Castile soap made of lard and olive oil, employing procedures developed and used in the last half of the nineteenth century. Lightly scented with essential and natural floral oils. Jasmine, milk and honey, mint, oatmeal, and unscented soaps are not colored; others contain FD&C cosmetic colors. ☺ ⊞ Four unwrapped bars in a paper box; individual bars in paper bags. ⬇ Except for some small mechanical stirrers driven by small electric motors, all operations are done by hand, including cutting of soap into bars.

Thursday Plantation Tea-Tree Oil Soap (Teaco International). *InterNatural, Teaco International.*

Tonialg Soap and Linen Net (Tonialg). French hand-milled seaweed soap in handmade linen net applicator. Promotes increased cell renewal. Natural fragrance. ① *EveryBody Ltd.*

Walnut Acres Natural Soap (Walnut Acres). Pure edible tallow and coconut oil, water, lanolin, aloe vera, and vitamin E. Floral scent. *Walnut Acres.*

SPONGES

Harmful ingredients: dyes, plastics (polyurethane foam).

At the Store/By Mail

Natural sponges can be purchased at drug, hardware, art-supply, and natural-food stores.

🌿 Natural sponges and other bath items

Aubrey Organics Spungies Natural-Fiber Facial Cleanser Squares (Aubrey Organics). Disposable three-by-three-inch cellulose squares for cleansing and gentle exfoliation. ⊞ ☺ ⊘ *Aubrey Organics.*

Brooks Fitness Mitts & Bands (Traditional Products Company). Woven sisal. They clean the pores, promote improved breathing of the skin, massage, and invigorate. *Earth Herbs, Traditional Products Company.*

EveryBody Ltd. Mexican *ayate* body cloths.

Fluir Herbals. Natural sea sponge.

InterNatural. Sea-wool bath sponge, vegetable-fiber bath brush, loofah bath brush, sea-silk cosmetic sponges, natural pumice, and a bath strap with loofah on one side and cotton terry on the other.

Karen's Nontoxic Products. Natural cellulose and sea sponges, wooden bath brushes with boar or vegetable-fiber bristles or loofa scrubber, terry/loofa mitts, and sea-wool bath sponges.

Maguey Weaves Ayate (Maguey Weaves). Agave fiber skin buffer and body bath cloth. *Earth Herbs.*

Meadowbrook Herb Garden. Sisal washcloths; genuine sea sponges.

Mountain Rose Herbs. Loofah terry mitt.

Natural Lifestyle Supplies. Soft boar bristle bodybrush in a contoured wooden handle and a natural loofa bath pad with a loofa on one side, terry on the other.

Simmons Handcrafts. Bath brushes with wooden handles and natural boar bristles, and large sea sponges for the bath. Also Mexican *ayate* washcloths, loofa scrubbers, and pumice stones.

SUNTAN LOTION

Harmful ingredients: ethanol, fragrance, glycols, mineral oil.

With the thinning of the ozone layer, it is now more important than ever to protect your skin from the sun. Sun damage is irreparable. It breaks down collagen and elastin fibers in the skin, and its effects don't show up for thirty years.

There are a number of natural sunscreens on the market, but there is some concern that regular use of even natural sunscreen can interfere with your skin's ability to produce vitamin D, a vital nutrient we do not get from food (except for fortified milk), but which is produced

when the sun shines on our bare skin. The *Journal of Clinical Endocrinologic Metabolism* reports that scientifically controlled studies of skin untreated with sunscreen versus skin treated with sunscreen (SPF 8) demonstrated a large difference in vitamin D production. The sunscreened skin showed no change in vitamin D, while the unscreened subjects had blood-level increases of 1,600 percent.

The most prudent way to shield your skin from the sun's harmful rays is to wear protective clothing such as windbreakers, scarves, gloves, and wide-brimmed hats.

HOMEMADE ALTERNATIVES

• Use plain sesame oil, which screens about 30 percent of the sun's ultraviolet rays in addition to softening the skin with natural vitamin E.

• Use cocoa butter.

• Use a mixture of olive oil and cider vinegar.

• Boil three quarters cup of pure water and brew strong tea with three black-tea bags. Put one quarter cup tea into a blender with one quarter cup lanolin and one quarter cup sesame oil. Blend at low speed. Add remaining tea steadily.

At the Store/By Mail

Natural suntan lotions are sold at natural-food stores.

⊕ *Earthwise suntan lotion*

Alexandra Avery Sun Oil (Alexandra Avery). Contains PABA and sesame oil as natural sunscreens; natural scent of biodynamically grown herbal ingredients. ☺ Ⓢ *Alexandra Avery, Earthen Joys, InterNatural*

🌿 *Natural suntan lotion*

+ Annemarie Börlind Sunless Bronze (Börlind of Germany). Self-tanning skincare lotion. ☺ *Earth Herbs.*

+ Jurlique Bronzer (Jurlique). Enhances skin's color, moisturizes, and offers light sun protection. Contains plant materials grown organically. ☺ *Jurlique.*

Allergy Resources. Pure cocoa butter.

Aubrey Organics Bronzer/Sun Shade 15/Tanning Cream (Aubrey Organics). Sunshade contains collagen. ☺ *The Allergy Store, Aubrey Organics, Motherwear.*

Aura Cacia 100% Pure Cocoa Butter/ Body Butter/Sun Butter (Aura Cacia). ☺ ⊘ *Aura Cacia, Earth Herbs, InterNatural.*

Mountain Ocean Sun Screen SPF-8 and Sunblock SPF-15 (Mountain Ocean). Active ingredient is ethylhexyl p-methoxycinnamate, derived from leaves of the cinnamon plant.

Orjene Suntan Lotion (Orjene Natural Cosmetics). With PABA, cocoa butter, and allantoin. ☺ *The Compassionate Consumer.*

Thursday Plantation Tea-Tree After-Sun Lotion (Teaco International). With aloe vera gel. *InterNatural, Teaco International.*

Wysong Sunscreen & Sun Block/Tanning Lotion (Wysong Corporation). PABA-free formulations. *Ecco Bella, InterNatural, Wysong Corporation.*

TOILET PAPER & FACIAL TISSUES

Harmful ingredients: dyes, formaldehyde, fragrance.

In addition, trace amounts of dioxin can be present from the bleaching process.

While I don't know of any formal scientific studies linking toilet paper or facial tissues with adverse health effects, there have been many published anecdotal reports. Several years ago, "Dear Abby" ran a number of letters describing complaints, which included reports of herpes-type flare-ups, itching, and burning. In each case, a switch to unscented, white toilet paper solved the problem.

The production of toilet paper and facial tissues also poses environmental prob-

lems. The pulp to make these products comes from clear-cut forests; the dioxins produced in the bleaching processs escape into the air and are dumped into local waterways. In addition, toilet paper is frequently packaged in plastic.

SPECIAL TIPS
Use cotton handkerchiefs in place of facial tissues.

At the Store/By Mail
At the very least, toilet paper should be undyed and unscented, and preferably packed in paper. There is only one brand of consumer-quality toilet paper packaged in paper sold in supermarkets, but if you go to a cash-and-carry store or janitorial supply house you should be able to buy a cardboard case of toilet paper, with each roll individually wrapped in paper.

The next step would be to buy toilet paper made from recycled paper. I was told by one manufacturer that most companies use some percentage of recycled pulp in their toilet papers but do not advertise this because consumers perceive it as unsanitary. Fortunately, a few manufacturers are getting braver and putting toilet paper made from recycled paper on the supermarket shelves. If you can't find it in your local area, ask your supermarket manager to stock the brands listed below, or order by mail.

Toilet paper made from recycled paper
2nd Opinion. Toilet paper and facial tissue made from 100-percent recycled paper and containing no bleaches or dioxins.

C.A.R.E. Paper Facial and Bathroom Tissue (Ashdun Industries). 100-percent recycled paper. No inks, dyes, or fragrances. ⊞

Envision Facial Tissue/Toilet Paper (Fort Howard Corporation). 100% recycled post-consumer waste. *Atlantic Recycled Paper Company.*

Green Forest Toilet Paper (Fort Howard Corporation). 100% recycled. "Bleaching method doesn't create dioxin. May contain small percentage of post-consumer waste."

Seventh Generation. Two-ply facial and toilet tissue made of pre-and post-consumer recycled paper.

Vegan Street. Recycled, dioxin-free toilet paper.

TOOTHBRUSHES

Harmful ingredients: plastics (nylon, PVC/vinyl chloride).

At the Store/By Mail
Choose a natural-bristle toothbrush, preferably one with a handle of a natural material, at your natural-food store, or order one by mail.

Natural toothbrushes
Brooks Pearwood Toothbrush (Traditional Products Company). Natural bristles, edible-plant finish. *Earth Herbs, Janice Corporation, Mountain Rose Herbs, Natural Lifestyle Supplies, Traditional Products Company.*

Janice Corporation. Natural white-bristle brushes with bone handles, from England.

Karen's Nontoxic Products. Wood handles, natural bristles.

TOOTHPASTE

Harmful ingredients: ammonia, benzyl alcohol/sodium benzoate, colors, ethanol, flavors, fluoride, formaldehyde, mineral oil, plastic (PVP), saccharin.

HOMEMADE ALTERNATIVES
• Brush regularly with plain water, and floss to remove food particles.
• Use plain baking soda, or mix baking soda with a few drops of peppermint extract or oil, or other extract or oil of your choice.

• Use plain salt or mix one part salt with two parts baking soda.
• Mash strawberries. Freeze them in cubes when in season and use during the winter months.
• Run dried lemon peel in a blender to make a half cup of powder and mix with one quarter cup baking soda.

At the Store/By Mail

Natural toothpaste
Beehive Botanicals Propolis Toothpaste (Beehive Botanicals). Includes antibacterial propolis and spearmint, fennel, and menthol oils. *Home Health Products.*

Dent-A-Kleen Tooth Drops (4-D Hobe). Has antiseptic and germicidal properties to help remove plaque. *Earth Herbs.*

Desert Essence Tea-Tree Oil Toothpaste/Dental Floss/Dental Pics (Desert Essence Cosmetics). Contains tea-tree oil, a natural antiseptic and fungicide. *Desert Essence Cosmetics, Natural Life-style Supplies.*

Eden Dentie Tooth Powder/Dentie Toothpaste (Eden Foods). Made from eggplant pickled in salt and roasted to a fine charcoal. *Simply Delicious.*

Home Health Salt 'N Soda Tooth Powder (Home Health Products). Contains baking soda, salt, and peppermint oil. *Home Health Products.*

Ipsab Tooth Powder (Heritage House). Herbal gum treatment. *InterNatural, Karen's Nontoxic Products.*

Merfluan Tooth Powder (American Merfluan). Base of baking soda and sea salt that remineralizes as it cleans. Anise, peppermint, and cinnamon and mint. *InterNatural.*

Mitoku Dentie Tooth Powder and Paste (Mitoku Company). Black tooth powder made from charred eggplant and sea salt. *Natural Lifestyle Supplies.*

Mountain Rose Herbs. Tooth powder with

mineral clay, sea salt, myrrh, and propolis powder, with spearmint and anise oils.

Nature's Gate Natural Toothpaste (Levlad). Herbal mint flavor. ☺ *Amberwood, EveryBody Ltd., Janice Corp., Karen's Nontoxic Products, Vegan Street.*

Ohsawa Dentie Tooth Powder (Ohsawa America). Made from carbonized eggplant. *Mountain Ark Trading Company.*

Peelu Tooth Powder/Toothpaste (Peelu Products). From the Salvadoran *persica* tree. *Earth Herbs, Home Health Products, InterNatural.*

Rainbow Natural Toothpaste (Rainbow Research Corporation). ☺ ⊘

Tart-X (Tart-X Products). Sugar-free chewing gum that contains microfibers of the *peelu* plant, which helps prevent the buildup of tartar and plaque. *Tart-X.*

Tom's Natural Toothpastes/Natural Flossing Ribbon (Tom's of Maine). Also flossing tapes in "cinnamint" and spearmint. *Carole's Cosmetics, The Compassionate Consumer, Ecco Bella, Eco-Choice, Humane Alternative Products, Mountain Ark Trading Company, My Brother's Keeper, Natural Lifestyle Supplies, Naturally Ewe, Seventh Generation, Simply Delicious.*

Vicco Herbal Toothpaste (Auromere). ☺ ⊘ *Allergy Resources, Auromere, Basically Natural, Earth Herbs, Home Health Products, Karen's Nontoxic Products, Simply Delicious, Vegan Street.*

Weleda Toothpastes (Weleda). Natural salt, pink, and plant-gel formulas, *Amberwood, The Compassionate Consumer, Deer Valley Farm, Earth Herbs, EveryBody Ltd., Humane Alternative Products, InterNatural, Janice Corp., Meadowbrook Herb Garden, Natural Lifestyle Supplies, Naturpath, Sunrise Lane, Weleda.*

10 ❧ Textiles

When I wore synthetic fabrics, I was distracted by
unwelcome sensations: clammy skin, static cling, and a
vague feeling that something wasn't right. When I wear a
cotton shirt, I don't have to think about the shirt—it is an
extension of me. The fabric breathes like my skin breathes;
I can feel the air and the radiant warmth of the sun.

CAROL VENOLIA

One of my greatest pleasures is wearing natural fibers. In addition to being healthful and good for the Earth, they feel good. Unlike fibers made from plastic, natural fibers breathe, keeping you warm in the winter and cool in the summer. They get softer the more you wash and wear them. And they come clean in plain soap, instead of requiring synthetic detergents, fabric softeners, and anticling sprays. There are so many attractive and functional textile items made from natural fibers that I haven't worn a synthetic fiber in ten years.

HOW TEXTILE PRODUCTS AFFECT OUR HEALTH AND THE EARTH

Since World War II, hundreds of synthetic fibers—such as polyester, acrylic, and nylon—have been developed and are now in popular use. Although there is little scientific evidence to prove that these fibers themselves are harmful to health, research shows that chemicals such as phenol, vinyl chloride, and other plastics that are used to make them can be absorbed by the skin.

From an environmental viewpoint, though, synthetic fibers do more harm than good. They are made of nonrenewable crude oil (every time there's an oil spill I think of polyester shirts), they produce toxic waste in their manufacture, they don't biodegrade, and they can't be recycled. When you stop and think about it, nylon pantyhose are almost as bad for the environment as disposable diapers: they're made of plastic, you wear them once or twice and they run, and then you throw them into a landfill, where they don't biodegrade.

Synthetic fibers aren't very comfortable, either. As a group, none absorb moisture very well, making you hot, sticky, and clammy in warm weather and providing an ideal environment for bacteria growth. They are also poor choices for winter wear, as they are not good conductors of heat.

Synthetic fibers are also difficult to clean because they tend to absorb oil from the skin and hold oil stains that can be effectively removed only with specially developed synthetic detergents (which also pollute and cause health problems).

Static cling is another problem unique to synthetic fibers. It is caused by an electric charge created by the friction of the synthetic fiber against your body. To solve this problem, even more synthetic chemicals are used in fabric softeners and antistatic agents.

Many textile products are treated with formaldehyde. Even if not stated on the label, all polyester/cotton-blend fabrics have formaldehyde finishes. Polyester/cotton bed sheets have a particularly heavy finish because of their continuous use and frequent laundering. Formaldehyde is also used on nylon fabrics to make them flameproof. Some pure-cotton fabrics have also been treated with formaldehyde finishes for easy care. Even though it is not required by law, clothing labels will usually reveal a finish that makes them "easy care," "permanent pressed," "no-iron," "crease resistant," "durable pressed," "shrink proof," "stretch proof," "water repellent," "waterproof," or "permanently pleated," since these are qualities considered desirable to the consumer. These finishes combine formaldehyde resin directly with the fiber, making the formaldehyde irremovable. At the end of processing, new textile products often contain free-formaldehyde levels of eight hundred parts per million to one thousand parts per million. Simple washing can lower these levels to one hundred parts per million, but formaldehyde continues to be released as the resin breaks down during washing, ironing, and wear.

Flame retardants are another problem, especially since most polyester fibers are treated with them. Even though carcinogenic TRIS, a leading flame retardant, was banned by the Consumer Product Safety Commission in children's sleepwear, it is still legally used in adult sleepwear, hospital gowns, industrial uniforms, wigs, and other textile products we use daily.

Dyes might also pose a problem. Usually fabric dyes are colorfast, but some dyes do bleed: we've all ended up with colored armpits or with some white clothes turned pink because we accidentally washed them with red clothes. If the dye comes out in water, it can be absorbed by the skin. Many dyes add heavy metals to the environment.

ON THE LABEL

Fibers are easy to identify because the Textile Fiber Products Identification Act, passed in 1960, requires that each textile product be labeled with the generic names of the fibers from which it is made. The generic names are established by the Federal Trade Commission (FTC) and include twenty-one manmade-fiber groups, plus the natural fibers. This law applies to all yarns, fabrics, household textile articles, and wearing apparel. Imported goods must also adhere to this law, and the label must also reveal the country of origin. This labeling appears along with the name of the manufacturer, the size of the garment, and cleaning instructions, and is usually attached to the seam of a garment near the waist or hemline.

This is what is required on the label:

• Fibers must be listed in descending order according to percentage by weight (e.g., "80 percent polyester, 20 percent cotton").
• Trademark names are permitted but must be capitalized if listed ("100 percent Fortrel polyester").
• If a fiber makes up less than 5 percent of a fabric's total weight, it must be listed as "other fiber" unless it has a specific purpose ("4 percent spandex added for elasticity").

• Fibers of unknown origin (miscellaneous scraps, rags, textile by-products, second-hand materials, and waste materials) are listed as "undetermined fiber."
• Fibers making up less than .5 percent of the total weight need not be revealed. Technically, this would allow a manufacturer to make a fabric labeled "100 percent cotton" that is actually .5 percent polyester, but the National Cotton Council feels that no manufacturer would go to the trouble of making a fabric containing .5 percent polyester because an amount of synthetic fiber that small would not affect the performance of the fabric. So we can safely assume that fabrics labeled 100 percent natural fiber most probably are.

Label information seems to apply only to the fibers used in the body of the garment or item. Sometimes labels will read "100 percent natural fiber, exclusive of decoration," without revealing the fabric of the decoration. Sweaters labeled "100 percent cotton" often have nylon threads running through the bottom edge and sleeve cuffs to help retain their shape. Cotton chamois shirts sometimes have nylon interfacings behind the buttons. Polyester thread may be used in natural-fiber garments, as well as synthetic zippers, elastic, trims, linings, and interfacings, and plastic buttons and hooks. Many less-expensive cotton undergarments have synthetic elastic and trim.

Exempt from this regulation are upholstery stuffing; outer coverings of furniture, mattresses, and box springs; linings, interlinings, stiffenings, or paddings incorporated for structural purposes and not for warmth; sewing and handicraft threads; and bandages and surgical dressings.

In addition to government regulations, independent organizations sell logos to manufacturers, giving information about the fiber content or performance of the textile products that bear them. The use of these logos is regulated, and products are tested to make sure they live up to their claims.

The *Seal of Cotton* is a trademark of Cotton, Inc. and can be used only with its permission. Created in 1973, this brown-and-white logo indicates that the item is made from 100 percent domestic cotton. It is used on fabrics, garments, bed linens, and towels.

The *Natural Blend* seal, in use since 1974, is also a trademark of Cotton, Inc., and can be used only on fabrics that contain 60 percent cotton or more.

The *Woolmark* is a registered certification owned by the Wool Bureau, Inc., a division of the International Wool Secretariat. Labels are purchased by manufacturers for apparel, knitwear, floor covering, upholstery materials, blankets, and bedspreads. Since 1964, over fourteen thousand companies in over fifty countries have been licensed to use it. Items bearing this logo must be of pure wool and be labeled "100 percent pure wool," "100 percent virgin wool," "all pure wool," or "all virgin wool."

The *Woolblend Mark* was introduced in 1972 by the Wool Bureau, Inc. Products displaying this logo must contain at least 60 percent wool and identify all nonwool components by their generic names.

Superwash is a registered certification mark used in conjunction with the Woolmark and the Woolblend Mark. This logo indicates that the wool product has been chemically treated to make it felt resistant.

NATURAL FIBERS

There are a number of wonderful natural fibers and stuffing/insulation materials that can be used, but because of current growing and manufacturing practices, the health, environmental, and animal-rights issues should also be considered. Even with these drawbacks, I prefer natural fibers and recommend them because basically they are a good choice—a better alternative to synthetic fibers—and we need to keep up the market demand while we are working to get growers to change their methods.

Fibers and stuffing materials that come from natural plant or animal sources are cotton, linen, silk, all the various types of wool, ramie, down, feathers, kapok, and natural-fiber blends: cotton/silk, linen/cotton, and wool/cotton (commonly known as Viyella).

A second choice would be to wear rayon, a man-made fiber that, unlike other synthetic fibers, is composed of cellulose, a substance found in all plants. Cellulose used in making rayon is taken from cotton linters, old cotton rags, paper, and wood pulp. The cellulose is broken down with petrochemicals and then re-formed into threads resembling cotton or silk.

Here's a quick review of natural fibers, their origins, and their processing, to help you choose those that best suit your needs.

Cotton

Cotton is a natural cellulose fiber, taken from fibers that develop around the seed pod of the cotton plant. After it is picked, the pod is placed in a cotton gin, which separates the seed, the lint, and the linters. The lint is then spun into yarn, and the shorter linters are used for cotton batting, in making rayon, and in the production of paper.

Cotton quality is determined by the length of the fiber around the seed pod. Long-staple varieties, such as Sea Island, Egyptian, and Pima, are the highest quality.

Two terms that you will frequently find on labels of cotton items are "sanforized" and "mercerized." Sanforized fabrics have been precompressed to the size to which they would shrink after washing by way of a mechanical process that controls shrinkage, involves no chemicals, and is considered harmless. Mercerized fibers have undergone a nontoxic process by which they have been immersed under tension in a strong solution of lye, which is then washed off. This permanently improves the strength, absorbency, and appearance of the fabric as well as providing excellent colorfastness.

Most cotton as presently grown, however, presents environmental problems. Cotton is the most contaminated of all the natural fibers; seeds are treated with fungicides, herbicides are used repeatedly, and the heavy use of pesticides is common practice worldwide. Whatever pesticide residues might remain in cotton fabrics after processing seem to be harmless, but we must also consider the environmental contamination of our air, land, and water, and the illnesses these pesticides cause to the cotton growers and their families. The good news is that there are a few growers who are experimenting with organically grown cotton, and while this isn't yet available as fabric in the United States, we can buy organically grown cotton batting and sliver for spinning.

Linen

Linen is made from fibers from the inner bark of the flax plant and is possibly the first fiber used by man. The bark is removed from the plant and left in the field so natural bacterial action can loosen the fibers. The stems are then crushed mechanically and the fibers removed. At the mill, the fibers are combed to separate the different lengths and align them in preparation for spinning.

Flax has relatively few insect pests, but if they are present they are controlled with pesticides such as parathion, dieldrin, and heptachlor.

Linen is often used in its natural beige shade, or bleached to make it a lighter color, but it can also be dyed.

Ramie

Ramie is a stingless nettle indigenous to mainland China. A soil-depleting crop, it needs large quantities of fertilizer to produce good yields. Most ramie is grown in Asia, where the fiber is extracted by hand. The usual procedure is to hand-cut green plants, remove the leaves, then pull ribbons of fiber from the woody stem. If the fiber is to be exported, it is sometimes exposed to sulfur fumes to bleach it to a uniform light straw color.

Ramie is used as a textile fiber in Asian countries. In America it is generally blended with cotton for use in knit sweaters.

Silk

A protein fiber, silk is taken from the cocoon of the silkworm caterpillar. Each cocoon is spun from one continuous silk filament extruded from the caterpillar's body.

Most silk is produced by cultivated silkworms. The cultivation process begins with the laying of eggs by silk moths. After incubation, young silkworms are fed mulberry leaves until they are ready to begin spinning their cocoons. The cocoons are made of silk filaments and a gummy substance that holds them together. After the cocoons are harvested, the gum is softened with warm water, allowing the silk filaments to be separated and formed into strands of yarn. The gum is then removed entirely with a soap solution.

Some people who support animal rights prefer not to wear silk because the worms inside the cocoons do not survive the silk-making process.

Wool

The term *wool* is a general one, referring to protein fibers spun from the fleece of over two hundred different breeds of sheep and from the hair of the angora rabbit, the cashmere goat, the camel, the alpaca, the llama, and the wild vicuña.

Highest-quality sheep's wool and exotic wools are generally taken from the animals by seasonal shearing or by combing the animal and collecting the hair as it naturally sheds. However, much lower-quality sheep's wool is removed from slaughtered animals with chemicals or natural bacteria action. This is generally blended with other types of wool, and not noted on the label. For this reason, many people who boycott meat from factory farms also do not wear wool. By choosing carefully, it is possible, especially through catalogs mentioned later in this chapter, to buy sweaters and other items made from sheared wool.

After shearing, the wool fleece is washed a number of times in a soapy alkaline solution. This "scouring" removes the lanolin, a natural oil that keeps the fleece soft and waterproof. "Unscoured" wool retains the natural water repellency of the lanolin.

If significant amounts of dirt, burrs, sticks, and other vegetable matter remain after scouring, the fleece is carbonized with sulfuric acid to remove the extraneous matter.

The wool is then carded and combed, the fibers separated with fine wire teeth in preparation for spinning.

Because wool is highly susceptible to attack by moths, many companies treat their woolens with chemical mothproofing. Because this is considered to be a positive selling point, the fact that an item has been mothproofed is likely to appear on the label. It is best to buy unmothproofed products.

Most wool imported from the British Isles, South America, Iceland, and Greece is unmothproofed. Domestic stores and distributors often treat woolens on the premises to prevent problems with moths. Check with the retailers before purchase to see if mothproofing has been done. Often, by advance request, retailers will hold for you an unmothproofed garmet from a future shipment.

If you consider yourself allergic to wool, try a softer variety of a natural unbleached wool; your allergy may be to the bleaches and dyes.

One special advantage of wool is that it is naturally fire resistant and could be used (though it currently isn't) to make beds and sleepwear, which are by law required to be fireproof.

Leather

Most leathers are taken from animals that have been slaughtered for meat, and are treated with toxic tanning agents and dyes. Although many people prefer not to use leather for these reasons, it is much more comfortable than plastics and has an environmental advantage: making good use of a durable, natural material that would otherwise create an immense waste-disposal problem.

Down and Feathers

All are taken from the bodies of ducks and geese; goose down is the highest quality and most expensive. Down and feathers are processed only by washing and sanitizing, as chemicals would break down the proteins in the feathers and destroy them.

Ducks and geese raised for down and feather production are plucked four or five times during their lifespan; then they are butchered for meat, and their final feathers are removed by machine. The use of down and feathers, as of other animal products, comes into question by those who endeavor to live a cruelty-free lifestyle.

Kapok

A fiber taken from the seed pod of the tropical kapok, or silk-cotton tree, it is used as a natural stuffing material.

HOW I CHOOSE TEXTILE PRODUCTS

The most important thing for me is that the fiber be natural: cotton, linen, silk, ramie, or wool. Then I make sure that it doesn't have a toxic finish. Cotton especially often has a permanent-press finish, and cotton upholstery fabrics are often treated with a stain- and water-resistant finish. Last, I see if the dye is colorfast.

Here's how I rate textile products:

⊕ **Earthwise** textile products are:
• safe to wear;
• nonpolluting in their manufacture, use, and disposal;
• made from natural, renewable fibers (cotton, linen, silk, wool, or ramie) that are organically grown and do not contain petrochemical ingredients;
• biodegradable;
• natural in color or dyed with organically grown natural dyes; and
• free of fabric finishes.

🌿 **Natural** textile products are:
• safe to wear;
• made from natural, renewable fibers (cotton, linen, silk, wool, or ramie) that are not organically grown and may have residues of pesticides or other petrochemicals used in growing or processing;
• biodegradable;
• natural in color or dyed with natural dyes that are not organically grown (some bleached white fabrics are also included in this category); and
• free of fabric finishes.

⊕ **Nontoxic** textile products are:
• safe to wear;
• made from natural, renewable fibers (cotton, linen, silk, wool, or ramie) that are not organically grown and may have residues of pesticides or other petrochemicals used in growing or processing;
• biodegradable;
• dyed with petrochemical-based synthetic dyes; and
• free of fabric finishes.

Unfortunately, there are very few earthwise textile products, as most organically grown plants and wool from wild-range animals is made into yard or batting for stuffing. Some fabrics are available untreated and undyed, and you can dye them yourself with natural dyes. Most natural-fiber products are dyed with petrochemical dyes, but these are still preferable to plastic synthetic fibers.

SPECIAL TIPS

• Launder all textiles before use to remove any finishes or excess dyes that may be present (this includes fabric for beds or upholstery). If simple laundering is not sufficient, try several launderings or soaking the fabric in hot water with baking soda or vinegar for several hours or overnight. Sometimes several soakings are needed before all the excess chemicals are removed.
• To fireproof a fabric, dip it in a solution of one-fourth cup alum dissolved in one gallon water. Or use naturally flame-resistant wool.
• If you'd like to explore a new craft, try natural dyeing. See DYES for more information.

APRONS

Harmful materials: dyes, formaldehyde finishes, plastics (polyester and PVC/vinyl chloride).

At the Store/By Mail
Art-supply, cookware, and fine linen stores often sell cotton and linen aprons.

❦ Natural aprons
Cuddledown. Elegant linen hostess aprons.

Fiddler's Green Farm. Cotton aprons, in unbleached natural color.

Richman Cotton Company. Cotton aprons in natural color or white.

Testfabrics. Bib aprons of untreated cloth.

⊕ Nontoxic aprons
Clothcrafters. Big aprons for children and adults—white cotton duck or blue hickory-stripe denim with colored tie.

Lillian Vernon. Striped cotton apron (can be custom embroidered with name).

Mother Hart's Natural Products. Cotton all-purpose aprons with deep pockets in many colors.

Williams-Sonoma. Cotton cook's apron with Williams-Sonoma insignia.

BAGS, BAGS, BAGS

Harmful materials: dyes, formaldehyde finishes, plastics (polyester and PVC/vinyl chloride).

Natural-fiber bags of all shapes and sizes can be used and reused instead of paper or plastic bags.

At the Store/By Mail

❦ Natural bags
The Cotton Place. Laundry bags of unbleached duck.

Crocodile Tiers. Bags of many sizes made from heavy, unbleached, untreated, prewashed cotton, tested to be formaldehyde free.

Gem Cultures. Small fine-weave gauze drawstring tote bags.

Mother Hart's Natural Products. Untreated natural cotton drill laundry bag with sturdy draw cord.

Nichols Garden Nursery. Cotton string bags for shopping.

Seventh Generation. Cotton string bags for shopping.

⊕ Nontoxic bags
Buffalo Shirt Company. Cotton tote and other bags in an assortment of colors. Leather trim.

The *Cotton Place.* Cotton storage bags.

French Creek Sheep & Wool Company. Large cotton khaki carryalls with snaps.

Karen's Nontoxic Products. Cotton bags and pocketbooks in bright colors.

Lillian Vernon. Heavy-duty cotton tote bags. Can be custom embroidered with initials.

L. L. Bean. Cotton "boat and tote" bags in four sizes, made from heavy-duty canvas duck.

NOPE (Non-Polluting Enterprises). Cotton string bags.

Patti Collins Canvas Products. Cotton canvas purses in over a dozen colors, plus totes, saddlebags, backpacks, duffles, and tennis and school bags.

Port Canvas Company. Wide variety of hand-stitched bags made with cotton canvas and cotton webbing, including duffels, totes, handbags, briefcases, fanny packs, day packs, shave kits, camera cases, and tool wraps. Silk-screening and custom monogramming available.

Pueblo to People. Classic crocheted Guatemalan cotton totes with hand-loomed straps.

BARRIER CLOTH

Barrier cloth, a special type of fabric made from cotton, is reputed to act as a shield through which petrochemical vapors cannot penetrate. Many people who are sensitive to petrochemicals use this tightly woven fabric (three hundred threads per square inch) for mattress covers, auto-seat covers, furniture upholstery, and to cover any other item that may be giving off undesirable fumes. Barrier cloth is quite expensive, and though it may be helpful to many, it may not provide sufficient protection for everyone. It can also make either unbleached cotton batting or down and feathers more tolerable to those who are allergic to these natural materials.

Wash thoroughly before using, as barrier cloth has a very strong odor when new.

At the Store/By Mail
Order barrier cloth by mail; if you ask the salespeople at your local fabric store, they probably will not have heard of it.

⊕ *Nontoxic barrier cloth*
Allergy Resources. Barrier-cloth mattress, box-spring, and pillow covers.
Allergy Relief Shop. Barrier cloth-pillow covers, and mattress and box-spring covers. Also available in yardage. ·
The Cotton Place. Naturalguard barrier cloth, of pima cotton in an oxford weave with a 280-thread count. No permanent chemical finish. By the yard or in ready-made mattress and pillow covers, ironing-board covers, garment storage bags, and shoe bags.
The Living Source. Yardage, plus mattress covers, pillow covers and other specialty items upon request.

BATH MATS

Harmful materials: dyes, plastic (polyester).

At the Store/By Mail
Choose 100% cotton bath mats.

❀ *Natural bathmats*
Janice Corporation. Bath-rug and toilet-seat-cover set in natural cotton.

⊕ *Nontoxic bathmats*
Chambers. Bath mats of handwoven cotton from an age-old but still thriving Portuguese cottage industry. Also mats of cotton terry loop.
Garnet Hill. Heavyweight reversible cotton rugs.
Land's End. Cotton tub mats and reversible oval rugs.
Vermont Country Store. Cotton bath mats in assorted colors and sizes.

BATH TOWELS

Harmful materials: dyes, plastic (polyester).

At the Store/By Mail
Choose cotton towels.

❀ *Natural bath towels*
Chambers. Undyed, unbleached cotton terry loop towels and washcloths. Imported from West Germany.

⊕ *Nontoxic bath towels*
Cannon Towels. (Cannon). *Allergy Relief Shop.*
Chambers. Several patterns of fine pima-cotton bath towels. Also cotton terry towels from Scotland, cotton waffle-weave towels from Austria, and cotton Turkish towels. Linen guest towels from China. Cotton friction terry towels.
Clothcrafters. Cotton terry bath sheets, towels, and washcloths; cornflower blue or white.
The Cotton Place. Terry towels and washcloths.

Cuddledown. Austrian towels and wash-cloths of pure cotton. Solid colors.

Fieldcrest Towels (Fieldcrest Mills).

Garnet Hill. Towels of Egyptian and Austrian honeycomb cotton.

J. P. Stevens Towels (J. P. Stevens).

Janice Corporation. Cotton terry towels.

Land's End. Thick pima-cotton towels in assorted colors. Can be monogrammed.

Lillian Vernon. Cotton terry/velour bath sheets. Can be custom embroidered with name or nickname.

Martex Towels (Westpoint Pepperell).

Simmons Handcrafts. Cotton washcloths and hand towels handwoven on the northern California coast, with a weft of cotton chenille for texture and softness.

Vermont Country Store. Hotel-weight cotton towels in assorted colors.

BATTING

Harmful materials: plastic (polyester), pesticides.

Use cotton or wool batting. Choose cotton batting carefully, because it may contain contaminants, of which a petrochemical oil is the most common. Used on most batting to reduce cotton dust produced by the batting machines, it is not removed during later processing. The Occupational Safety and Health Administration (OSHA) has set strict standards for cotton dust, as excess amounts cause lung disease in factor workers. Some manufacturers say that applying oil to the batting is the only way to comply with this regulation; nevertheless, batting is available that is made without the oil.

Bleach is sometimes used to whiten batting. It also removes the natural cotton smell. Unbleached batting is light brown, flecked with cottonseeds, and can smell strongly of the cotton itself. Because the bleach is washed out after it has removed objectionable natural and chemical odors, some people may prefer bleached batting.

Pesticides are used heavily on cotton. The batting process is purely mechanical and does not cleanse the fibers of these chemicals.

Choose cotton batting that is free from pesticides, oil, and bleach. Individuals with chemical sensitivities should give batting careful tests before use in futons, mattresses, pillows, or quilts.

At the Store/By Mail

Look for natural-fiber batting in fabric stores.

⊕ Earthwise batting

Dona Designs. Organically grown cotton batting. ⊞

Pure Podunk. Batting made from wool from sheep raised on small New England farms. Wool is washed with hot water and pure, colorless, odorless soap, and air dried.

Natural batting

Janice Corporation. Cotton felt batting in rolls. Also precut cotton batts for quilts.

Xhaxhi. Batting of New Zealand Chanco wool, a mechanically crimped wool fiber with enhanced springiness.

Nontoxic batting

The Cotton Place. Bleached surgical-type cotton batting with no chemical finish.

BED LINENS

Harmful materials: dyes, formaldehyde finishes, plastic (polyester).

Natural bed linens

Chambers. Pure untreated-cotton bed linens made without chemical, dyes, or bleaches; from West Germany.

Janice Corporation. Combed, knit white

cotton sheets in crib, twin, and double sizes.

Testfabrics. Untreated 108-inch unbleached cotton muslin sheeting. Also available in bleached 180-thread-count percale cotton.

⊕ Nontoxic bed linens

Chambers. Fine sheets of cotton flannel, long-staple Egyptian cotton, linen, linen/cotton blend, and cotton sheeting woven with embroidered trim. From England, Belgium, France, Italy, and China.

Clothcrafters. Seamed cotton flannel sheets and pillowcases made of "high grade domestic flannel which comes in narrower than sheet widths." They call them Princess Sheets because "a princess would feel a pea under her mattress before she'd feel this seam." Pink, yellow, mint, and white. Can't beat these prices.

The Company Store. Cotton percale sheets and pillowcases, 195 thread count, in colors. Also cotton percale waterbed sheets, sofa-sleeper sheets, and oversize sheet in colors. Will monogram and do custom work.

The Cotton Place. Sheets and pillowcases of white muslin or linen. Italian linen sheets and pillowcases in white and colors, plus pillowcases of silk charmeuse.

Cuddledown. Belgian cotton flannel bedding in solids and plaids.

The Futon Shop. Belgian cotton flannel sheets.

Garnet Hill. Cotton sheets in floral, stripe, and paisley patterns from France, Belgium, and the United States, some with pillow shams, duvet covers, and pettiskirts to match. Also Italian linen and linen/cotton sheets, plus cotton flannel sheets from England. Handcrafted duvet covers, pillow shams, and blanket covers from China.

Janice Corporation. White cotton sheeting in two widths.

Land's End. Two hundred-thread-count cotton percale bed linens in pastel colors. Can be monogrammed. Also matching pillow shams and dust ruffles.

L. L. Bean. Belgian long-staple-cotton flannel sheets in solid colors.

Mother Hart's Natural Products. Cotton flannel duvet cover/sheet sets, with pillow shams included.

Vermont Country Store. Belgian cotton flannel sheets and duvet covers.

Wamsutta Supercale (Wamsutta). A 200-thread-count percale. *The Allergy Shop, Allergy Resources, Chambers, The Cotton Place, The Futon Shop, Garnet Hill, Janice Corporation, Vermont Country Store.*

Winter Silks. Silk pillowcases. White, pink, and blue.

BEDS

Harmful materials: dyes, flame retardants, plastics (polyester, polyurethane).

CREATING A NATURAL BED

Comfortable natural beds can be created by combining components made of natural materials. The least expensive such bed is a Japanese cotton futon. After trying many combinations, I've finally settled on a wood-slat frame topped with a cotton futon and a mattress stuffed with organically raised wool.

• *Cotton Mattresses and Box Springs.* These are stuffed with cotton batting and covered with cotton ticking. Well-made cotton innerspring mattresses are very comfortable and can last for twenty years.

• *Cotton Thermal Blankets.* A stack of at least eight blankets can serve as a mattress.

• *Feather beds.* These are large pillows the size of a mattress, filled with feathers and covered with all-cotton down-proof ticking. Not thick enough to be used alone as a mattress, feather beds are usually placed on top of a mattress or futon for added softness and warmth.

• *Futons.* These Japanese folding mattresses made of cotton batting have become quite popular in recent years. They are available in several thicknesses. Local futon stores are often willing to make them with your preferred materials.

Because futons cannot be washed, it is best to use a protective futon cover. Flip the futon frequently when making the bed and puff it up, as the cotton compresses over time. In Japan, futons are rolled up and stored during the day, then unrolled for sleep at night. They should be aired outdoors in the sun at least four times a year.

Note: Due to a recent ruling by the Bureau of Home Furnishings, *all* futons must now be treated with a boric-acid flame retardant. The futon industry is none too happy about this, and most futon makers will be happy to make you an untreated futon upon presentation of a doctor's prescription.

• *Hammocks.* Completely washable, portable, and inexpensive, hammocks make you feel as if you are floating on a cloud.

• *Rollaway Bed Frames.*

• *Wooden Slat Beds.*

Be very careful when choosing a cotton mattress or futon. It can be a big investment (in the price range of a high-quality synthetic mattress) and will usually not be returnable, so you'll want to make sure it is as free from chemicals as possible.

At the Store/By Mail

⊕ Nontoxic feather beds

Cuddledown. Down/feather-blend feather bed with all-cotton covering plus a removable protective cotton cover.

Feathered Friends. Heavy white pima-cotton ticking filled with a 10-90 down-feather mix, with a unique baffle construction to prevent shifting.

Garnet Hill. Cotton bed of lofty cotton batting (twenty ounces per square yard), channel-quilted inside a two hundred-thread-count cotton shell.

Warm Things. Cotton Cambric casing filled with small white goose feathers.

⊕ Earthwise futons

– Bright Future Futons (Bright Future Futons). Cotton stuffing organically grown. Cotton fabric is processed without oil sprays and washed three times in baking soda. By mail only. *Bright Future Futons, Karen's Nontoxic Products.*

– *Dona Designs.* Futons in all sizes, filled with organically grown cotton, and cotton covered. Also futon covers of unbleached muslin with ties. ⊞

– *Jantz Design & Manufacturing.* Futons of cotton of cotton/wool blend, with soft cotton covers.

– *Pure Podunk.* Futons made of wool from sheep raised on small New England farms. Wool is washed with wood heated hot water and pure, colorless, odorless soap, and air dried. Cover fabric is untreated cotton that is soaked in a vinegar-water wash, rinsed, soaked in a baking-soda-water wash, rinsed again, then dried in the Vermont air and sunshine. Sewn with linen thread.

✿ Natural futons

Allergy Relief Shop. Futons made to order and covered with barrier cloth.

A Very Small Shop. Handcrafted futons of cotton batting covered with natural cotton drill. Also kits to make your own.

Blue Heron. "Hypoallergenic" futons filled with cotton and encased in canvas that is washed and free from sizing and does not contain a flame retardant.

Bright Future Futon. Futons in standard and custom sizes made from unbleached cotton duck and non-flame-retardant cotton batting, or unbleached cotton duck prewashed three times in baking soda and stuffed with organically grown cotton.

Essential Alternatives. Futons with cotton batting encased in a heavy cotton muslin shell.

The Futon Shop. Filled with long-fiber cotton batting and encased in durable unbleached cotton drill. Batting treated with borate.

High Cotton Company. Hefty futons of cotton batting sewn mattress-style in boxed cotton ticking of the finest duck. Also custon mattresses to fit odd-sized bed frames.

Northwest Futon Company. Handmade futons of sturdy cotton shells stuffed with either raw cotton or Pacific Northwest wool.

Xhaxhi. Futons of cotton or a blend of cotton and New Zealand Chanco wool, a mechanically crimped wool fiber with enhanced springiness.

❧ *Natural hammocks*

Essential Alternatives. Handcrafted supple cotton rope hammock with hand-selected oak stringers.

Hangouts. Hand loomed in 100 percent cotton. Some have beautiful hand-crocheted ornamental edges. Natural color or dyed.

Heavenly Hammocks. Cotton woven Yucatán hammocks, natural or multicolored.

Langenbach. Each hammock has over one thousand feet of highest-quality cotton rope woven together without knots and held by steam-bent oak spreaders.

⊕ *Earthwise mattresses and box springs*

— *Dona Designs.* Innerspring mattresses filled with organically grown cotton and covered with unbleached cotton. ⊞

— *Pure Podunk.* Mattresses made of wool from sheep raised on small New England farms. Wool is washed with wood heated hot water and pure, colorless, odorless soap, and air dried. Cover fabric is untreated cotton. Sewn with linen thread.

❧ *Natural mattresses and box springs*

Allergy Relief Shop. Custom-made cotton mattresses and box springs, covered with barrier cloth.

The Futon Shop. Handcrafted cotton innerspring mattresses, custom made by the oldest mattress manufacturer in the U.S.

Janice Corporation. Custom-made innerspring mattresses with cotton filling and ticking.

See also FURNITURE for wooden-slat beds.

BEDSPREADS

Harmful materials: dyes, plastics (nylon, polyester).

At the Store/By Mail

Cotton bedspreads can be found in most department stores; bedspreads made of cotton and other natural fibers are also available by mail.

❧ *Natural bedspreads*

Allergy Relief Shop. Cotton bedspreads in natural and white.

Janice Corporation. Cotton Plymouth historic bedspread.

Laura Copenhaver Industries. Petticoat valances or dust ruffles made of hand-hemmed cotton muslin with or without hand-tied fringe. In natural cream and white. Hand-tied cotton fishnet canopies for four-poster beds; authentic copies of very old designs. In natural cream and white.

Vermont Country Store. Woven cotton bedspreads in natural or white.

⊕ *Nontoxic bedspreads*

The Company Store. Cotton bed ruffles and pillow shams in a good selection of styles and colors. Will also do custom work.

Country Curtains. Handwoven colonial bed covers in a cotton/wool blend.

Laura Copenhaver Industries. Coverlets of long-fiber cotton and virgin wool with handmade hems and fringes. Available in wool/cotton blend or all cotton; also available as yardage.

Shama Imports. Bedspreads made from natural hand-loomed cotton, hand embroidered in Kashmir with dyed wool.

BLANKETS & AFGHANS

Harmful materials: dyes, pesticides (mothproofing), plastics (acrylic, nylon, polyester).

At the Store/By Mail

Buy blankets and afghans made of natural fibers: cotton, silk, cotton/linen or cotton/wool blends, unmothproofed alpaca, and unmothproofed wool. Preferably, blankets should be white or a natural, undyed color. Cotton thermal blankets can be found in department stores; other fibers will probably have to be ordered by mail.

⊕ Earthwise blankets and afghans

Sajama Alpaca. Blankets made from alpaca yarns hand spun and dyed with plants indigenous to the highlands of Bolivia. The wool comes from animals who live in their own habitat on the open range, kept by local people who spin the yarn themselves.

✿ Natural blankets and afghans

Chule's. Undyed handwoven blankets of unbleached worsted lambswool in natural colors.

The Cotton Place. Unbleached cotton flannel "sheet" blankets.

Janice Corporation. Unbleached lightweight cotton blanket with stitched edges, and cotton double-thickness thermal blanket. Natural-color cotton knitted lap robe/afghan.

Vermont Country Store. Cotton throws in two sizes. Natural or colors.

Winter Silks. Generous knitted silk afghan. Natural color.

⊕ Nontoxic blankets and afghans

Allergy Relief Shop. Cotton thermal blankets.

Berea College Student Craft Industries. Soft wool throws in solids and plaids.

Chambers. Blankets from Switzerland, France, and the United States include a wool/angora blend, all wool, cotton thermal, a cotton/linen blend, and a blend of 70 percent Bactrian camelhair and 30 percent new wool. Throws include a heather mohair, lambswool, a silk/cotton blend, and an alpaca. Also cotton piqué bed covers.

The Cotton Place. Cotton thermal blankets.

Country Curtains. Cotton throw-style afghans.

The Futon Shop. Cotton thermal blankets, and wool/cotton-blend Pendleton Indian blankets with colorful Native American designs.

Garnet Hill. Cotton thermal and other woven blankets made of an Egyptian/domestic cotton blend or Supima cotton. Also blankets of merino wool.

Goodwin Weavers. Reasonably priced cotton afghans with traditional American designs.

Janice Corporation. Cotton thermal blankets in colors. Also wool Hudson's Bay point blankets.

Landau. Icelandic wool blankets/throws in soft plaids.

L. L. Bean. Luxurious blankets of silky, long-staple pima cotton in colors.

Mother Hart's Natural Products. Handloomed cotton throw blankets.

Richman Cotton Company. Woven cotton blankets in white and colors.

Warm Things. Cotton/wool blend throw blankets.

CLOTHING

Harmful materials: dyes, formaldehyde finishes, pesticides (mothproofing), plastics (acrylic, nylon, polyester, PVC/vinyl chloride, spandex).

At the Store/By Mail

Purchase clothing made from natural fibers and wash them before wearing to remove excess finishes and dyes. Switching to natural fibers will be a gradual process; as much as you might like to, you probably won't be able to discard your entire wardrobe and buy all new clothes. Start by sorting through your existing clothing to determine which of the pieces you already own are made from natural fibers. Wear these most often, and the next time you buy new clothes, look for natural fibers.

You should be able to find clothing made from natural fibers in better stores in metropolitan areas. If you can't, plenty of natural-fiber clothing of all types and sizes is available by mail.

All businesses listed here carry items made from 100 percent natural fibers, but not all their garments will necessarily be made from natural fibers. Check descriptions carefully. In addition, fabrics may contain finishes and dyes, be sewn with polyester thread, or be finished with polyester zippers, elastic, trim, linings, or interfacings.

Abbreviations used: (M) for men's clothing; (W) for women's clothing.

Earthwise clothing

Sajama Alpaca. Sweaters made from hand-spun alpaca yarns dyed with plants indigenous to the highlands of Bolivia. Wool comes from animals who live in their own habitat on the open range, kept by local people who spin the yarn themselves.

Natural clothing

Chambers. (MW) Thick, full-length robes of cotton terry loop pile made without chemicals, dyes, or bleaches.

Chico Fabric Designs. (W) Clothes made from mostly white natural fibers; some fabric imported from Third World countries.

Earthware. (W) A unique garment that converts from skirt to pantaloons to nursing dress—jumper. Handcrafted from your choice of natural-fiber fabric.

French Creek Sheep & Wool Company. (MW) Sweaters, skirts, mufflers. Also hand-knitted clothing from other natural fibers and sheepskin coats from their own farm. Elegant, classic styles.

Karen's Nontoxic Products. (W) Cotton knee-highs, stockings, and anklets.

Pantropic. (MW) Panama hats in a wide variety of styles.

Testfabrics. Untreated cotton T-shirts.

Nontoxic clothing

Allergy Relief Shop. (MW) Cotton underwear, flannel gowns, and coffee coats for women. Also men's cotton socks.

Amberwood. Military-style canvas belts in many colors.

Artventure. (MW) Cotton clothing made of authentic Javanese batik.

Berea College Student Craft Industries. (MW) Wool mufflers in muted colors. Also mohair stoles.

Brooks Brothers. (MW) High-quality, classic natural-fiber clothing—mostly for men, but a few items for women. Men's items include wool suits, sports jackets and trousers, cotton shirts, silk suspenders and neckwear, leather belts, wool or cotton sweaters, cotton/wool-blend shirts and robes, cotton raincoats, and more.

Buffalo Shirt Company. (MW) Basic cotton knits, primarily cotton sweat clothes in a full spectrum of colors.

Bullock and Jones. (M) Classic natural-fiber clothing with a modern flair. Sports jackets and trousers, cotton shirts, silk neckwear, wool sweaters, and more.

Cable Car Clothiers. (MW) Fine classic natural-fiber clothing. For women there is a selection of wool suits, cotton shirts, and cotton sleepwear; for men, traditional dress and sports attire.

Chi Pants. (MW) Specializing in Natural-Fiber pants and shorts with a "unique gusseted design that gives you total comfort with no tightness or binding." Many styles and fabrics, from jeans to slacks. Also other occasional natural-fiber items such as cotton web belts and shirts.

The Cotton Company. (W) Feminine, stylish clothing made primarily of cotton (watch out for the cotton/poly blends).

The Cotton Place. (MW) Lounge wear, swimsuits, cotton scarves and belts, linen handkerchiefs, cotton knit gloves, silk scarves, cotton and silk underwear, flannel nightgowns and pajamas, terry robes, cotton and silk stockings, cotton garter belts, socks, sweatshirts and sweaters, wool dress slacks. All-cotton laboratory and hospital wear, including white twill jackets, lab coats, scrub suits and gowns.

Crocodile Tiers. (MW) Custom-made clothing in simple styles, made from natural-fiber fabrics tested to verify they have no formaldehyde finishes.

Cuddledown. (W) A small collection of cotton lingerie items.

Darnell Design. (MW) Cotton T-shirts printed with designs that have messages relating to personal and environmental transformation. Their inks "contain no formaldehydes, lead, or PCBs."

Decent Exposures. (W) Cotton bras, camisoles, and panties for women of virtually every size and shape. All elastic is covered.

Deva. (MW) Handmade cotton clothing; some fabrics from Guatemala. Good, basic styles in attractive solid colors. Pants, jackets, shorts, skirts, vests, sweat clothes, T-shirts, shirts.

Eddie Bauer. (MW) Classic casual sportswear in natural fibers. Shirts, sweaters, dresses, skirts, pants, nightwear, silk underwear for men, cotton web belts.

Exotic Gifts. (MW) Cotton, silk, and wool clothing imported from Eastern countries. Some fabrics hand loomed, some in natural colors.

Garnet Hill. (MW) Wide variety of clothing in cotton, silk, wool, and linen. Nightwear, underwear, socks, and women's skirts, blouses, jackets, and pants.

Gothic Image. (MW) Cotton and wool clothing imported from Guatemala and the Andes. Most made from cotton fabric handwoven by mayans in traditional patterns. Includes sweaters and ponchos handwoven by village craftspeople made from natural-colored alpaca wool.

Harmony Moon. Colorful cotton T-shirts and knit dresses batiked with whimsical designs.

High Sierra Concepts. (MW) Cotton long johns and fleecy cotton sweat clothes in rainbow colors.

Howard Graphics. (MW) Short- and long-sleeved heavyweight cotton T-shirts, printed with designs reflective of Native American culture.

James River Traders. (MW) Classic casual sportswear in cotton, linen, and wool. Shirts, pants, skirts, shorts, dresses, and jackets.

Janice Corporation. (MW) Cotton robes, nightwear, underwear, hats, scarves, sweaters, sweater jackets, mittens, socks, and stockings. Also silk stockings for women and undersocks for men and women, plus wool/cotton dress socks for men.

J. Jill Ltd. (W) Pretty dresses and separates, mostly cotton, with generous fit and detailing. Many are exclusive designs with loose, flowing styles. Misses' and women's sizes.

Landau. (MW) Beautiful imported hand-knit wool sweaters—many of warm Icelandic wool. Also a classic loden cape for women, imported from Austria.

Land's End. (MW) High-quality, moderately priced sportswear and casual wear, mostly cotton, linen, and wool. Cotton rugby shirts, pants, knit dresses.

Laughing Bear Batik. (MW) Batik cotton knit shirts and pajamas with a variety of fanciful designs.

Lillian Vernon. (MW) Cotton terry or waffle-weave robes. Can be custom embroidered.

L. L. Bean. (MW) Basic outdoor sportswear of cotton and wool.

Mandala. Simple, flowing, elegant handcrafted cotton clothing made by artisans living in the Blue Ridge Mountains of Virginia. Blouses, skirts, capes.

Mother Hart's Natural Products. (MW) Odds and ends of cotton clothing, including cotton-blend leotards and tights. Unbelievably low prices.

One World Trading Company. (MW) Shirts, skirts, and jackets made from fabrics hand dyed and handwoven by Mayan artisans.

Orvis. (MW) Classic sportswear made mostly of cotton (watch out for poly/cotton blends). Small collection of knit silk turtlenecks and underwear.

Penthouse Gallery. (W) Flowing, contemporary styles in natural fibers.

Powers' Country Store. (MW) Rugged cotton clothing including bib-overall jumpers, flannel-lined jeans, cotton knee-high socks for women, cotton chamois robes, and cotton T-shirts with native designs.

Pueblo to People. (MW) hand-loomed cotton clothing. Blouses, skirts, jackets, shirts, shawls. Also alpaca sweaters and mittens, and Panama hats.

Richman Cotton Company. (MW) Basic cotton clothing, underwear, and socks. Available undyed, or dyed with "nontoxic" dyes.

Royal Silk. (W) Moderately priced silk and cotton separates—mostly blouses. Also lingerie.

Simply Divine. (W) Basic cotton solid-color knits: T-shirts with nature-oriented designs.

Strand Surplus Senter. (MW) A fine-print listing of cotton and wool surplus clothing from armed forces worldwide.

Tweeds. (MW) Simple, loose, elegant clothing in cotton, linen, silk, and wool. Sweaters, pants, shirts, dresses, shorts.

Vermont Country Store. (MW) Sweaters, skirts, jumpers, slacks, separates, socks, stockings, sock and glove liners, underwear, cotton garment shields, robes, pajamas, nightgowns, and sleep caps in cotton, flannel, wool, and silk. Also handkerchiefs of Irish linen or cotton batiste.

Victoria's Secret. (W) Between the synthetic satin and lace, there's quite a selection of cotton and lace lingerie, including nightgowns, robes, camisoles, and underwear. Also natural-fiber sportswear.

Winter Silks. (MW) Long johns, underwear, socks, pajamas, sweaters, turtlenecks, scarves, gloves—everything to keep you warm all winter. Made from silk and silk/cotton or silk/wool blends. Also silk stockings.

COMFORTERS & QUILTS

Harmful materials: dyes, plastics (nylon, polyester).

Many comforters are available, priced from twenty-five dollars for a polyester-filled model to five-hundred dollars or more for the highest-quality white goose down encased in a fine cotton fabric.

The least expensive natural-fiber comforters are filled with cotton or wool batting and are made much like an old-fashioned quilt. For a little more money, you can buy a silk-filled comforter, a down-and-feather comforter, or one made with duck down and/or feathers. Pure goose down is the most expensive. (If the label says simply *down,* you can assume it's duck down.)

The best (and most expensive and warmest) comforters are made with imported white goose down and are sewn together with baffles—strips of fabric sewn between the top and bottom layers to prevent any cold spots caused by sewn-through seams. If you live in a very cold climate or sleep alone, it probably would be worth the extra investment to buy a comforter with baffled construction. But if you live in a moderate climate or have someone else to help generate body heat, a sewn-through comforter will keep you quite warm. Placing a cotton thermal blanket between the top sheet and the comforter can add more warmth, if needed.

Comforters should frequently be aired outside in the sunshine. A washable comforter cover (an oversize pillowcase with zippers or snaps that also doubles as a top sheet) will help you avoid having to wash the comforter itself as frequently.

At the Store/By Mail

Purchase comforters and quilts made from cotton and stuffed with down, cotton, or wool batting at department or bedding stores, or at local specialty shops. All comforters listed here are covered with cotton fabric.

⊕ Earthwise comforters

− *Dona Designs.* Comforters and summer quilts filled with organically grown cotton and covered with unbleached cotton. ⊞

− *Pure Podunk.* Comforters stuffed with wool from sheep raised on small New England farms. Wool is washed with hot water and pure, colorless, odorless soap, and air dried. Cover fabric is untreated cotton.

♣ Natural comforters

Allergy Relief Shop. Cotton comforters with two-hundred-thread-count percale covers. Also available with barrier-cloth covers.

Chambers. A variety of comforters with fillings such as cotton, cashmere, and silk. A wool-filled duvet from West Germany is

made from wool that "is sheared and cleaned, but otherwise unprocessed in any way."

Cuddledown. Authentic European prime silver goose-down comforters. Also a summer-weight style.

Feathered Friends. Comforters with pima- or Egyptian-cotton casings filled with white goose down. Can also revitalize old comforters or sleeping bags.

Janice Corporation. Quilts covered with natural-color combed cotton or white barrier cloth and filled with cotton or lambswool.

Jantz Design & Manufacturing. Wool comforter made of pure, untreated layers of lambswool batting tufted in place between prewashed all-cotton sheeting. Wool is washed and carded but left othersise unprocessed.

Scandia Down Shops. European-style comforters filled with down, down/feather blend, and silk.

Xhaxhi. Comforters stuffed with New Zealand Chanco wool, a mechanically crimped wool fiber with enhanced springiness.

⊗ Nontoxic comforters

The Company Store. Goose-down comforters in a variety of colors and styles, including overstuffed and oversize. Also comforters made of 10 percent down and 90 percent feathers that are almost as warm and much less expensive. Cotton quilts, and cotton comforter covers, fitted sheets, and matching shams. Will also revitalize old comforters, and make custom comforters. Good prices.

Essential Alternatives. Comforters of goose down, covered with long-staple cambric cotton. Also quilts made with cotton or lambswool batting and covered with cotton prints or solid colors.

The Futon Shop. Comforters filled with either down or cotton batting.

Garnet Hill. Cotton-filled cotton patchwork quilts and solid-color comforters.

Also a silk-filled comforter covered in raw silk.

Hearthside Quilts. Precut kits for beautiful quilts in traditional and contemporary designs—cotton tops and unbleached muslin backing. Can be purchased without polyester filling material and filled with cotton or wool batting.

Laura Copenhaver Industries. Custom quilts are appliquéd, pieced, and quilted by hand in any combination of colors or materials desired.

L. L. Bean. Cotton patchwork-design comforter with cotton fill.

Mother Hart's Natural Products. Cotton-filled and 90/10 feather/down-filled comforters with cotton cambric two-hundred-thread-count covers. Solid colors.

Vermont Country Store. Comforters filled with white goose feathers and covered with fine-weave blue and white cotton ticking.

DYES

Harmful materials: dyes.

A number of natural dyestuffs are available that produce a whole rainbow of beautiful colors. All types of plants, including flowers, weeds, trees, roots, and bark, as well as various foods, herbs, and spices can be used. Fennel, for example, produces a brilliant yellow; eucalyptus, a deep red; walnut leaves, a whole spectrum of earthy browns. Certain animals and insects also provide natural dyes: mollusks yield a Tyrian purple, and for centuries tiny cochineal insects were the most widely used ingredient for red dye. In ancient times, nearly one thousand different natural sources provided dyestuffs.

Some materials for dyestuffs can be gathered in their natural habitat, while other, more exotic dyes can be purchased.

There is some concern about using natural dyes because of the toxic mordants (such as copper, chrome, and iron) that are used to fix the dyes, but I've been told by two natural dyers that mordants are unnecessary. Natural dyestuffs used alone create beautiful, soft, subtle shades of color that can't be duplicated with synthetic dyes. For brighter, deeper colors, toxic mordants must be used, but without them the dyes will still hold.

At the Store/By Mail

Look for natural dyestuffs in local stores that sell dyeing equipment, or order by mail.

Natural dyestuffs

Rumplestiltskin. Natural dyes, mordants, and instruction books.

Nontoxic dyestuffs

Cerulean Blue. Petrochemical-based procion, fibracron, and telana dyes for dyeing natural-fiber fabrics. "We have gradually eliminated catalog items possessing questionable safety records out of concern for our customers and staff. We have cut possible carcinogens, toxins, or other potentially harmful substances from our product line. They don't carry natural dyes because of toxic mordants.

Richman Cotton Company. Nontoxic dyes for direct dyeing of all natural fibers.

FABRIC

Harmful materials: dyes, formaldehyde finishes, pesticides (mothproofing), plastics (acrylic, nylon, polyester, PVC/vinyl chloride, spandex).

At the Store/By Mail

Better fabric stores will carry a large variety of natural-fiber fabrics. Wash all fabrics before use to remove any excess dyes and finishes.

Natural fabrics

Cerulean Blue. Basic cotton and silk fabrics prepared for dyeing.

The Cotton Place. Unbleached cotton duck, felt padding, sateen, muslin. Also linen and noil silk.

Crocodile Tiers. A wide variety of fabrics: cotton knits, terry, heavy duck, canvas, and more. Also unique handwoven fabrics. All untreated and formaldehyde tested; can be dyed to order. Will prewash fabrics.

Janice Corporation. A variety of cotton fabrics: barrier cloth, muslin, drill, duck, downproof fabric, plissé, denim, batiste, flannel in two weights, percale.

Sureway Trading Enterprises. Good prices on a comprehensive selection of natural-colored and white silk fabrics from corduroy to organza, plus silk/wool blends for suiting. many available dyed, or dye them yourself.

Testfabrics. Untreated fabrics ready to dye: linen, silk, wool, and over fifty varieties of cotton.

Thai Silks. Nearly one hundred silk fabrics—also some linen and wool—many in natural shades. Also dyed in many colors.

Utex Trading Enterprises. One of the largest Chinese-silk suppliers in America; they directly import over one hundred different varieties of silk fabric. Undyed, dyed, or print fabrics.

◉ Nontoxic fabrics

The Cotton Place. Cotton absorbent toweling, Swiss batiste, pima broadcloth, corduroy, interlock knit, organdy, plissé, and drapery fabric. Also silk charmeuse, crepe de chine, noil, and China silk.

Homespun Fabrics & Draperies. Neutral-colored and interestingly textured cotton fabrics up to ten feet wide; no chemical finishes. Can be used for draperies, upholstery, clothing, wall coverings, tablecloths, bedspreads.

Sew Natural. A variety of cotton fabrics.

Shama Imports. Natural hand-loomed cotton, hand embroidered in Kashmir with dyed wool.

IRONING-BOARD COVERS

Harmful materials: plastics (polyester, tetrafluoroethylene).

At the Store/By Mail

Buy all-cotton ironing-board covers at hardware stores.

❦ Natural ironing-board covers

Clothcrafters. Made from unbleached cotton sateen.

The Cotton Place. Made of bleached muslin or linen. Also felt ironing-board pads.

Janice Corporation. Cotton ironing board pad and cover, prewashed in vinegar and baking soda.

Mother Hart's Natural Products. All-around elasticized, hooded ironing-board cover of untreated heavy cotton, with attached thick cotton padding.

Tug o' War 100% Cotton Ironing-Board Covers and Pads (John Ritzenthaler Company).

Vermont Country Store. Cotton ironing-board cover with cotton-batting underpad.

KITCHEN TOWELS

Harmful materials: plastic (polyester).

At the Store/By Mail

Buy cotton or linen kitchen towels everywhere kitchen towels are sold.

◉ Nontoxic kitchen towels

Clothcrafters. Plain white cotton towels in ample sizes; red-and-white cotton towels.

The Cotton Place. Absorbent dish and hand towels with no permanent finish.

Country Curtains. Cotton terry kitchen towels.

Cuddledown. French cotton/linen-blend kitchen towels.

Janice Corporation. White cotton all-purpose towels: bird's-eye reverse weave and flour sacks. Also absorbent towels in blue.

Seventh Generation. Cotton waffle-weave dish towels in white and colors. Also paper towels made of recycled paper.

Vermont Country Store. Large cotton flour-sack towels

Williams-Sonoma. Cotton kitchen towels in a variety of patterns. Also glass-drying towels, cotton flour-sack towels and cotton/linen towels.

❉ **Paper towels made from 100 percent recycled paper**

2nd Opinion. Paper towels made from recycled paper with no bleaches or dioxins.

C.A.R.E. Paper Towels (Ashdun Industries). No inks, dyes, or fragrances.

Envision Paper Towels (Fort Howard Corporation). *Atlantic Recycled Paper Company.*

Green Forest Paper Towels (Fort Howard Corporation).

Vegan Street. Dioxin-free paper towels.

LUGGAGE

Harmful materials: plastics (nylon, polyester, PVC/vinyl chloride).

At the Store/By Mail
Order luggage made from cotton canvas by mail.

⊕ **Nontoxic luggage**
Buffalo Shirt Company. Cotton luggage, briefcases, and duffles in an assortment of colors, handcrafted in their own shop. Leather trim and insignia.

Lillian Vernon. Black cotton canvas attaché with inside pockets and pencil/pen holders. Leather trim.

Mother Hart's Natural Products. Rugged cotton canvas luggage, including wardrobe and duffle bags, and attachés.

Orvis. Tough Battenkill luggage, made from water-resistant cotton canvas duck. Leather trim.

Port Canvas Company. Hand-stitched cotton canvas luggage with cotton webbing in a variety of styles and sizes, including carry-on and garment bags. Custom work available.

MATTRESS PADS

Harmful materials: plastic (polyester).

HOMEMADE ALTERNATIVES
• *Mattress pad:* Sew together several layers of cotton flannel BLANKETS. You can also add a thin layer of cotton or wool batting between the blankets (be sure to quilt the pad if you do, to keep the batting in place).
• Waterproof mattress pad: Make one from BARRIER CLOTH (several layers if necessary) or from cotton-covered rubber sheeting, available by the yard from *Vermont Country Store.*

At the Store/By Mail
Various mattress pads are available, made from cotton or wool or a blend of the two. If you need a waterproof pad, use rubber pads covered with cotton flannel.

⊕ **Earthwise mattress pads**
– *Dona Designs.* Quilted unbleached-cotton mattress pads filled with organically grown cotton. ⊞ Packaged in cellophane.

– *Pure Podunk.* Thick mattress pad made of wool from sheep raised on small New England farms. Wool is washed with wood heated hot water and pure, colorless, odorless soap, and air dried. Cover fabric is untreated cotton that is soaked in a vinegar/water wash, rinsed, soaked in a baking soda/water wash, rinsed again, then dried in the Vermont air and sunshine. Sewn with linen thread.

❧ **Natural mattress pads**
Chambers. Wool mattress pad made in Canada of two-and-one-half-inch-thick natural wool pile stitched to cotton backing.

The Company Store. Cotton-filled and -covered mattress pads and pillow protectors, and wool-shag mattress pads.

Cuddle Ewe. "Cuddler underquilt" made of thick blended natural wool (minimally processed) in a cotton-ticking cover. Four and one half pounds of wool per square yard.

Essential Alternatives. Wool mattress pad with cotton backing.

Feathered Friends. Wool mattress pad imported from West Germany, filled with a generous amount of virgin wool. One side is a thick wool fleece for winter use; the other is cotton knit, for summer.

The Futon Shop. Cotton batting quilted between layers of cotton muslin.

Garnet Hill. Mattress pads of wool fleece with a backing of quilted merinowool batting and Egyptian cotton.

Janice Corporation. Flat mattress pads of unbleached, soft, fluffy felt; mattress and box-spring covers of muslin or barrier cloth.

Jantz Design & Manufacturing. Mattress pads with pure, untreated layers of lambswool batting nestled inside a prewashed cotton cover.

Mother Hart's Natural Products. Natural, unbleached mattress and box-spring covers of heavy-weight cotton muslin.

SelfCare Catalog. Handmade untreated wool mattress pad with prewashed cotton.

Vermont Country Store. Mattress pad with cotton cover, filled with cotton batting. Also zippered cotton muslin covers for mattress and box springs.

Xhaxhi. Wool mattress overlay with cotton casing stuffed with New Zealand Chanco wool, a mechanically crimped wool fiber with enhanced springiness.

NOTIONS

Harmful materials: plastic (latex, polyester, PVC/vinyl chloride).

At the Store/By Mail
Fabric stores generally carry buttons made from wood, metal, cloisonné, ceramic, pewter, shell, leather, horn, or stone, as well as Chinese silk frogs, cotton elastic, and cotton and silk thread. Other natural notions may need to be ordered by mail.

⛄ Natural notions
Crocodile Tiers. Unbleached bias tape and quilt binding of untreated, formaldehyde-tested fabric. Can be custom dyed.

Karen's Nontoxic Products. Shell and wood buttons.

Testfabrics. Untreated cotton tapes.

⊕ Nontoxic notions
The Cotton Place. Woven cotton cording and cotton/rubber elastic. Cotton and silk thread, cotton bias tape from Holland, piping, twill tape, rayon/rubber lingerie elastic, pajama drawstrings, felt and cotton shoulder pads, hook-and-eye tape, and cotton lace and trims.

Janice Corporation. Cotton thread, lace, bias tape, and elastic; zippers of metal and cotton.

Utex Trading Enterprises. Silk sewing and embroidery thread in many colors.

PILLOWS

Harmful materials: plastics (polyester, polyurethane).

HOMEMADE ALTERNATIVES
Make your own natural pillows by stuffing prewashed cotton pillow ticks (available in the pillow department of most department stores) with prewashed cotton TOWELS, DIAPERS, thermal BLANKETS, or cotton or wool BATTING. To stuff with batting, simply unroll batting, fold into pillow shape, and stitch around the edges to hold batting in shape.

At the Store/By Mail
Purchase ready-made pillows covered with cotton ticking and filled with cotton, wool, or silk batting, down or feathers,

kapok, or buckwheat hulls; available in department or home-furnishing stores or by mail.

Pillows filled with down and feathers are available in varying proportions: all down, all feather, or mixtures of the two. The larger the percentage of feathers in a pillow, the firmer it will be. Pillows filled with natural buckwheat hulls are traditional in the Japanese culture and are reported to offer good neck support.

Natural pillows

— Bright Future Futons (Bright Future Futons). Pillows stuffed with organically grown buckwheat hulls or organically grown cotton, with cotton casings prewashed three times in baking soda. *Bright Future Futons, Karen's Nontoxic Products.*

— *Dona Designs.* Pillows in sizes from baby to king, filled with organically grown cotton and cotton covered. ⊞ Packaged in cellophane.

— *Jantz Design & Manufacturing.* Cotton pillows filled with organic cotton staple batting and covered with unbleached cotton sheeting, prewashed three times in baking soda wash. Sizes from compact to king.

— *Pure Podunk.* Pillows made of wool from sheep raised on small New England farms. Wool is washed with wood heated hot water and pure, colorless, odorless soap, and air dried. Cover fabric is untreated cotton that is soaked in a vinegar/water wash, rinsed, soaked in a baking soda/water wash, rinsed again, then dried in the Vermont air and sunshine. Sewn with linen thread.

Natural pillows

A Very Small Shop. Natural cotton drill pillows filled with cotton batting.

Chambers. Goose-feather/down pillows with Egyptian-cotton twill ticking. Also cotton pillow protectors.

Cuddledown. All-down and down/feather combinations with Egyptian-cotton coverings, in several styles. "Tri-Pillows" have an inner pocket of goose feathers surrounded by a generous amount of white goose down.

Essential Alternatives. Goose-down and 10/90 down/feather-filled pillows with European cambric cotton ticking in standard and king sizes. Also buckwheat-hull-filled pillows for neck support.

Feathered Friends. Standard and European pillows of goose down, or down/feather fillings, covered with Egyptian cotton.

Garnet Hill. Premium down pillows available with either live plucked down, regular down, or down/feather blend, all with Egyptian cotton cambric covers. Down/feather balloon pillows have an inner core of small whole goose feathers surrounded by goose down.

Jantz Design & Manufacturing. Pillows of all cotton and wool covered with cotton, in four sizes. Also a custom-contour neck-support pillow with a sturdy cotton shell, filled with wool and kapok.

Scandia Down Shops. Pillows of white goose down, grey duck down/feather blend, or small goose feathers, all covered in cotton. Also cotton pillow protectors.

SelfCare Catalog. Three-part cervical pillow with a sturdy all-cotton shell, filled with wool and kapok.

Vermont Country Store. Pillows filled with goose down, goose feathers, or cotton, with cotton covers. Also cotton pillow covers.

Warm Things. Pillows in standard or European sizes with cotton covers, filled with goose down or 80/20 goose-feather/down blend.

Xhaxhi. Large variety of pillows with cotton covers, stuffed with Chanco wool (New Zealand wool mechanically crimped for enhanced springiness), kapok, or cotton. Also neck rolls stuffed with buckwheat hulls.

⊕ *Nontoxic pillows*

The Company Store. Cotton-covered down and feather pillows in every size and shape you can imagine, including neck-support and wedge pillows. They will also custom make pillows to your specifications.

Crocodile Tiers. Replacement pillow ticks made of standard blue-stripe ticking. Guaranteed formaldehyde free.

The Ecology Box. All-cotton pillows, including filling, ticking, and thread.

KB Cotton Pillows (KB Cotton Pillows). Completely handmade; stuffed so as to prevent lumping. Blue-striped cotton ticking is prewashed in baking soda. Independent laboratory tests confirm there are no harmful chemical residues in the cotton batting. From baby to king size. *Allergy Relief Shop, Allergy Resources, The Allergy Store. Clothcrafters, KB Cotton Pillows, Garnet Hill, The Living Source.*

Mother Hart's Natural Products. Pillows of down or feather/down mixture, with cotton-ticking covers. Three sizes. Also heavyweight-cotton zippered feather-proof pillow protectors.

The Sprout House. Cotton pillows; no mineral oils or fire retardants.

Winter Silks. Cotton stuffing, blue-stripe ticking, and thread.

POTHOLDERS

Harmful materials: dyes, plastic (polyester).

Old potholders lying around your house may contain asbestos; new ones do not.

At the Store/By Mail
Buy cotton potholders at hardware, cookware, and variety stores.

⊕ *Nontoxic potholders*
Berea College Student Craft Industries. All-cotton natural potholders in a variety of weaving patterns.

Clothcrafters. Heavy cotton terry oven glovelined with cotton fleece, thirteen inches long.

The Cotton Place. Potholders of thick felt padding covered with bleached muslin.

SHOES

Harmful materials: dyes, formaldehyde, plastics (acrylic, nylon, polyester, polyurethane, PVC/vinyl chloride).

Wear shoes made entirely of leather, or wear cotton espadrilles or Chinese rubber-soled cotton shoes.

To avoid formaldehyde, look for leather shoes that are stitched instead of glued. Most leather shoes are made from dyed leather, but according to leading dermatologists the dye is so firmly fixed to the leather that reactions to it would be extremely rare.

At the Store/By Mail
Brand-name shoes are not listed here because there are so many fine brands available. Look for them in better department, clothing, and shoe stores. Nonnatural materials will bear a "manmade" legend on the shoe or the box. Ask the salesperson.

Abbreviations used: (M) for men's shoes; (W) for women's shoes.

⊕ *Nontoxic shoes*
The Cordwainer Shop. (MW) Custom-fitted, hand-sewn leather shoes. Fully rebuildable and inscribed with your name. Expensive, but a good investment.

Hi-Tec Sierra Sneaker IV (Sports USA). (MW) Hiking boots made with canvas uppers, lug soles, tight-weave cotton linings, rubber insulation, and steel shanks. *Vegan Street.*

Janice Corporation. (MW) Classic Sperry Top-Siders made of cotton canvas duck with rubber sole.

Richman Cotton Company. (MW) Chinese cotton shoes in black, white, and a wide variety of other colors.

SHOWER CAPS

Harmful materials: plastics (PVC/vinyl chloride).

At the Store/By Mail
Janice Corporation. Shower cap made of untreated barrier cloth with encased elastic.

SHOWER CURTAINS

Harmful materials: plastics (polyester, PVC/vinyl chloride).

SPECIAL TIP
Enclose your shower stall with glass doors.

At the Store/By Mail

🌱 **Natural shower curtains**
Clothcrafters. White cotton, in sizes to fit normal and extrawide bathtubs and shower stalls.
The Cotton Place. White cotton duck shower curtains.
Janice Corporation. Shower curtain of either natural drill, white cotton duck, or white cotton barrier cloth.
Mother Hart's Natural Products. White cotton duck shower curtains.
NOPE (Non-Polluting Enterprises). Cotton shower curtains.
Vermont Country Store. Cotton duck shower curtain, in natural or white.

SLEEPING BAGS

Harmful materials: plastics (nylon, polyester).

At the Store/By Mail
Have a natural-fiber sleeping bag custom made, or put natural-fiber sleeping-bag liners inside your synthetic sleeping bag for a soft, absorbent touch.

🌱 **Natural sleeping-bag liner**
Clothcrafters. White cotton flannel sleeping-bag liners, in rectangular and tapered shapes, and single and double sizes.

SLIPPERS

Harmful materials: plastics (acrylic, nylon, PVC/vinyl chloride).

At the Store/By Mail
Purchase slippers made from natural sheepskin.

🌱 **Natural slippers**
Chambers. Slippers made in Austria of 95 percent virgin merino wool and 5 percent cashmere, with a durable wool felt sole.
Country Spirit Crafts. Genuine sheepskin slippers with double-thickness leather bottoms.
Janice Corporation. Sheepskin slippers.
Vermont Country Store. Cotton flannel booties.

TABLE LINENS

Harmful materials: dyes, formaldehyde, plastics (polyester, PVC/vinyl chloride).

At the Store/By Mail
Choose cotton or linen table linens. Import stores often carry colorful, inexpensive table linens. Department stores or linen shops carry fine, often imported, natural-fiber table linens. Also check antique shops for heirloom-quality tablecloths and napkins.

🌱 **Natural table linens**
Testfabrics. Napkins and place mats, plus tablecloths made to order, all of untreated cotton.

🌐 **Nontoxic table linens**
Berea College Student Craft Industries. All-cotton table runners, place mats, and

dinner napkins. Plain or with color band. Also napkin rings hand carved from walnut or cherry.

Clothcrafters. Blue pinstripe cotton denim place mats; white cotton napkins with varied colored trims.

Country Curtains. Cotton homespun tablecloths, place mats, and napkins. Assorted colors.

Cuddledown. Linen/cotton damask place mats and napkins in solids and floral patterns.

Janice Corporation. White cotton rag place mats.

Laura Copenhaver Industries. Cotton place mats, napkins, and table covers in natural and other colors.

Mother Hart's Natural Products. White Chinese place mats and napkin sets embroidered in assorted colors.

One World Trading Company. Place mat/napkin sets woven on a backstrap loom; tablecloth/napkin sets foot-loomed. Assorted colors.

Pueblo to People. Hand-loomed Guatemalan cotton tablecloths with matching napkins.

Shaker Shops West. Woven cotton Shaker place mats.

Vermont Country Store. Tablecloths and napkins of cotton damask. Also cotton mountain-weave tablecloths, napkins, mats, and runners in a reversible white-on-colored-background pattern; can also be purchased as yardage. Also a cotton silence cloth for use under your tablecloth.

Williams-Sonoma. Cotton tablecloths, place mats, and napkins in a variety of patterns.

Napkins made from 100 percent recycled paper

C.A.R.E. Paper Dinner & Luncheon Napkins (Ashdun Industries). No inks, dyes, or fragrances.

Envision Paper Napkins (Fort Howard Corporation). White dinner napkins. *Atlantic Recycled Paper Company.*

YARN

Harmful materials: dyes, pesticides (mothproofing), plastics (acrylic, polyester, nylon).

At the Store/By Mail

Purchase undyed, unmothproofed natural-fiber yarns at a yarn store or by mail.

⊕ Earthwise yarn

Cotton Clouds. Organically grown brown cotton for spinning.

Sajama Alpaca. Soft, beautiful hand-spun alpaca yarns and alpaca wool for spinning, dyed with plants indigenous to the highlands of Bolivia. The wool comes from animals who live in their own habitat on the open range, kept by local people who spin the yarn themselves.

Jamie Harmon. Hand-spun wool yarns in natural colors (white, gray, or brown) or dyed with natural dye.

Natural Cotton Colours. Organically grown, dye-free brown and green cotton yarn for knitting and weaving.

Pure Podunk. Unusual yarns from New England exotic wool producers and hand spinners. Write for information.

❧ Natural yarn

Bartlettyarns. Small company specializing in wool yarns that have their natural lanolin oils retained for softness and weather resistance. Four basic undyed wools. Also available in colors. Unmothproofed unless listed as such.

Cotton Clouds. Pima and Acala cotton for spinning.

The Cotton Place. Virgin-wool yarn in natural color.

Mandala. Hand-spun wool yarn in natural colors.

Schoolhouse Press. Unbleached, untreated sheep's-wool yarn in several whites, grays, and browns; different gauges. Also dyed wool yarns.

Straw into Gold. Alpaca/merino wool,

cotton, silk, silk/linen, silk/wool, and wool yarns in natural shades and a wide range of dyed colors. Also fibers for spinning: angora, camel hair, cashmere, flax, goat hair, ramie, silk, wool, and yak hair.

Testfabrics. Untreated, ready-to-dye natural-fiber yarns: natural, scoured, bleached, or mercerized cotton; spun silk; worsted wool.

⊕ **Nontoxic yarn**

Cotton Clouds. Over five hundred cotton yarns, plus weaving looms and equipment, cotton rug warp, wooden crochet hooks, and bamboo knitting needles.

The Cotton Place. Cotton yarn and aluminum crochet hooks.

Hearthsong. Peace Fleece—wool yarn spun in Maine, blending the fleeces of Soviet and American sheep.

Karen's Nontoxic Products. Cotton yarns. Also bamboo knitting needles.

Utex Trading Enterprises. Silk knitting and weaving yarns.

11 ❧ Babies & Children

> Above all else, the child must be a healthy animal. Let
> nature teach them the lessons of good and proper living.
> Plants should be given sun and air and the blue sky; give
> them to your boys and girls. I do not mean for a day or a
> month, but for all the years. By surrounding this child
> with sunshine from the sky and your own heart, by giving
> the closest communion with nature, by feeding this child
> well-balanced, nutritious food, by giving it all that is
> implied in healthful environmental influences, and by
> doing all in love, you can thus cultivate in the child and
> fix there for all its life all of these traits.
>
> LUTHER BURBANK

I haven't yet become a mother, so I don't write this chapter from personal experience, but I know that when I do raise children, I will want to surround them with things that are as natural as possible, and also impress on them, at an early age, their own connection with and responsibility for the Earth. Many parents are already raising their children in this way, so there are plenty of natural products for babies, children, and mothers-to-be.

HOW PRODUCTS FOR BABIES AND CHILDREN AFFECT OUR HEALTH, OUR CHILDREN'S HEALTH, AND THE EARTH

Infants' and children's products are in many ways smaller versions of adult products: baby-care products contains similar toxic ingredients; baby food is grown with pesticides; toys and diapers are made from plastics. The effect on the environment is the same, regardless of who the user of the product is.

Yet babies and children are more susceptible to the harmful effects of the products they use every day. Their immune systems are not fully developed, so they don't have the natural defenses that we do. One of the best ways we can give our children a healthy start in life is to allow their bodies to grow in as natural an environment as possible.

HOW I RATE PRODUCTS FOR BABIES AND CHILDREN

Products for babies and children are rated by the same standards I use to rate adult products. You'll probably have to order the natural and nontoxic products listed here by mail, as most are not available in local baby stores.

BABY-CARE PRODUCTS

Harmful materials: artificial colors, BHA/BHT, fragrance, talc.

At the Store/By Mail

❧ *Natural baby-care products*

+ *Fluir Herbals.* Balm for diaper rash. Contains wildcrafted herbs and beeswax. ⊞

+ Lindos Chamomile Baby Bath/Baby Creams/Baby Oil/Baby Powder/Baby Shampoo/Baby Soap (Walter Rau Gmbh & Company Speickwerk). All contain biological or biodynamically grown herbal extracts and are scented with essential oils. A few products contain beeswax. Baby powder contains talc. ☺ Ⓐ *The Allergy Store, Meadowbrook Herb Garden.*

+ *Oak Valley Herb Farm.* Herbal baby oil and aloe-E oil. ⊞

+ *Simplers Botanical Company.* Herbal baby oil, powder, and salve made with organically grown and wildcrafted herbs.

Aubrey Organics Natural Baby Bath Soap/Body Lotion/Shampoo (Aubrey Organics). Natural vanilla and almond-oil fragrances. ☺ Ⓐ *The Allergy Store, Amberwood, Aubrey Organics, The Compassionate Consumer, Green Earth Natural Foods, Humane Alternative Products, The Natural Baby Company, Natural Elements.*

Autumn Harp Comfrey Salve (Autumn Harp). Fresh-picked herbs and natural oils in an all-purpose topical salve good for diaper rash. *The Compassionate Consumer, Green Earth Natural Foods, InterNatural, My Brother's Keeper, Natural Elements, Natural Lifestyle Supplies, Sunrise Lane.*

Autumn Harp Earth Child Baby Lotion/Baby Oil/Talc-Free Baby Powder (Autumn Harp). ① *Amberwood, Carole's Cosmetics, The Compassionate Consumer, Green Earth Natural Foods, InterNatural, My Brother's Keeper, Natural Elements, Seventh Generation, Sunrise Lane, Vegan Street.*

Baby Bunz & Company. Baby brushes with goat hair or soft boar bristles and lacquered wood handles. Infant and toddler sizes.

Baby Massage Creme/Massage Gelly/Massage Lotion/Massage Oil/Tearless Conditioner/Tearless Gelly Wash/Tearless Shampoo (Mountain Fresh). Unscented. ☺ Ⓐ *Eco-Choice, Mountain Fresh, Motherwear, Terra Verde Products, Vegan Street.*

Country Comfort Baby Oil/Baby Powder/Herbal Baby Cream (Country Comfort). ☺ *The Allergy Store, Earth Herbs, Motherwear, Natural Elements.*

Dr. Bronner's Baby Mild Soap (All-One-God-Faith). ☺ Ⓐ *Green Earth Natural Foods, Karen's Nontoxic Products, Simply Delicious.*

Mountain Rose Baby's Balm/Baby's Body Oil/Baby's Body Powder (Mountain Rose Herbs). Body powder is talc free. *Mountain Rose Herbs, Simmons Handcrafts.*

Natural Lifestyle Supplies. Child's wooden comb with dolphin-shaped handle.

Nature de France White Clay Baby Powder (Nature de France). Talc free. ☺ Ⓐ *Amberwood, The Compassionate Consumer, Natural Lifestyle Supplies.*

Robin Evanosky. Elderberry-wood teething beads.

Seventh Generation. Dioxin-free baby wipes, bleached without chlorine. Contain lanolin, but no irritating alcohol or artificial fragrance. Made with 33 percent cotton fiber.

Sunfeather Vegetarian Baby Soap (Sunfeather Herbal Soap Company). Unscented. Made with olive, coconut, and apricot oils. ☺ Ⓐ ⊞ *Sunfeather Herbal Soap Company.*

Tom's Natural Honeysuckle Baby Shampoo (Tom's of Maine). *Amberwood, Green Earth Natural Foods, InterNatural, Naturally Ewe, Natural Lifestyle Supplies, Seventh Generation, Simply Delicious.*

Vegelatum (Mountain Fresh). Vegetable-oil-based jelly to protect baby from wet diapers. ☺ *Earth Herbs, Eco-Choice, Motherwear, Sunrise Lane.*

+ Weleda Calendula Baby Cream/Baby Oil/Baby Powder/Baby Soap (Weleda). Contains biodynamically grown herbs. Baby powder contains talc. ☺ ⊗ *The Allergy Store, Baby Bunz & Company, The Compassionate Consumer, Earth Herbs, EveryBody Ltd., Family Clubhouse, Forest Flower, Green Earth Natural Foods, Humane Alternative Products, InterNatural, Meadowbrook Herb Garden, Moonflower Birthing Supply, My Brother's Keeper, Natural Elements, Natural Lifestyle Supplies, Naturpath, Simply Delicious, Sunrise Lane, Vegan Street, Weleda.*

BABY CARRIERS

Harmful materials: dyes, plastics (polyester, polyurethane).

At the Store/By Mail

⊕ **Nontoxic baby carriers**

Comfey Carrier. Made of cotton velour.

Cozy Cradles. Made from cotton fabric. Seven beads are attached for baby's teething pleasure.

Maine Baby Carrier (Maine Baby). Cotton fabric stuffed with polyester batting—easily adjustable. Can carry baby in front or on the back; baby can face in or out. *Maine Baby, Motherwear.*

Mother's Wear. Sling-style cotton carriers in patterns.

BABY FOOD

Harmful materials: artificial colors, artificial flavors, BHA/BHT, pesticides.

I've listed only a few brands of baby food here.

Breast-feeding (see NATURAL BIRTHING & NURSING SUPPLIES), seems to be the best choice for newborns: not only is mother's milk the perfect food supplied by Nature, but it supplies a baby with important nutrients and immune factors not found in commercial infant formulas.

When your child is old enough to eat solid food, consider making your own baby food or choosing a brand of baby food made from organically grown foods. If this isn't possible, check the labels on the brands at your supermarket. Many major brands have removed additives, though they still contain pesticide residues.

At the Store/By Mail

⊕ **Earthwise baby food**

Earth's Best Baby Foods (Earth's Best Baby Food). Pureed vegetables and fruits, fruit juices, and organic mixed whole-grain cereal. ⊞ *Green Earth Natural Foods, Seventh Generation, Simply Delicious, Walnut Acres.*

Perlinger Naturals Baby Foods (Perlinger Natural Products) ⊞

Simply Pure Baby Foods (Simply Pure). Organic vegetable and fruit purees, plus organic hot cereals. ⊞ *Fiddler's Green Farm, Natural Lifestyle Supplies, Simply Pure.*

Summa Organic Baby Cereal (Purity Foods). Whole-wheat, five-grain, rice-and-wheat, and barley-and-rice instant cereals. ⊞ *Green Earth Natural Foods, Simply Delicious.*

❧ **Natural baby food**

Healthy Times All-Natural Biscuits for Teethers (Healthy Times). Whole wheat or wheat free. *Baby Bunz & Company, Green Earth Natural Foods.*

Baby-food-making aids

Motherwear. A complete set of items for feeding your baby, including two baby-food cookbooks, a baby-food grinder, and eating utensils designed especially for tiny hands.

BED LINENS

Harmful materials: dyes, formaldehyde finishes, plastic (polyester).

At the Store/By Mail

⊕ **Nontoxic bed linens**

Allergy Relief Shop. Soft nonallergenic cotton sheets.

Classics for Kids. White cotton flannel crib sheets and cotton receiving blankets.

Clothcrafters. Cotton-flannel-backed real-rubber waterproof bed pads. Cotton flannel crib sheets.

Cuddledown. Fitted crib sheets available in cotton and cotton flannel, in solids and patterns.

Garnet Hill. Crib sheets in Egyptian cotton knit and English cotton flannel.

The Company Store. Down comforters, cotton flannel cover/sheet/pillow-sham sets, feather- or cotton-filled cotton-covered bumper pads, cottoncrib ruffles and pillow shams, wool-shag mattress pads.

The Cotton Place. White cotton knit crib sheets. Also broadcloth pillowcases.

Vermont Country Store. Cotton-flannel-covered rubber sheeting by the yard.

BEDS

Harmful materials: dyes, flame retardants, plastics (polyester, polyurethane).

At the Store/By Mail

🌿 **Natural beds**

+ *Bright Future Futons.* Crib-sized futons with cotton muslin covers, filled with non-flame-retardant cotton batting or organically grown cotton batting.

BLANKETS

Harmful materials: dyes, pesticides (mothproofing), plastics (acrylic, nylon, polyester).

At the Store/By Mail

🌿 **Natural blankets**

Berea College Student Craft Industries. Wool baby blankets in regular and thermal weave. Natural color.

⊕ **Nontoxic blankets**

A Baby Is a Gift. Cotton crib-sized afghans with charming country-style designs.

Allergy Relief Shop. Receiving blankets in cotton flannel and thermal weave.

Baby Bunz & Company. Pure pima-cotton thermal blankets in white and soft colors. Also merino-wool blankets with cream-satin binding, in cradle and crib sizes.

Family Clubhouse. Cotton flannel striped receiving blankets, and cotton thermals.

Forest Flower. Cotton flannel blankets.

Garnet Hill. Baby blankets of woven cotton (some in pima), in solids and patterns.

M. Matthews Handwoven Fabrics. Baby blankets handwoven of cotton or a blend of cotton, wool, and angora.

Natural Elements. Cotton baby blanket with soft flannel outside and warm cotton batting inside.

Richman Cotton Company. Woven cotton blanket in receiving and crib sizes. White and dyed colors.

CLOTHES

Harmful materials: dyes, formaldehyde finishes, pesticides (mothproofing), plastics (acrylic, nylon, polyester, PVC/vinyl chloride, spandex).

About children's sleepwear: federal law requires garments sold as sleepwear for infants and children to be flameproof. In the past, cotton sleepwear was simply flameproofed with TRIS. When TRIS was found to be carcinogenic, other chemicals (which have unknown health effects) were used, or else the sleepwear was made from nonflammable synthetic fibers. Be creative. Many cotton garments can be used for sleepwear even though they cannot by law be described or recommended as sleepwear. If you are concerned about combustibility, make your own sleepwear from naturally flame-resistant wool.

At the Store/By Mail

🌐 Nontoxic clothing

After the Stork. Natural-fiber children's clothes. Long-lasting, quality clothes at budget prices.

Baby Bunz & Company. All-cotton clothing from Sweden. Shirts with tie closures, nightwear, leggings, coveralls, caps.

Bebitos. Small collection of sturdy, well-made, colorful cotton children's clothes from Guatemala.

Biobottoms. Colorful catalog of cotton clothes for babies and children. Coveralls, jumpsuits, dresses, and cotton sweats, plus a few look-alike items in larger sizes for mom and dad. Read descriptions carefully; some items made from cotton/polyester blends.

Classics for Kids. From maternity to children's size ten; many cute cottons mixed in with synthetics.

Cot'n Kidz. Good selection of basic play clothes and sleepwear for toddlers to age twelve. Everything in this catalog is cotton.

The Cotton Place. Cotton knit jumpsuits, shirts, long pants, and cardigans in infant sizes small to large.

Crayon Caps. Colorful cotton caps for children.

Elaine Aldrich. Traditional clothing, inspired by paintings and children's books, made from cotton or wool, designed to allow room for growth. ⊞

Forest Flower. Day gowns, wrap shirts, bear suits, caps for newborns.

Garnet Hill. Cotton basics for newborns to size twelve.

Hanna Anderson. Brightly-colored, high-quality infants' and children's clothes imported from Scandinavia. Stripes, plaids, and bold colors dominate. Sturdy cotton fabrics. Many "keep warm" items not in other catalogs—even cotton mittens.

Harmony Moon. Colorful cotton baby sacks, overalls, footies, long johns, skirts, and sweat clothes batiked with whimsical designs.

High Sierra Concepts. Cotton infant basics. Also cotton long johns and fleecy cotton sweat clothes in rainbow colors.

Laughing Bear Batik. Batik cotton baby sets, footsie sets, long johns, dresses, overalls, and T-shirts with a variety of fanciful designs.

Les Petits. Brightly colored European-style casual clothing for children. Made in France from fine cotton and wool.

Lillian Vernon. Cotton hooded terry robes; can be embroidered with name.

Motherwear. Natural-fiber snowsuit made of cotton flannel with cotton cover. Cotton terry bibs in solid colors.

The Natural Baby Company. Basic cottons for infants.

Natural Elements. A few basic cotton garments for infants and children.

Powers' Country Store. Rugged cotton overalls, jeans, shirts.

Richman Cotton Company. Basic cotton clothing, underwear, and socks available undyed or dyed with "nontoxic" dyes.

Sew Natural. A collection of whimsical cotton clothes for boys and girls.

Silly Goose. Simple cotton knits, hand dyed and airbrushed with flower and animal designs.

Simply Divine. Basic cotton solid-color knits, and T-shirts with nature-oriented designs.

Tillys. Quality handmade children's clothing, primarily cotton.

Tortellini. Small catalog of very attractive children's clothing—all cotton.

Traditions. Imaginative cotton and wool basics.

Wild Child. Basic cotton T-shirts, dresses, striped overalls, and socks, in 24 "nontoxic" colors. ⊞

World Wear. Long-lasting natural-fiber garments designed to allow a free range of movement and accommodate a child's rapid growth rate. Designs are adapted from clothing from around the world.

COMFORTERS

Harmful materials: dyes, plastics (nylon, polyester).

At the Store/By Mail

⊕ *Nontoxic comforters*

Garnet Hill. Cotton-filled crib comforter covered with two-hundred-thread-count cotton. Also cotton crib quilt, bumper and sham set.

DIAPERS

Harmful materials: dyes, fragrance, plastics (acrylic, polyester, polyethylene).

Disposable diapers have been in the news enough lately that we all know about their environmental effects: raw sewage leaching into the groundwater; dioxin pollution from manufacturing plants; landfills piled with diapers that take five hundred years to biodegrade.

The new so-called biodegradable and dioxin-free diapers are better, but they are not the best solution. Their "biodegradability" comes from mixing a small amount of cornstarch in with the plastic from which they are made. The cornstarch helps the plastic break apart—into tiny pieces of plastic. Whether or not it is environmentally safe is controversial, and,

biodegradable or not, they are still disposable products that waste resources.

In addition to their environmental effects, disposable diapers aren't very comfortable or healthful for babies. They cause more frequent and severe diaper rash than cloth diapers do. Problems reported to the Consumer Protection Agency also include chemical burns, noxious chemical and insecticide odors, reports of babies pulling the diapers apart and putting pieces of plastic into their mouths and noses, of plastic covers melting onto the skin, and of ink from the diapers staining the skin.

The solution, of course, is to use cotton cloth diapers with wool or cotton diaper covers. If you really need to use a disposable diaper (such as when you are away from home), there are now paper liners that can be used with natural-fiber diaper covers. Using these at least reduces waste. And if you don't want to purchase and wash diapers, use a diaper service—which is less expensive than using disposables.

SPECIAL TIP
To kill bacteria in cloth diapers, use the hottest water in your washing machine, and dry diapers for forty minutes on the hottest setting. Whenever possible, air the washed diapers outdoors in the sunlight, which acts as a natural disinfectant. Soaking soiled diapers in a mixture of a half cup borax added to a pail of warm water will help reduce odors and staining, and will make diapers more absorbent.

At the Store/By Mail
If your local baby store doesn't carry natural-fiber diapers and covers, order them by mail.

⊕ *Nontoxic cloth diapers and diaper covers*

Baby Bunz & Company. "Lovingly sewn by local seamstresses (mothers!)," styles include an hourglass shape with rainbow stitching on the edges, prefolded terry velour, and terry velour on one side, cotton flannel on the other, with rainbow-stitched edges.

Biobottoms. Breathable virgin-wool diaper covers with Velcro closures; let you use cotton diapers easily and painlessly. Help prevent diaper rash, too. Also Pin-Free Diapers by Curity: five layers of cotton gauze and a fiber inner layer for extra absorbency; Velcro fasteners.

Classics for Kids. Basic cotton prefolded diapers; cotton minidiapers that can be used with a regular diaper for extra absorbency.

Clothcrafters. Triple-layer cotton gauze diapers, prefolded cotton flannel diapers, single-layer cotton flannel diapers, four-layer cotton flannel diaper liners. Great prices.

The Cotton Place. Gauze diapers.

Cuddlers Cloth Diapers. Six-layer cotton flannel diapers, in newborn and regular sizes. Adjustable Velcro closures.

Forest Flower. Cotton diapers, prefold and flat. Also cotton canvas diaper bags.

Lillian Vernon. Cotton terry diaper covers. Can be custom embroidered with name or nickname.

Lovely Essentials. Pinless cotton flannel diapers with extra-absorbent layering on the inside. Preshaped with elastic at the leg for a snug fit, with Velcro tabs that adjust to baby's growth. Shaped like disposable diapers.

Motherwear. Fitted cotton diapers for use with any Velcro diaper cover. Also rectangular cotton flannel pads for newborns. Tiny cotton washcloths—an alternative to chemical baby wipes.

The Natural Baby Company. Prefolded cotton diapers.

Nikky's Diaper Covers (Nikky America). Available in wool, cotton, or cotton terry, with Velcro closures. *Baby Biz, Baby Bunz & Company, Family Clubhouse, Forest Flower, Garnet Hill, Moonflower Birthing Supply, Motherwear, The Natural Baby Company, Natural Elements, Natural Lifestyle Supplies, Naturpath, Richman Cotton Company, Seventh Generation, Traditions.*

The Portland Soaker. Untreated woven wool diaper covers, Undyed inner lining; colorful outer cover. Elastic in waist and legs is accessible for custom fit as child grows. Also kits.

Richman Cotton Company. A variety of diapers, from flat to hourglass to prefolded.

Seventh Generation. Prefolded and flat cloth diapers.

Traditions. Diapers that fit neatly inside Nikky's Diaper Covers (see above). Made with two layers of very soft cotton flannel with a cotton terry pad sandwiched in between and rainbow stitching on edges. Also baby wipes of white cotton terry with rainbow trim.

"Disposable" Diapers

Dovetails (Family Clubhouses). Biodegradable; made of fluffed paper with a thin coating of rayon. Fit in Velcro diaper covers. Contain no plastic, chemicals, perfumes, or deodorants. *Baby Biz, Baby Bunz & Company, Family Clubhouse, Moonflower Birthing Supply, Natural Lifestyle Supplies, Naturpath.*

Diaper-cover Patterns

Sew Natural. An ingeniously simple pattern for pinless diaper covers with side bows.

Soaker Pattern. A simply designed pattern for making your own natural-fiber diaper covers.

MATTRESS PADS

Harmful materials: plastic (polyester).

At the Store/By Mail

⊕ **Nontoxic mattress pads**

Allergy Relief Shop. Mattress covers made of cotton barrier cloth.

The Cotton Place. Rubber sheeting covered on both sides with white cotton flannel. Also cotton felt mattress pads.

NATURAL BIRTHING & NURSING SUPPLIES

Research has shown that babies are fully aware when they are being born and that children and adults can and do remember their births. Some therapists believe that the quality of the birth experience has psychological effects that can last throughout a person's lifetime. Even hospitals are promoting natural birth methods and environments.

Nursing your baby has important emotional as well as physical benefits, and there are many resources available to help this be a positive experience for you and your baby.

At the Store/By Mail

Natural birthing and nursing supplies
+ *Oak Valley Herb Farm.* Belly oil with traditional pregnancy and birthing herbs. Herbs are organically grown or wildcrafted. ⊞
Bosom Buddies. Cotton nursing bras and nursing gowns in a number of pretty styles, plus breast-milk pump and expresser, instructional books, and a video.
Garnet Hill. Nursing bras of pima-cotton knit and cotton nursing pads. Also nursing gowns and shirts in patterned cotton.
Great Beginnings Lanolin (Landcare Laboratories). *Naturpath.*
Moonflower Birthing Supply. General birthing and parenting supplies; with many informative books.
Mother's Wear. Nursing bras with cotton cups; cotton jersey knit nursing gowns.
Motherwear. General supplies for the nursing mother, including many instructional books. Also unique, stylish clothing

with discreet nursing openings, most made of cotton, in a variety of styles. Wrap skirts, nursing bras, and washable cotton breast pads.
Naturpath. A general birthing-supply catalog with an extensive collection of books on natural birth and child rearing.
The Natural Baby Company. Cotton knit nursing gowns and pima-cotton nursing bras. Also cotton flannel nursing pads.
Traditions. Cotton flannel nursing pads.

PILLOWS

Harmful materials: plastics (polyester, polyurethane).

At the Store/By Mail

🌿 *Natural pillows*
Allergy Relief Shop. Cotton pillows. Also pillow covers of barrier cloth.
Cuddledown. Down and down/feather-blend throw pillows for the crib; cotton covers.

SHEEPSKINS & LAMBSKINS

Mothers use sheepskins for a variety of purposes. They provide a soft, clean, warm surface for playing or changing diapers, and they provide a familiar item when babies are away from home. Studies show that babies sleep longer and more peacefully on a lambskin, grow faster, and cry less. Lambskins and sheepskins are, however, animal products—a consideration for some.

At the Store/By Mail

🌿 *Natural sheepskins and lambskins*
Baby Bunz & Company. All-natural Australian merino lambskin.
Garnet Hill. Baby-care lambskin from New Zealand.
The Natural Baby Company. Machine-washable lambskin rugs for sleeping and many other uses.

Richman Cotton Company. Soft natural sheepskins tanned wth nontoxic materials. Machine washable.

Spencer's. Lambskins for babies and children.

SHOES & SLIPPERS

Harmful materials: dyes, formaldehyde, plastics (acrylic, nylon, polyester, polyurethane, PVC/vinyl chloride).

At the Store/By Mail

⊕ *Nontoxic shoes and slippers*

Bear Feet. Leather shoes that allow full room for toes to stretch. Handcrafted from soft cowhide, with a choice of vegetable-tanned leather or natural plantation rubber soles.

Biobottoms. Leather or cotton/rubber shoes in cute styles for kids.

Country Spirit Crafts. Totmocs. Do not bind, misshape, or restrict the bone growth of the foot or alter natural agility and balance. Made of soft, strong, elastic natural deer and elk; take the shape of the foot and stretch as the foot grows. Also genuine sheepskin slippers with double-thickness leather bottom.

Soft Star Shoes. Baby shoes made from soft, pliable cowhide and shearling lamb. Cotton laces.

Soft Steps. Flexible leather baby shoes with leather or crepe soles.

TOYS

Harmful materials: dyes, plastics (polyester, polyurethene, PVC/vinyl chloride).

At the Store/By Mail

❧ *Natural toys*

Hans Schumm Woodworks. Toys have smooth, flowing designs giving the impres-sion they are "shaped and finished by the elements—sand, water and wind." Hand made from carefully selected fir, pine, cedar, and redwood. Finished with natural plant oil.

Kemp Krafts. Fine wooden toys made by a group of individual craftspeople. Selection includes an unpainted wooden rocking horse, wooden whistles, blocks, and trucks.

⊕ *Nontoxic toys*

Animal Town Game Company. Carries cooperative and noncompetitive games, outdoor playthings, books on cooperation and family activities, and board games about environmental protection.

The Ark. An enchanting selection of toys and books that awaken the wonder of childhood. Wooden animals, dwarves, flower fairies, toys; shells, crystals, a flower press; child-sized garden tools, nature-oriented board games.

Banbury Cross. Musical instruments designed specifically for children to use with little or no instruction. Most are hand-made of fine natural materials. Chosen "with careful consideration for parents' ears."

Berea College Student Craft Industries. Games and puzzles made of wood and using marbles or stones. Also a toy train made entirely of wood.

Child Life Play Specialties. Wooden backyard swing sets, gyms, and other play equipment.

Childcraft. Amid pages of plastic toys, a wonderful set of wooden blocks made from northern maple in almost thirty different sizes and shapes. Also a set of wooden "castle blocks" of unusual and intricate shapes, that resemble medieval castles.

Dollies & Company. Simple, enchanting dolls, made of cotton stuffed with sheep's wool. Your choice of skin, hair, eye color, and eye shapes. Moderate to expensive.

Earth Care Paper Company. Paper by Kids by Arnold E. Grummer provides both simple and sophisticated papermaking techniques that kids can use to make paper by recycling junk mail.

Ethan's Wooden Toy & Doll Company. Wooden toys finished with nontoxic paint or food-grade mineral oil enriched with vitamin E, plus dolls clothed in cotton.

Garnet Hill. Fascinating wood rattles handcrafted in Vermont from white rock maple.

The Gingerbread Cat. An assortment of reasonably priced American and European wooden toys, finished in bright, colors.

Hearthsong. A wondrous and magical catalog filled with forty pages of natural playthings. Everything from a block-and-marble set and European village blocks to kits for making dolls and unusual, inspiring children's books, including one on making toys with kids. Contains many natural toys imported from Europe, and the handiwork of cottage industries.

Karen's Nontoxic Products. Classic folk toys from American toy makers.

Kreations by Kristen. "Baby Bunting" cotton dolls, stuffed with virgin lambswool.

The Marvelous Toy Works. Wooden toys, particularly trains and other vehicles, and many creative wooden blocks.

Meadowbrook Herb Garden. Small assortment of toys, including dolls made of cotton fabric stuffed with carded wool fleece, elves made of colorful felt, wooden climbing bears, and finger puppets.

Mountain Craft Shop. Largest source of authentic American folk toys, reproductions of the toys once made at home and handed down from one generation to another. The toys' names—such as Jack-in-the-Box (springs up when opened) and

Skyhook, (gravity-defying device)—are traditional and most are descriptive of their functions. Most are made of native hardwoods.

Natural Lifestyle Supplies. Hardwood toys by an American toy maker.

Night Sky Star Stencil (Ursa Major). Stencil and nontoxic luminous paint allow kids to place each star in its right place, at its true brightness. *SelfCare Catalog.*

North Star Toys. Wooden toys and puzzles, including all kinds of little rolling animals and vehicles, and cutouts of animals of the jungle and sea.

Papa Don's Toys. A variety of toys for babies and children, including crib, floor, pull, and push toys, block sets, rainbow ring stackers, rolling letters, train sets, and rolling ball ramps.

Pueblo to People. Mayan dolls handmade by Mayan women living in the Mexican state of Chiapas. Dolls have authentic, hand-loomed clothes.

Shaker Shops West. Traditional wooden Shaker toys.

Traditions. Bunnies and balls made of felted wool in a variety of colors.

Tree Top Toys. Colorful wooden rattles, toys, and puzzles. ⊞

Truth's Dolls. Girl, boy, and baby dolls made from natural materials chosen for their beauty, texture, and durability. Each is stuffed with wool. The hair is a wool/mohair blend, and the body is of skin-toned cotton knit. Four skin colors; six hair colors.

Tryon Toymakers. Handcrafted, hand-painted wooden toys. Rocking horse, magic wand, many cutouts, rattles, puzzles, moon-and-star mobile. Also a paper-making kit.

Tully Toys. Delightful wooden rocking animals, including a giraffe, hippopotamus, armadillo, and dinosaur.

Under the Willows. Handmade toys of soft, natural materials—cotton, wool,

wool fleece, Swiss lace. Simple forms and faces are "made to joyfully inspire love, creativity, and imagination." Collection includes sprites, angels, gnomes, elves.

Vermont Country Store. Three-hundred wooden-log building set. Also woods whistles that sound like train whistles, original 1956 ant farm, push-pull wagon, pogo stick made of steel with a heavy spring, and a rocking horse of maple with red steel rockers.

World Wide Games. Handcrafted, wooden games: chess, Chinese checkers, backgammon. Also unusual puzzles.

12 ❧ Office & Art Supplies

Every genuine work of art has as much reason for being as the earth and the sun.

RALPH WALDO EMERSON

Most of us have office and art supplies around the house, especially things like glue, paper, pens, and markers. If you are creatively inclined, or have children, you probably have paints and craft supplies around, too. In addition, most people also come into weekly, if not daily, contact with computers and copy machines.

HOW OFFICE AND ART SUPPLIES AFFECT OUR HEALTH AND THE EARTH

Although scientific documentation is incomplete, there is significant epidemiological and toxicological evidence that some ingredients in professional art materials and craft supplies may cause human health problems ranging from organ damage to birth defects and cancer. Although these effects have been observed under conditions of more prolonged and higher levels of exposure than would normally occur in your home, there is a legitimate concern about the safety of these materials even at lower levels of exposure.

Common symptoms that have been associated with exposure to art materials and office supplies through ingestion, inhalation, or skin absorption include dizziness, headaches, blurred vision, general fatigue, nausea, nervousness, loss of appetite, chronic cough, skin problems, depression, and shortness of breath.

While the environmental effects of office and art supplies have not been fully tested, these products do contain toxic substances that pollute air, land, and water in their manufacture, use, and disposal. The amount of paper we use when we copy, print with computers, and send faxes also has a major impact.

READING LABELS

The labels of office supplies carry very little information about their ingredients or dangers. Though it has recently been reformulated, typewriter correction fluid, for example, contained toxic chemicals for many years with no indication on the label that they were even present in the product.

The labels on art materials, on the other hand, are beginning to improve. There are two types of art materials—the usually less toxic consumer products designed for general use, and the frequently more toxic professional/industrial products intended for use by trained professionals in controlled environments. Since both are widely available to consumers in art-and office-supply stores, it's important to learn how to read the labels in order to choose less toxic products.

The labeling of art materials is supervised by the Consumer Product Safety Commission (CPSC), which administers three laws: the Federal Hazardous Substances Act (1970), the Poison Prevention Packaging Act (1970), and the Consumer Product Safety Act (1972). Under the Federal Hazardous Substances Act, the CPSC may require precautionary labeling of hazardous substances or ban substances for which labeling is determined to be insufficient to protect the public health.

Despite these laws, many art materials have insufficient labeling, which is a result not of inadequate regulations but from lack of enforcement of these laws. California, New York, Massachusetts, Illinois, Tennessee, and Oregon all have more detailed state laws that attempt to improve art-product labels.

Some common problems encountered in choosing art supplies include:

• Unlabeled products. Artists and craftspeople can purchase ceramic chemicals, clays, dyes, pigments, solvents, plastic resins, and other hazardous materials in paper sacks with no ingredient information.
• Improperly labeled products. Many product labels are missing information such as the manufacturer's address or precautions.
• Foreign product labels. Many products are imported from our countries whose labeling requirements are different from our own.

To avoid the more stringent regulations for consumer-product labeling, some product manufacturers label their products "for professional use only" or "for industrial use only." As a consumer, it is wise to stay away from these products.

Not all products are poorly labeled. At least twenty-nine companies have joined the Arts and Crafts Materials Institute, an industry group that has developed voluntary standards for the safety and quality of both consumer and professional/industrial art supplies. In evaluating the safety of a product, the institute's toxicologist considers both the concentration and the potential acute and chronic health effects of the ingredients, as well as possible uses and misuses of the products.

Manufacturers of safe products are allowed to pay the institute a fee to display certain certification seals such as the CP Nontoxic (Certified Product) seal, the AP Nontoxic (Approved Product) seal, and the Health Label. These seals represent that the product has been "certified in a program of toxicological evaluation by a medical expert to contain no materials in sufficient quantities to be toxic or injurious to humans or to cause acute or chronic health problems."

AP and CP Nontoxic labels are used on children's art supplies. CP products additionally meet specific requirements of material, workmanship, working qualitites, and color standards. The Health Label is used on adult art materials to assure that they are properly labeled with health and use information, and includes a line that states "Nontoxic" or "Warning: Contains [name of the hazardous substance]." One drawback to this system is that the toxicologist's assessment of the safety of a product is based on a literature review, and not actual testing of the product itself.

As with any product, read and follow instructions, and follow any precautionary advice. "Use with adequate ventilation" does *not* translate to "Open the window"; it means that sufficient ventilation must be provided to keep airborne concentrations of the product's mist, dust, fumes, or vapors below the levels considered hazardous for the user. Since proper ventilation can be complex to arrange, the average consumer should choose products without such precautions. In case of accidental ingestion of an art material, or if symptoms arise during use, call your local poison-control center immediately. Don't follow the antidote on the label, as many are incorrect. Again, when possible, products should be chosen that will not produce symptoms during use or accidental ingestion.

Last but not least, don't make the mistake of choosing a product without a warning label over a product with a warning label, assuming that no warning label implies that no warning is necessary. Whenever possible, choose products that list ingredients or give some other clear indication of their safety.

HOW I RATE OFFICE AND ART SUPPLIES

When I evaluate office and art supplies, I first want to choose supplies that are made from natural materials, if possible. If there are no natural supplies available, I look for the least toxic product that will do the job.

⊕ **Earthwise** office and art supplies are:
• safe to use;
• nonpolluting in their manufacture, use, and disposal;
• made from natural, renewable ingredients that are organically grown or otherwise grown and harvested in a sustainable way—devoid of petrochemical ingredients; and
• biodegradable.

� **Natural** office and art supplies are:
• safe to use;
• made from natural, renewable ingredients not organically grown and may have residues of petrochemicals used in growing or processing, may have trace amounts of nontoxic petrochemical ingredients, or may be nonpetrochemical synthetic formulations; and
• biodegradable.

⊕ **Nontoxic** office and art supplies are:
• safe to use;
• made mainly of synthetic formulations from petrochemical sources; and
• biodegradable.

At this point, I know of no earthwise office or art suppies. The few natural art supplies that are currently on the market need to be ordered by mail. Of course, there are many nontoxic art supplies available wherever art materials are sold. I haven't listed these because they are so common, and they are easily identifiable by their AP, CP, or Health Label seals. If you want a list of nontoxic art supplies, contact the Art and Craft Materials Institute (see Recommended Resources).

COMPUTERS

Harmful materials: plastic.

There has long been a debate over the safety of sitting in front of a computer screen. Many studies have linked using cathode-ray-tube (CRT) video display terminals to eye irritation, double vision, face rash, headaches, irritability, stress, and neck and back pains. The FDA, the American Academy of Ophthalmology, the National Institute of Occupational Safety and Health, and the National Academy of Sciences all agree that the amount of radiation given off is too small to pose a threat to health, but new studies seem to confirm the danger of being so close to a source of electromagnetic radiation.

Research reported in 1989 in many of the major newsmagazines found that there was a higher rate of leukemia in children who lived in homes near high-voltage power lines. The magnetic fields found routinely within a radius of about two feet from the average CRT computer terminal can be as strong as or even stronger than the magnetic fields found inside homes where children were dying of cancer. The evidence against CRTs seems to be mounting.

While the new liquid-crystal display (LCD) screens found on portable computers also produce radiation, it extends out from the computer a shorter distance and operates on a less powerful voltage than CRTs.

Beyond the radiation issue, there is also a problem with the static electricity, generated by high voltages, in the air that surrounds computers and the bodies of the people sitting at keyboards. The positively charged field around a computer neutralizes the negative ions in the air, creating an area that is high in positive ions. High concentrations of positive ions have been associated with fatigue, metabolic disorders, irritability, headaches, and respiratory problems. In addition, dust, tobacco smoke, and chemical pollutants become positively charged and seek out the nearest grounded or oppositely charged surface, which is usually the operator's face. The particles clinging to your face can cause rashes, itchy eyes, and dry skin.

Many of the eye problems associated with computer use are caused by glare from improper lighting. Bodily aches and pain are generally the result of poor posture, sitting in one position for too long, or the wrong furniture.

WHAT YOU CAN DO TO MINIMIZE COMPUTER HEALTH RISKS

• Get a lap-top computer with an LCD screen. To make it even safer, use the battery for power only while you're working on it, then recharge the battery when you're in another room.

• Block electrical fields with a grounded glare screen attached to your computer and plugged into a properly grounded plug (glare screens without ground wires are worthless from an electrical standpoint). These screens block only the electrical radiation, though; as of now there is no effective way to block magnetic radiation. To protect yourself from magnetic radiation, stay thirty inches from the front of your computer, and forty inches from its back and sides. Unplug computers when not in use to completely eliminate magnetic fields.

• To eliminate static electricity, try leafy houseplants and open windows. A negative-ion generator will also work if it is of good quality and proper design and positioned properly with respect to the computer, the operator, and the air flow in the room. The optimal placement could be overhead, or nearby on a table. It is important not to generate *too many* negative ions because there is a possibility that your body will absorb negative ions faster than they can be discharged, resulting in a buildup of negative ions on your skin. When this happens, you will begin to attract positive ions, which is just what you don't want. If you want to experiment with this, try a variable-output negative-ion generator and place it in different locations. You should be able to feel the difference as you search for its optimal spot. You can order negative-ion generators by mail from *Nigra Enterprises.*

• For glare control, diffused lighting is best. Make sure sunlight or bare bulbs are not shining directly on your screen. If you are inputting text and need brighter lighting, use a small work light that shines on the paper but not on the screen. Use the minimum contrast setting at which you can comfortably see the text; you may be able to work longer with less eyestrain at lower settings.

• Place your computer equipment on a table that allows you to adjust the screen and keyboard to proper heights to fit your body. Sit in a comfortable position and then adjust the screen so you are looking down at it slightly. To adjust the keyboard height, sit in a normal position and bend your arms at the elbow to form right angles. Your hands should fall comfortably onto the keyboard.

• Prevent bodily aches and pains by taking frequent breaks. Sitting motionless for long periods slows circulation, reduces muscle tone, and causes fatigue. Take a break every ninety minutes to stretch and walk around, and if you can, do some other type of work for a short period of time. Hit your "save" key every few paragraphs or at the end of each page; not only will you have your work protected in case of a power failure, but you can take a few moments to squirm in your chair.

At the Store/By Mail

Radiation test kit
Radiation Safety Corporation. An extremely sensitive test kit for your computer.

Radiation-free computer screen
Safe Computing Company. Carries the Safe Monitor, which it claims is "the world's first and only computer monitor with no radiation to the user." Special attention to wiring helps balance the magnetic fields from this backlit LCD display, and electric fields are shielded. Can be attached to almost any computer.

Computer-screen shield
NoRad Shield (NoRad Corporation). Mesh screen. Each strand has a monofilament core with a nickel-copper coating that is designed to block electrical fields more than 99 percent. Eliminates glare, increases contrast, and eliminates static electricity—but does not reduce the magnetic radiation. *Baubiologie Hardware.*

Personal electrical-field shield
Baubiologie Hardware. Polyester/cotton blend apron with a thin, lightweight copper-allow insert that blocks up to 98 percent of electrical fields and microwaves.

COPY MACHINES

Harmful materials: ammonia, ethanol, kerosene, plastics.

Most problems from copy machines come from older models that use a variety of volatile chemical toners that produce the copy image. Copied pages continue to smell of these toners for long periods of time. I doubt you can even buy one of these today.

Nowadays, all copiers make the copy image by electronically fusing odorless carbon powder to the paper. The new little personal copiers, which you may want to use at home, should be operated in a well-ventilated area, as they do give off some fumes.

Have empty toner cartridges refilled to reduce waste; they can be recycled up to ten times. Buy two; then you'll always have one in the machine, and one to refill.

At the Store/By Mail

Copier-cartridge recycler
Hartman Associates. Recycles toner cartridges for copy machines and for laser printers.

CRAYONS

Harmful materials: paraffin.

Children's crayons are generally considered quite safe. The Clinical Toxicology of Consumer Products gives them a rating somewhere between "practically nontoxic" and "slightly toxic," which means that a seventy-five pound child would have to eat between one and two cups of crayons for a toxic effect to occur.

Even so, standard crayons are made from nonrenewable petrochemical products.

At the Store/By Mail
Look for beeswax crayons with natural pigments at your local stores, or order them by mail.

🐞 Natural crayons
Auro Crayons (Auro). Crayons made from pure plant wax. Sinan Company.

Livos Stebio Crayons (Livos). Pigments derived from plants, bound primarily in beeswax and other natural waxes. Livos Plantchemistry.

Stockmar Wachsfarben (Stockmar). Beeswax crayons imported from West Germany, in block and pencil styles. The Ark, Hearthsong, Meadowbrook Herb Garden, Natural Lifestyle Supplies, Seventh Generation, Traditions.

GLUE & TAPE

Harmful materials: ammonia, ethanol, formaldehyde, hexane, naphthalene, phenol, plastics (acrylonitrile, epoxy resins, polyurethane, PVC/vinyl chloride, PVP).

Warning labels: Depending on the type of adhesive, the following warnings may appear on the label:

"DANGER: Extremely flammable. Vapor harmful. Harmful or fatal if swallowed. Skin and eye irritant. Keep out of reach of children. Bonds skin instantly. Toxic."

"CAUTION: Do not use near sparks or flame. Do not breathe vapors. Use in well-ventilated room. Keep away from small children."

HOMEMADE ALTERNATIVES

Paper Glues
• Blend four tablespoons wheat flour and six tablespoons cold water to make a smooth paste. Boil one and a half cups water and stir into paste, cooking over very low heat for about five minutes. Use when cold.
• Blend three tablespoons cornstarch and four tablespoons cold water to make a smooth paste. Boil two cups water and stir into paste, continuing to stir until mixture becomes translucent. Use when cold.
• Combine one-quarter cup cornstarch, three-quarters cup water, two tablespoons light corn syrup, and one teaspoon white vinegar in a medium saucepan. Cook over medium heat, stirring constantly, until mixture is thick. Remove from heat. In a separate bowl, stir together one-quarter cup cornstarch and three-quarters cup water until smooth. Add a little at a time to

the heated mixture, stirring constantly. Will keep two months in a covered container.

At the Store/By Mail

Order natural adhesives by mail or use a nontoxic glue stick (a solid, very-low-odor white glue made from petrochemical derivatives), white glue (made from polyvinyl acetate plastic), or yellow glue (made from aliphatic plastic resin). All have a slight odor when wet, but dry quickly. These can be purchased at office-supply, hardware, drug, and variety stores.

When you need tape, use brown paper tape, available at all office-supply stores.

❀ Natural adhesives

Auro Children's Craft Glue (Auro). *Sinan Company.*

Livos Bave Children's Paper Glue (Livos). *Livos Plant Chemistry.*

MAILING SUPPLIES & PACKAGING MATERIALS

Harmful materials: plastics.

Most mailing supplies and packaging materials today are made out of plastic—plastic tape, plastic bubble wrap, plastic bubble-wrap-lined envelopes, polystyrene "peanuts." And when we open packages, we throw all the packaging away, putting piles of nonbiodegradable material into the environment.

SPECIAL TIPS

• Reuse packaging materials and mailing supplies. Virtually every envelope and box can be sent out again. You might want to have some personalized mailing labels printed or use a rubber stamp that says "recycled" to make a statement when you cross out old addresses and patch packages together with tape. Some of the mail-order companies listed in this book have been reusing plastic "peanuts" for years.

• Make package-stuffing material out of discards you have around the house. Crumple old newspapers, paper bags, magazine pages.

At the Store/By Mail

Encourage your local office-supply store to stock recycled mailing supplies and packaging materials. Until it does, order them by mail.

Recycled mailing supplies and packaging materials

Bio-Pax. Specializes in recycled and biodegradable packaging products. Carries everything you need to mail or ship a package, including recycled shredder paper, postconsumer cushioning materials, wood excelsior cushioning material (this is what we used before we had plastic), 60 percent recycled padded mailing bags, recycled Kraft wrapping paper, recycled sturdy corrugated shipping boxes in almost two hundred sizes, and gummed Kraft sealing tape, which allows boxes to be recycled. ⊞

Quill Corporation. Sixty percent recycled padded mailing bags and unbleached Kraft paper envelopes in many sizes.

MODELING CLAY

Harmful materials: colors, fragrance, talc.

Clay in dry form contains free crystalline silica, which can be inhaled. Inhalation may result in silicosis, a permanent scarring of the lungs, which may not develop for fifteen or twenty years. Some talcs also contain asbestos.

HOMEMADE ALTERNATIVES

To make modeling dough, mix together one cup flour, half cup salt, and two tablespoons cream of tartar. Add one cup water, two tablespoons vegetable oil, and a natural coloring such as beet juice, blueberry juice, or the juice from other bright foodstuffs, or the water from boiling red cabbage, yellow-onion skins, marigolds, petunias, or other flowers and foodstuffs. Cook until mixed thoroughly. Cool and store in an airtight container. Lasts two months.

At the Store/By Mail
Choose a natural modeling beeswax imported from West Germany.

❧ *Natural modeling beeswax*
Auro Modeling Wax (Auro). *Sinan Company.*
Livos Mera Modeling Wax (Livos). *Livos Plantchemistry.*
Stockmar Modeling Beeswax (Stockmar). *The Ark, Hearthsong, Meadowbrook Herb Garden, Natural Lifestyle Supplies, Traditions.*

PAINTS (ART)

Harmful materials: Acrylic paints: ammonia, formaldehyde, pigment, plastic (acrylonitrile). Best avoided by home artists. The Arts and Crafts Materials Institute has not rated any brand CP.

Tempera paints and watercolors: formaldehyde, phenol, pigment, plastics (acrylonitrile, PVC/vinyl chloride). Moderately to very toxic.

Finger paints are generally made from "nontoxic colors," with formaldehyde added as a preservative.

HOMEMADE ALTERNATIVES
Mix a half cup cornstarch and three-quarters cup cold water in a saucepan. Soak one envelope gelatin in one-quarter cup cold water. Add two cups hot water to the cornstarch mixture and cook over medium heat until it comes to a boil and is clear, stirring constantly. Remove from heat, stir in the gelatin, add a half cup soap flakes, and stir until thickened and soap is dissolved. Tint with natural colors (see MODELING CLAY for suggestions).

At the Store/By Mail
Order natural art paints by mail.

❧ *Natural paints*
Auro Lasur Emulsion Paints/ Plant Watercolor Paints/Plant Color Set (Auro). *Sinan Company.*
Livos Children's Watercolors/Salis Finger Paints (Livos). Colors derived from earthen and mineral pigments, with all-natural binders. *Karen's Nontoxic Products, Livos Plantchemistry.*
Stockmar Aquarellfarben (Stockmar). Watercolor paints in six colors, imported from West Germany. *The Ark, Hearthsong, Meadowbrook Herb Garden, Natural Lifestyle Supplies.*

PAPER & ENVELOPES

There is a wide variety of papers on the market; some are plain, some have plastic finishes, some are bleached, some are dyed. While paper is not a health concern for most people, the manufacture of paper can cause severe environmental harm as forests are clear cut to make paper pulp, the bleaching process produces dioxin, and the general manufacturing process creates much toxic waste that often ends up polluting rivers.

The most environmentally sound paper would be made of recycled paper, unbleached or bleached with a nonchlorine bleach such as hydrogen peroxide, without finishes, and without coloring. While this type of paper may not be appropriate for every need, it is perfect for office paper, children's drawing paper, personal and environmentally oriented business stationery and envelopes, and many other uses.

While there are some 100 percent recycled paper products, most are a blend of recycled and virgin pulp to capitalize on strengths of both. Blends generally contain 40 to 80 percent recycled fibers. In recent years, the quality and selection of recycled paper has increased dramatically. Some recycled papers have an off-color, speckled, "recycled" look, while others are virtually indistinguishable from comparable grades made from virgin pulp fiber. Recycled papers lie flatter, have more strength, shrink and stretch less, and resist moisture and curling, making them in some ways superior to virgin papers for many uses.

Fine writing papers are also made from recycled materials. When the first papermill in the United States was established in 1690 near Philadelphia, paper was made exclusively from fibers taken from recycled cotton and linen rags. Today, the finest writing paper is 100 cotton, made from recycled cotton rags and virgin cotton linters that are too short to be spun into cotton thread.

More and more recycled paper is becoming available as we are showing manufacturers there is a market. Recycled paper is now being used to print greeting cards, wrapping paper, note pads, and other novelty items.

HOMEMADE ALTERNATIVES

You can make your own paper. Of course, handmade paper can't begin to fill your daily paper needs, but it's a nice creative art form that recycles paper. In England, home papermaking kits are a popular item, though I haven't seen them here. Check your local library for books on papermaking, and your local arts-and-crafts shop for supplies.

At the Store/By Mail

Ask your local office-supply store to stock recycled paper.

Recycled papers, envelopes, and novelty papers

Acorn Designs. Note cards made from recycled paper, printed with nature motifs. Also stationery, notepads, gift cards, and handmade paper "made entirely from locally gathered, hand-dipped, hand-pressed recycled paper with envelopes lined with locally crafted marbled paper. ⊞ Wrapped in cellophane.

Atlantic Recycled Paper Company. Unbleached, standard white, and bright white copier paper, green-bar and white computer paper, and letterhead.

Bio-pax. White bond copy paper and ruled white legal pads made from 100 percent preconsumer recovered waste paper. ⊞

Brush Dance. Wrapping paper, greeting cards, and stationery, with Oriental-style nature motifs.

Conservatree Paper Company. One of the largest distributors of recycled office and printing paper and envelopes. It sells by the carton only, with a one-hundred-dollar minimum; ideal for office or group ordering.

Creative Printing & Publishing. Will print letterhead on paper with recycled logo watermark, matching envelopes, and business cards.

Earth Care Paper Company. A good selection of office and printing papers, green-bar and continuous-form computer paper, recycled minimum-impact unbleached paper, and matching envelopes in several sizes for most papers, plus ruled and plain pads. Also note cards, stationery, wrapping papers, and holiday greeting cards.

Ecco Bella. High-speed-copier paper, green-bar and continuous-form computer paper, recycled minimum-impact unbleached paper, and an assortment of white business envelopes. Also writing papers and note cards with animal motifs, oak-tree postcards, and wrapping paper.

Eco-Choice. Gift wrap.

Graham-Pierce Printers. Custom-printed letterhead, envelopes, business cards, brochures, newsletters, and other general printing on a variety of recycled papers. Paper can also be purchased without printing.

Natural Lifestyle Supplies. Notes, stationery, holiday cards, and gift wrap.

The Paper Project. Stationery, plain envelopes, blank or lined pads, and paper for both copiers, and computers.

The Recycled Paper Company. Basic selection of white and colored office papers and matching envelopes for small-quantity purchase. Samples attached to information card.

Seventh Generation. Wrapping paper, brightly colored notepaper with envelopes, an artistic journal with the look of fine handmade paper, desk pads in rainbow colors, note cards with various designs, stationery made from unbleached recycled newspaper, and two sizes of ruled pads. Also fan-fold computer paper, copier paper, and telephone-message pads. All one-hundred percent recycled.

Women's Studio Workshop. Handmade papers of cotton with other natural fibers such as corn husks, cattails, and onion skins. Letter and note-card sets, and self-mailers.

Fine papers

Crane's Papers (Crane & Company). All papers made from 100% cotton. *The Vermont Country Store* (sells boxes of 250 sheets or envelopes).

Strathmore Papers (Strathmore Paper Company). Parchment, Strathmore Writing 100%, Alexandra Brillant, and Strathmore Script are made from 100% cotton.

PENCILS, PENS, & MARKERS

Harmful materials: acetone, ammonia, cresol/ethanol, naphtha, phenol, toluene, xylene.

The greatest danger from pens and markers is their solvent-based indelible inks. You can easily tell which markers contain solvents because they give off a strong smell when you open the cap. The ink in solvent-based ball-point pens have a more subtle odor; you can smell it slightly, but the real clue is that the ink globs around the tip or on the paper.

A wide variety of pens that come in many colors and thickness of line now have water-based ink. There are so many that I haven't even listed them here. Some have ballpoint tips, others plastic or felt tips.

Water-based markers are available now at most art-supply stores. I have listed my favorite brands below. Often variety stores will carry basic colors. If the label on a marker says "nontoxic" or *does not* say "permanent ink," the ink is probably water-based.

In addition to the toxic-waste issues around the manufacture of inks and plastics used to make pens and markers, there is the question of waste: we all go through copious numbers of disposable pens and pencils. I have invested in several refillable pencils and fountain pens. Now all I do is add lead to my mechanical pencil (instead of sharpening down all the wood in a wood pencil), or drop a cartridge into my fountain pen. High-quality pens even have refillable cartridges that use bottled ink. The trick with refillable pens and pencils is to keep track of them.

At the Store/By Mail

Look for pencils and water-based pens and markers at your local office and art-supply stores. If they don't stock them, ask them to.

PRINTING

According to the National Association of Printing Ink Manufacturers, about 80 percent of ink ingredients are made from petrochemicals and another 15 percent from forest products.

When you have stationery, newsletters, and anything else printed, it is likely that the printer will use a toxic ink. But there is a better alternative: the petroleum oil used in the ink can be replaced by soybean oil.

In 1986, research by the American Newspaper Publishers Association led to the introduction of soybean oil instead of petroleum oil as the base for news ink. Many newspapers have switched to soy-based ink for color reproduction, including the *Los Angeles Times, the Boston Globe,* and the *St. Petersburg Times.* Printers report brighter and sharper color reproduction, safer pressroom conditions, easier press cleanup, and less rub-off on reader's hands.

Soy-based inks are just now being developed for the rest of the printing industry. The cost is 5 to 10 percent more for most colors, including black, but the extra cost is a small price to pay for a healthier world, and these costs will become even more competitive as usage increases. The price of ink is actually a small percentage of total printing costs.

Soy-based inks are not completely environmentally safe. They may still use a small percentage of petroleum products, and the soybeans probably are not grown organically. They still use the same pigments as petroleum-based inks, which have varying degrees of toxicity according to colorant. The new "Right to Know" Act requires customer notification of the percentage of certain hazardous chemicals in a company's products. If you want to avoid the most toxic pigment colors, ask your printing company for the list of hazardous materials used in its inks.

With all the advantages they have in both quality and safety, soy-based inks are a definite step in the right direction, moving us away from nonrenewable and hazardous petroleum to safer, renewable plant oil.

At the Store/By Mail

Ask your printer to order soy-based ink for your next printing job.

Soy-based ink

Soy XL (Sinclair & Valentine). Soybean ink for sheet-fed presses used in commercial printing. Printers who have used the ink report that the press is easier to clean up after a run and that they get substantial increase in mileage and a little better gloss.

Tuttle Lithography. Professional-quality stationery, business cards, brochures, and direct-mail pieces printed on first-quality recycled papers with soy-based inks.

13 ❦ Building & Furnishing

In many ways, our homes act as extensions of our senses and, like a "third skin," also serve to protect us from the world around us. Internally, the home can be likened to the human organism, with organs to process energy, water, food, and wastes. The house can be made "intelligent," too—not by expensive complicated high-technology computers, electronic monitors, and control devices, but much more simply—by using the natural mechanisms of air, sun, water, and materials. These, together with the best computer available—your own brain—and the most sensitive monitors yet devised—your own senses—complete the process.

DAVID PEARSON

Because the list of products needed to build a house fills a book in itself, I will focus here on the finishing products used on the inside of the building structure that we come into most frequent contact with and affect us most directly—paints and finishes, flooring, carpeting, and the like.

HOW BUILDING AND FURNISHING MATERIALS AFFECT OUR HEALTH AND THE EARTH

The same issues raised about other products apply here as well—methods of growing, harvesting, and mining raw materials, toxins used and created in the manufacturing process, and the safety of the product during use and when it is discarded. These issues are especially important for several reasons: our homes and workplaces use a lot of both renewable and nonrenewable resources, we spend almost all of our time in them, and they can be a great health hazard when filled with the materials often used today.

DESIGNING OUR HOUSES AND COMMUNITIES

The goal of ecological design is to observe and work with Nature, to use her principles in running our homes and businesses. Resources are to be used as sustainably and efficiently as possible, nontoxic products and processes are a priority, and any waste is recycled, and safely detoxified if needed.

There are many new and old approaches that can help us in designing new buildings or communities or in transforming existing ones. Here's a brief description of some of them.

Baubiologie. Literally, "building biology." This approach from West Germany and now throughout Europe takes into consideration both the impact of buildings on the health of people and the holistic interactions between life and our living environment. Baubiologie combines many older traditions with the new to bring balance and harmony to people, buildings, and nature. One of its features is to build houses of natural materials (such as brick, stone, wood, and plaster) in a way that allows the entire shell of the house to expel pollutants while still maintaining good insulation. This ventilation by diffusion also has the advantage of absorbing and releasing excess moisture, which helps regulate indoor humidity.

Feng shui. A Chinese Taoist practice of harmonious placement of buildings and arrangement of rooms and furnishings. Literally meaning "wind and water," it sees natural elements and the alignment of cosmic and terrestrial forces as important in creating a healthy, prosperous, and beautiful place to live. There is a similar Hindu system of sacred siting and building placement called *vastuvidya,* currently being revived by Maharishi Mahesh Yogi as stapatya-ved.

Geomancy. In many ways the Western equivalent of feng shui. Stemming from old European traditions, geomancy is a blend of science and the sacred that considers the various energetic and natural patterns of the land to develop healthy and balanced buildings attuned to Nature.

Cohousing. A new concept pioneered mainly in Denmark and now being adapted in other countries. It reestablishes some of the advantages of traditional village life within the context of our current needs. Instead of the isolation of single-family houses and apartments, this approach combines the autonomy of private dwellings with the advantages of sharing common facilities with a large group.

In order to live in an earthwise manner, perhaps above all else we need to bring natural beauty back into our lives. All new construction could be required to have good landscaping, garden space, and trees. "Regreening" our cities and our land is gaining recognition as an important goal among grassroots movements all across the country. In addition to providing beauty and harmony in our lives, regreening will help to restore the ecosystem if done with natural methods.

HOW I RATE BUILDING AND FURNISHING MATERIALS

⊕ **Earthwise** building and furnishing materials are:
• safe to use;
• nonpolluting in their manufacture, use, and disposal;
• made from recycled materials or natural, renewable ingredients that are organically grown/wildcrafted and do not contain petrochemcial ingredients; and
• biodegradable.

▨ **Natural** building and furnishing materials are:
• safe to use;
• made from natural, renewable ingredients that have not been harvested sustainably and/or have been grown using fertilizers/pesticides, which may leave residues; and
• biodegradable.

⊕ **Nontoxic** building and furnishing materials are:
- safe to use;
- made mainly of synthetic formulations from petrochemical or natural sources; and
- biodegradable.

CARPETING & AREA RUGS

Harmful materials: formaldehyde, pesticides (mothproofing), plastics (acrylonitrile, latex, nylon, polyester, polyurethane, PVC/vinyl chloride).

After a 1987 incident at the offices of the Environmental Protection Agency during which more than 10 percent of the employees reported symptoms after exposure to new carpeting, both the EPA, and the Consumer Product Safety Commission, as well as other groups, have been investigating the toxicity of synthetic wall-to-wall carpeting.

Reported symptoms were as diverse as burning eyes, memory problems, chills and fever, sore throats, joint pain, chest tightness, cough, numbness, nausea, dizziness, lightheadedness, blurred or double vision, nervousness, depression, and difficulty in concentrating. Many reported newly acquired chemical sensitivity after a few days to a few weeks of exposure, and some required hospitalization.

EPA employees made their own analysis of the air-quality data. Based on information from a 1987 University of Arizona study on carpeting that isolated the chemical compound 4-phenylcyclohexene (4-PC), they began to monitor for this chemical and found it to be the culprit.

It is a by-product of the process used to make the latex backing for carpets. No one knows how to eliminate its production from the current manufacturing process. Its creation is unpredictable; it may be in one sample and not another.

While the carpeting industry claims that animal tests show 4-PC to be harmless, an EPA risk-assessment group predicted that it could create nervous-system and genetic problems.

Levels of 4-PC of up to twenty parts per billion have been measured in new carpet (this is the chemical that creates "new carpet smell"). Four days after installation, levels fall to about ten parts per billion, and after about two months levels decrease to approximately one to two parts per billion. You can smell 4-PC down to about .5 parts per billion.

This chemical is only one of a number of potentially harmful substances in carpets. In addition to not being good for our health, carpeting isn't good for the environment, either. Besides polluting the air with toxic contaminants, synthetic carpets are made from nonrenewable petrochemicals. And because they are made to wear and wear, year after year, they are not biodegradable. Synthetic carpets persist in the ecosystem just like any other plastic.

Do you need to be concerned about your carpet? If your carpet is over five years old, chances are the majority of the toxic components have already gassed out. If you suspect your carpet is affecting your health, or if you are in the market for buying a new one, here are a few things you can do.

- Apply a vapor-barrier sealant (see below).
- Install another type of flooring (see FLOORING).
- Choose natural-fiber area rugs or wall-to-wall carpeting (see below).

At the Store/By Mail
Use area rugs made of cotton, cotton/wool blend, sheepskin, or unmothproofed wool,

without jute or latex backing. Cotton, cotton/wool-blend, or unmothproofed-wool wall-to-wall carpets can also be used over a natural wood subfloor.

Natural-fiber carpeting is rare in stores, but many natural-fiber area rugs can be found in local import and department stores (sometimes they are in the bath department, but they can be used in other rooms as well). Some of these rugs have strong-smelling finishes that you may or may not be able to remove. Be sure to check the label on wool rugs to confirm that they have not been mothproofed.

⊕ Earthwise carpeting and area rugs

Sajama Alpaca. Rugs made from alpaca yarns hand spun and dyed with plants indigenous to the highlands of Bolivia. The wool comes from animals who live in their own habitat on the open range, kept by local people who spin the yarn themselves.

❧ Natural carpeting and area rugs

Carousel Carpet Mills. Carries a wide selection of natural-fiber carpets, and can make almost anything. Most carpets made of mothproofed wool with latex backing, but also has unique hand-loomed natural-color linen and cotton woven rugs, without latex backing, in a wide variety of patterns. Ask for "Casual Trends" and "Cotton Trends," both about two-hundred dollars per square yard.

Dellinger. Cotton carpet at about seventy dollars per square yard. Plush and thick, can be dyed to match any color or purchased in a natural, unbleached shade. No latex backing. Ask for style "3333 Linwood."

Sinan Company. Untreated, undyed, unmothproofed wool carpet with natural latex backing (no plastic). Three neutral variegated natural colors. Imported from Europe; around ninety dollars per square yard.

Southwest Collection. Investment-quality rugs handwoven by Zapotec Indian artisans in a native pueblo in Southern Mexico.

⊕ Nontoxic carpeting and area rugs

Berea College Student Craft Industries. Rugged multicolored cotton rag rugs.

Chambers. Multicolored rugs of Kashmir wool stitched by hand to cotton duck backing. White cotton dhurrie rugs.

The Cotton Place. Reversible cotton throw rugs.

Laura Copenhaver Industries. Hand-hooked wool rugs available in traditional or custom designs, in any size or color.

NOPE (Non-Polluting Enterprises). Handwoven cotton rag rugs, made with recycled blue jeans.

Sears Catalog. Room-sized cotton pile rugs in ancient tribal designs and English country floral prints. Also washable cotton rag rugs in white and five solid colors.

Vermont Country Store. Cotton rugs in two sizes for heavy-traffic areas.

❧ Natural carpet adhesive

AFM Carpet Adhesive (AFM Enterprises). Adhesive for installation of textiles and many types of carpets. ☺ By mail only: AFM *Enterprises, Baubiologie Hardware, The Ecology Box, The Living Source, Nigra Enterprises.*

❧ Natural carpet vapor barrier

AFM Carpet Guard (AFM Enterprises). Nonflammable water-soluble siliconate that reacts with moisture and carbon dioxide in the air to form an insoluble water- and odor-resistant barrier within twenty-four hours. ☺ By mail only. *AFM Enterprises, Allergy Relief Shop, Allergy Resources, The Allergy Store, Baubiologie Hardware, The Ecology Box, The Living Source, Nigra Enterprises.*

FLOORING

Harmful materials: formaldehyde, plastics (acrylonitrile, latex, nylon, polyester, polyurethane, PVC/vinyl chloride).

At the Store/By Mail

Use ceramic tile, solid hardwood, brick, marble or other stone tiles, or terrazzo, available at your local flooring and building-supply stores. Natural-fiber CARPETING & AREA RUGS and natural linoleum (see below) can be ordered by mail.

If you need to install new hardwood floors, buy prefinished hardwood floor tiles that have a baked-on finish, of which there are several types on the market. Choose those that come in six-inch squares and are held together with wire; avoid the twelve-inch squares that are glued together or have foam padding underneath. Remove the tiles from the box and air them outside in the sun for one day before installing. Lay the tiles on a particleboard or cement subfloor with white or yellow glue. Be sure to seal the particleboard subfloor and allow it to dry throughly before applying glue: it is not yet known whether dried glue and wood alone form an adequate seal from the formaldehyde gases coming from the particleboard.

Alternatively, you could also install a conventional hardwood strip floor, hammering the nails diagonally in the groove of the tongue-and-groove wood to avoid the need for toxic solvent-based wood filler.

❧ Natural linoleum

Forbo Nairn Natural Linoleum (Forbo North America). Linoleum made from linseed oil, pine-tree resins, wood flour from deciduous trees, and cork, mixed with chalk, clay, and colored mineral pigments, on a jute backing. Comes in sheets or tiles. *Baubiologie Hardware.*

FURNISHINGS

Harmful materials: formaldehyde, plastics (polyester, polystyrene, polyurethane, PVC/vinyl chloride).

One study showed that the addition of furniture to an otherwise empty room tripled formaldehyde levels.

At the Store/By Mail

Solid-wood furniture can be found at many unfinished-furniture stores; it can be protected with a natural finish.

Wood furniture should be checked carefully to make sure it is indeed solid wood. Often the front will be wood and the backs, sides, inside shelves, and drawer bottoms will be particleboard or plywood. Particleboard can be very convincingly veneered, but this wood veneer poses no barrier to formaldehyde.

Metal furniture is available in a number of styles: modern, high-tech functional, outdoor, and office. It can be the least toxic furniture available, if care is taken to avoid such components as synthetic seat pads and soft vinyl finishes. Check carefully to avoid particleboard in metal furnishings, especially under plastic-laminate desktops.

Consider buying used furniture. There are many attractive and functional pieces that can be recycled into your home or office and inexpensively refinished or re-covered. Look in the Yellow Pages under "Furniture Dealers—Used" and "Office Furniture and Equipment—Used," or check at flea markets and storage auctions.

Upholstered furniture should be covered with a prewashed natural-fiber fabric and stuffed with cotton or wool batting or feathers. An economical way to have custom-upholstered furniture is to buy used sofas and chairs and have the frames re-covered and restuffed.

⊕ *Earthwise furnishings*

Oak Art of Kentucky. Handmade chairs, coffee tables, loveseats, and recliners made "exclusively with native Kentucky oak. . . . Our goal is to plant oak trees to replace those we harvest, and replenish our own forests." Can be used indoors and out. Basic chair design dates back to the pre-Civil War period and provides excellent back support. All pieces fold and stack conveniently.

Willsboro Country Furniture. Rustic, simple furniture made in the Adirondacks from knotty native cedar, which has great weathering properties. Chairs, rockers, tables, loveseats, bedframes, dressers, desks. Dowel-in-hole construction. Unfinished.

🍃 *Natural furnishings*

These following are made with natural materials but in many cases have unknown finishes.

+ *Dona Designs.* Pillows (including bolsters and innerspring deck cushions) filled with organically grown cotton and cotton covered. Furniture made of solid poplar, including convertible sofas, bed bases, end tables, and lawyer's bookcases, are glued with Elmer's white glue and finished with beeswax. ⊞

Bales Furniture Manufacturing. "Chesttrunk beds," bedroom storage units, and complete shelving and wall-storage units made from hardwood covered with a wood veneer, oil, wax, and a sealer.

Berea College Student Craft Industries. Furniture handcrafted from solid Appalachian hardwoods—black walnut, wild cherry, poplar, white oak, and maple. Mahogany is also available. Will also do custom work. Desks, chests, secretaries, tables, chairs, hutches, beds, mirrors.

Blue Heron. Seven sleeper-sofa frames that turn a futon into a sofa, slatted bed frames (including bunk beds), and a variety of occasional tables. Made of maple, oak, cherry, walnut, or bubinga, or metal.

Also square cotton-covered kapok-filled throw and floor pillows.

Cohasset Colonials. Fine museum-reproduction furniture and furniture kits. "We use the same wood used in the originals, for the same reasons it was selected by the original artisans," such as pumpkin pine and New England hardwood.

The Company Store. Cotton-covered accent and chair pillows filled with small white waterfowl feathers. Also cotton pillow protectors and slip covers. Will also do custom work.

Cuddledown. Four-poster bed of traditional Shaker design, in cherry or mahogany and finished with natural oil and English wax. Throw pillows of white goose down or down/feather combination.

Essential Alternatives. A good selection of handcrafted futon frames constructed from selected oak and cherry, with a hand-rubbed oil finish. Many can convert into a sofa or chair. Plus a wide variety of pillows, including couch and floor pillows, bolsters, and ruffled and nonruffled throws, filled with cotton, wool, or a cotton/wool blend and covered with cotton. Many patterns. Can also be custom covered.

The Futon Shop. Furniture of solid cherry, red oak, and other hardwoods and finished with Watco Danish Oil, including sofas, beds, daybeds, tables, and convertible futon frames. Decorative pillows in many styles including throws, back cushions, and bolsters made of natural-fiber fabrics with a wide range of natural fillings, in standard sizes. Also custom-made futon cushions in a wide range of natural fillings and coverings.

High Cotton Company. Furniture handcrafted from North American hardwoods, including converter sofas, loveseats, chairs, tables, ottomans, loungers, and futons and other bed frames. Finished with natural oil. Can build to your own design. Also custom cotton-filled cushions to fit oddsized sofa frames.

Laura Copenhaver Industries. Traditional handmade furnishings crafted of solid mahogany. Designs include chests, bedside tables, chairs, and beds.

Northwest Futon Company. Futon bed frames, both regular and convertible, made from a variety of woods and finished with oil and beeswax. Also a variety of pillows including bolsters filled with kapok.

Outer Banks Pine Products. Clear pine colonial corner cabinets. Come fully assembled or in partially assembled kits.

Shaker Shops West. Traditional Shaker wooden furniture and accessories. Prefinished, kits, or custom assembly and finishing.

Shaker Workshops. A comprehensive collection of fine Shaker furniture and accessories.

🌐 Interior decorators

Ecology by Design. Offers interior-design services to help you create a beautiful safe, and nourishing home or work environment using nontoxic furnishings and ecology-based concepts.

Lawlor/Weller Design Group. Susan Weller is an award-winning designer who takes a holistic approach, integrating an ancient science of building with nontoxic and natural materials, in accord with her clients' personal approaches to living.

PAINTS, FINISHES, SEALANTS, CAULKS, AND ADHESIVES

Harmful materials: aerosol propellants, ammonia, benzene, ethanol, formaldehyde, glycols, kerosene, lead, pentachlorophenol, phenol, plastics (acrylonitrile, latex, phenolformaldehyde resin, polyester, polyurethane, tetrafluoroethylene), toluene, trichloroethylene, xylene.

Warning labels:
There are many kinds of warnings to be found on paint products, depending on their uses and formulas. Generally they are quite lengthy and explain in detail what to do in case of ingestion or overexposure to fumes. Here are two examples:

"WARNING: Harmful or fatal if swallowed. May cause slight skin irritation and eye irritation. Vapor and spray mist may be harmful if inhaled."

"CAUTION: Use with adequate ventilation. Where ventilation is inadequate, use a suitable respirator. In case of eye contact, flush eyes immediately with plenty of water for at least 15 minutes. Do not take internally. Keep out of reach of children."

A John Hopkins University study found that over 300 toxic chemicals and 150 carcinogens may be present in paint.

HOMEMADE ALTERNATIVES

Whitewash
Apply in very thin coats to a damp surface so the wash will dry gradually. For best results, apply the wash so thin that you can see through it while it is wet.

• For wood, glass, or metal, dissolve fifteen pounds salt or five pounds dry calcium chloride in five gallons water. In a separate container, soak fifty pounds of hydrated lime in six gallons of water. Combine the two mixtures thoroughly and thin with plain water to the consistency of whole milk. Makes a little over ten gallons.

• For masonry only (brickwork, concrete, cinder block, stone masonry, stucco), mix twenty-five pounds white portland cement and twenty-five pounds hydrated lime in eight gallons water. Mix thoroughly, then add more water until the mixture is the consistency of heavy cream. Do not mix more than you can use in a few hours. Makes a little over ten gallons.

• To make colored interior whitewash, stir five pounds hydrated lime into one gallon water and let sit overnight. The next morning, add powdered pigment (buy this from the paint store, or natural earth pigments from *Sinan Company* or *Livos Plantchemistry*) to the lime water until you reach the desired shade. Remember that the mixture will be further diluted and the paint will dry to a lighter color. Dissolve one and a half pounds salt in two quarts warm water and add to the lime mixture. Stir thoroughly and continue to stir every ten minutes or so while applying the wash. Makes about two and a half gallons. Store leftovers in a tightly closed container.

• For colored exterior whitewash, stir five pounds hydrated lime into one gallon water and let sit overnight. The next morning, add powdered pigment to the lime water until you reach the desired shade. Keep in mind that the mixture will be further diluted and that the paint will dry to a lighter color. Dissolve one and a half pounds salt and one pound alum in three quarts warm water, add to the lime mixture, and place on stove to heat. In a separate pot, melt one pound tallow. When both are hot, stir together and apply while still hot. Makes about three gallons.

Milk Paint

• Pour just enough hot water in instant nonfat dry milk to reconstitute it into a smooth syrup. Add powdered pigment in small amounts until the desired shade is reached. Apply several coats to raw wood with a brush or rag for a flat finish much like that of latex wall paint.

• Put six ounces of hydrated lime into a bucket and add enough milk to make it the thickness of cream (you will need one half gallon of milk in all). Stir in four ounces linseed oil, a little at a time, and add the rest of the milk. Sprinkle three pounds finely powdered calcium carbonate over the top and let it sink in before stir-

ring it well into the mixture. Add powdered pigment for color, if desired.

Paint Removers

Wear rubber gloves when mixing and using these formulas.

For general removal, mix one pound trisodium phosphate (TSP) into one gallon hot water. Mop or brush it on, let it sit for about thirty minutes, then remove the softened paint with a scraper or putty knife.

For walls, mix one part TSP with two parts calcium carbonate; then add enough water to make a thick paste. Using a putty knife or trowel, apply to walls, to a thickness of three-eighths inch. Leave on for about thirty minutes, then scrape off, taking the paint with it. Rinse with plain water.

For old brushes:

• Mix four ounces TSP in one quart hot water. Press the bristles of the brush against the bottom of the can to work the solution all the way into the brush, separating the bristles as the paint softens and continuing until all the paint has been removed. Rinse thoroughly with plain water.

• Place brushes in an old saucepan and cover with white vinegar. Bring to a boil, then turn the heat down and simmer for a few minutes. Remove the brushes and wash in soap and warm water.

SPECIAL TIP

To dry paint faster (and reduce your exposure to fumes), use heat. Close doors and windows and open the vents of your central heating system, or use an electric space heater. One week of heating is equivalent to about six months of air drying.

At the Store/By Mail

At the very least, use a water-based latex paint instead of an oil- or solvent-based paint. While these are made from non-renewable toxic substances, they are less toxic and wash out with water instead of paint thinner. And you can dispose of latex paint by letting any residue dry in the can and then throwing it in the trash (instead of taking it to a hazardous-waste collection site). Water-based latex paints can be purchased at any paint store.

A better idea would be to use a paint made from natural materials, or one that is specially formulated to be less toxic. These are somewhat higher in price, but worth using. Soon you will probably see these paints in hardware stores, but for now you will probably have to order them by mail.

The most natural wood finish is shellac, made from a natural resin secreted by the insect *Laccifer lacca,* mixed with alcohol. It is available at any hardware or paint store. It has the disadvantage of a long drying period and requires alcohol for cleanup, but noticeable fumes generally dissipate within one week.

🐞 Natural paint and finishing products

Auro Products (Auro). These are the only plant-based natural paint and finishing products I know of; they contain no petrochemical ingredients of any kind. Paints, oil finishes, varnishes, lacquers, glues, floor polishes, adhesives, tile grout, cleaners. *Sinan Company.*

Old-Fashioned Milk Paint (The Old-Fashioned Milk Paint Company). A casein-based paint that is great for furniture, wood, and walls (may tend to mold in damp locations such as kitchens or bathrooms). By mail only. *The Old-Fashioned Milk Paint Company, Shaker Workshops West.*

☻ Nontoxic paints and finishing products

AFM Products (AFM Enterprises). A variety of nontoxic water-based products: paints; sealers for concrete, masonry, wood, metal, tile, grout. Paints come in only formulations from petrochemical sources. Paints come in only two colors—white and off-white—but can be tinted with pigments to any color you want. ☻ By mail only: AFM *Enterprises, Allergy Relief Shop, The Allergy Store, Baubiologie Hardware, The Ecology Box, The Living Source, Nigra Enterprises.*

Livos Products (Livos). Paints, oil finishes, shellac, spackles. Generally made from natural ingredients, but paints and some other products contain a nontoxic petrochemical solvent. ⊘ By mail only: *Karen's Nontoxic Products, Livos Plant Chemistry.*

Miller Paints (Miller Paint Company). By mail only: *Miller Paint Company.*

Murco Paints (Murco Wall Products). Flat wall paint. By mail only: *Murco Wall Products.*

WINDOW COVERINGS

Harmful materials: plastic (polyester).

At the Store/By Mail

Choose natural-fiber curtains or drapes (available at some curtain shops or by mail), wooden shutters painted with a natural finish, metal blinds, or rice-paper shades (purchase at your local import store).

🐞 Natural window coverings

Country Curtains. Many styles of country-style curtains made of unbleached natural-color or white cotton muslin. Also wooden curtain rods.

Crocodile Tiers. Ready-made curtains and valances of damask, heavy carded cotton (which provides excellent sun protection and privacy), linen, cotton duck, white cotton lace, or unbleached medium-weight cotton. Also banded, gathered curtains for traverse rods. All fabrics untreated and formaldehyde tested; can by dyed to order.

Essential Alternatives. Roll-up window shades, including rice-paper, wooden-slat, and matchstick blinds.

The Futon Shop. Roman shades, Austrian shades, balloon shades, rod pocket curtains, and café curtains in natural-fiber fabrics.

Laura Copenhaver Industries. Curtains and valances of cotton muslin; coverlet materials of cotton or a wool/cotton blend. Available in natural color and white.

Deerfield Woodworking. Wooden curtain-rod and bracket sets.

Homespun Fabrics & Draperies. Neutral-colored, textured cotton draperies—made to almost any style. Also wooden curtain and drapery rods.

WOOD PRODUCTS

Harmful materials: formaldehyde, plastics (phenol-formaldehyde resin and urea-formaldehyde resin), pentachlorophenol, phenol.

Warning labels: This warning appears on particleboard used for subflooring. The same particleboard is sold in lumberyards for home use or already made into furniture but does not carry this caution.

"WARNING: This product is manufactured with a urea-formaldehyde resin and will release small quantities of formaldehyde. Formaldehyde levels in the indoor air can cause temporary eye and respiratory irritation and may aggravate respiratory conditions or allergies. Ventilation will reduce indoor formaldehyde levels."

Most wood products today are made of particleboard or plywood instead of solid wood. Particleboard, made from small wood shavings saturated with urea-formaldehyde resin and pressed into a wood-like form, is easily recognizable because you can see the pressed-together shavings on all sides. Plywood is more difficult to recognize because it has a wood grain on the outside. A cross-section, however, reveals several sheets of wood sandwiched together with phenol-formaldehyde resin.

While real, solid wood is a healthful alternative, much of our lumber, unfortunately, comes from unsustainable forestry practices: clear-cutting; tree farms in which all trees are the same species and age; using toxic chemicals for weed control and for the pest and disease problems that increase because of these unecological practices. We can have a wood-abundant economy only if we re-tree the earth and create ecological rules that will allow us to manage our forests in a truly sustainable way. This is true not only for rain forests, but for all our forests.

Cerro Gordo Forestry Cooperative is one of a handful of groups practicing sustainable forestry in the United States. Using a system called Individual Tree Selection Management, which was pioneered in the 1950s by forester Richard Smith, the cooperative cuts scattered individual trees which releases shaded trees for further growth and allows natural regeneration from seedlings that are already present on the forest floor. It harvests no more than the equivalent of the annual growth of the forest, thus perpetually maintaining the forest. Since the thinning process was begun in 1986, the growth rate in the forest has actually increased 50 percent.

At the Store/By Mail
Ask your lumberyard about the source of the lumber it sells. Are the trees being selectively and sustainably thinned from a forest while maintaining the ecosystem? Chances are they won't know (there are but a few places in the country where this is done, unfortunately), but we need to start demanding ecologically harvested wood.

If you use plywood, ask for a brand with low formaldehyde emissions.

14 ॐ Pet Care

> Holistic living is living in harmony with ourselves, each
> other, and nature as a whole; it is knowing that the quality
> of relationships influences our state of health as much as
> our temperament, perceptions, genetic constitution, and
> such. The same holds true for the health of our pets. In
> fact, there are many physical, social, and emotional
> "nutrients"—such as exercise and play, proteins, vitamins,
> affection, touch, and companionship—that are vital com-
> ponents of total health care for man and beast alike.
>
> MICHAEL W. FOX, VETERINARIAN

Anyone who has spent time with a pet learns, among other
things, a great deal about unconditional love and affection. Psychologists have found
that young adults who owned pets during early childhood scored higher on tests of
socialization, independence, responsibility, and tolerance than kids raised without animals. Another study by a team of medical researchers from the University of Pennsylvania and the University of Maryland showed that, a year after initial hospitalization for
heart disease, the survival rate of patients with pets was three times higher than that of
patients who had no pets.

Pets have been blessing us with their companionship and devotion throughout history. It is important that we give to them the best that we have, too. This includes
healthy food, natural pest controls, and our own unconditional love.

HOW PET-CARE PRODUCTS AFFECT OUR HEALTH, OUR PET'S HEALTH, AND THE EARTH

Pet-care products are no different than products for people: they can be grown or made
in ways and with ingredients that are harmful to the environment and to our pet, or
they can be grown or made in harmony with Nature's principles and can benefit both
pet and the Earth. The issues I've discussed throughout this book—organic food,
nontoxic pest control and cleaning products, natural first-aid remedies, and so on—also
apply to our pets. Using healthy products is good not only for pets, but for the rest of us
as well, since we come into contact with things like flea collars and other chemicals used
on pets that can harm our own health.

A social and environmental issue to consider is the food consumed by pets. Very
little pet food is grown organically or harvested in a sustainable way. The giant blue bass
was hunted to near extinction to feed our dogs and cats, and current tuna-harvesting
practices for cat food (and human food) have killed hundreds of thousands of dolphins.

We manufacture and throw away billions of pet-food cans each year, adding to our garbage problem.

HOW I RATE PET-CARE PRODUCTS

Pet-care products are rated by the same standards I used to rate human-care products. There are very few earthwise pet-care products but many natural ones.

BEDS FOR PETS

Harmful materials: plastics (polyester, polyurethane).

At the Store/By Mail
Mail-order pet beds made and filled with natural materials.

🌐 *Nontoxic pet beds*
Fuller Brush. Natural burlap beds filled with aromatic cedar shavings
The Company Store. Cotton-covered feather beds filled with small white waterfowl feathers; rectangular or round.
Cuddledown. Feather beds of 10/90 goose down/feathers. Removable washable cover in solid colors.

FIRST AID FOR PETS

Like humans, even the best-fed and best-cared-for animals will occasionally need first aid. Fortunately, there are some natural remedies formulated specifically for animals. You might also consider taking your pet to a natural-oriented veterinarian.

At the Store/By Mail
Check your local natural-food store for natural first-aid products for your pet, or order them by mail.

🌼 *Natural first-aid products for pets*
Dr. Goodpet Natural Medicines (Very Healthy Enterprises). *All The Best, Inter-Natural, Very Healthy Enterprises.*
Ellon Bach Homeopathic Remedies for Pets (Ellon Bach USA). Homeopathic medicines for cats, dogs, and other animals. *Ellon Bach USA.*
Homeopathic First-Aid Kits (Boiron Borneman). *Boiron Borneman.*
Royal Herbal Skin Ointment (The Pet Connection). Jojoba, aloe, and vitamins A, D, and E in a natural oil base; soothes and heals infected areas. *Meadowbrook Herb Garden.*

FLEA CONTROL

Harmful materials: pesticides.

Warning labels:
Impregnated flea collars:
"CAUTION: Do not allow children to play with this collar. Dust will form on this collar during storage. Do not get dust or collar in mouth, harmful if swallowed. Do not get dust in eyes, will cause temporary pupillary constriction. In case of contact, flush eyes with water. Wash hands thoroughly with soap and water after handling collar. The dust released by this collar is a cholinesterase inhibitor."
Insecticidal powders and shampoos:
"WARNING: Causes eye irritation. Do not get in eyes. Harmful if swallowed. While washing pets, avoid getting shampoo in animal's eyes. Do not use on kittens or puppies under six weeks of age."
Aerosol flea bombs:
"CAUTION: USE ONLY WHEN AREA TO BE TREATED IS VACATED BY HUMANS AND PETS. Harmful if swallowed or absorbed through skin. Avoid breathing vapors or spray mist. Avoid contact with skin and eyes. Do not apply directly to food. In the home, all food-processing surfaces should

be covered during treatment and thoroughly washed before use. Remove pets and cover fish aquariums and delicate plants before spraying. Remove all motor vehicles before use in garages."

Active-ingredients include pesticides DDVP, propoxur, diazinon, and carbaryl are nerve poisons that are toxic to pets and humans and may cause long-term health problems.

Some flea collars and powders can cause severe conditions such as contact dermatitis on the skin of your pets. Pets breathe the vapors given off by these products, cats lick the material from their fur when they clean themselves, and powders can fall off onto kitchen counters and other surfaces where food is prepared or eaten. Children who pet dogs and cats may pick up the chemicals on their hands.

Flea bombs are particularly dangerous, as they fill your entire house with a poisonous, flammable cloud. In one case reported in the Seattle area, a woman forgot to turn off the pilot light in her stove before using over a dozen flea bombs. The bombs ignited, blowing out all the windows and shifting the roof—yet the fleas survived.

HOMEMADE ALTERNATIVES

Flea Management
Flea control is an ongoing process. Even though you may kill all the adult fleas, there are still flea larvae waiting to hatch. As with any other insect, it will be impossible to eradicate fleas completely, but you can keep the flea population low enough that they don't bother anyone.

• Keep your pet healthy. Insects tend to be attracted to both unhealthy plants and unhealthy animals.
• Establish one regular sleeping area for your pet that can be cleaned easily and regularly. Fleas tend to accumulate where

animals sleep, so this will make it easier for you to collect them. Bedding materials such as blankets or rugs should be removed and washed frequently.
• Vacuum every week, with a strong canister-type machine, all areas to which your pet has access. Use a crevice tool for corners and out-of-the-way places and vacuum thoroughly—not just rugs, but floors, upholstered furniture, and pillows. Empty vacuum bag immediately, outside the house. Severe flea infestations may require an initial shampooing or steam cleaning of rugs and upholstered furniture.

Flea Repellents
• Sprinkle two ounces of lavender-oil extract over two or three quarts of rock salt and let the salt absorb the oil. Sprinkle lavender salt under dressers, couches, and rugs, and in other areas that don't move a lot. Dried pennyroyal can also be used (do not use pennyroyal oil, since in rare instances this more potent form has caused abortion in cats).
• Plant pennyroyal around the outside of your house and your lawn or garden during the spring or summer.
• Feed your pet (and yourself, if necessary) plenty of brewer's yeast. The yeast gives an odor to the skin that fleas find unpleasant. Use twenty-five milligrams per ten pounds of the animal's body weight, beginning in the spring and continuing through the warm season. To prevent intestinal gas, feed the yeast to your pet in small amounts with moist food. If you or your pet is allergic to yeast, try rice-based B-complex vitamins, available in natural-food stores.

Flea Killers
• Bake fleas out of your house: remove children, plants, and pets, close up your house, and turn up the heat to the highest setting. Go on an outing for the day; when you return, the fleas will be killed.

• Use a flea comb. Run the comb through your pet's fur, and drop the fleas that remain on the comb into a nearby container of soapy water (which should be flushed down the toilet when you're through).

• Shampoo your animal to knock off fleas and drown others. Use an ordinary soap, or a special insecticidal soap or shampoo.

At the Store/By Mail

Look for natural flea controls at your local pet store, or order them by mail.

❀ Natural flea controls

+ *Jeanne Rose Herbal BodyWorks.* Herbal flea repellents for dogs and cats using organically grown herbs when available. Beauty Without Cruelty Seal of Approval. ☺

+ *Willow Rain Herbal Goods.* Cedar animal spray contains tinctures of many herbs along with glycerin and biodegradable soap. For tick, flea, and fly control on dogs, cats, horses, and other animals.

Allergy Resources. Flea comb.

Amberwood. Herbal flea collars made of cotton cord impregnated with oils of pennyroyal, eucalyptus, cedar, citronella, and rue.

Aubrey Organics Dip and Creme Rinse for Dogs (Aubrey Organics Natural Organic Products). Natural ingredients, highly concentrated. ☺ Ⓐ *Aubrey Organics, The Compassionate Consumer, Humane Alternative Products, My Brother's Keeper.*

Aubrey Organics Shampoo for Dogs (Aubrey Organics). Cleans and deodorizes your pet's coat. ☺ Ⓐ *Aubrey Organics, The Compassionate Consumer, Humane Alternative Products, My Brother's Keeper.*

Avena Botanicals. Flea Be-Gone Soap, made from Dr. Bronner's eucalyptus castile soap, pure pine oil, and herbal extracts. No pesticides or harmful chemicals.

Breeders Equipment Company. Wood-and-metal flea comb; thirty-two teeth per inch. Also a flea trap and attractant.

Cedar-Al Products. Cedar products that can be used together to repel fleas. Pet pillows are covered with cotton and filled with western-red-cedar excelsior (long, thin shavings). Pet shampoo is made of pure castile soap with oil of cedar. Cedar-oil spray and carpet freshener help reduce fleas and pet odors around your home. ☺

Color & Herbal Dog & Cat Flea Collars (Color & Herbal Company). Cloth covered. *Color & Herbal Company.*

Color & Herbal Renewal Oil (Color & Herbal Company). Pure, concentrated herbal oils for all herbal collars. *Color & Herbal Company.*

Color & Herbal Spray Away (Color & Herbal Company). Herbal spray for your pet, its bedding, and around the home. *Color & Herbal Company.*

D. Flea. Flea kit includes diatom dust, applicator, mask, and flea collar. Dust is not for use on your animal and not for use by anyone with lung dysfunction such as emphysema, severe asthma, or lung cancer.

Flea & Tick Attack (Ringer). Comes in sprayer bottle. *Karen's Nontoxic Products, Ringer.*

Gardens Alive! Herbal shampoo and dip; dry-bath coat spray; and indoor flea guard with fresh, natural fragrance, to spray on carpet or upholstery.

Green Ban for Pets (Green Ban). Made of ground mint and talc, with essential oils. For dogs and cats. *Basically Natural, Baubiologie Hardware, Eco-Choice, Harmony Farm Supply, InterNatural.*

Harmony Farm Supply. Natural herbal flea collar. Also coat-enhancer spray that contains a citrus deodorizer and ingredients to repel fleas and ticks.

Karen's Nontoxic Products. Organic sprays for cats and dogs.

Mountain Ark Trading Company. Tea-tree-oil dog shampoo.

Pet Organics Kleen Pet Flea Shampoo (Pet Organics). *The Living Source.*

PetGuard Herbal Flea Collar (Pet-Guard). Pennyroyal, eucalyptus, cedar, and other aromatic herbs. *The Compassionate Consumer.*

Royal Herbal Pet Powder (The Pet Connection). Use in conjunction with flea collar on pet, pet bedding, and carpeting. *Meadowbrook Herb Garden.*

Royal Herbal Rechargeable Flea Collar (The Pet Connection). Adjustable rawhide collar impregnated with oils. For cats and dogs. *Meadowbrook Herb Garden.*

Royal Herbal Shampoo (The Pet Connection). Oils of eucalyptus, citronella, pennyroyal, and spearmint to repel fleas. *Meadowbrook Herb Garden.*

Safer Flea Indoor Flea Guard (Safer). For carpet and pet bedding. *All The Best, Eco-Choice, Harmony Farm Supply.*

Safer Flea Shampoo for Cats & Dogs (Safer). Pleasant scent. *Harmony Farm Supply.*

Safer Flea Soap for Dogs and Cats (Safer). Kills fleas on contact and grooms your pet at the same time. Fresh natural scent.

Safer Timed Release Indoor-Outdoor Pest Control (Safer). Contains microencapsulated pyrethrum. *Harmony Farm Supply.*

Mountain Rose Herbs. Pennyroyal repellent oil.

Natural Animal Pow (EcoSafe Products). Herbal flea powder that contains only dried pyrethrum flowers. *Baubiologie Hardware, Earth Herbs, EcoSafe Products, Karen's Nontoxic Products, Mountain Rose Herbs, Natural Lifestyle Supplies.*

Natural Animal Rechargeable Flea Collar (EcoSafe Products). Cotton collar with recharging solution made of essential oils of citrus, cedar, citronella, eucalyptus, and bay. *Baubiologie Hardware, Earth Herbs, EcoSafe Products, InterNatural, Karen's Nontoxic Products, Lost Prairie Herb Farm, Mountain Rose Herbs.*

Nature's Gate Herbal Pet Shampoo (Levlad). Blend of freshly cured herbs and pennyroyal. 🙂 🚫 *Amberwood.*

Nitron Industries. Herbal products include powder, shampoo, and leather flea collars pretreated with herbal formula.

Noah's Park Flea Products (Noah's Park). Herbal dip and powder, plus herbal collars. For dogs and cats. *Noah's Park.*

Pet Organics Dog-Ex & Cat-Ex Flea Treatment (Pet Organics). *The Living Source.*

Thursday Plantation Tea-Tree Oil Anti-Itch Pet Shampoo (Teaco International). Effective for fleas, ticks, rashes, cuts, and itches. *Teaco International.*

Wysong Py2 (Wysong Corporation). Concentrated source of natural pyrethrins. *Wysong Corporation.*

Zampet Herbal Pet Collars and Reactivating Herbal Oil (Zampet Manufacturing). Made of eucalyptus buds, ceramic beads, and carved wood, with oils of pennyroyal, eucalyptus, and citronella. Can be reactivated. *Zampet Manufacturing.*

FOOD FOR PETS

Harmful ingredients: artificial colors, artificial flavors, BHA/BHT, lead, nitrates/nitrosamines, pesticides.

I used to feed my cat canned or dry pet food, but now I prepare her food from fresh ingredients. She thrives on raw meat. She will eat canned or dry food if it is a natural brand, but if I give her pet food from the supermarket, she paws around it like she's trying to cover up something in her litter box.

Most large corporations that manufacture commercial pet food are concerned about providing an "adequate" product at a low price. They get their protein from cheap "4-D meats"—from animals that are already dead, dying, diseased, or disabled when they're sold. Then they add sugar so your pet will like it and artificial color so you'll think it looks fresh.

Many pet foods claim to be "100% nutritionally complete and balanced." This claim can legally be made and printed on commercial products based on information studies using *isolated nutrients* and not whole foods, or by feeding the complete pet food to animals for several weeks to determine whether it prevents obvious disease or malnutrition. Although motivated by an interest to assure quality for the consumer, these tests ignore important nutritional issues and give both producer and consumer a false sense of knowledge and security.

Measuring a food's merit by levels of isolated nutrients tells only a partial story. There are over forty known, essential nutrients, and over fifty other nutrients are under investigation. Thus making sure a food contains appropriate amounts of only a dozen of these nutrients can't possibly assure that a food is "complete."

Many pet nutritionists recommend adding fresh raw food (meat, vegetables, and whole grains) to your animal's diet. According to Anita Frazier, author of *The Natural Cat,* "You can't build resistance without some raw food. After three generations on a canned-food diet, the immune system is gone."

Studies by Dr. Francis M. Pottenger over forty years ago showed the superiority of raw food for cats. Dr. Pottenger noticed that cats fed raw meat were healthier, reproduced more easily, and had healthier kittens than cats fed cooked meat. This inspired him to embark on a carefully controlled set of scientific studies that spanned ten years and over nine hundred generations of cats.

In the study of raw versus cooked meat, the raw-meat-fed cats were friendly, even-tempered, well coordinated, and resistant

to infections, fleas, and parasites. Miscarriages were rare, and each generation showed striking uniformity in size and skeletal growth. Cause of death was generally old age, and autopsies revealed normal internal organs. The cooked-meat group, in contrast, showed many health problems that became worse with each successive generation—many of the same problems humans get from eating refined foods, such as arthritis and heart problems. After the third generation, all the cooked-meat-fed cats had died out.

In another experiment, Pottenger tested four kinds of milk: raw, pasteurized, evaporated, and sweetened condensed. The groups fed evaporated and sweetened condensed milk showed the most severe degeneration, those fed pasteurized milk had problems similar to the cooked-meat-fed cats, while the cats fed raw milk produced many generations of healthy cats.

Should you feed your pet a vegetarian diet? All the health and environmental reasons humans should reduce or eliminate their meat intake also hold true for animals. Yet I feel that animals' natural instinct is to eat meat. My cats love mice and flying insects. On the other hand, cats have been reported to be very fond of almonds, sunflower seeds, avocados, peas, corn, spinach, raisins, dried bananas, potatoes, yams, and sweet potatoes. Whether you choose to feed your pet meat or vegetables, the more fresh, unprocessed food you can give them the better.

A word of warning about canned tuna: in addition to the fact that hundreds of thousands of dolphins are being needlessly slaughtered as a result of current tuna-catching methods, a study at Cornell University has shown that cats fed tuna cat food daily are less active, less playful, and less vocal than cats fed beef cat food. The problem stems from methyl mercury, which accumulates in many fish; over five times more is found in tuna cat food than is generally found in beef cat food.

I discovered an ironic cruelty-free twist about pet food while I was reading labels: one major brand of natural pet food is owned by a major animal-testing corporation (Science Diet is owned by Colgate-Palmolive). So read those labels for more than just the ingredients.

HOMEMADE ALTERNATIVES

• Raw organically grown meat. When my cat was sick, that's all she would eat; she wouldn't even take milk. In *Keep Your Pet Healthy the Natural Way*, Pat Lazarus recommends that one-third to one-half of a dog's daily food should be meat and that for cats, meat should make up three-fourths of the daily diet. The rest should be fruits, vegetables, and grains, which contain essential nutrients that are not present in meat. Fruits and vegetables should be cut up and eaten raw; use cooked whole grains such as brown rice. Proper food combining is also recommended for animals to aid in digestion: feed fruit separately, protein with vegetables, and starch with vegetables.

• A pamphlet by world-famous herbalist-veterinarian Juliette de Bairacle Levy makes food recommendations based on observing what animals eat and how they behave in nature, and then applying these observations to home and kennel care. For adult cats, she suggests two meals a day of milk thickened with uncooked rolled oats or other grains and one protein meal each day composed of several teaspoons of raw, finely cut meat or lightly steamed, finely cut fish, a pinch of seaweed mineral powder, and a half teaspoon or so of very finely cut herbs such as parsley, mint, dandelion greens, or cress, covered with a teaspoon of light oil. Sprouted grains are also recommended. Five days a week give meat or fish, one day milk and cereals only, and one day very little food in order to rest the digestive system.

• Maryanne Hoag and Lisa Goldsmith, who raise purebred dogs in California, use this diet: the first meal (to be given after noon) is a cereal feed consisting of raw barley flakes or oats that have been soaked in raw goat's or cow's milk for about four hours (to make them digestible to a carnivore), mixed with a tablespoon of cold-pressed oil, some cornmeal, kelp, and sprouts or fresh green herbs such as parsley. About three times a week they put a raw egg into the cereal. The second meal of the day comes at least four hours after the first and consists of raw meat cut in large chunks with a couple of tablespoons of raw bran flakes sprinkled on top. They believe that 75 percent of the diet should be raw meat and 25 percent cereal; in addition, they recommend lots of raw garlic, raw bones, and pure water, and a fast of one day each week.

• Give your pet purified water to drink. Chlorine, fluoride, and other water pollutants are no better for animals than they are for us.

At the Store/By Mail

Look for natural pet foods at your natural-food store, or order them by mail.

❧ Natural pet food

+ Wow Bow Vegan Health Biscuits for Dogs (Wow-Bow Distributors). Ingredients include organically grown whole-wheat flour, bulgur, cornmeal, nutritional yeast, fresh garlic and parsley, and vegetable broth. Dairyless and eggless. ☺ Ⓧ *The Compassionate Consumer, Humane Alternative Products, Wow-Bow Distributors.*

Abady Dog and Cat Foods (Abady). Abady's system is based on the theory that different groups of ingredients often require opposite processing techiques. The heat and pressure of pelletizing and extruding can improve the starches in grains, but can impair the nutrients in animal meal. Therefore, Abady uses a two-step process.

Cornucopia Dog and Cat Foods (Veterinary Nutritional Associates). *Veterinary Nutritional Associates.*

Health Valley Pet Foods (Health Valley Natural Foods). Canned food, in two flavors for dogs, three for cats.

Lick Your Chops Dog and Cat Foods (Lick Your Chops). Contain USDA-inspected fresh meats, vegetable oils, fish fillets, and brown rice.

LifeSource Holistic Pet Foods (Wysong Corporation). A rich blend of whole fresh, natural foods, formulated by veterinarians. *Mountain Ark Trading Company.*

Natural Life Pet Foods (Natural Life Pet Products). Dog and cat food that uses fresh-milled grains, quality beef, fish, poultry, herbs, eggs, dairy products, and chelated minerals. A generous dose of linoleic acid, a fatty acid necessary for healthy coats, is added. Only the natural preservatives vitamins C and B are used. *All The Best.*

Natural Pet Liver Pet Treats (EcoSafe Products). *Earth Herbs, EcoSafe Products.*

Nature's Recipe Pet Foods (Nature's Recipe). *All The Best, Wow-Bow Distributors.*

Noah's Park Dog, Cat, and Bird Foods and Treats (Noah's Park). Dog and cat food uses USDA meat as its primary ingredient, plus organic brown rice and other human-consumption-quality ingredients. Also food for finches, parakeets, canaries, cockatiels, and parrots. *All The Best, Noah's Park.*

North Farms New-Process Dog Food (North Farms Cooperative). *Mountain Ark Trading Company.*

PetGuard Dog and Cat Foods (PetGuard). Dry and canned.

Science Diet Pet Foods (Hill's Pet Prod-

ucts). Largest alternative pet-food line. Dry and canned varieties; the canned line consists of five formulas.

Tyrrell's Pet Food (Tyrrell's). Meat combined with cracked wheat. Dog food contains more than 10 percent protein; cat food has even more. Both with no added preservatives or artificial color.

Wysong Dog and Cat Foods (Wysong Corporation). Wide variety of diets for cats and dogs. *All The Best, Wysong Corporation.*

GROOMING

Harmful ingredients: artificial colors, BHA/BHT, fragrances (this is an estimation; there are no ingredients lists on animal grooming products).

At the Store/By Mail

Check your local natural-food store for grooming products for your pet, or order them by mail.

☘ *Natural grooming products for pets*

Aubrey Organics Grooming Spray for Dogs (Aubrey Organics). For skin irritation between shampoos. ☺ Ⓐ *Aubrey Organics, Humane Alternative Products, My Brother's Keeper.*

Color & Herbal Conditioning Shampoo (Color & Herbal Company). Aloe herbal shampoo for a shiny coat. Fresh herbal scent. *Color & Herbal Company.*

Green Ban Dog Shampoo (Green Ban). Coconut-oil-based shampoo with herbs. *Basically Natural, Baubiologie Hardware, Harmony Farm Supply, InterNatural.*

Karen's Nontoxic Products. Shampoos for cats and dogs.

KSA Jojoba. Jojoba oil for skin and coat of dogs and cats.

Lightning Pet Sprays (Lightning Pet Products). Natural blend of citrus oils and aloe vera that combats skin irritations caused by fleas and ticks, and fungus-related dry flaky skin. For dogs. ☺ ⊘ *All The Best, Humane Alternative Products.*

Natural Animal Herbal Shampoo and Dip/Animal Spritz (EcoSafe Products). *Baubiologie Hardware, Earth Herbs, EcoSafe Products, Mountain Rose Herbs, Natural Lifestyle Supplies.*

Noah's Park Grooming Aids (Noah's Park). Salve, shampoo, and ear wash made from herbs, minerals, and oils. For dogs, cats, and birds. *Noah's Park.*

PetGuard Shampoo with Conditioner (PetGuard). For skin irritations and coat care.

Vetcair CoatCair (Protech). Environmentally safe, all-natural formula that cleans and conditions pet's coat. Works by naturally biodegrading the molecules of offending substances.

Widupet (DCM Industries). Wood-bristle brush with wooden handle. *Inter-Natural.*

KITTY LITTER

Most kitty litters contain very strong deodorants and are generally poured into plastic pans.

HOMEMADE ALTERNATIVES
• If you live in an appropriate area, train your cats to go outside.
• Cats can also be trained to use the bathroom toilet. Ask at your pet store for training equipment.
• Instead of using a plastic pan, buy the cheapest big enameled turkey roasting pan at your hardware store. It works great, can be easily washed, and lasts forever.

SPECIAL ODOR-CONTROL TIPS
• Add baking soda or powdered zeolite (order from G & W Supply) to kitty litter to control odor.
• In her book *The Natural Cat,* Anita Frazier suggests putting only a slight cover-

ing of litter in the bottom of the box and removing all the soiled litter, not just the feces. Smelly boxes come from several inches of old soiled litter, and changing the litter frequently solves the problem.
• If there is a lot of odor, you might consider changing what you feed your cat.

At the Store/By Mail
Buy plain ground corncobs or ground walnut shells at your pet store.

❖ *Natural kitty litter*
EverClean Cat Litter (A & M Pet Products). Made of crushed ground minerals, this soft, unscented litter completely absorbs and captures urine in easy-to-remove balls. By completely removing all waste daily, you eliminate the source of the odor. *All The Best.*

Nature's Miracle Cat Litter Treatment (Pets & People). Guaranteed to eliminate urine odors and at least double litter life or your money back. *Ecco Bella.*

Safer Pet Odor Eliminator (Safer). Clean, fresh scent.

Wysong Litter Lite (Wysong Corporation). Natural, biodegradable litter-box filler. *Wysong Corporation.*

Zampet Dry Herb Deodorizer (Zampet Manufacturing). All-natural deodorizer for cat litter box or doghouse. *Zampet Manufacturing.*

NUTRITIONAL SUPPLEMENTS FOR PETS

Animals have the same need for essential nutrients that humans do, and unless you're feeding your pet homemade meals of organically grown food, your pet's diet may need to be supplemented. You can give your pet the same whole-food-type supplements you use in your own diet, such as brewer's yeast and kelp, or choose nutritional supplements especially formulated for animals.

HOMEMADE ALTERNATIVES

• Anita Frazier, author of *The Natural Cat*, advocates a special vitamin/mineral mix that can be made at home. Mix one-and-one-half cups brewer's yeast (for quality of fur), two cups bran (to keep intestines healthy), one cup lecithin granules (for hair texture and skin quality), one-quarter cup kelp (for minerals), and three-fourths cup bone meal (for strong bones and nerves). "Add a teaspoon per cat per meal," she says, "and you'll see a difference in a month!"

At the Store/By Mail

Nutritional supplements especially formulated for animals can be found at your natural-food store or ordered by mail.

◆ Natural nutritional supplements for pets

+ *Avena Botanicals.* Powdered herbal daily food supplement balances nutritional needs and provides natural resistance to fleas. Also liquid daily herbal tonic. ✚ ☺ ⊗

Dr. Goodpet Nutritional Supplements (Very Healthy Enterprises). Variety of hypoallergenic vitamins and trace minerals. *All The Best, Very Healthy Enterprises.*

Natural Animal Supplements (EcoSafe Products). All-natural supplements also discourages worms and fleas. *Earth Herbs, EcoSafe Products, Gardens Alive!*

Naturally Chelated Trace-Mineral Supplement (Wow-Bow Distributors). For both cats and dogs. *Wow-Bow Distributors.*

Noah's Park Manna Multi-Vitamin and Mineral Supplement (Noah's Park). blended from human-consumption-quality herbs, minerals, and oils. For dogs, cats, and birds. *Noah's Park.*

PetGuard Supplements (PetGuard). Yeast-and-garlic, multivitamin-and-mineral, and skin-and-coat supplements.

Vegepet (Harbingers of a New Age). Add these supplements to specially developed recipes to meet the nutritional requirements of cats and dogs without meat. Formulas for dogs, cats, and kittens. ⊗ *Amberwood, Harbingers of a New Age.*

15 ❧ Garbage

I never met a garbage I didn't want to recycle.
ANONYMOUS

Every product, eventually, becomes garbage. For most of my life, I never had any awareness beyond the garbage can. If I didn't want something anymore, I simply threw it away, like we all do. Sure, I knew our city had a dump—I even went there on a few occasions—but I never made the connection that what I put in my garbage can actually ended up in a landfill. And I never considered what would happen if those landfills filled up.

We're running out of room in our current landfills. Garbage now washes up on beaches, wildlife is killed when it eats or is strangled by our garbage, and hazardous waste from our household products is leaching through piles of garbage to contaminate land and water supplies.

HOW GARBAGE AFFECTS OUR HEALTH AND THE EARTH

It is becoming increasingly difficult and costly to dispose of the more than 365 billion pounds of solid waste we generate each year—about four pounds a day for every man, woman, and child in this country. Between 1950 and 1988, the amount of waste thrown out per person in the United States doubled. Other industrial countries such as West Germany and Japan generate only half as much waste per person as we do.

Our garbage cans are filled with a diverse mix (by weight):

paper and paperboard (36 percent)

yard wastes (19 percent)

glass (8 percent)

metals (9 percent)

food (9 percent)

plastics (8 percent)

wood/fabric (4 percent)

rubber and leather (3 percent)

textiles (2 percent)

other (1.6 percent)

household hazardous waste (.4 percent)

The items that constitute the greatest portions by weight are cardboard (7 percent), newspapers (6 percent), beverage containers (6 percent), and disposable diapers (3 percent). Overall, packaging accounts for 30 percent of the weight of all municipal waste.

The picture is a bit different when you look at the figures in terms of volume—which may be more important in relation to landfill space. Packaging contributes 50 percent of the volume. Plastics (including packaging such as bottles, containers, and wrappings) make up almost 30 percent of the volume.

Currently, approximately 80 percent of our garbage goes into landfills, 10 percent is incinerated, and 10 percent is recycled, but this can't continue. About half the cities in the United States will be unable to use their current landfills by the time this book is published. More than two thousand landfills have closed in the last five years for environmental reasons, and another seven hundred for lack of space.

In some communities, incinerators are being promoted as a way to reduce the amount of garbage sent to landfills. But incinerators, even if they produce some usable energy as a by-product, have many problems: they are extremely expensive to build and operate (and are less cost-effective than other solutions while at the same time creating only about one-sixth the jobs), they inhibit recycling because to operate daily they require a minimum of garbage which otherwise might have been recycled, and they have many environmental health consequences.

Incinerators emit roughly twenty-seven different metals, over two hundred organic chemicals, and a variety of acidic gases. One average sixteen-hundred-ton-a-day incinerator blows out over twenty-one-thousand pounds of toxic waste every *day*.

The ash from the incinerator stack (fly ash) is poisonous, as is bottom ash, the burned remains of the garbage. The ash that remains is still 30 percent by weight of the original garbage and still must be disposed of, often at a cost greater than that of disposing the original garbage. EPA studies have shown pollutants to exceed hazardous-waste safety levels in many instances, with ash from state-of-the-art plants being just as hazardous because toxics scrubbed out of smokestacks end up in the bottom ash instead of in the air. Although nine out of eleven ash samples from garbage incinerators have proven to be toxic, the EPA hasn't yet classified contaminated incinerator ash as hazardous waste. Most of it is being landfilled as if it were household garbage, stored in open piles, or even used to de-ice roads. Dioxins and toxic metals in the ash are readily absorbed and retained in the tissues of living organisms and will move up the food chain.

Depending on whether you're talking to somebody in the incinerator industry or an environmental group, toxic ash in landfills either hardens into impenetrable concrete or stays a soft mass. So rainwater either runs right off, or it trickles through buried ash; taking toxic pollutants down into aquifers and streams, and into local water supplies. Even if we could absolutely contain toxic ash, future generations will eventually face landfill limitations and may be poisoned by our errors.

REDUCING THE AMOUNT OF GARBAGE WE PRODUCE

Solid-waste-management experts, environmentalists, and administrators at all levels of government agree that the only sensible thing to do to solve our garbage problem is to reduce the amount of garbage we produce. The EPA has established a national goal of 25 percent reduction by 1992.

That means each of us needs to participate in this process in our own homes. Once you start becoming aware of the garbage you produce, you'll find ways to produce less and less. If you throw away a lot of cans, see if you can prepare more meals from fresh ingredients. I decided to invest in a citrus juicer after I watched all the plastic bottles from my lunchtime organic orange juice piling up, and I started feeding my kitten fresh food so I wouldn't have to deal with the empty cans. It's become a fun and interesting game for me to see how empty I can keep my garbage can.

Here are some general tips:

1. Buy fewer products. This might be easier than you think. Buy only one or two general nontoxic housecleaning products, for example, rather than a different product for each cleaning job (see Chapter 7).

2. Buy durable, reusable items instead of disposables: for example, refillable fountain pens and razors, cotton kitchen towels, cloth napkins, and the like. When you go to the market, take a cloth carryall (see BAGS, BAGS, BAGS in Chapter 10) or bring along paper and plastic bags from your previous purchases that can be reused. Try a soap mug and brush instead of buying shaving cream in disposable cans. Each time a product is reused, a new one need not be manufactured, purchased, and ultimately disposed of.

3. Buy used or refurbished items. Antique stores, flea markets, garage sales, storage auctions, classified advertisements, and community bulletin boards are filled with products that may be of interest to you.

4. Sell or give away items you no longer use. Perodically clean out your garage, cabinets, and closets, and put things you no longer use back into circulation.

5. Rent or share things you use only occasionally.

6. Reduce the amount of packaging you buy:
   • Look for products with no packaging.
   • Buy a large size or buy in bulk. If you need only small amounts, shop with a friend, buy a larger size, and split it.
   • Choose packaged items that are wrapped once. A product needs to be covered and identified only once, so a jar, a box, or a bag will do. There is no need to have bags inside boxes, wrapped in plastic. Sometimes there is more wrapping than product.

7. Stop junk mail. According to the U.S. Postal Service, every man, woman, and child in the United States receives an average of 248 pieces of unsolicited, third-class advertising each year. To reduce this amount:
   • Clearly state that you do not want your name and address sold or traded whenever you write for a catalog or make a mail-order purchase.
   • Return mailing labels on junk mail in their postage-paid return envelope along with a note (written on reused waste paper) asking to be removed from their mailing list.
   • Write to the Mail Preference Service at the Direct Marketing Association, 6 East 43rd Street, New York, NY 10017. They can stop your name from being sold to most large mailing-list companies. The amount of *new* junkmail sent to you will be reduced by up to 75 percent.

WHAT TO DO WITH YOUR (REDUCED) GARBAGE

Beyond reducing the amount of our garbage as much as we can, we need to recycle the rest. At least ten states and six hundred communities have mandatory-recycling laws, and these numbers will grow. The primary materials we recycle now are aluminum and other metals, glass, and paper. Only about 2 percent of plastic is currently being recycled.

The United States now recycles about 12 percent of its waste, but the EPA hopes to double that figure within four years. This is a modest aim, for we actually have the ability to recycle over 80 percent of our waste using existing technology. Nature, of course, recycles 100 percent—our ultimate goal.

But where will all this recyclable material go? Already a discrepancy is developing between the amount of recyclable materials collected and the demand for products made from recycled materials. Prices are dropping for recycled materials, jeopardizing existing programs. We have to begin to buy more recycled products, and industry needs to invest in recycling plants.

Food and yard wastes, which make up almost 30 percent of our garbage, can be recycled by composting. In the natural world, 100 percent of all plant and animal material goes through the process of breaking down into humus and natural fertilizer. Composting is a great way to reduce the amount of our garbage, and build up soil fertility the natural way at the same time. You can even compost your food wastes under your kitchen sink or in the basement using earthworms, one of nature's best composters (for more information on composting, see COMPOST, FERTILIZERS, AND OTHER SOIL AMENDMENTS in Chapter 6).

Products made with nonrecycled resources generally create up to *ten* times as much toxic pollution in our air, land, and water, use *twice* as much energy, create fewer jobs, and of course, waste precious resources. For every million Americans who recycle, some fifteen hundred manufacturing jobs are created.

Aluminum

Send aluminum cans, foil, foil products such as pie plates, and tin cans to the recycling center.

Aluminum can be made from a mined ore called bauxite, or it can be made from old aluminum cans. Enough aluminum is thrown away by U.S. consumers and industry to rebuild our entire commercial air fleet every three months. The aluminum we do recycle has already created thirty thousand new jobs.

Every ton of recycled aluminum:

• Reduces energy use 95 percent (28,860 kilowatt hours—enough to power the average home for three and a half years).
• Reduces air and water pollutants 95 percent.

It takes six weeks for an average recycled container to come from the store, be melted into a new container, and get back on the shelf. We recycled 55 percent of our aluminum cans in 1988; however, the 55 million cans we threw away that year would circle the Earth 104 times if laid end to end.

Batteries

Use rechargeable batteries, and take old ones to a household hazardous-waste collection. Do not throw batteries in the dump, as they are filled with heavy metals. Return all car batteries to gas stations or battery dealerships, where they will be recycled.

Throwaway batteries are one of the largest sources of toxic lead, cadmium, zinc, manganese, and nickel in municipal solid waste in the United States. In 1973, 31 percent of all mercury released into the environment came from improper disposal of household batteries, with a typical community of five hundred thousand putting almost thirty thousand pounds of mercury into its landfills each year.

Ideally, household batteries should be recycled, but this is not economically feasible right now due to the difficulty of collection and separation of the various types. Perhaps a recycling tax or returnable-battery deposit fee (similar to what is used for returnable bottles) should be used to enable a recycling market to exist.

Automotive batteries each contain about eighteen pounds of lead and a gallon of corrosive sulfuric acid. Car batteries account for about 71 percent of the lead consumed in the U.S. Due to increased pollution-control regulations for recycling centers and a decline in the price of lead, the total number of batteries recycled has declined from a peak of 97 percent in 1965 to 80 percent at present.

Fabrics

Compost natural fibers, or recycle fabric items. I was surprised to find out that about 13 percent of all cloth fibers are recycled. Textile-recycling processes are similar to those for paper, and cloth can be recombined into clothes, blankets, padding, carpeting, fine paper, and other products.

Once synthetic fibers go to the landfill, they do not biodegrade.

Food Wastes

Compost, and feed local animals. Also, support local food-exchange programs that pick up daily leftover food from businesses (restaurants, bakeries, and local farms) and deliver it to free-food programs.

Glass

Any type or color of glass bottle or jar can be recycled. It should be clean and free of metal, but it's acceptable to leave a paper label on. Recycling centers will not accept light bulbs, ceramic glass, dishes, or plate glass because these items consist of materials other than those found in bottles and jars.

Glass can be reused and recycled an infinite number of times. It is 100 percent recyclable, and the process produces much less waste and fewer by-products. In addition, glass containers offer the benefit of not imparting tastes or leaching contaminants into the products they contain.

We throw away enough glass bottles and jars to fill the 1,350-foot twin towers of New York's World Trade Center every two weeks. Bottle bills that require returnable deposits have resulted in 90 percent return rates in the states that have them.

Simply refilling glass jars and bottles a second time reduces litter by 40 to 50 percent, reduces resource consumption and solid-waste generation by 70 percent, and reduces energy consumption by 40 percent.

Household and Building Materials

Take lumber, doors, windows, plumbing fixtures, and other reusable buiding items to your local salvage yard.

Household Hazardous Waste

According to an article in *National Geographic,* we throw away eight billion pounds of hazardous waste each year; that's thirty-two pounds per person.

Some communities have days set aside when they collect household hazardous wastes and take them to a reprocessing center (some chemicals can be reproccessed into usable products) or to a special hazardous-waste dump for disposal. While it is much better to take your household hazardous waste to a collection site than to throw it into the garbage can, these waste-collection days are not the long-term answer. In my county, they cost three hundred dollars per drum of waste collected, plus the cost of labor, publicity, and administrative work to run the program. Each car typically brings in about a third of a drum of hazardous waste, making the disposal costs over one hundred dollars per car.

Hazardous-waste collection days should be used as a last resort, after citizens have reduced their use of toxics by as much as possible. They should include a strong campaign to promote safe alternatives.

If you have household toxics to dispose of, call your local public- or environmental-health department, department of health services, or sanitation department to see if you have a hazardous-waste-disposal program in your community. If you don't have a local program, ask your local authorities how best to dispose of your toxics. It may be *illegal* to dispose of certain products with your normal household garbage.

First, take an inventory of your home and identify household products that should be disposed of as hazardous waste with the following list. *Use these products up, and find alternatives to as many as you can so you don't need to buy them again.*

Hazardous Household Products

The following Hazardous Household Products list is from the San Francisco Household Hazardous Waste Program.

Do not dispose of these products in your household garbage.

Housecleaning supplies
Ammonia cleaners
Chlorine bleach
Cleansers
Disinfectants
Drain openers
Furniture and floor polish
Lye
Metal polish
Oven cleaner
Rug cleaners
Tub, tile, shower-stall cleaners

Laundry supplies
Dry-cleaning solvent

Mothballs and flakes
Spot remover

Cosmetics
Cuticle remover
Depilatory cream
Hair-permanent solutions
Hair-straightener solutions
Nail polish
Nail-polish remover

Medicines
Chemotherapy drugs
Liquid medicine
Mercury from a broken thermometer

Prescription medicine

Rubbing alcohol

Shampoo for lice

Other household products

Aerosol cans containing *any* pressure or fluid

Butane lighters

Flea powder

Lighter fluid

Pet shampoo

Shoe dye and polish

Automotive supplies

Aluminum cleaner

Auto-body filler

Automatic-transmission fluid

Brake fluid

Carburetor cleaner

Car wax

Chrome polish

Diesel fuel

Engine degreaser

Gasoline

Kerosene or lamp oil

Lubricating oil

Motor oil, used (see if you can find a place that will accept this for recycling)

Building and woodworking supplies

Asbestos

Fluorescent lamp with ballasts and tubes

Glues and cements

Wood preservatives

Garden supplies

Fungicides

Herbicides

Insecticides

Rat, mouse, and gopher poison

Snail and slug poison

Soil fumigants

Weed killer

Hobby and pet supplies

Artist's mediums, thinners, fixatives

Acrylic paint

Chemistry sets

Oil paint

Photographic chemicals/solutions

Resins, fiberglass, and epoxy

Rubber-cement thinner

Painting supplies

Latex-based paint

Model-airplane paint

Oil-based paint

Paint stripper

Paint thinner, turpentine, mineral spirits

Metals

All metals should be recycled. Larger items can be sold as scrap metal. Rinse cans and remove labels.

Recycling of metals currently provides about half of all the lead, 40 percent of all copper, 35 percent of all gold, and 25 percent of all silver used in the United States. Recycling lead reduces energy use by 60 percent, recycling copper, 87 percent.

Even though we generally do a better job at recycling scrap metal than other materials, we still throw away enough iron and steel to continuously supply all of the nation's automakers. The U.S. scrap industry has the ability to process 280 billion pounds of iron and steel each year (much less than is currently being recycled), while studies estimate there are over 1.6 trillion pounds of scrap in this country waiting to be recycled.

Motor Oil

Recycle used motor oil at any gas station (some will charge, others will not) or at a dump that will accept it.

Used oil contains toxics such as lead, chromium, cadmium, naphthalene, chlorinated hydrocarbons, and other dangerous chemicals. Less than 10 percent of the 200 million gallons of used motor oil drained from cars each year in the United States is recycled, even though it is a valuable resource that can be reused as fuel or re-refined as a lubricant.

Paper and Paperboard

Any kind of paper can be recycled, but check with your local recycling center to see if they want you to separate different types of paper for pickup. Office paper fetches a much higher price than newspapers, for example, and every collection center has a different method of sorting. Some magazines, however, cannot be recycled because they use slick paper, hot-melt glues for bindings, and mailing labels that are not water soluble. Recycle these by passing them along to interested friends, rest homes, doctors offices, or schools for art projects, or consider canceling your subscription. Pull the little plastic window coverings out of window envelopes before recycling them.

Approximately 30 percent of paper "waste" is now recycled (during World War II we recycled 43 percent). Instead of piling up in a landfill, paper can be recycled seven to ten times before the fibers become too soft to hold together.

Recycling half the paper used throughout the world today would free 20 million acres of forest land from paper production.

Every ton of recycled paper:

- Saves approximately seventeen trees.
- Saves half the energy (forty-one hundred kilowatt hours—enough to power the average home for six months).
- Saves half the water (seven thousand gallons).
- Eliminates 70 percent of air pollutants (sixty pounds), fifty percent of water pollutants (eighteen pounds), and 50 percent of solid wastes (ninety pounds)
- Saves over three cubic yards of landfill space.
- Creates five times as many jobs as the manufacture of virgin paper.

Manufacturing *unbleached* recycled paper uses even less water, fewer chemicals, and produces much less solid waste than manufacturing bleached recycled paper.

Plastics

Don't buy them in the first place. If you have to dispose of them, try to recycle; otherwise they stay around for hundreds of years.

As a nation we throw away 60 million plastic bottles and 50 million plastic disposable diapers *each day*. That is enough diapers each year to stretch back and forth to the moon seven times. Worldwide, we dump 90 million pounds of plastics into the oceans each year.

While there has been a growing interest in the past few years in recycling plastic, it does have its disadvantages. One big problem is that every time plastic gets recycled, it moves down a step in quality. What starts out as a plastic soda bottle or container for a cleaning product ends up as fence posts, paint brushes, fiberfill for pillows, park benches, fencing, and landscape items. Recycled plastics are not allowed for food packaging because the recycling process does not sanitize them. Some uses of recycled plastics may be appropriate, such as making lighter-weight, strong plastic car fenders to replace metal. But how many plastic park benches do we need? General Electric is planning on recycling plastic into modular plastic houses. Do we want plastic houses that may outgas toxic fumes?

To maintain the recycling loop, virgin material must still be used to make the recyclable plastic. We must still deplete nonrenewable petrochemicals, toxic waste is still produced, plastics (recycled or not) are still harmful to human health, and after plastic is recycled only a very few times we still need to dispose of it, and it is not biodegradable. By encouraging the recycling of plastics we encourage their continued production.

The best long-term solution for most plastics is simply to eliminate them entirely, especially throwaway items such as food packaging and containers, which account for about half of all plastic used. For the moment, though, plastic is an inescapable part of our lives. Buy as little as possible, and when you do buy a plastic item, choose one that is made of recycled plastic or that is recyclable. Reuse plastic items as many times as you can, then pass them on to others or recycle them. Encourage your town or county to ban throwaway plastic.

Tires

The best solution is to recycle them. Only about 5 percent of the estimated 240 million car and truck tires discarded each year are currently recycled. The huge stockpiles, often in private junkyards, are breeding grounds for mosquitos and are susceptible to fire.

Rubber (40 percent of the tire) can be recycled to make building materials, irrigation piping, and paving material, and recycled rubber can be added to virgin rubber and plastics to produce a variety of products such as laundry baskets, mud flaps, athletic and door mats, truck-bed liners, grocery-cart wheels, and retreaded tires. The remainder of the tire—steel belts, bead wire, and sidewall—can also be recycled. If you don't have a rubber-recycling plant in your area, you might want to start one.

GARBAGE BAGS

Although there has been a lot of publicity about so-called biodegradable plastic bags, they aren't really what their name suggests.

Almost all "degradable" plastics sold are made with a mixture of plastic and about 6 percent cornstarch. They are either photodegradable (which means they break down when exposed to sunlight) or biodegradable (which means they are broken down by microbes in the soil). There is controversy over whether they do break down (even some of the companies that make these bags admit that they don't), how long it may take, and if any toxic products are produced in the process.

Even if these issues are resolved, however, the main problem remains: only the small percentage of cornstarch actually breaks down, leaving plastic dust. This dust can contain toxic additives that easily seep into the water table and contaminate streams and soils, perhaps causing more damage than if the plastic had stayed intact.

A writer to *Organic Gardening* magazine's letters column asked some important questions about this plastic residue. Can these small bits of plastic create problems for the delicate membranes of small animals? Are they small enough to be taken in by the roots of plants? Will they clog the gills of fish? What will be the cumulative effect of plastic in our soils and water? We don't know the answers.

Use paper garbage bags, preferably ones made from recycled paper.

At the Store/By Mail

Paper garbage bags

Dano Enterprises. 30-gallon bags.

Seventh Generation. 8-, 13-, and 30-gallon bags.

Set Point Paper Company. 9- and 13.5-gallon bags made from 100 percent recycled paper; 30-gallon bags made from 50 percent recycled paper.

Walnut Acres. 9-, 13-, and 30-gallon bags.

RECYCLING BINS

To collect newspapers and other paper, metal, glass, and plastic for recycling, you'll need a container for each and a place to put the containers. You can be as simple or creative about setting up your collection space as you want to be. The point is to do whatever makes it easy for you to put the recyclables in their proper places at the time you dispose of them. In my household, we rarely use cans, so we need only a small collection box for them. Glass bottles and jars go in a cardboard box under the sink; newspapers go in a special pile so everyone in the house can read them (one subscription for four people); and since I use the wastebasket in my office only for paper, it's easy to dump it into our paper-collection box at the end of the week.

Call your local recycling center to find out about curbside collections or drop-off places and hours. Some recycling companies provide recycling bins free to customers.

At the Store/By Mail

Recycling bins

Advanced Recycling Systems. Sells a residential recycling cart—a metal-frame cart on wheels that holds six different bins for trash separation.

Flowerfield Enterprises. Labels to attach to your own recycling containers: tin cans, trash, glass, milk jugs, junk mail, aluminum, beverage containers, newspaper, and worm food.

Home Recycling Catalogue. Carries an assortment of containers useful for collecting recyclables.

Rubbermaid Stack 'n Cycle Containers (Rubbermaid). Made from postconsumer and industrial recycled plastic.

Seventh Generation. Furniture-quality hardwood newspaper recycler whose special design makes it a snap to tie up newspapers because the cord wraps around the bundle without your having to lift the papers. Also stackable sorting bins (black bins made from 100 percent recycled plastic and tires; colored bins from 50 percent recycled plastic), cardboard recycling units for the office, plus an inexpensive cardboard home unit. Crushers for aluminum cans.

The Trashcycler (Better Environment). An epoxy-coated wire cabinet that holds two trash containers and has a shelf for newspapers. Comes with optional casters and butcher-block top. *Better Environment.*

Appendix

❧ Harmful Effects of Common Substances

Included here is a representative list of harmful substances most commonly found in consumer products, along with their potential health effects. This is not to suggest that everyone will experience these symptoms upon any amount or type of exposure to these chemicals; this is simply to condense the toxicological data available on these substances.

Everyone reacts differently, individually, to all things. Some people can tolerate exposure to large amounts of chemicals with no ill effects, while others develop complex symptoms to even small exposures—very much as some people can eat like a horse and remain slender, while others gain weight even though they consume less food.

The harmful substances listed here fall into two categories. The first covers those ingredients found in consumer products that are classified as and known to be hazardous. Fourteen of these (indicated with an asterisk) are so dangerous that they are included on the Environmental Protection Agency's list of sixty-five "priority pollutants" recognized as being hazardous to human health. The second category includes substances that may appear safe for many people but that pose a problem to those who are sensitive to petrochemical derivatives or have specific other reactions (such as an allergy to perfume or hyperactivity related to food additives). Read the descriptions of the possible health effects, and then decide which of these substances you want to avoid.

If you have health problems, avoiding any of these chemicals may make a difference.

Aerosol Propellants

Heart problems, birth defects, lung cancer, headaches, nausea, dizziness, shortness of breath, eye and throat irritation, skin rashes, burns, lung inflammation, and liver damage. If misdirected, aerosol sprays can cause chemical burns and eye injury.

The most commonly used aerosol spray is Freon, a lung irritant and central-nervous-system depressant. In high concentrations, Freon can cause coma or even death.

Aerosol gases can also turn into other, more toxic gases, including fluorine, chlorine, hydrogen fluoride, hydrogen chloride, and phosgene (military poison gas).

Many aerosol products also contain other toxic ingredients that can get into eyes and lungs more easily than they could were these products dispensed by some other method. This can lead to high particle retention in the lungs and cause respiratory problems.

Ammonia (including Ammonium Chloride, Ammonium Hydroxide, Benzalkonium Chloride, and Quarternary Ammonium Compounds)

Irritation of eyes and respiratory tract, conjunctivitis, laryngitis, tracheitis, pulmonary edema, pneumonitis, and skin burn.

Asbestos*

Autopsy reports show that 100 percent of urban dwellers have asbestos in their lung tissue. Asbestos exposure can affect almost every organ of the body. Illnesses: asbestosis, a chronic lung disease; and mesothelioma, an often fatal form of cancer. Asbestos diseases can result from very brief exposures and even exposure to other people who have been exposed (who may have asbestos fibers in their hair or clothing), and may take up to forty years to appear. The EPA announced in 1972 that there is no safe level of asbestos exposure, as *any* exposure to the fibers involves some health risk.

Aspartame (Nutrasweet)

According to a letter from Dr. Richard J. Wurman to the *New England Journal of Medicine*, NutraSweet, an FDA-approved natural sweetener made from amino acids, can change levels of chemicals in the brain that affect behavior, especially affecting people with underlying brain disorders such as Parkinson's disease and insomnia. Aspartame may also cause brain damage in children suffering from phenylketonuria. Because it has not been widely used, its long-term effects are unknown.

Nevertheless, scientific tests performed on aspartame to establish its safety prior to FDA approval resulted in brain tumors and grand mal seizures in rat studies, and depression, menstrual irregularities, constipation, headaches, tiredness, and general swelling in human test groups. Furthermore, during human evaluations, two of the subjects underwent cancer operations. (Aspartame has not been tested yet for carcinogenicity.)

When exposed to heat, aspartame breaks down into toxic methyl alcohol. This may occur even at temperatures reached by diet sodas during regular storage.

Benzene*

Carcinogenic. Can also cause drunken behavior, lightheadedness, disorientation, fatigue, and loss of appetite.

Benzyl Alcohol/Sodium Benzoate

Intestinal upsets and allergic reactions. Although these substances are usually considered relatively safe, clinical observation by medical doctors has shown them to cause adverse reactions in people who are sensitive to petrochemical derivatives.

BHA (Butylated Hydroxyanisole)/BHT (Butylated Hydroxytoluene)

BHT is a suspected human carcinogen. Studies not only show that BHT is carcinogenic to mice, but also indicate that it promotes existing tumors. Moreover, animal studies reveal that BHA and BHT cause metabolic stress, depression of growth rate, loss of weight, damage to the liver, baldness, and fetal abnormalities.

Clinical observation by medical doctors has shown that BHA and BHT can cause adverse reactions in those who are sensitive to petrochemical derivatives. The late Dr. Benjamin Feingold, of Kaiser-Permanente Medical Center, widely publicized BHA and BHT as a cause of hyperactivity and behavioral disturbances in children. Although it has been very difficult to substantiate this claim with scientific studies, the observations of parents and doctors for over fifteen years confirm that avoidance of BHA and BHT has significantly improved their children's condition.

Chlorine (including Chlorine Dioxide and Sodium Hypochlorite)

Pain and inflammation of the mouth, throat, and stomach and erosion of mucous membranes, vomiting, circulatory collapse, confusion, delirium, coma, swelling of the throat, severe respiratory-tract irritation, pulmonary edema, and skin eruptions. Exposure has been linked to high blood pressure, anemia, diabetes, and heart disease, and causes a 44 percent greater risk of gastrointestinal or urinary-tract cancer.

Clinical observation by medical doctors has shown that reactions to chlorine can also occur from chlorine fumes rising from hot or cold running tap water, including such symptoms as red eyes, sneezing, skin rashes, and fainting or dizziness while taking a shower or washing dishes.

Colors

Colors that can be used in foods, drugs, and cosmetics (and hence are known as FD&C colors), as well as U.S. certified colors and artificial colors, are made from coal tar. There is a great deal of controversy about their use, because animal studies have shown almost all of them to be carcinogenic.

The FDA determines the safety of coal-tar colors by testing for acute oral toxicity, primary irritation, sensitization, subacute skin toxicity, and carcinogenicity by skin application. There are six coal-tar colors permanently listed as being "safe" (even though most are animal carcinogens), and others in current use are on an FDA provisional list awaiting further proof of safety of toxicity. Technical materials on FD&C colors warn, "CAUTION: Consult the latest government regulations before using this dye in foods, drugs, and cosmetics."

Food colors were widely publicized by the late Dr. Feingold as a cause of hyperactivity and behavioral disturbance in children. While it has been very difficult to substantiate this claim with scientific studies, the observations of parents and doctors for over fifteen years confirm that avoidance of artificial colors has significantly improved their children's conditions.

FD&C Yellow No. 5 causes allergic reactions in those sensitive to aspirin. The World Health Organization estimates that half the aspirin-sensitive people in the world, plus nearly one hundred thousand others, are sensitive to this color, which can cause many different symptoms including life-threatening asthma attacks. Because of this, all foods produced after July 1, 1982 must list this color on the label separately from any other artificial colors.

D&C colors are coal-tar colors that can be used only in drugs and cosmetics. "Ext. D&C" on a label before a color listing means that it is approved for exterior use only in drugs and cosmetics and may not be used on the lips or mucous membranes. "Traces of D&C" before a color indicates that a form of aluminum, calcium, barium, potassium, strontium, or zirconium has been added to the coal-tar dye.

There are several different types of D&C colors. Azo dyes are made from phenol and are easily absorbed through the skin. Anthraquinone dyes, which are currently being studied for carcinogenicity, are made from benzene. Aniline dyes cause intoxication, lack of oxygen in the blood, dizziness, headaches, and mental confusion.

HC colors are approved only for hair coloring. They include aniline, azo, and peroxide dyes. Symptoms from peroxide dyes include skin rash, eczema, bronchial asthma, gastritis—and occasionally, from complications arising from the above, death.

Colors in cleaning products are regulated by the Consumer Product Safety Commission (CPSC), which oversees the makeup of all cleanup products. All the commission requires is that products display warning labels if they contain "hazardous" ingredients; it is not necessary to list what those ingredients are. According to the CPSC, no laws exist regulating the type of dye that may be used to color cleaning products.

Cresol

Affects the central nervous system, liver, kidneys, lungs, pancreas, and spleen, and can be fatal. Can be absorbed through the skin and mucous membranes. Symptoms: dermatitis, digestive disturbances, faintness, vertigo, mental changes, sweating, pallor, weakness, headache, dizziness, ringing in the ears, shock, delirium, and skin numbness and discoloration.

Detergents

Detergents are responsible for more household poisonings than any other substance. Dermatitis, flulike and asthmatic conditions, severe eye damage; severe upper-digestive-tract damage if ingested.

Dyes

Direct dyes (the do-it-yourself, at-home type) contain highly carcinogenic dichlorobenzidene, which is very easily absorbed through the skin. Can also cause anemia, jaundice, and damage to the central nervous system, kidneys, and liver, as well as death. Azo, basic, disperse, fiber-reactive, and vat dyes all can cause allergic reactions, as can fluorescent whitening agents.

Ethanol

Central-nervous-system depression, anesthesia, feelings of exhilaration and talkativeness, impaired motor coordination, diplopia, vertigo, flushed face, nausea and vomiting, drowsiness, stupor, coma, dilated pupils, shock, hypothermia, and possible death.

Flame Retardants

TRIS, a leading flame retardant, has been proved to be both mutagenic and carcinogenic to animals. Studies have shown that TRIS can be absorbed through the skin from garments washed more than fifty times. Materials treated with tetrakis hydroxylmethyl phosphonium chloride (THPC), another retardant, release formaldehyde when the fabric is wet. Additional flame retardants include tetrakis hydroxyl-methyl phosphonium (THP), phenol, polybrominated biphenyls (PBBs), and polychlorinated biphenyls (PCBs).

Flavors

More than fifteen hundred different petrochemical-derivative flavoring agents are currently in use. Usually they are listed as a group as artificial or imitation flavors, although occasionally a particular flavoring, such as vanillin, will be listed separately.

Most artificial flavorings are considered safe, but clinical observation by medical doctors has shown that artificial flavors can cause adverse reactions in those who are sensitive to petrochemical derivatives.

The late Dr. Feingold widely publicized artificial flavors as a cause of hyperactivity and behavioral disturbances in children. While it has been very difficult to substantiate this claim with scientific studies, the observations of parents and doctors for over fifteen years confirm that avoidance of artificial flavors has significantly improved their children's condition.

Fluoride

Carcinogenic. Over ten-thousand cancer deaths per year are linked to fluoridated water. Can also cause tiredness and weakness, mottling of the teeth, wrinkled skin, a prickly sensation in the muscles, kidney and bladder disorders, constipation, vomiting, itching after bathing, excessive thirst, headaches, arthritis, gum diseases, nervousness, diarrhea, hair loss, skin disorders, stomach disorders, numbness, brittle nails, sinus problems, mouth ulcers, vision problems, eczema, bronchitis, and asthma. Excessive fluoride can also reduce blood vitamin-C levels, weaken the immune system, and cause birth defects and genetic damage. The use of fluoride has been banned in ten European countries.

Formaldehyde

Suspected human carcinogen. Has been related to teratogenic and mutagenic changes in bacteriological studies. The National Academy of Sciences estimates that 10 to 20 percent of the general population may be susceptible to the irritant properties of formaldehyde at extremely low concentrations. Symptoms from inhalation of vapors: cough, swelling of the throat, watery eyes, respiratory problems, throat irritation, headaches, rashes, tiredness, excessive thirst, nausea, nosebleeds, insomnia, disorientation, bronchoconstriction, and asthma attacks. Symptoms from ingestion: nausea, vomiting, clammy skin and other symptoms of shock, severe abdominal pain, internal bleeding, loss of ability to urinate, vertigo, and coma, possibly leading to death. Symptoms from skin contact: skin eruptions. Long-term exposure can cause allergic sensitization. A preliminary scientific study speculates that formaldehyde may be a contributing factor in sudden infant death syndrome.

Fragrance

"Fragrance" on a label can indicate the presence of up to four thousand separate ingredients that are not listed at all. Most or all of them are synthetic. Symptoms reported to the FDA have included headaches, dizziness, rashes, skin discoloration, violent coughing and vomiting, and allergic skin irritation. Clinical observation by medical doctors has shown that fragrances can cause all types of central-nervous-system symptoms including depression, hyperactivity, irritability, inability to cope, and other behavioral changes.

Hexane
Cough, depression, heart problems, nausea, vomiting, abdominal swelling, and headache.

Hydrogenated oil
The hydrogenation of oil into hard fat (margarine, vegetable shortening) destroys or deforms the essential fatty acids in the oil. Lack of essential fatty acids can contribute to neurological disease, heart disease, arteriosclerosis, skin diseases, cataracts, arthritis, high blood-cholesterol levels, and cancer.

Kerosene
Intoxication, burning sensation in chest, headaches, ringing in the ears, nausea, weakness, uncoordination, restlessness, confusion and disorientation, convulsions, coma, burning in the mouth, throat, and stomach, vomiting and diarrhea, drowsiness, rapid breathing, tachycardia, low-grade fever, and death.

Lead*
Early symptoms of lead poisoning: abdominal pains, loss of appetite, constipation, muscle pains, irritability, metallic taste in the mouth, excessive thirst, nausea and vomiting, shock, muscular weakness, pain and cramps, headache, insomnia, depression, and lethargy. Chronic low-level exposure has been found to produce permanent neuropsychological defects and behavior disorders in children, including low IQ, short attention span, hyperactive behavior, and motor difficulties. In high doses, lead can cause brain damage, nervous-system disorders, and death. Can also affect the kidney, liver, gastrointestinal system, heart, immune system, nervous system, and bloodforming system, and can cause malformations in sperm and low sperm counts. There is no demonstrably safe level for lead.

Because of the overuse of lead products in the past, virtually all air, water, food, and living beings are contaminated. Lead exposure can be lessened, but not completely avoided.

Methylene Chloride
Suspected human carcinogen. Mutagenic.

Mineral Oil
Suspected human carcinogen. Interferes with vitamin absorption in the body. Forbidden as a food coating in Germany. Is less dangerous if inhaled than if ingested or rubbed on skin.

MSG (Monosodium Glutamate)

Symptoms: "Chinese-restaurant syndrome"—numbness, weakness, heart palpitations, cold sweat, and headache. Animal studies show that MSG can cause brain damage, stunted skeletal development, obesity, and female sterility. It is also on the FDA list of additives that need further study for mutagenic, subacute, and reproductive effects. Pregnant woman and people on sodium-restricted diets should not use MSG.

Naphthalene*

Suspected human carcinogen. Skin irritation, headache, confusion, nausea and vomiting, excessive sweating, urinary irritation; in sufficient quantity can lead to death.

Nitrates/Nitrosamines

Relatively harmless, naturally occurring nitrates are changed within the body to nitrites, which cause a lowering of blood pressure, headache, vertigo, palpitations, visual disturbances, flushed skin, nausea, vomiting, diarrhea, methemoglobinemia in infants, coma, and death. They can also turn into nitrosamines, which are carcinogenic.

Nitrobenzene*

Symptoms include bluish skin, shallow breathing, vomiting, and death.

Paraffin

Impurities in paraffin are carcinogenic. In addition, clinical observation by medical doctors has shown that paraffin can cause adverse reactions in those who are sensitive to petrochemical derivatives.

Pentachlorophenol*

Carcinogenic. Can also cause central-nervous-system depression, lightheadedness, dizziness, sleepiness, nausea, tremor, loss of appetite, disorientation, and liver damage.

Pesticides, Herbicides, Fungicides*

Over fifteen hundred pesticides, herbicides, and fungicides are used in consumer products, combined with approximately two thousand other possibly toxic substances to make nearly thirty-five hundred pesticide products. Over one hundred of these in common use are thought to be carcinogenic, mutagenic, or teratogenic.

Some pesticides are extremely long lasting in the environment. An EPA study detected residues of chlordane inside homes twenty years after application. These pesticides also tend to be stored in the fatty tissue, and can accumulate over time to high levels in the body.

Health effects of some commonly encountered pesticides include paralysis, neuritis, sterility, convulsions, dizziness, weakness, tiny pupils, blurred vision, muscle twitching, slowed heartbeat, aplastic anemia, nausea, cough, diarrhea, tremors, damage to the liver, kidneys, and lungs, headaches, respiratory difficulty, coronary edema, coma, suppression of immune function, depression, irritation to ear, nose, and throat, hyperirritability, brain hemorrhages, central-nervous-system effects, decreased fertility and sexual function, and altered menstrual periods.

Phenol

Suspected human carcinogen. Can also cause skin eruptions and peeling, swelling, pimples, hives, burning, gangrene, numbness, vomiting, circulatory collapse, paralysis, convulsions, cold sweats, coma, and death.

Plastics

All plastics present a problem due to "outgassing"—the constant release of sometimes undetectable fumes, especially when heated. A good example of this effect occurs in new cars. That new-car smell is caused by the outgassing of the plastic materials used in the interior of the car. As well as smelling it, you can see it in the scum that forms on the inside of the windshield. In a study done by the National Aeronautics and Space Administration, polyester was found to be the synthetic material that released the most fumes.

*Acrylonitrile** (Lucite/Plexiglas) is a suspected human carcinogen. Can also cause breathing difficulties, vomiting, diarrhea, nausea, weakness, headache, fatigue, and increased incidence of cancer in humans.

Epoxy resins are a suspected human carcinogen.

Latex is one of the least toxic plastics. Though it is usually considered relatively safe, clinical observation by medical doctors has shown that latex can cause adverse reactions in those who are sensitive to petrochemical derivatives.

Nylon is usually considered relatively safe, but clinical observation by medical doctors has shown that nylon can cause adverse reactions in those who are sensitive to petrochemicals. Both benzene and phenol are used to make nylon, and minute amounts of these substances that might still be present in the finished product may account for these adverse reactions.

Phenol-formaldehyde resin ("Bakelite") releases minute amounts of formaldehyde when new.

Polyester can cause eye and respiratory-tract irritation and acute dermatitis.

Polyethylene is a suspected human carcinogen.

Polyurethane can cause bronchitis, coughing, and skin and eye problems. It also releases toluene diisocyanate, which can produce severe pulmonary effects and sensitization.

Polyvinyl chloride (PVC) releases *vinyl chloride,** especially when the product is new. Vinyl chloride is carcinogenic, mutagenic, and teratogenic, and can cause mucous-membrane dryness, numbness in the fingers, stomach pains, hepatitis, indigestion, chronic bronchitis, ulcers, Raynaud's disease, and allergic skin reactions.

Polyvinylpyrrolidone (PVP) is carcinogenic and can also cause thesaurosis, a lung disease affecting some users of hairspray, causing enlarged lymph nodes, lung masses, and changes in blood cells. The disease is reversible if hairspray is avoided.

Tetrafluoroethylene (Teflon) can be irritating to eyes, nose, and throat, and can cause breathing difficulty. Tetrafluoroethylene produces poisonous gases when burned and may also produce these gases to a lesser degree when heated.

Saccharin

Label warning: "Use of this product may be hazardous to your health . . . Contains saccharin, which has been determined to cause cancer in laboratory animals."

*Sucrose (Sugar, Corn Sugar/Syrup, Dextrose, Glucose Syrup, Invert Sugar/
Syrup, Maple Sugar/Syrup)*
Symptoms: nutritional deficiencies, lowered resistance to disease, tooth decay, diabetes,
hypoglycemia, coronary disease, obesity, ulcers, high blood pressure, vaginal yeast infections, and osteoporosis.

*Sulfur Compounds (including Potassium and Sodium Bisulfate and
Metabisulfite, Sulfur Dioxide, and Sulfuric Acid)*
Can cause fatal allergic anaphylactic shock and asthma attacks, destroys vitamin B1
(thiamin), has mutagenic effects on viruses, bacteria, and yeast, and can act synergistically with carcinogens to make them more potent.

Talc
May be contaminated with carcinogenic asbestos.

*Toluene**
Nervous-system and mental changes, irritability, disorientation, depression, and damage
to liver and kidneys.

*Trichloroethylene**
Suspected human carcinogen. Mutagenic. Symptoms: gastrointestinal upsets, central-
nervous-system depression, narcosis, heart and liver malfunctions, paralysis, nausea,
dizziness, fatigue, and psychotic behavior.

Xylene
Nausea, vomiting, salivation, cough, hoarseness, feelings of euphoria, headaches, giddi-
ness, vertigo, ringing in the ears, confusion, coma, and death.

❧ Recommended Resources

There are many, many things each one of us can do to make ourselves and our environment healthier. I could fill another book just with lists of recommended publications and organizations that need support in their efforts to improve our health and the environment. Obviously, they cannot all be covered in depth or even all mentioned in a single book. Because this book's focus is consumer products, my list of resources is limited to those providing additional information to consumers about products or services.

I continue to do research on consumer products and write about my findings in various publications. My newsletter, *The Earthwise Consumer*, will keep you up to date on the best of the products, as well as environmental issues that relate to consumer choices. I also offer a list of books, and will consult, privately, over the phone. Send $20.00 for a one-year, eight-issue subscription, or a self-addressed, stamped envelope for more information to: *The Earthwise Consumer*, P.O. Box 279, Dept. NNE, Forest Knolls, CA 94933, 415/488-4614. Other publications that have related information include:

Buzzworm, P.O. Box 6853, Syracuse, NY 13217, 800/825-0061
Country Life (formerly *Harrowsmith*), The Creamery, Charlotte, VT 05445,
   800/344-3350
E—The Environmental Magazine, P.O. Box 6667, Syracuse, NY 13217, 800/825-0061
East West, P.O. Box 1200, Brookline, MA 02147, 617/232-1000
Garbage, P.O. Box 56519, Boulder, CO 80322-6519, 800/274-9909
In Business, P.O. Box 323, Emmaus, PA 18049, 215/967-4135
NewAge Journal, P.O. Box 53275, Boulder, CO 80321-3275
Solstice, 310 East Main Street #105, Charlottesville, VA 22901, 804/979-4427
Yoga Journal, 2054 University Avenue, Berkeley, CA 94704, 415/841-9200

CHAPTER 1: NONTOXIC, NATURAL, & EARTHWISE

Toxics

Publications

Clinical Toxicology of Consumer Products by R. E. Gosslin et al. (Baltimore: The Williams & Wilkins Company, 1984). A product-by-product guide to possible toxic substances in products and their effects on health.

Organizations

Citizens' Clearinghouse for Hazardous Waste, P.O. Box 926, Arlington, VA 22216, 703/276-7070.

Household Hazardous Waste Project, P.O. Box 108, Springfield, MO 65804, 417/836-5777.

The National Toxics Campaign, 37 Temple Place, 4th Floor, Boston, MA 02111.

Animal rights

Publications

Vegetarian Times, P.O. Box 570, Oak Park, IL 60303, 800/892-0735. The primary magazine reporting on vegetarian lifestyles, new vegetarian and cruelty-free products and all aspects of living well without harming animals.

Organizations

Animal Protection Institute of America, P.O. Box 22505, Sacramento, CA 95822, 916/422-1921. Has a *Shopper's Guide to Cruelty-Free Products.*

Beauty Without Cruelty USA, 175 West 12th Street, New York, NY 10011-8275, 212/989-8073. Has extensive lists of cruelty-free and nonanimal products. Publishes *The Compassionate Shopper* quarterly, which contains product updates and gives a "Beauty Without Cruelty Seal of Approval."

National Anti-Vivisection Society, 53 West Jackson Boulevard, Chicago, IL 60604-3795, 312/427-6065. Publishes a guide of cruelty-free cosmetics and household products from major manufacturers.

People for the Ethical Treatment of Animals (PETA), P.O. Box 42516, Washington, DC 20015, 202/726-0156. Publishes lists of products not tested on animals and no animal ingredients, and products known to be tested on animals that they recommend avoiding.

Social responsiblity

Publications

Economics as If the Earth Really Mattered by Susan Meeker-Lowry (Philadelphia: New Society Publishers, 1988).

Shopping for a Better World: A Quick and Easy Guide to Socially Responsible Supermarket Shopping (New York: Ballantine Books, 1990).

Organizations

Co-op America, 2100 M Street NW, Suite 310, Washington, DC 20063, 800/424-2667, 202/872-5307. Works toward environmental quality, workplace democracy, and a peaceful society. Publications and services include an Alternative Marketplace Catalog of products from socially responsible groups, a Directory of Responsible Businesses, insurance plans that invest premiums in socially responsible ways, a Responsible Travel Agency, access to investment funds, and a quarterly magazine.

Council on Economic Priorities, 30 Irving Place, New York, NY 10003, 212/420-1133. An independent, nonprofit public-interest research organization whose goal is to educate the American public. Also provides incentives for corporations to be good citizens.

National Boycott News, 6506 28th Avenue NE, Seattle, WA 98115, 206/523-0421. Keeps you up-to-date on product boycotts called for reasons of animal testing, cigarette company subsidiaries, nuclear weapons subsidiaries, etc. At almost 200 pages, the quarterly publication is hefty, but it explains the boycott issues thoroughly.

Nuclear Free America, 325 East 25th Street, Baltimore, MD 21218, 301/235-3575. International clearinghouse and resource center for Nuclear Free Zones that tracks products made by nuclear weapons contractors and their subsidiaries.

Oxfam America, 115 Broadway, Boston, MA 02116, 617/482-1211. Encourages funding socially responsible businesses throughout the world.

Simple living

Publications

In Search of the Simple Life: American Voices, Past and Present by David E. Shi (Layton, UT: Gibbs M. Smith, 1986).

Living More With Less: A Pattern of Living with Less and a Wealth of Practical Suggestions from the Worldwide Experiences of Mennonites by Doris Janzen Longacre (Scottsdale, PA: Herald Press, 1980).

Voluntary Simplicity: Toward a Way of Life that is Outwardly Simple, Inwardly Rich by Duane Elgin (New York: William Morrow, 1981).

CHAPTER 2: AIR

Organizations

The Greenhouse Crisis Foundation, 1130 Seventeenth Street NW, Washington, DC 20036, 800/ECO-LYNE. Publishes a citizen's guide of solutions.

Rainforest Action Network, 301 Broadway, Suite A, San Francisco, CA 94133, 415/398-4404. Alerts the public of the need to save rainforests and works with developing nations to create environmentally sound ways to preserve the rainforest as a renewable resource. Newsletter gives little-known facts about how we foster rainforest destruction and what we can do to stop.

World Peace University Rain Forest Preservation Project, P.O. Box 10869, Eugene, OR 97440, 503/741-1794. Lets you buy a piece of Costa Rican rainforest, adding to a land trust preserve run by Quakers. Each purchase includes a certificate of ownership and visitation rights.

Smoking

Organizations

Action on Smoking and Health (ASH), 2013 H Street NW, Washington, DC 20006, 202/659-4310.

Americans for Nonsmokers Rights, 2530 San Pablo Avenue, Suite J, Berkeley, CA 94702, 415/841-3032.

Group Against Smokers' Pollution (GASP), 25 Deaconess, Boston, MA 02115, 617/266-2088.

CHAPTER 3: WATER

Publications

H_2O: *The Guide To Quality Bottled Water* by Arthur von Wiesenberger (Santa Barbara, CA: Woodridge Press, 1988). The complete guide to bottled waters, with advice on what to look for and what to avoid, and an encyclopedic list of bottled waters from around the world, including background information and water analysis. Also has a directory of major bottled water companies in the United States.

Organizations

Clean Water Action, 317 Pennsylvania Avenue SE, Washington, DC 20003, 202/547-1196. A national citizens organization working for affordable clean and safe water, controlling toxic chemicals, and protecting our nation's natural resources.

Food & Water, Inc. 3 Whitman Drive, Denville, NJ 07834, 800/EAT-SAFE, 201/625-3111. Nonprofit group dedicated to clean food and water resources.

Rocky Mountain Institute, 1739 Snowmass Creek Road, Snowmass, CO 81654-9199, 303/927-3128. A leader in water resource-efficiency research and policy. Publications include *Water Efficiency for Your Home.*

Safe Water Foundation, 6439 Taggart Road, Delaware, OH 43015, 614/548-4458. Fights against fluoridation and offers information on its bad health effects.

CHAPTER 4: ENERGY

Publications

Cross Currents: The Perils of Electropollution, The Promise of Electromedicine by

Robert O. Becker, MD (Los Angeles: Jeremy P. Tarcher, 1990). Details the dangers of electromagnetic pollution and how to reduce exposure.

Energy Unbound: A Fable for America's Future by L. Hunter Lovins, Amory Lovins, and Seth Zuckerman (San Francisco: Sierra Club Books, 1986). An easy-to-read story about a housewife appointed national Secretary of Energy, this book explains clearly how America can maintain energy abundance and lower energy costs.

Home Power Magazine, P.O. Box 130, Hornbrook, CA 96044-0130, 916/475-3179. Published bimonthly, full of information about home alternative energy systems.

Organizations

American Council for an Energy-Efficient Economy, 1001 Connecticut Avenue NW, Suite 535, Washington, DC 20036, 202/429-8873. Publishes an annual list of the most energy-efficient residential appliances that are widely distributed.

Conservation and Renewable Energy Inquiry and Referral Service, P.O. Box 8900, Silver Spring, MD 20904, 800/523-2929. Provides basic information on renewable energy technologies and energy conservation. Operated by the U.S. Department of Energy.

Massachusetts Audubon Society, South Great Road, Lincoln, MA 01773, 617/259-9500. Eight booklets that describe energy solutions clearly and simply. Includes weatherization, solar, insulation, financing tips, and more.

National Appropriate Technology Assistance Service, P.O. Box 2525, Butte, MT 59702-2525, 800/428-2525, 800/428-1718. Toll-free service answers technical questions on wood stoves, insulation, wind, furnaces, appliances, water heaters, and renewable energy economics.

Natural Food Institute, P.O. Box 185

WMB, Dudley, MA 01570. *Alternative Electricity* tells where to buy devices that run off wind, water, or solar power, with simple, clear explanations of how they work.

Rocky Mountain Institute, 1739 Snowmass Creek Road, Snowmass, CO 81654-9199, 303/927-3128. A leader in energy resource-efficiency research and policy. Publications include *The Resource-Efficient Housing Guide.*

Solar Box Cookers International, 1724 Eleventh Street, Sacramento, CA 95814, 916/444-6616. Sells educational materials on building and using your own solar cooker.

Synerjy, P.O. Box 1854, Cathedral Station, New York, NY 10025. Publishes *Synerjy: A Directory of Renewable Energy,* which lists articles, books, plans, patents, and government reports and over 3000 manufacturers and distributors, organized geographically.

Windstar Foundation, 2317 Snowmass Creek Road, Snowmass, CO 81654-9198, 800/669-4777, 303/927-4777. Sells their booklet *Energy: 101 Practical Tips for Home and Work.*

CHAPTER 5: FOOD

Publications

A Consumer Dictionary of Food Additives by Ruth Winter (New York: Crown Publishers, 1989). Alphabetical listing of thousands of food additives, how they're used, and their health effects.

Diet for a New America by John Robbins (Walpole, NH: Stillpoint Publishing, 1987). Why being a vegetarian is a humane choice, good for both our health and the Earth's.

The Goldbeck's Guide to Good Food: Your Complete Shopping Guide to the Best, Most Healthful Foods Available in Supermarkets, Natural Food Stores and By Mail by Nikki and David Goldbeck (New York: New American Library, 1987). A thick reference of food product information—how to read labels, how to get good nutrition. Contains extensive lists of the name brand natural products available in 1987.

The Green Earth, 2545 Prairie, Evanston, IL 60201, 708/864-8949. A quarterly journal about food and environment that "hopes to provide a forum where we can all learn more about the foods we eat and grow." Printed on recycled paper with a castor oil-based ink.

Nature's Kitchen: The Complete Guide to the New American Diet by Fred Rohé (Pownal, VT: Storey Communications, 1986). A practical guide to making the transition to a natural diet.

Organically Grown Food: A Consumer Guide by Theodore Wood Carlat (Los Angeles: Wood Publishing, 1990). Overview of the differences between organic and chemical growing practices. Notes related books and publications and provides a comprehensive list of related-industy organizations.

Pesticide Alert: A Guide to Pesticides in Fruits and Vegetables by Lawrie Mott and Karen Snyder of the Natural Resources Defense Council (San Francisco: Sierra Club Books, 1987). A list of pesticides commonly used on produce, and their health effects.

Traditional Foods Are Your Best Medicine: Health and Longevity with the Animal, Sea and Vegetable Foods of Our Ancestors by Dr. Ronald F. Schmid (Stratford, CT: Ocean View Publications, 1987). Examines the natural diets of native peoples and presents evidence for including healthful meat and fish in our food choices.

True Food, P.O. Box 87, Woodstock, NY 12498, 914/679-8561. The latest word on food and health from Nikki and David Goldbeck, authors of *The Goldbecks' Guide to Good Food, American Wholefoods Cuisine,* etc. Contains updates and articles on name brand organic foods and their preparation.

Organizations

Americans for Safe Food, 1501 Sixteenth Street NW, Washington, DC 20036, 202/332-9110. A coalition of over 80 safer-food groups. Publishes lists of mail-order sources for organic food.

The American Vegan Association, 501 Old Harding Highway, Malaga, NJ 08328, 609/694-2887. Information on veganism, including books and cookbooks, conferences, and quarterly *Ahisma* newsletter.

California Organic Wine Alliance, 7740 Fairplay Road, Somerset, CA 95684, 209/245-3248. Lists of organic wines.

The Humane Farming Association, 1550 California Street, Suite 6, San Francisco, CA 94109, 415/771-2253. Campaigns against factory farming. Sells books and provides consumer information.

Mothers and Others for Pesticide Limits (a project of the Natural Resources Defense Council), 40 West 20th Street, New York, NY 10011, 212/727-4474. A national organization that presses for reforms in pesticide regulations to ensure the availability of safe produce. Publishes *For Our Kids' Sake: How to Protect Your Child Against Pesticides in Food.*

North American Vegetarian Society, P.O. Box 72, Dolgeville, NY 13329, 518/568-7970. Dedicated to promoting the life-enhancing possibilities of vegetarianism. Publishes *Vegetarian Voice* quarterly newsmagazine; distributes books and educational materials.

The Soyfoods Center, P.O. Box 234, Lafayette, CA 94549-0234, 415/283-2991. An international resource on soy usage. Promotes soy as a viable alternative to meat using booklets, pamphlets, and a computerized database of soy foods.

CHAPTER 6: LAWN & GARDEN SUPPLIES

Publications

A Garden of Wildflowers: 101 Native Species and How to Grow Them by Henry W.

Art (Pownal, VT: Storey Communications, 1986).

Attracting Backyard Wildlife: A Guide for Nature-Lovers by Bill Merilees (Stillwater, MN Voyageur Press, 1989).

The Biodynamic Farm: Agriculture in the Service of the Earth and Humanity by Herbert H. Keopf (Hudson, NY: Anthroposophic Press, 1989).

The Bug Book: Harmless Insect Controls (Pownal, VT: Storey Communications, 1974). The gardener's classic natural pest control book tells you almost everything you need to know about bugs.

Building a Healthy Lawn by Stuart Franklin (Pownal, VT: Storey Communications, 1988). Written by a professional landscaper, this book shows how to "achieve the emerald green lawn of the American dream."

Companion Plants and How to Use Them by Helen Philbrick and Richard Gregg (Old Greenwich, CT: Devin-Adair, 1966).

Designing and Maintaining Your Edible Landscape Naturally by Robert Kourick (Santa Rosa, CA: Metamorphic Press, 1986). A complete guide to growing beautiful, edible plants.

The Garden Doctor, 1684 Willow, Denver, CO 80220. Literally a one-of-a-kind publication (each of its 24 pages is handcolored), *The Garden Doctor* dispenses common sense organic gardening and environmental information with entertaining, offbeat humor.

The Heirloom Gardener by Carolyn Jabs (San Francisco: Sierra Club Books, 1984). How to collect and grow old and rare ("heirloom") varieties of vegetables and fruits.

How to Grow More Vegetables Than You Ever Thought Possible on Less Land Than You Can Imagine and *The Backyard Homestead Mini-Farm and Garden Log Book,* both by John Jeavons (Berkeley, CA: Ten Speed Press, 1974 and 1983).

The Natural Garden by Ken Druse (New York: Clarkson N. Potter, 1989).

The New Organic Grower: A Master's Manual of Tools and Techniques for the Home and Market Gardener by Eliot Coleman (Chelsea, VT: Chelsea Green, 1989).

The Organic Garden Book: The Complete Guide to Growing Flower, Fruit, and Vegetables Naturally by Geoff Hamilton (New York: Crown Publishers, 1987).

Organic Gardening, 33 East Minor Street, Emmaus, PA 18098, 215/967-5171. The classic, practical magazine on the subject.

Shepherd's Purse: Organic Pest Control Handbook by Pest Publications (Summertown, TN: The Book Publishing Company, 1987). A guide to pest identification and control. Includes color illustrations.

Worms Eat my Garbage by Mary Appelhof (Kalamazoo, MI: Flower Press, 1982). Instructions for setting up and maintaining a worm-based composting system.

Organizations

Acres, U.S.A., P.O. Box 9547, Kansas City, MO 64133, 816/737-0064. A one-of-a-kind organization that explores ecological agriculture, as well as general environmental, political, and health issues. Publishes a monthly newspaper, *Acres, USA,* and catalog of ecogardening books.

Bio-Dynamic Farming and Gardening Association, P.O. Box 550, Kimberton, PA 19442, 215/935-7797. Founded in 1938, this is the oldest group advocating an ecological, sustainable approach to agriculture. Publishes *Biodynamics,* a quarterly magazine and a catalog (printed on recycled paper) of books and biodynamic compost preparations. Provides an advisory service, training programs, and conferences.

Committee for Sustainable Agriculture, P.O. Box 1394, Davis, CA 95617, 916/753-1054. Promotes agricultural methods that are ecologically sound, economically viable, socially just and humane. Offers yearly Ecological Farming Conference, tours of successful organic farms, and one-day programs on sustainable agriculture. Publishes *Organic Food Matters*, a quarterly newspaper.

Ech$_2$O$_2$, P.O. Box 126, Delano, MN 55328. Publishes information about the use of hydrogen peroxide in health and agriculture/gardening.

Ecology Action, 5798 Ridgewood Road, Willits, Ca 95490. A leader in bio-intensive gardening. Researches, develops, and educates people in small-scale bio-intensive food-raising. Has a catalog of books, research papers, organic seeds, and gardening supplies.

Elfin/Yankee Permaculture, 2126 South Madison, Wichita, KS 67211. Dedicated to permaculture design, which naturally integrates people into nature's design for the bioregion. Publishes a journal, *The International Permaculture Species Yearbook*.

G.R.O.W., 38 Llangollen Lane, Newtown Square, PA 19073, 215/353-2838. Grass Roots the Organic Way is a non-profit organization providing information about harmful pesticides and offering safe and effective alternatives for protecting lawns and landscapes.

The Invisible Gardener's Organic Home and Gardening Club, 29169 Heathercliff Road, Suite 216-408, Malibu, CA 90265, 213/457-1893. Offers resources for natural gardening products and services and publishes a great newsletter of organic gardening tips. Helps members solve organic gardening problems.

CHAPTER 7: CLEANING PRODUCTS

Publications

Clean & Green: The Complete Guide to Nontoxic and Environmentally-Safe Household Cleaning by Annie Berthold-Bond (Woodstock, N.Y.: Ceres Press, 1990). Over 500 recipes for natural, homemade cleaning products.

CHAPTER 8: HOUSEHOLD PEST CONTROL

Organizations

Bio-Integral Resource Center, P.O. Box 7414, Berkeley, CA 94707, 415/524-2467. The very best source for practical information on the least toxic methods for managing pests. Members can get advice by mail or phone for virtually any pest problem. Publishes the *Common Sense Pest Control Quarterly* and booklets on almost every pest you'll find in your house.

National Coalition Against the Misuse of Pesticides, 530 Seventh Street SE, Washington, DC 20003, 202/534-5450. Groups and individuals seeking to better protect the public from toxic pesticides. Holds yearly conference on pesticide issues.

Northwest Coalition for Alternatives to Pesticides, P.O. Box 1393, Eugene, OR 97440, 503/344-5044. Provides information packets on pesticide issues and fact sheets on pesticides commonly used.

Rachel Carson Council, 8940 Jones Mill Road, Chevy Chase, MD 20815, 301/652-1877. Maintains an extensive library on chemical contamination and its health impact.

CHAPTER 9: PERSONAL CARE

Publications

A Consumer's Dictionary of Cosmetic Ingredients by Ruth Winter (New York: Crown Publishers, 1984). Complete information about the ingredients found in cosmetics.

Back to Eden by Jethro Kloss (Loma Linda, CA: Back to Eden Books). The easy-to-read guide to herbal medicine, natural foods, and home remedies since 1939. Expanded edition contains the original text plus new, updated material. Tried-and-true advice.

Everybody's Guide to Homeopathic Medicine: Taking Care of Yourself and Your Family with Safe and Effective Remedies by Stephen

Cummings, FNP and Dana Ullman, MPH (Los Angeles: Jeremy P. Tarcher, 1990). Basic instructions for treating common ailments with homeopathy.

The Way of Herbs by Michael Tierra (New York: Pocket Books, 1983). A guide to herbal health care, blending Eastern, European, and American Indian healing traditions.

CHAPTER 11: BABIES & CHILDREN

Publications

Childbirth Wisdom by Judith Goldsmith New York: Congdon & Weed, 1984). The customs, practices, and lore about childbirth that has been passed from woman to woman in the world's traditional societies.

Mothering, P.O. Box 1690, Santa Fe, NM 87504, 505/984-8116. The most comprehensive, widely-distributed magazine on natural mothering. Includes articles written by mothers and resources for all types of natural products used by babies, children, and mothers. Strong environmental ethic and general alternative attitude.

The Natural Baby Food Cookbook by Margaret Elizabeth Kenda and Phyllis S. Williams (New York: Avon Books, 1982).

WiseWoman Herbal for the Childbearing Years by Susan S. Weed (Woodstock, NY: Ash Tree Publishing, 1986). Natural remedies for before, during, and after pregnancy.

Organizations

American Academy of Husband-Coached Childbirth, P.O. Box 5224, Sherman Oaks, CA 91413-5224, 800/423-2397, 800/42-BIRTH, California.

American College of Nurse-Midwives, 1522 K Street NW, Suite 1000, Washington, DC 20005, 202/289-0171.

ASPO/Lamaze, 1840 Wilson Boulevard, Suite 204, Arlington, VA 22201, 800/368-4404.

Informed Homebirth/Informed Birth & Parenting, P.O. Box 3875, Ann Arbor, MI 48106, 313/662-6857.

La Leche League International, P.O. Box 1209, Franklin Park, IL 60131-8209, 800/LA-LECHE.

National Association of Parents & Professionals for Safe Alternatives in Childbirth, Route 1, Box 646, Marble Hill, MO 63764, 314/238-2010. Catalog, books, support groups, and the *Directory of Alternative Birth Services.*

CHAPTER 12: OFFICE & ART SUPPLIES

Publications

Artist Beware: The Hazards and Precautions in Working with Art and Craft Materials by Michael McCann, Ph.D., CIH. (New York: Watson-Guptill Publications, 1979). Provides information on toxic substances found in art materials, and how you can set up a non-toxic studio.

Children's Art Hazards by Lauren Jacobsen. Natural Resources Defense Council, 40 West 20th Street, New York, NY 10011, 212/727-2700. A basic overview of children's art materials and health hazards, and art precautions for children under 12 years of age.

Organizations

The Art and Craft Materials Institute, 715 Boylston Street, Boston, MA 02116, 617/266-6800. Certifies children's and adult's art materials with "CP Nontoxic," "AP Nontoxic" and "Health Label" seals. For a list of approved products, send a self-addressed, stamped envelope.

The Center for Occupational Hazards, 5 Beekman Street, Suite 1030, New York, NY 10038, 212/227-6220. A national clearinghouse for information on hazards in the arts. Answers written and telephone inquiries, and distributes over 70 books, pamphlets, articles and data sheets.

CHAPTER 13: BUILDING & FURNISHING

Publications

Bioshelters, Ocean Arks, City Farming: Ecology as the Basis of Design by Nancy Jack Todd and John Todd (San Francisco: Sierra Club Books, 1984). A new approach to design based on pioneering research at New Alchemy Institute.

Cohousing: A Contemporary Approach to Housing Ourselves by Kathryn McCamant and Charles Durrett (Berkeley, CA: Habitat Press/Ten Speed Press, 1989). Describes a new European housing concept, successfully combining the privacy of individual housing with the advantages of shared community resources.

Design Spirit, 438 Third Street, Brooklyn, NY 11215, 718/768-9756. Reports on the activities of people working, through art and design, on environmental and social issues. Information on architects, building projects, design in harmony with nature, geomancy, and alternative building techniques.

Healing Environments: Your Guide to Indoor Well-Being by Carol Venolia (Berkeley, CA: Celestial Arts, 1988). How the buildings you inhabit can influence your well-being, and what you can do to turn a healthy house into a nurturing home.

Healthful Houses: How to Design and Build Your Own by Clint Good with Debra Lynn Dadd (Bethesda, MD: Guaranty Press, 1988). Complete architectural specifications for nontoxic building materials.

The Healthy House: How to Buy One, How to Cure a "Sick" One, How to Build One by John Bower. Complete instructions for nontoxic building, including name brand building materials.

The Natural House Book: Creating a Healthy, Harmonious, and Ecologically-sound Home Environment by David Pearson (New York: Simon & Schuster, 1989). Designs and ideas for using natural materials in home construction.

The Smart Kitchen: How to Design a Comfortable, Safe, Energy-Efficient, and Environment-Friendly Workspace by David Goldbeck (Woodstock, NY: Ceres Press, 1989). Ideas for designing a non-toxic gourmet kitchen.

The Timeless Way of Building, A Pattern Language and other books by Christopher Alexander (New York: Oxford University Press). A theory of architecture, building, and planning that has at its core the age-old process by which people understand their world through their own existence and their relationship with the environment.

Organizations

Housing Resource Center, 1820 West 48th Street, Cleveland, OH 44102, 216/281-4663. Along with Environmental Health Watch, they sponsor the Healthy House Project. Has a yearly conference and publishes the *Healthy House Catalog.*

International Institute for Baubiologie and Ecology, P.O. Box 387, Clearwater, FL 34615, 813/461-4371. An independent organization run by architects with close ties to American and European consultants in fields related to natural living. Researches the manufacture and use of natural products in home and workplace construction. Offers a correspondence course on Baubiologie.

CHAPTER 14: PET CARE

Publications

The Complete Herbal Book for the Dog and Cat by Juliet D. Bairacli-Levy (New York: Arco Publishing, 1986).

Dogs and Cats Go Vegetarian by Barbara Lynn Peden (Swisshome, OR: Harbinger House, 1988).

Dr. Pitcairn's Complete Guide to Natural Health for Dogs & Cats by Richard H. Pitcairn D.V.M., Ph.D. & Susan Hubble

Pitcairn (Emmaus, PA: Rodale Books, 1982).

Keep Your Pet Healthy the Natural Way by Pat Lazarus (New Canaan, CT: Keats Publishing, 1983).

The Natural Cat: A Holistic Guide for Finicky Owners by Anita Frazier (New York: Kampmann & Company, 1985).

Vegepet Gazette, P.O. Box 146, Swiss-home, OR 97480, 503/268-4880. A quarterly newsletter providing answers and support for people who are feeding their pets a vegetarian diet.

American Holistic Veterinary Medical Association, 2214 Old Emmorton Road, Bel Air, MD 21014, 301/838-7778. A professional organization of veterinarians who use nontraditional techniques, including nutrition, homeopathy, and acupuncture. Send a self-addressed, stamped envelope for a list of holistic veterinarians in your area.

CHAPTER 15: GARBAGE

Organizations

The Windstar Foundation, 2317 Snowmass Creek Road, Snowmass, CO 81654-9198, 800/669-4777, 303/927-4777. Publishes *Recycling: 101 Practical Tips for Home and Work,* a book of fact, resources, and tips for reducing waste and recycling at home.

❧ Mail-Order Sources

Be very specific when dealing with mail-order companies. A letter asking about organically-grown whole wheat bread might get an immediate response, while a simple catalog request may not be answered until the next catalogs are printed (sometimes six months later). Also, because companies are constantly changing and rotating their products, you could read about an item in this book, yet not see it in the catalog. If you mention one item in particular, the company could find there's a few still sitting on the warehouse shelf.

Always write your full name and address on your request letter; the envelope on which you wrote your return address will have long parted from its enclosure.

While most of the catalogs are free, some companies charge a small fee, often refundable with your first order. Others ask that you enclose a SASE—a self-addressed, stamped #10 letter-sized envelope—with your catalog request to ensure a prompt reply.

Each address is followed by the code Dept. NNE. Please use this code so the businesses know you read about them in this book.

A Baby is a Gift
623 South Street, Dept. NNE
Roslindale, MA 02131
617/327-3227
Free catalog

Abundant Life Seed Foundation
P.O. Box 772, Dept. NNE
Port Townsend, WA 98368
206/385-5660
$1.00 catalog
Sponsors the World Seed Fund, which sends seeds to agencies working to end hunger.

Acorn Designs
5066 Mott Evans Road, Dept. NNE
Trumansburg, NY 14886
607/387-3424
Free catalog printed on recycled paper. Participates in 1 percent for Peace and suggests an optional "green tax" (9% of sub-

total of the purchase is donated to non-profit environmental groups involved in environmental protection to offset environmental costs of products).

Acres, U.S.A.
P.O. Box 9547, Dept. NNE
Kansas City, MO 64133
816/737-0064
Free catalog

Advanced Recycling Systems
P.O. Box 1796, Dept. NNE
Waterloo, IA 50704
319/291-6007
Free catalog

AFM Enterprises
1140 Stacy Court, Dept. NNE
Riverside, CA 92507
714/781-6860
Free catalog

After the Stork
1501 12th Street NW, Dept. NNE
Albuquerque, NM 87104
800/333-5437   505/243-9100
Free catalog

agAccess
P.O. Box 2008, Dept. NNE
Davis, CA 95617
916/756-7177
Free catalog

Ahlers Organic Date & Grapefruit
P.O. Box 726, Dept. NNE
Mecca, CA 92254
619/396-2337
Free catalog

Aireox Research Corporation
P.O. Box 8523, Dept. NNE
Riverside, CA 92515
714/689-2781
Free catalog

Alexandra Avery
68183 Northrup Creek Road, Dept. NNE
Birkenfeld, OR 97016
503/755-2446
Free catalog
Refuses to buy raw materials from suppliers promoting animal testing. Reuses styrofoam packing pellets; includes note encouraging receiver to reuse pellets.

Allen's Naturally
P.O. Box 514, Dept. NNE
Farmington, MI 48332-0514
313/453-5410
Free catalog

Allergy Relief Shop
2932 Middlebrook Pike, Dept. NNE
Knoxville, TN 37921
800/678-2028   800/280-2028
TN/KY 615/522-2795
Free catalog

Allergy Research Group
P.O. Box 489, Dept. NNE
San Leandro, CA 94577-0489
800/782-4274
Free catalog

The Allergy Store
P.O. Box 2555, Dept. NNE
Sebastopol, CA 95473
800/950-6202   707/823-6202
Free catalog

AllerMed Corporation
31 Steel Road, Dept. NNE
Wylie, TX 75098
214/422-4898
Free catalog

All The Best
2713 East Madison, Dept. NNE
Seattle, WA 98112
800/962-8266
Free catalog

Alpine Spirit Company
P.O. Box 8064, FDR Station, Dept. NNE
New York, NY 10150-1917
212/268-5399
Free catalog

Alternative Energy Engineering
P.O. Box 339, Dept. NNE
Redway, CA 95560
707/923-2277
$3.00 catalog

Alternative Health Insurance Services
22704 Ventura Boulevard, Suite 506,
Dept. NNE
Woodland Hills, CA 91364
818/702-0888
Free catalog

Amberwood
Route 1, Box 206, Dept. NNE
Milner, GA 30257
404/358-2991
Free catalog
No products in this catalog have been animal-tested. Statements from the manufacture reaffirm that products do not contain any animal ingredients.

American Environmental Laboratories
60 Elm Hill Avenue, Dept. NNE
Leominister, MA 01453
800/522-0094   508-534-1444
Free catalog

Animal Town Game Company
P.O. Box 485, Dept. NNE
Healdsburg, CA 95448
707/431-7575
Free catalog

Aqua Associates
P.O. Box 1251, Dept. NNE
West Caldwell, NJ 07007
201/227-0422
Free catalog

Aquaculture Marketing Service
356 West Redview Drive, Dept. NNE
Monroe, UT 84754
800/634-5463, ext. 230
800/542-7981, ext. 230 in Iowa
Free catalog

Arco Iris
Dept. NNE
Ponca, AR 72670
No Phone
SASE for catalog
A group of women striving to create a self-supporting community in the Ozark Mountains.

Arjoy Acres
HCR Box 1410, Dept. NNE
Payson, AZ 85541
602/474-1224
Free catalog

The Ark
4245 Crestline Avenue, Dept. NNE
Fair Oaks, CA 95628
800/872-0064   916/967-2607
Free catalog

Aroma Vera
3384 South Robertson Place, Dept. NNE
Los Angeles, CA 90034
213/280-0407
Free catalog

Arrowhead Mills
P.O. Box 2059, Dept. NNE
Hereford, TX 79045
806/364-0730
Free catalog

Artventure
2547 8th Street, #18B, Dept. NNE
Berkeley, CA 94714
800/234-1898   415/548-3030
$1.00 catalog

Atlantic Recycled Paper Company
P.O. Box 11021, Dept. NNE
Baltimore, MD 21212
800/323-2811   301/323-2676
Free catalog printed on recycled paper

Aubrey Organics
4419 North Manhattan Avenue,
Dept. NNE
Tampa, FL 33614
813/876-4879
$3.00 catalog

Aura Cacia
P.O. Box 399, Dept. NNE
Weaverville, CA 96093
916/623-3301
Free catalog

Auromere
1291 Weber Street, Dept. NNE
Pomona, CA 91768
800/735-4691   714/629-8255
Free catalog

Auro Trading Company
18 A Hangar Way, Dept. NNE
Watsonville, CA 95076-2485
800/225-6111   408/728-4525
Free catalog

Avena Botanicals
P.O. Box 365, Dept. NNE
West Rockport, ME 04865
207/594-0694
$2.00 catalog

A Very Small Shop
P.O. Box 425, Dept. NNE
Saunderstown, RI 02874
401/295-8569
Free catalog
A family-based cottage industry.

Aztec Secret Health & Beauty Products
P.O. Box 19735, Dept. NNE
Las Vegas, NV 89132
702/369-8080
Free catalog

Baby Biz
1840 Commerce Street #E, Dept. NNE
Boulder, CO 80301
303/449-3988
Free catalog

Baby Bunz & Company
P.O. Box 1717, Dept. NNE
Sebastopol, CA 95473
707/829-5347
Free catalog

Backwoods Solar Electric Systems
8530 Rapid Lightning Creek Road,
Dept. NNE
Sandpoint, ID 83864
208/263-4290
Free catalog

Baldwin Hill Bakery
Baldwin Hill Road, Dept. NNE
Phillipston, MA 01331
508/249-4691
Free catalog

Bales Furniture Manufacturing
153 Utah Avenue, Dept. NNE
South San Francisco, CA 94080
415/742-6210
Free catalog

Banbury Cross
1408 Kerper Street, Dept. NNE
Philadelphia, PA 19111
215/745-5121
Free catalog
A family-run home business, inspired
by the owners' children.

Bandon Sea-Pack
P.O. Box 5488, Dept. NNE
Charleston, OR 97420
800/255-4370   503/888-4600
Free catalog

Bartlettyarns
P.O. Box 36, Dept. NNE
Harmony, ME 04942-0036
207/683-2251
Free catalog

Basically Natural
109 East G Street, Dept. NNE
Brunswick, MD 21716
301/834-7923
Free catalog

Basilo Lepuschenko
RFD 1, Box 589, Dept. NNE
Richmond, ME 04357
No phone
Free catalog

Baubiologie Hardware
207 #B 16th Street, Dept. NNE
Pacific Grove, CA 93950
408/372-8626
Free catalog

Bear Creek Nursery
P.O. Box 411, Dept. NNE
Northport, WA 99157
509/732-6219
2 stamps or $.50

Bear Feet
1911 Austin Avenue, Dept.NNE
Brownwood, TX 76801
No phone
Free catalog

Beauty Naturally
P.O. Box 429, Dept. NNE
Fairfax, CA 94930
800/432-4323   415/459-2826
Free catalog

Bebitos
Suite 161, 105 Charles Street,
Dept. NNE
Boston, MA 02114
617/354-1432
Free catalog

Bee Beyer
1154 Roberto Lane, Dept. NNE
Los Angeles, CA 90077
213/472-8961
SASE for catalog

BeeDazzled Candleworks
6289 River Road, Dept. NNE
Benzonia, MI 49616
616/882-4456
Free catalog

Bellerose Vineyard
435 West Dry Creek Road, Dept. NNE
Healdsburg, CA 95448
707/433-1637
Free catalog

Beneficial Insectary
14751 Oak Run Road, Dept. NNE
Oak Run, CA 96069
800/477-3715   916/472-3715
Free catalog

Berea College Student Craft Industries
P.O. Box 2347, Dept. NNE
Berea, KY 40404
800/824-4049   800/432-1960
606/986-9341
$2.00 catalog
Since 1893, the Berea College Student Crafts Program has combined the talents of student and fulltime craftspeople in a unique sharing of heritage and crafts production.

Better Environment
480 Clinton Avenue, Dept. NNE
Albany, NY 12206
518/426-4987
Free catalog

BioBin
8407 Lightmoor Court, Dept. NNE
Bainbridge Island, WA 98110
206/842-6641
Free catalog

Biobottoms
P.O. Box 6009, Dept. NNE
Petaluma, CA 94953
707/778-7945
Free catalog

Bioforce of America
P.O. Box 507, Dept. NNE
Kinderhook, NY 12106
800/645-9135   518/758-6060
Free catalog

Bio-Pax
1265 Pine Hill Drive, Dept. NNE
Annapolis, MD 21401
$2.00 catalog printed on recycled paper. 1½ percent of gross sales goes to the Bio-Pax Fund, to be used for research to develop environmentally-sound new products.

Bio-Safe
P.O. Box 1216, Dept. NNE
Georgetown, TX 78627
512/863-4694
Free catalog

Black Bat Soil Conditioner
P.O. Box 876, Dept. NNE
Ruidosos, NM 88345
No phone
Free catalog

Blessed Herbs
Route 5, Box 1042, Dept. NNE
Ava, MO 65608
417/683-5721
Family-run, home-based business.
Free catalog

Blue Corn Trading Company
P.O. Box 951, Dept. NNE
Taos Pueblo, NM 87571
No phone
Free catalog
Native American corn (from original seed form) and herb products traditionally grown and hand-gathered on Indian lands. Sales benefit Native Americans maintaining traditional lifestyles. Supports the Deertrack Foundation.

Blue Heron
937 Massachusetts, Dept. NNE
Lawrence, KS 66044
913/841-9443
Free catalog

Blue Heron Farm
P.O. Box 68, Dept. NNE
Rumsey, CA 95679
916/796-3799
Small, family farm.
Free catalog

Boericke & Tafel
1011 Arch Street, Dept. NNE
Philadelphia, PA 19107
800/272-2820   215/922-7467
Free catalog

Boiron Borneman
1208 Amosland Road, Dept. NNE
Norwood, PA 19074
800/BLU-TUBE   215/532-2035
Free catalog

Bosom Buddies
P.O. Box 6138, Dept. NNE
Kingston, NY 12401
914/338-2038
Free catalog

Boston Wine Company
840 Summer Street
Boston, MA 02127
617/268-5770
Free catalog

Botanical Pharmaceuticals
P.O. Box 10235, Dept. NNE
Bainbridge Island, WA 98110
206/842-1985
Free catalog

Brae Beef
100 Greyrock Place, Dept. NNE
Stamford, CT 06901
800/323-4484   203/323-4482
$3.00 catalog

Bread Alone
Route 28, Dept. NNE
Boiceville, NY 12412
914/657-3328
Free catalog

Breeders Equipment Company
P.O. Box 177, Dept. NNE
Flourtown, PA 19031
215/233-0799
Free catalog

Bricker's Organic Farms
824-K Sandbar Ferry Road, Dept. NNE
Augusta, GA 30901
404/722-0661
Free catalog

Brier Run Farm
Route 1, Box 73, Dept. NNE
Birch River, WV 26610
304/649-2975
Family-owned and run.
Free catalog

Bright Future Futons
3120 Central Avenue SE, Dept. NNE
Albuquerque, NM 87106
505/268-9738
Free catalog

Brody Enterprises
9 Arlington Place, Dept. NNE
Fair Lawn, NJ 07410-3506
800/GLU-TRAP   201/794-3616
Free catalog

Brooks Brothers
350 Campus Plaza, Dept. NNE
Edison, NJ 08818
800/274-1815
Free catalog

Brush Dance
218 Cleveland Court, Dept. NNE
Mill Valley, CA 94941
415/389-6228
Free catalog

Buffalo Gal
Rt. 1, Dept. NNE
Houston, TX 55943
605/342-6434
Free catalog

Buffalo Shirt Company
315 Main Street, Dept. NNE
Half Moon Bay, CA 94019
800/752-4402   800/762-4400
Free catalog

Bullock & Jones
401 Forbes Boulevard, Dept. NNE
South San Francisco, CA 94080
800/227-3050
Free catalog

Burbank Gourmet Gardens
Box 11360, Graton Road, Dept. NNE
Sebastapol, CA 95472
707/829-7546
Free catalog

Butte Creek Mill
P.O. Box 561, Dept. NNE
Eagle Point, OR 97524
503/826-3531
Free catalog

Butterbrooke Farm
78 Barry Road, Dept. NNE
Oxford, CT 06483
203/888-2000
SASE

Cable Car Clothiers
One Grant Avenue, Dept. NNE
San Francisco, CA 94108
415/397-4740
Free catalog

Cal Ben Soap Company
9828 Pearmain Street, Dept. NNE
Oakland, CA 94603
415/638-7091
Free catalog
Family owned and operated, they have been making "ecology" soaps for over 40 years. Literature printed on recycled paper.

Carole's Cosmetics
7678 Sagewood Drive, Dept. NNE
Huntington Beach, CA 92648
714/842-0454
Free catalog

Carousel Carpet Mills
1 Carousel Lane, Dept. NNE
Ukiah, CA 95482
707/485-0333
Free catalog

Cascadian Farm
P.O. Box 568, Dept. NNE
Concrete, WA 98237
206/853-8175
Free catalog

Cat Holler Farm
Route 1, Box 300, Dept. NNE
Olive Hill, TN 38475
901/925-5910
Free catalog
A small, family industry.

Cedar-Al Products
HCR 63, Box 6, Dept. NNE
Clallam Bay, WA 98326
800/431-3444   206/963-2601
Free catalog

Cell Tech
1300 Main Street, Dept. NNE
Klamath Falls, OR 97601
800/321-1301
Free catalog

Cerulean Blue
P.O. Box 21168, Dept. NNE
Seattle, WA 98111-3168
206/443-7744
$4.50 catalog

Chambers
P.O. Box 7841, Dept. NNE
San Francisco, CA 94120-7841
800/334-9790
Free catalog

Charis Company
P.O. Box 2422, Dept. NNE
San Rafael, CA 94912-2422
415/454-8191
Free catalog

Chartrand Imports
P.O. Box 1319, Dept. NNE
Rockland, ME 04841
207/594-7300
SASE for catalog

Chico Fabric Designs
Box 152, Cohasset Stage Route,
Dept. NNE
Chico, CA 95926
916/342-9178
Free catalog

Childcraft
20 Kilmer Road, Dept. NNE
Edison, NJ 08818
800/367-3255
Free catalog

Child Life Play Specialties
55 Whitney Street, Dept. NNE
Holliston, MA 01746
800/462-4445   508/429-4639
Free catalog

Chi Pants
125 Walnut Avenue, Dept. NNE
Santa Cruz, CA 95060
800/331-2681
Free catalog

Chule's
2044 Redondela Drive, Dept. NNE
San Pedro, CA 90732
213/320-1351
Free catalog
Chule, a fifth-generation weaver, says, "we want only to make enough to live simply and to see others enjoy our work."

Classics for Kids
P.O. Box 614, Dept. NNE
Silver Spring, MD 20901
301/949-3128
Free catalog

Clean Country
P.O. Box 448, Dept. NNE
Willmar, MN 53201
800/448-1999   612/235-1975
Free catalog

Clean Environments
P.O. Box 17621, Dept. NNE
Boulder, CO 80308
303/494-1770
Free catalog

Clear Light, the Cedar Company
Box 551, State Road 165, Dept. NNE
Placitas, NM 87043
505/867-2381
Free catalog

Clothcrafters
P.O. Box 176, Dept. NNE
Elkhart Lake, WI 53020
414/876-2112
Free catalog
A family-run business. They send only one catalog each year and encourage customers to save it.

Coast Filtration
142 Viking Avenue, Dept. NNE
Brea, CA 92621
714/990-4602
Free catalog

Cohasset Colonials
38 Parker Avenue, Dept. NNE
Cohasset, MA 02025
617/383-0110
$3.00 catalog

Color & Herbal Company
P.O. Box 5370, Dept. NNE
Newport Beach, CA 92662
800/284-PETS   714/723-1700
Free catalog

Comfey Carrier
P.O. Box 447, Dept. NNE
Santa Cruz, CA 95061
408/338-2017
Free catalog

Community Mill & Bean
RD 1, Route 89, Dept. NNE
Savannah, NY 13146
315/365-2664
Free catalog

Companion Plants
7247 North Coolville Ridge, Dept. NNE
Athens, OH 45701
614/592-4643
$2.00 catalog

The Company Store
500 Company Store Road, Dept. NNE
La Crosse, WI 54601
800/356-9367 608/785-1400
Free catalog

The Compassionate Consumer
P.O. Box 27
Jericho, NY 11753
715/445-4134
$1.00 catalog

Composting Toilet Systems
1211 Bergen Road, Dept. NNE
Newport, WA 99156-9608
509/447-3708
$2.00 catalog

Conservatree Paper Company
10 Lombard Street, Suite 250,
Dept. NNE
San Francisco, CA 94111
800/522-9200 415-433-1000
Free catalog

Co-op America Health Insurance
2100 M Street NW, Dept. NNE
Washington, DC 20063
800/255-4432
Free catalog

Cooperative Trading
611 West Wayne Street, Dept. NNE
Fort Wayne, IN 46802-2125
219/422-1650
Free catalog
The Ikwe Marketing Collective is an out-
growth of land rights organizing on the
White Earth Reservation. They support
and enhance traditional economic activities and economy on the reservation. Pro-
ceeds are retained by the Collective and
support work on economic development
and the Native ricers.

The Cordwainer Shop
67 Candia Road, Dept. NNE
Deerfield, NH 03037
603/463-7742
Free catalog

Corns
Route 1, Box 32, Dept. NNE
Turpin, OK 73950
No phone
Free catalog

Cot'n Kidz
P.O. Box 620159, Dept. NNE
Newton, MA 02162
617/964-2686
Free catalog printed on recycled paper

Cotton Clouds
Route 2, Desert Hills #16, Dept. NNE
Safford, AZ 85546
800/322-7888
$9.00 for catalog and samples

The Cotton Company
P.O. Box 23057, Dept. NNE
Chattanooga, TN 37422
800/421-4548
Free catalog

The Cotton Place
P.O. Box 59721, Dept. NNE
Dallas, TX 75229
800/451-8866 214/243-4149
$3.00 catalog

Coulee Region Organic Produce Pool
Main Street, Dept. NNE
La Farge, WI 54639
608/625-2602
Free catalog

Country Curtains
At the Red Lion Inn, Dept. NNE
Stockbridge, MA 01262
913/483-6163
Free catalog

Country Life Natural Foods
Oak Haven, Dept. NNE
Pullman, MI 49450
616/236-5011
Operated as an educational facility in a
Seventh-Day Adventist community.
Free catalog

Country Spirit Crafts
P.O. Box 320, Dept. NNE
Talent, OR 97540
No phone
Free catalog

Covalda Date Company
P.O. Box 908, Dept. NNE
Coachella, CA 92236
619/398-3441
Free catalog

Cozy Cradles
P.O. Box 514, Dept. NNE
Tahlequah, OK 74465
No phone
Free catalog

Crayon Caps
P.O. Box 1809, Dept. NNE
Mendocino, CA 95460
707/964-7549
Free catalog
A home-based industry employing mothers who want to work at home.

Creative Printing & Publishing
712 North Highway 17-92, Dept. NNE
Longwood, FL 32750
800/780-4447   407/830-4747
Free catalog

Crocodile Tiers
402 North 99th Street, Dept. NNE
Mesa, AZ 85207
602/373-9823
$1.50 catalog
Home business run by the chemically sensitive, for the chemically sensitive.

Cross Seed Company
HC-69, Box 2, Dept. NNE
Bunker Hill, KS 67626
De Bary, FL 32713
407-668-6361
Free catalog

Cuddledown
P.O. Box 66, Dept. NNE
Yarmouth, ME 04096
207/846-9781
Free catalog

Cuddle Ewe
10650 County Road 81, Suite U,
Dept. NNE
Maple Grove, MN 55369
800/328-9493   612/424-3344
Free catalog

Cuddlers Cloth Diapers
3020 Cheyenne Drive, Dept. NNE
Woodward, OK 73801
No phone
Free catalog

Czimer Foods
13136 West 159th Street, Dept. NNE
Lockport, IL 60441
708/301-7152
Free catalog

Dach Ranch
P.O. Box 44, Dept. NNE
Philo, CA 95466
707/895-3173
SASE

Dakota Lean Meats
136 West Tripp, Dept. NNE
Winner, SD 57580
800/727-5326   605/842-3664
Free catalog

Dano Enterprises
75 Commercial Street, Dept. NNE
Plainview, NY 11803
516/349-7300
Free catalog

Darnell Design
P.O. Box 4691, Dept. NNE
Medford, OR 97501
503/773-5782
$1.00 catalog

**David Feldman
Drug-Free (Organic) Meats**
402 North Pine Meadow Drive,
Dept. NNE
800/937-1237
Free catalog

DeBoles Nutritional Foods
2120 Jericho Turnpike, Dept. NNE
Garden City Park, NY 11040
516/742-1818
Free catalog

Decent Exposures
2202 NE 115th Street, Dept. NNE
Seattle, WA 98125
206/364-4540
Free catalog

Deer Valley Farm
RD 1, Dept. NNE
Guilford, NY 13780
607/764-8556
$.50 catalog

Deerfield Woodworking
420 Dwight Street, Dept. NNE
Holyoke, MA 01040
413/532-2377
Free catalog

Dellinger
1943 North Broad, Dept. NNE
Rome, GA 30161
404/291-7402
Free catalog

Denise Blythe
511 Sir Francis Drake #357, Dept. NNE
Greenbrae, CA 94904
415/456-9132
Free catalog

Desert Essence Cosmetics
P.O. Box 588, Dept. NNE
Topanga, CA 90290
213/455-1046
Free catalog

Deva
P.O. Box F83, Dept. NNE
Burkittsville, MD 21718
301/663-4900
$1.00 catalog
Operates in the classic cottage industry style, with an administrative "headquarters," and the sewing taking place in the stitchers' homes.

Deva Magic
P.O. Box 280, Dept. NNE
Bearsville, NY 12409
No phone
Free catalog

D. Flea
P.O. Box 8461, Dept. NNE
Emeryville, CA 94662
415/655-3928
Free catalog

Dial Herbs
P.O. Box 39, Dept. NNE
Fairview, UT 84629
800/288-4618   801/427-9476
Free catalog

Diamond K Enterprises
RR 1, Box 30-A, Dept. NNE
St. Charles, MN 55972
507/932-4308
Free catalog

Dirt Cheap Organics
5645 Paradise Drive, Dept. NNE
Corte Madera, CA 94925
415/924-0369
Free catalog

D. Landreth Seed Company
180–188 West Ostend Street, Dept. NNE
Baltimore, MD 21230
301/727-3922
$2.00 catalog

Dollies & Company
P.O. Box 17804, Dept. NNE
Boulder, CO 80308
303/444-8686
$1.00 catalog

Dona Designs
825 Northlake Drive, Dept. NNE
Richardson, TX 75080
214/235-0485
Free catalog

Dry Creek Herb Farm
13935 Dry Creek Road, Dept. NNE
Auburn, CA 95603
906/878-2441
Free catalog

D. Senften
6843 Myakka Valley Trail, Dept. NNE
Sarasota, FL 34241
No phone
$3.75 catalog

Dutch Mill Cheese Shop
2001 North State Road 1, Dept. NNE
Cambridge City, IN 47327
317/478-5847
Free catalog

Eagle Agricultural Products
2223 North College, Dept. NNE
Fayetteville, AR 72701
501/442-6792
Free catalog

Earth Care Paper Company
P.O. Box 14140, Dept. NNE
Madison, WI 53714-0140
608/277-2900
Free catalog

Earthen Joys
1412 Eleventh Street, Dept. NNE
Astoria, OR 97103
503/325-0426
Free catalog
Use recycled paper as much as possible.

Earth Herbs
40 North Fir Street, Dept. NNE
Ventura, CA 93001
805/641-9820
$1.00 catalog

Earth Science
P.O. Box 1925, Dept. NNE
Corona, CA 91720
800/222-6720   714/524-9277
Free catalog

Earthware
RD 1, Box 75-C1, Dept. NNE
Carlton, PA 16311
A woman who is a midwife and mother
home-schooling her children runs this one-
person home business.
Free catalog

Ecco Bella
6 Provost Square, Suite 602, Dept. NNE
Caldwell, NJ 07006
800/888-5320   201/226-5799
Free catalog
"Our products have not been tested on
animals. We sell products that we have
determined to have minimal impact on
the environment. We believe in recyclable
and biodegradable packaging. Where we
can we have substituted glass or paper
packages. We donate 20% of our profits
from the catalog to animal and environment protection organizations."

Eco-Choice
P.O. Box 281, Dept. NNE
Montvale, NJ 07645-0281
201/930-9046
Free catalog

Ecological Water Products
102 Aldrich Street, Dept. NNE
Providence, RI 02905
401/461-0870
Free catalog

Ecology Action
19550 Walker Road, Dept. NNE
Willits, CA 95490
Free catalog

The Ecology Box
425 East Washington, #202, Dept. NNE
Ann Arbor, MI 48104
800/735-1371   313/662-9131
Free catalog

Ecology By Design
801 Second Street, Suite 402, Dept. NNE
Santa Monica, CA 90403
213/394-4146

Ecology Sound Farms
42126 Road 168, Dept. NNE
Orosi, CA 93647
209/528-2276
Free catalog

EcoSafe Products
P.O. Box 1177, Dept. NNE
St. Augustine, FL 32085
800/274-7387
Free catalog

Eddie Bauer
P.O. Box 3700, Dept. NNE
Seattle, WA 98124-3700
800/426-8020
Free catalog

Elaine Aldrich
RR 2, Box 2675, Dept. NNE
Westford, VT 05494
802/879-4869
Free catalog

Electro Automotive
P.O. Box 1113, Dept. NNE
Felton, CA 95018-1113
408/429-1989
$5.00 catalog

Elemental Enterprises
P.O. Box 1036, Dept. NNE
Seaside, CA 93955
408/394-7077
Free catalog

E. L. Foust Company
Box 105, Dept. NNE
Elmhurst, IL 60126
800/225-9549
Free catalog

Ellon Bach USA
644 Merrick Road, Dept. NNE
Lynbrook, NY 11563
800/433-7523   516/593-2206
Free catalog

Environmental Purification Systems
P.O. Box 191, Dept. NNE
Concord, CA 94522
800/829-2129   415/682-7231
Free catalog

Equal Exchange
101 Tosca Drive, Dept. NNE
Stoughton, MA 02072
617/344-7227
Free catalog

Erth-rite
RD 1, Box 243, Dept. NNE
Gap, PA 17527
800/332-4171   717/442-4171
Free catalog

Erwin's Bee Farm
33618 Jenkins Road, Dept. NNE
Cottage Grove, OR 97424
503/942-7061
Free catalog

Essential Alternatives
22 Center Street, Dept. NNE
Rutland, VT 05701
802/773-8834
$1.00 catalog

Ethan's Wooden Toy & Doll Company
22333 Nancy Avenue, Dept. NNE
Southfield, MI 48034
313/355-0606
Free catalog

Everybody Ltd.
1738 Pearl Street, Dept. NNE
Boulder, CO 80302
303/440-0188
Free catalog

Exotic Gifts
P.O. Box 842, Dept. NNE
Hermosa Beach, CA 90254
213/374-2570
Free catalog

Fairfax Biological Laboratory
P.O. Box 300, Dept. NNE
Clinton Corners, NY 12514
914/266-3705
Free catalog

Family Clubhouse
6 Chiles Avenue, Dept. NNE
Asheville, NC 28803
800/876-1574   704/254-9236
Free catalog

Feathered Friends
1417 First Avenue, Dept. NNE
Seattle, WA 98101
206/622-0974
Free catalog

Fiddler's Green Farm
RFD 1 Box 656, Dept. NNE
Belfast, ME 04915
207/338-3568
Free catalog

Fitzpatrick Winery
7740 Fairplay Road, Dept. NNE
Somerset, CA 95684
209/245-3248
$5.00 catalog

Flowerfield Enterprises
10332 Shaver Road, Dept. NNE
Kalamazoo, MI 49002
616/327-0108
Free catalog

Fluir Herbals
P.O. Box 25, Dept. NNE
Minisink, PA 18341
No phone
Free catalog

Foothill Agricultural Research
510½ West Chase Drive, Dept. NNE
Corona, CA 91720
714/371-0120
Free catalog

Forest Flower
RFD 2 Box 500, Dept. NNE
Tilton, NH 03276
No phone
Free catalog

Four Chimneys Farm Winery
RD 1, Hall Road, Dept. NNE
Himrod, NY 14842
607/243-7502
Free catalog

The Fragrant Path
P.O. Box 328, Dept. NNE
Fort Calhoun, NE 68023
No phone
$1.00 catalog

French Creek Sheep & Wool Company
Dept. NNE
Elverson, PA 19520
800/345-4091   215/286-5700
$2.00 catalog
Family-owned farm.

Fuller Brush
P.O. Box 1020, Dept. NNE
Rural Hall, NC 27098-1020
800/522-0024
Free catalog

The Futon Shop
491 Broadway, Dept. NNE
New York, NY 10012
212/226-5825
Free catalog

G & W Supply
1441 West 46th Avenue #31, Dept. NNE
Denver, CO 80211
303/455-8834
Free catalog

Gaeta Imports
141 John Street, Dept. NNE
Babylon, NY 11702
516/661-2681
Free catalog

Gaia Herbs
62B Old Littleton Road, Dept. NNE
Harvard, MA 01451
508/456-3049
$2.00 catalog

Garden City Seeds
1324 Red Crow Road, Dept. NNE
Victor, MT 59875-9713
406/961-4837
$2.00 catalog

Gardener's Supply
128 Intervale Road, Dept. NNE
Burlington, VT 05401
802/863-1700
Free catalog

Gardens Alive!
P.O. Box 149, Dept. NNE
Sunman, IN 47041
812/623-3800
Free catalog

Garden-Ville of Austin
6266 Highway 290 West, Dept. NNE
Austin, TX 78735
512/892-0006
$3.00 catalog

Garnet Hill
262 Main Street, Dept. NNE
Franconia, NH 03580
800/622-6216   603/823-5545
Free catalog

Gem Cultures
30301 Sherwood Road, Dept. NNE
Fort Bragg, CA 95437
707/964-2922
Free catalog
Small, family-owned business. Reuses styrofoam packaging and encourages customers to reuse also.

Gemma Wenger
1154 Roberto Lane, Dept. NNE
Los Angeles, CA 90077
213/471-3984
Free catalog

The Gingerbread Cat
12083 Weiman, Dept. NNE
Hell, MI 48169
313/878-2411
$1.00 catalog

Gingerich Small Engines
Route 2, Dept. NNE
Jamesport, MO 64648
No phone
Free catalog

Golden Pride
P.O. Box 21109, Dept. NNE
West Palm Beach, FL 33416
407/586-7778
Free catalog

Gold Mine Natural Food Company
1947 30th Street, Dept. NNE
San Diego, CA 92102
800/475-FOOD   619/234-9711
Free catalog

The Good Earth Seed Catalogue
P.O. Boxs 5644
Redwood City, CA 94063
415/595-2270
Free catalog

Good Seed Company
Star Route Box 73A, Dept. NNE
Oroville (Chesaw), WA 98844
No phone
Free catalog

Goodwin Creek Gardens
P.O. Box 83, Dept. NNE
Williams, OR 97544
503/846-7357
$1.00 catalog

Goodwin Weavers
P.O. Box 16, Dept. NNE
Blowing Rock, NC 28605
800/445-4437   704/295-3577
Free catalog
A family business run by seventh generation weavers.

Gothic Image
Box 609, Dept. NNE
Buffalo, NY 14226
716/832-7460
$1.00 catalog

Graham-Pierce Printers
P.O. Box 1866, Dept. NNE
Fairview Heights, IL 62208
618/632-5600
Free catalog

Granny's Old Fashioned Products
P.O. Box 256, Dept. NNE
Arcadia, CA 91066
818/577-1825
Free catalog

Greek Gourmet
George & Diane Nassopoulos & Family
195 Whiting Street, Dept. NNE
Hingham, MA 02043
617/749-1866
Free catalog

Green Earth Natural Foods
2545 Prairie, Dept. NNE
Evanston, IL 60201
800/322-3662   708/864-8949
Free catalog
"Whenever possible we support socially responsible and environmentally safe companies; likewise, we have discontinued products for ethical considerations, either related to their product line or their policies."

Green Knoll Farm
P.O. Box 434, Dept. NNE
Gridley, CA 95948
916/846-3431
Free catalog

Halcyon Gardens
P.O. Box 124, Dept. NNE
Gibsonia, PA 15044
412/935-2233
Free catalog

Hangouts
P.O. Box 148, Dept. NNE
Boulder, CO 80306
800/HANGOUT   303/442-2533
Free catalog

Hanna Anderson
1010 NW Flanders, Dept. NNE
Portland, OR 97209
800/346-6040
Free catalog
Can return children's clothes purchased from them in "good used condition" for a 20 percent credit voucher. Returned used clothes are donated to local charities.

Hans Schumm Woodworks
RD 2, Box 233, Dept. NNE
Ghent, NY 12075
518/672-4685
Free catalog

Harbingers of a New Age
12100 Brighton Street, Dept. NNE
Hayden Lake, ID 83835
208/772-7753
Free catalog

Hardscrabble Enterprises
Route 6, Box 42, Dept. NNE
Cherry Grove, WV 26804
304/567-2727
Free catalog

Harmonious Technologies
26 North Mentor Avenue, Dept. NNE
Pasadena, CA 91106
818/792-2798
Free catalog

Harmony Farm Supply
P.O. Box 460, Dept. NNE
Graton, CA 95444
707/823-9125
$2.00 catalog

Harmony Moon
P.O. Box 91212, Dept. NNE
Long Beach, CA 90809
213/439-4716
Free catalog

Hartman Associates
26211 Central Park, Suite 102, Dept. NNE
Southfield, MI 48076
313/353-8120
Free catalog

Hartmann's Plantation
P.O. Box E, Dept. NNE
Grand Junction, MI 49056
616/253-4281
Free catalog

Hawkhaven Greenhouse
Route 3, Box 143, Dept. NNE
Wautoma, WI 54982
800/326-1558   414/787-4544
Free catalog

Hearthside Quilts
P.O. Box 429, Dept. NNE
Shelburne, VT 05482-0429
800/451-3533   802/985-8077
$3.00 catalog

Hearthsong
P.O. Box B, Dept. NNE
Sebastopol, CA 95473-0601
800/325-2502   707/829-0900
Free catalog

Heavenly Hammocks
P.O. Box 25, Dept. NNE
Santa Cruz, CA 95063
408/335-3160
Free catalog

Heavenly Soap
5948 East 30th Street, Dept. NNE
Tucson, AZ 85711
602/790-9938
Free catalog

Heirloom Gardens
P.O. Box 138, Dept. NNE
Guerneville, CA 95446
707/887-1215
$2.00 catalog

Heirloom Seeds
P.O. Box 245, Dept. NNE
West Elizabeth, PA 15088
No phone
$1.00 catalog

Heliodyne
4910 Seaport Avenue, Dept. NNE
Richmond, CA 94804
415/237-9614
Free catalog

Helios
P.O. Box 2153, Dept. NNE
Carmel, CA 93921
800/444-5157   408/624-9973
Free catalog

Helmuth Country Bakery
6706 West Mills Road, Dept. NNE
Hutchinson, KS 67501
316/567-2301
Free catalog

Herbalist & Alchemist
P.O. Box 63, Dept. NNE
Franklin Park, NJ 08823
201/545-1979
$1.00 catalog

Herb-Pharm
P.O. Box 116, Dept. NNE
Williams, OR 97544
503/846-7178
Free catalog

The Herb Shop
188 South Main, Dept. NNE
Springville, UT 84663
800/453-1406   801/489-8787
Free catalog

High Altitude Gardens
P.O. Box 4238, Dept. NNE
Ketchum, ID 83340
800/874-SEED   208/726-3221
$2.00 catalog

High Cotton Company
39 Broadway, Dept. NNE
Asheville, NC 28001
704/253-1138
Free catalog
A woman-run and -owned business that
hires visually-impaired workers and dis-
placed textile workers.

High Sierra Concepts
P.O. Box 3477, Dept. NNE
Sparks, NV 89432
702/356-1719
Free catalog

Home Health Products
1160 A Millers Lane, Dept. NNE
Virginia Beach, VA 23451
800/284-9123
Free catalog

Home Recycling Catalogue
2141 P Street NW, Suite 204, Dept. NNE
Washington, DC 20037
202/331-9578
Free catalog

Home Service Products Company
P.O. Box 269, Dept. NNE
Bound Brook, NJ 08805
201/356-8175
Free catalog

Homespun Fabrics & Draperies
P.O. Box 3223, Dept. NNE
Ventura, CA 93006
805/642-8111
$2.00 catalog

Howard Graphics
P.O. Box 7208, Dept. NNE
Loveland, CO 80537
303/667-8477
Free catalog

Humane Alternative Products
8 Hutchins Street, Dept. NNE
Concord, NH 03301
603/224-1361
Free catalog

Humboldt Composting Company
5685 Holland Loop Road, Dept. NNE
Cave Junction, OR 97523
503/592-4753
Free catalog

The Hummer Nature Works
Reagan Wells Canyon Box 122,
Dept. NNE
Uvalde, TX 78801
512/232-6167
Free catalog

Hydro-Analysis Associates
620 Noble Street, Dept. NNE
Kutztown, PA 19530
215/683-7474
Free catalog

Illuminee du Monde
22 Main Street, Dept. NNE
Bristol, VT 05443
802/453-3952
Free catalog

Integral Energy Systems
105 Argall Way, Dept. NNE
Nevada City, CA 95959
916/265-8441
$4.00 catalog

Integrated Fertility Management
333 Ohme Gardens Road, Dept. NNE
Wenatchee, WA 98801
800/332-3179   509/662-3179
Free catalog

Integrated Health Network
P.O. Box 27275, Dept. NNE
Tempe, AZ 85282
800/548-2710   602/921-1188
Free catalog

InterNatural
P.O. Box 680, Dept. NNE
South Sutton, NH 03273
800/446-4903   603/927-4776
Free catalog

Interpro
P.O. Box 1823, Dept. NNE
Haverhill, MA 01831
508/373-2438
Free catalog

Jack's Honey Bee Products
2602 East Foothill Boulevard, Dept. NNE
Pasadena, CA 91107
213/681-5275
Free catalog

Jade Mountain
P.O. Box 4616, Dept. NNE
Boulder, CO 80306
303/449-6601
$2.00 catalog

Jaffe Brothers
P.O. Box 636, Dept. NNE
Valley Center, CA 92082-0636
619/749-1133
Free catalog
A 40-year-old family business.

James River Traders
James River Landing, Dept. NNE
Hampton, VA 23631
800/445-2405   804/827-6000
Free catalog

Jamie Harmon
RR 1, Box 391 Plains Road, Dept. NNE
Jericho, VT 05465
802/434-2350
$3.50 catalog includes yarn samples

Janice Corporation
198 Route 46, Dept. NNE
Budd Lake, NJ 07828
800/JANICES   201/691-2979
Free catalog

Jantz Design & Manufacturing
P.O. Box 3071, Dept. NNE
Santa Rosa, CA 95402
707/823-8834
Free catalog printed on recycled paper

Jeanne Rose Herbal BodyWorks
219 Carl Street, Dept. NNE
San Francisco, CA 94117
415/564-6785
$2.00 catalog
"We recycle everything. Plastic containers
are all reuseable."

J. Jill Ltd.
P.O. Box 3004, Winterbrook Way,
Dept. NNE
Meredith, NH 03253-3004
800/642-9989
Free catalog

J. L. Hudson, Seedsman
P.O. Box 1058, Dept. NNE
Redwood City, CA 94064
No phone
$1.00 catalog

Johnny's Selected Seeds
Foss Hill Road, Dept. NNE
Albion, ME 04910
207/437-9294
Free catalog

Jurlique
37 Commercial Blvd., Suite 110,
Dept. NNE
Novato, CA 94949
800/462-0666   415/883-4966
Free catalog

Kansas Wind Power
Route 1, Dept. NNE
Holton, KS 66436
913/364-4407
$3.00 catalog

Karen's Nontoxic Products
1839 Dr. Jack Road, Dept. NNE
Conowingo, MD 21918
301/378-4621
Free catalog printed on recycled paper with
soy-based ink

KB Cotton Pillows
P.O. Box 57, Dept. NNE
De Soto, TX 75115
214/223-7193
Free catalog

Kemp Company
160 Koser Road, Dept. NNE
Lititz, PA 17543
800/441-5367   717/627-7979
Free catalog

Kemp Krafts
275 Main Street, Apt. 11, Dept. NNE
Winooski, VT 05404
802/655-9563
Free catalog

Kettle Care Products
1145 2nd Avenue East, Dept. NNE
Kalispell, MT 59901
406/756-3485
Free catalog

Kickapoo Diversified Products
Main Street, Dept. NNE
La Farge, WI 54639
608/625-4431
Free catalog

Kim Supply Company
1407 Kansas Avenue, Dept. NNE
Kansas City, MO 64127
800/444-2783   816/241-6000
Free catalog

The Kinsman Company
River Road, Dept. NNE
Point Pleasant, PA 18950
215/297-5613
Free catalog

Kiss My Face
P.O. Box 224, Dept. NNE
Gardiner, NY 12525
914/255-0884
Free catalog

K Lighting Company
3509 Elizabeth Lake Road, Suite 103,
Dept. NNE
Pontiac, MI 48054
313/683-1290
Free catalog

Knorr Beeswax Products
14906 Via de la Valle, Dept. NNE
Del Mar, CA 92014
619/755-2051
Free catalog

Kreations by Kristen
9050 West Waters Road, Dept. NNE
Ann Arbor, MI 48103
No phone
Free catalog

Krystal Wharf Farms
RD 2, Box 2112, Dept. NNE
Mansfield, PA 16933
717/549-8194
Free catalog

KSA Jojoba
19025 Parthenia Street, Suite 200,
Dept. NNE
Northridge, CA 91324
818/701-1534
SASE/45¢

L. L. Bean
Casco Street, Dept. NNE
Freeport, ME 04033
800/221-4221   207/865-3111
Free catalog

Land's End
One Land's End Lane, Dept. NNE
Dodgeville, WI 53595
800/356-4444
Free catalog

Landau
P.O. Box 671, Dept. NNE
Princeton, NJ 08542-0671
800/932-0709   800/257-9445
Free catalog

Langenbach
P.O. Box 453, Dept. NNE
Blairstown, NJ 07825
201/362-5886
Free catalog

Lanocare Laboratories
10305 Dutchtown Road, Dept. NNE
Knoxville, TN 37932
800/292-4794   615/675-0436
Free catalog

Laughing Bear Batik
P.O. Box 732 Studio, Dept. NNE
Woodstock, NY 12498
914-246-3810
Free catalog

Laura Copenhaver Industries
P.O. Box 149, Dept. NNE
Marion, VA 24354
800/227-6797   703-783-4663
$2.00 catalog
Founded in 1916 to help the mountain
people and sheep farmers of Southwest
Virginia overcome economic hardships,
the company still shares its founder's vision of preserving traditional mountain
crafts.

Lawlor/Weller Design Group
200 East Briggs Avenue
Fairfield, IA 52556
515/472-4561

Lean and Free Products
5265 Rockwell Drive NE, Dept. NNE
Cedar Rapid, IA 52402
800/383-BEEF   319/395-9636
Free catalog

Leslie Manufacturing
Route 1, Box 286, Dept. NNE
Lawrence, KS 66044
913/842-1943
Free catalog

Les Petits
6510 Eastwick Avenue
P.O. Box 33901, Dept. NNE
Philadelphia, PA 19142-0961
800/333-2002   215/492-6328
Free catalog

Le Tan
236 South 3rd Street, Suite A,
Dept. NNE
Montrose, CO 81401
800/937-5433
303/240-1500 (Alaska/Hawaii)
Free catalog

Lett Company
P.O. Box 2222, Dept. NNE
Mill Valley, CA 94942
415/381-0352
Free catalog

Lillian Vernon
510 South Fulton Avenue, Dept. NNE
Mount Vernon, NY 10550
914/633-6300
Free catalog

Living Farms
P.O. Box 50, Dept. NNE
Tracy, MN 56175
800/533-5320   507/629-4431
Free catalog

The Living Source
3500 MacArthur Drive, Dept. NNE
Waco, TX 76708
817/756-6341
Free catalog

**Livingstone's Living Earth Topsoil
Production Centers**
P.O. Box 2910, Dept. NNE
Santa Cruz, CA 95062-2910
408/426-0384
Free catalog

Living Tree Centre
P.O. Box 10082, Dept. NNE
Berkeley, CA 94709
415/528-4467
$7.00 catalog

Livos Plantchemistry
1365 Rufina Circle, Dept. NNE
Santa Fe, NM 87501
800/621-2591   505/438-3448
Free catalog

Longevity Pure Medicines
9595 Wilshire Boulevard, Suite 706,
Dept. NNE
Beverly Hills, CA 90212
800/327-5519   213/273-7423
Free catalog

Lost Prairie Herb Farm
805 Kienas Road, Dept. NNE
Kalispell, MT 59901
406/756-7742
$1.00 catalog

Lovely Essentials
P.O. Box 27D, Dept. NNE
St. Francis, KY 40062
502/865-5501
Sewn at home by women; sold wholesale
by a grandmother; shipped in recycled card-
board boxes.
Free catalog

Lundberg Family Farms
P.O. Box 369, Dept. NNE
Richvale, CA 95974
916/882-4551
Free catalog

Magic Garden Produce
Route 3, Box 304, Dept. NNE
Edinburg, VA 22824
No phone
Free catalog

**Maharishi Ayur-Veda Products
International**
P.O. Box 541, Dept. NNE
Lancaster, MA 01523
508/368-1818
Free catalog

Maine Baby
P.O. Box 910, Dept. NNE
Morrill, ME 04952
207/342-5055
Free catalog

Maine Coast Sea Vegetables
Shore Road, Dept. NNE
Franklin, ME 04634
207/565-2907
Free catalog

Mandala
Route 3, Box 117, Dept. NNE
Floyd, VA 24091
703/745-4479
Free catalog

Maplewood Seed Company
311 Maplewood Lane, Dept. NNE
Roseburg, OR 97470-9236
No phone
Free catalog

Marine Minerals
P.O. Box 237, Dept. NNE
Roy, UT 84067
800/444-8077   801/731-7036
Free catalog

Marvelous Toy Works
2111 Eastern Avenue, Dept. NNE
Baltimore, MD 21231
301/276-5130
A family-run business.
Free catalog

Maskal Forages
1318 Willow, Dept. NNE
Caldwell, ID 83605
208/454-3330
Free catalog

McCracken Solar Company
329 West Carlos, Dept. NNE
Alturas, CA 96101
916/233-3175
Free catalog

Meadowbrook Herb Garden
Route 138, Dept. NNE
Wyoming, RI 02898
401/539-7603
$1.00 catalog

Medina Agriculture Products Company
P.O. Box 309, Dept. NNE
Hondo, TX 78861
512/426-3011
Free catalog

Memphremagog Heat Exchangers
P.O. Box 456, Dept. NNE
Newport, VT 05855
802/334-5412
Free catalog

Mia Rose Products
1374 Logan, Unit C, Dept. NNE
Costa Mesa, CA 92626
714/662-5465
Free catalog

Micro Balanced Products
25 Aladdin Avenue, Dept. NNE
Dumont, NJ 07628
800/LAVILIN   201/387-0200
Free catalog

Miller Paint Company
317 SE Grand Avenue, Dept. NNE
Portland, OR 97214
503/233-4491
Free catalog

Millstream Natural Health Supplies
1310-A East Tallmadge Avenue,
Dept. NNE
Akron, OH 44310
216/630-2700
Free catalog

M. Matthews Handwoven Fabrics
21 Hillcrest Drive, Dept. NNE
Rochester, NH 03867
603/332-6779
Free catalog

Monda Belle de Vienne
1121 King's Road #12, Dept. NNE
West Hollywood, CA 90069
213/656-2484
Free catalog

Montana Naturals International
19994 Highway 93, Dept. NNE
Arlee, MT 59821
800/872-7218   406/726-3214
Free catalog

Monterey Bay Gourmet Natural Foods
P.O. Box 689, Dept. NNE
Freedom, CA 95077
800/274-8778
$1.00 catalog

Moonflower Birthing Supply
P.O. Box 128, Dept. NNE
Louisville, CO 80027
800/747-8996   303/665-2120
Free catalog

Moon Mountain
P.O. Box 34, Dept. NNE
Morro Bay, CA 93443
805/772-2473
$2.00 catalog

Morningland Dairy
Route 1, Box 188, Dept. NNE
Mountain View, MO 65548
417/469-3817
Free catalog

Mother Hart's Natural Products
P.O. Box 4229, Dept. NNE
Boynton Beach, FL 33424-4229
407/738-5866
Free catalog

Mother's Wear
1738½ Topanga Skyline Drive,
Dept. NNE
Topanga, CA 90290
800/322-2320   213/455-1426
Free catalog

Motherwear
P.O. Box 114, Dept. NNE
Northampton, MA 01061
413/586-3488
Free catalog

Mountain Ark Trading Company
120 South East Avenue, Dept. NNE
Fayetteville, AR 72701
800/643-8909
Free catalog

Mountain Butterfly Herbs
P.O. Box 1365, Dept. NNE
Hamilton, MT 59840
406/363-6683
Price list printed on recycled paper.
Free catalog

Mountain Craft Shop
American Ridge Road, Route 1,
Dept. NNE
New Martinsville, WV 26155
304/455-3570
Employs about 40 local artisans.
Free catalog

Mountain Fresh
P.O. Box 40516, Dept. NNE
Grand Junction, CO 81504
303/434-8434
Free catalog

Mountain Rose Herbs
P.O. Box 2000, Dept. NNE
Redway, CA 95560
800/879-3337   707/923-3941
Free catalog
"We use recycled materials as much as we can, from our packing materials (such as boxes, styrofoam pellets, and shredded paper), to our gift wrapping printed on recycled paper."

Mountain Spirit
P.O. Box 368, Dept. NNE
Port Townsend, WA 98368
206/385-4491
Free catalog

Mountain Springs
356 West Redview Drive, Dept. NNE
Monroe, UT 84754
800/542-2303   801/527-4528
$1.00 catalog

Murco Wall Products
300 NE 21st Street, Dept. NNE
Fort Worth, TX 76106
817/626-1987
Free catalog

My Brother's Keeper
211 South 5th Street, Dept. NNE
Richmond, IN 47374
317/962-5079
Free catalog

National Testing Labs
6151 Wilson Mills Road, Dept. NNE
Cleveland, OH 44143
800/458-3330   216/449-2525
Free catalog

Native Seed Foundation
Star Route, Dept. NNE
Moyie Springs, ID 83845
208/267-7938
$1.00 catalog

Native Seeds/SEARCH
2509 North Campbell Avenue, #325,
Dept. NNE
Tucson, AZ 85719
602/327-9123
$1.00 catalog

The Natural Baby Company
RD 1, Box 160, Dept. NNE
Titusville, NJ 08560
800/388-BABY   609/737-2895
Free catalog printed on recycled paper

Natural Cotton Colours
P.O. Box 791, Dept NNE
Wasco, CA 93280
805/758-3928
Free catalog

Natural Elements
P.O. Box 3299, Dept. NNE
Santa Cruz, CA 95063
408/425-5448
Free catalog

The Natural Gardening Company
217 San Anselmo Avenue, Dept. NNE
San Anselmo, CA 94960
415/456-5060
Free catalog

Natural Lifestyle Supplies
16 Lookout Drive, Dept. NNE
Asheville, NC 28804
800/752-2775   704/254-9606
Free catalog
"For trees' sake, our catalog will be printed twice a year (rather than seasonally) on recyclable newsprint. All orders are shipped in paper packing materials we 'recycle' from a local natural food store."

Natural Pest Controls
8864 Little Creek Drive, Dept. NNE
Orangevale, CA 95662
916/726-0855
Free catalog

Naturally Ewe
14662 SR 574 West, Dept. NNE
Dover, FL 33527
813/681-6787
Free catalog

Nature House
Purple Martin Junction, Dept. NNE
Griggsville, IL 62340
217/833-2393
Free catalog

Nature's Colors
424 LaVerne Avenue, Dept. NNE
Mill Valley, CA 94941
415/388-6101
Free catalog

Nature's Control
P.O. Box 35, Dept. NNE
Medford, OR 97501
503/899-8318
Free catalog

Nature's Way Products
P.O. Box 2233, Dept. NNE
Springville, UT 84663
801/489-3631
Free catalog

Naturpath
1410 NW 13th Street, Dept. NNE
Gainesville, FL 32601
800/542-4784
Free catalog

Necessary Trading Company
P.O. Box 305, Dept. NNE
New Castle, VA 24127
703/864-5103
$2.00 catalog

NEEDS
602 Nottingham Road, Dept. NNE
Syracuse, NY 13224
315/446-1122
Free catalog

The New Alchemy Institute
237 Hatchville Road, Dept. NNE
East Falmouth, MA 02536
508/564-6301
Free catalog

New Cycle
P.O. Box 3248, Dept. NNE
Santa Rosa, CA 95402
707/571-2036
Free catalog

Nichols Garden Nursery
1190 North Pacific Highway, Dept. NNE
Albany, OR 97321
503/928-9280
Free catalog
"We have been in the seed and nursery business for 40 years. Our purpose during these years has been to bring people closer to nature through gardening." A family business.

Nick Sciabica & Sons
P.O. Box 1246, Dept. NNE
Modesto, CA 95353
209/577-5067
Free catalog

Nigra Enterprises
5699 Kanan Road, Dept. NNE
Agoura, CA 91301
818/889-6877
Free catalog

Nitron Industries
P.O. Box 1447, Dept. NNE
Fayetteville, AR 72702
800/835-0123
Free catalog

Noah's Park
13600 Wright Circle, Dept. NNE
Tampa, FL 33626
800/VIA-NOAH   813/854-5757
Free catalog

Nokomis Farms
3293 Main Street, Dept. NNE
East Troy, WI 53120
414/642-9665
Free catalog

NOPE (Non-Polluting Enterprises)
P.O. Box 333D, Dept. NNE
Smethport, PA 16749
800/782-NOPE
Free catalog

North Country Soap
7888 County Road 6, Dept. NNE
Maple Plain, MN 55359
800/776-7627   612/479-3381
Free catalog

Northern Lakes Wild Rice Company
P.O. Box 592, Dept. NNE
Teton Village, WY 83025
307/733-7192
Free catalog

Northplan/Mountain Seed
P.O. Box 9107, Dept. NNE
Moscow, ID 83843-1607
208/882-8040
Free catalog

North Star Toys
617 North Star Route, Dept. NNE
Questa, NM 87556
505/586-0122
Price list printed on recycled paper.
Free catalog

Northwest Futon Company
400 SW 2nd Avenue, Dept. NNE
Portland, OR 97204
503/242-0057
Free catalog
Price list printed on recycled paper. They recycle extensively.

Northwoods Nursery
28696 South Cramer Road, Dept. NNE
Molalla, OR 97038
503/651-3737
Free catalog

Nuclear Free America
325 East 25th Street, Dept. NNE
Baltimore, MD 21218
301/235-3575
Free catalog

Nutra-Min
Box 212, 600 South 400 West,
Dept. NNE
Smithfield, UT 84335
No phone
Free catalog

Nu-World Amaranth
P.O. Box 2202, Dept. NNE
Naperville, IL 60567
708/369-6819
Free catalog

Oak Art of Kentucky
P.O. Box 181, Dept. NNE
Ravenna, KY 40472
606/723-7498
Free catalog

Oak Valley Herb Farm
14648 Pear Tree Lane, Dept. NNE
Nevada City, CA 95959
No phone
Free catalog
"Our intention is to serve you and the planet by producing ecologically sound products that promote life and health."

The Old-Fashioned Milk Paint Company
P.O. Box 222, Dept. NNE
Groton, MA 01450
508/448-6336
Free catalog

One World Trading Company
P.O. Box 310, Dept. NNE
Summertown, TN 38483
800/445-1991   615/964-2334
Free catalog

Organic Cattle Company
P.O. Box 355, Dept. NNE
White Plains, NY 10605
914/684-6529
Free catalog

Organic Foods Express
11003 Emack Road, Dept. NNE
Beltsville, MD 20705
301-937-8608
Free catalog

Organic Pest Management
P.O. Box 55267, Dept. NNE
Seattle, WA 98155
206/367-0707
Free catalog

Organic Vintages
Somerstown Turnpike, Route 100,
Dept. NNE
Somer, NY 10589
800/877-6655   707/462-4258
Free catalog

The Organic Wine Company
54 Genoa Place, Dept. NNE
San Francisco, CA 94133
415/433-0167
Free catalog

Original Swiss Aromatics
P.O. Box 606, Dept. NNE
San Rafael, CA 94915
415/459-3998
Free catalog

Ornamental Edibles
3622 Weedin Court, Dept. NNE
San Jose, CA 95132
408/946-SEED
$1.00 catalog

Orvis
P.O. Box 12000, Dept. NNE
Roanoke, VA 24022-8001
800/541-3541
Free catalog

Ott Light Systems
306 East Cota Street, Dept. NNE
Santa Barbara, CA 93101
800/234-3724   805-564-3467
Free catalog

Outer Banks Pine Products
P.O. Box 9003, Dept. NNE
Lester, PA 19113
215/534-1234
$1.00 catalog

Pantropic
7330 Lynch Road, Dept. NNE
Sebastopol, CA 95472
707/823-2033
Free catalog

Papa Don's Toys
Walker Creek Road, Dept. NNE
Walton, OR 97490
503/935-7604
Free catalog

The Paper Project
P.O. Box 12, Dept. NNE
Arcata, CA 95521
707/822-4338   415/540-1127
Free catalog
Now an independent business, the Project
was started by students who wanted to
make recycled paper more readily available
to the community.

Pascalite
P.O. Box 104, Dept. NNE
Worland, WY 82401
307/347-3872
Free catalog

Patti Collins Canvas Products
167-B Throckmorton, Dept. NNE
Mill Valley, CA 94941
415/388-4934
Free catalog

Paul's Grains
Route 1, Box 76, Dept. NNE
Laurel, IA 50141
515/476-3373
Free catalog
A family-owned farm business.

Peaceful Valley Farm Supply
P.O. Box 2209, Dept. NNE
Grass Valley, CA 95945
916/272-4769
Free catalog

Peace Seeds
2385 Southeast Thompson Street,
Dept. NNE
Corvallis, OR 97333
No phone
Free catalog

Penthouse Gallery
116 East 16th Street, Dept. NNE
New York, NY 10003
800/221-7611   212/673-7070
Free catalog

People's Energy Resource Cooperative
354 Waverly Street, Dept. NNE
Framingham, MA 01701
508/879-8572
Free catalog

Photocomm
P.O. Box 649, Dept. NNE
North San Juan, CA 95960
800/544-6466   916/292-3754
Free catalog

Pines International
P.O. Box 1107, Dept. NNE
Lawrence, KS 66044
800/642-PINE
Free catalog

Pinetree Garden Seeds
Route 100, Dept. NNE
New Gloucester, ME 04260
207/926-3400
Free catalog
Uses recycled materials, primarily newspaper, in their packaging. "When we use
those plastic peanuts they have been sent
to us by someone else."

Plants of the Southwest
930 Baca Street, Dept. NNE
Santa Fe, NM 87501
505/983-1548
$2.00 catalog

Ponce Bakery
116 West 12th Street, Dept. NNE
Chico, CA 95928
916/891-8654
Free catalog

Port Canvas Company
P.O. Box H, Dept. NNE
Kennebunkport, ME 04046
207/985-9767
Free catalog

The Portland Soaker
P.O. Box 19827, Dept. NNE
Rochester, NY 14619
No phone
Free catalog

Powers' Country Store
Route 120, Dept. NNE
Cornish, NH 03746
603/542-7703
Free catalog

Pronatec International
P.O. Box 193, Dept. NNE
Peterborough, NH 03458
603/924-9452
Free catalog

Pueblo to People
1616 Montrose, #3100, Dept. NNE
Houston, TX 77006
800/843-5257   713/523-1197
Free catalog

Founded in 1979, this nonprofit organization works at the grassroots, supporting
the craft and agricultural cooperatives of
very low income Latin American peoples.

Pure Podunk
RR 1, Box 69, Dept. NNE
Thetford Center, VT 05075
802/333-4256
Free catalog

The Pure Water Place
P.O. Box 6715, Dept. NNE
Longmont, CO 80501
303/776-0056
Free catalog

Quality Health Products
409 South Main, Dept. NNE
Waldron, MI 49288
No phone
Free catalog

Quill Corporation
P.O. Box 4700, Dept. NNE
Lincolnshire, IL 60197-4700
708/634-4800
Free catalog

Radiation Safety Corporation
140 University Avenue, Dept. NNE
Palo Alto, CA 94301
800/443-0100 Ext. 624   415/321-8986
Free catalog

Real Goods Trading Company
3041 Guidiville Road, Dept. NNE
Ukiah, CA 95482
800/688-9288   707/468-9214
$5.00 catalog

The Recycled Paper Company
185 Corey Road, Dept. NNE
Boston, MA 02146
617/277-9901
Free Catalog

Redwood City Seed Company
P.O. Box 361, Dept. NNE
Redwood City, CA 94064
415/325-7333
$1.00 catalog

Reggio Register Company
P.O. Box 511, Dept. NNE
Ayer, MA 01432-0511
508/772-3493
Free catalog

Resource Conservation Technology
2633 North Calvert Street, Dept. NNE
Baltimore, MD 21218
301/366-1146
Free catalog

Rex & Susan Mongold
HCR 15, Dept. NNE
Dyer, NV 89010
No phone
Free catalog

Richman Cotton Company
529 Fifth Street, Dept. NNE
Santa Rosa, CA 95401
800/992-8924   800/851-2556
Free catalog
"We try to consider the whole cost to the environment of an article from manufacture to disposal."

Riehs & Riehs
501 George Street, Dept. NNE
New Bern, NC 28560
919/636-1615
Free catalog

Rincon-Vitova
P.O. Box 95, Dept. NNE
Oak View, CA 93011
800/248-BUGS   805/643-5407
Free catalog

Ringer
9959 Valley View Road, Dept. NNE
Eden Prairie, MN 55344-3585
800/654-1047
$1.00 catalog

Rising Sun Enterprises
Box 586, Dept. NNE
Old Snowmass, CO 81654
303/927-8051
$5.00 catalog

Rising Sun Organic Produce
P.O. Box 627, Dept. NNE
Milesburg, PA 16853
814/355-9850
Free catalog

Robert Kacher Selections
3015 V Street NE
Washington, DC 20018
202/832-9083
Free catalog

Robin Evanosky
Box 105, Hix Route, Dept. NNE
Hinton, WV 25951
304/466-5109
Free catalog

Ronniger's Seed Potatoes
Star Route, Dept. NNE
Moyie Springs, ID 83845
208/267-7938
$1.00 catalog

Roseland Farms
27427 M-60 West, Dept. NNE
Cassopolis, MI 49031
616/445-8987
Free catalog

Rosetta Teas
P.O. Box 4611, Dept. NNE
Berkeley, CA 94704-0611
No phone
Free catalog

Royal Silk
Royal Silk Plaza, 45 East Madison, Dept. NNE
Clifton, NJ 07011
800/321-SILK   201/772-4100
Free catalog

Rumpelstiltskin
1021 R Street, Dept. NNE
Sacramento, CA 95814
916/442-9225
Free catalog

Safe Computing Company
368 Hillside Avenue, Dept. NNE
Needham, MA 02194
800/222-3003   617/444-7778
Free catalog

Sajama Alpaca
P.O. Box 1209, Dept. NNE
Ashland, OR 97520
503/482-0233
$3.00 catalog

Santa Barbara Olive Company
1661 Mission Dr.
Solvang, CA 93463
805/688-9917
Free catalog

Santa Fe Fragrance Company
P.O. Box 282, Dept. NNE
Santa Fe, NM 87504
505/473-1717
SASE

Scandia Down Shops
1546 California Street, Dept. NNE
San Francisco, CA 94109
415/928-5111
Free catalog

Schoolhouse Press
6899 Cary Bluff, Dept. NNE
Pittsville, WI 54466
715/884-2799
$2.00 catalog and all other materials
printed on recycled paper.

Schoonmaker/Lynn Enterprises
4619 NW Barnes Road, Dept. NNE
Portland, OR 97210
503/222-5435
Free catalog

Scientific Enterprises
708 119th Lane NE, Dept. NNE
Blaine, MN 55434
612/757-8274
$2.00 catalog

Sears
Check local store for catalog.

2nd Opinion
P.O. Box 69046, Dept. NNE
Portland, OR 97201
800/979-6922   503/228-0711
Free catalog

Seeds Blüm
Idaho City Stage, Dept. NNE
Boise, ID 83706
208/342-0858
Free catalog

Seeds of Change
621 Old Santa Fe Trail, #10, Dept. NNE
Santa Fe, NM 87501
505/983-8956
Free catalog

Select Seeds
180 Stickney Hill Road, Dept. NNE
Union, CT 06076
No phone
$1.50 catalog

SelfCare Catalog
349 Healdsburg Avenue
Dept. NNE
Healdsburg, CA 95448
800/345-3371
Free catalog

Set Point Paper Company
31 Oxford Road, Dept. NNE
Mansfield, MA 02048
508/339-9300
Free catalog

Seventh Generation
49 Hercules Drive, Dept. NNE
Colchester, VT 05446-1672
800/456-1177
Free catalog
Has plastics recycling center and accepts
Seventh Generation containers returned
for recycling. One percent of their gross
product sales are put into a fund to support projects that benefit the planet.

Sew Natural
Route 1, Box 635, Dept. NNE
Middlesex, NC 27557
919/235-2754
Free catalog

Shaker Shops West
P.O. Box 487, Dept. NNE
Inverness, CA 94937
415/669-7256
$3.00 catalog

Shaker Workshops
P.O. Box 1028, Dept. NNE
Concord, MA 01742
617/646-8985
Free catalog

Shama Imports
P.O. Box 2900, Dept. NNE
Farmington Hills, MI 48333
313/478-7740
Free catalog

Shelburne Farms
Dept. NNE
Shelburne, VT 05482
802/985-8686
Free catalog
Preserve, maintain, and adapt the historic
buildings and landscape for teaching and
demonstrating the stewardship of natural
and agricultural resources.

Shiloh Farms
P.O. Box 97, Dept. NNE
Sulphur Springs, AR 72768
501/298-3297
Free catalog

Sierra Legacy
P.O. Box 563, Dept. NNE
Lotus, CA 95651
916/622-6587
Free catalog

Sill House Bakery
Coxe Farm, Dept. NNE
Old Lyme, CT 06371
203/434-9501
Free catalog

Silly Goose
P.O. Box 671, Dept. NNE
Brisbane, CA 94005
No phone
A small, home-based business.
Free catalog

Simmons Company
P.O. Box 3193, Dept. NNE
Chattanooga, TN 37404
800/533-6779   615/622-1308
Free catalog

Simmons Handcrafts
42295 Highway 36, Dept. NNE
Bridgeville, CA 95526
707/777-3280, Ext. 6074
Free catalog

Simple Wisdom
775 South Graham, Dept. NNE
Memphis, TN 38111
901/458-4686
Free catalog

Simplers Botanical Company
P.O. Box 39, Dept. NNE
Forestville, CA 95436
707/887-2012
$1.00 catalog

Simply Delicious
P.O. Box 124, Dept. NNE
Pennsville, NJ 08070
609/678-4488
Free catalog

Simply Divine
1606 South Congress, Dept. NNE
Austin, TX 78704
512/444-5546
Free catalog

Simply Pure
RFD 3, Box 99, Dept. NNE
Bangor, ME 04401
800/IAM-PURE   207/941-1924
Free catalog

Sinan Company
P.O. Box 857, Dept. NNE
Davis, CA 95617-0857
916/753-3104
Free catalog printed on recycled paper

Smoot Honey Company
P.O. Box 158, Dept. NNE
Power, MT 59468
406/463-2227
Free catalog

Soaker Pattern
P.O. Box 3527, Dept. NNE
Wichita, KS 67201
No phone
Free catalog

The Soap Factory
3 Burlington Road, Dept. NNE
Bedford, MA 01730
617/275-8363
Free catalog

Soft Star Shoes
P.O. Box 1629, Dept. NNE
Wimberley, TX 78676
512/847-3460
A home-based, family business.
Free catalog

Soft Steps
P.O. Box 827, Dept. NNE
Corvallis, OR 97339
No phone
Free catalog

Solahart
11855 Sorrento Valley Road, Suite B,
Dept. NNE
San Diego, CA 92121
800/233-7652   800/762-SOLA
Free catalog

Solar Components Corporation
121 Valley Street, Dept. NNE
Manchester, NH 03103
800/258-3072   603/668-8186
$2.00 catalog

Solar Electric
175 Cascade Court, Dept. NNE
Rohnert Park, CA 94928
707/586-1987
$5.00 catalog

Sonoma Antique Apple Nursery
4395 Westside Road, Dept. NNE
Healdsburg, CA 95448
707/433-6420
$1.00 catalog

Sourdough International
P.O. Box 1440, Dept. NNE
Cascade, ID 83611
800/888-9567
Free catalog

South River Miso Company
South River Farm, Dept. NNE
Conway, MA 01341
413/369-4057
Free catalog

Southern Exposure Seed Exchange
P.O. Box 158, Dept. NNE
North Garden, VA 22959
No phone
$3.00 catalog

Southern Oregon Organics
1130 Tetherow Road, Dept. NNE
Williams, OR 97544
503/846-7173
$1.00 catalog

Southwest Collection
P.O. Box 1337, Dept. NNE
Mill Valley, CA 94942
415/381-0707
Free catalog

Special Foods
9207 Shotgun Court, Dept. NNE
Springfield, VA 22153
703/644-0991
Free catalog

Specialty Grain Company
P.O. Box 2458, Dept. NNE
Dearborn, MI 48124
313/535-9222
Free catalog

Spencer's
1759 Old Baxter, Dept. NNE
Chesterfield, MO 63017
314/537-3389
Free catalog

Spotlight Marketing
4609 Seagraves, Dept. NNE
Joplin, MO 64804
417/624-8923 or 548-2121
Free catalog

Spring Valley Gardens
6143, Spring Valley Road, Dept. NNE
Loganville, WI 53943
608/727-5397
Free catalog

Sprout Delights
13090 NW Seventh Avenue, Dept. NNE
Miami, FL 33168-2702
800/334-BAKE   305/687-5880
Free catalog

The Sprout House
40 Railroad Street, Dept. NNE
Great Barrington, MA 01230
413/528-5200
Free catalog

Standard Homeopathic Company
P.O. Box 61067, Dept. NNE
Los Angeles, CA 90061
800/624-9659   213/321-4284
Free catalog

Starr Organic Produce
P.O. Box 561502, Dept. NNE
South Miami, FL 33256
305/262-1242
Free catalog

Stock Seed Farms
RR 1, Box 112, Dept. NNE
Murdock, NE 68407
402/867-3771
Free catalog

Stone Flour Products
Route 1, Dept. NNE
Horatio, AR 71842
501/832-2444
Free catalog

Strand Surplus Senter
2202 Strand, Dept. NNE
Galveston, TX 77550
800/231-6005
$1.00 catalog

Straw Into Gold
3006 San Pablo Avenue, Dept. NNE
Berkeley, CA 94702
415/548-5247
SASE/45¢

Suburban Water Testing Laboratories
4600 Kutztown Road, Dept. NNE
Temple, PA 19560
800/433-6595   215/929-3666
Free catalog

Summerfield Farm
HCR 4, Box 195A, Dept. NNE
Brightwood, VA 22715
703/948-3100
Free catalog

Sunelco
P.O. Box 1499, Dept. NNE
Hamilton, MT 59840
406/363-6924
$3.95 catalog

Sunfeather Herbal Soap Company
RD #3, Box 102A, Dept. NNE
Potsdam, NY 13676
315/265-3648
They support 1% for Peace.
Free catalog

Sun Mountain
35751 Oak Springs Drive, Dept. NNE
Tollhouse, CA 93667
209/855-3710
$25-per-year membership includes
monthly newsletter

Sunnybrook Farms
P.O. Box 6, Dept. NNE
Chesterland, OH 44026
216/729-7232
$1.00 catalog

Sunrise Enterprises
P.O. Box 10058, Dept. NNE
Elmwood, CT 06110-0058
No phone
$1.00 catalog

Sunrise Lane
780 Greenwich Street, Dept.NNE
New York, NY 10014
212/242-7014
Free catalog

Sun Watt Corporation
RFD Box 751, Dept. NNE
Addison, ME 04606
207/497-2204
Free catalog

Sureway Trading Enterprises
826 Pine Avenue, Suites 5 and 6,
Dept. NNE
Niagra Falls, NY 14301-1806
416/596-1887
SASE

Sustane Corporation
1107 Hazeltine Boulevard, Dept. NNE
Chaska, MN 55318
612/448-8828
Free catalog

Synergy Seeds
P.O. Box 5, Dept. NNE
Rumsey, CA 95679
916/757-5767
Free catalog

Talavaya Seeds
P.O. Box 707, Santa Cruz Station,
Dept. NNE
Santa Cruz, NM 87507
505/753-5801
Free catalog

Talisman
68 Tinker Street, Dept. NNE
Woodstock, NY 12498
914/679-7647
Free catalog

Tart-X Products
6224 Madison Court, Dept. NNE
Morton Grove, IL 60053
708/470-9100
$1.00 catalog

Teaco International
P.O. Box 17628, Dept. NNE
Fountain Hills, AZ 85269
602/252-0855
Free catalog

Terra Firma Botanicals
28653 Sutherlin Lane, Dept. NNE
Eugene, OR 97405
503/485-7726
A woman-owned business.
$1.00 catalog

Terra Verde Products
P.O. Box 1353, Dept. NNE
Clifton, CO 81520
No phone
Free catalog

Territorial Seed Company
P.O. Box 27, Dept. NNE
Lorane, OR 97451
503/942-9547
Free catalog

Terry Theise Selections
9070 Maier Road
Laurel, MD 20723
301/490-9190
Free catalog

Testfabrics
P.O. Box 420, Dept. NNE
Middlesex, NJ 08846
201/469-6446
Free catalog

Texas Ruby
1505 Doherty, Dept. NNE
Mission, TX 78572
512/585-1712
Free catalog

Thai Silks
252 State Street, Dept. NNE
Los Altos, CA 94022
800/722-SILK   800/221-SILK
415/948-8611
Free catalog

Threefold International Company
Dept. NNE
New York, NY
800/456-3490
Free catalog

Three Sisters
8624 South Chestnut Avenue,
Dept. NNE
Fresno, CA 93725
209/834-2772 or 834-3150
Free catalog

Thunderstorm Corporation
P.O. Box 150, Dept. NNE
Hingham, MA 02043
607/749-7622
Free catalog

Thurmond Air Quality Systems
P.O. Box 23037, Dept. NNE
Little Rock, AR 72221
800/AIR-PURE   501/227-8888
Free catalog

Tillys
P.O. Box 18864, Dept. NNE
Denver, CO 80218
303/832-4904
A home-based business.
Free catalog

Timber Crest Farms
4791 Dry Creek Road, Dept. NNE
Healdsburg, CA 95448
707/433-8251
Free catalog

Tinmouth Channel Farm
P.O. Box 428B, Dept. NNE
Tinmouth, VT 05773
802/446-2812
Free catalog

The Tomato Seed Company
P.O. Box 323, Dept. NNE
Metuchen, NJ 08840
No phone
Free catalog

Tortellini
23 East 17th Street, Dept. NNE
New York, NY 10003
800/527-8725   212/645-4266
Free catalog

Totally Organic Farms
2404 F Street Suite 101, Dept. NNE
San Diego, CA 92102
619/231-9506
Free catalog

Traditional Products Company
P.O. Box 564, Dept. NNE
Creswell, OR 97426
No phone
Free catalog

Traditions
P.O. Box 409, Dept. NNE
Fairfield, IA 52556
515/472-6909
Free catalog

Tree Top Toys
RR 2, Box 223D, Dept. NNE
Stone Ridge, NY 12484
914/687-0708
A family business.
Free catalog

Trianco Corporation
14 Buchanan Road, Dept. NNE
Salem, MA 01970
508/745-9766
Free catalog

Trinity Herb
Phone orders only
707/874-3418
Free catalog

Trout Lake Farm
149 Little Mountain Road, Dept. NNE
Trout Lake, WA 98650
509/395-2025
Free catalog

Truth's Dolls
P.O. Box 42, Dept. NNE
Fulton, CA 95439
No phone
Free catalog

Tryon Toymakers
1851 Redland Road, Dept. NNE
Campobello, SC 29322
803/457-2017
Free catalog

Tulikivi Group North America
30 Glen Road, Dept. NNE
West Lebanon, NH 03784
800/843-3473   603/298-8388
Free catalog

Tully Toys
4606 Warrenton Road, Dept. NNE
Vicksburg, MS 39180
601/638-1724
Free catalog

Tuttle Lithography
919 East Broadway, Dept. NNE
Madison, WI 53716
608/221-3531
Free catalog

Tweeds
One Avery Row, Dept. NNE
Roanoke, VA 24012-8528
800/999-7997
Free catalog

21st Century Foods
30A Germania Street, Dept. NNE
Jamaica Plain, MA 02130
617/522-7595
Free catalog

Uncle Joel's Maple Syrup
1580 35th Avenue, Dept. NNE
Hammond, WI 54015
715/796-5395
Free catalog

Unco Industries
7802 Old Spring Street, Dept. NNE
Racine, WI 53406
800/666-8626   414/886-2665
Free catalog

Under the Willows
P.O. Box 866, Dept. NNE
Edmonds, WA 98020
206/775-8900
Free catalog

Unique Insect Control
5504 Sperry Drive, Dept. NNE
Citrus Heights, CA 95621
916/961-7945
Free catalog

The Urban Farmer Store
2833 Vicente Street, Dept. NNE
San Francisco, CA 94116
800/666-DRIP   415/661-2204
$1.00 catalog

Utex Trading Enterprises
710 9th Street, Suite 5, Dept. NNE
Niagra Falls, NY 14301
716/282-4887
Free catalog

Valley Cove Ranch
P.O. Box 603, Dept. NNE
Springville, CA 93265
800/548-4724   209/539-2710
Free catalog

Van Dyke Ranch
7665 Crews Road, Dept. NNE
Gilroy, CA 95020
408/842-5423
Free catalog
Fourth generation family farm. All processing done by hand labor on the farm.

Vegan Street
P.O. Box 5525, Dept. NNE
Rockville, MD 20855
301/869-0086
Free catalog

Vermont Country Store
P.O. Box 3000, Dept. NNE
Manchester Center, VT 05255-3000
802/362-4647
Free catalog

Very Healthy Enterprises
P.O. Box 4489, Dept. NNE
Inglewood, CA 90309
800/222-9932   213/672-3269
Free catalog

Veterinary Nutritional Associates
229 Wall Street, Dept. NNE
Huntington, NY 11743
516/427-7479
Free catalog

Victoria's Secret
P.O. Box 16589, Dept. NNE
Columbus, OH 43216
800/888-8200
Free catalog

Vineyard Brands/ Robert Haas Selections
Haywood Road, Dept. NNE
Chester, VT 05143
802/875-2139
Free catalog

Wachters' Organic Sea Products
360 Shaw Road, Dept. NNE
South San Francisco, CA 94080
800/682-7100   800/822-6565
Free catalog

Wade Manufacturing Company
9995 SW Avery Street, Dept. NNE
Tualatin, OR 97062
503/692-5353
Free catalog

Wahatoya Herb
P.O. Box 169, Dept. NNE
Gardner, CO 81040
719/746-2370
Free catalog

Walnut Acres
Dept. NNE
Penns Creek, PA 17862
800/433-3998   717/837-0601
Free catalog

Walt Nicke Company
P.O. Box 433, Dept. NNE
Topsfield, MA 01983
508/887-3388
Free catalog

Warm Things
180 Paul Drive, Dept. NNE
San Rafael, CA 94903
415/472-2154
Free catalog

Water Conservation Systems
Damonmill Square, Dept. NNE
Concord, MA 01742
800/462-3341   508/369-3951
Free catalog

WaterTest Corporation
33 South Commerical Steet, Dept. NNE
Manchester, NH 03101
800/H2O-TEST
Free catalog

Wax Orchards
22744 Wax Orchard Road SW,
Dept. NNE
Vashon, WA 98070
800/634-6132
Free catalog

Weiss Brothers Nursery
11690 Colfax Highway, Dept. NNE
Grass Valley, CA 95945
916/272-7657
$1.00 catalog

Weiss's Kiwifruit
594 Paseo Companeros, Dept. NNE
Chico, CA 95928
916/343-2354
Free catalog

Weleda
P.O. Box 769, Dept. NNE
Spring Valley, NY 10977
914/352-6145
Free catalog

Wendy & Cindy Originals
4010 West Douglas Avenue, Dept. NNE
Milwaukee, WI 53209
414/438-1000
Free catalog

Westwind Seeds
2509 North Campbell, #139, Dept. NNE
Tucson, AZ 85719
No phone
Free catalog

Weygant-Metzler Importing
Box 56, Dept. NNE
Unionville, PA 19375
215/932-9113
Free catalog

Wild Child
1813 Monroe Street, Dept. NNE
Madison, WI 53711
608/251-6445
Free catalog

Williams-Sonoma
P.O. Box 7456, Dept. NNE
San Francisco, CA 94120-7456
415/421-4242
Free catalog

Willow Rain Herbal Goods
P.O. Box 5, Dept. NNE
Grubville, MO 63041
314/285-3697
Free catalog

Willsboro Country Furniture
P.O. Box 336, Dept. NNE
Willsboro, VT 12996-0336
800/342-3373
Free catalog

Wilton's Organic Certified Potatoes
P.O. Box 28, Dept. NNE
Aspen, CO 81612
No phone
Free catalog

Winter Silks
P.O. Box 130, Dept. NNE
Middleton, WI 53562
800/648-7455   608/836-4600
Free catalog

Wolfe's Neck Farm
2 Burnett Road, Dept. NNE
Freeport, ME 04032
207/865-4469
Free catalog

Women's Studio Workshop
P.O. Box 489, Dept. NNE
Rosendale, NY 12472
914/658-9133
Free catalog

World Wear
123 Alder Lane, Dept. NNE
Boulder, CO 80304
303/938-8404
Free catalog

World Wide Games
P.O. Box 517, Dept. NNE
Colchester, CT 06415-0517
800/243-9232
Free catalog

Wow-Bow Distributors
309 Burr Road, Dept. NNE
East Northport, NY 11731
800/326-0230   516/499-8572
Free catalog

Wysong Corporation
1880 North Eastman, Dept. NNE
Midland, MI 48640
517/631-0009
Free catalog

Xhaxhi
25 Holden Street, Dept. NNE
Providence, RI 02908
800/345-6480   401/861-6480
Free catalog

Zampet Manufacturing
3274 Mission Street, Dept. NNE
San Francisco, CA 94110
415/285-0209
Free catalog

& *Manufacturers, Importers, & Distributors*

The following reference list contains the names of the companies that manufacture, import, and distribute the brand name products mentioned throughout this book. If you cannot find the products locally, ask store managers to order them or contact the manufacturer for the retailer nearest you. An asterisk means the company is included in Mail-Order Sources.

A & M Pet Products, Houston, TX
Abady Company, Poughkeepsie, NY
Abkit, New York, NY
Abracadabra, Guerneville, CA
AFM Enterprises, Riverside, CA*
After the Fall, Brattleboro, VT
Air-Crete, Weedsport, NY
Aireox Research Corporation,
    Riverside, CA*
Alba Botanica Cosmetics,
    Santa Monica, CA
Alexandra Avery, Birkenfeld, OR*
All-One-God-Faith, Escondido, CA
Allen's Naturally, Farmington, MI*
Allergy Research Group,
    San Leandro, CA*
Allergy Resources, Monument, CO
AllerMed Corporation, Wylie, TX*
Almond Sun, Trumbull, CT
Aloe Products, Kerrville, TX
Alpine Spirit Company, New York, NY*
Alpursa, Salt Lake City, UT
Alvarado Street Bakery,
    Rohnert Park, CA
American Image Marketing, Nampa, ID
American Merfluan, San Francisco, CA

American Orsa, Redmond, UT
American Solar Network, Herndon, VA
American Standard, Piscataway, NJ
Appleseed Orchards, Sebastopol, CA
Artesian Plumbing Products,
    Perrysville, OH
Arrowhead Mills, Hereford, TX*
Ashdun Industries, Fort Lee, NJ
Aubrey Organics, Tampa, FL*
Aura Cacia, Weaverville, CA*
Auro, West Germany
Auromere, Pomona, CA*
Autumn Harp, Bristol, VT
Azome-Utah West, San Francisco, CA
Aztec Secret Health & Beauty Products,
    Las Vegas, NV*
Bandon Sea-Pack, Charleston, OR*
Barbara's Bakery, Petaluma, CA
Bare Escentuals, Los Gatos, CA
Baudelaire, Marlow, NH
Baugher Ranch, Artois, CA
Bee Beyer, Los Angeles, CA*
Beehive Botanicals, Hayward, WI
Beh Housewares Corporation,
    New York, NY
Bellerose Vineyard, Healdsburg, CA*

Better Environment, Albany, NY*
BioBin, Bainbridge Island, WA*
Bio-Botanica, Hauppauge, NY
Bioforce of America, Kinderhook, NY*
Biological Homeopathic Industries,
    Albuquerque, NM
Bio-Safe, Georgetown, TX*
Biosys, Palo Alto, CA
Biotec Foods, Honolulu, HI
Bioterra, Independence, OR
Bobalee Originals, West Jordan, UT
Body Love, Petaluma, CA
Boericke & Tafel, Philadelphia, PA*
Boiron Borneman, Norwood, PA*
Börlind of Germany, New London, NH
Botanical Pharmaceuticals,
    Bainbridge Island, WA*
Boyle-Midway, New York, NY
Brant Corporation, Concord, CA
Brier Run Farm, Birch River, WV*
Briggs, Tampa, FL
Bright Future Futons, Albuquerque, NM*
Brookside Soap Company, Seattle, WA
Burns-Milwaukee, Milwaukee, WI
C. C. Pollen Company, Phoenix, AZ
Cafe Tierra, Portland, OR
California Ecology, San Marcos, CA
CAM2 Oil Products Company,
    Denver, CO
Cannon, Cannon, NY
Care-Free Water Products,
    Santa Ana, CA
Cascadian Farm, Concrete, WA*
Cell Tech, Klamath Falls, OR*
Cemac Foods Corporation, New York, NY
Chase Organics, England
Chronomite Laboratories, Carson, CA
Church & Dwight Company,
    Princeton, NJ
Clean Environments, Boulder, CO*
Clear Light, the Cedar Company,
    Placitas, NM*
Clearly Natural, Petaluma, CA
Cloudworks, Contoocook, NH
Cloverdale, West Cornwall, CT
Coast Filtration, Brea, CA*
Col. Sanchez Foods, Santa Monica, CA

Coleman Natural Beef, Saguache, CO
Color & Herbal Company, Newport
    Beach, CA*
Colton Wartsila, Colton, CA
Community Soap Factory, Washington, DC
Controlled Energy Corporation,
    Waitsfield, VT
Country Comfort, Nuevo, CA
Crane & Company, Dalton, MA
Crane Plumbing, Evanston, IL*
CRSI, Michigan City, IN
Cuno, Meridian, CT
Dacopa Foods/California Natural
    Products, Manteca, CA
D-Con Company/Sterling Drug,
    Montvale, NJ
David's Goodbatter, Bausman, PA
DCM Industries, Boston, MA
DeBoles Nutritional Foods,
    Garden City Park, NY*
Deep Sea, Battleboro, VT
Del-Rain Corporation, Niagara Falls, NY
Desert Essence Cosmetics, Topanga, CA*
Deva Magic, Bearsvile, NY*
Dr. Hauschka Cosmetics, Wyoming, RI
Dr. & Mrs. J. M. Summers, Waco, TX
Duggan's, Eugene, OR
Duro-Lite Lamps, Fair Lawn, NJ
E. L. Foust Company, Elmhurst, IL*
E. McCormack & Company, Dublin,
    Ireland
Earth Science, Corona, CA*
Earth's Best Baby Food, Middlebury, VT
Earthen Joys, Astoria, OR*
Eclectic Institute, Portland, OR
EcoSafe Products, St. Augustine, FL*
EcoWorks, Baltimore, MD
Eden Foods, Clinton, MI
Edna's, McCall, ID
Elemental Enterprises, Seaside, CA*
Eljer Plumbingware, Plano, TX
Ellon Bach USA, Lynbrook, NY*
Enro Manufacturing, Riviera Beach, FL
Environmental Purification Systems,
    Concord, CA*
Enzyme Health & Beauty Products of
    Hawaii, Flagler Beach, FL

Equal Exchange, Stoughton, MA*
Erth-rite, Gap, PA*
Etex, Las Vegas, NV
Evergreen Bin, Seattle, WA
Faith Products, Edinburgh, Scotland
Family Clubhouse, Asheville, NC
Farnum Companies, Omaha, NE
Faultless Starch/Bon Ami Company,
    Kansas City, MO
Fieldcrest Mills, New York, NY
First American Marketing Group,
    East Rochester, NY
Fitzpatrick Winery, Somerset, CA*
Flora Laboratories, Lynden, WA
Forbo North America, Richmond, VA
Fort Howard Corporation, Green Bay, WI
4-D Hobe, Chandler, AZ
French Meadow Bakery, Minneapolis, MN
French Transit, Burlingame, CA
Frey Vineyards, Redwood Valley, CA
Gaeta Imports, Babylon, NY*
The Gajee Company, San Francisco, CA
Garden Empress, Bridgeville, CA
Garden of Eatin', Los Angeles, CA
General Ecology, Lionville, PA
Gerber Plumbing Fixtures Corporation,
    Chicago, IL
Gingerich Small Engines, Jamesport, MO*
Giovanni Cosmetics, Reseda, CA
Grain & Salt Society, Magalia, CA
Grandpa Soap Company, Cincinnati, OH
Granny's Old Fashioned Products,
    Arcadia, CA*
Great Eastern Sun, Asheville, NC
Greek Gourmet, George & Diane
    Nassopoulos & Family, Hingham, MA*
Green Ban, Norway, IA
Green Foods Corporation, Carson, CA
H. Coturri & Sons, Glen Ellen, CA
Harbingers of a New Age,
    Hayden Lake, ID*
Harvest Moon Mochi Company,
    Boulder, CO
Health Valley Natural Foods,
    Montebello, CA
Healthy Times, San Diego, CA
Heinke's, Paradise, CA

Heliodyne, Richmond, CA*
Helios, Carmel, CA*
Helix Corporation, Boulder, CO
Herb-Pharm, Williams, OR*
The Herb Shop, Springville, UT*
Heritage Store Products,
    Virginia Beach, VA
Hi-Bar, Oroville, CA
Hi-Tec Sports USA, Modesto, CA
Hidden Cellars, Ukiah, CA
Hill's Pet Products, Topeka, KS
Holly Solar Products, Petaluma, CA
Home Health Products,
    Virginia Beach, VA*
Homesteader & Arnold Company,
    Middle Falls, NY
Huish Chemical Company,
    Salt Lake City, UT
I. Rokeach & Sons, Farmingdale, NJ
Indian Creek Naturals, Selma, OR
Infinity Herbal Products, Toronto, Canada
Integrated Health Network, Tempe, AZ*
International Food Specialty Company,
    Santa Rosa, CA
Interpro, Haverhil, MA*
Island Spring, Vashon Island, WA
Isothermics, Anaheim, CA
J. L. Price, New Berlin, WI
J. P. Stevens, New York, NY
J. R. Liggett, Cornish, NH
J. T. Eaton Company, Twisburg, OH
Jack's Honey Bee Products, Pasadena, CA*
John Ritzenthaler Company,
    West Conshohochen, PA
Johnson & Johnson, New Brunswick, NJ
Jurlique, Novato, CA*
Kachelofen Group, Ashland, OR
KB Cotton Pillows, De Soto, TX*
Kickapoo Diversified Products,
    La Farge, WI*
Kim Supply Company, Kansas City, MO*
Kiss My Face, Gardiner, NY*
Knorr Beeswax Products, Del Mar, CA*
Knudsen & Sons, Chico, CA
Kohler Company, Kohler, WI
Kress & Owens Company,
    Dobbs Ferry, NY

La Maison De Soba, Montreal, Quebec, Canada

Lanocare Laboratories, Knoxville, TN*

Las Montanas, Glen Ellen, CA

Laurel Canyon Herbs, Hayward, CA

Lean and Free Products, Cedar Rapids, IA*

Lennox Industries, Dallas, TX

Leslie Manufacturing, Lawrence, KS*

Le Tan, Montrose, CO*

Levlad, Chatsworth, CA

Lick Your Chops, South Norwalk, CT

Life Tree Products, Sebastopol, CA

Lifeline Natural Soaps, Fairfax, CA

Lifestream Natural Foods, Richmond, BC Canada

Lightning Pet Products, Clearwater, FL

Lightning, Kansas City, MO

Lip Shtick, Beverly Hills, CA

Little Bear Organic Foods, Pacific Palisades, CA

Livos, West Germany

Loanda Products Corporation, Novato, CA

Longevity Pure Medicines, Beverly Hills, CA*

Loriva Supreme Foods, Hauppauge, NY

Lumiram Electric Corporation, Mamaroneck, NY

Lundberg Family Farms, Richvale, CA*

Magick Mud, Santa Ana, CA

Maguey Weaves, El Paso, TX

Maharishi Ayur-Veda Products International, Lancaster, MA*

Maine Baby, Morrill, ME*

Maine Coast Sea Vegetables, Franklin, ME*

Mansfield Plumbing Products, Perrysville, OH

Maranatha Natural Foods, Ashland, OR

Marine Minerals, Roy, UT*

Maskal Forages, Caldwell, ID*

Maxicrop USA & Company, Arlington Heights, IL

McCracken Solar Company, Alturas, CA*

McZand Herbal, Santa Monica, CA

Medina Agriculture Products Company, Hondo, TX*

Melior, Los Angeles, CA

Melitta North America, Cherry Hill, NJ

Mendocino Sea Vegetable Company, Navarro, CA

Mercantile Food Company, Georgetown, CT

Mexi-Snax, Hayward, CA

Mia Rose Products, Costa Mesa, CA*

Micro Balanced Products, Dumont, NJ*

Microlight Nutritional Products, Bay Center, WA

Microphor, Willits, CA

Miller Paint Company, Portland, OR*

Miracle of Aloe, Westport, CT

Mitoku Company, Seattle, WA

Monda Belle de Vienne, West Hollywood, CA*

Montana Naturals International, Arlee, MT*

Mountain Butterfly Herbs, Hamilton, MT*

Mountain Fresh, Grand Junction, CO*

Mountain Ocean, Boulder, CO

Mountain Rose Herbs, Redway, CA*

Mr. Bee Pollen, Scottsdale, AZ

Muramoto, Escondido, CA

Murco Wall Products, Fort Worth, TX*

Myson, Falmouth, VA

Naace Industries, Tucker, GA

Nasoya Foods, Leominster, MA

Natrol, Chatsworth, CA

Natural Bodycare, Camarillo, CA

Natural Brew Coffee Filters, Sheboygan, WI

Natural Life Pet Products, Minneapolis, MN

Natural Way Mills, Middle River, MN

Naturall, Farmington, MI

Nature de France, New York, NY

Nature House, Griggsville, IL*

Natureland Teas, South Croydon, Surrey, England

Nature's Colors, Mill Valley, CA*

Nature's Herbs, Orem, UT

Nature's Own, Weehawken, NJ

Nature's Path Foods, Blaine, WA

Nature's Recipe, Orange, CA

Nature's Sunshine, Spanish Fork, UT

Nature's Way Products, Springfield UT*
Naturopathic Laboratories,
    St. Petersburg, FL
New Cycle, Santa Rosa, CA*
NHC, Morrisville, VT
Nick Sciabica & Sons, Modesto, CA*
Nigra Enterprises, Agoura, CA*
Nikky America, New York, NY
No Common Scents, Yellow Springs, OH
Noah's Park, Tampa, FL*
NoRad Corporation, Santa Monica, CA
Norimoor Company, New York, NY
North Country Soap, Maple Plain, MN*
North Farm Cooperative, Madison, WI
O'Naturel, Oakland, CA
Octopus Mountain Wines, Boonville, CA
Ohsawa America, Chico, CA
The Old-Fashioned Milk Paint Company,
    Groton, MA*
Old World Honey Company, Arlee, MT
Olson Vineyards, Redwood Valley, CA
Open Sesame, Santa Cruz, CA
Organic Milling Company,
    San Dimas CA
The Organic Wine Company,
    San Francisco, CA*
The Organic Wine Works, Felton, CA
Original Swiss Aromatics,
    San Rafael, CA*
Orjene Natural Cosmetics,
    Long Island City, NY
Pacific Resources International,
    Summerland, CA
Paloma Industries, Elk Grove Village, IL
Para Labs, Hempstead, NY
Patricia Allison, La Mesa, CA
Paul Penders, Seffner, FL
Paul Thomas Wines, Bellevue, WA
Peelu Products, Morton Grove, IL
Peerless Pottery, Evansville, IN
Penn Herb Company, Philadelphia, PA
Perlinger Natural Products,
    Sebastopol, CA
Perlite Institute, Chicago, IL
The Pet Connection, Mountain View, CA
Pet Organics, Fullerton, CA
PetGuard, Orange Park, FL
Pets & People, Rancho Palos Verdes, CA

Pines International, Lawrence, KS*
Ponce Bakery, Chico, CA*
Porcher, Chicago, IL
Pratima, New York, NY
Premier One Products, Omaha, NE
The Prepared Gourmet, Northridge, CA
Preston-Brock Manufacturing Company,
    Cambridge, Ontario, Canada
PRH & Associates, Peachtree City, GA
Prince of Peace Enterprises,
    San Francisco, CA
Pronatec International,
    Peterborough, NH*
Protech, Stamford, CT
Purity Foods, Okemos, MI
Pyro Industries, Everett, WA
Rainbow Light Nutritional Systems,
    Santa Cruz, CA
Rainbow Research Corporation,
    Bohemia, NY
Rathdowney Ltd., Bethel, VT
Real Purity, Ypsilanti, MI
The Reggio Register Company, Ayer, MA*
Rejuvenative Foods, Santa Cruz, CA
Resources Conservation, Greenwich, CT
Richter Bros., Carlstadt, NJ
Riehs & Riehs, New Bern, NC*
Ringer, Eden Prairie, MN*
The Rockland Corporation, Tulsa, OK
Rubbermaid, Wooster, OH
Safer, Newton, MA
Sage Advance Corporation, Eugene, OR
Santa Barbara Olive Company,
    Solvang, CA*
Santa Cruz Natural, Freedom, CA
Santa Fe Fragrance Company,
    Santa Fe, NM*
Satori, Santa Cruz, CA
Schoonmaker/Lynn Enterprises,
    Portland, OR*
Scientific Enterprises, Blaine, MN*
Scientific Glass, Albuquerque, NM
Señor Felipe's, Chico, CA
Seven Stars Farm, Phoenixville, PA
Shelton's Poultry, Pomona, CA
Shikai Products, San Francisco, CA
Sigma Pharmaceutical Corporation,
    New York, NY

Similasan Corporation, Kent, WA

Simmons Handcrafts, Bridgeville, CA*

Simple Soap, England

Simplers Botanical Company,
    Forestville, CA*

Simply Pure, Bangor, ME*

Sinclair & Valentine, St. Paul, MN

Solahart, San Diego, CA*

South River Miso Company,
    Conway, MA*

Spectrum Naturals, Petaluma, CA

Springwell Dispensers, Atlanta, GA

Sprout Delights, Miami, FL*

Standard Homeopathic Company,
    Los Angeles, CA*

Stockmar, West Germany

Strathmore Paper Company,
    Westfield, MA

Sun Frost, Arcata, CA

Sunfeather Herbal Soap Company,
    Potsdam, NY*

Sun-Mar, Canada

Sunrider International, Torrance, CA

Sustane Corporation, Chaska, MN*

T & A Gourmet, Middlebush, NJ

Talisman, Woodstock, NY*

Tambrands, Lake Success, NY

Tart-X Products, Morton Grove, IL*

Teaco International, Fountain Hills, AZ*

Tecnu Enterprises, Albany, OR

Terra Flora, Montague, MA

Terra Nova, Ojai, Ca

Thermal Energy Storage Systems,
    Randolph, VT

Third Day Botanicals, Yellow Springs, OH

Threefold International Company,
    New York, NY*

Thunderstorm Corporation,
    Hingham, MA*

Thurmond Air Quality Systems,
    Little Rock, AK*

Timber Crest Farms, Healdsburg, CA*

Tom's of Maine, Kennebunk, ME

Tonialg, Atlanta, GA

Traditional Products, Mahwah, NJ

Traditional Products Company,
    Creswell, OR*

Tree of Life, St. Augustine, FL

Trianco Corporation, Salem, MA*

Tropical Soap Company, Dallas, TX

Tulikivi Group North America,
    West Lebanon, NH*

21st Century Foods, Jamaica Plain, MA*

Tyrell's Seattle, WA

U.S. Brass (division of Eljer), Plano, TX

U.S. Mills, Omaha, NE

Unco Industries, Racine, WI*

Universal-Rundle, Newcastel, PA

Ursa Major, Ashland, OR

Ventre Packing Company, Syracuse, NY

Very Healthy Enterprises, Inglewood, CA*

Veterinary Nutritional Associates,
    Huntington, NY*

Vibrant Life, Burbank, CA

Vita Wave Products, Canoga Park, CA

Viva Vera, Garland, TX

Wachters' Organic Sea Products,
    South San Francisco, CA*

Wahatoya Herb, Gardner, CO*

Wakunaga of America Company,
    Mission Viejo, CA

Walnut Acres, Penns Creek, PA*

Walter Rau Gmbh & Company
    Speickwerk, Stuttgart, West Germany

Wamsutta, New York, NY

Water Conservation Systems,
    Concord, MA*

Wax Orchards, Vashon, WA*

Weeds of Worth, Great Barrington, MA

Weleda, Spring Valley, NY*

Westbrae Natural Foods, Emeryville, CA

Westpoint Pepperell, Westpoint, GA

White Wave Soyfoods, Boulder, CO

Whole Food Marketing Company,
    Rancho Palos Verdes, CA

Willert Home Products, St. Louis, MO

Wirsbo, Apple Valley, MN

Withers Mill Company, Hannibal, MO

Wow-Bow Distributors,
    East Northport, NY*

Wysong Corporation, Midland, MI*

Zampet Manufacturing,
    San Francisco, CA*